Hoover Institution Publications 122

FROM PROTEST TO CHALLENGE

Volume 2

Hope and Challenge
1935-1952

From Protest to Challenge

A DOCUMENTARY HISTORY OF AFRICAN
POLITICS IN SOUTH AFRICA
1882-1964

Volume 1: Protest and Hope, 1882-1934

Volume 2: Hope and Challenge, 1935-1952

Volume 3: Challenge and Violence, 1953-1964

From Protest to Challenge
A DOCUMENTARY HISTORY OF AFRICAN
POLITICS IN SOUTH AFRICA
1882-1964

Edited by

Thomas Karis and Gwendolen M. Carter

———————

Volume 2

Hope and Challenge

1935-1952

by Thomas Karis

Hoover Institution Press
Stanford University
Stanford, California

Hoover Institution Publications 122
International Standard Book Number 0-8179-1221-5
Library of Congress Card Number 72-152423
© 1973 by the Board of Trustees of the
   Leland Stanford Junior University
All rights reserved
Printed in the United States of America

To the African People of South Africa

For the role they have played "during the last 50 years to establish, peacefully, a society in which merit and not race would fix the position of the individual in the life of the nation."

Albert J. Lutuli
Nobel Peace Prize Address
December 10, 1961

CONTENTS

The Authors   xiii

The Documents   xv

Preface   xvii

PART ONE
AFRICANS UNITED UNDER THE THREAT
OF DISENFRANCHISEMENT, 1935-1937

Leaders and Chiefs Oppose Government Plans   4

The All African Convention   6

Documents – Part One

Leaders and Chiefs Oppose Government Plans   13

1. "A National Convention." Statement by the Rev. Z. R. Mahabane, in the *Bantu World*, May 18, 1935   13

2. News Report and Resolution of the Conference called by the Transvaal African Congress, June 8, 1935   14

3. Resolution of the Executive Committee of the Cape Native Voters' Convention, July 13, 1935   14

4. Introduction to pamphlet, *Native Views on the Native Bills*. By Professor D. D. T. Jabavu, August 1935   15

5. "The African Liberator, Our Message." Editorial by Gilbert Coka, in *The African Liberator*, October 1935   16

6. News Report and Resolution of the Conference of Chiefs and Leaders in the Transvaal and Orange Free State Convened by the Government, September 6-7, 1935   18

7. News Report and Resolution of the Conference of Chiefs and Leaders in the Cape Province Convened by the Government, September 18, 1935   20

8. Proceedings and Resolution of the United Transkeian Territories General Council, March 30, 1936   23

The All African Convention   31

9. The All African Convention Proceedings and Resolutions of the AAC, December 15-18, 1935   31

10. Resolution of the Executive Committee of the AAC, February 15, 1936   46

11. "Presidential Address" by Professor D. D. T. Jabavu, AAC, June 29, 1936   48

12. Proceedings and Resolutions of the AAC, June 29- July 2, 1936   54

13. "The Challenge" and "The Alternative." Extracts from pamphlet, *The Crisis*, by Selby Msimang, 1936 [?]   57

14. "Policy of the AAC." Statement issued by the Executive Committee of the AAC, December 1937   61
15. Constitution of the AAC, December 1937   64

PART TWO
MODERATION AND MILITANCY, 1937-1949

Overview   69
White Grounds for Nonwhite Hope and Despair   73
Urban Trends and Popular Protest   79
The African National Congress, 1937-1949   81
The Failure of the Natives' Representative Council, 1946-1947   92
The Rise of the ANC Youth League and the Programme of Action, 1943-1949   98
The All African Convention, Non-European Unity, and the Left Wing   107
Notes   120

Documents — Part Two

The Revival of the African National Congress, 1937-1945   131
16. "Presidential Address" by the Rev. J. A. Calata, Cape African Congress, July 4, 1938   131
17. Report of a Deputation from the ANC and Congress of Urban Advisory Boards to the Minister of Native Affairs, May 15-17, 1939   138
18. "Presidential Address" by the Rev. J. A. Calata, Cape African Congress, June 25-27, 1939   145
19. Resolutions of the ANC Conference, December 15-18, 1939   154
20. Minutes of the ANC Annual Conference, December 15-17, 1940   155
21. "An Address at the Mendi Memorial Celebration, Bantu Sports Grounds, Johannesburg." by Dr. A. B. Xuma, February 23, 1941   162
22. "Mass Meeting, Africans Shot in Cold Blood." Flyer issued by Transvaal African Congress, for meeting on June 26, 1941   166
23. Report of a Deputation from the ANC to the Minister of Justice, on July 8, 1941, [n. d.]   166
24. "The Policy and Platform of the African National Congress." Statement by Dr. A. B. Xuma in *Inkululeko (Freedom)*, August 1941   168
25a-25c. ANC Annual Conference of December 14-16, 1941   172
25a. "Presidential Address" by Dr. A. B. Xuma   172
25b. Report of the Secretary-General   184
25c. Resolutions   186
26. Report of a Deputation from the ANC to the Deputy Prime Minister and Others on March 4, 1942, by Dr. A. B. Xuma [n.d.]   188
27. Letter from Paul R. Mosaka, Newly-elected Member of the Natives' Representative Council, to Dr. A. B. Xuma, November 11, 1942   198
28. Resolutions of the ANC Annual Conference, December 20-22, 1942   199
29a-29b. ANC Annual Conference of December 16, 1943   204
29a. Constitution of the ANC   204

29b. *Africans' Claims in South Africa*, Including "The Atlantic Charter from the Standpoint of Africans within the Union of South Africa" and "Bill of Rights," Adopted by the ANC Annual Conference   209

30. "Africans and San Francisco." Statement by Dr. A. B. Xuma, May 8, 1945   223

The Failure of the Natives' Representative Council, 1946-1947   224

31. *Reasons Why the Native Representative Council in the Union of South Africa Adjourned [on August 14, 1946]*. Pamphlet by Professor Z. K. Matthews, published in November 1946   224

32. Report of Interview by Some NRC Members with Prime Minister Jan C. Smuts; Verbatim Report of the Proceedings; Press Conference Remarks by Paul R. Mosaka and Professor Z. K. Matthews; and statement by Professor Matthews, May 8-9, 1947   233

33. Statement on the Prime Minister's Proposals, by Dr. A. B. Xuma for the ANC, May 11, 1947   257

34. Statement on the Prime Minister's Policy toward the NRC, by the Caucus of the NRC, November 1947   258

The Postwar African National Congress Under Dr. Xuma, 1946-1949   261

35. Statement on the African Worker, by Dr. A. B. Xuma, January 14, 1946   261

36. Cable to the United Nations Opposing Incorporation of South-West Africa, by Dr. A. B. Xuma, January 1946   262

37. Resolutions of the ANC Annual Conference, December 14-17, 1946   263

38. Minutes of the National Executive Committee of the ANC, February 1-2, 1947   266

39. "Joint Declaration of Cooperation." Statement by Dr. A. B. Xuma of the ANC, Dr. G. M. Naicker of the Natal Indian Congress, and Dr. Y. M. Dadoo of the Transvaal Indian Congress, March 9, 1947   272

40. "To All Africans and Friends of Justice." Flyer issued by Dr. A. B. Xuma, March 21, 1947   273

41. Statement at Press Conference on Coming General Election, by Dr. A. B. Xuma, April 5, 1948   274

42. "Presidential Address" by the Rev. J. A. Calata, ANC (Cape), July 1948   278

43. Cable to the United Nations, by Dr. A. B. Xuma, November 25, 1948   284

44. Joint Statement on the Durban Riots, by A. W. G. Champion of the ANC (Natal) and Dr. G. M. Naicker of the Natal Indian Congress [n.d.]   285

45. Statement on the Durban Riots, by the Working Committee of the ANC, signed by Dr. A. B. Xuma, January 20, 1949   286

46. "Statement Issued by Joint Meeting of African and Indian Leaders" [For Closer Co-operation], February 6, 1949   287

47. Minutes of the Annual Conference of the ANC, December 15-19, 1949   288

The Rise of the African National Congress Youth League and Adoption of the Programme of Action, 1943-1949   300

48. "Congress Youth League Manifesto." Issued by the Provisional Committee of the Congress Youth League, March 1944   300

49. "Trumpet Call to Youth" [announcing meeting of September 10, 1944]. Flyer issued by the Provisional Executive Committee of the Congress Youth League   308

50. Constitution of the ANC Youth League, 1944   309

51. "Some Basic Principles of African Nationalism." Article by A. M.
Lembede, in *Inyaniso*, February 1945   314

52. Letter from the ANC Youth League (Transvaal) to the Secretary
[Ruth First] of the Progressive Youth Council, March 16, 1945   316

53. "Policy of the Congress Youth League." Article by A. M. Lembede,
in *Inkundla ya Bantu*, May 1946   317

54. "The African Mine Workers' Strike—A National Struggle." Flyer
issued by the ANC Youth League, August 1946   318

55. Letter on the Youth League, from A. P. Mda to G. M. Pitje,
August 24, 1948   319

56. Letter on the Youth League, from A. P. Mda to G. M. Pitje,
September 10, 1948   321

57. "Basic Policy of Congress Youth League.' Manifesto issued by the
National Executive Committee of the ANC Youth League, 1948   323

58. Address on Behalf of the Graduating Class at Fort Hare College,
delivered at the "Completers' Social," by M. R. Sobukwe, October 21,
1949   331

59. Prayer delivered at the Annual Conference of the ANC Youth League,
by the Rev. I. C. Duma, December 15, 1949   336

60. "Programme of Action." Statement of Policy adopted at the ANC
Annual Conference, December 17, 1949   337

The All African Convention and Efforts at Wider Unity   339

61. Resolution on the War. Adopted by the National Executive Committees of the AAC and the ANC, July 7, 1940   339

62. Address by I. B. Tabata, AAC Conference, December 16, 1941   340

63. Statement on the Atlantic Charter, by Professor D. D. T. Jabavu,
June 26, 1943   347

64. "A Call to Unity." Manifesto adopted by the National Executive
Committee of the AAC, August 26, 1943   347

65. "Draft Declaration of Unity" [including 10-point Programme]. State-
ment Approved by the Continuation Committee of the Preliminary
Unity Conference of Delegates from the AAC and the National Anti-
C.A.D., December 17, 1943   352

66. "A Declaration to the Nations of the World." Statement of the Non-
European Unity Movement, signed by the Rev. Z. R. Mahabane, Dr.
G. H. Gool, and E. C. Roberts, July 1945   357

67. Letter ["On the Organisations of the African People"], from I. B.
Tabata to Nelson Mandela, June 16, 1948   362

68. "A Call for African Unity." Statement signed by Xuma, Jabavu,
Moroka, Matthews, Bokwe, Godlo, Mosaka, Baloyi, Champion,
Selope Thema, Ntlabati, and Mahabane, October 3, 1948   368

69. Minutes of the Joint Conference of the ANC and the AAC, December
16-17, 1948   370

70a-70c. Joint Meeting of the National Executive Committees of the ANC
and the AAC, April 17-18, 1949   378

70a. Minutes, signed by C. M. Kobus [of the AAC], Recording Secretary   378

70b. Letter reporting on this meeting, from Moses Kotane to Professor
Z. K. Matthews, May 8, 1949   386

70c. Review of this meeting, in Minutes of the Annual Conference of the
      AAC, December 1949   388

Other Non-European or Left-Wing Activity

71. "Arms for Non-Europeans." Flyer issued by the Non-European United
     Front of South Africa, March 18, 1942   389
72. "Non-European Peoples' Manifesto." Adopted at Non-European Con-
     ference Convened by the Non-European United Front, June 28, 1942   390
73. Manifesto of the African Democratic Party, September 26, 1943   391
74. Resolution of the National Anti-Pass Conference, May 20-21, 1944   396
75a-75b. First Transvaal-Orange Free State People's Assembly for Votes
          for All, May 22-24, 1948   398
75a. "Manifesto." Call to attend the People's Assembly, [n.d.]   398
75b. "The People's Charter." Manifesto adopted at the People's Assembly   399

PART THREE
JOINT ACTION AND THE DEFIANCE
CAMPAIGN, 1950-1952

A Crucial Period   403
The Programme of Action in 1950   405
Moving toward Defiance   410
The Defiance Campaign   416
Notes   428

Documents – Part Three

The Programme of Action in 1950   441

76. "Post-Mortem on a Tragedy." Editorial on the events of May 1, by
     Jordan K. Ngubane, in *Inkundla ya Bantu*, May 20, 1950   441
77. Resolution adopted at a Conference of Representatives of the Execu-
     tive Committees of the ANC, South African Indian Congress, African
     People's Organisation, ANC Youth League, Communist Party, and
     Transvaal Council of Non-European Trade Unions, May 14, 1950   442
78. Statement of the National Executive Committee of the ANC in an
     Emergency Meeting on May 21, 1950   443
79. "United Anti-Fascist Rally." Flyer announcing rally in Durban on
     May 28, 1950, to be addressed by Dr. J. S. Moroka, [n.d.]   444
80. Statement on a National Day of Protest, by the Central Executive
     Committee of the ANC Youth League (Transvaal), May 31, 1950   445
81. Letter on plans for June 26, from the Rev. J. J. Skomolo to Pro-
     fessor Z. K. Matthews, June 16, 1950   447
82. "Monday 26th June, National Day of Protest and Mourning." Flyer
     issued by the Natal Co-ordinating Committee, [n.d.]   448
83. "National Day of Protest and Mourning, Stay at Home on Monday,
     26th June!" Flyer issued by [twelve persons], June 15, 1950   449
84. "Report on the National Day of Protest, June 26, 1950." Issued by
     the Secretary-General of the ANC and initialed by Nelson R. Mandela,
     June 26, 1950   450

85. Draft Report of the National Executive Committee of the ANC, submitted to the Annual Conference, December 15-17, 1950   452

Moving Toward Defiance   458

86. Report of the Joint Planning Council of the ANC and the South African Indian Congress, signed by Dr. J. S. Moroka, J. B. Marks, W. M. Sisulu, Dr. Y. M. Dadoo, and Y. Cachalia, November 8, 1951   458

87a-87b. ANC Annual Conference of December 15-17, 1951   466

87a. Draft Report of the National Executive Committee   466

87b. "Presidential Address" by Dr. J. S. Moroka   471

88. Letter calling for Repeal of Repressive Legislation and Threatening a Defiance Campaign, from Dr. J. S. Moroka and W. M. Sisulu to Prime Minister D. F. Malan, January 21, 1952   476

89. "Opening Address" at Annual Conference of the South African Indian Congress, by Dr. S. M. Molema, January 25, 1952   477

90. Letter replying to letter from the Prime Minister's office and statement of intention to launch defiance campaign, from Dr. J. S. Moroka and W. M. Sisulu to Prime Minister D. F. Malan, February 11, 1952   480

The Defiance Campaign   482

91. "April 6: People's Protest Day." Flyer issued by the ANC (Transvaal) and the Transvaal Indian Congress   482

92. Statement in court by W. M. Sisulu before sentencing for pass offence, July 21, 1952   484

93. Statement on violence in New Brighton, Port Elizabeth on October 18, by local ANC leaders, in the *Eastern Province Herald*, October 20, 1952   484

94. "Police Shootings Must Stop!" Flyer issued by the National Action Committee, ANC, and South African Indian Congress, November 1952   485

95. "The Road to Freedom Is Via the Cross." Statement by Chief A. J. Lutuli, issued after the announcement on November 12, 1952, of his dismissal as chief [n.d.]   486

96. "Circular Letter to All Congress Branches of the Province." Review of 1952 by the Working Committee of the ANC (Cape), December 1952   489

NEUM and SOYA   494

97. "A Declaration to the People of South Africa from the Non-European Unity Movement." Statement by the NEUM, April 1951   494

98. "Opening Address" at First Conference of the Society of Young Africa, by I. B. Tabata, December 20, 1951   506

Chronology   509

Bibliographical Data   516

Index of Names   519

Index of Organizations   531

The Authors

Primary responsibility for the selection of documentary material and the accompanying text for Volume I and for Part I of Volume II was undertaken by Dr. Sheridan Johns III, of Duke University. He is particularly well-equipped to handle the material in this period, having written his doctoral dissertation on early left-wing movements in South Africa, and published lengthy articles on the Industrial and Commercial Workers' Union.

Professor Thomas Karis, of City College, City University of New York, undertook comparable responsibility for the remainder of Volume II and for Volume III, covering most of 1935-1952 and 1953-1964. He is author of the section on South Africa in *Five African States: Responses to Diversity,* Gwendolen M. Carter, ed., (Cornell University Press, 1963), and *The Treason Trial in South Africa: A Guide to the Microfilm Record of the Trial* (Hoover Institution, 1965). He is also coauthor with Gwendolen M. Carter and Newell M. Stultz of *South Africa's Transkei: The Politics of Domestic Colonialism* (Northwestern University Press, 1967).

Professor Gwendolen M. Carter of Northwestern University has aided throughout as collaborator, critic, and editor. She brings to bear her research and writings on South Africa, which include most relevantly *The Politics of Inequality: South Africa since 1948* (Praeger, 1958, rev. 1959), "African Nationalist Movements" in *Southern Africa in Transition,* edited by John A. Davis and James K. Baker (Praeger, 1966), pp. 3-19, *African Concepts of Nationalism in South Africa* (Melville J. Herskovits Memorial Lecture, University of Edinburgh, March, 1965), and her share in preparing *South Africa's Transkei.*

Gail M. Gerhart has assisted in the preparation of Volume III and is the author of the introductory essays on the Africanist movement and the Pan Africanist Congress in that volume. She is a graduate of Radcliffe College. Her doctoral dissertation for Columbia University is an analysis of the development of the Pan Africanist Congress and the problem of change in South Africa. Now living in Nairobi, she has made a number of research trips to South Africa since 1963.

The Documents

In the following documents inconsistencies may occur in punctuation, format, spelling of certain words and proper names, and manner of speech. Because we believe that these variations enhance rather than detract from the value of the papers, we have made no attempt to edit beyond the correction of obvious typographical errors.

Preface

The general preface to the three volumes of *From Protest to Challenge*, which appeared in Volume I, noted that these bulky volumes provided only a selection of the rich materials that should be used when a definitive political history of modern South Africa is eventually written. The validity of this observation has been strikingly apparent in the preparation of Volume II. In comparison with the first volume, far more primary material was available as were many more interviews which the editors had been able to conduct with persons active during the period 1935-1952. At the same time, as the general preface pointed out, we are painfully aware that our documentary holdings do not include many of the records we would like to have. We are also aware of the invaluable oral history that remains to be recorded and of the problems of evaluation that that history presents.

Despite the amount of material now on hand, the introductory essays have a limited aim: to provide a broad setting for the selected documents, to comment on their significance, and to describe the main developments in African politics in South Africa. The volume includes documents dealing with political activities in which whites and Indians and Coloureds were closely involved with Africans, but not documents which illustrate the independent efforts of Indians and Coloureds and of both liberal and left-wing whites. One additional caveat: the space given to particular organizations and personalities is not necessarily a measure of our evaluation of their historical importance in South Africa. Although we have generally been guided by our view of such importance, we have also given substantial space to material that was illustrative of divergent trends of thought and would be of special interest to students of African political attitudes and ideas and, indirectly, to students of American race relations.

Primary responsibility for the selection of documentary material for Part One of Volume II and its introductory essay was undertaken by Sheridan W. Johns III, Associate Professor of Political Science at Duke University. The remainder of the volume is the responsibility of Thomas Karis, Professor of Political Science at the City College of the City University of New York. Both were fortunate to be recently at the University of Zambia, Mr. Johns in 1968-1970 and Mr. Karis in 1968-1969. In Lusaka, they had valuable opportunities to review the manuscript and to discuss recent political history with South Africans who played a role in that history or were close observers of it. Throughout the preparation of Volume II,

Gwendolen M. Carter, Professor of Political Science and Director of the Program of African Studies at Northwestern University, has continued to serve as collaborator, critic, and editor.

Again we express our great debt to the many South Africans who have granted us lengthy interviews about the past, responded patiently to our many questions, and commented on early drafts of the manuscript. Their warm cooperation and friendship have been among the deep satisfactions of our work on this documentary history. We wish also to record the debt that scholarly researchers owe to Benjamin Pogrund, who has for years been providing both the Hoover Institution and the Center for Research Libraries with microfilm copies of historical materials.

Thomas Karis

August 1970 Gwendolen M. Carter

NOTE: The introductory essays in this volume use "nonwhite" as an inclusive term for Africans, Coloureds, and Indians since this (like "non-European") was used during the period 1935-1952 by the leaders of these groups themselves. By the early 1970's, "Black consciousness" decried "nonwhite" and "non-European" as negative and derogatory terms, coined by whites. The term now preferred is "Black."

PART ONE

Africans United under the
Threat of Disenfranchisement
1935-1937

The years 1935-1937 mark a major turning point in African politics in South Africa. In 1936, the strengthened white government, backed by the combined political forces of Prime Minister J. B. M. Hertzog and Jan Smuts, removed Cape African voters from the common voters' roll. That action, advocated by Hertzog for at least a decade, was the most far-reaching political blow to African aspirations since Union. Africans of widely differing political convictions, from tribal conservatism to urban radicalism, united to protest against the renewed threat to the real though limited rights of enfranchised Africans in Cape Province and to the symbolic importance of these rights for all Africans. At the same time they renewed their demands for greater participation in the government of South Africa. Their protests and demands were in vain, but the heightened political agitation of 1935-1937 shaped the organizational and tactical issues of subsequent African politics. More important, the loss of special status for Africans in Cape Province laid the basis for more effective cooperation in the future among Africans nationally.

The formation of the Hertzog-Smuts coalition government in early 1933 and its endorsement by the white electorate in the general election held later that year was followed in mid-1934 by fusion of the two coalition parties into the new United Party. With economic recovery from worldwide depression under way, the new government began to reconsider the "Native Question" that had preoccupied the two previous Nationalist-dominated governments headed by Hertzog. Hertzog now for the first time commanded a two-thirds majority of the joint membership of both houses of Parliament, the number required by the Act of Union to amend the entrenched clause protecting the nonwhite franchise in Cape Province.

In May 1935 a Joint Select Committee of Parliament tabled two measures: the Representation of Natives Bill and the Native Trust and Land Bill. The first bill, a modified version of Hertzog's original proposals of 1926, provided for the exclusion of future African voters from the common roll while allowing the 11,000 Africans already on the roll to remain there. As compensation, all Africans in South Africa were to elect four white senators (and possibly later two additional white senators) through a cumbersome indirect process. Only later did the government offer the compromise proposal that was finally enacted: a separate roll on which qualified Cape Africans voted for three white members of the House of Assembly and two white members of the Cape Provincial Council. (This roll was abolished in 1959.)

In addition, a Natives' Representative Council (NRC) was to be created in which twelve Africans, indirectly elected by Africans throughout the Union, would sit

3

with four Africans chosen by the government and with white Native commissioners under the chairmanship of the secretary for Native affairs. The new body was to be purely advisory, however, and concerned only with matters affecting Africans. (It was abolished in 1951.) Thus the proposed legislation dealt a final blow to the hopes of many Africans that the Cape franchise could be a useful lever for the eventual extension of the franchise to all Africans.

The second bill offered to redeem the promise of the Natives Land Act of 1913 to increase the area of land which Africans could occupy. The act of 1913 had scheduled about 7½ percent of the country's land for African occupation; the bill, by "releasing" white-owned land for purchase by a government trust, which was to have control over all scheduled and reserve lands, provided for an eventual increase to about 13.7 percent. (By 1972 the total land available for African occupation was still less than 13.7 percent.) The 1913 act also prohibited Africans—but not those in Cape Province—from buying land outside the scheduled areas except with official consent. (In 1937, however, as the step-by-step process of restriction continued, new legislation virtually barred all Africans, including those in Cape Province, from buying land in towns.)

Although seeking to meet African demands to a limited degree, the proposed legislation also contained repressive labor sections, including a section, Title IV, providing for a system of registration and licensing which would force African squatters from white-owned land into the already overcrowded Native reserves or into the cities, where they would swell the pool of cheap African labor.

LEADERS AND CHIEFS OPPOSE GOVERNMENT PLANS

Hertzog announced that a special joint sitting of Parliament would be held in 1936 to consider the new versions of his "Native Bills." African reaction to the bills was unequivocal in its opposition and Unionwide in its expression. Articulate Africans of differing viewpoints and from all parts of the country condemned the Representation of Natives Bill. So also did white liberals and radicals. Although many Africans sympathized with the principle in the Native Trust and Land Bill that more land should be released to Africans, they attacked the bill's specific provisions—in particular, Title IV. In the common concern to devise means to fight the proposed legislation, previous political differences were submerged.

Echoing the African response in 1909 to the impending Act of Union, there was immediate and extensive support for a 1935 proposal to convoke a national meeting of Africans. The *Bantu World* took the initiative in suggesting a national convention; in mid-May the idea was enthusiastically seconded by the Rev. Z. R. Mahabane, a former president-general of the ANC (Document 1). At a June meeting called by the Transvaal African Congress, representatives of African groups, including locally based vigilance associations, elected advisory boards, remnants of the ICU (Industrial and Commercial Workers' Union), and the Communist Party, endorsed the calling of a national convention of representatives of

4

existing African organizations and urged the subordination of all political differences to the overriding necessity for African unity (Document 2). Thus the stage was set for a broadly representative gathering to consider ways to organize further opposition to the Native Bills.

Meanwhile, other African organizations and publicists added their protests and suggestions for strategy. In Cape Province the executive committee of the Cape Native Voters' Convention, representing the group most directly affected by the proposed legislation, met in emergency session to issue a public appeal for retention of the existing franchise and to request a year's delay to enable Africans to offer "constructive criticism" (Document 3). D. D. T. Jabavu, professor of Bantu languages at Fort Hare Native College and the most prominent member of the convention, contributed his journalistic skills to the opposition movement through publication of a pamphlet containing statements by Africans of diverse political persuasions. He coupled his efforts to present a broad range of African views with an appeal to the government to give adequate time for consideration of the proposals through the established machinery for consultation. The pamphlet's introduction is reproduced in Document 4. In it, Jabavu noted that the legislation had not yet been translated into the vernacular languages. "It is fortunate for the Government," he said later in the pamphlet, "that the masses of our people are not aware of what is going on in Parliament as they do not read the papers. This, however, is no security for the European race; for the intelligent Blacks have a way of passing on the information and thus act as an agency to create distrust in the rule of White people."

Taking a different tack, Gilbert Coka, editor of the short-lived newspaper, *The African Liberator*, focused upon the potential for coordinated African activities in the economic sphere (Document 5). Writing at the start of the Italo-Ethiopian War before Italian victory became evident, Coka hailed the opening of a new era in which Africa would regenerate itself. A former member of the ICU, who had just been expelled from the Communist Party for attempting to organize a "counter-revolutionary" African party, he drew upon his own experiences to urge Africans to end their internal feuds and to organize themselves through economic cooperation and trade unions.

The Hertzog government seemingly ignored the agitation. It neither called a national conference of African leaders in accordance with the Native Affairs Act of 1920 nor postponed consideration of the legislation as Jabavu and others requested. The government, however, did convene a hastily organized series of five regional conferences and some smaller ones to which African chiefs and other selected Africans were invited. But these Africans endorsed many of the protests put forth earlier by others. At the government-sponsored meeting of Africans from the Transvaal and the Orange Free State held in Pretoria in early September 1935, the delegates deplored the government's haste and pleaded for more time in which to consider its proposals (Document 6). At another meeting in King William's Town in mid-September, the African delegates were more definite; they unequivo-

5

cally opposed the removal of the Cape African franchise, buttressing their opposition with a careful enumeration of the benefits which that franchise had brought (Document 7). Not only had it given enfranchised Africans protection against curfew regulations, exemption from customary law, and property rights in towns; it also had influenced the adoption of some advantageous policies and helped stave off some oppressive policies—for example, the extension to Cape Province of the pass laws in force elsewhere in the Union.

THE ALL AFRICAN CONVENTION

The center of African protests remained, however, within the Africans' own organizations. In response to a call from Jabavu and Pixley ka I. Seme, president-general of the African National Congress, Africans from all shades of the political spectrum and from all sections of South Africa converged upon the African township of Bloemfontein in mid-December 1935 at the same time that Afrikaners were celebrating the ninety-eighth anniversary of the Voortrekker victory over the Zulus. On the site where the South African Native Convention had met in 1909 to formulate its vain protests against the Act of Union and where the South African Native National Congress had been launched in 1912 as a Unionwide political organization, the most broadly representative group of Africans since those gatherings met in the All African Convention (AAC). Under the chairmanship of Professor Jabavu, the delegates drafted comprehensive resolutions on African grievances and resolved to constitute the AAC as "an organized body" that was to meet again (Document 9).

The All African Convention provided a new national umbrella organization within which all existing African political groups could be linked. A number of moderates, in particular the enfranchised voters of the Cape Province, who, like Professor Jabavu, had previously remained aloof from national bodies, joined for the first time with leaders of the ANC, members of the Communist Party, and others who had been active in the once powerful ICU.

Dr. John Dube and the Rev. Z. R. Mahabane, past presidents-general of the ANC, Dr. A. B. Xuma and Dr. J. S. Moroka, future presidents-general of the ANC, J. B. Marks and Edwin Mofutsanyana of the Communist Party, and Clements Kadalie of the ICU were all present. Among the delegates were tribal chiefs (some of them members of the Transkei Bunga), respected church dignitaries, professional men (some recently returned from study in Europe and America), elected members of urban advisory boards, prominent women, and representatives of a score of local organizations, including Coloureds from left-wing study circles in Cape Town. The more than 400 delegates included about 200 from Cape Province, 100 from the Transvaal, 70 from the Orange Free State, 30 from Natal, 10 from Basutoland, and one (representing the paramount chief) from Swaziland. "It is noteworthy," said the report of the proceedings, "that the delegates included six graduates from the University of South Africa, six from the United States of

6

America, one from the University of Budapest, one from Glasgow, two from Edinburgh, and two from the University of London."

The diversity of the delegates made the unanimity of their views all the more striking. Discussion focused upon the pending Native Bills, but antagonism to the entire post-Union trend of government policy ran deep. The delegates paid particular attention to the franchise, arguing, as had the King William's Town meeting, that the common franchise had furthered harmony between the races. The proposed NRC was rejected as an unacceptable substitute for the franchise. In the same vein, the proposals contained in the Native Trust and Land Bill were rejected as inadequate for the satisfaction of African demands for land. The AAC also demanded reconsideration of "oppressive laws" such as the Riotous Assemblies Act, the Native Service Contract Act, the Poll Tax Act, and the pass laws. In every instance, resolutions on African grievances were carried unanimously.

Although the AAC declarations were uncompromising in their opposition to the direction of government policy, which was under right-wing pressure from Malan's opposition Nationalists and English-speaking racialists in Natal, they were punctuated by affirmations of loyalty to South Africa and the British Crown. Seeking some understanding response, the AAC appealed to the House of Assembly and to the four senators appointed for their "thorough acquaintance with the reasonable wants and wishes of the coloured races." It also stressed the importance of appealing to the governor-general, the King, and the British Parliament. The government was again urged to use the existing consultative machinery available under the Native Affairs Act of 1920. Moreover, in keeping with past practice, the AAC called for a national "day of universal humiliation and intercession" during which "prayers must be offered up for the Almighty's guidance and intervention in the dark cloud of the pending disfranchisement of the Cape Natives by the Parliament of South Africa." This resort to traditional tactics in the charged atmosphere of the meeting highlighted the peaceful and constitutional nature of African protests on the eve of a historic defeat for African political representation.

Yet the delegates were also receptive to proposals for more militant action. They unanimously accepted a proposal by a Cape Town Coloured Communist, John Gomas, that mass protest meetings be organized throughout South Africa. Dr. G. H. Gool, another Cape Town Coloured delegate, posed more ambitious aims when he urged that the AAC "lay the foundations of a national liberation movement to fight against all the repressive laws of South Africa." Although the delegates did not accept Gool's formulation, they endorsed a proposal made initially by Clements Kadalie that the convention remain in existence. Thus, there were signs that the AAC would be not merely a platform from which to protest the Native Bills but a potential springboard for further political action.

In its statement of principles the AAC sought a policy of "political identity" and "full partnership" in which no one racial group would be dominated by another. These aspirations were qualified, however, by an indication that Africans were willing to accept a "civilization test" as a qualification for the franchise. At the same time, the AAC proposed that while "various racial groups may develop on

7

their own lines, socially and culturally, they will be bound together by the pursuit of common political objectives." Thus, while accepting "separate development" in the social sphere, the AAC stood in sharp contrast to the apartheid policy of the opposition Nationalist Party by its insistence that Africans and whites held a common citizenship and should participate in common political institutions. By endorsing both the Cape liberal ideal and united African action, the AAC fused the traditions established by the Cape African liberals and the leaders of the ANC.

The AAC's deputation to Cape Town in early 1936 had the same experience as had earlier African deputations: it met with politeness but received no satisfaction of its demands. Composed of members of the executive committee and led by Jabavu, the deputation met with Prime Minister Hertzog and other government officials. Hertzog offered a compromise: retention of the Cape African franchise but removal of all registered African voters from the common voters' roll, where they voted for the same candidates as did whites, to a separate roll which would elect three white members to the House of Assembly and two white members to the Cape Provincial Council. Under pressure from the government and some white sympathizers to accept this compromise formula, the deputation showed signs of wavering in its unequivocal opposition. Reports differ, particularly about the role of Professor Jabavu: apparently some members gave the impression that they would accept the compromise if given time to discuss it within the Convention. (The identity of the Africans who gave this impression has remained unsettled to the present day. Many Africans at the time suspected that Jabavu had supported compromise, but he vigorously denied this.) The prime minister refused to allow a postponement; and, in a statement presented to him before it left Cape Town, the deputation reaffirmed its opposition to the bills in the same strong terms that had been expressed by the AAC at its meeting in December 1935 (Document 10).

Subsequently, white members of Parliament from the eastern Cape Province met with a group of African voters for further consultation. Confronted with the government's determination not to offer further concessions, some of the group yielded and endorsed the compromise proposals, thus lending some justification to the government's contention that its spirit of conciliation had found support among "responsible" Africans. The large majority of politically active Africans, however, refused to end their opposition.

Although the AAC did not organize the mass protest meetings throughout the country that it had endorsed, its supporters reiterated their rejection of the government's policy. Rejection was evident, for example, in the lively discussion of the pending bills in the United Transkeian Territories General Council, the Bunga. African members of the oldest representative body recognized by the government unequivocally supported retention of the Cape African franchise and its extension throughout the country (Document 8). Thus Africans regarded by the government as moderates put themselves on record as supporters of no compromise.

Nonetheless, despite continuing protests, which were supported by white liberals and other sympathizers, the Representation of Natives Bill was passed at a

8

joint sitting of Parliament in April 1936 as amended in accord with the limited compromise offered by Prime Minister Hertzog. Only eleven dissident members of Parliament, including Jan Hofmeyr, a member of the Cabinet, broke ranks to vote against the top-heavy majority of 169. The Native Trust and Land Bill, as originally submitted, became law during the following month.

Meanwhile, events elsewhere in Africa were heightening the tension felt by Africans in South Africa. The Italian attack on Ethiopia, the oldest independent African state, aroused feelings of oneness with the rest of Africa. Interest was intense, and everywhere Africans, including tribally oriented individuals, talked about the war in Ethiopia. Some Africans (for example, Gilbert Coka—Document 5) hoped that an Ethiopian victory over the Italians would spur new united action by Africans, but such optimism quickly gave way to pessimism as the rapidity and extent of the Italian takeover became known.

The double impact of the events in Ethiopia and the action of the white South African Parliament jolted Africans throughout the country. When the AAC reconvened in June, two months after the passage of the Native Bills, Professor Jabavu delivered a presidential address which conveyed, in a singular manner, the prevailing climate of feeling (Document 11). He began: "All Africans, as well as all other non-White races of the world have been staggered by the cynical rape by Italy of the last independent state belonging to the indigenous Africans." He underlined the feeling of frustration caused by the apparent indifference of the white world to Ethiopia. Referring to the vaunted attributes of "European civilization," he continued, " . . . the brief history of the last eight months has scratched this European veneer and revealed the White savage hidden beneath." Thus the most distinguished of African professional men, one who had been long associated with African acceptance of the Cape liberal promise, not only through the part played by his father in African politics but also through his own activities in the Cape Native Voters' Convention, now questioned the legitimacy of the claims by whites to a "civilizing mission."

Following Jabavu's address, the AAC denounced the Italian attack upon Ethiopia in a resolution condemning European imperialism on the African continent (Document 12). The resolution also supported a continental and worldwide liaison among people of African descent. It declared: "The All African Convention recognizes the value and desirability of establishing contacts with Africans and African organizations in other parts of the world. To this end the All African Convention believes that a call to international conference of Africans and overseas peoples of African descent should receive the serious consideration of the Executive Committee." In this way the AAC added a pan-African dimension to its outlook.

The focus of AAC attention, however, revolved around Jabavu's major concern—the strategy that Africans within South Africa should adopt now that the Native Bills had become law. Selby Msimang, the long-time publicist for the ANC and one-time trade union leader in Bloemfontein, who had been elected general secretary of the AAC, expressed his views in a pamphlet, *The Crisis* (Document

9

13). He argued that " . . . Parliament and the white people of South Africa have disowned us, flirted and trifled with our loyalty. They have treated us as rebels, nay, they have declared we are not part of the South African community." Since white South Africans denied the Africans political participation within the country, Msimang suggested rhetorically that the Africans had no choice but to demand the complete partition of South Africa "on a fifty-fifty basis." A minor strain in African political thought thus, once again, found expression. With ironic references to a statement by Smuts on the necessity of freedom, Msimang urged Africans to unite for renewed struggle and even hinted at the possibility of revolutionary action.

Professor Jabavu had agreed in his presidential address that an equitable partition was a possible alternative if segregation and color bars continued. But he concentrated particularly on the means for conducting an effective African struggle for political integration. Taking a slightly different approach to that of Msimang, Jabavu placed great value on a new racial emphasis. Echoing arguments made by Coka in 1935 and reminiscent of Marcus Garvey (the American Negro who had urged African self-reliance), Jabavu urged Africans to buy from Africans "out of a patriotic spirit of African nationalism." He argued that African organizations must be revitalized so that educated Africans could lead the masses in the continuing struggle for African rights. Since he doubted that African organizations had the discipline and cohesion to undertake forceful revolution or boycott, he rejected the arguments of those who urged total boycott and "using the fear of a bloody revolution as a weapon of propaganda." Equally, however, he rejected a policy which had no support in the conference: full acceptance of the new laws. Instead, Jabavu counseled Africans "to evolve an intermediary policy of using what can be used and fighting against all that we do not want."

On the floor of the convention a small but vocal minority—the delegates associated with left-wing study circles in Cape Town—argued against Jabavu and urged a boycott against the segregatory institutions established by the Representation of Natives Act: the NRC and the "Native" seats in Parliament and in the Cape Provincial Council. The delegates as a whole rejected the boycott strategy and accepted the more flexible tactics proposed by Jabavu; yet the tone of the "Programme of Action" which they adopted indicated continued strong opposition to government policy (Document 12). While the "Programme" used restrained language to record its "profound disappointment" at the action of Parliament, it also authorized the executive committee "to explore all effective avenues of action" with the organizations affiliated with the AAC in order to achieve its goal of common citizenship rights for all. In conclusion, the Programme stated: "Now therefore this All African Convention solemnly resolves to pick up the gauntlet thrown before it by the White Parliament of South Africa." But what specific measures Africans were to take were not enumerated.

Eighteen months were to elapse before the next meeting in December 1937. During that time delegates were expected to strengthen the organization through intensive activity in their own localities. But in the interim it became clear that the cohesion of the new organization did not extend beyond coordinated action on the Native Bills. When the government established the machinery for implementing the Representation of Natives Bill, the center of African political activity shifted to include the new forms of representation. Despite continuing agitation by proponents of boycott, the large majority of politically active Africans appeared to believe in making use of the new forms. Many Africans who had associated themselves with the AAC, including ANC politicians, Communists, leaders of the Location Advisory Boards' Congress, members of the Transkei Bunga, and other local leaders, competed in June 1937 for the NRC's twelve indirectly elected seats. Six of the seats were won by members of the AAC Executive Committee: R. V. Selope Thema, T. M. Mapikela, the Rev. John Dube (the three of them leaders of the ANC in the Transvaal, Orange Free State, and Natal, respectively), A. M. Jabavu (brother of Professor Jabavu), R. H. Godlo, and C. K. Sakwe. Prominent AAC members also became active on behalf of various white candidates contesting the new Native seats in Parliament and the Cape Provincial Council. Thus, although the AAC had not taken an official position with regard to the separate institutions created by the Representation of Natives Act, it found itself deeply enmeshed in them through the activities of its members.

The new situation was evident at the December 1937 meeting of the AAC. Among the official delegates were six of the white "parliamentary members" elected by Africans: one member of the House of Assembly, three senators, and two provincial councillors. At least four of the new members of the NRC were in attendance (Selope Thema, A. M. Jabavu, Mapikela, and Godlo), and three of them (all except Godlo) were elected to the new executive committee. A new statement of policy, written by Jabavu and Msimang and adopted by the AAC, explicitly stated that "all the candidates returned as members at the elections held during June 1937 under the 1936 Representation of Natives Act are hereby recognized as the accepted mouthpiece of Africans in their various representative State Chambers of the (i) Senate, (ii) House of Assembly, (iii) Provincial Council, and (iv) Native Representative Council" (Document 14). The statement also asserted that the representatives would be expected to attend AAC meetings "for the purpose of ascertaining the opinion of African views on various questions, securing a mandate for expressing African views on matters arising from time to time, and of giving an account of their stewardship." Thus the AAC formally accepted the new institutions as part of its machinery of representation to white South Africa. The middle-of-the-road policy which it had adopted in June 1936 was extended to include the very institutions which the AAC had initially opposed.

Despite the shift of policy, the AAC did not weaken its commitment to agitate upon a broad range of African grievances. Indeed, its proceedings were mainly concerned with economic and social disabilities, including land rights, inadequate social facilities, and high taxation—a concentration perhaps reflecting the removal of the Native Bills as matters of contention. Its December 1937 statement of policy

11

reaffirmed long-standing aims and, in effect, rejected the desperate flirtations with the alternative of partition.

The AAC also moved to convert itself into a permanent federal organization. Some African leaders, particularly President Seme of the ANC and those close to him, vigorously opposed making the AAC a permanent body that would claim allegiance from all African organizations. Nevertheless, the delegates to the December 1937 meeting (representing thirty-nine organizations, including three provincial sections of the ANC), adopted a constitution which invited the affiliation of "all African religious, educational, industrial, economic, political, commercial and social organizations" (Document 15). The emphasis was to be upon the creation of African unity in the economic and political sphere, the formulation of a national program for Africans, and the revival and establishment of affiliated organizations to include all Africans. Through further detailed provisions, the constitution provided the structure for the continuation of the AAC as a policy body, meeting triennially in a national conference and linking groups throughout the country.

The passage of the Native Bills in 1936 had created a new situation for African politics in South Africa. The agitation against those measures had spurred greater political consciousness among Africans, including groups, such as students, who were to produce important leaders in the future. With the conversion of the originally ad hoc AAC into a permanent Unionwide federal body, a new focus for African political activity was created, and a potential national rival to the ANC was launched.

The new organization brought together Africans from widely different political persuasions, from the still tribally oriented to the educated Cape African voters who had previously kept aloof from Unionwide political organizations. One result of the 1936 legislation was a new common ground between Africans in the Cape and in the north. The AAC did not mount the coordinated mass protests which it had endorsed but used the traditional techniques of African pressure group politics used by the ANC. Under its umbrella, the major issues which had engaged Africans since the advent of Union were debated anew. New thought was given to the establishment of contact with Africans outside the country. And the contentious question of boycott was added to the regular agenda. As the crucial years of 1935-1937 came to a close, Africans faced the prospect of further repressive policies and fundamental questions of tactics. Yet, despite intimations of radical action, the prevailing outlook regarding tactics continued to be essentially conservative, concerned with the long-standing effort to build a national African patriotism, and unready—for more than a decade—for mass action in concert with other nonwhites.

DOCUMENTS — PART ONE

LEADERS AND CHIEFS OPPOSE GOVERNMENT PLANS

Document 1. "A National Convention." Statement by the Rev. Z. R. Mahabane, in the *Bantu World*, **May 18, 1935**

The proposals embodied in the Report and the Draft Bills constitute a direct challenge to the African community of the Union. How long shall the African people who form the integral and inseparable part and parcel of the population of the Union be contented with a position of political inferiority and political helotry and of exclusion from the civil organism of this land of their birth? The present occasion calls for the summoning of what should prove to be the largest, most important and representative National Convention of chiefs, leaders and other representatives of all shades of religious, educational, economic and political thought among the African people of the four Provinces of the Union of South Africa. This National gathering should be held at a centrally situated locality which should be easily accessible to delegates from all parts and all corners of the Union.

It would also be most fitting that an assemblage of this colossal character should be held this year when South Africa is celebrating the Silver Jubilee of the consummation of Union of the four Colonies. The Africans should gather together on this occasion, take stock of the position as a race of people in the country, consider the whole Native policy that has been inaugurated since Union and prosecuted during the last period of twenty-five years, study the culmination of this policy as adumbrated in the draft Bills that are now before the country, "reason together" and publish a statement of their views on the whole situation.

The proposed National Convention should be preceded by local District, Divisional or parochial Conferences, the object of which would be to make preliminary pronouncements, suggest items of the Agenda of the National Convention and elect Representatives to the latter.

13

Document 2. News Report and Resolution of the Conference called by the Transvaal African Congress, June 8, 1935

An important gathering held under the auspices of the Transvaal African Congress took place last Thursday and Friday at Pimville Native Township, Johannesburg, over 100 delegates attending from all parts of the Province.

The Congress discussed Native grievances, the Native Bills, and the problem of the Protectorates. The following significant resolution was passed:

"That this meeting unanimously resolves that a national convention of all African chiefs, leaders and organisations, namely, the African National Congress, Native Advisory Boards' Congress, Ikaka la Basebenzi, Communist Party, Cape Voters Association, Bantu Union, Bantu Women's League, African Vigilance Associations, Independent I.C.U., United I.C.U., I.C.U. yase Natal, Interdenominational African Ministers' Association, Joint Council of Native Ministers, African Dingaka Association, Non-European Conference, African People's Union, and other bodies, as well as representatives from Basutoland, Swaziland and Bechuanaland, be held at Bloemfontein on December 16, 1935, to consider the Government's new Native policy and the incorporation of the Protectorates."

Mr. T. M. Mapikela, the veteran speaker of the African National Congress moved this resolution as an unopposed motion after a most appealing speech to African leaders and masses to unite, and to bury all political differences in this time of national crisis. He said that too much fault-finding and criticism impeded the forward march of the African. As a result they were losing even the meagre rights they once had. It was time to put the African house in order.

Among the many Reef leaders who met in conference were Messrs. L. T. Mvabaza, C. S. Mabaso, D. T. Mweli Skota, C. Dunjwa, the Reverends S. Mdolomba, J. Mdelwa Hlongwane and Twala, all representing the T.A.C.; G. S. Mabeta, Western Native Township, African Vigilance Association; E. Mahlanza, Benoni, African Vigilance Association; S. P. Mqubuli, the Native Advisory Boards' Congress; J. B. Marks and J. Ngedlane, the Communist Party; M. M. Kotane and A. Chuenyane, Ikaka la Basebenzi; I. B. Muroe, I.C.U.; and representatives of other bodies.

Mr. Matseke, President of the T.A.C., presided.

Document 3. Resolution of the Executive Committee of the Cape Native Voters' Convention, July 13, 1935

At an emergency meeting of the executive committee of the Cape Native Voters' Convention held in East London on Saturday, July 13, for the purpose of examining the franchise proposals contained in the new Native Bills, it was unanimously resolved: —

"That the Government be asked to preserve the existing Cape Native franchise unaltered on the following grounds: —

"(1) It has always been wisely used as a voice of the Bantu people since 1854, when it was first granted.

"(2) It will be a backward step for the present Government to annul this privilege, which has never been abused at any time.

"(3) The confiscation of citizenship without rebellion or treason is an irregular and unprecedented course on the part of any modern State.

"(4) The entrenchment of the Native vote in the Union Act was a gentlemen's agreement, implying the duty of honour that is be left untouched as a privilege for future Bantu generations.

"(5) Apart from all considerations of political influence, this vote is a dearly prized symbol of citizenship—highly appreciated by its individual possessors on the lines of the dignity attaching to the traditional court of all Bantu peoples.

"(6) Its retention will make for peace and satisfaction among the various non-European elements that constitute the Union population, being, as it is, held in trusteeship for the future for all other races in the Union who aspire thereto as the consummation of true citizenship.

"(7) The representatives of the Native voters humbly request the Government authorities to give at least 12 months' time to the Native voters and other sections of the Bantu population to study the Native Bills as a whole and to be able to offer constructive criticism to the Government upon them."

Document 4. Introduction to pamphlet, *Native Views on the Native Bills*. By Professor D. D. T. Jabavu, August 1935

The Union Government has taken ten years (1925-1935) to evolve its "Native Bills" that are intended to be a permanent model for ruling its subject non-White peoples in the Union and the prospective Protectorates. The majority of the Africans vitally touched by this proposed piece of legislation have not yet seen it as it was published in English only a couple of months ago. They will understand its contents only when the latter are translated into Xhosa, Zulu, Sotho and Tswana and circulated town by town and village by village in the land. This implies that each headman, blockman and chief will have a copy of these bills in his mother-tongue, and the same done for groups like Advisory Boards and organisations of teachers, ministers, agriculturists, farmers, vigilance associations and the numerous economic and political units falling outside of tribal society. In all probability the Native Affairs Department will need four months to translate and publish these documents in the vernacular languages, and several more months during which to explain them analytically to the Bantu people concerned. The latter will thereafter require time to hold their own meetings for discussion so as to furnish their respective spokesmen with agreed views which will be tabled at a Government conference that will be summoned by the Minister for Native Affairs in 1936 or 1937 under Act 23 of 1920, the "Native Affairs

Act" that provides for Government conferences to ascertain Native opinion on all important contemplated legislation affecting Natives. This was the sensible procedure adopted in 1922 in connection with the promulgation of the 1923 Urban Areas Act; and the present bills are of much greater significance.

Our Government, like all other civilised legislative bodies, is supported by influential daily journals that defend and justify its measures good or otherwise. The case for the inarticulate Bantu is either never heard or is severely handicapped by the lack of a strong press to educate public opinion, and the only public opinion that matters for parliamentary purposes in this country is European public opinion.

This publication is a humble attempt to readjust the balance in order that the weaknesses, the injustice and the defects of the bills under consideration may be better understood. The spearpoint of these bills is universally admitted to be the abolition of the Cape Native franchise. In the name of civilisation it will be a pity if these proposals reach enactment in the statute books in their present form without their framers fully realising the political obliquity that will be reflected therefrom upon South African history. We Bantu are as much exercised as any Europeans about the prestige of South Africa in the eyes of the world of Christendom. Many Whites mistakenly think that to be their exclusive concern. The Blacks may conceivably pity the Union Government when it unwittingly embarks on a policy censured by the rest of modern civilisation, because and only because of not knowing the evil repercussions of such a policy upon the future of South Africa and Africa as a whole. And the future of South Africa will not be a happy one if it is built to-day, even through the pretext of protecting the political supremacy of the White races, on legislation designed to be unfair to the weaker Black and Coloured races.

In this pamphlet, and other successive numbers of the series, we hope to get together some expressions of views that deserve the notice of our legislators, views excerpted from various publications. Our aim in doing this is to invite co-operation, willing co-operation between the African subjects of the King and the Union Government in the construction and evolution of a policy that will make for future peace, loyalty and contentment among the diverse peoples that constitute the Union of South Africa.

Document 5. "The African Liberator, Our Message." Editorial by Gilbert Coka, in *The African Liberator*, **October 1935**

War is on. Fascism has let loose the hounds of hell. Greed and envy have their little hour. International conventions and treaties have been treated like a scrap of paper. Wars and rumours of war, are in the air. But the divinity that shapes our ends, has also brought forward the opportunity of liberty to the captive, freedom to the oppressed and opportunity to those who struggle. Of course there will be suffering and woes, but that is the rule of nature that there must be death in order that life must be. Africa is opening another era in human history. As she started the era of knowledge, culture, education, civilisation and worship, so today she commences a new era of goodwill, magnanimity and triumph.

The hour of African freedom has struck. That for which Toussaint L'Ouvertue suffered and died, that for which Frederick Douglas and Booker Washington lived and died, that for which Menelik, Shaka, Makana, Lewanika, Lobengula, Langalibalele and other great sons of Africa, lived, suffered and died for. The complete liberty of Africans to shape their own destiny in their own way, has come. The light of liberty has broken in great splendour. In the present confusion of class and national interests, the African underdog is coming to his own. Justice will have her way. Africans must be ready to take their great opportunity towards freedom. They must be prepared to act the part of men. The dreams and prophecies of Marcus Garvey, the solidarity of Africans throughout the world, is becoming a fact. And but for a few traitors, Africans had reached the land of Promise— liberty, equality, opportunity and justice.

But this good time coming, will not come of its own volition. It will be brought by Africans themselves when they purge themselves free of envy, jealousies and other manifestations of the inferiority complex which debar them from unity and solidarity. The African Liberator teaches Africans to free themselves from the bondage of poverty, prejudice and injustice. It teaches them self reliance and self help not only in one essential but in all those things that contribute towards human happiness and wellbeing. However, the unfortunate thing about us is that we take the monkey apings of our so-called distinguished men for progress. There is no progress in Africans aping Europeans and telling us that they represent the best in the race, for any ordinarily well trained monkey would do the same. The slave mentality still holds our people in chains and they firmly believe that they can only exist through the good graces of their "Masters". Before doing anything worthwhile, they must have the stamp of approval, from some European, otherwise they have no confidence in their work, thoughts and ideas. It is this spirit of "defeatism and Boyishness" secured as "good servants," rather than as independents, which makes our "men who represent their coats, suffer from lack of initiative, inferiority complexed, lying, backbiting, envious, backstairs-creepers and abject cringers" fight to death any and all independent ideas and actions calculated to uplift Africans without consulting the "good master" first. But in the bottom of their hearts, Europeans as well as other men respect Africans who work out their salvation, than throughout the whole of eternity they could ever respect the groups of helpless apes and beggars who make a monopoly of undermining themselves and their people by being "Good Boys" instead of able men. But such spineless creatures who live by deceit will not forever remain deceiving Africans and therefore cannot permanently impede African progress towards unity, liberty, justice and freedom.

The present war is destroying the Old Africa, which has been undermined for over three centuries. The new Africa is being born. The pangs of suffering attendant upon new birth will follow the bringing forth of a New Africa. But where there is courage there will be a way. Africans must unite and co-operate in their enterprises. They must spend their money where they will get fair returns. As long as they are buyers they will remain despised and powerless, but when they become sellers they will be respected. It is therefore time that Africans reorganized their economic life in order to enter into the new era. They must face the realities of life which are that Nothing can be obtained for nothing and that Money at present is the ruling power of the world. Consequently as workers, they must struggle and obtain higher wages. As buyers they must spend it for tangible returns and that can only be best done by organising consumers cooperatives in every locality. Time has come for Africans to supply themselves with the necessities of life. Our reply to War, oppresive legislation, discrimination, injustice, pauperisation, unemployment and oppression, must be "Let all African money circulate through African friends". An economic boycott against unjust and tyrannical employees, coupled with a persistent struggle for more wages and shorter working conditions, as part of a national consumers league, supplying all African buyers with the necessities of life, a national liberation movement for equal democratic rights for all South Africans irrespective of colour, creed or race and an independent National newspaper of Africans for Africans by Africans to tell truth about our conditions in the Union, will be worth tons of pious hopes.

Africans! rescue yourselves from degradation, poverty and oppression. Let every African worker be a Trade Unionist. Let every African consumer be a cooperator. African workers unite into your Trade Unions and fight for your rights. African buyers, buy from African traders, put up your cooperatives and get your biggest returns from your monies. Kill envy. Work together. Unite for the greater common good of a free Africa. Mobilise Public Opinion and struggle for "equal citizen rights", justice, liberty, freedom and opportunity of all inhabitants of South Africa irrespective of colour, creed or race. But, fellow Africans! Put your house in order. Sink petty selfish jealousies. Organise your consumers cooperatives, Organise your Trades Unions, demand your "Citizen rights," cooperate with all lovers of justice and fair play and make of Africa a land fit for the dwelling of the brave, the just, the humane, the loving, the rich, the powerful, the free and the honest as it was in ancient [times]. Smother internal jealousies, prejudice, injustice and exploitation. To be fit for a new Africa, Unite and cooperate, think and act, struggle and win.

Document 6. News Report and Resolution of the Conference of Chiefs and Leaders in the Transvaal and Orange Free State Convened by the Government, September 6-7, 1935

The conference of chiefs and leaders of the Native peoples of the Transvaal and Orange Free State, which has been in session at Pretoria on the two Native

Bills of the Prime Minister, has declined to express any definite opinion on the Bills. The conference adopted a policy of caution and passed a resolution asking for more time to consider the Bills and consult their people.

The conference, which was convened by the Government to hear the views of the Natives on the Bills, was opened yesterday morning by the Acting Minister of Native Affairs (Mr. R. Stuttaford). The morning and early afternoon were taken up by explanations of the Bills by members of the Native Affairs Commission. The conference then went into committee and discussed the Bills.

Late yesterday afternoon and yesterday evening a committee was appointed and deliberated further. This morning at noon the committee presented the following resolution: —

"As the chiefs and delegates to this conference were only given two weeks notice of the conference and were not supplied with copies of the Bills in advance, and as the policy underlying the Bills is one of political, territorial and economic segregation, and it is the intention of the Government to further amend the Natives Urban Areas Act to complete its general policy, and in view of the importance and gravity of the situation and the very limited time at the disposal of the conference, and the fact that this policy affects posterity, this conference is unable at the moment to give a matured and considered decision on the fundamental principles and details involved for the following reasons:

"(a) The chiefs and delegates were not conversant with the principles involved.

"(b) They had not time to obtain the mandate of the people they represented.

"(c) The Bills are not available in the vernacular and are, therefore, beyond the comprehension of the majority of the chiefs and delegates.

"(d) The chiefs and delegates are not at the moment in a position to visualise or locate the proposed released areas, nor do they know to what extent the released areas are occupied or owned by missionaries, Africans, or private bodies.

"(e) It is the intention of the Government to take a Native census next year and in the opinion of this conference the Native Bills should be held over until the Native population in the scheduled and released areas, and on private farms, has been ascertained through the census.

This conference therefore respectfully asks the Government: —

"(1) To translate the Bills into the various Native languages;

"(2) To appoint a mixed commission to investigate the scheduled and released areas with a view to assuring the chiefs and the public as to what areas are really and actually granted to them under the Native Trust and Land Bill;

"(3) To convene a Union conference of African chiefs and leaders during the next year to consider the whole policy of the Bills."

Three members of the conference who drafted the resolution—Chiefs Sekukuni and Manope, of the Transvaal, and Chief Charles Mopedi, of the Free State—spoke in support of the resolution and explained how they had reached the conclusions contained in the resolution.

19

"Let us not rush this thing or we will make serious mistakes," said Chief Mopedi.

Other delegates expressed themselves in complete agreement with the attitude of the committee. One of them made an appeal for the incorporation in the Government's general Native policy of a progressive education policy.

The resolution was passed unanimously.

In closing the conference Mr. D. L. Smit (Secretary for Native Affairs) said the conference had served a very useful purpose and he thought there should be similar meetings every year to consider matters concerning the welfare of the Native people. The requests contained in their resolution would be conveyed to the Government and he would use his personal influence in support of them. The resolution would receive careful consideration and they would be informed later of the Government's decision. He could quite understand that they had some difficulty in following the Bills and it was just as well that they should first discuss them with their people.

Document 7. News Report and Resolution of the Conference of Chiefs and Leaders in the Cape Province Convened by the Government, September 18, 1935

The Native Affairs Commission conference with Cape Province Natives on the Native Bills terminated when the delegates, who represent the whole Cape Province proper, passed the following resolutions, which were moved by the Paramount Chief of the Ciskei, Velile Sandile, seconded by R. H. Godlo and J. M. Dippa:

This conference welcomes the gesture of the Government in consulting Bantu opinion on the proposed legislation, and reaffirms its loyalty to the Government. On the principle placed before this conference by the Native Affairs Commission of the abolition of the Cape Native Franchise, the unanimous opinion of the conference is the unequivocal rejection of the proposal to take away the existing right to the vote. In the words of the Duke of Newcastle in 1853, 'It is the earnest desire of Her Majesty's Government that all her subjects at the Cape, without distinction of class or colour, should be united by one bond of loyalty and a common interest.' We cannot, for any consideration whatever, depart from that principle, and we see no reason for the necessity for its repeal nor making any bargain therewith. We earnestly hope the Government will refrain from its intention to remove the existing right to the franchise on the part of future descendants of the possessors of this franchise. We humbly beseech the authorities to proceed with their long overdue programme of raising the political and economic standard of the Bantu throughout the Union without stipulating that the abolition of this franchise is a quid pro quo therefor.

In answering some of the arguments advanced against our franchise, we humbly submit that

(a) Those who, in 1926, alleged that this vote was a menace to the security

20

of the White race by reason of its likelihood to swamp White voters when it was 16,000 to 185,000 White voters, while now it has dwindled to 11,000 to 400,000, are clearly in error, because the machinery regulating voting qualifications rests at all times with Parliament.

(b) It is argued now that it is being abolished because it is ineffective. We feel no need for commiseration as we are perfectly contented with it as it is.

(c) It is alleged that it engenders disrespect for Whites. This is not borne out by experience. On the contrary, loyalty to the Whites in the Cape is unsurpassed.

(d) We are told it causes irritation. Local evidence in this regard is conspicuously to the opposite.

(e) It is being abolished in order to attain uniformity. Our reply is that even in the Act of Union there are concessions to each province to retain its pre-Union traditions.

(f) We are accused of being swayed by false promises of candidates. This weakness, which is sometimes found among all electors, need not be exclusively stressed as against us.

In reply to the statement that our vote is useless, we wish to point out—

(1) That in the first instance it caused the first advance by the Whites to the Blacks, and this contact, unattained elsewhere in South Africa, produced masses of friendly Europeans acquainted with our interests by reason of this contact and common bond.

(2) It has given us an effective right and power to secure protection against much unjust projected legislation.

(3) It is directly responsible for the framing of the Native Affairs Act of 1920 with its Native conference, local councils and commission.

(4) It is the influence of this vote that secured the ear-marking of one-fifth of the poll tax for direct allocation to Native development.

(5) It has saved the Cape from the Lands Act and its harsh operation so luridly depicted in Sol. T. Plaatje's book, *Native Life in South Africa.*

(6) It killed the 1917 Native Administration Bill and thus saved all the Bantu of South Africa from a second ill-digested Lands Act.

(7) It has hung up the present Native Bills since 1926, thus keeping the door open for a future genuine franchise for the Northern Bantu.

(8) It successfully prevented the Maori system of separate representation in the Cape election of 1904 from being applied in this country with its inferior franchise based on colour discrimination.

(Note: Under the Maori system of separate Representation from which this Bill purports to be copied, the New Zealand constitution provides for a Maori native member in its Cabinet; but the South African government's proposal makes no such provision).

(9) It saved many Native farms situated in so-called neutral areas.

(10) It has kept out the pass laws when it was sought to have them introduced in 1887.

(11) It has effectively protected its possessors from the pin-pricks of the Curfew Bell Laws.

(12) It has saved us from evictions from towns and enabled us to own property therein.

(13) It has been a standing legal recognition of the fact that the citizens of one and the same country have their economic interests intertwined though they are racially and socially separate.

(14) It is a true reflex of Bantu tradition in that every man has a voice in his court (*kgotla, inkundla*), where children and females are barred.

(15) Its qualifications of property, education and money have induced us to rise in our level of civilisation generally.

(16) We have always regarded it as an honourable "gentlemen's agreement," and when we have said "thank you" for a gift we never expect the giver to return and take back what he has freely given, according to Bantu tradition.

(17) It secured and guaranteed White leadership and supremacy in that we have always been contented to follow the advice of Europeans in our exercise of the franchise and never abused it, and have never been a danger to the Whites. On the contrary, we have embellished the House of Parliament with illustrious personages like Sir James Rose-Innes, W. P. Schreiner, Merriman, Sauer, Saul Solomon, Frost, Sir Charles Crewe, Garret, Sir Bisset Berry, Fuller and Molteno.

(18) It gave us higher education and generous grants for education where those without the vote had to rely entirely on the mercy of charity and accidental benefactors.

(19) It has given us representation for our taxation exactly where our money goes.

(20) Behind this vote lie the principles of freedom, education, full-blooded citizenship, Christian benignity, and a vast loyalty to those in power, confidence in government, elimination of rebellion (for the last Xosa war was in 1853, the bestowal of the franchise in 1854 effectively abolishing all war between us and Whites), and a liberality that gave the Union Act to South Africa with its concomitants of peace and goodwill, and a definite *tertium quid* between segregation and assimilation.

(21) It forms a constitutional exemption certificate from customary law for those brought up outside of tribal law, giving a qualification that is not subject to the caprice of officials.

(22) Its conditions of a money or property qualification render it superior to manhood or womanhood suffrage because it vests power only on citizens with something to lose, a responsibility of value.

(23) The biggest danger to South Africa as a whole is not the political freedom of the Africans, but the creation to-day of a disgruntled ex-voter population in future generations, better educated than their present fathers. They will feel more grieved than we who in all conscience feel sore consternation at the gloomy prospect.

(24) The removal of this vote will resuscitate bitter feelings against the White race as a whole and compel us to identify ourselves with all anti-White propaganda, especially that already generated in all Africa by the Italo-Ethiopian conflict, this probably being the thin end of the wedge that alarmed South African White voters in the 1929 Kafir Manifesto prognostications.

(25) The abolition of our franchise will be a signal for the political declassing or degrading of the Bantu race as a whole into a sort of semi-slave or helot group of the South African population. From every conceivable point of view, this is not a step forward, but a step backward towards primitive stagnation.

With reference to Native Representative Council of the Union and the Land and Trust measures, we humbly pray that these be postponed for at least a year pending the supply of translated copies in all the vernacular tongues and the taking of the census in order that these be submitted to a Union conference under the Native Affairs Act, and that next year this conference include members returned by popular election.

Document 8. Proceedings and Resolution of the United Transkeian Territories General Council, March 30, 1936

CR. J. MOSHESH moved: "That this Council views with grave concern the Government's intention by its proposed legislation to abolish the existing form of franchise to Natives and thereby tamper with the rights of citizenship, and as this can only have the effect of undermining the good feeling between European and Native which has hitherto existed, this Council therefore expresses its profound disapproval."

The mover: Before speaking on the motion I wish to thank the Chairman very much for having shown us the picture of our beloved Queen Victoria the Good on Thursday last. I wish all to bear in mind that we are to-day dealing with a great gift that was given to us by our beloved Queen Victoria the Good, and that now the Union Parliament wishes to abolish it. I therefore call upon you one and all to think of that picture which you saw and to remember that that Queen would never give you anything that would harm you but rather that which would be for your good. I will not now go into anything new. These Bills have been before Parliament for a very very long time, but there was no way by which they could be pushed through. All sorts of plans were tried, but they seemed to fail, until at last they hit upon the idea of forming in Parliament what they call a United Party. That United Party, as the word implies, was to move as one body. That is a most unsatisfactory state of things, but there it is. Well, Government this year, or rather late last year, sent out members of Parliament to go through their districts preaching what was to take place. Gen. Smuts went through the country, and Mr. Heaton Nicholls went through the country, telling the story of the wolf and lamb, as we saw it in these parts. Government, again

23

called upon Mr. Smit, Secretary for Native Affairs, to come to Umtata and call a big meeting. Natives of all classes were called. The members of this Council were called together so that the Native mind might be properly represented. We met here in this very hall. The Secretary for Native Affairs, after having explained everything to us, retired and left us to deal with the subject. As is well-known we came to one conclusion. It is on record that we decided that we would have nothing that would shake our franchise, that we would not sell it for anything. We were willing to take what Government offered us in the way of councils and land, but those two things were not in any way to interfere with our franchise. To that was added a most remarkable speech by the Rev. Mazwi to be conveyed to Government. That was the first meeting we had called by the Secretary for Native Affairs on behalf of the Government. Our views then expressed were, I believe, placed before the Government. We were not satisfied with that. A meeting was again called by the Natives themselves which met at Bloemfontein and there were Natives there from all parts of South Africa. I am glad to say that all parts were represented, and I must here thank the three Northern provinces who said that they would not accept anything which would tamper with the Native franchise existing in the colony, though they were quite willing to take anything else that Government offered them. The resolution passed was taken to Capetown by delegates appointed by that meeting and was presented to Gen. Hertzog himself. His replies are well-known. He refused to listen to anything that was suggested to him by these delegates of ours and told them he would push on with the Bill. The delegates retired. Then came a change. The delegates came home and told us what had happened. After they had got home they were recalled to Capetown. They were not then sent down by us who sent them originally; they were called by a quite different body of people. A compromise was suggested in Capetown which was put to the Natives who were down there. The money which took these delegates there was not ours; they were not sent down by us. We therefore do not recognise them. They did not go on our behalf but on behalf of those who called them. And here, sir, I have a letter from Mr. L. D. Gilson, M. P. for Griqualand, reading:

"Dear Chief,—You will have seen by now that we have arrived at a compromise on the vital clause of the Native Franchise Bill; that is, clause I, which practically took away the franchise, as we know it now, from the Natives. The position a fortnight ago was that these Bills would definitely have been passed in their original form and the individual vote would have been gone forever. Three or four of us, including Mr. Payn and Mr. van Coller, got together and on meeting Professor Jabavu and other representative Cape Native voters we found them in full agreement with our suggestion that we should try and effect a compromise on the lines of Native constituencies being formed in the Cape whereby three European representatives in the House of Assembly with full voting powers will be elected."

24

From this you will understand that the suggestion of a compromise came from white parliamentarians and not from us. Then how can it be said that the compromise came from us? Here is a letter written to me by Mr. Gilson wherein he says the suggestion came from them. He mentions three names. They were people who were thought to be standing for the Natives in Parliament. Is it possible that they could make such a suggestion knowing very well that this compromise was going to take away our franchise, for they have been laboring all these years in order to obtain this? Is it possible for us Natives to say we are represented by these gentlemen? I say the compromise is not ours and that the people who agreed to it were not sent by us. After they had presented our views to the Prime Minister and come back they ceased to act for us. They were called down by those who called them. I therefore call this a white compromise, not a Native compromise, and this will bring about misunderstanding between European and Native. The one will not be able to trust the other, and whose handiwork is it? We are not willing under any circumstances to hand over our franchise to anybody. The only one to whom we could have given it was the giver, knowing that if she took it away she would replace it with something far better, not something that was inferior and worthless. I therefore call upon you councillors when dealing with this subject to know that the most sacred gift that we have is about to be taken away. But let it be taken honestly, not under false pretensions. Our minds are well-known; they have not changed and they will never change.

CR. L. BAM: I second. We stand up knowing full well that the matter we are dealing with is a delicate one, and we know the matter has been under consideration for a long time. But on account of its importance it does not matter how often it is discussed—it will bear it. Native opinion is like this: We were given the franchise 80 years or more ago, and Natives used it in a proper manner. We found that the vote represented two or three things which we can mention now and which are very important to us and on which the British Government depends. The vote or franchise gave us the right of citizenship in this country. Citizenship we understand to mean this, that whether you are white or black you vote for a representative who goes to Parliament; and whether you are a European or a Native, if you are qualified you become a voter and because you are a common citizen of the country you gain all the privileges so that you can make progress. To-day, with the franchise being taken away from us it means that that door is being closed against us. We think that a great privilege is being tampered with for the first time in the history of the British Government. We find that if the Government wants to force a change in this great principle it can do so on its own, but we cannot assist the Government to do that. To-day people are talking about a compromise. This compromise is a new thing suggested just recently. People were given only ten days to think over this compromise and to decide whether it was a good thing or not, and we cannot forget that it took the Government ten years to think over these

Bills. I do not think it is necessary to analyse this compromise. If there is any suggestion of a compromise Government should carry it on itself, but we will have nothing to do with it, because we hold on to our vote and cannot speak with two voices, agreeing to one thing to-day and to another the next day. It is said that under the compromise there will be a separate register for Native voters and that there will be three members of Parliament to represent our interests. We are not told that there are 150 members of Parliament altogether, and I would ask what three members will avail against 150 men? There is no provision made for an increase in the number of members to represent Native interests as the number of Native voters increases. That is why I say we are satisfied with the little we have had. We know that our minds have been confused in this matter of the vote by mixing several things not at all associated with one another. The suggestion was made to take away the vote and replace it with Native Councils and it was clear to us after examining this proposal that the councils might be even beneficial to us, but we are troubled over one difficulty, that these councils will not be given to us unless the vote is taken from us. Then we were surprised and wondered why the Government, if they aim at improving Native administration, cannot go on with the council system and leave the vote alone. We told our member of Parliament that we were grateful for the Council system, but that the vote should be allowed to remain. Again, certain suggestions are made to vote certain sums of money for us to buy land. That also interferes with us in this matter because in 1913 the Government promised to give us additional land. But the Government did not do that. Several commissions were appointed to investigate land matters but their recommendations were shelved and no action taken on them. To-day when a promise is made of additional land, it is brought along with the proposal to take away our vote, whereas we are still waiting for the Government to carry out its original promise of land and to give us that land because, as we claim to be common citizens with Europeans, we are entitled to land. Government should give us land in a good position and on suitable conditions. We are very depressed that the promises made have not been fulfilled, and we do not know whether there is any truth in the latest promise to provide land. We know that the motive behind all this is segregation, but it seems to us that this segregation is discriminating. It deprives one section, but not the other section, and thus it ceases to be complete segregation. It becomes class legislation and we, being the under-dogs, are the sufferers. We do not understand why the Government should make all these conditions and take away all these rights from us. If Government is sincere in its segregation scheme we contend that on the Native side the Government should open higher positions to Natives so that they can advance as far as they can. Some who hear us speak like this will say we are only being ambitious. We know from reading books and from what people have told us that South Africa is not the only British colony. There are other British colonies in the world and we understand that the Governments of these colonies are different from what it is in this country. We know that in the Gold Coast a

26

Native with the required qualifications can rise to be even a judge. But that does not obtain in this country. We can go on and make comparisons, for instance the treatment of Natives in French colonies. The Government must give us what is suitable for us and leave intact what we have already got and which we prize highly. One of the Empire builders, Cecil Rhodes, said this: "Equal rights for all civilised men south of the Zambesi."

CR. E. QAMATA: Much has been said in connection with this Bill, and I do not want to touch on points that have been already raised. What is it that makes Government and the European public act in this way? The answer is given by the white nation themselves. They say they fear the black man. I am surprised that after hundreds of years of working together the white man should say he is afraid of the Native. The Prime Minister says they have to take away the Native vote in order to protect the white people, yet he has every reason to know that their position would never be interfered with and he quotes from the Bible to support his intention. I do not know whether what he says from the Bible is correct, but Jesus Christ who brought Christianity into the world said we must love one another. What did Jesus Christ do when one of His disciples cut off the ear of one of the servants of the high priests? He ordered His disciple to put it back; if it were necessary he would get his protection from God. This is the view of Christ, who introduced Christianity. That being the case I cannot see how Western civilisation and Christianity can be defended at the expense of other people. And I fail to see how one in this connection can hide behind Holy Scripture. What does the Government say it is going to give us? It says it will give us money to buy land, but we do not know the value of the land it is going to give us. If one looks at the areas scheduled they will find they have already been inhabited by Natives. The Prime Minister was asked to give us time to think things out, but that request was refused. What can we say that will move them not to take away our rights? I appeal to the white people of this country, as we were told by General Smuts that it was the white people's intention that this vote should be taken away. We have had this right for a good many years. What is wrong that the franchise should now be taken away? Even European women have the right to vote. Is it not sufficient protection that in order to vote a Native must have certain educational and other qualifications? I appeal to the white people in this respect. Let us view this from another angle and ask, are we not loyal enough to the Government? Even in voting Natives have never made any trouble. In a matter of this kind it is difficult to find words to express what we want to say. Whatever else the Government may do we will never agree to have our rights taken away.

CR. G. DANA: When we discuss this matter it is well that we go back to the convention from which resulted the Union of South Africa before we can deal with things that are happening to-day. Everyone knows what happened at the National Convention. The Native vote in the Cape Colony was a great pact at the convention and everyone knows what the European statesmen who attended

27

that convention did. If they had known that the Union Government in 1926 would produce these Native Bills, the Cape Colony would never have joined the Union. I quote from a statement made by the late Mr. J. W. Jagger. When we ask what was the meaning of the provision of the two-thirds majority, I would reply by saying a petition was sent from this country to England to present the draft constitution before the British Parliament. The late King Edward made recommendations that if any law should be introduced affecting the Cape Native franchise that it would be reserved for him so that he could use his powers of veto. But the Union proceeded to deal with this matter with great wisdom by combining the two big parties and passing the Status Act of 1934, which states that on all matters South African the King would be advised by his South African ministers. The King's power of veto was taken away by that provision and the door was open for the Union Government to do what it liked with the Native vote. To-day the Native vote is being separated from the European vote. That means that the interests of Natives and Europeans are different, and that is not true. It is proposed to give us four senators, three members of Parliament and a Union Native Council in place of the Native vote. We pay direct and indirect taxes and those monies are in the hands of the House of Assembly. How are these senators going to represent us when our money is in the hands of the House of Assembly? The period of tenure of the senators is fixed by law. They are not appointed by the people. To come to the Native Council promised us, I liken it to a can that is said to contain water when it is practically empty. This Union Council will have no funds like the United Transkeian Territories General Council, and there is nothing to bind future parliaments to carry on the traditions of the present Parliament. No people will reach the standard we have reached by exercising the powers only of advisory boards. Gen. Smuts said that this council was not going to be made a legislative body but only a body advisory to the Government in regard to Native matters, but that in time the Government would consider whether to give it legislative powers or not. Natives are in a majority compared with Europeans. This Union Government is known as a democratic government. If that is true it is strange that we should be represented by three members when the Europeans are represented by 150. That could never satisfy the Natives of South Africa. The decision of the conference held at Bloemfontein was to reject these Native Bills, and I am sure that the opinion of the Native people expressed at Bloemfontein is the opinion of the Native people at home.

THE CHAIRMAN: I would like to remind councillors, that this is not a political meeting. I have allowed discussion on this matter not so that you could give expression to your political convictions but to enable this Council as representing the people of these territories, to send its message to the Government. I think it would be better if members confined themselves to that aspect of the matter.

CR. T. NTINTILI: All the points have been mentioned by the previous speakers and we should not make any more long speeches. We should only deal with a few points in order to show that we are of one opinion in this matter. Many years ago Queen Victoria, whose picture, sir, you showed us the other day, sent out instructions. Even if they were not issued directly by herself, yet she signed them. They told the people in this country that whatever steps they took should be such as to place all the people on one level, and we are of opinion that the Union Government has deviated from those instructions, for the reasons stated by previous speakers. At the time of the visit of the Secretary for Native Affairs to Umtata to interpret the aims and objects of the Native Bills, in our reply we asked for time in order that we could consider the Bills and we even stated that a year thereafter a convention should be called for us. The All-Africa convention held at Bloemfontein made a similar request and we sent delegates to interview the Prime Minister. This is what surprised us. When we asked for time to consider the request it was not granted. Is it right that when you give a man something that is good you do not give him time so that he can think over it? We ask ourselves the question, what interests of Government will suffer if Government gives us time to think over the Bills? Probably that is why we think that Government is prompted by fear. We are only guessing from what we see in the papers. We have read the speeches delivered on this matter. Another thing that surprised us was spoken by the councillor on the other side of the chamber, when we were thinking that these Bills were made in the interests of Natives and to protect their interests. We find the statement that these Bills were made to protect European civilisation so that it may not be swept away by the Native people. We are surprised and wonder why the Bills are being hurried through. We should have understood if Government had given the Native people time to consider. When the Government introduces legislation affecting our votes it combines it with Native councils and land. We do not know where we stand. We are not complaining about Native Councils and the land proposals, because we know these things are what we require and that they will be of benefit to us. We are expressing the opinion that we are not prepared to associate ourselves with the present Bill. We are restraining ourselves in our speeches because we feel we must not become heated with the Government.

CR. J. XAKEKILE: I am glad to have the opportunity to say something on this matter. A great deal has been said already by members of the Council. I will only deal with a few points that they have not touched on. This is a painful matter to the Native. A matter like lands is bound up with certain entrenched privileges conferred on us by Queen Victoria, who found it fit to give the right to vote to Native and European alike. I know from experience that this country has advanced a great deal from very humble beginnings. Since the time the Cape Parliament was first constituted it has been composed of members elected by both European and Native voters. The Native carried out all his duties in trying to advance this country, and when it was sought to appoint representatives to further the work of civilisation the Native also had a share. No one can deny the fact that the Native never abused his vote, but used it properly. They appointed European men like Rose Innes, Sauer, Molteno, Solomon, and Native votes assisted in their election. Those were the men who bore the burden trying to uplift this country. How can people be deprived of their rights without any reason? It is clear that the suggested compromise has not emanated from the Natives. When the Government sent a certain commission round the country it seemed that Government was trying to find means to make the Natives speak with different voices. Again it is clear that the Government undertook the matter in the assurance that it would have a two-thirds majority if it formed the United Party. Therefore there is nothing to lead to the conclusion that it was the Native people who suggested the compromise. Government should be clear on this matter, because this is class legislation. Only people of a certain colour are discriminated against. The Native is not to blame for being black; if anybody is to blame it is God. We should be very glad if the Government could find another way to deal with this matter.

CR. P. XABANISA: We complain about being deprived of the vote because it gave the right to Natives to appoint a European as a member of Parliament whom they knew was a man of justice. Even to-day we still have Europeans full of justice and who have sympathy with the Native. That is our complaint that we are being ousted from the main voters' roll. To say it is being exchanged for something else is not true, because we have been given nothing. This council that we have been promised is already in existence under Act 23 of 1920, where it is stated that Councils would be introduced in all the provinces in South Africa. All that we were expecting was offered when that law was to be applied. We are surprised that Government should suggest an exchange or purchase price because we already had what was proposed. What sort of a man would he be who came to buy an ox and gave you in payment a horse that was already yours? Again, this vote is sought to be purchased with land. We already have a law about land—the 1913 Act. The Beaumont Commission was sent out to divide the land so that Natives would be on one side and Europeans on the other side. The Scully Commission was sent out for the same purpose and the Stanford Commission came to this country to do the same work. The Government must know our natural right in the land as being the Native people of this country, and that is why we say that an Act for the diversion of land is already in existence. How can it be proposed to pay us with that for our vote? The Native in this country finds it hard to follow the policy in this regard. I could have spoken much longer on this subject. Cr. Sakwe was present at the conference at Umtata and at the convention at Bloemfontein and was sent to be our representative at Capetown, and if I am in order to make the request I would ask that he address the Council.

THE CHAIRMAN: I think we have discussed the motion at quite sufficient length, and it might be embarrassing to Cr. Sakwe to mention things dealt with at Capetown. The discussion is not on what has taken place but to bring to the notice of Government what are the feelings of the people of these territories.

The motion was carried unanimously.

THE ALL AFRICAN CONVENTION

Document 9. The All African Convention Proceedings and Resolutions of the AAC, December 15-18, 1935

(1) THE FRANCHISE BILL

On Clause 1 of the Representation of Natives Bill, the following Resolution was moved by Mr. H. Selby Msimang (Transvaal), seconded by Rev. A. Mtimkulu (Natal), that:—(Preamble)

"In the opinion of this national convention of African chiefs and other leaders, the policy of political segregation of the White and Black races embodied in the Representation of Natives in the Senate Bill is not calculated to promote harmony and peace between the two races, for the logical outcome of its operation will be the creation of two nations in South Africa, whose interests and aspirations must inevitably clash in the end and thus cause unnecessary bitterness and political strife. The political segregation of the two races can only be justly carried out by means of the creation of separate States, and this, besides being undesirable and impracticable, is not contemplated under the Land and Trust Bill.

"The denial to the African people of participation in the government of the country of which they are an integral part, on the basis of common citizenship, is not only immoral and unjust, but will inflame passions and fertilize the soil on which propagandists will sow the seeds of discontent and unrest.

"The danger of denying to a people the right to work through constitutional channels for the improvement of its conditions is supported by the history of European countries, particularly in the first half of the nineteenth century.

"Another principle of these Native Bills is to set up the White man as the trustee of the African people, and to relegate the African people permanently to the position of a child race.

"This ought to mean that the Europeans are exercising, in the interests of the African, a disinterested tutelage for as long as this population is itself unable to take care of its welfare. The principle further implies that the trustee himself has no interest in the affairs he is administering, beyond the welfare of the ward. But where the White man forms part of the permanent population, as is the case in South Africa, the conflict of interests militates against the utmost good faith which a trustee ought to show in the discharge of his duties and responsibilities.

"Under such circumstances this convention is convinced that the only policy which will adequately safeguard the vital interests of both sections is one based

31

on the principle of partnership. This principle of partnership should find expression in all the councils of the State.

"The common assumption that the South African conception of trusteeship is identical with that evolved and pursued in her colonies by Great Britain we believe is erroneous and misleading. The policy followed by Great Britain in her possessions and protectorates is that of trusteeship, to be eventually superseded by full partnership, viz., responsible government and Dominion status, as is instanced by the development of the relations between Great Britain and India. This is the direction in which British administration in Nigeria, the Gold Coast, Uganda and Tanganyika has moved and is moving. In these territories, where African interests are paramount in theory and very largely in practice, there are no rights, duties and obligations which are closed to Africans merely on the grounds of race or colour.

"The hope that the paramountcy of African interests will be achieved in the segregation areas dotted all over the country is diametrically opposed to the facts of the South African situation. In a country like South Africa, where the interests of the racial groups are inextricably interwoven, the attempt to deal with them separately is bound to defeat its own objects, and the placing of the destinies of the under-privileged groups in the hands of one dominant group, however well intentioned, is fundamentally wrong and unjust.

"In the light of the above considerations, the convention is convinced that the only way in which the interests of the various races which constitute the South African nation can be safeguarded is by the adoption of a policy of political identity. Such a policy will ensure the ultimate creation of a South African nation in which, while the various racial groups may develop on their own lines, socially and culturally, they will be bound together by the pursuit of common political objectives.

"The convention contends that this object can only be achieved by the extension of the rights of citizenship to all the groups.

"The idea that the granting of full political rights to the African people would constitute a menace to the peaceful development of the Union of South Africa is disproved by the history of the Cape Colony prior to Union. In that Colony the wars and racial friction which prevailed between White and Black prior to the enfranchisement of the non-Europeans may be contrasted with the harmonious and peaceful relations which had characterised the contact of the racial groups during the last seventy-five years.

"We recognise that the exercise of political rights in a democratic State demands the possession, on the part of those who enjoy them, of a reasonable measure of education and material contribution to the economic welfare of the country.

"The convention is therefore not opposed to the imposition of an education or property or wage qualification, as a condition for the acquirement of political privileges, and believes that such measures would adequately protect the interests of the White population in whose favour the dice are already heavily loaded

32

in view of the extension of adult suffrage to White men and women. In short, we believe that a civilisation test, such as was contemplated at the National Convention in 1909-1910, is equitable; but that the criterion of race or colour, which is implied in these Bills, is contrary to democratic government and is calculated to engender and provoke feelings of hostility and ill-will between White and Black.

"This convention is therefore opposed to the abolition of the Cape Native franchise and reiterates its firm conviction that the Cape Native franchise is a matter of such vital importance to all the African people of South Africa that it cannot bargain or compromise with the political citizenship of the African people by sacrificing the franchise, as is proposed in the Representation Bill. On the contrary, the Convention believes that the time has arrived for the immediate granting of the individual franchise to Africans in the northern provinces.

"The Convention enjoins all African inhabitants of the Union to observe Sunday, January 19, as a day of universal humiliation and intercession in their places of worship, public gatherings and private abodes. Prayers must be offered up for the Almighty's guidance and intervention in the dark cloud of the pending disfranchisement of the Cape Natives by the Parliament of South Africa.

"This convention makes a direct appeal to the honourable members of the Senate of the Union legislature, nominated by the Government for their special knowledge of the reasonable wants and wishes of the Native population, and to the members of the House of Assembly to make strenuous efforts in opposing the passage of the clause that disfranchises the Cape Natives in the Representation of Natives in Parliament Bill and otherwise to use their vote to defeat other objectionable features in the Native Bills.

"Furthermore, that the Governor-General, in his capacity as chief executive officer of His Majestys' Government in this country, be requested to refrain from assenting to the passage of this clause, if passed by the joint session of Parliament.

"This convention feels that it is imperative to appeal to His Majesty King George V and the Parliament of Great Britain, as the present representatives of the original beneficent donors of the Cape Native franchise, for an expression of their opinion in the event of such treasured gift being abrogated by His Majesty's Government in the Union of South Africa without reason.

"This convention commends the policy adumbrated in the present Native Bills to the close study of African inhabitants in the protectorates of Basutoland, Bechuanaland and Swaziland, particularly in regard to the proposed future incorporation of such protectorates in the Union."

The resolution on the franchise question was put to the convention and carried unanimously.

The following resolution, moved by Mr. L. T. Mtimkulu, was carried:—

"This convention resolves:—

"(1) That the resolutions on the Representation of Natives Bill and Native Land and Trust Bill be submitted to Parliament by a deputation of Africans during the next session of Parliament.

33

"(2) The said deputation to present the viewpoint of the African National Convention held at Bloemfontein on December 16 at the bar of the House of Assembly.

"(3) That it be an instruction to the deputation to submit to Parliament the contention that, in the opinion of this convention, no permanent or peaceful solution of the franchise or land question is possible unless it is the result of mutual agreement between representatives of White and Black races, which is only possible by means of a round-table or similar conference.

"This conference therefore respectfully requests the Government to consider the advisability of taking steps in the direction of calling together such a conference."

Mr. C. Kadale [Kadalie] (East London) said that past experience had shown that it was futile to ask for deputations to meet the Government. In case another failure should be met with, he suggested that at the conclusion of the convention the meeting should not be closed, but stand adjourned. Thus the convention would be in a position to deal with any eventuality that might arise in future.

Mr. J. Gunas [Gomas] (Cape Town) moved that the delegates to the convention should be instructed to form committees in the towns and villages to organise protest meetings. Success could only be obtained on the basis of the mass organisation of the people to carry on the struggle for the rights and liberties of the non-Europeans of South Africa.

N.B.—All the above resolutions were passed with absolute unanimity, there being not a single dissentient, in the Convention sessions. In the committee on the Council bill the voting was 26 in favour of the resolution with 3 against. The harmony of the Convention was remarkable, when one considers its conflicting elements of extremists, die-hards, moderates and those who actually favoured the Bills. (President)

(2) UNION NATIVE REPRESENTATIVE COUNCIL

On the Union Representative Council Bill the following finding of the convention's committee dealing with resolutions was submitted to the convention in the form of a resolution:

"The proposals for the establishment of the Union Representative Council are not acceptable to this convention, for they are a substitute for the Cape Native franchise. This convention holds that the Government has the machinery provided for by the Native Affairs Act No. 28 of 1920, which is capable of improvement, through which the Government has power to consult the African people on matters and legislation affecting their interests.

"The convention urges the Government, therefore, to proceed with the establishment of the local councils in the Union under the 1920 Act and any amendments thereof."

Mr. R. H. Godlo (East London), moving the adoption of the resolution, said

34

that the Natives had found much that was good in the existing local council movement, which could be extended; but the establishment of a new national council as contemplated in the Native Bills could not be accepted as a quid pro quo for the vote.

Dr. P. ka I. Seme seconded.

Mr. L. Mtimkulu (Lady Frere) pointed out that the formation of local councils was dependent on the wishes of local communities. He advocated the deletion of the last sentence of the committee's finding. To this the convention agreed.

The resolution was carried with the following in place of the deleted portion: "This convention is strongly opposed to the creation of another colour bar in the Provincial Councils under the guise of the Provincial Council representation of Natives, as contemplated under the proposed Representation of Natives in Parliament Bill. The system of representation in vogue in the Cape Provincial Council, where there are no restrictions on the participation of non-Europeans in Provincial Council matters is, in the opinion of this convention, a model which might well be adopted in the provincial systems of other provinces, as well as by the Union Parliament itself."

(3) NATIVE LAND AND TRUST BILLS

In introducing a number of proposals in connection with the Native Land and Trust Bill, Dr. A. B. Xuma said that the Bills were a thorn in the side of South Africa. Land was the most important item in the life of a nation, and even aeroplanes, in spite of the wonders they performed, had to come down to the ground. The proposals he had to make were the outcome of the consideration of the executive committee of the convention.

The proposals, which were passed without opposition, were as follows:—

"This national convention of chiefs and other representative leaders of the Bantu people regards the proper adjustment of the land problem as fundamental to the so-called 'Native question,' and therefore welcomes the attempt of the Government to deal with this matter.

"At the same time the convention wishes to point out that the efforts of the Government in this direction are vitiated by the gross inadequacy of the morgenage of seven and a quarter millions which it is proposed to set out as a maximum amount of land to be acquired by the Natives' land trust to be established under the Bill.

"When it is further borne in mind that, even if this morgenage were to be made available under the Bill, it would secure to the Native population only about 17 million morgen of the total morgenage of 143,000,000 in the Union, the failure to take into account the future needs of an increasing Native population will be realised.

"The true aim of land adjustment, we maintain, should be to provide the bulk of the Native population, which is predominantly rural, with sufficient land to allow of their making a livelihood.

"The fact that this aim is ignored by the Native Land and Trust Bill can only be interpreted by the African people as a vague attempt to force them out of their reserves into a position of economic dependency.

"In connection with chapter IV of the Native Land and Trust Bill, this convention desires to point out that the problems of labour, tenancy, squatting, and so on, are a direct result of the inadequacy of the amount of land set aside for Native occupation.

"Further, this convention is convinced that the restrictive provisions of this chapter are not only unnecessary but negative in effect, and the convention urges the Government to drop this whole chapter in the Bill and to take as a first step:—

"(a) A Union census of the Native population in order to ascertain the distribution and number of the Native people in the following areas: (1) The Native reserves and privately-owned Native lands; (2) Squatters, labour tenants or servants on European farms; (3) The proposed released areas;

"(b) The convention urges the Government to appoint a mixed commission to investigate the ownership of the proposed released areas.

"This convention is of the opinion that only after these facts have been ascertained would it be possible to determine with any degree of accuracy the actual amount of land which is being made available for African occupation under the Land Bill.

"This convention welcomes the suggestion of the establishment of a South African Native trust, but recommends that the powers of such a trust be definitely defined, and further urges the Government that, in the event of the Bill becoming law, definite financial provision be made to enable the trust to secure sufficient land for the needs of the African people within five years from the date of the commencement of the Act, and also adequate additional funds to enable the proposed South African Land Trust to carry out its functions."

In seconding the motions, Mr. H. Selby Msimang (general secretary) claimed that the Native legislation had been undertaken in the dark and there was no intention on the part of the Government to grant more land to the Natives. The 7¼ million morgen of land had been set aside without any knowledge of the size of the population affected. In 1926, he stated, General Smuts had said that the reserves were over-crowded and that there were up to 9,000 squatters who would have to leave the land they occupied. He asked what had the 7¼ million morgen been released for and how many African families would be able to get accommodation there? If the scheduled areas were crowded where would the surplus population go? There was not sufficient ground to accommodate the Native population.

Mr. Msimang hoped that some relief would follow the release of the 7¼ million morgen, but he claimed that this area would be given to the Natives, for land that had been placed on the schedules before 1913 as being Native-owned was now being released for Native occupation under the Bill. He mentioned a case in the Transvaal where a chief's farm—property which had been bought by the tribe and scheduled before 1913—was being released today. He requested that a commission be appointed to find out if the Natives were really getting any new land.

There seemed to have been a conspiracy against the Native people, Mr. Msimang continued, with the object of condeming them to everlasting economic slavery.

More than a million Natives were living on the farms of Europeans under conditions bordering on slavery. They were called squatters, labour tenants or servants, but they received no pay. The labour tenants received strips of land to plough instead of payment and the farmers made sure that each received not more than ten bags of grain out of the land. This they accomplished by keeping the tenants busy with their work, with the result that the Natives either had to plough very late at night, or early in the morning. When weeding had to be done, the tenant's wives were needed by the employer for housework.

Chapter four of the Bill stated that the squatters would have to leave the land within ten years and after that period each farmer who wished to keep a squatter would have to pay a licence fee. The labour tenant, however, only had to be registered under the name of the farmer. The Bill did not say what protection would be granted to the interests of the labour tenant. The farm owner would have the right to use the tenant's oxen without payment (chorus of dissent from the gathering) and he would also be able to take the milk from the tenant's cows. All this tended to drive the labour tenant off the land.

Where would this man go, Mr. Msimang asked. Would he try to enter service in the towns? A Government Commission had been appointed to seek means of driving the Native out of the towns and to keep him out.

There was no room in the scheduled areas. No land could be given by the Trust. The result would be that the Native would have to surrender to the nearest person who would give him food.

The Rev. Z. R. Mahabane predicted the outbreak of a revolution in South Africa. The Europeans, he said, underrated the intelligence of the Natives and although there were only about two million White people in the Union they were appropriating 80 per cent of the land—the land that had been the birthright of the Natives. In addition the Europeans were creating further reasons for discontent among the Natives.

Speaking as a man who occupied a position of grave responsibility among the community, Mr. Mahabane claimed that the trend of Native legislation in South Africa was definitely going to lead to a Native revolution. He could see a revolt coming unless the policy with regard to the Natives was drastically altered.

Other speakers claimed that the Government was taking the land of the Natives and returning it to them as a gift. It was true that under the Native

37

Lands Bill nothing had been given to the people in the Free State. Others again suggested that the poll tax should be written off, as had been done in the case of the debts of the farmers.

(4) GRIEVANCES FROM OPPRESSIVE LAWS

Mr. F. H. M. Zwide (Port Elizabeth) seconded by Mr. Marks (Johannesburg) moved the following omnibus resolution on repressive legislation:—

"(1) That, as a direct result of repeated and unfair declarations by members of the Government and others to the effect that Africans are a menace in this country, a stigma has been cast and gullibly received in South Africa, to the detriment of the aborigines.

"(2) That since then and until today the trend of legislation has been inclined to oppression and repression. Laws like the Riotous Assemblies Act, the Native Service Contract Act, the Poll Tax Act and the Pass Laws are oppressive.

"(3) The convention feels that the Union Government has not regarded the Union Africans as part and parcel of the community of South Africa.

"(4) That the continual discrimination, politically and economically, has tended to emasculate the Africans and to relegate them to a position bordering on slavery.

"(5) That, whereas compensation and consideration have been extended towards the White community by way of pensions, a White labour policy, the remission and alleviation of taxation, Land Bank assistance to farmers, the supply of milk to White children out of public revenue, the minimum wage determinations, compensation for South African War losses, and facilities for White education, very little of the legislation in this country has been devoted to assure Union Africans of their citizenship in a democratic country like South Africa.

"(6) That Union Africans have been treated like aliens in their own country.

"(7) That this attitude of the Government has grievously violated and injured our susceptibilities, and we now pray, as His Majesty's loyal subjects who have been patient 'like asses' and loyal despite all these disabilities, that His Majesty's Government should consider the redress of these grievances and alleviate the Black man's lot.

"(8) That this convention fully and firmly believes that the prosperity and progress of South Africa lies solely in the contentment of each and every one of its population, irrespective of colour or creed."

This was passed unanimously.

(5) PROPOSED WOMEN'S ORGANISATION

During the congress the women delegates met and adopted a resolution expressing admiration of the stand taken by the convention. "We feel," the resolution continued, "that the time has come for the establishment of an African Council of Women on lines similar to those of the national councils of other races, in order that we may be able to do our share in the advancement of our race."

This was adopted and registered as a Convention Resolution.

(6) CONVENTION ORGANISATION

It was further resolved and unanimously agreed that

"(a) This Convention is from henceforth an organised body.

(b) That the present Executive Committee is empowered to act until the next meeting of the Convention.

(c) That the present Executive Committee draft a Constitution to be circulated among the delegates, the constituent organisations, and the African press in preparation for discussion, amendment and adoption at the next Convention meeting.

(d) That in the hands of the Executive Committee be left all Convention matters such as the collections of Convention funds, the appointment and despatch of necessary delegations to the Government, and the summoning of next Convention meeting.

(e) That collections be made from the public in lists endorsed by the signature of the President and all such funds to be sent to and deposited with the Convention Treasurer, Dr. J. S. Moroka, P.O. Thaba Nchu, O.F.S., cheques being crossed 'All African Convention per Dr. J. S. Moroka.'

(f) That the total funds aimed at be five million shillings—to correspond to the five million Bantu people—for the propagation of the purposes of the Convention as described in the Regulations."

[The delegates hereupon paid a shilling each, amounting to £17 and it was urged that shilling collections be made at home in all towns and villages, specially by Chiefs, from all sympathisers with the movement.]

(7) URBAN AREAS

Another resolution adopted was as follows:—

"The projected amendment of the Natives (Urban Areas) Act threatens to disorganise everything already initiated by urban Africans in the way of self-development. This is occurring at a time when no real efforts are being made to remove the causes of the drift to the towns of the rural African families. Therefore this convention respectfully and yet strongly urges the Government to desist from introducing further legislation that disturbs the progress already initiated by Africans in the urban areas."

(8) THE PERMIT SYSTEM

Another resolution read:—

"The convention learns from reliable sources that wholesale arrests are being made in Reef municipal locations as a result of the unexpected reintroduction of the permit system. The convention respectfully requests the Minister of Native Affairs to order a halt of these arrests until the leaders of the people have had the opportunity of studying the situation and making representation to the authorities." This was passed.

(9) DISEASES

Dr. G. H. Gool, of Cape Town, proposed that the Government investigate the health position of non-Europeans in South Africa, as reflected in the high death-rate from certain preventable diseases and take the necessary steps to remedy this state of affairs. The convention also recommended the establishment of National Councils of African Women in all parts of South Africa. Agreed.

(10) DEPUTATION

A deputation consisting of a representative from each province will go to Cape Town to interview the Minister of Native Affairs (Mr. P. G. Grobler) and to present to him the resolutions of the convention. Agreed.

SUMMARY OF PROCEEDINGS

The attendance numbered about 400 delegates, there being 30 from Natal, 70 from the Orange Free State, 100 from the Transvaal, 200 from the Cape (including British Bechuanaland and the Transkei Territories), 10 from Basutoland and one from Swaziland.

The delegates arrived on Sunday morning, 15th December, 1935, and registered with the local committee at the office of Mr. T. M. Mapikela, the Chief Headman of all the Bloemfontein locations.

At 11 a.m. the Convention religious service was conducted by the Rev. Abner Mtimkulu of Durban, and at noon Professor Jabavu was unanimously elected Chairman of the preliminary meetings in preparation for the official commencement on Dingaan's Day, and the sub-committees started straightway to work at the four draft bills.

The committees, confirmed on Monday, were the following:—

1. *Executive Committee of the Convention :—*

President :   Professor D. D. T. Jabavu (Fort Hare, Cape).
Vice-President :   Dr. A. B. Xuma, M.D., B.Sc. (Johannesburg).
General Secretary: H. Selby Msimang (Johannesburg).

Record Secretary :	R. H. Godlo (East London).
Clerk-Draughtsmen :	Z. K. Matthews, M. A., LL.B., (Amanzimtoti, Natal).
	S. D. Ngcobo, B.A. (Amanzimtoti, Natal).
Treasurer :	Dr. J.S. Moroka, M.B., Ch.B., (Thaba Nchu, O.F.S.).
Committee Members :	All Chiefs ex-officio, and
(a) Natal :	Rev. J. L. Dube (Phoenix).
	Rev. A. S. Mtimkulu (Durban).
	W. W. Ndlovu (Vryheid).
	A. W. G. Champion (Durban).
	J. Kambule (Ladysmith).
(b) O.F.S. :	C. R. Moikangoa (Bloemfontein).
	Keable Mote (Kroonstad).
	R. A. Sello (Kroonstad).
	R. Cingo, B.A. (Kroonstad).
	T. M. Mapikela (Bloemfontein).
(c) Transvaal :	R. V. Selope Thema (Johannesburg)
	L. T. Mvabaza (Johannesburg)
	P. A. M. Bell (Johannesburg)
	T. D. Mweli Skota (Johannesburg).
	E. T. Mofutsanyana (Pretoria).
(d) Cape :	Rev. Z. R. Mahabane (Kimberley).
	C. K. Sakwe (Idutywa).
	Alex. M. Jabavu (King William's Town).
	J. M. Dippa (Port Elizabeth).
	P. Mama (Cape Town).

2. *Franchise Committee:* A. M. Jabavu (Convener), C. K. Sakwe, R. H. Godlo, J. S. Mazwi, J. M. Dippa, Ch. Jer. Moshesh, L. G. E. Bam, Z. R. Mahabane, Dr. Molema, Rev. A. Mtimkulu, Rev. E. Mdolomba, Dr. Xuma, T. M. Mapikela, Ch. H. Bikitsha, A. W. G. Champion.

3. *Land Committee:* Ch. W. Kumalo (Convener), Dr. Moroka, Dr. Seme, Ch. C. Mopeli, L. T. Mvabaza, P. A. Bell, A. Mazingi, W. M. Ndlovu, Rev. J. L. Dube, T. Poswayo, P. T. Xabanisa, J. Madupuna, H. Msimang, Dr. Moroka, W. P. Mlandu, J. Marks.

4. *Council Committee:* E. C. Bam (Convener), G. Dana, M. Balfour, H. Ntintili, Rev. R. M. Tunzi, N. S. P. Matseko, S. D. Ngcobo, J. Mpanza, Ch. I. Mgudlwa, S. P. Mqubuli, Rev. J. Likhong, C. Moikangoa, Tsala, Kambule, G. Dana, Tsoai, Motshabi, Lebere, Molaltou, Ramailane.

The Convention was officially opened at 9:30 a.m. by His Worship the Mayor of Bloemfontein, Mr. A. C. White, who, after welcoming the delegates to Bloemfontein, expressed the hope that they would find time to inspect the amenities offered to the Natives of Bloemfontein's locations. He referred to the seven schools in the location, the Y.M.C.A., the thirty churches and the bioscope. He told of the Town Council's decision to spend £1,000 on a new Native dispensary, and £20,000 on the improvement of the sanitary conditions of the locations and the negotiations now in progress between the Town Council and the Provincial Administration for the allocation of £20,000 to be used for the erection of new schools in the locations....

In a brief address to the delegates, Mr. J. R. Cooper, superintendent of Bloemfontein's Native Administration Department, who had been called on by the Chairman and described as the most popular location superintendent in the Union, expressed the opinion that the failure to administer Native affairs with satisfactory success in some centres could be attributed to three facts: (a) A need for machinery to enable consultation and co-operation between the location inhabitants and the local authorities; (b) the fact that many location inhabitants did not take a lively interest in their own welfare; (c) the absence of support for the members of the Native Advisory Board after their election.

Thanking the Mayor and Mr. Cooper, Professor Jabavu said that the delegates to this, the most representative convention of Natives in the history of South Africa, had not come on a joyful errand, but "with sorrow deeply embedded in our hearts."

The tendency today was to enforce legislation on the Natives without consulting them as citizens of the Union. The object of the convention was to give expression to Native opinion and to show the need for consulting it. Members of Parliament, sitting in comfortable chairs in Parliament, thought of the Natives only in connection with matters such as the vote and other theoretical things and ignored the economic straits into which the Natives had fallen and their famines and hardships. The convention was intended to show that the Native was sufficiently developed and educated to be worthy of consultation on matters affecting his own well being and existence.

The convention got down to business in the afternoon when Professor Jabavu gave his address from the chair....

On the conclusion of this address, some telegrams were read to the convention, loud applause being evoked by one from Moscow exhorting the Natives of South Africa to set about their historic task and assist in the struggle of the Negro peoples against exploitation and oppression.

The following submitted as an unopposed motion by Mr. Keable Mote (Kroonstad), was carried: "This convention vigorously protests against the predatory war carried on by Fascist Italy against the relatively unarmed Abyssinian people, and pledges itself to do all in its power to support Abyssinia in her gallant and heroic struggle against the Italian invasion. Further, the convention calls upon the League to impose all sanctions, even up to the point of forming a military bloc against the aggressive Fascist Italy. The convention feels that the present war may serve as a prelude to an Imperialist world war. Thus it appeals to the Africans to realise the imminence of a world war, and to do all they can to struggle against such a danger."

The Rev. John Dube (Natal) said that the Natives of South Africa were passing through a crisis. These Bills were supposed to be the basis of the Government's policy towards the Natives. They were thus of vital importance. In Natal the Natives had passed a resolution urging that their introduction should be deferred, pending their being submitted to a national Native council for full consideration. It had taken a Select Committee of Parliament eight to nine years to come to its recommendations; the Natives were being given only three months to consider them. On that Select Committee no Bantu had served.

He trusted that the convention would not be productive of inflammatory oratory, and that the best brains would be used in drafting its resolutions.

Mr. T. McLeod (Kimberley), vice-chairman of the African People's Organisation, said that all the non-Europeans should stand together, whether Bantu or Coloured. Both had their rights restricted. It had been said that the Government was trying to improve the lot of the non-Europeans. And yet the Government proposed taking away the franchise from the Coloured. He challenged the wisdom of this action, and claimed that the best parliamentarians in the Union had come from constituencies in which the Coloured people had the vote—men who had been elected by Europeans and non-Europeans together. . . .

The Rev. Z. R. Mahabane (Kimberley) said that while some Natives were concerned about the land question, others were concerned about the franchise, for the Bill in this connection was a challenge to the non-European. . . .

The Natives must not be reduced to a position of political inferiority. As permanent inhabitants who had made their contributions to the general welfare and progress of the country, they claimed the right of partnership in the management of the affairs of the country and in determining and shaping its course. Otherwise the Natives would have to raise the cry of the American colonists: "No taxation without representation."

The European vote had been strengthened by the granting of the franchise to women—and now the Native was to be disfranchised. By what right did the White man claim to rule the Native, unless it was by the out-of-date doctrine of the divine right of kings reincarnated as the divine right of the White man? He hoped the convention would claim Cecil Rhodes's policy of equal rights for all civilised men, irrespective of colour, and the doctrine of no government without the consent of the governed.

Dr. A. B. Xuma (Johannesburg) said that in the northern provinces of the Union there had been manhood suffrage, limited to Europeans, for some years, whereas in the Cape there had been manhood suffrage irrespective of colour. In 1930-1931 the franchise had been given to European women, but not to the non-European women in the Cape. He desired to show that there were non-European women quite fit to have the vote and called on Mrs. Charlotte Maxeke, B.Sc. (Cape Province), "the mother of African freedom in this country," to speak.

Describing the convention as a wonder conference, Mrs. Maxeke drew attention to it being representative not only of the various parts of the country, but of the two sexes. The non-Europeans were uniting because something was threatening their very lives. The Natives had no other country to which they could go. . . .

The non-Europeans, while thanking their European friends for their support, had to go ahead themselves. The Natives were not a peculiar people who had to be carried on the backs of others for ever. They had to be helped to help themselves. They would have to give their all so that the Europeans could realise that the Natives were here.

She reminded them of the saying *Eendrag Maak Mag* (Unity is Strength) and exhorted the Natives to live up to it.

On this note, the convention adjourned until Tuesday.

For three days the committees on Resolutions worked twelve hours a day right into midnight of each day, while the draughtsmen and typists worked without cessation.

Monday evening, for the unemployed delegates, was devoted to a grand reception function organised by Mr. T. M. Mapikela and his local hospitality committee.

On Tuesday morning the President called upon the Convention to discuss the Franchise question in the light of the Bills and the draft resolution tendered by the Committee on the Native Representation Bill. . . .

The following is a selection from the speeches delivered:

Mr. S. P. Matseke contended that at the Treaty of Vereeniging the assurance had been given that the question of granting the franchise to the Natives of the Free State, Natal and the Transvaal would be considered after South Africa had obtained responsible government. But nothing had been done to implement that promise. Even in the Cape, where non-Europeans had the vote, they had been deprived of their right, for it had been laid down in the South Africa Act that members of Parliament had to be of European descent.

Mr. T. M. Mapikela (Bloemfontein) said that no promise had been given at the Treaty of Vereeniging, though it had been said that the matter should be left to the South African Government. The Natives had been deprived of all their rights by the Act of 1909, when they had not raised a voice in protest. They had been defeated, and they should now make a big bid to obtain the rights they wanted.

Mr. G. G. Coka (Johannesburg) said that Natives were being robbed of rights they had possessed for 80 or 90 years. The Government policy was Imperialism— to keep the Natives in slavery by giving authority to reactionary chiefs. It was nothing but open bribery. He wanted the chiefs to know one thing. If they were going to serve their people they must throw aside these gifts. If they were not going to work for their people they had to be the good boys and lackeys of the Whites. The granting of representation to the Natives in the Senate was a sop. It was the duty of the chiefs, if they wished to do their people good, to organise and struggle to secure the franchise for the Native people.

44

Mr. S. P. Akena (Cradock) said that the object in transferring Native representation from the House of Assembly to the Senate had been to enable the Europeans to present a united front, which meant that trouble was brewing for the Natives. Another instance of this had been the two great White parties—the South African and National Parties—had come together in Fusion.

As evidence of the obstacles put in the way of the Natives, Mr. P. T. Xabanisa (Idutywa) said that in 1852 the qualification for the Native voter in the Cape had been the ownership of a house worth £25. Subsequently this was increased to £50 and then to £75. The Natives had worked and sold their stock to build such houses.

The Rev. R. M. Tunzi (Kokstad) said that the Natives should not have to go on bended knees for what they were entitled to. They should have equal rights in this country.

Mr. B. S. Ncwana (Port Elizabeth) said he also wanted to register his protest against a policy of permanent retrogression. Some people seemed to think that there was something in the council system of representation. Such a system was operative in the Cape Province, but it excluded the thousands of Natives in the urban areas. What hope, therefore, had the urban Natives in the northern provinces in the Government's council system?

Mr. R. H. Godlo (East London) said that there could be no substitute for the right of citizenship. On it there could be no compromise. The franchise, he contended, had been virtually conferred on the Natives under the fiftieth ordinance of the Cape, 1828, which had granted the Natives a legal and economic status. The Natives should tell the Government they were not prepared to compromise on the franchise.

It was not satisfactory, Mr. Godlo said, to give the Natives a separate franchise and separate representation. That would still debar them from the rights of citizenship.

Mr. I. B. Mbelle (Pretoria) declared that in 1926 General Smuts had said that if the Natives of the Cape were deprived of the vote, it would be a direct violation of the constitution. General Smuts had also said that no change should affect those already registered as voters. The Natives, if given the vote, would never be able to swamp the White man, because the White man and the White woman both had the vote.

Dr. G. H. Gool, an Indian of Cape Town, said that in the Cape the colour bar had been smashed and it was up to the Convention to smash the colour bar in the rest of the Union. The Cape delegates were not present to discuss the Native Bills, but to reject them *in toto* and lay the foundations of a national liberation movement to fight against all the repressive laws of South Africa. The position of the Bantu people in South Africa was like that of the worker in Britain during the industrial revolution when, in 1832, the workers were deprived of their vote. It took the workers many years to regain that vote.

Mr. B. Mashologu (Basutoland) contended that the Cape vote was not the franchise, for the Natives there could not send the people they wanted to Parliament, but were bound to send European candidates elected by other people. No race could be adequately represented by another. The Cape Natives had the shadow but not the substance.

Mr. J. Marx [Marks] (Johannesburg) said it was time that a halt was called to the blundering exploitation of the Natives. The time had arrived for the consolidation of the African people against their offenders. The present policy of subordinating the Natives and chiefs was bound to end in bloodshed. An active policy should be adopted by the Natives, who should refuse to pay taxes until their rights were recognised.

The resolution was then submitted to the convention—and unanimously passed.

On Wednesday the Council and Land Bills were discussed and resolutions thereanent adopted. . . .

In the evening numerous votes of thanks were proposed and passed.

In bidding the delegates farewell, the vice-chairman, Dr. Xuma, said that the Bantu had reached a higher stage of civilisation than most people realised. At this session of the convention they had retained their dignity, which was a tradition of the African people. They had behaved as ladies and gentlemen of Africa and true sons and daughters of the soil. More august bodies had not behaved so well when faced with such grave circumstances. He thanked the delegates for their decorum.

Votes of thanks were passed to the Chairman and all the office-bearers; all the committees; to Mr. Mapikela and the local committee that organised the boarding and lodging arrangements; all helpers; the Bantu Press; the local Press, especially the Reuter service; and everyone else concerned.

The Convention came to a close with the singing of the Bantu National Anthem *Nkosi Sikelel i-Afrika* (God Bless Africa).

Document 10. Resolution of the Executive Committee of the AAC, February 15, 1936

Whereas the All-African Convention, held at Bloemfontein on December 16, 1935, had resolved that it was opposed to the abolition of the Cape Native Franchise and had reiterated its firm conviction that the Cape Native Franchise was a matter of such vital importance to all the African people of South Africa that it could not bargain or compromise with the political citizenship of the African people by sacrificing the franchise as is proposed in clause one of the Representation of Natives Bill;

And whereas the said Convention had appointed a fully representative executive committee, inclusive of Africans from the four Provinces of the Union, and had empowered this body to investigate and to use all possible methods of persuading the Government and the Hon. Prime Minister and the House of Assembly to refrain from passing this clause of the Bill;

And whereas the members of the executive committee of the Convention had assembled in Cape Town since the opening of Parliament in January to initiate and negotiate with the Hon. the Prime Minister, the members of the Senate and the Parliamentary representatives most concerned with the native vote;

And whereas the result of the interview of the All-African Convention executive with the Hon. the Prime Minister on February 15, 1936, was the absolute refusal of the Prime Minister to withdraw Clause One of the Bill and the substitution of an offer by him to retain the Cape franchise in an atrophied form of separate rolls for native voters and the right to elect three members for the Assembly and two European members for the Cape Provincial Council and an additional two European Senators;

And whereas the Hon. the Prime Minister had refused our pressing request to refer the Prime Minister's new proposal to our people in convention; now, therefore, we have no alternative but to adhere to our mandate to oppose any alteration of the present Cape native franchise.

The All-African Convention Committee feels that the blame for the deadlock thus created must not be placed on them for any national repercussions that may result from the indiscretion of ill-conceived and one-sided legislation.

The executive committee is convinced that the fundamental principle of full political equality hitherto entrenched in the Cape native franchise will be wilfully and unjustly violated by the passage in Parliament of Clause One of the Bill, a violation that would perpetuate the discrimination against the natives of South Africa by reason of their colour, throughout all future legislation by Parliament.

Further, the executive committee is convinced that this differentiation in electing the law-makers of the country of which the natives form an integral part, cannot, in any circumstances whatsoever, receive their support, sanction or ratification.

The committee is firmly convinced that the policy of common citizenship, as expressed in the Cape Native franchise, is the only one that would ensure harmony between the races and make South Africa the palladium of racial peace in Africa.

The committee further considers that the proposal embodied in Clause One of the Bill constitutes a departure from the spirit of the Treaty of Vereeniging in which provision was made for the consideration of the granting of the franchise to natives in the north after the introduction of self-government to the Orange Free State and the Transvaal.

The committee is convinced that the only safe form of franchise would be one which, regardless of race or colour, is based upon a common form of qualification.

Document 11. "Presidential Address" by Professor D. D. T. Jabavu, AAC, June 29, 1936

All Africans, as well as all other non-White races of the world, have been staggered by the cynical rape by Italy of the last independent State belonging to indigenous Africans. After hearing a great deal for twenty years about the rights of small nations, self-determination, Christian ideals, the inviolability of treaties, humane warfare, the sacredness of one's plighted word, the glory of European civilisation, and so forth, the brief history of the last eight months has scratched this European veneer and revealed the White savage hidden beneath.

Two decades ago, millions of human lives were sacrificed at the altar of Belgian neutrality; to-day nothing has been done to stay Italy's determination to butcher in cold blood and asphyxiate our peaceful fellowmen of Ethiopia. Italy's defiance of solemn pledges has been met by hesitation, prevarication, caution, dialectics and pusillanimity, in turn. In 1914 it was a case of a White European nation, Belgium; to-day it is only Black Abyssinia.

As on other occasions, the Churches of the countries concerned claimed that God was fighting on their side, and invoked His blessing to prosper their imperialistic ambitions. Organised Christianity has so far failed to curb the animal propensities of rapacity and selfishness in the hearts of men who rule empires. The present world muddle seems to be exactly what it was two or three thousand years ago. Take away our scientific knowledge of tools and we are where we were then. One man did paint and illustrate a better way of living, but was murdered by his Jerusalem contemporaries for doing so. His professed followers have ended in lip service to Him, so far as war goes. They have partly wished to effect the change, and partly failed to take the necessary risks. Our Prime Minister, if I interpret his Parliamentary speech rightly, has disowned or superseded Christianity as a working proposition in politics. The governing ideal in human history is once more the Law of the Jungle. The modern system centres round the glorification of national empires. In so far as we are included as subjects within and under these empires, we share the blame for their tragic obliquity even against our will.

The structure of European political morality has suddenly tottered and collapsed from above our heads down to its pristine level of the jungle that obtained two thousand years ago.

Might is still right, though it is no longer the might of the sword but the vaunted science of aeroplanes raining dynamite bombs and poison gas. That, in short, is the pride of so-called White civilisation. It constitutes a moral challenge to the rest of humanity.

During the debate on the Colour Bar Bill at Cape Town in 1926 one member triumphantly asserted that he supported the Bill because self-preservation was the first law of nature, and defended the policy of repressing the non-Europeans of this land. Early this year Parliament again endorsed this policy by backing the Prime Minister who declared:—

"I do not understand at all what you mean by Christian principles. Christian principles count for very much, but there is a principle of self-preservation for a nation, the principle which causes everybody to sacrifice his life in time of war . . . I place that principle still higher. It is the only principle, that of self-preservation, of self-defence, by which humanity itself and Christianity itself will ever be able to protect itself."

This astounding declaration rules out Christianity very clearly from the politics of the Cape Town House of Assembly, because, as one well-known writer puts it,

"Politicians are men of the world – of a world so close and familiar to them that they can no longer descry either its wonder or its horror. That familiarity beclouds the wider and deeper aspects of truth and corrodes the spiritual instruments that apprehend them, it is no rare thing to find its victims mistaking a balance of conflicting selfishnesses for justice, and supposing freedom to exist wherever active revolt is not."

Guided by this philosophy of self-preservation as a basis for discrimination, the Union Parliament has, since its existence from 1909, registered no less than thirty-six pieces of colour bar legislation against us, and this seems the only basis on which such laws can be justified. Parliament has grown accustomed to passing differential laws at our expense as a matter of course. They have fallen into a rut, as it were, from which they are unable to emerge try as they will. Out of sheer habituation they take it for granted that segregation laws are morally right *per se* even where the rights of those on the opposite side of the colour line are interwoven with theirs, as, for example, the indirect taxes through which we circulate millions of pounds over which we have a mathematical and moral claim to have a say on terms of equality. To be denied the equal right to dispose of money we equally contribute is the absurd logic of segregation. We have been legislated out of our equal right to sit in the Provincial Council by reason of our black colour, segregation and self-preservation.

When we interviewed the Prime Minister last February as a deputation representing the All African Convention, all our instructions from you were inflexibly rejected on the ground that Parliament only wanted this, and not that. No heed was paid nor reference made to our answers given through the five official regional conferences at Maritzburg, Pretoria, Mafeking, King William's Town and Umtata, that cost the State £4,000 ostensibly for the purpose of ascertaining our opinion. We asked for bread, but got a stone. We asked for the preservation of the political *status quo*, but got, instead, a new Bill embodying our political inferiority and segregation plus a new colour bar in the Provincial Council. On asking for the postponement of the Land and Trust Bill till we had the chance to visit the released areas *in loco*, the Prime Minister gave us to understand that the Land Bill would not be proceeded with straightway after the first Bill; but, to

49

our amazement, it was taken and pushed through without further reference to us. No regard was paid to our request for the excision of the Squatters' Section Four. The few members who loyally fought for our cause (all thanks be to them, the courageous eleven who worthily challenged the course of ruthless injustice) at the Joint Sitting were made to count for nothing, the proceedings at one stage being steam-rollered in dictatorial fashion, concluding with a photograph and festive celebrations, I believe, elsewhere.

The impression one got of Parliamentary methods in South Africa was that only the interest of White men is considered by the majority of members. Everything is rigidly subordinated to that interest. Outside the walls of Parliament one found a large section, both articulate and silent, who fearlessly espoused our cause by press propaganda, public meetings and lobbying, and they represented the old liberal tradition that is dwindling.

Inside Parliament, however, there is one paramount interest, that of the White man. To demonstrate this, let us, for instance, take the Budget. Most State budgets in the world normally show some degree of lopsided incidence of taxation burdens as between those able to pay and those too indigent to pay, groups known as "the haves" and the "have-nots." This year's Union budget has astounded everybody in its totally callous neglect of consideration for the poorest section of the population who have silently shouldered their taxation without getting anything from the vast wealth they help produce for this country. Indeed the Black man planteth the vineyard but eateth not of the fruit thereof.

For us the budget speech affords but little joy. Its gifts are lavished among the rich in such profusion that some of the white beneficiaries have actually declined to accept the gifts out of a sense of shame and fear of their constituents. The Minister of Finance, perplexed to find ways of scattering his phenomenal surplus derived from cheap Black labour, a surplus that has recurred for years in succession, chose to relieve the opulent groups from income tax, leaving the lucky White farmers, because of their omnipotent franchise power, free from all direct taxation that cannot be labelled nominal. These farmers were privileged to feed their cattle and pigs at a cost of only 5/- per bag of maize during the drought while starving Natives had to pay 18/- a bag to save life from death, as the Government had made a law for the convenience of White farmers to sell mealies in England for about half-a-crown, feed their animals for 5/6 but charge the hungry Africans 18/-, and turn round to us and say it is the law, and the law cannot be changed! That is the meaning of the new policy of "Trusteeship" so-called. I think it stands self-condemned *ab initio*.

No wonder our neighbours of Rhodesia have characterised it as being "distinctly ungenerous." Just think of the ghastly fact that the Black races have enabled the Government to reap profits of over six million pounds per annum through their cheap labour at the mines, labour that would cost four million pounds more if it were White labour, especially when working profits have risen by 100%, and dividends swelled by 70%, the Treasury will not let go the one odd

50

million pounds of Poll Tax sucked out of the blood of our people under distressing circumstances of poverty and even penury. Nobody in Parliament so far as I am aware suggested the reduction or abolition of this draconian tax of blood. I think it is fair to be taxed according to income and ability to pay, but the Native Poll Tax of £1 all round is a savage anachronism. On the one hand the pensions for aged White men of sixty, who never pay Poll Tax as we do, have been increased, while on the other hand the Black men of sixty who are too poor to pay any tax but have always paid it, get no pension whatever and are forced by law to find £1 or go to prison. Parliament genuinely does not know that this tax absorbs the wages of two full months each year in the case of thousands of our people. Such things will be known only when we are represented on an equality by Black men in Parliament, and there are many in this hall who are good enough for that position. We have no choice but to keep on agitating for this equality. Otherwise we shall never be rescued from this travesty of justice.

Last December in this hall we held a mammoth and epoch-making gathering representative of every conceivable African organisation in the Union and parts of our adjoining Protectorates, for the purpose of giving our reply to the Native Bills such as they were then. We framed a unanimous answer and your committee proceeded to carry out your instructions, it is hoped, to your satisfaction. We must now make plans for the future and consider

(a) What to do with the new Acts, (b) how to consolidate this organisation and promote its unity and efficiency, and (c) devise schemes for improving our economic welfare by self-help.

We are thus confronted with a greater problem than ever, a problem demanding prevision or foresight instead of precipitate impetuosity; sanity in place of hysteria, and combined action rather than mutual wrangling. Your discussion will, I hope, result in a sensible agreement as regards our attitude to the new legislation and towards the future of the Convention.

You will have to examine a number of possible courses along with their advantages and disadvantages. Among these will be:—First, to declare a complete boycott on all the new Acts, adopting a policy of retaliative reprisals and bottled revenge.

In favour of this, we could startle White South Africa, attract the notice of the rest of the world and win our rights by using the fear of a bloody revolution as a weapon of propaganda.

Against this, one cannot calculate what the end of it would be. It might end in disaster. It presupposes that every single person literate and illiterate will obey our word of command. It presupposes a perfect organisation where there are no blacklegs. It will be hard to apply it to the Land and Trust Bill. Its collapse would make the last state worse than the first, because it would preclude all possibility of our unity thereafter. It rests on the use of force.

(b) To make an unconditional acceptance. This course offers no advantage whatever, for it would mean we accept all these laws as being just.

51

(c) To evolve an intermediary policy of using what can be used and fighting against all that we do not want. The advantage here is that we can keep the goal we are striving for constantly in view before us and work for the repeal of these colour bars backed by the strongest supporting forces in the country. We would keep our self-respect, get new opportunities to initiate fresh efforts, educate backward followers and ensure loyalty. Its drawback is that it will prolong the battle and exasperate those who are burning for quick results.

(d) There will possibly be other alternatives that will emerge from your discussions. Whatever be the diversity of opinions you hold, you will be well advised to be mutually tolerant, remembering that we are all working for the same end, to save Africa from virtual serfdom.

There will be no divergence of opinion as to the need of self-help and a more effective mobilisation of our economic forces for that purpose. Here I shall venture a few suggestions.

We should find a solution for an escape out of poverty by all practicable means within our power. So long as we are an impoverished community we shall never rise and scale the heights of success to which our mental and physical capacity entitles us to attain. We should burst our way into the vocations that create wealth among our communities. Those of us who secure a better education must abandon the idea of confining our ambition to Teaching and the Ministry, necessary as these are in all life. It is time for us to take up Law, Medicine, Commerce and progressive Farming. Business and Commerce must be stressed and much propaganda carried out to further them. Let us learn how to support our own traders however humble they may be, out of a patriotic spirit of African nationalism. Nationalism or race-pride has been rightly condemned in so far as it is a sentimental abstraction and an isolated ideal, but it is a ncessary preliminary step for people in our stage of development to attain commercial effectiveness, especially because we have often been criticised for being bad business men as a race. I do not subscribe to that condemnation, and it is for us to disprove it by deeds. In America I found a slogan among the Negroes "Keep your money within the colour," meaning that a Black man should do all his shopping at another Black man's shop whenever possible. If a Negro trader supplies good sugar, then all the Negroes in the town or district buy their sugar at his store, making him flourish and provide employment to others of his race. Following that example, we could multiply the number of our humble shoe-makers, tailors, grocers, taximen, bus contractors, butchers, farmers, co-operative stores, adopting a scheme of self-upliftment to counter the Government's anti-Black and repressive "Civilised Labour" policy.

Among our tasks is that of educating our Union rulers on our view of affairs and our reason for claiming equal rights, because our situation here is but symptomatic of the world-wide travail of all repressed communities and dominated classes even apart from the local colour problems that complicate and obscurify the true issue of class repressing class. Our ways of thinking have to be

52

revised till we dispassionately apprehend the general problem of our failure to live amicably as an evil facing all mankind, and as such needing concerted effort by all nationalities. We must be agreed and determined upon certain fundamental principles such as these: —

(a) Segregation and colour bars must go; alternatively we want a separate State of our own where we shall rule ourselves freed from the present hypocritical position.

(b) Economic repression must go. We can do that partially ourselves; for if we but knew our power we could hold up the industries that depend on our labour in one day and secure terms approximating fairplay. We are not so powerless as we often imagine ourselves to be.

(c) Selfishness must go. In our primitive African tradition we used to smell out and destroy all abnormally acquisitive individuals as a danger to society. By this crude method we guaranteed all men a chance to have food, shelter and clothing without prejudice. This is a lesson we Africans can teach Christendom, for Christendom still needs a change of heart from selfishness.

The supreme task of this Convention is to protect the interest of Africans not only in the Union but in all Africa. It is our duty to protect our fellow Africans in the Protectorates against being forced into the Union of South Africa contrary to their wish, until the policy of the Union is changed and made more liberal than it is at present. One eminent European press writer in this country last February flattered us in the following words: —"This All African Convention is to-day to the Natives of the Union what the India Congress is to the people of India. It is recognised by the Parliament of this country as the mouthpiece of the Natives of South Africa, and any resolution which it takes on Native questions will carry great weight not only with the Black peoples of the whole of Africa, but also with the Government and Parliament in Great Britain."

That is the outcome of unity and unified organisation which we must jealously guard against losing. In order to retain this unity, we, leaders, must avoid mental stagnation. Our minds should be kept refreshed by the breezes of fresh knowledge gotten from the vast available literature concerning what other leaders in the rest of civilisation are doing in facing problems similar to ours.

For example, a stirring Presidential Address was delivered last April in Lucknow by Mr. Jawaharlal Nehru, head of the All India Congress, a perusal of which (in its full version) gives much food for thought. In the course of that address he indicated that the efficiency of Congress organisation means little if it has no strength behind it, "and strength, for us, can only come from the masses." He emphasised the fact that the vital section of the Indian population was that of labour and the peasantry, and that the leaders must protect these classes from suppression and exploitation; for the most important question was appalling poverty, unemployment and indebtedness. Hence the need for closer contact with the masses.

These exhortations are applicable to us. Whatever we do or decide upon, we

53

must not lose touch with our backveld masses. The time is ripe for us leaders to reconstruct and rehabilitate all our mass organisations to fight starvation, poverty and debt.

Says Nehru, "Let us not indulge in tall talk before we are ready for big action." I think this wise advice is worth following.

Once we emancipate our people from the servitude of poverty we shall be able to accomplish great deeds. The stumbling blocks placed in our path are for us to remove. If we do not work hard to remove them we shall get only what we deserve to get. If we succeed in removing them we shall be in a position to render to the world the contribution due from Africa.

Document 12. Proceedings and Resolutions of the AAC, June 29-July 2, 1936

(24) Programme of Action.

After a full dress debate on the Programme of Action, the Convention passed the following set of resolutions, submitted by the Executive Committee:

1. This Convention of African chiefs and other leaders desires to record its profound disappointment with the Government in its enactment of the Representation of Natives Act and the Native Trust and Land Act without due regard to the views of the African people as expressed both in the regional conferences held by the Government ostensibly for the purpose of consultation and in the resolutions of the All-African Convention presented by a deputation to the Prime Minister at the beginning of the recently concluded session of the Union Parliament.

2. In brief the objects of the Native Trust and Land Act is presumably to improve the economic position of the African people. We believe, on the contrary, that the result of the application of this Act, in so far as it will drive large numbers of Africans now on European farms and in urban areas into the already congested Native Reserves and into the meagre released areas set aside for, and already largely in Native occupation, will accentuate the precarious economic status of the African people and will be prejudicial to the interests of all sections of the African population, the White no less than the African, the Coloured and the Indian. We are convinced that the Poor White Problem cannot be solved by doing what is calculated to lower the economic level of any section of the people.

3. The Representation of Natives in Parliament Act purports to provide, through the Native Representative Council, machinery for the ascertaining of Native Views on legislative measures affecting their welfare. The method of election of the members of this Council will not give adequate scope for the representation of the various interests and aspirations of the African people—an object which can only be achieved by broadening the basis of voting for its members. This convention re-affirms its conviction that the only way in which the interests of the various races which constitute the South African population

54

can be safeguarded is by the adoption of a policy of political identity. Such a policy will ensure the ultimate creation of a South African State in which, while the various groups may develop on different lines socially and culturally they will be bound together by the pursuit of common political objectives. The Convention contends that this object can only be achieved by the extension of the rights of citizenship to all the groups. This latter objective—common and citizenship rights for all—we make no apology for reiterating, and we are determined in no way to relax our efforts in working for this end.

Therefore we instruct our Executive Committee to call upon all organisations affiliated to the Convention to devise ways and means of co-operating with it in this task. In the struggle for the attainment of these objectives the Executive is authorised to explore all effective avenues of action.

Now therefore this All-African Convention solemnly resolves to pick up the gauntlet thrown before it by the White Parliament of South Africa.

Thursday
July 2.

After discussion by Messrs. Mapikela, Ramutla, Mbete, Tunzi, Klaaste, Mrs. Godlo, Mrs. Gool, Mrs. Bhola, Mrs. Lesabe, Mapitsa, Chief Chuene, Mancoba, Nyezi, Msimang, Leepile, Kabane, the motion was adopted unanimously on the proposal of Mr. L. Mfeka seconded by Mr. Rajuili.

(27) On Abyssinia.

(a) The All African Convention hereby expresses its utmost condemnation of the savage, unprovoked and unwarranted attack made by Italy upon Abyssinia and declares as its considered opinion that the ruthless action of Italy can only be regarded as large scale violence against fundamental human rights.

(b) Further this Convention sees in this action of Italy a continuation of the game of grab which the imperialist nations of Europe have played in this continent whereby millions of inhabitants have been deprived of their land, exploited and robbed of their labour.

(c) This Convention hereby declares its conviction that imperialism which has thus resulted in the ruthless destruction of life, in violent acts of robbery, in increasing exploitation and in the destruction of African culture is an evil force to be exposed, condemned and resisted.

(d) The All African Convention recognises the value and desirability of establishing contacts with Africans and African organisations in other parts of the world. To this end the All African Convention believes that a call to international conference of Africans and overseas peoples of African descent should receive the serious consideration of the Executive Committee.

(28) Overseas Contacts.

Having in mind the desirability of establishing and maintaining contacts with other African peoples and organisations and overseas peoples of African descent and other races, the Convention hereby instructs the Executive Committee to appoint a secretary for their purpose in terms of its authority provided in Clause 4 section (c) of the Constitution and that the committee make the appointment—passed unanimously.

(29) The Protectorates.

With reference to the Protectorates of Basutoland, Bechuanaland and Swaziland, the following resolution moved by Miss Janub Gool, B.A., seconded by Mr. C. R. Moikangoa, was unanimously adopted: —

(a) That the Convention heartily supports the struggle of the Africans in the Protectorates against incorporation in the Union, as such incorporation would not be in the best interests of the people of the Protectorates.

(b) This Convention pledges itself to supply all information to the Africans in the Protectorates through the press and otherwise, giving facts regarding conditions and the Native policy of the Union Government, with a view to assisting them to come to a proper conclusion if and when they are consulted by the British Government with regard to the question of their inclusion in the Union.

(c) In terms of Clause 4, Section (c) of the Draft Constitution, the Executive Committee is instructed to arrange for the secretariat necessary for the prosecution of this resolution (Number 29) as well as that of Number (28), and that the appointment of the secretariat be effected immediately.

(It may now be pointed out that the secretariats for each of these two objects were straightway appointed by the Executive, and that the necessary instructions to implement the Programme of Action under Resolution number 24 were duly framed and forwarded to the Provinces by the General Secretary.)

(30) Executive Activity.

This resolution was carried unanimously: —

That the Convention authorises the Executive Committee, pending the next meeting of the Convention, to conduct the work of the All African Convention such as the raising and disposal of funds in terms of the Draft Constitution as well as carrying into effect the programme of action agreed upon at this Convention.

(31) Date of next Convention.

After a long and interesting discussion it was moved and unanimously decided that the next meeting of the All African Convention be held in December, 1937, beginning on Monday 13th and terminating on Dingaan's Day 16th.

The object is to ratify the Draft Constitution, as well as to give the ample time of eighteen months for the delegates to conduct intensive work in their constituencies in the interests of the Convention. This will allow time for our work to percolate in all the rest of Africa and overseas countries where we should work hand in hand with people of African descent, other non-White folks and all White people who, being in sympathy with our cause, have identified themselves with our objectives.

(32) The term "non-European."

During the discussions, a rather novel idea of designating Europeans in South Africa was mooted, with appreciable effect. One delegate strongly contended that it was erroneous to describe the Africans in South Africa as "Non-Europeans" when to all intents they formed the indigenous population of the continent of Africa. He urged the Convention in all sincerity to adopt the nomenclature of "Non-Africans" for all Europeans as distinct from Africans, arguing that here they lived in Africa, and not in Europe where the term "Non-European" is conceivable and tolerable for strangers in the continent of Europe. This sign of an awakening race-consciousness may well be discussed next year in December.

(33) Closure.

In closing the Convention, the President gave an exhortation saying the delegates must bear in mind the motto "No cross, no crown" which meant they must be prepared to face hard work and cast away racialism. The only evidence we can see from anyone professing sympathy with us is the arrival of his shilling or more as proof of his loyalty. By this Convention we may create as many friends as enemies, but let us not look to the right or left but go onward undaunted till we reach our goal.

The Convention was finally closed at 6:30 p.m., Thursday 2nd July with the singing of the African National song *Nkosi sikelel' i-Afrika.*

Document 13. "The Challenge" and "The Alternative." Extracts from pamphlet, *The Crisis*, by Selby Msimang, 1936 [?]

THE CHALLENGE.

My friends and countrymen, let us now admit, both publicly and in our conscience, that Parliament and the white people of South Africa have disowned us, flirted and trifled with our loyalty. They have treated us as rebels, nay, they have declared we are not part of the South African community. Whatever it means, I am satisfied in my mind that if we do no longer form part of the community which constitutes Parliament and the Government of the Union of South Africa, we have to belong to some authority other than the present, or we shall have to admit that we are slaves and outcasts in our fatherland. If we refuse to be made slaves then we should seek emancipation by such means as the dictates of self-preservation may lead us to.

In one of our resolutions, we have expressed a desire "to appeal to the King and Parliament of Great Britain as the present representatives of the original beneficent donors of the Cape Native Vote, for an expression of their opinion in the event of such treasured gift being abrogated by His Majesty's Government in the Union of South Africa without reason." That resolution has not been transmitted, for its terms convey the meaning that such an appeal will be made immediately the Executive Committee is assured that the measure approaches its final stages. In any event, it is not my business nor my place to decry, but to act in faith and honesty as directed. What is uppermost in my mind is that we have reached a point in our national life where and when we should have recourse to the law of self-preservation, which is in the hands of the highest tribunal of our conscience as a race. I believe it is nothing but right, as we did with the Union Government, to protest as never before and say, whatever is the result of this colossal blunder, we wash our hands of it and accept the challenge.

What do we mean or what should we mean when we say we accept the challenge? What is the meaning of this challenge to us? General Smuts, in his rectorial address at St. Andrews University in Scotland, told the world that "to suppose that in the modern world you can dispense with freedom in human government, that you can govern without the free consent of the governed, is to fly in the face of decent human nature as well as of the facts of history." To me, therefore, it means that we have been thrown out of the purview and tutelage of the Union Government. The idea of a trusteeship, even of the kind a stepmother may possess, has been abrogated. It is therefore for us to choose whether or not we shall approach the situation thus created for us in a cringing attitude, begging to be taken over once more like unrequired foster children to be dealt with anyhow by the callous and iron-hearted stepmother. Or accept the challenge by demanding our freedom as completely as it is the privilege of people who do not form part of the community to which the Government of the day belongs. In other words, if we accept that we are a separate community from that represented by the Union Government, are we willing to be dependent on its grudging benevolence? General Hertzog has told the world that the first duty of the white man is to himself, and that we have no right to ask the Government or Europeans of South Africa to do anything that may jeopardise their supremacy.

My candid and conscientious reply to the question is that we can no longer loyally serve and be subject to a government which has openly disowned us and told us in brutal language that we can never, never be free. The choice therefore is not ours. The law of self preservation demands that we should seek avenues likely to lead us out of this incubus to which we have been thrust against our will. We have it on the authority of General Smuts, the present Minister of Justice, that "freedom is the most ineradicable craving of human nature; without it peace, contentment, and happiness, and even manhood itself, are not possible." If we feel we are sufficiently human to have the craving for freedom, and feel that we cannot surrender our freedom whatever it is or give up what chances we had heretofore for eventually reaching the highest pinnacle of our manhood, then it behoves us to accept General Hertzog's challenge by declaring our refusal to be made slaves and to suffer him to traffic with our freedom in order to uphold the white man's supremacy. If we feel we cannot conscientiously accept the challenge, all I can say, as a man and patriot, is that it were better to die now

58

than to live to see our children carried into economic bondage and into a dungeon to perish of hunger. For me, it is better indeed to spend the remaining years of my normal life behind prison bars than witness with my own eyes the misery of the children I swore before God to protect, love and cherish as a gift more precious than life.

I am under no illusion. I know that behind this brutal injustice is the reliance of the powers-that-be on the stupendous and murderous modern weapons of war and the advantage they have thereby against us—defenceless people. In spite of a well organised defence force, of all the deadly instruments of war and the most pagan militarism that can be given play, if my countrymen are possessed of a soul which can never perish by machine guns and artificial war devices, that soul will fight a righteous battle under the invincible captaincy of the gods who made our worthy forefathers what they were. We owe it to them that we have so far, in humility and self-sacrifice, made ourselves indispensable in every walk of life and refused to be extinct as the Red Indians and other aborigines who no longer are. If we have the soul to resist the machinations of the oppressor, I know of no power in the world and under the sun to conquer us; I know of no influence capable of persuading us to suffer degradation and shame and to suffer ourselves to be made the pawn in the big game of "topdoggism" and arrogance. That, my countrymen, is the challenge.

THE ALTERNATIVE.

I see in the horizon two alternatives indicating the way to freedom. The vision which gave to the Colonists a century ago the determination, the will and self-denial on the emancipation of their slaves to search more land for them to be free, makes me feel its presence and power in this crisis. I am able to see that we have no alternative but to accept the position as created by the Native Bills, that is, that we are not part of the South African community and that the interests of the Europeans are not bound together with our own. In other words, that between the European and ourselves there is no longer any community of interests.

This means to me that, that being the case, and as we share the country with the Europeans who have chosen to segregate us from them territorially, economically, politically and otherwise, it behoves us to demand a complete segregation on a fifty-fifty basis to enable us to establish our own State and government wherein to exercise our political, economic and social independence without the inconvenience of islands dotted all over the country. This alternative has already been advanced in our resolution on the Representation of Natives Bill, viz.: "The political segregation of the two races can only be justly carried out by means of the creation of separate States." I repeat, it is not our choice and of our own volition. We have in our resolution informed the Government that this creation of two States is undesirable. But the Government has decided that we should

59

think about it and agitate for it as never man sought his freedom. No sacrifice, however bitter, should deter us from seeing to it that we ultimately gain this objective. For my part I do not see why the Government should not seize on it since it is by way of completing its programme for making this a white man's country.

Another alternative is contained in the book, "Bayete," by the distinguished champion of the Native Bills, Chairman of the Native Affairs Commission and the Honourable Member for Zululand, Mr. G. Heaton Nicholls, M.P., to whom we owe an irredeemable debt of gratitude for this book. In this book, Mr. Nicholls indicates to us the way and method we should adopt to seize the reins of government and regain all the freedom we have lost since the advent of the white man in this country. It is the only way short of the creation of two States. It calls for no machine guns, no bombs nor aeroplanes. That weapon is a power in itself in that it is the power of the soul, the indestructible something that is in man—the Sword of God. It is the will and determination to be free, the ineradicable craving of human nature, without which we certainly must agree to perish or be made slaves.

I have used elsewhere the expression that we should agitate. But what type of agitation do I mean? Agitations may serve to create mob psychology, but may not rouse and fire the soul, create determination and self-denial for the cause of freedom. Yet in the end, mob psychology is an element for good, and simplifies the task of the leaders whose soul is fired with the desire to disarm the enemy. We must have intense organisation and persistent education of the masses along systematic and persuasive lines, capable of removing mental inactivity and usher in knowledge of the dangers of our existing relationship with the Europeans who seek domination and economic subjection. When that knowledge has increased and our people are conscious of their fate, then shall we hope and begin to see visions and to dream the dreams of freedom. Let us not forget that the white man, who has made us believe he is better civilised than we are, has had to descend so low as to resurrect century-old memories that he may find a pretext with which to appease his conscience when he avenges himself upon us for the "wrongs" alleged to have been committed by Great Britain against his fore-fathers. We have in the past succeeded in aping him in many things—some extremely undesirable. Why cannot we emulate him now in this crisis and make ourselves a free people?

The practicability of the first alternative depends on the government and the white people who feel that this country is not safe for them if they live side by side with us. To achieve the ideal of a White South Africa which does not entail the enslavement of the African race, they need not hesitate to establish two territorial States on an equal basis. Their sense of justice (if there be any left) should persuade them to release one-half of the area of the Union and have "Whiteman Territory" and "Blackman Territory." They cannot have it both ways. We should therefore demand that the present Native Land Bill be withdrawn and another introduced forthwith giving effect to a vertical territorial

60

segregation. I used the word "demand" advisedly, for is not this loaf baked by the white man? If we have to accept it, let us have the whole. There should be no halves about it.

The second alternative depends upon ourselves. I see in this crisis the hand of Fate stretching out to free us. General Hertzog and all his lieutenants may prove yet the instruments by which we will forge our liberation. Bantudom now sees the clouds gathering in the horizon and seeks to gather her children under her strong wings. Shall we prove cowards and flee from her strength? God forbids. Perhaps in this crisis we may live, if we dare, to witness the fulfilment of General Smuts's philosophy broadcast to the world in these great words:

"To suppose that in the modern world you can dispense with freedom in human government, that you can govern without the free consent of the governed, is to fly in the face of decent human nature as well as of the facts of history."

We may live to see, if we have the soul and the righteous determination to do and dare, the history of the overthrow of the Russian Empire by the governed, repeated in this our dear Fatherland.

NKOSI SIKELELA I AFRIKA

Document 14. "Policy of the AAC." Statement issued by the Executive Committee of the AAC, December 1937

1. *Segregation:* (a) Segregation in all its forms is to be opposed.

(b) All Colour-Bar laws are to be fought.

(c) Africans demand the freedom to organise trade-unions, unemployed councils, the right to strike, the abolition of racial barriers in existing trade-unions and in industry, as well as race prejudice generally; the stoppage of police terrorism against African workers.

(d) Opposition must be organised against those sections of the Urban Areas Act and the Native Laws Amendment Act that provide for the compulsory removal of Natives from towns merely by reason of unemployment and of being "redundant." The position of those Africans whose homes are in the towns and have never been in touch with rural areas must be safeguarded.

2. *Political Rights:* A vigorous agitation must be conducted for (a) the right to the franchise for the Africans; (b) representation by indigenous Africans in all State councils, particularly the House of Assembly; (c) the appointment of an African member on the Native Affairs Commission as well as other commissions that are periodically appointed to inquire into various aspects of Native affairs.

3. *Land Rights:* (i) The allocation of land sufficient for the needs of an ever-growing African population.

(ii) Acceleration of the acquisition of the "released areas" and of the economic development of existing reserves.

61

(iii) Opposition to the eviction of Africans who are called "squatters" or who are dwellers on lands outside of reserves and released areas.

(iv) The settlement of Africans on the land under such favourable conditions as will obviate the necessity to leave their land and seek employment on unjust terms.

(v) Maintenance of the right to purchase land on freehold title for those African individuals or communities that desire so to do.

(vi) The abolition of all restrictions placed in the way of Africans in purchasing land anywhere.

(vii) The multiplication of agricultural schools for Africans in order to foster adaptability to make a success of rural life.

(viii) That the appointment of a Native member to the Land Board for the released Areas be made legally compulsory instead of being left optional as at present in the Native Land Trust Act.

4. *Unemployment:* Government financial relief, freedom from Poll Tax and abolition from rent dues for all unemployed Africans must be pressed for.

5. *Wages:* The All African Convention demands

(a) equal pay for equal work irrespective of race or colour.

(b) an eight-hour day in all industries;

(c) a more liberal wage-scale for African labourers in all classes of urban and rural employment;

(d) that Native workers be brought legally within the protective scope of the Wage Act and Industrial Conciliation Act because much of the prevailing poverty, under-nourishment and low degree of health is directly traceable to the deplorable low rates of wages obtaining universally among African employees.

6. *Taxation:* (a) The abolition of the Native Poll Tax.

(b) The reduction of the Poll Tax as a first step towards its abolition.

(c) The substitution of a tax based on a reasonable proportion of a man's income in place of the Poll Tax.

7. *Pass Laws:* The radical abolition of all Pass Laws and of the substitution thereof of an income tax receipt as proposed in 6 (c) above.

8. *Education:* The All African Convention endorses the resolutions and statements issued by the South African Native Teachers' Federation in December 1936, and specially stresses the axiomatic fact that the education of the African is essential to his efficiency in employment and his progress in agriculture.

The first step towards improving the present inadequate system of Native education is to put into force the recommendations made in the Inter-Departmental Report on Native Education (1936) as analysed and criticised by the South African Native Teachers' Federation, especially the points suggesting

(a) that Native education be financed on a per caput basis, instead of the present fixed and inadequate subsidy;

(b) equal pay for African and European teachers in Native schools or colleges whenever qualifications are equal;

(c) and a general improvement in the salary scales of African teachers.

9. *Health:* (a) The widest publicity and inquiry into the present appalling state of malnutrition and incidence of disease among Africans generally;

(b) the employment of more nurses in urban areas and reserves;

(c) scholarship facilities to enable promising young Africans to enter the medical profession and improve the health of their people;

(d) the establishment in the Union of South Africa of a fully equipped medical school for Africans granting a recognised and registrable medical certificate.

10. *Chiefs:* The improvement of status and financial allowances for African chiefs and headmen in view of their serious responsibilities in maintaining law and discipline in extensive and populous districts.

11. *Protectorates:* In re-affirming Minute 29 of its 1936 session, the All African Convention decisively opposes all proposals to incorporate the Protectorates of Basutoland, Bechuanaland and Swaziland into the Union of South Africa on the ground that such incorporation will not be in the best interests of the Africans in those Protectorates, especially while the Native policy of the Union Government continues to be that of Segregation, Colour Bars and all sorts of political and economic discriminations at the expense of the Natives.

12. *Economic Policy:* The Convention stands for:—

(a) The advancement of the economic interests of Africans in the belief that this is the key to all progress;

(b) encouraging Africans to serve Africans in mutual exchange of living stock and agricultural products by means of central depot links that will bring producers and consumers into touch with one another;

(c) developing associations of farmers, credit societies and cooperative systems of buying and selling agricultural products;

(d) inculcating individual thrift and frugality in every community, especially by means of deposits in Saving Banks accounts;

(e) training Africans in founding trading shops, grain stores, and factories to supply goods to African centres and communities or reserves, thus incidentally widening the scope of the employment of Africans by Africans in all phases of work;

(f) stressing the need of an education on the lines of book-keeping and business methods, thereby promoting economic uplift, initiative, and efficiency;

(g) and urging successful business men and women to provide frequent public lectures calculated to rouse the national conscience and to stimulate African latent gifts in trading and business capacity.

13. *Representation:* (a) All the candidates returned as members at the elections held during June 1937 under the 1936 Representation of Natives Act are

hereby recognised as the accepted mouthpiece of Africans in their various representative State Chambers of the (i) Senate; (ii) House of Assembly, (iii) Provincial Council, and (iv) Native Representative Council.

(b) These representatives will be expected to attend the plenary sessions of the All African Convention at Bloemfontein for the purpose of ascertaining the opinion of African views on various questions, securing a mandate for expressing African views on matters arising from time to time, and of giving an account of their stewardship.

Document 15. Constitution of the AAC, December 1937

Preamble: Whereas it is expedient in view of the situation created by the "Native" Policy of segregation, discrimination and other repressive measures definitely adopted by the Government and Parliament of the Union of South Africa that the African races of South Africa as a national entity and unit should henceforth speak with one voice, meet and act in unity in all matters of national concern,

This Convention resolves that a Central Organisation shall be formed with which all African religious, educational, industrial, economic, political, commercial and social organisations shall be affiliated,

And to give effect to this purpose, the following Constitution shall form the basis of the organisation to be and which is hereby established, namely:—

1. *Name:* The name of the organisation shall be the All African Convention.

2. *Composition:* (a) The Convention shall be composed of accredited organisations and organised bodies duly registered with the General Secretary and which organisations and organised bodies shall be represented by accredited delegates at all meetings of the Convention.

(b) Any duly organised body with a constitution that expresses its objects shall be eligible for registration.

3. *Objects:* (a) To act in unity in developing the political and economic power of the African people.

(b) To serve as a medium of expression of the united voice of the African people on all matters affecting their welfare.

(c) To formulate and give effect to a national programme for the advancement and protection of the interests of the African people.

(d) To assist in rehabilitating dormant and moribund African organisations and bringing together unorganised Africans into societies. communities or bodies affiliated to the All African Convention.

4. *Officers:* (a) The Officers of the Convention shall consist of a president, a vice-president, a general secretary, a recording secretary, a treasurer and an assistant treasurer.

(b) The General Secretary shall be a paid official whose salary shall be determined by the Executive Committee, from time to time.

5. *Executive Committee:* (i) The Executive Committee shall consist of (a) the officers, (b) five representatives from each province.

Chiefs and, in their absence, their duly accredited representatives shall be *ex-officio* members of the Executive Committee.

(ii) The Executive Committee shall have power to meet any further organisational needs of the Convention.

(iii) In case of emergency the Officers shall have power to act on behalf of the Convention subject to review by the Executive Committee.

(iv) If a member of the Executive Committee fails to attend two consecutive meetings without giving satisfactory reasons for his absence he shall forfeit his position.

6. *Election:* The Officers of the Convention (a) shall be elected by ballot at an ordinary general meeting of the Convention;

(b) shall hold office for three years, and

(c) shall be eligible for re-election.

The other members of the Executive Committee nominated in special meetings of provincial delegates at the Convention shall be elected at the time of the election of the officers.

7. *Vacancies:* The Executive Committee shall be competent to fill any vacancy occuring between meetings of the Convention.

8. *Finance:* (a) The general funds of the Convention shall be made up of (i.) an initial registration fee of ten shillings and six pence (10/6) payable by each affiliating organisation for the first year; (ii.) an affiliation fee of five shillings (5/-) per annum payable by each registered organisation for every consecutive year thereafter; (iii) public or private donations and funds raised by such other means as the Convention may deem fit to devise.

(b) All Convention moneys shall be deposited with the treasurer.

(c) The treasurer shall deposit all Convention funds in an approved bank in an account styled the "All African Convention."

(d) All cheques in favour of the Convention funds should be crossed "All African Convention."

(e) All disbursements from the Convention funds shall be made by cheque payments and must be signed by the treasurer, the general secretary and the president, or, in the absence of the President overseas, the Vice-President.

(f) The budget of expenditure must have been previously approved of by the Executive Committee.

(g) The travelling expenses of the executive committee shall be paid out of the Convention treasury when funds permit.

9. *Audit:* The Executive Committee shall arrange for an audit of the Convention books by an *ad hoc* committee of the Convention, and shall present a report to the Convention.

10. *Conference:* The Convention shall meet every three years, provided:—

(a) That the Executive Committee shall have power to convene a special meeting of the Convention whenever it deems it fit and necessary so to summon it.

(b) That on the requisition of at least three registered organisations submitted to the general secretary at least three months before the date suggested for the meeting and embodying the subject matter for discussion, the Executive Committee, at their discretion, shall convene, through the president, a special meeting of the Convention.

(c) That the Executive Committee shall meet at least once a year and may at its discretion invite each registered organisation to send one representative to a meeting for purposes of consultation.

11. *Quorum:* The quorum of a Convention meeting shall be one third of affiliated organisations and that of an Executive Committee meeting shall be eight members.

12. *Venue:* The venue of the Convention shall be Bloemfontein unless the Executive Committee or the Convention itself especially decide otherwise.

13. *Amendments:* This Constitution may be amended at any ordinary Convention meeting by a two-thirds vote of the members in session, provided that twelve months notice of such amendment shall be given by the general secretary to all registered organisations prior to the Convention meeting at which such amendment is to be registered.

PART TWO

Moderation and Militancy
1937-1949

OVERVIEW

The year 1937, the twenty-fifth or "Silver Jubilee" year of the African National Congress, marked the beginning of a transitional period in African politics. The ANC began slowly to revive while continuing to employ tactics of representation through resolutions, deputations, and meetings. Seeking to salvage some hope of future advance, both the ANC and the recently established All African Convention looked to the June 1937 election of "Natives' representatives" (under the 1936 legislation) to establish a new channel of expression. During the dozen years that followed, and particularly during World War II, African leaders were torn between renewed hope for liberal change and new frustrations. They participated in efforts to build African national consciousness and also nonwhite unity, debated tactics of expediency and those of total boycott, and were increasingly impelled toward militancy and polarization in their relations with the dominant whites.

The end of the war was followed in 1946 by the beginning of Indian passive resistance (the first sustained defiance of laws by nonwhites since Gandhi's time in South Africa), the revolutionary omen of the largest African strike (involving some 70,000 mine workers), and the breakdown of the Natives' Representative Council. The period culminated in two events that are landmarks in the rise of Afrikaner and African nationalism: the coming to power in 1948 of the first Union government composed exclusively of Afrikaners, that of the Nationalist Party in control ever since, and, secondly, the adoption by the ANC in 1949 of a program of direct action—boycotts, strikes, and civil disobedience—and election of a new leadership.

The white political leadership which Africans confronted during this period appeared in three guises, each committed to white supremacy yet differing in tone and outlook. During Prime Minister J. B. M. Hertzog's leadership of the United Party, Native policy was considered "settled" after 1936. Removal of Africans from the common voters' roll epitomized Hertzog's policy of political segregation, yet the representation of Africans in Parliament by a few specially elected whites and the establishment of a nationally based Natives' Representative Council were tacit recognition that the African voice should be heard in national policy-making. With the split in the United Party on the issue of entering World War II alongside Great Britain—the House of Assembly voted 80 to 67 to enter the war on September 4, 1939—General Jan Christiaan Smuts again became prime minister, with the liberally inclined Jan H. Hofmeyr as his deputy. Abroad a rhetorician of freedom although at home a white supremacist, Smuts left open the door of expectation that the direction of South African policy might change. The unexpected victory

69

of Dr. Daniel F. Malan's Reunited National Party on May 26, 1948 closed that door, however, for as long as the Nationalists remained in power. Their course of policy moved steadily toward abolition of the Natives' Representative Council, removal of the vestiges of African and other nonwhite representation in Parliament, and the establishment of a comprehensive and rigid racial separation, or apartheid, which denied that Africans were a national group with national spokesmen.

Wartime and postwar economic developments not only strengthened the indigenous roots of a resurgent liberalism among a small number of whites but also broadened the social basis for African nationalism. Urban and industrial life provided a common milieu for intertribal contact and also growing opportunities for contact among Africans, Coloureds, and Indians.[1]

For most urban Africans, the level of living was near, or even below, the poverty line, which white social investigators defined as a level below which subsistence was hardly possible. In the cities Africans sometimes lived in areas adjacent to or overlapping those inhabited by poorly skilled and poorly educated Afrikaners. The latter were themselves fairly recent arrivals from unproductive farms but were the beneficiaries of white trade union pressures, apprenticeship regulations, and customary and legislative color bars. In these combustible circumstances, police enforcement of the pass laws—the most persistent and widely felt African grievance—and raids to prevent home brewing of beer or to search for liquor always ran the risk of violent eruptions. The African National Congress and other bodies often protested the actions of the police in dealing with such eruptions, and whites reacted to African defiance with anger and fear as well as with calls for official inquiry. The most terrible rioting of the period, however, was not directed against whites. In January 1949, Zulus gave vent to accumulated grievances against Indians in and around Durban, with some initial encouragement from white bystanders. The 1940s also demonstrated the capacity of Africans, responding to immediately critical problems such as intolerable congestion in housing and higher bus fares, to act quite spontaneously under local African leaders who were acting independently of any broader political program. On several occasions Africans boycotted buses in the Johannesburg area with some success.

The African potential for organized activity to win economic gains was evident, furthermore, in the renewed efforts of vigorous leaders to form or to enlarge African and nonwhite trade unions. A wave of illegal strikes occurred during the war; but the largest strike took place only after the war, which had inhibited Communist trade union leaders from undertaking large-scale action. In August 1946, South African whites were shaken by the most threatening spectacle of African labor protest in South Africa's history: some 70,000 mine workers, politically the least advanced group of urban workers, left or refused to enter the gold mines in response to the call of the African Mine Workers' Union, which was led by John B. Marks, a long-time member both of the Communist Party and the ANC. The violent handling and breaking of the strike by white authorities contributed to the decision of the Natives' Representative Council to adjourn indefinitely.

The strike also resulted in the beginning of systematic efforts to prosecute the Communist Party's leadership or to restrict individual leaders, efforts culminating in the party's self-dissolution shortly before the Suppression of Communism Act was passed in 1950.

In the late 1930s, on the eve of these wartime years of urban turmoil and change, the ANC slowly revived from the nearly moribund state in which it had been unable alone to challenge the Hertzog bills. Its animators were a cross-section of African leaders, including most of the moderate old-timers and a small number of Communists. South Africa's entrance into the war in 1939 generated new hope and excitement, and the ANC's leadership felt growing pressures for African assertion.

With the election in December 1940 of Dr. A. B. Xuma to the first of his three three-year terms as president-general, the ANC entered a period during which sustained efforts were made to transform it from a loosely bound federal movement whose major activity was its annual conference into a more tightly functioning and centralized national organization that would attract "graduates" and other intellectuals. A major event of the Xuma era of December 1940-December 1949 was the preparation and adoption of the most important statement of African aims since 1919, *Africans' Claims in South Africa* (Document 29b). The Bill of Rights incorporated in this document was a careful restatement of long-standing African opposition to racial discrimination, but on the key issue of the franchise it took a stronger position and apparently endorsed unqualified universal suffrage. Dr. Xuma retained his predilection for deputations and statements. He built up the ANC's dues-paying membership and treasury, raised standards of public financial accounting, and asserted presidential authority over provincial and branch misconduct. In December 1949, however, the ANC still had far to go to become a strong mass organization.

The year 1943 saw not only the high-water mark of assertion by the ANC's older generation in *Africans' Claims* but also the formal authorization of an ANC Youth League. During the remaining years of Dr. Xuma's presidency, a younger generation of potential leaders, impatient with tactics of protest by petition and suspicious of Xuma's readiness to enter into agreements with Indian leaders and left-wing whites, rose to power within the ANC. The Youth League was inaugurated with the cooperation of Dr. Xuma, who welcomed somewhat cautiously the infusion of new energy despite old-guard apprehension that a separate organization might undermine the established leadership. The new group accepted the older generation's 1943 statement of goals, but its driving interest was in generating among the African masses a spirit of militant nationalism and self-reliance and in pressuring the ANC to adopt new tactics to reach its goals.

Three other developments in 1943 each represented a different kind of challenge to the ANC's caution and its reluctance to merge its own activities with those organized by others. First, the AAC, which from its inception had allowed all nonwhites to become members, came to be dominated by Coloured and African radicals in the Cape Town area. The Coloureds had reacted vehemently early in the year to the establishment of a Coloured Affairs Department (C.A.D.), which was seen as a significant turn toward further segregation of the Coloured community. They also sought to move into positions of leadership and influence over a new nonwhite liberation movement that would include all Africans. Their Anti-C.A.D. organization linked with the AAC in a federal body, the Non-European Unity Movement (NEUM), which condemned all forms of participation in segregated forms of representation.

Secondly, Paul Mosaka, a member of the Natives' Representative Council who was impatient with the ANC's lack of dynamism, as he saw it, formed the African Democratic Party (ADP) in 1943 with other young Africans and the aid of Senator Hyman M. Basner, a former Communist and the most radical of the white members of Parliament elected by Africans. The party called for "mass support," readiness to use "mass passive resistance," if necessary, and cooperation with progressive whites. (Document 73). And thirdly, Communists—including an Indian leader— were instrumental in launching a National Anti-Pass Campaign of conferences, petition-signing, and deputations during 1943-1945.

Xuma was ambivalent toward the AAC, hostile to the ADP, and willing (acting in the role of the paramount African leader) to accept the national chairmanship of the Anti-Pass Campaign. The ADP, which was opposed as a divisive influence, proved to be abortive. Joint meetings of delegates of the ANC and the AAC during 1940-1949 resulted neither in the predominance of the NEUM nor in the creation (through fusion) of an "All African National Congress." The ANC's united front activity in the long-drawn-out and sporadic Anti-Pass Campaign, however, and Xuma's so-called pact in 1947 with the Communist and Gandhian leaders who had recently won power in the Indian congresses were precursors of the multiracial alliance entered into by the ANC in the 1950s. The Indian passive resistance campaign that began in mid-1946 against the Smuts government's Asiatic Land Tenure and Indian Representation Act was particularly important as one inspiration for the decision to adopt the Programme of Action in 1949 and to undertake African passive resistance in 1952.

Meanwhile, the ANC Youth League, the Unity Movement, and the experiences of the NRC also contributed to the resolution of the debate between pragmatic collaboration and total boycott that bedeviled African politics, particularly after 1943. The NRC's impotence was starkly revealed in 1946, at the time of the African mine workers' strike, and relations between the council and the government deadlocked and then broke down. Smuts's last-moment suggestion that the council might develop into a "Native Parliament" came to nothing. In consequence, moderate and even conservative African members of the council—who had had no illusion that the body was more than purely advisory but had hoped it might serve usefully as a platform—became almost hopelessly frustrated and moved uncertainly toward acceptance of the tactic of boycott. The gesture of those who finally resigned was fruitless since the Nationalist government already planned to abolish the council.

The victory of the Afrikaner Nationalist Party in the general election of May 1948 challenged all politically minded Africans to intensify their activity. The ANC had vacillated in its attitude toward the boycotting of segregatory institutions; but mainly under the influence of the Youth League, in December 1949 it adopted the "Programme of Action," which specifically set forth tactics of direct action—boycotts, strikes, and civil disobedience—in "the struggle for national liberation." Dr. Xuma presided at the conference and, without enthusiasm, accepted the Programme. But because of his unwillingness to defer to the Youth Leaguers, who asked him to be their candidate, and his identification with nearly a decade of moderation, he was defeated for reelection to a fourth three-year term. Dr. Xuma accepted membership in the new national executive committee, but it now also included leading members of the Youth League. With Dr. James S. Moroka as president, the ANC entered a period of direct challenge to white domination.

WHITE GROUNDS FOR NONWHITE HOPE AND DESPAIR

So long as Smuts was prime minister, African leaders could make use of his rhetoric and even find hope in his relative open-mindedness about long-range developments. During the fluid period of 1939-1948, African leaders who were disposed to retain hope in the historic promise of liberalism (roughly synonymous in South Africa with nonracialism) were able to find grounds for doing so. At the same time, they recognized that the actions of Smuts were designed to maintain white supremacy. Although the volume of segregationist legislation during these years was small compared with the spate of Nationalist legislation that followed, the Smuts government not only stiffened or extended the segregationist policies already in existence but also laid the groundwork for some of the major acts of apartheid.

Smuts was severely limited in his freedom of action by white fears and prejudices; but he continued to rely on Hofmeyr, who had dissented from the 1936 franchise policy, and did not put a stop to recurrent speculation that Hofmeyr might be his successor. In 1937 at the University of Cape Town, which was attended by nonwhites, Smuts spoke of "racial indifference." Later as prime minister, he spoke often in the spirit of Roosevelt and Churchill's Atlantic Charter of August 14, 1941, which had expressed "hopes for a better future for the world" and respect for "the right of all peoples to choose the form of government under which they will live." (The Atlantic Charter gave rise in 1943 to the ANC'S *Africans' Claims*—Document 29b.) In a public meeting in Cape Town on February 21, 1942, during dark days in the war as the Japanese moved into the Indian Ocean, he declared dramatically that "segregation has fallen on evil days" and envisaged white and black as "fellow South Africans, standing together in the hour of danger."[2] If Japan's aggression made it necessary, he said at about the same time, " . . . every native and coloured man, who can be armed, will be armed."

Smuts was also considering, he said in 1942 and hinted at in succeeding years, including African workers by law within the system of industrial conciliation, thus officially recognizing their rights to organize and bargain collectively. Industrialization and urbanization, he told the United Party Congress in 1944, required a "profound change" in traditional policies and better use of manpower. Smuts's most memorable promise of "larger freedom" came in June 1945, when the San Francisco Conference adopted the United Nations Charter. The Charter included a preamble of which Smuts was the main author, calling for a "larger freedom" and reaffirming "faith in fundamental human rights, in the dignity and worth of the human person, in the equal rights of men and woman. . . ."

Smuts's grandiloquent words were matched by what Alan Paton has called "little niggardly concessions"; nevertheless, the underlying premise of these ameliorations, instituted by Hofmeyr as minister of finance, was that nonwhites shared a common national interest even though social benefits were paid on a racially discriminatory scale. The wartime Social and Economic Planning Council prepared valuable studies on the development of a national economy in which all races would benefit. Social welfare benefits were extended to children, the blind, invalids, and the aged of all races.

More revealing of differing outlooks was policy toward education. Whereas the Nationalists favored transferring African education from the provinces to the central government's Department of Native Affairs, Hofmeyr (who preferred control by the Department of Education if it were to be shifted to the central government) retained provincial control and slowly increased its financial support. In 1945, for the first time, legislation provided for financing African education out of general revenue rather than from African tax revenue although government expenditure for each white student remained about seven times that for each African student.

Still more important were the underlying differences in attitude toward so-called Bantu education and Western education. Neither Smuts nor Hofmeyr had any doctrinaire objection to African educational opportunities that opened doors into the white community and, for that matter, into a universe of liberal individualism. Although supporting social and residential segregation, they appeared to accept the trend of the 1930s and 1940s that resulted in 1946 in 72 Africans among 143 nonwhites sharing classrooms with whites at the University of the Witwatersrand in Johannesburg, and 107 nonwhites (mostly Coloureds) similarly associated with whites at the University of Cape Town. Some 239 nonwhites (mostly Indians) attending college in Durban and Pietermaritzburg had separate classes but shared the same instructors. Hofmeyr himself supported the admission of African students to all-white medical schools.

Potentially the most solid basis for African hope that the direction of policy might change lay in the facts of wartime and postwar economic developments: the continued influx of African workers into the cities, the expansion of secondary industry, and the further growth of white dependence on black labor. Africans could hope that white recognition and acceptance of movement toward racial integration in the economy might mean eventual acceptance of the political and social implications of such integration.

An important step toward recognizing the degree of interaction and interdependence of whites and Africans came with the appointment of the Native Laws Commission headed by Judge Henry Fagan, whose terms of reference were made public on August 16, 1946. The Fagan Commission was to study not only the pass laws but also, generally, the problems of Africans in urban areas and migratory labor. Its report in 1948 disclosed a situation of which few whites had been aware. Noting that the Native reserves were seriously overcrowded, the Fagan Report pointed out that more than half the Africans were outside the reserves at any given time and that there was "a settled, permanent Native population" in the urban areas. In its view, the process of integration could not be reversed.[3] The report, which was widely expected to influence future Native policy, was presented to Smuts and publicly endorsed by him on the eve of the 1948 election. The new Nationalist government shelved the report, however, and in 1949 appointed its own commission. (Six years later the Tomlinson Commission on the Socio-Economic Development of the Bantu Areas rejected movement toward "ultimate total integration." It proposed to reverse existing trends to move toward "ultimate separate development," and it recommended extraordinary financial expenditure for the Native reserves. The Nationalist government accepted the recommendations for separate political development but disagreed with the size of the financial estimates.)

With the maturing of South Africa's industrial revolution and the growth of a permanently urbanized and Western-oriented class of Africans, conditions became more auspicious for the growth of a new liberalism among whites. On April 4, 1938 *The Forum* appeared, a new journal which was to be an organ of Hofmeyrian liberalism. During the Afrikaner Nationalist celebration of the centenary of the Great Trek, later in the year, young liberals and progressives organized the Libertas Bond in Johannesburg and the Libertas League of Action in Durban.

The number of whites actively involved in those and similar small groups, in the Institute of Race Relations, and in *The Forum* was small but included distinguished sympathizers of African aspirations: for example, Margaret Ballinger, Donald B. Molteno, J. D. Rheinallt Jones, and Edgar Brookes—who were Natives' Representatives in the House of Assembly or the Senate—Professor Alfred Hoernle, Leo Marquard, Leslie Rubin, John Cope, and René de Villiers. From time to time and with varying degrees of enthusiasm in the years after 1937, they looked to Hofmeyr for leadership in the formation of a new liberal party. But such action was deferred in the face of arguments for working within the United Party and, after September 1939, preoccupation with the war. Whether or not Hofmeyr as leader of the United Party could have held it together is doubtful. His publicly stated expectation that eventually nonwhites would be represented by nonwhites in Parliament was used relentlessly by the Nationalists during the general election campaign of 1948 to prove that he favored total abolition of the color bar. In the election, the Nationalists came to power with only a minority of the white vote and a narrow parliamentary majority of only five votes (the latter based upon the support of a minor party). Anti-Nationalist whites retained some confidence, therefore, that the Nationalists might be defeated at the next election. Hofmeyr's premature death on December 3, 1948, six months after the Nationalist Party's electoral victory, deprived liberal whites of an orthodox political leader of national stature. However, not until the Nationalist Party's second and third electoral victories in 1953 and 1958, respectively, did some of those referred to above organize the Liberal and subsequently the Progressive parties, groups interested in maintaining contact with politically minded Africans.

For most African leaders, the signs of liberalism were negated by legislative and governmental action that confirmed South Africa's dominant trends of segregation and repression. The United Party government before 1948 was only a lesser evil in comparison with the continuing threat of the rise to power of a doctrinaire Afrikaner nationalism that would bar all opportunities for African entrance into a common society. And even after 1948 Africans did not give any serious consideration to preparations for violent tactics, since opportunities remained for exerting extraparliamentary pressure. Furthermore, they still faced an unfinished agenda of organization, political education, and action needed to achieve nonwhite unity.

During the decade before the Nationalists came to power, the United Party government laid the groundwork for some of the later acts of apartheid. The Native (Urban Areas) Act of 1923, which gave municipalities power to control the influx of Africans, was amended in 1937 so as virtually to bar Africans—in practice, only a very few—from buying urban property from non-Africans. Also during the same year, Parliament enacted the Native Laws Amendment Act without waiting to consult the Natives' Representative Council at its first session. To meet the problem of municipal acquiescence in the building of schools and churches attended by Africans in so-called white areas, the act strengthened the central Government's control over such developments. It also enlarged the powers of both urban and rural officials, including those in Cape Province, to control the townward movement of Africans and their residence in the towns, particularly in the case of Africans not required as laborers. (Influx controls were imposed in Cape Town by proclamation in 1939; this was a restrictive policy of the kind that Africans claimed was prevented before 1936 through the influence of the African vote.) Urban areas legislation was consolidated in 1945, again without allowing the NRC an opportunity to comment; together with legislation affecting Indians, the ground was laid for the comprehensive Group Areas Act of 1950.

Nor was there any liberalization of official policy regarding African trade unions. The Industrial Conciliation Act of 1937, like the 1924 act of the same name, excluded Africans from the definition of employees whose trade unions could be officially registered and could make use of machinery for arriving at enforceable agreements on labor standards. African workers had long been subject to criminal penalities—under the Master and Servant Acts and the Native Labor Regulation Act of 1913—for breaking a labor contract; but late in 1942, after a wave of strikes by African workers, War Measure 145 defined existing restrictions in detail. In the words of Margaret Ballinger, the measure made "all strikes of all African workers in all circumstances illegal."[4] Two years later, when the African Mine Workers' Union was organizing thousands of workers, War Measure 1,425 forbade meetings of more than twenty persons on mine property. In August 1946 the African mine workers' strike was crushed by soldiers and police. In 1947, when the Industrial Conciliation (Natives) Bill was drafted, the Smuts government gave signs of being prepared to move toward a qualified but official recognition of African unions; but the bill, severely criticized within the United Party and by white labor, did not pass.

The government anticipated other apartheid legislation when it empowered itself in 1941, in the Factories Act, to prescribe racially separate accommodations and facilities for workers. Also noteworthy was its adherence during the war to the policy of not arming nonwhite soldiers (other than with assegais) so long as the Union itself was not directly threatened.

Coloureds and Indians were also subjects of discriminatory action that not only pointed toward post-1948 legislation but also had a major impact on Coloured and Indian politics and stimulated renewed efforts to create nonwhite unity. In 1943, ironically in expectation of a grateful response, Smuts set up a Coloured Affairs Department on an experimental basis for two years. (It was periodically extended until 1949.) Its purely advisory functions were to be performed by twenty Coloureds appointed by the government. Traditionally the impoverished Coloureds, who were often described by whites (not invidiously) as an "appendage" of the white community, had received relatively favorable official treatment although in practice they were subjected to many economic and social restrictions. Liberalization of franchise qualifications in 1930 and 1931 had not applied to Coloureds, but Coloured males were still on the common voters' roll in Cape Province (about 53,100 were registered in 1945). Coloured leaders were bitter, however, in their reaction to the new and racially discriminatory body, which they saw as comparable to the Native Affairs Department and the first step toward their removal from the common voters' roll and greater segregation.

Three years later, in June 1946, the Asiatic Land Tenure and Indian Representation Act (or "Ghetto Act") was passed, the culmination of intensive white pressures, especially from English-speaking members of the United Party in Natal, to prevent Indian "penetration" of white residential areas and the expansion of Indian trading. The legislation was both an extension to Indians of many of the principles of the 1923 Urban Areas Act affecting Africans and a precurser of the Group Areas Act of 1950, which also affected Coloureds and whites. Legislation in 1939 had sought to "peg," or prevent change in, the status quo in the Transvaal for two years.[5] Other legislation proposed in 1939—to allow a three-fourths majority of whites in a particular residential area to exclude nonwhites from it—was dropped after multiracial protests led by Dr. Y. M. Dadoo, an Indian physician and Communist in Johannesburg.

In 1943 another temporary "pegging" act extended to Natal restrictions on the ownership of land and provided for the prohibition of interracial property transactions. Natal, where most of South Africa's Asians live (477,000 in the Union in 1960), had previously not had restrictions on the ownership of land comparable to those in the Transvaal. Finally, in 1946, legislation dealt comprehensively with land ownership and occupancy and provided for the demarcation of Natal into exempted and unexempted areas. As partial compensation for new restrictions and as a gesture that might strengthen South Africa's case in the United Nations, the 1946 act also provided for the first Indian representation in Parliament. Two whites were to be elected to the House of Assembly and one to the Senate by Indian males in Natal and the Transvaal who met educational and economic qualifications. Indians were also allowed to elect two representatives in the Natal Provincial Council, and the representatives could themselves be Indians. At the same time, Indians who had qualified for the common voters' roll in Natal before 1896—only one or two by 1946—were removed from the common roll. Indians boycotted the communal vote, and it was repealed by the Nationalist government in 1948.

During the period under review, Africans and other nonwhites were constantly aware of the continuing threat that Malan's "Purified National Party" might rise to power. In 1934, rejecting reconciliation with Hertzog and Smuts, Malan had led a small and militant wing of Nationalists into the new party, which aimed at Afrikaner predominance and the establishment of a Christian National Republic. Renewed efforts were made to promote Afrikaner separatism in the social, economic, and educational life of the country. Nationalist fervor reached its highest emotional peak in 1938 during the centennial celebrations of the Great Trek. The climax came with the laying of the foundation of the Voortrekker monument outside Pretoria on Dingaan's Day, December 16, the date when Afrikaner Nationalists celebrate the defeat of the Zulus at Blood River, a time of year when the ANC coincidentally held its annual conference. The split in the United Party in 1939, when South Africa entered the war, gave new hope for Afrikaner reunification. Almost one-third of the United Party's members in Parliament followed Hertzog into opposition, and in 1940 he merged with Malan in the "Reunited National Party."

The years of opposition during the war revealed the political strength of parliamentarians like Malan and the Nazi-minded extremism of some other Nationalists. Attitudes varied widely: Hertzog, essentially neutralist in the war and insistent on equality between Afrikaner and English-speaking South Africans; Malan, sympathetic to Germany and aiming at predominance for Christian National Afrikaner ideals; militantly authoritarian groups like the Ossewa Brandwag (OB or ox-wagon guard) and Oswald Pirow's New Order, which admired the Nazis; and a few men whose intransigence led them to commit treason or sabotage. In June 1941, at the height of Nazi victories, supporters of Malan, of the OB, and others drafted an authoritarian constitution for a future republic. Meanwhile, Hertzog and his followers had already split from Malan. The OB became increasingly militaristic, organizing storm troopers and scorning parliamentary institutions.

In the general elections of May 30, 1938, July 7, 1943, and—a historic watershed in South African politics—May 26, 1948, Malan's Nationalists increased their parliamentary and popular strength. Their estimated percentage of the popular vote in those elections (including minor party support in 1948) was 29.6, 33.7, and 40.0. Owing to the geographical distribution of their support, giving them an edge in marginal districts, and to overrepresentation of rural areas, the Nationalists achieved disproportionate strength in the House of Assembly, winning in the three successive elections 18.0, 28.7 and—despite the lack of a popular majority—52.7 percent of the seats. In 1943 Malan took a more moderate approach than was desired by many Nationalist leaders and offered full guarantees to the English-speaking section. Nevertheless, his electoral appeal continued to be directed almost exclusively to Afrikaners. In 1948, the Nationalists voiced economic grievances and under the banner of "apartheid," exploited white racial fears in inflammatory attacks on vaguely liberal pronouncements of the United Party. In winning practically every district that was predominantly Afrikaans-speaking, the Nationalists laid the basis for a consolidation of political power that was intended to endure indefinitely.

URBAN TRENDS AND POPULAR PROTEST

In entering urban and industrial life, Africans became more receptive than before to nationalist appeals. The new and common milieu provided opportunities for intertribal contact at work, in official advisory bodies, in schools, and in voluntary associations such as trade unions, churches, and sports clubs. Africans in Cape Province, after being virtually disenfranchised in 1936, came to share political aspirations with other Africans in the Union. The grounds for nonwhite unity were also strengthened with the growth of opportunities for contacts among Africans, Coloureds, and Indians and of awareness that all nonwhites were commonly threatened by a white oppressor.

Despite their common disabilities under white rule, Africans developed widely varying outlooks and interests in the changing conditions of urban life. During the 1930s and 1940s, a small middle class of teachers, professional men, and businessmen—serving Africans—grew slowly. The mass of urban Africans, however, were unskilled or semiskilled laborers, members of a landless proletariat whose movement out of the reserves was due, historically, to overcrowding, the pressure of taxation, and the attractions of economic opportunity. During the fifteen years after 1936, the number of Africans resident in urban areas increased from about one million to over 2.3 million. By 1949, as the Fagan Report had disclosed, more than half the African population was in the urban and rural working force of the white economy, with Africans who remained in the Native reserves (covering about 12.9 percent of South Africa's land) depending largely on remittances from relatives to maintain subsistence levels. By the early 1950s, according to the Tomlinson Commission, about two-thirds of the Africans working in urban areas were "permanently" urbanized. (In the mid-1960s, perhaps 2.6 million were permanently urbanized.)

Increasing numbers of Africans aspired to Western material standards and culture, although the values and institutions loosely described as tribal continued to have some local importance. That importance was especially marked in the case of Africans whose labor was migratory, that is, who moved periodically between town and the reserve where their families lived. Permanently urbanized Africans, on the other hand, were sharply aware of the barrier to economic advancement that was represented by lower-class Afrikaners who were the beneficiaries of official and unofficial discrimination.

In the combustible circumstances of poverty and insecurity, police action directed at Africans sometimes resulted in violent eruptions.[6] On September 19, 1937, in Vereeniging, for example, a defiant African mob beat one African and two white policemen to death, while a number of the mob were wounded. A statement made later by the white superintendent of the African "location" was to be remembered and quoted by Clements Kadalie in 1944: "Young and inexperienced officers," said the superintendent, "were called upon to administer the harsh and oppressive laws relating to beer, taxes, and passes."[7]

On another occasion, a police raid in the African township of Sophiatown, Johannesburg, on June 18, 1941, resulted in the fatal shooting of two Africans, the serious wounding of another, and —according to a Transvaal African Congress circular calling a mass protest meeting (Document 22)—a "savage assult" on a woman who was "in the family way." Dr. Xuma sent telegrams of protest to the prime minister and the minister of justice and led a deputation to the latter to discuss this and other recent raids (Document 23).

On December 28, 1942, 17 persons were killed and about 111 wounded in a riot in the Pretoria municipal compound after stones were thrown and a white soldier killed by an African crowd, angry about delays in carrying out promises to raise wages. In November 1944, scattered fighting between Africans and whites in Johannesburg was sparked when a trolley car ran over an African; about 100 Africans were injured, and a white mob destroyed the *Bantu World* printing plant and back files of the *Bantu World*. The bloodiest episode of the period, however, was the rioting of Zulus against Indians and shooting by police in Durban in January 1949.

During the war, tens of thousands of Africans in the Johannesburg area reacted to intolerable congestion by moving as squatters to vacant land, where they built and organized shanty towns. Other grass roots action, more in the form of confrontation than of self-help, were the boycotts carried on by the workers of Alexandra, a suburb outside Johannesburg where about 60,000 Africans lived. In protest against increases in fares, there were brief bus boycotts in August 1940 and October 1942. In August 1943, thousands of Africans walked some eighteen miles a day for nine days. On November 14, 1944, they began to walk for a period of seven weeks.

The later boycotts attracted the organized help of African organizations, the Communist Party, and some white sympathizers. The most prominent figure was Gaur Radebe, a trade union organizer who lived in Alexandra and was a leading member of the Transvaal African Congress and a local leader of the Communist Party. The boycotts brought about some improvement. Much later, during three months early in 1957, they were precedents for the successful boycott of Johannesburg buses by more than 50,000 Africans.

Africans were also responsive to trade union leaders who voiced their immediate economic grievances. Early attempts to organize Africans had taken place with varying degrees of success after World War I, most notably in the spectacular rise during the 1920s of Kadalie's Industrial and Commerical Workers' Union. In the mid-1930s only a very few African unions were still flourishing. Although they were not officially recognized, and their members faced severe penalties for striking, which was against the law, the unions themselves were not illegal, and they sometimes succeeded in winning an employer's de facto recognition. In the renewed activity of the late 1930s and 1940s, the organization of African mine workers, in the face of almost crippling restrictions, was remarkable. At a conference on August 3, 1941, a new effort was begun to build up the African Mine Workers' Union, existing in embryo for a decade, under the leadership of Gaur Radebe and John B. Marks, who later became president.

Africans moving into private manufacturing industry—126,000 in 1939, rising to 292,000 in 1949—were particularly responsive to militant leadership.[8] Militancy erupted in a wave of strikes late in 1942. Even after War Measure 145 of that year, Africans took part in some sixty illegal strikes during the next two years. The largest strike, led by the African Mine Workers' Union in August 1946, has already been described. At about this time, the Council of Non-European Trade Unions claimed an affiliation of 119 unions, about 59 of them being African unions on the Witwatersrand, with 158,000 members. Most of the African unions were chronically in financial distress and in 1949 only about 38,000 Africans (according to an official inquiry) were paid-up members; but the number who considered themselves to be union members was far larger.

THE AFRICAN NATIONAL CONGRESS, 1937-1949

By the mid-1930s, during the presidency of the conservative Dr. Pixley ka I. Seme, the founder of Congress and a busy attorney in Johannesburg, the African National Congress became nearly moribund. Unlike the Industrial and Commercial Workers' Union in the 1920s, the ANC had failed to win a mass following, nor had it built an effective organization or an independent financial base. The All African Convention meetings, which Seme was urged to call jointly with Professor D. D. T. Jabavu, who had kept aloof from the ANC, attracted such wide representation and enthusiasm that the ANC seemed to be in serious danger of being declared dead in order to make way for a new organization. A new organization, it was

81

argued, would be unencumbered by a legacy of passivity and internal quarrels.

In 1936, the Rev. James A. Calata of Cradock in the eastern Cape Province, the conservative but vigorous president since 1930 of the Cape African Congress, became the national secretary-general. Traveling to Bloemfontein, Johannesburg, and Pretoria, mainly on his own meager resources but with occasional assistance from local Africans and white friends, he discussed whether or not new efforts should be made to resuscitate—the word often used—the ANC. Veteran members argued that the ANC was "in the hearts of the people," that it had survived while other movements had risen and fallen.

A special meeting of members in the Pretoria-Johannesburg area was called. R. V. Selope Thema, editor of the *Bantu World*, was so pessimistic about the ANC's future that he failed to attend after promising to come. J. B. Marks, the Communist trade unionist, came and made a pro-ANC speech regarded by Calata as "brilliant." Calata habitually distrusted "leftists" like Marks and Moses Kotane; but although he had opposed having Kotane, who lived in Cape Town, hold any ANC office in Cape Province, Calata judged him to be "very loyal to the ANC."[9] The small group of members, of widely differing political temperaments, finally decided that the ANC should be revived and that a Silver Jubilee conference should be held in December 1937.

The NRC was indirectly useful in reviving the Congress. After 1937, Thema, R. G. Baloyi, Thomas Mapikela, and other members of the NRC were able to arouse interest in the ANC by using their position as councillors, traveling sometimes at government expense and holding meetings in tribal areas. Marks traveled as private secretary to Baloyi and has recalled that "we toured both the Transvaal and the Orange Free State, visiting almost every village or dorp and took the message that the ANC had come back." Though the ANC was "literally dead," according to Marks, he discovered that remnants existed all over South Africa and that there was a favorable response to the Silver Jubilee appeal.[10]

The ANC under Mahabane

Meanwhile, the question of Seme's successor faced the December 1937 conference. Calata believed the ANC needed a younger leader who could, above all, appeal to "the graduates." He should also be able to overcome the federal weaknesses of the ANC, unify the Cape Province—divided between rival leaders of the western and eastern Cape Provinces, excluding the Transkei reserve, which was an autonomous ANC area—and bring Dr. John Dube's independent Natal Native Congress back into the fold. Calata's candidate was Dr. A. B. Xuma, the American-educated physician who had a successful medical practice and therefore financial means in the key center of Johannesburg. But Dr. Xuma was in England late in 1937 and during most of 1938. "I have a great hope," Calata wrote to him in August 1938, "that in you the African people have found the leader they are looking for."[11] In Xuma's absence, Calata and others turned to the Rev. Z. R. Mahabane, a Methodist minister and one of the respected older leaders who had once before been president-general during the mid-1920s. He could "speak strongly," Calata has said, though he "wasn't a fighter at all." [12]

With Mahabane in the small town of Winburg in the Orange Free State and Calata in Cradock, with virtually no money for travel, functioning within a cumbersome constitutional framework and lacking a small executive or working committee whose members lived within easy commuting distance of each other, the ANC revived slowly. The AAC, of which Mahabane was a vice-president, was even less active since its constitution provided for a plenary conference only once every three years. Although emergency conferences could be called, the AAC did not meet again until December 1940. During this period, ANC members, some of them also active in trade unions, advisory bodies, or other organizations, made uncoordinated local efforts to present grievances to the authorities, to hold demonstrations, or to challenge in the courts various official actions against individuals. Nationally, the main activity of the ANC, aside from its conferences of 1938 and 1939, was to send a thirteen-man deputation to meet with the minister of Native affairs and the parliamentary Natives' representatives in May 1939. The ANC men were joined by three representatives of the Congress of Advisory Boards, the government-subsidized annual meeting of boards provided for by the Urban Areas Act of 1923 (Document 17).

During Mahabane's presidency of the ANC, the key official was Calata; indeed, his role as national secretary-general covered the much longer period of 1936-1949. He was also president of the Cape African Congress from 1930 to June 1949, when he was succeeded by Professor Z. K. Matthews. Calata's presidential addresses of 1938, 1939, and, shortly after the coming to power of the Nationalists, 1948 (Documents 16, 18, and 42) illustrate the depth of his conservative African nationalism, his appreciation of the chiefs, and his desire for African unity. He displayed a persistent hope that moderate appeals to high officials of good will and African cooperation with whites in movements like that of the Joint Councils (groups of whites and middle class Africans who began during the 1920s to meet informally in the major cities) could improve the immediate lot of his people. He demonstrated a devotion to ideals of racial reconciliation and a united South Africa in which ultimately Africans would attain "full citizenship in the land of our fathers." Calata also emphasized his debt to missionary education and Christian upbringing—"we love the people of British descent because of what we owe them," he said in 1948. [13] "Many Nationalists," he also said in the same year, " . . . are good men and women" and their government should be given a chance. But he concluded that he was "beginning to wonder" whether white religious ministers like Prime Minister Malan were preaching to their people, as he was to his, "that Christianity is a world brotherhood." [14]

With South Africa's entrance into the war, the ANC's leadership became more assertive. At the December 1939 conference in Durban, which Dr. Dube attended, the annual conference accepted "the principle of the Non-European United Front," the nonwhite popular front whose leader in the Transvaal was Dr. Dadoo, but made no move to affiliate with the Front itself. The conference also resolved that the ANC would not advise Africans to participate in the war "in any capacity" until the government granted "full democratic and citizenship rights" (Document 19). Six months later, having learned that the executive committee of the AAC was to meet at Bloemfontein on July 7, 1940, Calata summoned the ANC's national executive committee to meet in the same place on the preceding day—"before other organisations step into our shoes"[15]—to discuss the issuance of a joint statement with the AAC. On July 7, the joint executive committees issued a more respectfully worded statement than the ANC statement of December 1939 but one warning of "mischievous doctrines that are being disseminated among Africans," of "the expediency of admitting the Africans of this country into full citizenship," and of fully arming those who served in the military forces, if South Africa was to be effectively defended (Document 61).

Xuma as Organizer

In the election of a new president-general in December 1940, only 41 delegates were present to vote, and the vote was surprisingly close: 21 for Xuma to 20 for Mahabane (Document 20). Nine years later, Dr. Xuma accepted nomination for a fourth term but was defeated. (The exact results are not reported in the minutes, but his defeat was not a close one.) He then recollected the number of delegates in 1940 and the fact that he had taken over an organization with nothing in the treasury. In December 1949, 101 delegates attended the conference, and £491 was in the bank (Document 47).

Comparison of delegates and money does not indicate the extent and pervasiveness of Dr. Xuma's leadership. Proudly independent, suspicious of any activity that appeared to threaten his authority, temperamentally averse to mass demonstrations or militancy in the streets, he was, nevertheless, the hoped-for and vigorous new personality who did attract "the graduates." He succeeded also in asserting national authority over the provincial congresses, in beginning the construction of an organization having paid-up members, functioning branches, and a functioning central executive committee, and in extending lines of communication to all levels. Those elements of organization were all present in the 1919 constitution; but they existed mainly on paper, with activity occurring only wherever and whenever leaders appeared. Xuma was decisive in his oversight of provincial organizations, for example, in September 1942, by suspending officials in western Cape Province who had disregarded national policy against the official endorsement of white candidates seeking election as Natives' representatives, and in August 1943 by taking over the administration of the Transvaal Congress at a time when competing groups both claimed to be the legitimate provincial leaders.[16]

The urgent need for more effective organization was the note struck by Xuma immediately following his election, and at the same conference he was given a committee and a mandate to revise the 1919 constitution (Document 20). That document had been extraordinarily long, detailed, and legalistic, establishing a

84

body supposedly patterned after the bicameral American Congress, with a Lower House of representatives from a large number of districts and the British High Commission Territories and an Upper House of chiefs. On its face, the constitution had much to say about membership, branches, meetings, finances, and communication. But in practice it had earned the reputation of providing for a federal or decentralized parliament that spoke for a movement of affiliated bodies as well as for individual members. Many felt, however, that what was needed was a more centralized mass organization prepared to educate the people and to be continually ready to challenge the government. Thus, despite the nostalgia of some old-timers who were unhappy to see the scrapping of the old document, Dr. Xuma succeeded in having the conference of December 1943 adopt a new and drastically simplified constitution to replace the old one (Document 29a). [17]

In providing that "any person . . . willing to subscribe to the aims of Congress" could become a member, the new constitution was nonracial, whereas the old constitution had limited membership to persons "belonging to the aboriginal races of Africa." The new constitution still provided for affiliated bodies but eliminated the Upper House of chiefs. Although Xuma himself had a high respect for chiefdom, most chiefs had long ago drifted away under government pressures, and the House had become defunct with only the position of its president kept filled.

Formerly the treasurer and secretary were elected by the conference on the nomination of the president; henceforth they were to be directly elected. Thus, the new constitution was considered more democratic. More important was a new provision for a working committee composed of persons living within fifty miles of national headquarters. The committee, acting for the national executive committee, was in practice to meet almost weekly with Dr. Xuma. Despite a significant shift in emphasis from annual parliament to year-round organization, the constitution was generally regarded as being merely a more workable and simpler—some thought too abbreviated—version of the old.

Membership statistics during 1937-1949 reveal both the smallness and slow growth of the membership (presumably the dues-paying membership) and the inadequacy of reporting from the branches to provincial headquarters and from the provinces to national headquarters. The minister of Native affairs is reported to have asked Calata in May 1939, after meeting with the thirteen-man deputation referred to earlier, how many members the ANC had. Calata replied, "4,000." [18] But in December 1941, at the end of the first year of Xuma's presidency, Calata reported that none of the provincial congresses had sent in statistics of numerical and financial strength; nevertheless, he knew that the Cape Province had six branches with at least twenty-five fully paid members and estimated a total membership of about 200 (Document 25b). A year later, the annual conference authorized Xuma and his national executive committee to campaign for a membership of 1 million in southern Africa (Document 28).

In 1945, the Transvaal, Orange Free State, and Natal reported 69 branches (three-fourths of them in the Transvaal) and 4,176 members (nearly half of them in the Orange Free State). [19] In 1947, the ANC claimed a total membership of 7,000 (Document 42). But the national executive committee complained again in 1949 that many branches had failed to report to the provincial secretaries. Only 46 branches, out of a much larger number of known branches, were alive, with 2,755 members. [20] At the conference of that year, there was some sentiment for a policy of nondisclosure of membership statistics, but a motion to discuss this matter in committee was defeated. (See Document 47, which is reproduced in this volume without the foregoing matter.) Despite these meager statistics of formal membership, ANC leaders could believe with justification that they expressed African grievances and aspirations more truly than did any other organized group in the country.

Before Xuma's presidency, the ANC's reputation was tarnished by charges of financial irresponsibility. In part, this was due to the problem referred to by Calata in his July 1938 address (Document 16), when he warned of "irresponsible agitators who go about the country . . . taking our ignorant people's money under our name." In the Cape provincial conference of that year, the treasurer submitted a detailed statement of income, fully reported in the *Eastern Province Herald* (July 3, 1938), amounting to £13, 11 shillings, and 3 pence. Almost half of this amount was donated by whites, and only 15 shillings were contributed by members. Applause greeted the promise of one of the white senators elected by Africans that he would contribute £5 annually to the Congress. [21] Two months before Xuma's election, Calata described the ANC as "an organisation which depends upon white donations for finances." [22]

As president, Xuma made the first systematic effort within the ANC to keep a public financial accounting as well as to build up the treasury. He also sought to confine participation in conferences to dues-paying members in good standing, thus implementing the 1919 constitution. But traditionally, as Professor Z. K. Matthews has recalled, an ANC weakness was reluctance to insist that a man who had not paid his annual dues of two shillings and sixpence was not entitled to speak or to vote. "Let him have his say!" was the usual cry. Funds, therefore, were usually lacking, and leaders had to pay their own expenses. In addition to stressing the importance of paying dues, Xuma also sought white financial support, at one point securing a donation of about £2,000 from the Donaldson Fund, an African welfare fund, and also money from the Chamber of Mines. [23] On the other hand, Xuma's cooperation with Indians and left-wing whites produced rumors and suspicion of unaccounted financial aid and undue influence. Such feelings were expressed by Africans like Selope Thema, who distrusted the Indians, and I. B. Tabata of the AAC, who distrusted the Communists.

For the period from December 1945 to October 1946, Xuma produced a printed and audited account, showing a balance sheet of about £848, with income that included donations of £283 and membership dues of £132. The conference of December 1946 resolved that the constitution should be amended to raise individual dues to one shilling a month in urban areas and three shillings a year in rural

86

areas and that an additional levy of one shilling a month in urban areas and sixpence a month in rural areas be imposed for a "fighting fund" (Document 37). Soon afterward, the national executive committee suspended the constitutional amendment but adopted the special levy and resolved to campaign for a fighting fund of £10,000 (Document 38).

The annual conference in December 1947 refused to accept the financial statement presented by R. G. Baloyi, the treasurer-general, since it had not been audited. In the 1948 conference, Baloyi, under a cloud because of his support of a Nationalist Party candidate for the Senate, was not even present; and an acting treasurer was appointed. In 1949, the conference was informed that an audited statement would be forthcoming. Meanwhile, the Cape Congress had not forwarded to the national executive committee its share of dues because of lack of confidence in "the Treasury Department."

Two needs, requiring money, that were frequently recognized during the period were support for an ANC newspaper and for full-time, paid organizers. The 1937 annual conference resolved that a new newspaper should be established to take the place of *Abantu-Batho*, the official organ which had begun publication in 1912 but had declined and died by 1935 (Document 16). But at no time before the ANC was banned in 1960 did it manage once again to publish its own national organ, although newsletters and bulletins were issued from time to time.

Resolutions passed during Xuma's presidency had called for paid organizers at both national and provincial levels (Documents 28 and 37). ("The I.C.U. [in Natal] is the only organization that has a whole-time Secretary," Champion wrote of himself in July 1941. [24]) Xuma hired various part-time employees for the national office, but not until December 1949 did the annual minutes report the presence of a full-time employee, a typist (Document 47). And not until that time did the ANC acquire a secretary-general, Walter Sisulu, who was to work full time, but supported by his wife's earnings rather than by payment by the ANC. [25]

Xuma and "Africans' Claims"

One accomplishment of the Xuma era was the preparation and adoption of *Africans' Claims in South Africa*, the most important ANC statement since 1919 and one accepted by later ANC leaders as an authoritative statement of ANC aims (Document 29b). It was a sixteen-page printed booklet whose contents consisted mainly of two parts: a restatement of Roosevelt and Churchill's Atlantic Charter and explication "from the standpoint of Africans within the Union of South Africa" and a "Bill of Rights."

The document's precurser was "The Policy and Platform of the African National Congress," a short statement issued by Dr. Xuma during the first year of his presidency. (Document 24, published in August 1941 in *Inkululeko* [Freedom], the official organ of the Communist Party.) Six general aims appearing in the statement were lifted verbatim from the 1919 constitution, though in a different order, and quoted again in Xuma's first presidential address as aims that had been enunciated by the founders (Document 25a). The conference thanked Xuma for the August statement and resolved that a committee should be appointed to lay down further principles (Document 25c). A year later, the December 1942 conference empowered Xuma to appoint a committee to study the Atlantic Charter and to draft a bill of rights to be presented to the peace conference at the end of the war (Document 28).

Although Xuma was anxious to reach the mass of Africans, his special strength and predisposition lay in attracting intellectuals to Congress. In preparation for the 1941 annual conference, he appealed to "the best brains" to attend. [26] A year later, the conference congratulated Xuma on his "unique success" in achieving "the co-operation and the confidence of the leaders of all shades—distinguished University Graduates, and the most noted professional men among the African people today" (Document 28). In March 1943, Xuma invited thirty-four Africans, exclusive of representatives of chiefs in the Union and in the High Commission Territories, to join the Atlantic Charter Committee to study "post-war reconstruction in Africa with special reference to Southern Africa" and "to formulate a statement of principles and a programme of action." [27]

Those invited were assigned to subcommittees and also asked to submit essays or recommendations by May 15, 1943, a deadline that was several times deferred. The committee, numbering twenty-eight, met on December 13 and 14 in Bloemfontein. They were "leaders of African thought," Xuma wrote later in the preface to *Africans' Claims*, who had acted "without assistance or influence from others." The members of the committee were indeed a distinguished group, including physicians, attorneys, teachers, ministers, and one editor.

But more remarkable was the breadth of the political spectrum from conservative to Communist represented by the members, as had been the case in the AAC meetings of 1935-1937, and their unanimity in agreeing on aims. The committee also demonstrated the continuity of African leadership, although there were some notable absences. Professor Jabavu, Dr. Dube (who was not well), A. W. G. Champion, and Chief Albert Lutuli were invited but did not attend. Paul Mosaka, a member of the NRC, was also invited; but after becoming an organizer in September 1943 of the rival African Democratic Party, it is not surprising that he too was absent. The AAC's vice-president and its treaurer—Mahabane and Moroka—were present, however, as were many others who had played leading roles in the meetings held nearly a decade earlier. On the other hand, none of the younger AAC leaders who were hostile to the ANC, like I. B. Tabata, were invited.

Z. K. Matthews, who had been clerk-draughtsman in the first AAC meetings, was elected chairman of the Atlantic Charter Committee, Xuma serving as "secretary-organizer." In the committee, Matthews occupied a position probably near the center of the spectrum, between Seme, Calata, Selope Thema, and Godlo on one side and the Communists on the other: Kotane, Marks, and Mofutsanyana. Also on the committee was Gana Makabeni, who had been expelled from the Communist Party but was not antagonistic to it and was now president of the

88

Council of Non-European Trade Unions. The committee, including its left-wing members, was limited almost entirely to representatives of the older generation. Only J. C. M. Mbata and M. T. Moerane, who were on the committee, were also active in the informal meetings taking place about that time among men who were to found the ANC Youth League.

The document and its Bill of Rights, which emerged from this group, restated long-standing aims, but on the key issue of the franchise it appeared to take a more radical position than any taken by the ANC in the past. The 1919 constitution had called for "the removal of the 'Colour Bar' in political, education, and industrial fields and for equitable representation of Natives in Parliament. . . ." The 1923 "Bill of Rights" claimed " 'equal rights for all civilised men' " and "an equal share in the management and direction" of the country. The 1943 constitution called for "the freedom of the African people from all discriminatory laws whatsoever." Throughout the intervening years, the call had been made for "full citizenship," but the emphasis was on equal treatment with whites rather than, necessarily, the principle of one man one vote, although by 1931 legislation had extended that principle to all whites. The AAC, for example, accepted as "equitable" in 1936 a qualified but nonracial franchise, the franchise policy adopted by the multiracial Progressive Party more than two decades later. The AAC was willing to accept, in other words, "a civilization test" based upon "an educational or property or wage qualification," and it expressed its belief that "such measures would adequately protect the interests of the white population in whose favour the dice are already heavily loaded in view of the extension of adult suffrage to white men and women" (Document 9).

Sometimes wording was used that suggested an essentially unqualified franchise, that is, one man one vote. The March 4, 1942, deputation, for example, spoke of education as being essential in a democratic state if there was to be "intelligent participation . . . by every adult member" (Document 26). The 1943 Bill of Rights at last apparently endorsed unqualified universal suffrage in its call for "the extension to all adults, regardless of race, of the right to vote." (The Freedom Charter of 1955 was to declare that "every man and woman shall have the right to vote." Compare Document 75b, "The People's Charter" of May 1948.) Yet one could also read the Bill of Rights as being consistent with a qualified franchise so long as it was nonracial. Four years later, on the eve of the 1948 general election, Xuma spoke of a "return to the old Cape principle of a common voters' roll," thus suggesting that he himself was more concerned with non-racialism than with one man one vote (Document 41).

At any rate, *Africans' Claims* was a statement of objectives and was not concerned with timetables, nor did it propose any program of action. It was adopted by the annual conference of the ANC in December 1943 [28] and continued for some time to be sold widely and to be a minor source of revenue. Although proudly received by Africans, its reception by Prime Minister Smuts was sour. Xuma in his preface had counseled against discouragement by quoting "the wise

89

and encouraging words" of Smuts, to the irritation of some ANC men. Smuts had said, "Do not mind being called agitators," and had advised Africans to attend to matters of "Native . . . welfare." Xuma sent Smuts a copy of *Africans' Claims* and requested an interview. Smuts replied through his private secretary, who wrote that the document was "propagandist" and that Smuts was "not prepared to discuss proposals which are wildly impracticable." [29]

Xuma and Non-Africans

Xuma's ambivalent relations with the All African Convention, whose leadership joined with radical Coloureds in 1943 to form the NEUM, his hostility to the ADP, which called for both mass action and the enlistment of white supporters, and his acceptance of the national chairmanship of the Anti-Pass Campaign, launched by Communists, illustrate the complexity of his attitudes regarding the independence of the ANC and cooperation with whites and nonwhites. Xuma was both an Africanist, calling for African unity and self-reliance, and a multiracialist, welcoming cooperation by whites of goodwill but turning increasingly to cooperation with nonwhites. In the earlier years of his presidency, he emphasized his hope and faith in the future; in his later years, these attitudes tended to give way to expressions of frustration and even bitterness. In his 1941 speech commemorating the death of 615 Africans in the transport-ship Mendi in 1917, he expressed faith that South Africa would put into practice the ideals it was fighting for, though he added a veiled threat of the consequences if it did not do so (Document 21). Later in the year he spoke with enthusiasm at the opening of the Orlando High School in Johannesburg; Africans were "very grateful," he said, for the "generous" grant of money from the Native Affairs Department for the buildings. "There seems to be a welcome change of heart and awareness about the educational needs of the African community," he said. [30]

The reports of the deputations in 1941 and 1942 show the politeness and even cordiality of relations with high officials, although the 1942 deputation also bluntly warned that Africans did not have "the will and the heart to fight" in the war (Documents 23 and 26). A year later, in the preface to *Africans' Claims*, Xuma could say—again to the irritation of many—that he knew the prime minister would "represent the interests of the people of our country" at the peace conference and could express confidence that "all men and women of goodwill" would support the African struggle.

Xuma's tone changed after the war. In May 1945, he accepted "demonstrations on Victory Day" as a stage in the "fight for freedom" (Document 30). In his growing concern with trade union rights (Xuma gave the opening address in August 1945 to the "All-in Conference of the Non-White Trade Unions"), he issued a statement on January 14, 1946 which, again, accepted that South Africa's ideals were "Democracy, Christianity and human decency" but described "the African worker" as "bitter and sullen" (Document 35). Although not directly involved in preparation for the mine workers' strike of August 1946, Xuma and the ANC supported the strike; but Xuma's support fell short of endorsement of a general

90

strike. His lack of interest in such action was disillusioning to both younger and left-wing leaders.

During his absence in the United States, the December 1946 annual conference described the government's policy as "barbarous" and called for African boycott of welcoming festivities for the British Royal Family—a boycott that turned out to be almost invisible (Document 37). Following Xuma's return to South Africa and his pact with Dr. Dadoo and Dr. Naicker, noted below, he issued a flyer on March 21, 1947, addressed not only "to all Africans" but also to "friends of justice" declaring "the time has come" for the organization of mass meetings in the liberation struggle (Document 40). The following year, in a press conference before what he called "the queer general election," Xuma reviewed the "deterioration of race relations" under "a despotic colour oligarchy" and described both Smuts's "trusteeship" and Malan's "apartheid" as euphemisms for exploitation (Document 41). Europeans, he said, in a cable to the United Nations on November 25, 1948, have "the machine guns" (Document 43).

Accumulated frustrations, dramatized by the events within and outside the Natives' Representative Council in 1946, once again gave special importance to external allies. In October 1945, shortly after the end of the war, and also in 1947, ANC delegates attended the fifth and sixth Pan-African Congresses, in Manchester and in Dakar. At about the same time, the United Nations began to assume an importance for the South African opposition that the League of Nations never had. Xuma's cable in January 1946 to the chairman of the U.N. General Assembly opposed South Africa's bid to incorporate South-West Africa and linked the mandated territory to South Africa's domestic policy by concluding that "South Africa must first remove colour bar, restrictions, discriminations at home" (Document 36). During the latter part of 1946 Xuma attended the U.N. in company with two Indian leaders—H. A. Naidoo and Sorabjee Rustomjee of the South African Passive Resistance Council—and Senator H. M. Basner, who had played a key role in the organization of the ADP in 1943.

Xuma's readiness to cooperate with non-Africans was a sign of his self-assurance. Opinions differ, however, on whether or not he strengthened or weakened his prestige among Africans by the company he kept at the U.N. At any rate, the ANC conference of December 1946 congratulated Xuma, the Indian representatives, and Basner and also "the delegates of India, China and the Soviet Union and all other countries who championed the cause of democratic rights . . ." at the United Nations. The conference also paid tribute to participants in the Indian passive resistance campaign and instructed the national executive committee to consider closer cooperation with other non-European national organizations (Document 37).

The government's setting up of the Coloured Affairs Department in 1943 had already stimulated Coloured leaders in Cape Town to seek closer cooperation with Africans. But they expended their influence on the AAC and cut themselves off from any development of close cooperation with the oldest African body, the ANC, which they had hoped would come under the AAC. On the other hand, the radical Indians who later rose to leadership—Dr. Dadoo and Dr. Naicker—had close relations with some of the ANC's leaders in the Transvaal and Natal and, unlike the Coloured leaders, a similar flexibility of mind regarding tactics.

The resolution of the ANC conference suggesting closer cooperation with nonwhites met opposition in the national executive committee on February 1-2, 1947 (Document 38). But on March 9, 1947, Dr. Xuma, Dr. Dadoo, and Dr. Naicker, at a meeting in Johannesburg presided over by Dr. Xuma, issued "a joint Declaration of cooperation," the so-called "Doctors' Pact." It set forth common aims, expressed the view that "it is urgently necessary that a vigorous campaign be immediately launched," and resolved that future joint meetings would be held (Document 39).

Little progress was made in organizing any joint campaign. Indian passive resistance continued as an exclusively Indian effort. However, the terrible circumstances of the Zulu-Indian rioting set off in Durban when an Indian shopkeeper cuffed an African boy on January 13, 1949, gave a great emotional boost to closer cooperation between African and Indian leaders. Lasting several days, the rioting, and the shooting by police and military forces who intervened, resulted in the deaths of at least 137 Indians and Africans and injuries, many of them serious, to more than a thousand persons. [31] On the second day, despite his distrust of cooperation with Indians, A. W. G. Champion, president of the ANC (Natal), joined with Dr. Naicker in an appeal to their followers "to assist in trying to discourage the wild and false talk which brought about this trouble" (Document 44). Dr. Xuma traveled to Durban, and on January 20 he and his working committee in Johannesburg blamed the official policies of discrimination for the racial friction that led to the rioting and called for a round-table conference of African and Indian leaders (Document 45).

About a fortnight later, thirty-five men—leaders of the ANC, the SAIC, and "other leaders," notably including Professor Jabavu and the Rev. Z. R. Mahabane of the AAC—met in Durban. Their statement condemned "the preaching in high places of racial hatred and intolerance," called "for closer cooperation and mutual understanding" among Africans and Indians through their national organizations, and directed that joint councils of Africans and Indians be formed (Document 46). In December 1949, the ANC executive committee reported the formation of "Joint Councils of Goodwill consisting of Africans and Indians" (Document 47). The conference was more notable for the adoption of the Programme of Action, which called upon Africans to go their way alone, but precedents had been set for joint action in the future.

THE FAILURE OF THE NATIVES' REPRESENTATIVE COUNCIL, 1946-1947

The deadlock and then breakdown in relations between the Natives' Representative Council and the Smuts government, in the wake of World War II and the African mine workers' strike, provide an episode in frustration that deserves close examination. [32] To overcome the councillors' sense of impotence, Prime Minister Smuts attempted to give the NRC a renewed lease on life; but the unacceptability of his proposals testified to the gap that had arisen between the vaguely liberal promises of Smuts and the expectations of the moderate and even conservative members of the NRC. Their experiences helped shape the attitudes that brought about the adoption of the Programme of Action and its call for direct action and boycotts.

The twelve Africans elected indirectly to the council and the four—all tribal chiefs—appointed by the government were among the ablest Africans in the Union; in ability, many were undoubtedly the peers of the leading members of the white Parliament. [33] Among the elected members during its history were businessmen (for example, Thomas Mapikela, R. G. Baloyi, and Paul Mosaka, who had also been a teacher), farmers (Charles Sakwe and Saul Mabude), journalists (R. V. Selope Thema, A. M. Jabavu, and R. H. Godlo), teachers (Dr. John Dube and Z. K. Matthews, who was also a lawyer), a lawyer (B. B. Xiniwe), a trade unionist (A. W. G. Champion), a doctor (James S. Moroka), and at least one chief (Jeremiah Moshesh).

Professor D. D. T. Jabavu of the AAC did not become a member, although other members of the AAC, which did not adopt a pro-boycott position until 1943, were candidates both in 1937 and 1942. In the latter year, Dr. James Moroka, the AAC's treasurer, was elected. [34] Veteran members of the ANC were elected in 1937: Dube, Selope Thema, Mapikela, and Baloyi. Other prominent personalities in the ANC became members in 1942: Matthews, Mosaka, Champion, and Selby Msimang. [35] When Dr. Dube died in 1946, Chief Albert Lutuli won Dube's seat in a by-election, while Matthews succeeded Dube as chairman of the caucus of the sixteen African councillors.

Smuts himself attended the first session of the new council, which was widely reported, but this visit was also his last. Although proponents of participation recognized the council's purely advisory nature, they continued to feel during its first five-year term that it had some usefulness as a platform and provided opportunities for movement throughout the country and for meetings that otherwise might not exist. In a public symposium in 1942, Matthews, who was not yet a member, noted that the council was a statutory recognition of African representation in national affairs. It was an official platform that could show white and African interests to be complementary and at the same time promote the development of African national consciousness. However, he criticized the "ridiculously" small number of representatives and the fact that they were not elected directly or by secret ballot.

Writing in later years, Matthews suggested that the council deserved credit for some minor improvements in official policy—for example, the passage of the Native Education Finance Act of 1945, which for the first time provided for the financing of Native education out of general revenue and also provided for a Union Advisory Board on Native Education. Nevertheless, within the council, the feeling deepened that it was futile to expend energy in an enterprise that was virtually

93

ignored by the government and treated as an appendage of the Native Affairs Department. When Dr. Moroka joined the council in 1942, he did so (he later claimed) with the determination to expose and to smash it.

Wartime idealism did little to arouse new hopes. Jan H. Hofmeyr, the deputy prime minister, who embodied liberal white aspirations for change, invoked the Atlantic Charter of Roosevelt and Churchill when he opened a council session on December 1, 1943. Two years later the council adopted a motion of appreciation for Smuts and his war effort, Selope Thema saying, "The Natives participated in this war because they felt they must be on the side of democracy." [36] But meanwhile, the social and economic problems accompanying the wartime influx of Africans to the cities were becoming more severe; and in the words of Professor Matthews, "the increased output of restrictive and discriminatory legislative and administrative measures" and "the increasingly provocative utterances of Members of Parliament" in both government and opposition were producing "a sense of despair and frustration" (Document 31). Before the historic meeting of August 14, 1946 (described below), the conviction had spread within the council that it should adjourn until the government demonstrated that it was reconsidering the direction of its Native policy.

The last straw, the immediate provocation for the decision to adjourn indefinitely, was the government's attitude toward the council during the African mine workers' strike. This strike began in Johannesburg about two days before the council began its scheduled session in Pretoria on August 14, 1946. (The meeting was the first to be attended by Chief Albert Lutuli.) Some councillors on the way to the meeting talked with striking miners while waiting to change trains in Germiston. About 70,000 Africans stopped work, and on the day the council met, about 4,000 attempted to march on Johannesburg. The strike was broken by soldiers and police within a week, with some loss of life and many injuries. Meanwhile, in the midst of conflicting reports and confusion, the young official who had been brought in at short notice to chair the meeting, said nothing about the crisis in his opening speech. The African members made several requests and motions which were rejected or ruled out of order. As Alan Paton later commented: "The Council stood revealed in all its impotence." [37]

On the next day, Dr. Moroka offered the following resolution: [38]

This Council, having since its inception brought to the notice of the Government the reactionary character of the Union Native Policy of segregation in all its ramifications, deprecates the Government's post-war continuation of a policy of Fascism which is the antithesis and negation of the letter and the spirit of the Atlantic Charter and the United Nations Charter. The Council, therefore, in protest against this breach of faith towards the African people in particular and the cause of world freedom in general, resolves to adjourn this session, and calls upon the Government forthwith to abolish all discriminatory legislation affecting Non-Europeans in this country.

The presentation of important resolutions was regularly preceded by informal

94

meetings of the caucus, attended by all the African members, including the four appointed by the government. Discussion was always very frank and full, according to Professor Matthews, and on this occasion the chiefs, whose tribesmen were among the strikers, were particularly interested. Moroka's resolution was adopted unanimously. There were to be several more meetings of the council but never again a full session.

In a pamphlet circulated at the United Nations late in 1946 (Document 31), Matthews reviewed the deterioration in the relations between the council and the government and the reasons for the adjournment.

The final breakdown occurred three months later. The question whether or not the councillors should attend the next meeting, scheduled for November 20, 1946, or should resign, was debated on October 6-7 at an "Emergency Conference of All Africans" called by Dr. Xuma and attended by eight members of the council and some 500 delegates. [39] Anton Lembede, leader of the ANC Youth League, argued for immediate mass resignations. But a compromise resolution was adopted (495 to 16) which endorsed the council's adjournment in August and supported attendance at the meeting convened for November. [40] At the same time the resolution described the Representation of Natives Act of 1936 as a fraud and called on Africans to boycott future elections held under the act.

On November 20, 1946, Hofmeyr himself addressed the council, but his speech appeared to the councillors to have been written by the Department of Native Affairs. He received a unanimous vote of thanks for his courtesy, and the council adjourned. Five days later, Matthews replied. Hofmeyr's statement, he said, "seemed merely an apologia for the status quo."

> The statement [Matthews continued] makes no attempt to deal with some of the burning questions of the day such as the pass laws, the colour-bar in industry, the political rights of the non-European in the Union; and in effect it raises no hope for the future as far as the African people are concerned. . . . In his statement the Acting Prime Minister virtually denies that the Native Policy of the Union is in need of revision and proceeds to justify the policy of segregation and discrimination on the grounds of its supposedly protective character. [41]

The council unanimously approved Matthews' motion "That pending the receipt of a more reassuring reply from the Government the proceedings of this session of the Council be suspended—the Councillors remaining in Pretoria to await such reply."

The culmination came the next day. Hofmeyr's reply was read to the council: the government would not change its decision but hoped for continued cooperation. Again, during a midday recess, there was careful discussion within the caucus. When the councillors reconvened, they were unanimous (one chief was absent) in supporting Matthews' motion for adjournment so that they could consult with their people and the government could reconsider.

Prime Minister Smuts himself finally attempted, in his words, "to get things on the move again" (Document 32). His eyes were on the outside world and he wanted the council to work, Paton has written, while the Nationalists had their eyes on the forthcoming general election and favored abolishing the "impudent and truculent" council. [42] Smuts invited three elected members—Matthews, Selope Thema, and Mosaka—and three appointed members to meet with him, Piet van der Byl (the minister of Native affairs), and three officials on May 8, 1947. He had not met with the council or a deputation from it since the council's first meeting, ten years. earlier. With charm and apparent sincerity, he outlined his tentative thinking for enlarging the council and making it all-African and all-elective, giving it some responsibility and executive authority for developing the rural Native reserves, and perhaps linking local advisory boards to it. In short, he wanted to give the council (in his words) "a bone to chew at." He also expected to convene the full council as soon as possible, he said, in part to consult it regarding a bill for the recognition of Native trade unions. Racial separation of unions would be required, however; mine workers would be excluded; and the prohibition on strikes would be continued. Because Smuts's remarks were made directly to African representatives, who responded, and are particularly revealing of how retarded was his understanding of African aspirations, they are reproduced in full in Document 32.

The six Africans who met with Smuts for one hour and fifty-five minutes were impressed by his friendly and respectful manner and willingness for everyone to talk quite freely. But neither they nor other members of the council who were consulted by Matthews afterward were impressed by what the prime minister had said. Matthews found "a definite gain" in the fact of Smuts's personal intervention and his seeming admission that Native policy was out of date. But following a second meeting with Smuts on the following day, Matthews and Mosaka sought to dispel press enthusiasm for the prime minister's suggestions by holding a press conference in which they described them as constituting "no radical departure from the established Native policy." (This and the following quotations are from Document 32). Nevertheless, Matthews, in a memorandum to members of the council, warned against "a mere stubborn refusal to consider proposals put before us on their merits."

> We owe it to the people we represent to state without fear or favour
> precisely what it is we condemn or approve in schemes intended for them.
> We are engaged in delicate negotiations on behalf of our people and we
> must conduct them with a due sense of responsibility.

Others in the meeting with Smuts had also called attention to the importance of particular improvements that fell short of radical political change. Selope Thema, for example, remarked that "the majority of my people don't want to come to Parliament—I want that, but not the majority of my people." He argued that abolition of the pass laws rather than improvement of the council was the kind of change that the people understood.

There was little likelihood, however, that in 1947 the council would backtrack on the demand of its resolution of August 15, 1946, that the government abolish all discriminatory legislation "forthwith." Matthews in his 1946 pamphlet (Document 31), explaining the reasons for the resolution, moderately described indefinite adjournment as one lasting "until the Government showed evidence of its intention to give more serious consideration to the views of the Council." The literal meaning of the resolution for adjournment was quickly reaffirmed, however, by Dr. Xuma and the ANC's working committee two days after the conclusion of the meetings with Smuts. Their statement (Document 33) criticized Smuts for failure to respond to the council's demand that discriminatory legislation be repealed, and reendorsed the council's resolution to adjourn until that demand was met.

The demise of the council was a long-drawn-out anticlimax, and surprisingly the African members continued to be involved. Highlights of the late 1947-1951 period are as follows. Despite Smuts's assurance that a full meeting of the council would be convened as soon as possible, the government not only called no special meeting but also announced that the regularly scheduled meeting of November 1947 would not be held. The reason seemed obvious: the term of the councillors was expiring and new elections were soon to be held. They were held in March 1948, about two months before the general election and the victory of the Nationalist Party. All twelve elected members stood for reelection, and all but three were reelected. On January 4-5, 1949, in compliance with existing law, the new government called a meeting of the council, the first in over two years, and gave notice of its intention to abolish the council. Once the pro-boycott Programme of Action was adopted by the ANC in December 1949, the course for councillors who were ANC members was clear. Yet Matthews and Moroka did not resign until after the council's last meeting in November 1950, and even then they were in a minority in doing so. At last, by the Bantu Authorities Act of 1951, the council was abolished.

Perhaps most Africans who opposed boycott would say, today, in retrospect, that the Natives' Representative Council should have been boycotted from the start. But for men like Matthews and for some others further to the left, the tactical question was not simple. To prevent the council from becoming a useful front for the government, the boycott had to be universal,[43] and the councillors doubted that popular support had reached that stage. AAC spokesmen, however, were certain that such support existed and were vitriolic in their attacks on "opportunists," "quislings," and "agents of the herrenvolk."[44]

The issue of tactics attracted much attention late in 1947. In November, fourteen of the sixteen councillors met in caucus and issued a statement (Document 34) in which they suggested that the government was hoping for the election of a body of men more amenable to government control and guidance." The boycott movement deserved "sympathetic understanding and practical support," they said, but they were not prepared to advise the African people "at this stage . . . to refrain from voting." They did advise them, "if they do elect," to choose a council that would continue to work for the objectives of the adjournment resolution.

97

Meanwhile, the militant Youth League of the ANC was urging total boycott. But when Oliver Tambo made such a proposal at the ANC's annual conference in December 1947 it was defeated by 57 votes to 7. [45] Instead, backtracking on its earlier expression of support for boycott, the conference decided that ANC members should continue to be active in the council. [46] The AAC, at the same time, again attacked participation in "dummy institutions"—"the Native Representative Council, Advisory Boards, Bungas, etc."—since they diverted attention from the vital need of representation in Parliament. It called unsuccessfully on all Africans to boycott the forthcoming elections. [47]

The council's last meeting, in November 1950, provided the final frustration. Dr. Hendrik Verwoerd himself, the new minister of Native affairs, appeared and set forth the new government's policy. Dr. W. M. M. Eiselen, the secretary of Native affairs, who was acting as chairman, refused to allow discussion of the speech and insisted that the council proceed with the agenda. The council, in a procedural deadlock, adjourned until the next day; Dr. Verwoerd refused to see a deputation; and Dr. Eiselen refused a motion to adjourn. He finally accepted a motion to adjourn *sine die* in order that an appeal be made to the Transvaal Supreme Court regarding the council's procedure and functions. The case was argued before the court, but with the passage of the Bantu Authorities Act and the abolition of the council, the case became moot and no judgment was made.

For more than a decade, the council had been ineffectual and even the subject of derision, but at least it had represented Africans nationally in a dialogue, however unequal, with the white holders of power. Henceforth, the official dialogue was to be only with ethnically separate "Bantu authorities" approved by the government.

THE RISE OF THE ANC YOUTH LEAGUE
AND THE PROGRAMME OF ACTION, 1943-1949

The founders of the ANC Youth League were comparable in middle class status to the professional men who founded the ANC in 1912, although there were no professional churchmen among them. [48] They were an extraordinarily able group in their mid-twenties or early thirties, mainly teachers or students of medicine or law. For some of them, interest in politics originated in discussions at home with fathers who had taken part in earlier protest. For most of them, however, serious political discussion began during school days. Almost all—Walter Sisulu, who had to leave school at sixteen, is a notable exception—had secondary school or college training. Graduates of the Anglican (Episcopal) secondary school of St. Peter's in Johannesburg had especially close ties with each other and constituted a kind of old boys' association. Others were graduates of teacher-training schools at Lovedale or Healdtown or of Adams College, which was both a teacher-training school and high school, and many had graduated—or been expelled—from Fort Hare, the "South African Native College" in the eastern Cape Province. [49]

Many of the early Youth Leaguers had also been prominent members of provincial or local student associations. Although these organizations were mainly social and not connected with adult political organizations, they occasionally sponsored political talks and discussion. The Transvaal African Students' Association, for example, held such discussions at the Bantu Men's Social Center in Johannesburg during school holidays. Its Fort Hare branch was organized as early as 1928. In the mid-thirties at Fort Hare, political discussion was also sponsored by a so-called Social Studies Society. William Nkomo, who was there during 1935-1937 and was a founding member of the Youth League, has vivid memories today of the intense interest of students in following white Italy's war against black Ethiopia, an interest that stimulated concern not only for South African politics but for all of Africa. He himself was stimulated to think about political struggle when Hitler came to power in 1933.

The franchise crisis of 1935-1936 and the leading role taken by Professor Jabavu of Fort Hare in opposition to removing African voters from the common roll stimulated further student interest. Some of the men who were later to join the Youth League became active members of the ANC after 1937.

One of the early activists was Manasseh T. Moerane, secretary of the Natal Bantu Teachers' Association. After attending an ANC conference in Bloemfontein, Moerane returned to Natal and suggested to Jordan Ngubane, a journalist, that a youth league should be formed. With Moerane as head and Ngubane as secretary, they organized the National Union of African Youth in 1939. The organization attracted over a dozen members, mostly young teachers, who met every weekend and published a newsletter. A brief manifesto by Moerane asserted that the organization's goals were to stir the political consciousness of African youth and to set the pace of development toward freedom. Because he was a teacher, Moerane was forced to withdraw soon after the manifesto was issued. Shortly thereafter, Ngubane moved to Johannesburg, where he became assistant to R. V. Selope Thema, editor of the *Bantu World*, and the National Union of African Youth died.

"As the circle in which I moved in Johannesburg widened," Ngubane has written, "I realized that the ferment in me was in everybody else." [50] Wartime hopes for a new deal, the growth and new militancy of African trade unions, and Communist and other left-wing demonstrations and activity undoubtedly stimulated the political consciousness of the younger intellectuals. Another stimulus was the growing outspokenness of African teachers early in the 1940s, which was expressed in 1944 by the march of 4,000 to 5,000 teachers in downtown Johannesburg, led by the Transvaal African Teachers' Association, demanding higher pay and other improvements. Meanwhile, the All African Convention, which was especially strong among teachers in the Transkei, in the eastern Cape, took part at the end of 1943 in the organization of the Non-European Unity Movement. Its strong pro-boycott position served to increase the dissatisfaction felt by young articulate Africans with the ANC's leadership.

For those who were to enter the Youth League, however, the historic strand of exclusivism in African political thought and the desire to promote African self-reliance and national pride exerted a far stronger pull than did arguments for noncollaboration or non-European unity. Trade union activity was not an outlet for their energy except in a few cases; their desire was to remold the historic national organization, the ANC. Nor did the Communists attract much support; Nkomo was closely associated with them and Ngubane suspected a few other Youth Leaguers of having Communist sympathies. (Nkomo spoke from Communist Party platforms but not as a party member. Moses Kotane, J. B. Marks, and Edwin Mofutsanyana were African Communists who were of the older generation and not among the founders of the Youth League.) Indeed, notes of the committee which drafted the Youth League manifesto recorded the "need for vigilance against Communists and other groups which foster non-African interests."

The immediate origins of the Youth League lie in the effort that took place in mid-1943 to mobilize support among youth for the candidacy of Self Mampuru for the presidency of the ANC in the Transvaal. Oliver Tambo and J. C. (Congress) M. Mbata—both teachers—met with Mampuru and afterward brought together a group of eight or ten in the office of William Ballinger, later to be elected by Africans to the Senate. At a second meeting a draft manifesto was prepared. However, by August, Mampuru, who was not himself a personality of political appeal for youth, shifted his interest to cooperation with Paul Mosaka and Senator Hyman Basner, who were organizing the African Democratic Party. Many of the younger African Nationalists opposed the ADP as a splinter organization that competed with the ANC and also lacked an exclusively African appeal. At the same time, they sought opportunities for initiative like those offered by the ADP to younger men.

Youthful interest then shifted toward recruiting a broader circle and organizing a permanent youth league within the ANC. In October 1943, movement in that direction was spurred by a meeting in Johannesburg presided over by Peter Raboroko, who was active in the Transvaal African Students' Association and years later was to be one of the founding members of the Pan Africanist Congress. [51] Among those joining the circle were Ngubane and Anton Lembede. Lembede was a law clerk for Dr. Seme; he earned an LL.B. degree and became a full partner, the firm becoming "Seme and Lembede" in 1946. Lembede was recruited by A. P. (Ashby Peter) Mda, who was then a teacher and later a lawyer. They met informally either in the offices of the ANC, or of Dr. Seme, or of Walter Sisulu, who was an estate agent. More important were meetings with Dr. Xuma before the December 1943 annual conference of the ANC which sought to forestall his opposition by embracing him as one of the initiators of a youth league.

At the conference, the veteran and self-educated A. W. G. Champion of Natal warned Dr. Xuma publicly that a youth league would bring about his downfall.

100

But Dr. Xuma's presidential address included a call to youth, and the conference adopted a resolution providing "that Congress Youth Leagues and Women's Leagues be formed."

During the conference, a latent difference between Xuma and the younger men became evident in the unsuccessful effort by Lembede and Sisulu to oppose what has been called (by a later Youth Leaguer) the "collaborationist" bias of the nonracial provision in Dr. Xuma's new constitution for the ANC. That is, the new constitution provided that "any person over 17 years of age who is willing to subscribe to the aims of Congress and to abide by its Constitution and rules may became an individual member. . . . " (The 1919 constitution provided that membership was open to men of 18 or over "belonging to the aboriginal races of Africa" [Paragraph 83] . Women were "auxiliary members.") The Constitution of the Youth League (Document 50) later, however, largely conformed with this nonracialism by making eligible for full membership "young members of the other sections of the community who live like and with Africans and whose general outlook on life is similar to that of Africans."

Supported by the authorization of the annual conference, a deputation visited Dr. Xuma at his home in Sophiatown (Johannesburg) on February 21, 1944, to review in detail the draft of a constitution and a manifesto, the latter written by a committee composed of Lembede, Mda, and Ngubane. Members of the deputation were Lembede, who was to be elected the first president of the Transvaal Youth League later in the year, William Nkomo, a medical student and chairman of the provisional executive committee before Lembede's election, Mbata, Sisulu, Ngubane, and Nelson Mandela, a law student at the University of the Witwatersrand. Although Dr. Xuma reacted warily at this and later meetings, particularly expressing his concern over the young men's criticism of the ANC, he extended his general blessing on their activities.

Lembede was the most outstanding personality in the early Youth League. He died in July 1947 at the age of 33 and was succeeded by Mda.[52] There have been few personalities in African politics in South Africa who may be called charismatic. Clements Kadalie was probably one of them. But for the later Africanist movement whose leaders founded the Pan Africanist Congress, Lembede has taken on this quality, at least in retrospect.

In the early months of the Youth League, others who stood out—in addition to Mda—were Oliver Tambo (who later became general secretary), Victor Mbobo (vice-president) and David Bopape—all teachers although Tambo and Mbobo later became lawyers; Lionel Majombozi, Wilson Zami Conco, and Arthur Letele—medical students; B. Masekela, a social worker; Dan Tloome, a trade unionist; and Johannes Matlou and Robert Matji. Professional men or those preparing for professional careers predominated among those who became prominent in the next few years: Godfrey Pitje, a teacher and later a lawyer; Joseph Matthews and Duma Nokwe, who were to become lawyers; and Robert

101

Sobukwe, a teacher—all of whom were active in founding the students' Youth League at Fort Hare in 1948; M. B. Yengwa, a bookkeeper and later a student of law in Durban; and Dr. James Njongwe in Port Elizabeth.

The manifesto (Document 48) was intended to be an expansion of the constitution's preamble and was issued by "the Provisional Committee of the Congress Youth League" in March 1944. On Easter Sunday in April 1944 the Youth League was "established" (according to Document 57) at an inaugural meeting held at the Bantu Men's Social Centre in Johannesburg. [53] A conference held on September 10, 1944—announced by a flyer, "Trumpet Call to Youth" (Document 49)—elected Lembede as president and endorsed both the manifesto and the constitution (Document 50).[54] In 1948 one of the most important Youth League documents was issued, the "Basic Policy" (Document 57).

Not until December 17, 1949, when the annual conference of the ANC unanimously adopted the Programme of Action (Document 60), did the Youth League endorse a statement that specified tactics of direct challenge to the white regime. The 1944 manifesto, while speaking in generalities about "fighting" and "struggle," said nothing about methods of struggle but was concerned entirely with goals and a three-year interim program designed to strengthen African national unity so that Africans might approach or attain a position from which they could challenge white domination effectively. The manifesto did not tell leadership what to do but what to be: "the personification and symbol of popular aspirations and ideals" (Paragraph "e" of "Our Creed"). It described the dual roles of the Youth League: to work privately as a pressure group within the ANC and to work publicly "in rousing popular political consciousness." Furthermore, Youth Leaguers themselves were exhorted to maintain "high ethical standards" in order to "combat moral disintegration among Africans." (A typical example of Christian prayer in behalf of "the African race" is the prayer opening the ANC Conference of December 1949—Document 59.)

Although the original intention of at least some of the founders of the Youth League was to do its more important work privately, the public role of the Youth League was prominent almost from the beginning. (Bopape, for example, became secretary of the Transvaal ANC in April 1944.) "The intention was to establish a pressure group inside the ANC ... " Ngubane has written. [55] Dr. Xuma also wanted such a group, according to Ngubane, but one "amenable to his type of reason and discipline." Many of the early Youth Leaguers thought of themselves not only as "the backroom boys of the ANC," Congress Mbata has recalled, but as a group comparable to the Broederbond, the secret Afrikaner society. In the manner of Broederbonders, they thought they would infiltrate and capture other African organizations.

Documents following the 1944 manifesto were concerned, similarly, with closing ranks ("Trumpet Call"), reinforcement of the ANC "in its struggle" and "educational, moral and cultural advancement" (constitution), and "basic principles" (Lembede, Document 51). A letter in March 1945, apparently written by

Lembede, replied to an invitation to cooperate with the left-wing Progressive Youth Council "in promoting unity among the youth of this country" (Document 52). The letter supported "the cooperation of all Non-Europeans on certain issues" but dismissed cooperative action at that time as "premature" since "Africans can only cooperate as an organized self-conscious unit."

Those themes were repeated by Lembede early in 1946 (Document 53). He also stated, as did the September 1944 "Trumpet Call," that the national movement was "gaining strength and momentum." "Events are moving toward a climax," a Youth League flyer announced at the time of the August 1946 mine strike (Document 54). But the flyer's call to "all Africans . . . to lend active support to the mine workers' struggle" was unexplained, although it noted that while Africans are "physically unarmed ... spiritual forces ... lead the world."

Meanwhile, in mid-1946, the Indian congresses in Natal and in the Transvaal, under new and militant leadership, had embarked on the first South African passive resistance campaign since the days of Gandhi. Their campaigns attracted thousands of new members and impressed some of the younger African nationalists, like Nelson Mandela. Speaking much later Professor Matthews described the 1946 passive resistance movement as "the immediate inspiration" for the ANC's decision in 1949 to employ civil disobedience.[56]

Discussion of methods of struggle took place continually, of course, and pressures for action grew.[57] Shortly after the May 8-9, 1947, meeting of Prime Minister Smuts with a deputation from the NRC, Lembede and Mda were among the speakers at a meeting in Vereeniging which endorsed their call to boycott white-sponsored elections. Pressures for action intensified after the Nationalist Party's victory in the general election of May 26, 1948. Two letters by Mda written in August and September 1948 to Godfrey Pitje, a lecturer at Fort Hare, where a Youth League branch was being organized, were concerned not with tactics but with "laying a solid foundation for creating a revolutionary national front. . . ." (Documents 55 and 56). A month later, at a widely representative African meeting in Bloemfontein, Mda—now president of the Youth League—supported the call of David Bopape: "We must use our atom weapon, withdrawal of labour."[58]

The "Basic Policy," issued in 1948, reviewed the history of African nationalism in South Africa and described 1944 as "a historic turning point" when the Youth League sought to impose "the creed of African Nationalism" on the ANC. (Mda wrote the statement, which was approved by his working committee. His first task as president, Mda has recalled, was to clarify the League's stand in relation to liberalism and communism.) Only this creed could "give the black masses the self-confidence and dynamism to make a successful struggle. . . ." But the methods of struggle were still undefined although the statement noted that "the programme of organisation and tactics" depends on changing circumstances.

By 1948, sentiment for mass action was widespread, and the ANC at its

103

annual conference in December of that year decided that there should be a new program of action. (The resolutions committee, which made the recommendation, was composed of A. P. Mda, Moses Kotane, Z. K. Matthews, Selby Msimang, and L. K. Ntlabati.) Final adoption was postponed, however, until December 1949 to allow time for discussion in the branches and provincial congresses. There was, in fact, much serious discussion at all levels, and specific proposals were brought to the annual conference from all provinces. Recollections differ regarding the importance of various persons in the formulation of the Programme of Action. David Bopape has recalled that the Youth League executive committee—Mda, Mandela, Sisulu, Tambo, Njongwe, and himself—drafted a programme that was adopted by the Transvaal provincial conference and became, with some amendments, the Programme adopted by the ANC. Another early draft, discussed at the Cape provincial conference, was published in *Inkundla ya Bantu (Bantu Forum)* on July 30, 1949 over the signatures of the Rev. James Calata, G. M. Pitje, Mangaliso R. Sobukwe, G. B. Socenywa, and A. P. Mda. [59]

The earliest available speech by Robert Sobukwe, who headed the Students' Representative Council and had helped to found the Youth League branch at Fort Hare, was made about this time (Document 58). Speaking at the "completers' social" of October 21, 1949, an annual function for the graduating class, which had chosen him to give the main address, Sobukwe expressed as little concern with tactics as did the earlier Youth League statements; but he did say, in passing, that only through "non-collaboration" could those in power be forced to relinquish their position.

In the final formulation of the Programme of Action at the December 1949 ANC conference, the continuity of ANC aims was underlined by the active participation of leading representatives of both the older generation and the Youth League generation. Dr. Xuma referred the various drafts and suggestions that had been received to a drafting committee headed by Professor Z. K. Matthews. Particularly striking is the fact that Professor Matthews had also been chairman of the Atlantic Charter Committee, which formulated *Africans' Claims*. His committee included Selby Msimang, who had attended the 1912 meeting, Moses Kotane, and—from the Youth League—Oliver Tambo. Another measure of the extraordinary standing of the Programme of Action is the fact that in the years that followed both the Youth League members who were to lead the ANC into the multiracial Congress Alliance and those Youth League members who were to splinter from the ANC to form the Pan Africanist Congress (PAC) claimed to be the Programme's true exponents.

The Programme "suggested" that a council of action work for the boycott and abolition of "all differential political institutions" and "employ the following weapons: immediate and active boycott, strike, civil disobedience, non-cooperation and such other means as may bring about the accomplishment and realisation of our aspirations." [60] It called also for "a national stoppage of work for one day as a mark of protest. . . . " And it contained provisions for African economic, educational, and cultural advancement that were similar to provisions in the 1919 constitution.

As a theoretical exposition of African nationalism, the Programme, a rather unpolished statement of some 560 words, was hardly comparable in breadth or eloquence to earlier statements of the Youth League or of Lembede. Yet it did have an emphasis on "self-determination" that distinguished it from earlier official statements of the ANC. The objects of the 1919 constitution, as we have seen, had not only been "to bring together [all Africans] as one political people" but also "to enlist the sympathy and support of . . . European Societies, Leagues or Unions. . . . " The preface written by Dr. Xuma to *Africans' Claims* had referred not only to "struggle" and to the ANC as "the mass liberation movement" but also expressed confidence that "all men and women of goodwill of all races and nations will see the justice of our cause and stand with us and support us in our struggle." The Programme of Action, on the other hand, said nothing about interracial cooperation although its reference to the 1943 Bill of Rights may be read as a reaffirmation of the goal of equal citizenship with whites. The Programme rejected "trusteeship, or white leadership which are all in one way or another motivated by the idea of white domination" and concluded with an expression of confidence that "inspired leadership" would ultimately bring about unity "under the banner of African Nationalism."

The Programme of Action and, more importantly, the documents that illustrate the rise of the Youth League provide textual material of special interest in the light of later differences between the ANC and the PAC regarding the relationship of Africans to non-Africans. Leading members of the Youth League differed in their attitudes toward Marcus Garvey's exclusive slogan of "Africa for the Africans." Lembede, often described as the moving spirit of the Youth League, is remembered as the leading advocate of Garvey's outlook and, by Ngubane and Mda, as the coiner of the word "Africanism."[61]

Mbata, in recalling the writing of the 1944 manifesto, has said: "The question of multi-racialism came in. Lembede was out and out Africanist. His thesis was Africa for the Africans. Not all of us were fully convinced that way." Lembede felt that the Africans needed "something that they could feel. I remember his elaboration of this theme was that the African, the very color of the African, links him with the color of the soil of Africa. . . . His main cry was that the Africans should be taught that there was nothing to be ashamed of in being black. They should be proud of it because he [the African] is nearer to mother earth and feeding on the breast of mother Africa. . . . His main point was self-confidence, but he said that if it became necessary to exclude the other [i.e., multiracialism], then we must be prepared to do so. This led to some argument." The slogan of "Africa for the Africans" was finally accepted by the Youth League but "defined so that it ceased to be exclusive. . . . A formula . . . something to this effect—Africa for the Africans. The Africans for humanity. Humanity for God and for Africa." [62]

Although "Africa for the Africans" does not appear in any of the documents reproduced here, Lembede's first "cardinal principle" was that "Africa is a blackman's country. Africans are the natives of Africa . . . Africa belongs to them." " . . . the African spirit," he added, was " . . . unique and peculiar to Africans only." However, " . . . our ethical system today has to be based on Christian morals since there is nothing better anywhere in the world" (Document 51). Lembede, like Mda, was a Catholic, and had written a thesis on "The Conception of God as Expounded by, and as It Emerges from the Writings of Philosophers from Descartes to the Present Day" for a master's degree by correspondence at the University of South Africa. [63]

For Lembede, "Africanism" and "African Nationalism" were synonymous; but both Mda and Ngubane preferred to use the words "African Nationalism." Mda, whose influence as a correspondent was far-reaching, spoke of Africa as "the black man's continent"; but he took pains to affirm that African nationalists "only hate white oppression and white domination and not the white people themselves!" Statements by Robert Sobukwe in 1958 and 1959 were to reaffirm Mda's vision of a future democracy in which (in Mda's words) "all men shall have rights and freedom merely because they are men."

In the Youth League documents one can find not only the language of racial exclusiveness but also allusions to nonracialism (the right of each African "to be a free citizen in the South African democracy"–Document 48) and multiracialism (the constitutional guarantee of human rights for "all the nationalities and minorities"–Document 57). There is no doubt that racial exclusiveness was the distinctive appeal of the new spirit of nationalism, at least as a means of strengthening Africans in their struggle against white domination. It is also true, however, that the Youth Leaguers' view of the ultimate nature of the South African state was not consistently and fully developed. Though the 1944 manifesto spoke of "South Africa's progress to nationhood," a progress said to be hampered by racial conflict between white and black, its form was not defined. What is of outstanding importance is that in the 1940s and thereafter "Africa for the Africans" was generally acceptable only when redefined as a policy of accommodation with those whites who accepted majority rule.

In short, exclusive and nonexclusive approaches to the problem of change in South Africa were reconciled or at least blurred. "Africanism" did not come to denote a racially exclusive goal but remained indistinguishable from "African Nationalism" as a driving force or means. Pan-Africanism was a recurring theme. In the earliest of the official Youth League documents, the creed stated: "We believe in the unity of all Africans from the Mediterranean Sea in the North to the Indian and Atlantic Oceans in the South . . . and that Africans must speak with one voice." In the 1948 statement of "Basic Policy," however, an explicit distinction was finally made between "two streams of African Nationalism." Garvey's slogan of "Africa for the Africans" and its implication that whites must be driven into the sea was disavowed as "extreme and ultrarevolutionary." Instead, the statement identified the Youth League with the "moderate" stream of

106

African nationalism and declared: "We of the Youth League take account of the concrete situation in South Africa, and realise that the different racial groups have come to stay." Thus, while in tune with "Africa" and while expecting "a long, bitter, and unrelenting struggle for . . . national freedom," the Youth League recognized the special historical circumstances of South Africa and accepted the participation of whites in any future democracy.

THE ALL AFRICAN CONVENTION, NON-EUROPEAN UNITY, AND THE LEFT WING

During 1937-1949, new efforts were made to promote African unity or non-European unity ("non-European" being used rather than "nonwhite") or to build radical popular fronts of all races, including whites. The relations of African nationalists with white liberals, with the members of the nonracial Communist Party (whose African members were also nationalists), and with others on the left were extraordinarily complex. Opponents of white domination dealt with ideological and tactical issues both dialectically and with reference to personalities, displaying concern for principle or imputing selfish motives. Organizationally, they were involved in united fronts, schisms, and competition to wrest control from more conservative leaders. Earlier discussion has noted the AAC's participation in the formation of the NEUM in 1943 and its repeated failures to achieve unity, on its own terms, with the ANC. Before examining the major documents that are a part of these developments, we shall look at some earlier efforts to bring together whites, Africans, Indians, and Coloureds.

Before 1943

The Communist Party since its formation in 1921 was almost obsessed with the problem of the relation of a class party with national liberation movements and its effort to merge the two. The party itself rapidly became Africanized in the mid-1920s, although whites have always been of key importance in it. In 1929, 1,600 members out of a total membership of 1,750 were Africans.[64] James Gumede, president-general of the ANC in the late 1920s, favored unity with the Communist Party but was succeeded by the conservative Seme. The party was disrupted by expulsions at the beginning of the 1930s and was diverted from further activity among Africans by threats from the right and the attention given to united front tactics in the early and mid-1930s. When renewed efforts were made in 1937 and 1938 to revive the ANC, the party itself was at a low point, but with the shift of headquarters to Cape Town about 1939 under Moses Kotane as national secretary, it revived. At the time of its dissolution in 1950, it had about 2,000 dues-paying members; the great majority were Africans, about 150 were whites, and about 250, Indians.

Although the party was always small in numbers, its members played important roles in the organization of African trade unions and were active in the

ANC. During the 1930s and 1940s, Kotane, Edwin Mofutsanyana, and J. B. Marks came to be trusted as African nationalists by the established leadership of the ANC. This moderate leadership opposed the efforts of the Youth League after 1943 to purge the ANC of Africans who were thought to have a conflicting allegiance because of their membership in other organizations.

In seeking a base for mass action, the Communist Party involved itself in the National Liberation League, which had been formed in 1935 by Coloured radicals who were not Marxists but who aspired to lead a national liberation movement of nonwhites. In 1938 the party inspired the formation of the Non-European United Front, whose leader in the Transvaal was Dr. Dadoo, the Indian Communist. A Non-European United Front Conference in Cape Town in April 1939 was extraordinarily representative of radicals of all races and included both Communists and the small number of Trotskyists. [65] Non-Communist Coloured radicals, who disliked the whites in the Communist Party, attacked Communist support for the war effort and Stalinism after the invasion of the Soviet Union on June 22, 1941; they came to be identified with Trotskyism although the Communists considered the label to be misleading since they believed the Coloured intellectuals had only a superficial and polemical interest in Marxist and Trotskyist theory.

Dadoo described the war prior to the invasion of the Soviet Union as "an imperialist war, and therefore an unjust war," which could "only be transformed into a just war for the preservation of Democracy and the defeat of Fascism when full and unfettered democratic rights are extended to the Non-European people of this country. . . ."[66] He attracted nonwhite support, not so much for his attitude toward the war as for his eloquent denunciation of racial discrimination, especially during his trials in 1940 and 1941 for incitement of nonwhites. [67]

The government's use of nonwhites in the military forces and their unequal treatment were issues on which the nonwhite opposition could focus. For Communists, including Dadoo, the entry of the Soviet Union into the fighting brought about a change from demands for stopping the recruitment of nonwhites to demands for "Arms for Non-Europeans." A flyer with this heading announced a "mass meeting" sponsored by the Non-European United Front on March 18, 1942, in Cape Town, featuring speakers from the four major racial groups (Document 71). A few months later in 1942, a Non-European Conference of some 300 delegates from nonwhite organizations in the Transvaal, including many non-Communist Africans, was convened by Dr. Dadoo. The presiding officer was W. B. Ngakane, secretary of the Orlando (Johannesburg) advisory board. The Non-European People's Manifesto adopted at the conference was keyed more to immediate circumstances than was true of some later statements, for example, the ANC's Bill of Rights of 1943 and the Freedom Charter of 1955, which were intended to become historic charters of popular aims. "Our hearts," it declared, were with the Soviet Union and China, and "our main demand" was full participation in the war by nonwhites "with our fellow South Africans of European descent" (Document 72).

During the early years of the war, representatives of the ANC (that is, all provincial branches except the Transvaal but not the national ANC itself), the Cape Voters' Association, the Communist Party, other left-wing groups, and a varied assortment of African bodies met in two conferences of the All African Convention. The AAC constitution provided for triennial meetings, and the conference of December 1940 was the first since 1937. In response to a proposal by "the progressives," [68]—those who were to form the NEUM three years later—the 1940 conference decided to meet in a special or emergency session in December of the following year. The participants in both conferences represented a political spectrum as wide as that of the meetings of the mid-thirties. But despite the presence of radicals, the AAC's policy was moderate, that is, the AAC continued to be ready to participate in the separate forms of representation established in 1936. The 1940 conference was attended by members of the NRC and addressed by two of the whites elected to Parliament by Africans, and in 1941 there was unanimous agreement on the formation of an "African Parliamentary Committee" of lobbyists to be in contact with the NRC and with "our Parliamentary Representatives" on "legislation affecting our Non-European groups." [69] The 1941 meeting also endorsed slates of candidates for the 1942 elections in which Africans were to elect whites to Parliament and representatives to the NRC.

The resumption of the AAC conferences and Dr. Xuma's accession to power in the ANC stirred up the latent rivalry between the two movements. The conferences provided a platform for those who dismissed the ANC as ineffectual and wished to recover the exciting promise of the mid-thirties that the AAC might become an effective federal "Parliament" representative of all African organizations and therefore the voice of all Africans. Older African personalities like Professor Jabavu and the Rev. Z. R. Mahabane, who (like the ANC leaders) were devoted to the quest for African unity and remained aloof from disputes and recrimination about African failures, professed to find no conflict between the ANC and the AAC. The AAC was to meet again in December 1943 and, after amendment of the constitution, in regular annual meetings thereafter; Jabavu continued as president until December 1948, when he stepped down for W. M. Tsotsi, a graduate of Fort Hare and a teacher. Mahabane was both president-general of the ANC and vice-president of the AAC from December 1937 through 1940. He was senior chaplain of the ANC during at least the first of Xuma's terms and continued as vice-president of the AAC throughout Jabavu's presidency and also under Tsotsi. [70] Mahabane also served as president of the NEUM until 1956. Both men were obviously useful as figureheads for the younger Africans and Coloureds who came to dominate the AAC and who formed the NEUM, but they were also independent personalities who stood ready throughout the 1940s to enter into joint meetings with ANC leaders. [71]

In the December 1941 conference of the AAC, the leaders of "the progressives" spoke bitterly of past failures, but both policies and leadership continued unchanged. The most articulate African in the group was thirty-two-year-old I. B. Tabata, who had attended Fort Hare for a short time. He had worked in Cape Town since the early 1930s, had been active in the Cape African Voters' Association, and in 1941 was officially a delegate to the AAC from the Young Men's Ethiopian Society of Cape Town. His counterpart among the Coloureds was Dr. G. H. Gool, ably supported by Jane Gool, his sister, and by B. M. Kies, a teacher and later a lawyer. Gool, who had been active in the Non-European United Front, later became closely associated with the Trotskyists but was primarily a non-Marxist radical. In the 1941 AAC conference, he and Miss Gool and Kies were delegates from the New Era Fellowship.

Both Tabata and Gool spoke at length at the conference, condemning both the ANC and the leadership of the AAC. Nevertheless, said Tabata, "the Convention is and remains the most suitable organization for the Africans in the struggle for liberation"; unlike either the ANC or the ICU in the past, it could become a "parliament" that represented all Africans. Tabata's advocacy of the boycotting of separate elections was less absolutist than in later years; if boycott could not be agreed upon, he said, nominations should at least be made by "a united people" (Document 62).

The 1941 AAC conference also rejected the recommendations that had been made a year earlier by a joint ANC-AAC committee, which had been formed in response to an ANC invitation. At that time, the committee's unanimous recommendation had appeared as a step toward unity, which was not surprising in light of the six-man committee's composition: Mahabane (vice-president of the AAC), Marks, and Calata, representing the ANC, and Z. K. Matthews (whose energies were to shift to the ANC) and two others representing the AAC. The committee unanimously recommended that the AAC be a "co-ordinating and consultative committee," mainly of national organizations that would be represented only by their top officials, and that the ANC confine itself mainly to "the political aspirations" of Africans.[72] Within the AAC conference of 1940, however, Tabata apparently expressed fears that the AAC was being denigrated and moved that the recommendations be deferred until December 1941, when they were rejected.[73]

African Democratic Party—1943

Younger Africans who found Dr. Xuma's leadership autocratic or who criticized the ANC for lacking militancy and failing to win a mass following had various courses of action open to them in 1943: to act as a pressure group within the ANC—the course followed by the Youth League; to reinvigorate another existing organization—the AAC; or to set up a new competing organization—the African Democratic Party. The Youth League, active initially in Johannesburg, committed to African nationalism, and eschewing non-African ideologies, was to have the strongest impact on African politics. Opposed to the role of Communists in the ANC during the 1940s and distrustful of non-African Communists, the Youth League excluded as premature the possibility of cooperation with other nonwhites. Young Africans working within the AAC, on the other hand, were concentrated mainly in Cape Town and among teachers in the Transkei. Their association with Coloured intellectuals in Cape Town—mainly teachers and a few professional men—involved them in a movement for non-European unity, full acceptance of the Coloured tactic of boycott, and a rhetorical Trotskyism in their opposition to the Communist Party and the ANC. While less activist than the Youth League, the AAC from 1943 onward was to be a continual goad to the ANC and a stimulus to the Youth League in its acceptance of boycott. The ADP, inaugurated at a meeting held on September 26, 1943, was less distinctive in its orientation and appeal than were the Youth League and the post-1943 AAC, and had the least impact (Document 73). Like the AAC, though to a much lesser degree, the ADP attracted Trotskyist support; [74] but unlike the AAC it did not formulate a policy of boycott nor place its main emphasis upon non-European unity. The AAC insisted that it was not antiwhite; but the ADP, in welcoming the cooperation of all racial groups, emphasized the importance of white allies. In endorsing "the method of the STRIKE . . . MASS PROTESTS and MASS DEMONSTRATIONS," the ADP's manifesto promised more immediate action than future pronouncements of the AAC and the NEUM were to do. But the ADP's manifesto not only lacked the occasional Marxist premises of the latter; it affirmed the nonviolent nature of its weapon of "last resort . . . mass passive resistance." Indeed, the tone of the manifesto was moderate in its favorable reference to the Joint Councils, the Institute of Race Relations, and similar organizations, which it saw as evidence of growing white sympathy for African aspirations. [75]

Only one of the "convenors" of the ADP, Dan Koza, had been involved in left-wing politics. Its leading figure and chairman was thirty-two-year-old Paul R. Mosaka, one of the first Transvaal graduates of Fort Hare College, a businessman and former teacher who had edited the journal of the Cape African Teachers' Association, and a recently elected member of the NRC. The secretary was thirty-five-year-old Self Mampuru, who campaigned for the presidency of the Transvaal ANC in 1943 and was "African Consultant" for a white liberal organization, the Friends of Africa. Others were S. J. J. Lesolang, president of the Transvaal African Teachers' Association; G. R. Kuzwayo, a businessman; and Koza, an able trade unionist with Trotskyist connections. [76] All were residents of Johannesburg. Closely allied to the convenors was Hyman Basner, a lawyer, former Communist, and one of the senators elected by Africans. Basner was a "guest speaker" on "the present political situation" at the inaugural meeting, where he spoke of "an unholy alliance" between the Communist Party and the ANC. [77]

Mosaka's attitude to the ANC was ambivalent, however. Xuma's earlier relations with Mosaka had been cold; nevertheless, following his election to the

111

NRC, Mosaka had written to Xuma to assure him of "my willingness . . . to act on the instructions of . . . the one and only organisation that can serve and save the African people, the African National Congress" (Document 27).[78] The ADP's manifesto criticized the ANC's "disorganisation, political stagnation and general inaction. . . . The leaders quarrel while the people die." But shortly afterward, Mosaka and Mampuru described the ADP as "a political party that will work within [the] parliamentary framework of the National Congress" and declared that no one known to be either a Communist or a member of the Fourth International would be allowed in the ADP.[79]

Xuma scornfully attacked the ADP as a divisive force that was inspired by "Non-Africans," and R. V. Selope Thema, editor of the *Bantu World*, repeatedly attacked it as a tool of the Trotskyists.[80] Speaking at a conference of the Transvaal African Congress on October 3, 1943, Dr. Xuma called for loyalty and recalled that a year earlier he had rejected joining the Non-European United Front because African organizations should join such fronts only as "a complete equal."[81] The conference approved a six-month extension of Dr. Xuma's administration of the Transvaal provincial organization, thus deferring a provincial election that some members feared might be exploited by the ADP or even won by a candidate favorable to it.[82] The Transvaal's endorsement of Dr. Xuma, who had announced that the ANC had £800 in the bank, and Xuma's reelection as president-general in December 1943 dampened the prospects of the ADP. It continued to exist until about 1948, issuing statements, sponsoring some demonstrations, and taking part in meetings of the AAC and the NEUM, but failed to make headway.[83]

NEUM–1943

Meanwhile, during 1943, the stage was set for the formation of the NEUM. The government's setting up of the segregationist Coloured Affairs Department (C.A.D.) was countered early in the year by the formation of the National Anti-C.A.D. by Dr. Gool and others. The new organization was a federal body of Coloured groups which agreed to boycott the C.A.D., began to arouse the political consciousness of the usually apathetic Coloureds, and sought common ground with Africans and Indians. In June 1943, Tabata's Western Province Committee of the AAC distributed a leaflet, "Calling All Africans," that drew attention to the importance for non-European unity of the forthcoming conference of the South African Indian Congress (SAIC) and the AAC conference in December. During the same month, however, Professor Jabavu, although he had not joined other AAC leaders in responding favorably to Dr. Xuma's invitation to join the Atlantic Charter Committee, displayed the orientation of the older generation when he issued a somewhat hopeful statement regarding the Atlantic Charter and referred to "our representatives" in the NRC (Document 63).

Soon afterward, the AAC executive committee adopted a manifesto, "A Call to Unity" (Document 64), whose tone was that of Tabata in December 1941. It recommended that the AAC follow the example of both the Anti-C.A.D. and the

SAIC. The latter had resolved that "the time has arrived" for cooperation with other non-European organizations "on specific questions." [84] The committee invited the SAIC and the Anti-C.A.D. to send delegates to attend the December 1943 AAC Conference as guests and to meet immediately afterward in a Unity Conference. [85] At its conference, the AAC adopted its executive committee's manifesto. [86] On December 17, delegates from the AAC and the Anti-C.A.D., but with the SAIC absent, adopted a "Draft Declaration of Unity" and a "10-Point Programme" (Document 65). Thus these delegates, comprising the "Continuation Committee of the Preliminary Unity Conference," provisionally founded the Non-European Unity Movement. The "10-Point Programme" was adopted by the National Anti-C.A.D. Conference in January 1944 and the AAC conference in December 1944.

Henceforth, the NEUM was to refer to the "10-Point Programme" as the "principled" basis upon which to build unity. The preamble to the "10-Points" was notably lacking in Marxist formulations. Non-Europeans, it declared, suffered "National Oppression." "The main cause" of their poverty was their "lack of political rights." Justice could be won only through "democracy," defined as "the rule *of* the people, *by* the people, *for* the people." The "10-Points" themselves, presented as "minimum demands" and expressed in lackluster style, began with a demand for universal franchise and were followed by ten paragraphs of "explanatory remarks." One of the most radical remarks referred to "a new division of the land." Also remarkable was the absence of any program of action. Unity at all levels—not against whites but against segregation—was described as the prerequisite for what was "chiefly a political struggle." Not until July 7, 1944, when the AAC Executive Committee issued a statement entitled "Along the New Road," was a detailed program of "noncollaboration" set forth, including "as a first practical step" the resignation of all elected members of the NRC. [87]

NEUM and SAIC

On the following day, July 8, 1944, representatives of the SAIC met with representatives of the AAC and the Anti-C.A.D. in the Second Unity Conference. The Indians had been too busy in December 1943, dealing with anti-Indian legislation, to attend the First Unity Conference but had sent a telegram expressing "wholehearted agreement with the Unity Movement" (as summarized in the Minutes).

Accordingly, the preamble to the "10-Point Programme" had begun with a reference to "these three organisations"; and A. I. Kajee of the SAIC was tentatively listed as a vice-chairman of the provisional committee with Dr. Gool as another vice-chairman, under the chairmanship of Professor Jabavu. (The SAIC was also expected to supply one of the three joint secretaries and four committee members; four other committee members were to be Coloured and eight, African.)

113

But the frank discussion at the Second Unity Conference made it clear that unity with the conservative leadership of the SAIC on the basis of the "10-Points" was impossible. Kajee and seven colleagues were prepared, after further consultation with the SAIC, to cooperate on "specific questions." But SAIC policy was one of gradualness and compromise, they said, and they had already accepted a communal franchise based on educational and property qualifications. Professor Jabavu counseled against embarrassing the Indians, and even Mrs. Z. Gool (sister-in-law of Dr. Gool) expressed the feeling that the conservative Kajee leadership was with them in principle. But Tabata, Kies, Koza, and others found the positions irreconcilable. Indian radicals who opposed Kajee and were organized as the Anti-Segregation Council of Durban attended the Third Unity Conference of January 1945. Nonetheless, when then took over the leadership of the Indian congresses later in the year, they did not form an alliance with the NEUM. Their future ally was to be the ANC.

Indian radicals defeated the Kajee leadership, representative of Indian merchant interests, and won control of the Natal Indian Congress (NIC) and the South African Indian Congress (the latter, a federal body) during the crisis produced by the "Ghetto Bill." This bill was introduced in 1945 and enacted in June 1946. Indians differed over whether or not to protest by means of passive resistance. Dr. Naicker, a Gandhian, took over the leadership in Natal in October 1945. In the Transvaal, some months later, Dr. Dadoo became president of the Transvaal Indian Congress and of the SAIC.

On June 13, 1946, both groups embarked on a passive resistance campaign, and their members courted arrest. The Indians acted alone, though with the praise of the ANC. The campaign, designed to last until the legislation was repealed, was conducted intermittently for about two years, with over 2,000 Indian resisters going to jail. The government did not repeal the legislation, but the organizations increased their working class membership, the NIC growing from a few hundred to about 35,000. (The communal representation provided for in the act was boycotted, repealed in 1948 by the Nationalist government, and never went into effect.) Both Dr. Naicker and Dr. Dadoo reached out for nonwhite support and on March 9, 1947, signed the so-called pact with Dr. Xuma (Document 39). The Reverend Z. R. Mahabane, still uninterested in nonwhite rivalries, described Dadoo and Naicker in March 1948 as "two of the most outstanding leaders of Indian opinion," whereas Dr. Gool described their pact with Dr. Xuma as "despicable," since it confused the people, and the passive resistance campaign as an effort to use nonwhites "to gain concessions only for the Indian merchant class." [88]

Other Developments—1943-1948

Much longer drawn out than relations with the SAIC and far more important for the building of unity were the repeated efforts made by Africans to achieve

114

unity themselves, that is, between the ANC and the AAC. Not until 1949 did the failures become final. The recommendations of a joint ANC-AAC committee of 1940 were rejected by the AAC Conference of 1941. Under Dr. Xuma, the ANC lost interest and sent no representatives to the AAC conference of December 1943, which immediately preceded the formation of the NEUM. However, the ANC at that time again proposed a joint committee. Tabata opposed its formation as a waste of time, arguing that the 1941 AAC conference had reaffirmed the constitutional description of the AAC as the mouthpiece of the African people. But the conference decided that Jabavu and nine elected representatives, including Tabata, should meet with ten ANC delegates. On December 17, Jabavu "reported the final decision arrived at by majority vote that A.A.C. should be the recognised political mouthpiece of the African people." [89] Despite Jabavu's understanding of the agreement, the ANC continued to look upon the AAC as a federal, coooordinating body and upon itself as the only national mouthpiece of the African people.

During 1944 through 1947, the NEUM made futile efforts to engage Dr. Xuma in consultation. [90] Meanwhile, the AAC sought to enlarge its support. Its constitution had been amended in 1943 to provide for individual membership; and an executive committee statement of July 7, 1944, "Along the New Road," called for immediate steps to form provincial, district, and local branches. But the AAC continued to be concentrated in Cape Province. [91] Especially acclaimed within the AAC was the affiliation of the Cape African Teachers' Association (CATA) in 1948 after several years during which some branches had affiliated and others had resisted affiliation as unprofessional. CATA was the first African body of major importance to affiliate with the AAC. Little effort was made to expand into areas of ANC strength; the AAC continued to hope that the ANC would be won over. Furthermore, the intellectuals who were most prominent in the AAC's ranks and in the Anti-C.A.D. had little time for organizational work and mobilizing support, and their emphasis on political education and "principled" opposition to the white regime left little room for demonstration and other "stunts." Once all Africans were won to noncollaboration, the day would come when the machinery of oppression would stop.

During the later years of the war, two movements arose which attempted to bring together persons and groups of all races as extraparliamentary pressure groups: the Anti-Pass Campaign whose inaugural conference was in November 1943, and the Campaign for Right and Justice, inaugurated on December 4-5, 1943. In inaugurating the former, Communists played a leading role—Dr. Dadoo was the first chairman—in cooperation with nonwhite trade unionists and some ANC members. White liberal churchmen were in the forefront of the latter campaign, notably the Rev. Michael Scott; and Communists (including Dr. Dadoo), and white and nonwhite trade unionists were among its supporters. The campaign was diffuse in its aims—it proposed the abolition of racially discriminatory legislation—and sponsored conferences and deputations; but its development was abortive. Because the Communists came to dominate it, Scott, who had what he has called "a furious controversy" with Dr. Dadoo about the role of liberal whites, resigned after two years. [92]

Almost equally abortive but more spectacular was the single-issue Anti-Pass Campaign. Its conference of May 20-21, 1944, which resolved "to launch a nation-wide Anti-Pass Campaign for the repeal of the Pass Laws" (Document 74), was attended by 540 delegates claiming to represent 605,222 people and was followed by a march of 20,000 demonstrators in Johannesburg. [93] Of all instruments of white rule, that which has been most persistently hated by Africans has been the pass system, and opposition to it tended to override personal suspicion and enmity. Dr. Xuma, at first reluctant to join the campaign, apparently was impressed by the popular response to meetings held in preparation for the conference and accepted the chairmanship of the Anti-Pass Council. Selope Thema and Mosaka were also members of the council along with Kotane, Marks, and Dadoo. [94] Even the Anti-C.A.D. resolved that it "in practice will support any effort to have them [pass laws] abolished" (after deleting from the original draft of the resolution a favorable reference to the ANC).[95]

The campaign was expected to culminate in a general strike and burning of passes, but the conference and the march that followed marked the climax of popular enthusiasm. Pass-burning was deferred to an indefinite date, pending the gathering of a million signatures on a petition, a tactic that was adopted as an organizational device and means of winning the support both of conservative Africans and whites. The ambitious deadline of August 31, 1944, for completing the petition was not met. The ANC conference of December 1944 called on all branches to continue collecting signatures. [96] Not until mid-1945 was an incomplete petition (Bopape has claimed 850,000 names) presented to officials in Cape Town. In demonstrations outside Parliament, Selope Thema and Dadoo were among those arrested. Neither Hofmeyr nor, after the war's end, Smuts would meet with a deputation.

Later in the year, the Anti-Pass Campaign sponsored protest meetings on Armistice Day, November 11; and more than half a year later, on June 23, 1946, the Second National Anti-Pass Conference was held. Dr. Xuma concluded his presidential address with a call for "intensive organization" for action rather than talk, and the conference resolved to work toward a "national stoppage of work and the burning of passes." [97] But popular enthusiasm for the long-drawn-out campaign had evaporated, and no date for action was set. Dr. Xuma himself received much blame for failing to provide dynamic leadership and to commit himself to a general strike.

Meanwhile, in July 1945, the NEUM marked the ending of the war by speaking "for the 8 million Non-Europeans . . . Bantu, Coloured and Indian" in "A Declaration to the Nations of the World" (Document 66). The statement, translated into all the major African languages, was an analytical exposition rather than a program of action, expanding upon the comparison with Nazism that had been made in the Draft Declaration of Unity of December 1943.

No large multiracial conference with a sponsorship similar to that of the Anti-Pass conferences again took place until the eve of the general election of May 26, 1948. African and Indian leaders in the Transvaal who had been active in the Anti-Pass Campaign saw the forthcoming election as an opportunity to dramatize the issue of the franchise. An ad hoc committee called for "delegates . . . who will represent more citizens than those voting in the General Elections" to attend the "First Transvaal-Orange Free State People's Assembly for Votes for All" on May 22-24 (Document 75a). Unlike the Anti-Pass Campaign, the planning of the People's Assembly encountered suspicion and opposition within the ANC. A deputation had invited Dr. Xuma to become a sponsor, and he had responded by holding a press conference on the coming election and calling on South Africans of all races to work for "a common franchise" (Document 41). But, as national president, he had declined to sponsor a provincial assembly and did not attend. C. S. Ramohanoe, the ANC'S provincial president, thought that working outside the ANC was unnecessary. Some members of the Youth League who were now on the ANC's provincial executive committee were apathetic or hostile though ready to support the conference if the organizing committee was limited to persons who represented the ANC, the Transvaal Indian Congress, and the [Coloured] African People's Organisation.[98]

Over 300 delegates of all races attended the People's Assembly, which was opened by the Rev. Michael Scott, and adopted "The People's Charter" (Document 75b), calling for equal political rights for "all adult men and women of all races." The charter resembled the later Freedom Charter, which was to be adopted on June 26, 1955, at a mass rally of the multiracial alliance known as the Congress of the People. Like the Freedom Charter, the People's Charter attempted no historical explanation of the status quo, suggested no philosophy of social change, and proposed no program of action. Though radical in the South African context, it was as old-fashioned as the preamble to the NEUM'S "10-Points" and, like it, called for government "of the people, by the people, and for the people."

The People's Assembly was itself a precursor of the Congress of the People in several respects: its tactic of popular meetings held first in localities and then progressively covering wider areas, the selection of delegates for a representative conference, its multiracialism, the important (but often exaggerated and not controlling) role of the Communists, and the adoption of a proclamation of aims. Anticipating steps that were to culminate in the Congress of the People, the People's Assembly also adopted a resolution calling for a joint meeting of the executive committees of the ANC, the SAIC, and the APO to plan for "a National Assembly of the South African peoples." [99]

ANC-AAC–1948-1949

During the year that followed the general election of 1948 and the Nationalist Party's victory, ANC and AAC leaders met together on three occasions; they seemed to make progress toward unity, but they finally gave up, believing that unity was impossible so long as the other side continued under its existing leadership.

The distrust to be overcome by Tabata and his group in agreeing to any formulation of unity that was supported by Dr. Xuma was evident in a letter of June 16, 1948, from Tabata to Mandela (Document 67).[100] Professing to be un-patronizing, Tabata reviewed African political history for the younger man, attacked Communists and "careerists and opportunists," and accused Xuma of being a tool of the white press and a deliberate fomenter of disunity. Tabata, an exponent of a federal organization of all non-European bodies, also opposed as "racist" the African nationalist argument that Africans should be appealed to "on the basis of colour" and described proposals for a single and unitary national organization of Africans as resembling "fascism." Tabata only hinted at these attitudes in his letter to Mandela and (on the face of the record) during the later joint meetings, but he expressed them in his 1950 book with reference to A. P. Mda, one of the leaders of the Youth League.[101]

Xuma's efforts for unity, which he later said had been actively going on since August 1943 (Document 69), appeared to have won notable success when he convened a meeting of twelve of the older leaders in Bloemfontein on October 3, 1948. Jabavu, Mahabane, and Dr. James S. Moroka of the AAC and also Paul Mosaka met with eight leaders of the ANC and signed "A Call for African Unity" (Document 68). "Differences of the past" should be put aside in "a period of crisis," the statement said; and the ANC and the AAC should become unified as the "All African National Congress" at a joint conference to be held on December 16.

The Tabata group (the Western Province Committee of the AAC), pointing out that six of the signatories were members of the NRC, repudiated Professor Jabavu's action and denounced the proposal as "a manoeuvre."[102] They repeated their opposition at the ANC-AAC conference on December 16-17, when Dr. Xuma and Professor Jabavu presided jointly over about 160 delegates (Document 69). Both Jabavu (saying "I am desperate") and Mahabane (saying that he would "chuck up the sponge" if not listened to) urged the adoption of the October 3 statement. The conference unanimously adopted "the principle of unity," but the AAC delegation insisted on acceptance of the "10-Points" and "noncollaboration." Among ANC responses was a declaration by A.P. Mda that the "10-points" were included in the ANC's constitution and by R. H. Godlo that they were included in *Africans' Claims*. The conference ended with agreement that the two executive committees would meet jointly.

The committees met under the joint chairmanship of Xuma and Tsotsi on Sunday, April 17, 1949, in the meeting room of a Bloemfontein advisory board. Beginning at 10:00 a.m., the meeting went on for over seventeen hours, until 3:30 a.m. The minutes (or at least one set of minutes) were prepared by C. M. Kobus, general secretary of the AAC (Document 70a). The conclusion of Moses Kotane that "we cannot come to an understanding with the Conventionites, especially if they still have Dr. Gool, Mr. Tabata and Mr. Tsotsi as their leaders" was expressed in a letter to Z. K. Matthews, who left the meeting early (Document 70b). In a summary of the meeting prepared by Kobus for the 1949 AAC conference, a similar conclusion was expressed: "it is not likely that unity will be effected in the near future with the ANC, at least as long as it has its present leadership" (Document 70c).

The differences were far wider, however, than differences in personalities. Much discussion revolved around the old question of a unitary organization or a federal one. The real question, said Kotane at the meeting, was which body should be the mouthpiece. But the question involved far-reaching considerations related to the form of organization: which form would be more effective in rallying the people (taking into account the existence of many local organizations and the needs of the struggle), more open to divisiveness, more effective in challenging the regime? Would a single, unified national organization be a mass political party, as the AAC feared, or a movement united for liberation, like the Congress of India? In the formulation that led finally to breakdown, the question became: should the proposed "All African National Congress" be "a unitary form of organization with federal features" or an "organization federal in character with unitary features"? (Document 70b). For the AAC delegates, the latter description meant that any organization which accepted national policy had a right to affiliate with the national organization; thus, they objected to the ANC's insistence that national leadership should have discretion in allowing affiliation.

The delegates differed also in their estimates of the situation, in the assessment of priorities, and in timetables for various kinds of action. Thus they differed on the readiness of the people for total boycott and the need for political education, on the priority of radical political demands as opposed to particular demands (for example, the demand for land or for an end to the pass system), on the priority to be given to African unity rather than to non-European unity and to African nationalist appeals as opposed to appeals to all persons subjected to white domination. Underlying those differences were differences of approach and temperament: the leaders of the AAC tended to be doctrinaire, in their reading of the "objective" historical facts, and absolutist; the ANC, more open to differing theories, expedient and pragmatic; thus, the delegates could not agree on the definition of "collaborator" and there was even uncertainty about what were ends or "policy" and what were means or "program."

Negotiations collapsed, but at the end of the year the ANC adopted the weapon of boycott in its Programme of Action. The AAC and the NEUM became, even more, peripheral organizations as the ANC began to gird itself for the Defiance Campaign of 1952. Some of the differences expressed in joint ANC-AAC meetings, in particular the emphasis to be placed on exclusively Africanist priorities, remained to be fought out within the ANC. Meanwhile, the Nationalist government was both defining its apartheid policies for all nonwhites and investigating communism. The minister of justice reported in February 1949 that Communists were undermining "our democratic institutions and our West-

119

ern philosophy." [103] The government was not only contributing to the building of nonwhite unity; but, in moving toward its broadly defined "Suppression of Communism" Act of 1950 (seen by Africans as a threat to their political action), it was also fostering the radicalization of the rising African generation.

NOTES

1. For an analysis of the effects of a common milieu, see Leo Kuper, "African Nationalism in South Africa—1910-1964," to be published in Monica Wilson and Leonard Thompson (eds.), *The Oxford History of South Africa*, Volume II.

2. Much of the review of white politics and policies is based on Alan Paton, *Hofmeyr* (London: Oxford University Press, 1964), with special reference to pages 333, 353-354, 397 and 399, and Eric A. Walker, *A History of Southern Africa* (London: Longmans, Green and Co., 1957). See also Edward Roux, *Time Longer than Rope: A History of the Black Man's Struggle for Freedom in South Africa* (Madison: University of Wisconsin Press, 1964), p. 306. Some material is taken from Thomas Karis, "South Africa," in Gwendolen M. Carter (ed.), *Five African States: Responses to Diversity* (Ithaca: Cornell University Press, 1963). See also Gwendolen M. Carter, *The Politics of Inequality: South Africa since 1948* (New York: Frederick A. Praeger, 1958).

3. *Report of the Native Laws Commission, 1946-1948*, U.G. 28/1948.

4. Roux, *op. cit.*, p. 339.

5. Asiatics (Transvaal Land and Trading) Act. The 1943 legislation referred to in the following paragraph was the Trading and Occupation of Land (Transvaal and Natal) Act.

6. The main source for this and the following six paragraphs is Roux, *op. cit.*

7. Clements Kadalie to Chairman, Anti-Pass Committee, May 9, 1944.

8. See Alex Hepple, *South Africa: A Political and Economic History* (London: Pall Mall Press, 1966), pp. 239-241.

9. Conversation with Calata.

10. Conversation with Marks.

11. Calata to Dr. A. B. Xuma, August 18, 1938.

12. Conversation with Calata.

13. Although he often expressed debt to the British, Calata said in 1938, in referring to franchise rights, "I do not believe we can any longer look to the South African Britisher for our champion for these rights." (Document 16)

14. In 1962, two years after the outlawing of the ANC, Calata was charged under the Unlawful Organisations Act and sentenced to six months' imprisonment which was suspended for two years, because two twenty-year-old photographs of ANC deputations were found hanging on his living room wall.

15. ANC circular of June 19, 1940 from Calata to members of the ANC National Executive Committee.

16. "Suspension of Cape African Congress Officials," Statement by Dr. A. B. Xuma [n. d.]; "African National Congress Affairs in the Transvaal," Statement by Dr. A. B. Xuma [n. d.].

17. Calata has recalled that the new constitution was "completely African," that Dr. Xuma himself had drafted it with, so far as Calata knew, no outside help. Mary Benson, *The African Patriots: The Story of the African National Congress of South Africa* (London: Faber and Faber, 1963), p. 92, states that Xuma drafted the constitution with the help of Bram Fischer, a lawyer belonging to an illustrious Afrikaner family and a Communist.

18. Benson, *op. cit.*, p. 92.

19. Minutes of the Thirty-third Conference of the ANC. Statistics for Natal are particularly variable during this period; the number of members reported in 1945, 1946, and 1949, respectively, are 707 members, 3,000 members, and 1,226. With reference to the 3,000 members, A. W. G. Champion, president of the ANC in Natal, told the chief Native commissioner of Natal that membership meant the payment of two shillings and sixpence in annual dues. "Notes of Meeting with the Executive Committee of the ANC, Held at Pietermaritzburg on the 15.1.1947."

20. ANC National Executive Report, December 16, 1949.

21. Not until the December 1939 conference was Calata given a lump sum to help defray administrative and clerical expenses: £15, contributed mainly by African chiefs and partly by Indians. Conversation with Calata.

22. Calata to Champion, October 16, 1940.

23. Conversations with J. B. Marks and Dr. Silas M. Molema.

24. "Special Economic Conference to Study the Position of the Cost of Living

affecting Natives in Natal Held in Durban 5th, 6th, and 7th July 1941 at No. 19 Old Dutch Road, Durban," statement issued by A. W. G. Champion.

25. Benson, *op. cit.*, p. 162.

26. "Victory Congress Conference, December 14-16th, 1941," statement issued by Dr. A. B. Xuma (n.d.)

27. Circular letter of March 22, 1943, by Dr. A. B. Xuma. The letter spoke of "a demand for a Charter of Citizenship—a bill of rights for Africans who served King and Country with unswerving loyalty, devotion and courage, excelled by none irrespective of race or colour."

28. Dr. Xuma's preface to the printed booklet entitled *Africans' Claims in South Africa* ("Congress Series No. II") stated, "Their findings [those of the Atlantic Charter Committee] were unanimously adopted by the Annual Conference of the African National Congress at Bloemfontein, on the 16th of December, 1943." This date appeared as "1945" in many copies of the booklet, which was poorly printed and had pages out of order. In his presidential address on December 14, 1944, Dr. Xuma said that the findings had been adopted by the 1943 conference. Afterwards, the drafting committee had "put final touches and handed [it] to your National President for final editing and the writing of an introduction"; it was "now printed and available for sale at one shilling a copy."

In its report to the December 1944 conference, the national executive committee announced the availability of bulk orders of the printed document, which included "a bill of rights which was adopted in 1943." Two hundred copies of *Africans' Claims*, printed in October 1944, were sold at the December 1944 conference (according to Dr. Xuma, as reported in the minutes of the annual conference of December 1945).

29. Prime minister's private secretary to Dr. A. B. Xuma, September 29, 1944.

30. Address by Dr. Xuma at the opening of the Orlando High School, 13th August 1941.

31. See G. H. Calpin, *Indians in South Africa* (Pietermaritzburg: Shuter and Shooter, 1949), Chapter XIV, and Maurice Webb and Kenneth Kirkwood, *The Durban Riots and After* (Johannesburg: South African Institute of Race Relations, 1949—a 22-page booklet).

32. Analysis of the NRC is based to a large extent upon conversations with Professor Z. K. Matthews and an unpublished manuscript by Professor Matthews. Also particularly useful have been conversations with Dr. J. S. Moroka and A. W. G. Champion.

33. Election of the twelve was by so-called voting units (chiefs and headmen, urban advisory boards, district councils, electoral committees) except in the Transkei, where the United Transkeian Territories General Council, or Bunga, served as the electoral college. These units voted on behalf of male taxpayers under their jurisdiction. The Transkei returned three members, and three other electoral areas (Cape Province outside the Transkei, Natal, and the Transvaal and Orange Free State combined) each returned one representative of urban areas and two of rural areas. The six chief Native commissioners, who were white, belonged to the council as assessor members, and the minister of Native affairs or his deputy served as chairman.

34. Not until December 1948 did Professor Jabavu, as president of the AAC, rule that no member of the NRC could be a member of the AAC. I. B. Tabata, *The All African Convention: The Awakening of a People* (Johannesburg: People's Press, 1950), p. 96.

35. Dr. Xuma is mistakenly listed as a member by John Cope, *South Africa* (New York: Praeger, 1965), p. 146.

36. Paton, *op. cit.*, p. 405.

37. *Ibid.*, pp. 432-3.

38. *Ibid.*, p. 433

39. On September 8, Hofmeyr had written to Smuts in Paris: "It seems that the (hitherto) moderate intellectuals of the Professor Matthews type are now committed to an extreme line against colour discrimination, and have carried the Chiefs with them. We can't afford to allow them to be swept into the extremist camp, but I don't see what we can do to satisfy them, which would be tolerated by European public opinion." Smuts replied, characteristically: " . . . we must temporise for the present . . . "

On October 7, Hofmeyr, misjudging the temper of the council, wrote to Smuts: "You should know that Professor Matthews came to see me a week or two ago. He was at great pains to emphasize that they did not want the Council to be abolished, and hoped that we would be conciliatory. I told him that having regard to their resolution and the speeches that led up to it we could not do anything that would be interpreted as a surrender, and suggested that they should reconsider the question from that angle. He said he would take steps to consult his colleagues. As a result there may be something in the nature of a climb-down, in which event I shall of course let you know. It is clear that some of them at least are now frightened of the possible consequences of their action." Ibid, pp. 435-6.

40. Article by Moses Kotane, *Inkululeko* [Freedom], September-October 1947, quoted by Tabata, *op. cit.*, p. 139.

41. Paton, *op. cit.*, p. 439.

42. *Ibid.*, p. 454. The quoted words are Paton's.

43. Edward Roux has observed that "the most effective form of boycott" has never been tried in South Africa, that is, the technique of the Irish Nationalists, who won elections and then refrained from taking seats in the British Parliament. *Op. cit.*, p. 307.

44. I. B. Tabata, *op. cit., passim*. See also the documents below concerned with "The All African Convention and Efforts at Wider Unity."

45. Benson, *op. cit.*, p. 145, Benson notes that "even Marks, the Communist" agreed with continued participation. Matthews, however, recollected that at the December 1947 conference Marks favored boycott and thus differed with Moses Kotane, also a Communist, who followed the ANC line.

46. "That is when they [the ANC] invented the notorious meaningless slogan: 'Return the Boycott Candidates.' " Tabata, *op. cit.*, p. 142.

47. *Ibid.*, pp. 94, 102.

48. Discussion of the Youth League is based largely on conversations in 1963 and 1964 with Oliver Tambo, W. F. Nkomo, Jordan Ngubane (and an unpublished manuscript by him), M. T. Moerane, David Bopape, Z. K. Matthews, A. W. G. Champion, G. M. Pitje, and J. C. M. Mbata (and his notes of the February 21, 1944 meeting with Dr. Xuma). Mr. Mbata also reviewed the manuscript. Also valuable has been the conversation of Gail M. Gerhart with A. P. Mda, January 1, 1970.

49. Lovedale was the first establishment for African higher education in South Africa, founded in 1841 by the Church of Scotland. See Robert H. W. Shepherd, *Lovedale, South Africa: The Story of a Century, 1841-1941* (Lovedale, C. P., South Africa: The Lovedale Press, n.d.). Lovedale and Healdtown, a Methodist institution, were in eastern Cape Province; and Adams College, a Congregational school, was near Durban. When "The South African Native College" became affiliated to Rhodes University in 1952, it was re-named "The University College of Fort Hare." Alexander Kerr, *Fort Hare, 1915-48: The Evolution of an African College* (London: C. Hurst and Co., 1968), p. ix.

50. Unpublished manuscript.

51. "The ANC Youth League was born," Raboroko has claimed, "at a meeting held at the Domestic and Cultural Workers' Club Hall in Diagonal Street, Johannesburg, in October 1943; a meeting convened and presided over by the present writer." *Africa South*, April-June 1960, p. 29.
124

52. Just one year earlier, on July 20, 1946, Dr. Xuma and other leading Africans spoke at a public reception in honor of Lembede's "academic achievement"—he had been awarded the M.A. degree as well as the LL.B. degree and was professionally proficient in High Dutch and Afrikaans. *Inkundla ya Bantu*, August 1946.

53. Nkomo presided, and the speakers included Dr. Xuma, Selope Thema, Lembede, Mbobo, and J. Malepe. *Bantu World*, April 22, 1944.

54. The conference was held at the Bantu Men's Social Centre in Johannesburg and was presided over by Nkomo. Speakers included Dr. Xuma, Selope Thema, Bopape, Tambo, Tloome, J. Nhlapo, the Rev. Z. R. Mahabane, and Miss V. Ncakeni. Lembede's election was as president of the Youth League "in the Transvaal"—the only center of Youth League activity at that time— and the following were elected as executive committee members: Bopape, Masekela, Malepe, Mandela, Mbobo, Mda, Joseph Mokoena, Nxumalo, Sisulu, and Tambo. *Bantu World*, September 30, 1944.

55. Unpublished manuscript.

56. *Treason Trial Record* [of 1956-1961], p. 17, 891.

57. The role of the leaders of the Youth League regarding the NRC after August 1946 is noted in the discussion of the NRC.

58. Benson, *op. cit.*, p. 151.

59. The opening paragraph of the statement published in *Inkundla* was identical to that of the Programme of Action as adopted, and much of the remaining text of the statement was also incorporated. The statement endorsed the boycott of "differential institutions" but unlike the Programme of Action included no reference to strikes or civil disobedience.

60. Professor Matthews was asked in the treason trial in 1960 whether the final clause regarding "other means" was "put in to cover the possible use of violence." Matthews strongly denied that it was or that such a thought was expressed at any of the many conferences he attended. *Treason Trial Record*, p. 17, 895.

61. Ngubane has written in an unpublished manuscript, "It was from Anton Lembede that I first heard the word [Africanism] used seriously to indicate a way of life. Up to then, some of our friends had used the phrase 'Africanisation of the civil service' rather loosely, obviously borrowing it from Nigerian writings. My first reaction to Africanism was that it was too racially angular to make me feel comfortable. It laid too much stress on the African and ran the danger of producing a racially exclusive attitude among the Africans which would be similar to that of the Afrikaner nation-

125

alists." Ngubane adds that Mda "did not really like the word Africanism" but that his objections were not as strong as Ngubane's.

Ngubane has denied that Lembede was a "racialist." Rather, he has declared that Lembede criticized Ngubane's close association with whites because he feared it "might tone down my aggressiveness as a nationalist." Lembede was prepared to collaborate with other races but only when he could bargain as an equal.

62. Testifying at the treason trial in 1960, Professor Matthews stated that Marcus Garvey's "idea of Africa for the Africans . . . was never adopted by the African National Congress." *Treason Trial Record*, pp. 18, 244-5.

63. Mda recalls Lembede as a "tireless student" and himself (Mda) as his "testing ground." Together they read widely and had heated disagreements about writers such as Descartes, Nietzche, Marx, Engels, Ruskin, Russell, and Smuts (his *Holism and Evolution*). Lembede also read Mussolini, Hitler, and Verwoerd's newspaper columns in Afrikaans and was impressed by their conceptions of leadership. These were reflected in "Our Creed" in the manifesto (Document 48): "We believe that leadership must be the personification and symbol of popular aspirations and ideals." Lembede's intensity is indicated by an article in *Inkundla*, February 27, 1947, in which he wrote, "African Nationalism is to be pursued with the fanaticism and bigotry of religion. . . . "

64. H. J. and R. E. Simons, *Class and Colour in South Africa, 1850-1950* (Baltimore: Penguin Books, 1969), p. 406.

65. *Ibid.*, pp. 503-504.

66. "Statement of Dr. Y. M. Dadoo, Secretary, Non-European United Front (Transvaal), before the Court on Friday, 6th September, 1940 at his trial under the Emergency Regulations, Published by Authority of the Non-European United Front (Transvaal), Johannesburg."

67. Roux, *op. cit.*, pp. 316-317.

68. Tabata, *op. cit.*, p. 117.

69. *Minutes of the All African Convention*, December 1941, p. 11. The ten members of the committee included Moses Kotane, Clements Kadalie, I. B. Tabata and Dr. G. H. Gool.

70. Mahabane has recollected, in conversation in 1964, that "the ANC refused to have anything to do" with the AAC and the NEUM. "I don't know why. Their policies were absolutely the same."

71. Jabavu and Mahabane were severely criticized in the December 1948 AAC

conference for cooperating with Dr. Xuma in producing a joint statement in October 1948 (Document 69), but Jabavu was warmly extolled at the same meeting on his thirteen years as president. "Mr. I. B. Tabata, recalling memories of his school days under Professor Jabavu, said he had never known Professor to lose his temper except once, when Mr. Tabata could not conjugate a Latin verb." *Minutes of the All African Convention (1948)*, p. 17.

72. Appendix 3 to *Minutes of the All African Convention, December 1940* and Tabata, *op. cit.*, pp. 115-116.

73. The *Minutes* of the 1940 conference do not summarize Tabata's argument. His book, pages 116-117, accuses "those who framed" the recommendations of conceiving "a deliberate plan to emasculate the Convention and render it impotent."

74. *Workers' Voice, Organ of the Fourth International (Trotskyists) of South Africa*, in its issue of October 5, 1943, welcomed the formation of the ADP. On November 7, it stated that the Fourth International "has supported the A.D.P. and continues to support it, from within and without, as an organisation with possibilities . . . " and would continue "to criticise those elements inside the A.D.P. who . . . are tied up in their ideas with the present system of the Native Representative Council and collaboration with the European Liberals."

75. However, *Native Opinion of South Africa (Imvo Zabantsundu)*, in an editorial of October 9, 1943, condemning divisiveness, saw "militant fanatacism" in the ADP's manifesto. "Militant we must be, of course, but within reasonable limits."

76. *Inkundla ya Bantu (Bantu Forum)*, October 30, 1943, critically described the founding members. It identified Koza as "a diehard Trotskyist." The AAC Minutes of December 1943 listed him as a delegate from the Fourth International of Johannesburg. Koza apparently drifted away from the ADP.

77. Quoted in *Workers' Voice*, November 7, 1943. *Inkululeko ('Freedom)*, the official Communist Party organ, on October 9, 1943, carried a first-hand report of the inaugural meeting, attended by "only a few hundred people" who "yawned" as they listened to "the one-time Communist Basner" and others. Basner's billing for the inaugural meeting was in a flyer, "African Democratic Party," issued on September 6, 1943.

78. Professor Z. K. Matthews has recalled that Mosaka and Basner were optimistic about the ADP, because they had won their 1942 campaigns decisively in spite of opposition from various members of the ANC. He warned Mosaka that the people could not be won away from the ANC.

127

79. Letter from Mosaka and Mampuru to the *Bantu World*, October 9, 1943. Later letters were published on October 16 and November 13.

80. "Non-Africans," said Xuma, ". . . appear to be patrons and promoters of this disintegrating influence in the ranks of the Africans." "Rebels and Enemies of Congress," an article by Xuma in the *Bantu World*, October 30, 1943. Observing events in the Transvaal, *Inkundla ya Bantu (Bantu Forum)*, March 31, 1944, described Xuma as an African nationalist and Mosaka as an African liberal who, by allowing whites to join his party, "aims at splitting whites, while Congress aims at uniting Africans."

81. The *Bantu World*, October 16, 1943.

82. *Inkundla ya Bantu (Bantu Forum)*, October 30, 1943.

83. Mrs. Mampuru has claimed that the ADP was formed by 2,000 loyal and non-Communist ANC members who were "middle-aged" and well-educated, mainly teachers. Conversation with Mrs. Self Mampuru.
    A New Year's message by Mosaka and Mampuru announced that the ADP would seek African unity in the planning of a campaign for the observance of an "African Day of Prayer," which might also be observed as "Atlantic Charter Day." *Umteteli wa Bantu*, January 8, 1944.

84. The text of the SAIC resolution is Addendum IV of *Proceedings of the 2nd Unity Conference . . . 8th July, 1944*.

85. Minutes, "Unity Conference . . . 17th December, 1943," Addendum I to *Proceedings of 2nd Unity Conference . . . 8th July, 1944*.

86. One of the eight "decisions" in the manifesto, regarding "the form of representation to the coming Peace Conference," was not approved because the "Conference felt that no useful purpose would be served by sending delegates to a Peace Conference of Imperialist governments." Tabata, *op. cit.* p. 75.

87. *All African Convention, Executive Committee's Statement, 7th July, 1944, Along the New Road*. Extracts appear in Tabata, *op. cit.*, pp. 81-85.

88. Non-European Unity Movement, *Proceedings of 6th Unity Conference Held on 29th, 30th, 31st March, 1948*, pp. 1 and 15.

89. *Minutes of the All African Convention, Bloemfontein, 18th-19th December, 1943*, p. 9. The words "by majority vote" in the printed minutes do not appear in the typewritten minutes. On the other hand, the printed minutes omit some sentences of the typewritten minutes—for example, the suggestion that an appeal for funds be made "to certain lady European philanthropists."

90. In 1945, Xuma ignored letters and refused to see the Reverand Z. R. Mahabane or Dr. Gool. In 1947, Mahabane urged Jabavu and Xuma jointly to convene a conference of all African organizations in December 1947; Jabavu answered favorably but Xuma not at all. *Proceedings of the 6th Unity Conference Held on 29th, 30th, 31st March, 1948*, p. 10.

91. At the Third Unity Conference of the NEUM on January 4-5, 1945, the Credentials Committee reported that 214 delegates represented 102 organizations having about 59,520 members but that, for several reasons, this number of members was "a very conservative estimate." *Report of the 3rd Unity Conference . . . on 4th & 5th January, 1945*, p. 22. At this conference, Tabata spoke in detail of the need to rely on federal organizations of Africans, Coloureds, and Indians; he also emphasized that federal organizations should cooperate under a Head Unity Committee and in local coordinating unity committees.

92. Michael Scott, *A Time to Speak* (New York: Doubleday & Co., 1958) Chapter 7. In January 1944, a Communist delegate to the Anti-C.A.D. Conference spoke in "defence of the Liberals and the 'Rights and Justice' Conference" but was attacked for this by Tabata and leading members of the Anti-C.A.D. *Report of the Proceedings of the Second National Anti-C.A.D. Conference . . . January 4th and 5th, 1944.*

The Campaign for Right and Justice had at least a rhetorical impact on Dr. Xuma; prior to the general election of 1948 he called on nonwhites to "organise their respective communities for this campaign for right and justice" (Document 41).

93. Roux, *op. cit.*, p. 328. Bopape, in a 1964 conversation remembers 35,000 demonstrators.

94. Young Jordan Ngubane, always strongly anti-Communist, also supported the campaign and warned Dr. Xuma to counter rumors that the ANC was not sincerely behind it. Ngubane to Xuma, January 26, 1944.

95. *Report of the Proceedings of the Second National Anti-C.A.D. Conference . . . January 4th and 5th, 1944*, p. 11.

96. Resolution reproduced in *A.N. Congress Bulletin*, No. 3, June 24, 1945.

97. Roux, *op. cit.*, p. 330.

98. A resolution to this effect was adopted on May 6, 1948 by the ANC (Transvaal) executive committee. *Bantu World*, May 16, 1948.

99. *Assembly News: Official Bulletin of the First Transvaal-Orange Free State People's Assembly for Votes for All*, June 24, 1948.

100. The text reproduced in this volume is taken from an undated and mimeographed copy. The letter, along with a letter to A. P. Mda, was reproduced as a printed "Unity Movement Publication" in March 1965 in Zambia, with many minor but mainly explanatory changes.

The letter inaccurately referred to Dr. Xuma as a former president of the AAC; he was vice-president of the AAC until December 1937, when he was in London and was replaced by Mahabane. "I thought it was discourtesy," Jabavu wrote shortly afterward, "to drop you in your absence." Jabavu to Xuma, March 7, 1938.

101. *Op. cit.*, p. 154. See Document 70a for the remarks by Mda that Tabata characterizes in his book.

102. "All African Convention Committee (W.P.) Resolutions Rejecting Bloemfontein 'Unity' " [n.d.] Dr. Moroka, who was to join the ANC at the same time he became president-general in December 1949, supported the proposal for a single African organization as a necessary step before "we can go to the Indians, Coloureds and democratic Europeans . . . and together with them call a national convention. . . . " *The Guardian*, October 21, 1948.

103. Quoted in Carter, *op. cit.*, p. 63.

DOCUMENTS—PART TWO

THE REVIVAL OF THE AFRICAN NATIONAL CONGRESS, 1937-1945

Document 16. "Presidential Address" by the Rev. J. A. Calata, Cape African Congress, July 4, 1938

Mr. Chairman, Chapter VI of the Constitution of the African National Congress deals with matters relating to Provincial Congresses and states that in each of the four Provinces of the Union, to wit, Natal, Orange Free State, Transvaal, and Cape Province, there shall be a Congress to be held once in every year at such places within the Provinces as shall be appointed. The said Provincial Congress shall be composed of the Chiefs, delegates and officers of the Congress, and such other special delegates as may be approved. The Provincial Congress shall be subject in all and everything to the supreme authority of the National Congress.

After the Silver Jubilee of the African National Congress which was celebrated in Bloemfontein last year, at which the Cape African Congress was more strongly represented than any other Provinces, it is fitting for me as your President to give you a brief outline of the history of the Congress, more especially as the Congress in the Cape Province needs so much re-organising.

The introductory note to the constitution of the A.N.C. was that the inception of the National Congress was due to a crying need for a comprehensive machinery by which to manage and direct national affairs. . . . The Provincial Congresses entertained a spirit of self-control and exercised a defiant influence towards the Mother Congress which was powerless for lack of proper machinery.

It was not until 1915 when this intolerable position was fully realised, and the National Congress then passed a resolution for the revision of the constitution.

There were then five Provincial Congresses in existence: The Natal Native Congress, The Orange Free State Native Congress, The Transvaal Native Congress, The Cape Native Congress, and The Transkei Native Congress, as they were then called. It was these Congresses which were represented at the first National Convention held at Bloemfontein in January 1912, summoned by Dr. P. Ka I. Seme, B.A., L.L.B., and the first President was Dr. John L. Dube of Natal.

131

Among some of the names which figure prominently in the early history of the Congress are the following:

Cape: Dr. W. B. Rubusana, Rev. E. P. Koti, S. T. Plaatje, J. D. Ngojo.

Transkei: E. Tshongwana, R. W. Msimang.

Natal: J. T. Gumede, W. W. Ndlovu, Rev. J. L. Dube.

Transvaal: R. V. Selope-Thema, Dr. P. Ka. I. Seme, S. M. Makgatho, D. S. Letanka.

Orange Free State: J. B. Twayi, T. M. Mapikela, Rev. A. P. Pitso.

Swaziland: P. Nxumalo.

I can assure every one here present that when the history of the A.N.C. comes to be written pages and pages will be full of stories of heroic sacrifices of the leaders whose names I have mentioned. Can you imagine any body with sense suggesting that the Congress should be abolished!

Among the chief objects of the Congress as stated in the National constitution are: (a) To form a national vigilant association and a deliberative assembly or council without legislative pretensions. (b) To unite, absorb, consolidate, and preserve under its aegis existing political, and educational associations, vigilance committees, and other public and private bodies whose aims are the promotion and safeguarding of the interests of the aboriginal races. (c) To be the medium of representative opinion and to formulate a standard policy on Native affairs for the benefit and guidance of the Government.

The Cape African Congress as this brief review shows, existed before the National Congress, and the term "National" refers to the Congress of all Provinces combined. There are some among us who may remember a large conference or "Ngqungquthela" which met at Queenstown in 1908.

Owing to the fact that the Cape Africans enjoyed the franchise and other political rights which the Africans in other Provinces did not have, the Congress in the Cape kept itself more or less aloof and had its own constitution apart from that of the National Congress and although it recognised the authority of the National body yet it maintained rigidly its own identity as it still does today.

My predecessor, the late Rev. E. Mdolomba who, like myself was President of the Cape and also Secretary General of the National Congress told me that he found the Cape a much more difficult Province than the others because of its lack of cohesion among its people.

Please allow me to clarify one important point which I feel sure is not understood, and it is that an association of the Congress as laid down in the constitution, should consist of district and local branches, agricultural and educational societies, industrial and economic unions, and any other bodies formed for such specific purposes as are closely allied with the objects of the Congress.

The Congress recognises and honours all Chiefs by heritage and other persons of Royal blood and exhorts all its branches to foster and enlist the sympathy and practical support of the ministers of religion and their congregations.

I want the African People of the Cape to realise that the African Congress is comprehensive enough to accomplish the unity of our race, and now that we have lost the franchise we should rally round the congress and join up with our brethren in the north to plan out our salvation.

I beg to ask this conference to consider two serious draw backs: (1) The lack of funds to enable organisers to travel about. (2) The need for a newspaper that can be used for propaganda purposes. The National Congress passed a resolution in favour of a national paper under the control of the A.N.C. last year and we shall be asked to discuss the same proposal at this conference. At this stage I desire to take this opportunity and thank the existing African newspapers for their very generous attitude towards the Congress, as you will realise that they gave a great deal of assistance to the summoning of this conference. The executive is seriously considering the undertaking [of] some negotiations with one or two of them to see if for the present at any rate, until there is money, we could not come to some agreement by which we could co-operate to achieve our object.

AFRICAN LEADERSHIP

I feel it my duty to say a few words on Leadership. My mind is greatly exercised over the existence of much rivalry in the Cape and the easy way in which communists and other people use the name of the Congress to spread their doctrines among our people.

I regret that owing to unavoidable circumstances the National executive which was to have met on Wednesday after here has had to change its venue to Bloemfontein, for one of the questions to be discussed is how to put a stop to irresponsible agitators who go about the country without the authority, addressing meetings and taking our ignorant people's money under our name. I am afraid we shall be forced in certain cases to take drastic measures.

As your chief organiser I have made it a point of never addressing a public meeting anywhere unless I have first of all obtained the support of the local leaders, Advisory Board Members, Ministers and Teachers; but I have noticed that the rank and file prefer the man who comes from the outside and ignores their leaders, who in his speech, utters most extravagant criticism of local authorities and does not worry about what happens to the relations between masters and servants or the location residents and the municipal authorities as a result of his speech. I do not say that Congress Leaders should not assist local agitation on behalf of the wage earners, nor am I opposed to agitation for better conditions for our locations and farms. What I deplore is agitation not based on knowledge of conditions and such as only aims at making people pop out half crowns and then leave them in a worse state than before. My own opinion is that such leaders are not of the right sort and should not be encouraged. I feel that it is the duty of our Congress to protect its rank and file, and that no organizer should be allowed to address a meeting unless he produces a warrant

133

signed by a recognised official of the body he represents. I feel also that in order to educate the people to follow the right kind of leadership, our organisers should not start branches in opposition to local associations which meet the needs of the community but should seek to establish a relationship whereby that local association shall recognise the authority of the Congress and assist or be assisted by the Congress in some of its local difficulties. Where there are several bodies without any co-ordination of forces there perhaps a branch could be usefully started but with the consent of the local leaders.

We must also train our people to trust the leaders they know best and stick to them. It is a shame to see how some leaders for no reason whatsoever are undermined and rejected and inferior men and women take their places to the detriment of the National cause.

Unless we understand leadership and follow it well, we cannot look to our Parliamentary representatives for help for they can do nothing for us unless we have proper leaders with whom they could confer and obtain representative opinion. It has been very kind of them to come to this conference. It shows how zealous they are to learn from us and to understand all our ways.

THE POLITICAL SITUATION

Mr. Grobler, the retired Minister of Native Affairs, is quoted to have said, speaking at the Pretoria University on the 12th December 1936: "There can be no middle course in native policy. You must either have equality and assimilation on the one hand, or on the other the golden rule of Calvinism and of the old republics—No equality in church or state. Indecision can only lead us to an abyss".

We Africans of the Cape must be forgiven if we rebel against the golden rule policy, because we have been allowed for over 80 years to enjoy full citizenship rights, and for the Government to take those rights away from us without pointing out how we have misused them is to us a very unkindly act. It constitutes a grievance that will last for generations and may have serious repercussions, for those rights were cherished by our brethren in the north who had declared that they were prepared to wait for 50 years without a franchise than take anything lower than was enjoyed by the Cape Africans.

To explain what I mean let us go back exactly 100 years to 1828 when the Cape legislature instituted ordinance 50, generally known as the "Magna Charta" of the Hottentots, a system of government which equalised all His Majesty's subjects without regard to colour or race. Then go on to the principles laid down by the Duke of Newcastle, then British Secretary of State for the Colonies, in his despatch transmitting the approved constitution for the Cape Colony in 1852: "It is the earnest desire of Her Majesty's Government that all her subjects at the Cape without distinction of class or colour, should be united by one bond of loyalty and common interest".

134

Come nearer by another 50 years and hear Cecil Rhodes' declaration of "equal rights for all civilised people south of the Zambosi."

In the Cape Parliament we had the late Rev. Dr. W. B. Rubusana representing Tembuland, and the late John Tengo Jabavu as an active politican assisting some of the finest statesmen of English and Dutch descent to establish the Afrikander Bond Party.

Today we are told that in spite of all the educated men we turn out of our colleges and Fort Hare and those who have graduated overseas, that we are not sufficiently civilised to know how to exercise the franchise. I cannot understand Bishop Carey's attitude in England in advocating the Grondvet policy as the right policy for us in South Africa.

Some people do not even understand that the land that the Government is buying with such high prices is bought for the Trust and not for the natives which is a totally different thing. Mind you I think the Government has been generous towards us in passing the Land and Trust Act.

The reason why I have asked the Cape Parliamentary Representatives to attend this conference is simply that I want them to realise the tremendous responsibility we are putting on their shoulders, and what we expect of them as well as for us to be told by them what they can expect of us.

As your President I can say that I hope they will stay with us and hear the other members of the executive when they introduce discussions on Land, Labour, Education and health questions for which I have no time to discuss in this address. But I can say this, that we must sympathise with the representatives in their uphill work. We must not expect impossibilities from them just because we have sent them to Parliament. We must give them time to get used to Parliamentary ways. They have a very hard job to educate the European members of Parliament on the fact that we are not a menace to the interests of the Europeans of this country, and to show them as in fact they are already doing, how impossible it is to trust the African as if he was a different kind of creature from other South African human beings.

I say our Parliamentary representatives are already doing their job. Let me quote you extracts from the Rand Daily Mail: "The three representatives who have been sent to the assembly by the Native Voters of the Cape have already acquitted themselves with distinction. . . . It is not merely that Mrs. Ballinger and Messrs. Molteno and Hemming are fluent and convincing speakers, backed by an intimate acquaintance with the needs of their Native Voters and by a high sincerity of purpose. Nor is it because these new members have kept rigidly aloof from the party antagonism with which Parliament is so predominantly concerned. The real reason is to be found, rather, in the strong sense of national responsibility which they are bringing to their task. They have avoided the purely parochial and provincial issues and have approached the problems of Native well-fare from that broad perspective in [which] the needs of both Black and White in this country must ultimately be regarded as one."

For this impression alone our members deserve our most cordial thanks, for we realise that the plea that Mrs. Ballinger made for higher wages for Africans is not merely an appeal to the conscience but also to the self interest of the White people of this country. The second thing I want to place before you in connection with our political outlook in the Cape is this: Let us remember the story of the wise men who wanted to see the Holy Baby. They were told to return home by another road for fear of King Herod. Let us look for another political road back to our rights. Let our watchword for this conference be "ANOTHER ROAD" (NDLELA YIMBI). By that I do not mean we are to give up the idea of a common franchise. Oh no! But I see no possibility of our asking for a return to those rights within the next five or ten years; besides I do not believe we can any longer look to the South African Britisher for our champion for those rights.

Personally I am thankful that Mr. Heaton Nicholls was not appointed Minister of Native Affairs. I venture to suggest that the other road lies in agitation for the extension of the present franchise to the Northern Provinces. That is why the Congress has sent Mrs. Ballinger of Johannesburg to Parliament, and it is also for the same reason that the Congress calls her its leader.

We would, however, ask our Senators, Parliamentary Representatives and Provincial Councillors not to divide on matters of policy. While I say that, I want to impress it upon you that unless we, behind them, are united and speak with one voice, it is not possible for them to be united. Therefore the call of the Cape African Congress for closing ranks behind our Parliamentary representatives and our members of the Native Representatives Council is timely and must be responded to. The third thing I want to say is that time is ripe for us to look about for ways of self help. I endorse with all my heart the timely words which fell from the lips of Professor Jabavu at his presidential address of the All African Convention held on June 29th 1936 when he said "We should find a solution for an escape out of poverty. Business and commerce must be stressed and much propaganda carried out to further them. Let us learn to support our own traders however humble they be." I bid you all take these words from a leader of world wide experience. Let our department of commerce be the hardest working department. I know for a fact that Mr. W. G. Ballinger will only be too glad to help in this direction. Co-operative stores must be taken up as another line of action towards our national salvation. I would go further and say let us bring before the National Congress and the All African Convention the necessity of exploring ways and means by which we could co-operate in commercial enterprises with other non-Europeans overseas.

INTERNATIONAL OUTLOOK

I believe it sounds strange for me to talk of an International Outlook. I would not introduce the subject if I did not think it had some bearing on the 'other road' policy which I want us to follow. I am sure we all understand that our salvation does not just depend on our coming together, important though that itself may be.

We must be ready to co-operate with those Europeans who want to work with us. There is in this country, yes, even in our Parliament, a steady rise of liberalism, especially in the cities it is evident. The South African press with its international outlook is doing a lot of useful work in educating the public of South Africa through international politics to take a broader view of human questions.

The Joint Council movement with which we have agreed to co-operate has an international outlook. The Pathfinder Scout and Wayfarer Guide movements are international movements. Besides that we have individuals who represent us in international conferences overseas. The African Mine Labourers owe Mr. Ballinger a large debt of gratitude for fighting the question of the payment of travelling expenses of the South African Mine Labourers when they go to employment at the Mines. This he did at the International Labour Conference at Geneva. By cultivating an international outlook we shall find that we have more to be thankful for at the present time than we perhaps imagine. Take for instance the gift of Colonel Donaldson. You will find that all over the country we have many benefactors on a smaller scale, like Mr. Asher at Graaff Reinet, Mr. Metcalf at Cradock and others. Take our patron, the Rev. A. W. Blaxall. That man is simply giving himself away as a sacrifice for the sake of our blind, deaf and dumb, something that many of those among our people who are better privileged do not yet appreciate. With a little more international outlook we should rally round Mr. Blaxall and create a national fund to help him carry on his noble work for our handicapped people. I am sure we would earn more respect from other races. Look at the Abyssinian tragedy from an international stand point and you will be surprised to notice that it has drawn a lot of eyes towards Africa and has helped to draw non-European nations nearer each other in different parts of the world.

Today the leaders of the non-European races all over the world are conferring on the present world crisis. They realise that Great Britain in deciding to bargain with Fascist Italy has let down Abyssinia and in the event of a bust up she has practically lost power over the Mediterranean and so the Congress in India is pushing forward for sovereign independence.

The position has its parallel in South Africa. Great Britain is about to let go the Protectorates although she understands quite well that by doing so she will lose the prestige of her 50 million Africans in her empire in Africa.

Taking the population of the British commonwealth as a whole about 80 per cent are Black and 350 million of these are in India. Therefore I cannot see how England can be so short sighted as to play with her rights in South Africa more especially as the Cape Route is the only right of way she has to herself for looking after the Empire in event of war.

Now shouldn't that give us hope that England's interests in South Africa is

137

bound to re-awaken and perhaps that would be to our favour? I realise that looking at things from this point of view is apt to raise all sorts of false hopes, but I am convinced of the fact that Native Bills has brought England's eyes nearer South Africa and the eyes of the non-European races of the world nearer England.

It is a case of what will follow. I say let us not get despondent and think that we have lost all. Our poet, Mr. Mqhayi, has told us that the handle that turns the wheels of the universe is in the hand of God and a new world is about to be begotten.

NKOSI SIKELEL'I AFRICA.
JAMES A. CALATA.

Document 17. Report of a Deputation from the ANC and Congress of Urban Advisory Boards to the Minister of Native Affairs, May 15-17, 1939

A deputation representing the African National Congress and the Congress of Advisory Boards attended at Cape Town on May 15th, 16th and 17th to interview the Honourable the Minister of Native Affairs and to meet the parliamentary representatives of the African people. The deputation consisted of the following:— Representing the African National Congress: Reverend Z. R. Mahabane (President-General), Reverend J. A. Calata (Secretary-General and Senior Chaplain), Councillor R. G. Baloyi, M.R.C. (Treasurer-General); representing the Transvaal African Congress: Mr. S. P. Matseke, (President), Messrs. C. S. Ramohanoe (Provincial Secretary), J. M. Lekhetho and J. B. Marks; representing Natal Congress: Rev. A. S. Mtimkulu; representing Orange Free State Congress: Councillor T. Mapikela, M.R.C.; representing Cape Congress: Mr. J. D. Ngojo; representing Cape Western Congress: Messrs. M. Kotane, S. Oliphant and P. Sehloko; representing the Congress of Advisory Boards: Councillor R. H. Godlo, M.R.C. (President), Councillor A. J. Sililo, M.R.C., and Mr. J. Mafu.

The deputation had two interviews with the Minister of Native Affairs (the Honourable H. A. Fagan, K.C., M.P.) who was accompanied by the Secretary for Native Affairs (Mr. D. L. Smit) and altogether the interviews lasted nearly six hours.

By arrangement with the parliamentary representatives the deputation was introduced by Senator the Honourable J. D. Rheinallt Jones.

The Reverend Z. R. Mahabane, as leader of the deputation conveyed the greetings of the bodies represented to the Minister. The Native Affairs Department, he said, had a difficult position as it was a buffer between the European population and the African people. He wished to make clear that the deputation had not come to usurp the functions of the Natives Representative Council, which was an official mouthpiece of the African people. There are, however, he said, unofficial bodies which have useful functions to perform in providing opportunities for free discussion among the people themselves, and it is only right that voluntary organisations of this kind should come into touch with the

Minister. The deputation had come to present the views of the African National Congress (with its branches) and the Congress of Advisory Boards and to explain them. They dealt with a number of matters but the deputation would deal with the most important.

As regards wages, Mr. Mahabane said that low wages is one of the root causes of our problems, leading to juvenile delinquency, malnutrition, infantile mortality and even the Beer question. It is important that wages be raised to remove these evils.

The Congresses asked for an extension of the individual franchise so that the Africans in the northern provinces may be represented in the House of Assembly and in the Provincial Councils. Now that the supposed fear of the old Cape franchise has been removed there is no reason to refuse the extension of the representation now given to the Native voters in the Cape Province. There is now a large number of educated people—even graduates—in all the provinces, and others who own land or who work on their own account. Surely such people should be given citizen rights. "We are under the same flag", said the speaker, "we have the same government and out interests are identical. Contentment is the only basis of sound government", and there should be nothing to fear from this extended representation.

The Minister of Native Affairs said that he appreciated the greetings and congratulations extended to him and agreed that the Native Affairs Department is a buffer. "It is important in our country to recognise differences of outlook. We have had to recognise differences between the English and Afrikaans-speaking people, which is however still an urgent problem. Similarly in Native Affairs differences between Europeans and Natives must be recognised. The Department does try to see how matters affect the Natives and to adjust them accordingly. The Department is at all times glad to hear the views of the Natives and special steps were taken to do this in regard to the Native Bills. It must be remembered that in political matters nothing is final, decisions are changed, circumstances decide and the future may change. In all things public opinion must be reckoned with". His ambition, he said, was to earn the thanks of the Native people as his predecessor (Mr. Grobler) had done.

The Reverend A. Mtimkulu presented the resolution on Education which asked for Union control under the Union Education Department. "Education is of paramount importance to us", he said, "as it is the means of progress and the making of good citizens. We have to live side by side with the Europeans and we must have education to help us to live rightly with them. We want our education to be on the same basis and on the same lines as the education of other peoples, under the direction of a specialist body with the right attitude". He said that his people feared that if the education of their children is wrapped up with political policy that they will suffer. He considered that the poll tax is not the right way of financing eduction. It is subject to fluctuations and is not the right foundation. Besides, it is a departure from the principle of the common revenue to which all contribute through the Post Office, Railways, etc. The State should accept responsibility for the educational services of the Africans. The withdrawal of the present contribution of £340,000 from the general revenue would be unacceptable. A financial deadlock must follow any attempt to segregate the finances. "A grant per pupil is the only scientific basis which will permit of increases as the needs increase".

The speaker then made a strong plea for the raising of teachers' salaries. "Increments there are none and pensions are unknown", he said.

In making a final plea for education to be on educational lines, Mr. Mtimkulu said, "Education is a European institution and we know no other kind that will help us today".

Mr. J. M. Lekhetho supported. He said: "Education is a universal thing and should not be segregated". He claimed that low wages are a big contribution to the country's wealth. He also pressed for higher salaries for teachers. He complained that Europeans are put into good positions in secondary schools at salaries that are three or four times those of African teachers in those schools. Mr. Lekhetho expressed strong disagreement with the views of the Native Affairs Commission on the aim, scope and content of Native Education. Inasmuch as the Native Affairs Department depends on the views of the Commission, the transfer of Native education to the Department must be opposed.

Councillor R. H. Godlo, Deputy leader of the deputation, dealt with the question of wages. He emphasised the ill effects of low wages on the physical life of the African people. While he appreciated the efforts of the Union Health Department and the Department of Native Affairs to improve the people's health, he said that "Wages must also be tackled at the same time, otherwise it is like pumping a ship without stopping the leak". He acknowledged that the Wage Board and Industrial Councils are improving wages, but pointed out that Government Departments should be leading the way, and yet these departments are the worst offenders. He held that the drop in the proceeds of the poll tax are due to increased poverty and that no increase can be expected unless wages are increased. "We bring the tears of our people, and we hope the Minister will see these tears and redress our troubles".

Mr. J. D. Ngojo dealt with the beer question and pointed out that the law is sending people to prison for offences which they do not consider wrong. "Our people", he said, "cannot understand that what is wrong for them can be right for a municipality, and what is right for a municipality is wrong for them". He described the evils which arise from the break up of homes through the imprisonment of the parents. Loss of parental control of children arises from this.

Mr. C. S. Ramohanoe said that the people's opposition to the beer halls is growing fiercer. He complained that the beer halls are placed in the centre of urban locations (e.g. Witbank, Randfontein and Germiston) and often right in front of churches. On the Rand the municipalities now allow the Mine Natives to enter the canteens in the locations. The local residents do not care for these halls

140

and are opposed to women going to the beer halls. "If this municipal beer system is a sample of our development along our own lines, then these are not lines we want". He did not want to entertain his friends in a beer hall where every sort of person comes.

Mr. S. P. Matseke pressed for parallel beer systems where desired.

The Reverend Z. R. Mahabane held that the people are unanimous against municipal brewing because it encourages drinking as the municipality is considered to be a part of the government and gives prestige to drinking. In reply to a question from the Secretary for Native Affairs, Mr. Mahabane declared that the African churches and the Africans in European churches are in favour of home brewing.

The Minister of Native Affairs pointed out that all the profits from the municipal system go towards Native Welfare.

Councillor R. G. Baloyi spoke on the pass laws which he said made criminals of the people. He described the numerous passes a man has to carry. "You may have three and not have the one you are asked for. To evade the police men do not go out by day to look for work, but go out at night and then become criminals." He asked for one identification certificate.

Councillor Baloyi then spoke on the resolution which asked that members of chiefs' families only be appointed or recognised as chiefs.

The Minister of Native Affairs said that this is the practice of the Department and he would be glad if any case where this principle has not been observed could be brought to his notice.

Mr. S. P. Matseke supported Councillor Baloyi's remarks on the pass laws and recognition of chiefs. He gave a graphic account of what takes place at railway stations in regard to passes and asked: "Are we really foreigners in our own land? ". He also asked that there should be more representatives in Parliament and Natives Representative Council for the Transvaal and Orange Free State.

The Reverend Z. R. Mahabane explained a resolution asking that the members of the Natives Representative Council be elected by popular vote.

Councillor Godlo asked for further representation for urban advisory boards.

The Reverand J. A. Calata dealt with the Land question and asked several questions: (1) Why has there been so much delay in the administration of the new Land Act? (2) Will it not cost more than £10,000,000 to buy the land because the prices which the Government is paying are too high? (3) Is the Government going to take out the "black spots" (i.e. Native owned land in "European areas") before all the land has been bought? (4) Is there any guarantee that if a new Government comes in that the buying of land will not be stopped? (5) Is the Government going to set aside areas for individual tenure? (6) Why has the promise made on the White Paper in this matter not been carried out? (7) Will the land exchanged for the "black spots" be equal in agricultural or pastoral value? (8) Will the compensation in cash be the same as

141

that given to Europeans who are expropriated from released areas? (9) What tenure will these people have who are transferred to released area? (10) Why has no land been bought in Natal? (See later for the Minister's replies).

Councillor A. J. Sililo spoke on the need for social services. He pointed out that there are a number of institutions working for the African people which lack funds. Not only has there been an awakening among Europeans but the Africans also are organising social agencies. In ancient days the Africans carried their own burden of the helpless, but times have changed. In the country the land has decreased. In the towns the wages are less able to keep the families so that individual families cannot carry the helpless. For these reasons special organisations have come into being. "We have contributed to the wealth of the country", he said, "and this country is now prosperous through taxation and low wages. None of the wages we get goes out of the country. We think we should share in the social services, instead of being forced to go to the magistrate and Native Affairs Department for charity. Our people have worked hard and have earned a restful old age. Many of them have lost their health through working in damp places, they have been deformed through their work and they go to the towns to beg. They should get assistance where they are and not be compelled to go into the towns". He expressed thanks for the grants made to the blind, but regretted that they are segregated from the benefits of the Blind Persons Act. Referring to the rumours that child welfare work among Africans will not be supported by the Department of Social Welfare, Councillor Sililo showed how the child welfare societies are increasing and are not merely giving relief but bringing new life to despairing people. They have helped many poor mothers who have had no bread-winners to help them. They receive no grants for administration and now it is rumoured that they are to lose the grants for the maintenance of destitute children. He appealed for their continuance. He referred also to the probation system and the rumours that this is also to be segregated. "We ask", he said, "that our people be not shut out from social services provided in every civilised country. We cannot carry our own poverty. We will carry our share but we cannot carry the whole". He drew attention to the lack of old age pensions and the hardships under the Workmen's Compensation Act (which cuts off payments for the period an injured worker is in hospital and makes no provision for his family during that time).

Councillor Godlo dealt with the effects of the Natives (Urban Areas) Act as it stands today. He claimed that the original intention of Parliament, as shown in the preamble to the first Act, was to provide improved conditions for Africans in urban areas, and pointed out that under it, "a location is a place set aside for the residence and reasonable requirements of Natives". He held that "the Act is unequivocal in conferring the right to Africans to trade amongst their own people. The intention is made more clear because of the specific prohibition of Europeans from trading in the location. Yet the Orange Free State municipalities refuse to allow Africans to trade in their urban locations and also some towns in

142

other provinces. Why does the Government allow these municipalities to flout Parliament and the recommendations of Commissions? "

The speaker expressed fear over the expulsion of "redundant Natives" and urged that they be not forced on to the farms. He asked for the right to Africans to purchase land in Native villages and emphasised that most Africans in the towns have no other resting place and only ask to be allowed to own their own homes. "We are willing to co-operate with the Government," said Councillor Godlo, "where the provisions of the law aim at meeting the needs and requirements of our people, but we are frequently irritated by the actions of the Government when it legislates about us without adequate consultation with us".

The Honourable the Minister of Native Affairs then replied and dealt with the various subjects in turn as follows:—

(1) *Chieftainship*: . . . The Department does try to appoint the best man, but always with one regard to Native Law and Custom, and there is therefore no cause for complaint on this point.

(2) *Representation*: The question of representation is a very contentious one and it took a very long time to put the Natives Representation Act through Parliament, and the Minister therefore found himself unable to agree to reopen this question at the moment. . . .

(3) *Pass Laws*: . All the Minister could say was that the Department is considering in what way it can make the system as simple and at the same time as effective as possible for its purpose.

(4) *Kaffir Beer*: The Minister read a memorandum prepared by the Secretary for Native Affairs on this point. At the Minister's request the Secretary then addressed the meeting and explained how the present position has arisen. Both he and the Minister emphasised the fact that any profits which may accrue through the beer halls are paid into the Native Revenue Account and do not go to the municipalities. Councillor Mapikela asked that an enquiry should be held to see what the Natives really want, but Mr. Smit informed him that the matter is still in the experimental stage and that it is not advisable to institute a general enquiry now.

(5) *Released Areas*: The Minister gave the following replies to the questions asked by Reverend Calata:—

1. *Why has there been delay in the administration of the Native Trust and Land Act?* . . . The Department has been working at great pressure all the time and purchases have been going on as rapidly as possible.

2. *Criticism in regard to prices paid*: The prices are being settled by the Land Board, which is a competent Government body specially created for purchasing land on behalf of the Government. . . .

3. *Is the development work held up*? . . . Various factors have to be taken into consideration. Many farms have "bywoners" [sub-tenants or squatters] living on them. They cannot be evicted, and the farm cannot be prepared for occupation

by Natives until the Lands Department has made provision elsewhere for the "bywoners". When the land has been fenced and adequate water supplies provided and it is ready for occupation, the Natives cannot move on to it all in a moment. Care has to be exercised in deciding who should live there and how many can go on to it. All these matters take time, but the Department is working at high pressure both in buying and preparing the land and there is no question at all of intentional delay.

4. *Black Spots*: Each individual case will have to be dealt with on its merits. . . .

In reply to Mr. Matseke the Minister said that the urban locations have to be dealt with under the Urban Areas Act, but that Native Townships situated outside urban areas can be dealt with under the Natives Land Act.

He assured the deputation that the Department of Native Affairs exercises its powers in a judicious manner, always with an eye on the best interests of the Natives. The power of expropriation already existed with regard to European land. It will always be exercised with due regard to the interests of all sections concerned. . . .

5. *Is the Government going to set aside land for individual buyers?* In the short time that he has been Minister he has on various occasions approved of advances to individual Natives to assist them in keeping their land by paying off bonds. The greatest need is for more tribal lands, however, and the Department's first consideration at the moment is to buy land for relieving the congestion in tribal areas.

A suggestion has been made by the Commission that certain areas should be set aside for individual tenure, but as it was feared that individual Natives would acquire big pieces of land, with the result that there would ultimately not be sufficient land for accommodating the rest of the Native population, this suggestion was not adopted. The matter was left over and each individual application is being considered on its merits.

6. *Acquisition of Land in Natal*: . . . substantial purchases will shortly take place in that Province.

(6) *Wages*: . . . Government Departments do not employ so many people that they can upset the whole scale of wages that exists. They have to take the scales which they find in operation around them, and those scales are fixed by the laws of supply and demand. . . .

(7) *Native Locations*: The Orange Free State has received several requests from the Department to reconsider its decision not to allow Natives to trade in the urban locations, and although they did reconsider the question they have hitherto not been agreeable. There are two views on this question of Native locations, firstly that they are really Native areas in which Natives should as far as possible be allowed to serve their own people, and secondly that the Natives are in a European area purely for the purpose of serving the needs of the Europeans. The Orange Free State Municipalities have adopted the latter view. The Department has done what it could and cannot take the matter any further.

144

Councillor Mapikela asked whether this is not a "breach of faith". The Minister replied that all it could do was to send a request to them to reconsider the matter, and this it has done. . . .

(8) *Old Age Pensions and Social Services*: The Minister asked the deputation to take up a reasonable attitude and recognise the difference in circumstances between the Native and the non-Native population of the country, and also recognise the fact that the Government can easily cause a clash of interests between Natives and Europeans if they do not act carefully. The Department is trying to help the Natives in a way which will not cause political upheavals in South Africa in which the white and Native people are made the football. . . .

(9) *Education*: The Minister said that the Natives are arguing along theoretical lines and saying that because certain changes are contemplated it is proposed to segregate them.

In the first place he wished to point out that the Native community has its own problems quite distinct from those of the Europeans and they require different remedies. When these problems are dealt with by a special division it does not mean that the intention is to segregate them; it merely means that the problem is being tackled in the most practical way. . . .

He assured the deputation that he tries to keep in touch with Native opinion and the opinion of those who profess to speak for the Natives. Whenever a matter which concerns them is considered by another Department, the Secretary for Native Affairs goes along to represent the interests of the Natives. The whole Department is concerned with the upliftment of the Native people and is their friend, and this fact is becoming daily more widely recognised.

(10) *Extension of Franchise to the Northern Provinces*: The Minister warned the deputation that they must not go away with the idea that this is a matter which can be put forward. The Acts that were passed were the result of a very long effort to arrive at a solution on a question on which there were very strong conflicting ideas, and at the moment they must realise that it is quite impossible to consider changing these Acts radically. . . .

Document 18. "Presidential Address" by the Rev. J. A. Calata, Cape African Congress, June 25-27, 1939

Mr. Speaker, Ladies and Gentlemen:

Last year the Presidential address took up a great deal of time on the history and constitution of the Cape African Congress, and its relation to the African National Congress. This year I propose to begin with a short note to clarify one or two difficulties which affect the African National Congress in its relation to the All African Convention.

The A.N.C., which was originally known as the South African Native National Congress, was established in 1912, and one of its objects as stated in the Constitution was, that it should be the medium of representative African opinion, and that it should formulate a standard policy on Native Affairs for the benefit and guidance of the Government.

The Congress was not established in order to fight against the Government, but in order to co-operate with it as well as other European organisations which require its assistance. But that does not mean that the Congress is in any way under the influence of the Government or any European organisation.

The All African Convention as its name implies, is an organisation that is composed of "Accredited African Organisations".

It might help you if, at the outset, I tell you what led to the establishment of the A.A.C. In the history of the A.N.C. there was a time when Communism threatened to seize the reins of Congress leadership when its President after a visit to Russia came back imbued with communistic ideas. This was resisted by the majority of the leaders on the grounds that the policy and propaganda methods of the Communists in those days clashed with Congress' Constitution. This resulted in splits and resignations from among the ranks of the Congress and subsequent establishment of other organisations.

Whilst the Congress was losing its power as a national movement, the repressive Government Policy gained ground, until in 1935, some of the leaders of the A.N.C. proposed that a national Convention of all African Organisations should be called to protest against the Native Bills. At that time there was no thought of the Convention superseding the Congress. The A.A.C. drew about 300 leaders of Non-Europeans to Bloemfontein at its first meeting, and appointed a deputation to interview the Government and protest against the Government Native Bills.

The African leaders then saw that the A.A.C. was capable of drawing large numbers of representatives of many organisations including the Communists, who, in the Western Province and Transvaal, had a fairly strong organisation, and decided to draw up a Constitution putting the A.A.C. on the recognised national basis as a Convention of "Accredited African Organisations", which did not in any way interfere with the Constitutions of existing organisations, but rather intended to strengthen the membership of those organisations, as its own force depended on the representatives of the existing organisations.

The A.N.C. which meets annually and regards itself as the African Parliament has not revised its constitution to delegate its office to the A.A.C., nor has the A.A.C. passed a resolution curtailing the powers and lowering the national status of the Congress.

If the A.A.C. were to kill the Congress and supersede it, it would also suffer the fate of the Congress, and be rendered incapable of full national leadership.

The A.N.C. is fast regaining its former reputation and is re-organising itself well, especially in the Northern Provinces. The National Conference will be held at Durban this year, and I hope next year it will come to us. The A.N.C. within 27 years of its life, has done a great deal for the African people as a whole. It has sent deputations to the Government in this country and Overseas.

The Rev. Z. R. Mahabane, who is the President General of the African National Congress, is also the Vice President of the All African Convention.

He is finding no clash of interests between the two bodies, and when he was asked by the National Conference last year to lead a Congress deputation to interview the Minister of Native Affairs, he gladly did so and invited the co-operation of the Advisory Boards Congress. This joint deputation interviewed the Minister of Native Affairs last month and a full report will follow this address, but I crave your indulgence to deal in a general way with some of the main points which were brought before the Minister, and to give my impressions.

NATIVE TAXATION

You will remember that last year the Government appointed a Departmental Commission to enquire into the methods of collecting Native Taxes. That Committee has reported and Parliament acting in accordance with the wishes of the Commission has amended the Native Taxation Act to modify the methods of collecting the Poll Tax and reduce the hardship that was borne by our people. But to our surprise, the terms of reference constituting the functions of the Committee did not permit evidence to be given, objecting to the Poll Tax as a principle of Native Taxation. You will remember also that a petition signed by a large number of Europeans in this country, asking for the abolition of the Poll Tax was submitted before Parliament; the Cape African Congress also passed a unanimous resolution last year asking for the abolition of the Poll Tax. Our Parliamentary representatives also tabled a motion in the House on the same lines. To all these the Government has turned a deaf ear. Our Parliamentary representatives did not only receive a cold shoulder on this question, but they were warned that if they brought motions of that kind, they would lose the sympathy of the House.

We were surprised because the farmers of this Country disapprove of the Poll Tax and everybody should know that the Poll Tax contributes one of the chief causes for the shortage of Native farm labour. We as a Congress representing the four Provinces of the Union, while we have no objection to Africans being taxed, condemn the Poll Tax as unjust, cruel, and a constant source of irritation to our people, and the deputation emphatically objected to the Minister against the Government schemes of perpetuating the Poll Tax.

NATIVE WAGES

Although Port Elizabeth itself may perhaps be one town in the whole of the Union which sees eye to eye with us in the matter of Native Wages, it is true, however, to say that it was necessary for a deputation to approach the Government, for the Government employs a lot of Native labour in the Mines, on Railways and Harbours, and on National roads. We pointed out to the Government that the low wages paid to Africans were responsible for many of the evils which cause African social problems, such as child delinquency, malnutrition, infantile mortality, and even the Beer question. We asked the Government to set a good example, and pay its own employees better wages. The Minister thought it was impossible for the Government to pay higher wages than they were obtaining locally, as they did not like to interfere with local conditions of employment.

NATIVE EDUCATION

Another question on which the deputation made strong representations was that of Native Education. This is a question in which I have found every Province very much agitated, and the deputation was completely of one mind.

Congress is amazed at the attitude of the Government in ignoring the recommendations of its own Commission, the Interdepartmental Commission which was appointed to enquire into the subject of Native Education. This Commission was composed of educational experts, presided over by an ex-Magistrate who had knowledge of Native affairs, and who is now Senator representing the Transkeian Africans.

This Commission recommended that Native Education should be placed under the Union Department of Education. Mr. Grobler, the former Minister of Native Affairs, had declared himself in favour of this recommendation. The Right Honourable gentleman's views were, that the problems of the Native Affairs Department were already too numerous for them to increase their multiplicity by the addition of Native Education. He also realised the need of specialists to attend to such a matter as education, and as there already existed a Union Department of Education, there was little or no justification for setting up for the Union duplicate educational machinery under the Native Affairs Department. But it was the Native Affairs Commission in its yearly report of 1936 which recommended that Native Education should be placed under the Native Affairs Department, with ideas of Bantuization, and conforming to Native policy.

The Minister of Native Affairs, the Rt. Hon. Mr. Fagan, is strongly in favour of transferring Native Education to his department. His chief reason is, that Native Education would be better financed. It would be easier for him to ask Parliament to transfer the proceeds from the Poll Tax to his Department, and he would then be able to devote four-fifths of the Tax to Native Education instead of the present two-fifths plus the block grant of £340,000 which only amounted to £860,000. Four-fifths was estimated at about £1,040,000.

The Minister believes that by placing the Native Education under the Native Affairs Department it will be removed from politics, as he will not have to come to Parliament to ask for a vote. He states that he is already handicapped and requires funds very badly, which in his opinion is the first consideration with Native Education.

"This does not mean that all Native services will be paid for by themselves. Matters such as Native health, Native Administration, generally, including

Administration of justice, blind Natives, soil erosion, and salaries of Native chiefs, all big items, will still be financed out of general Revenue", said the Minister.

The Minister added that with regard to the fear that Natives would be given a different kind of education, it was the present tendency of all education to let the child specialise in the practical things he will require in life. Any education, whether designed for Europeans or Natives, ought to be such as to fit the people for the positions they are going to occupy.

Whilst we also understand that our education should have its practical value to be beneficial and not merely to be bookish, yet we do not believe that it is so different from forms of education of other races in South Africa that it needs to be segregated. We realise differences of language and customs, but these should only apply to elementary not higher and professional education. It is true to say that our education is already segregated under the Provincial Administration; but it is not placed in the hands of political agents, and in fact, if the Native Affairs Department takes it over, it will always be connected in the African mind with the Administration of repressive laws, and the policy of keeping the Native in his place.

Although we complain that under the present financial arrangement our education does not receive a square deal, we are satisfied that the Government should have to vote the money every year as that maintains and preserves an important connection as well as brings our education before the public eye of the State.

In view of the fact that Africans contribute in many direct and indirect ways to the upkeep of the state in general, we claim that we are entitled to be regarded as members of the State. South Africa is not likely to develop two parallel States, and even its system of indirect rule as practised in the Transkei and other parts through Bungas, will not rise to compare favourably with what obtains in Central Africa, Nigeria, Tanganyika, Northern Rhodesia, and even the Protectorates in our midst.

There are some people who think that Union control and Native Affairs control are one and the same thing under the same Government and will both carry out the same policy. Therefore let us ask the Government for a compromise, and accept the transfer of our education to the N.A.D. provided the Government will not take away the block grant of £340,000, and will give us back the whole of the Poll Tax for education and development of the reserves.

This idea emanates from outside Congress circles, and I am throwing it out to you for consideration. Personally, I do not think the Government would care to compromise with us in anything unless there would be some political gain by so doing.

Again a suggestion was made at the African National Congress Conference last year that Africans should make a beginning and establish funds for starting National Schools. The idea was warmly received, but as our Province was poorly represented I desire to ask you to give your opinion at this Conference. One

149

finds, as one moves about the Country that there is a great deal which calls for serious attention in the whole atmosphere surrounding African education.

A Conference has been summoned by the Institute of Race Relations to meet next Monday and Tuesday, and the heads of the Institutions have been invited. The Congress with its Provincial Branches has also been invited, but I am afraid we are not ready with any practical solution to any of the existing problems, for we are not united.

Those who believe that there is anything to be gained from financing Native Education from the Poll Tax alone, have not yet realised that the capacity of the Bantu to contribute to direct taxation is gradually falling away owing to his state of poverty, and in fact without the cruel force of imprisonment, I doubt if there is any other way by which the Poll Tax could be made to get anywhere near the estimated figure of £1,300,000. But those who study the condition of our people will bear with me when I say that a time is not far when the State will be bound to face a serious position with regard to the black people of this country, due to physical deterioration and disease infection, unless a change of policy takes place in time.

History tells us of many subject races that have perished and become extinct like the Mohicans. But after we have attained to such a high standard of civilisation and education, it will be our own fault if we perish and die out. For instance, if we only could realise what a force this Congress could be in rehabilitating and re-integrating our people, we would all join; but we do not want to think that way; also if we could know that unity means so much strength that our Parliamentary representatives would not need to fall on their knees in Parliament to ask for our rights, we would all unite like ants. But let me tell you, ladies and gentlemen, that no Government, however good and generous in South Africa, will forget the needs of its own racial group and put those of another first. If we want our Parliamentary representatives and our members for the Representative Council to carry any weight about with them, we shall first organise our Congress force behind them, so that when they speak, the Government will know that the Africans are speaking.

I say this because the Government knows that our Parliamentary representatives and Councillors do not approve of the transfer of Native Education, but the only opinion that counts in stopping them so far from transferring is that of the Natal Provincial Council which has not agreed, and they believe that when they win Natal over, they will simply proceed to carry out their intentions, all because the Government knows we black people are disunited, and our leaders are opposed to one another. What a shame!

THE LAND QUESTION

The Deputation also made strong representations on the Land Question. We remember that the Land and Trust Act of 1936 formed part of the so-called

Native legislation. In passing that Act, the Government made a solemn promise to buy additional land to relieve the terrible congestion that reigns in the Reserves and in some Urban locations. The Government promised to find some 10 million pounds and more if necessary, and release 7¼ million morgen of land for this purpose.

At that time it was believed that European public opinion would back the Administration of this Act if the Cape Province gave up the Native Franchise, and the Government anticipated no difficulty in buying the land for the Trust, and made everybody believe that the removal of the Cape Franchise would bring about a more liberal spirit among the Europeans of this country. No sooner were the two Bills, which were said to hang together, passed, than the Government gave complete effect to the Administration of the Disenfranchisement of Natives Act, so much so that when the third Bill, which was also said to be part of the Native Legislation (The Native Laws Amendment Bill) was before the House, the Africans were not represented in the House in any form whatsoever. The Government had further promised to give full effect to its promise in five years' time.

Now three years have lapsed and the Government has only been able to buy 998,339 morgen and spent £3,413,676 to acquire that land.

The Deputation asked the Minister several questions to show him that our logical conclusion is that if it took the Government 3 years to buy one million morgen, it will certainly take them more than 5 years to buy 7¼ million morgen, and if one million morgen costs the Government four million pounds, it certainly is going to cost the Government a good deal more than £1,000,000 to buy 7¼ million morgen, and seeing that already the political trend of the country is making it difficult for the Government to get the money required from Parliament, we wanted to know just how the Minister proposed to overcome the obstacles, and as we could see that there is a possible change of Government within the near future, what guarantee could we have that the whole of this land would be acquired.

We felt it our duty to tell the Minister that the confidence of the Bantu of South Africa was seriously shaken owing to the fact that the Government was already taking steps to amend the Act to expropriate about 250,000 morgen of our land without first fulfilling its promise to provide land.

We asked the Government not to expropriate any of the existing land but to hasten the buying of Released Areas. We can hear the outcry from certain politicians that land is bought for Natives at the expense of the white people.

We are surprised to note that Natal, the home province of Mr. Heaton Nicholls, the father of the Land Act, has not yet released an acre of ground for Native occupation. I am informed that already in Natal certain Chiefs and Tribes have been given notice to leave their land, but nobody knows where they are going to be settled.

I fear the Government does not realize that unless the question of land is properly settled in South Africa, there is no hope for an adjustment of Race relations. There is no Native problem, but there is a problem of Race relations, and it centres round the land problem.

I am convinced that in South Africa there is plenty of land for everybody. The present population, both white and black, and even Asiatic, is yet too small for this country.

But in all questions of this kind, just as it is with our Franchise, our education, and our wages, so it is with land, the public need to be educated. The Government is afraid of doing what is right because the European public opinion of this country is against it. Who can believe such a story? Judging from what the Government has been able to do for our people within a comparatively short time in the agricultural sphere and the health department, is it really true to say that European public opinion is opposed to the Government doing what is right in every department for the African people? I think what the Government Officials mean when they say that they are afraid of European public opinion, is that they are afraid of the political opinion of the strongest opposing party in Parliament, backed up by the minority of the uninformed and unlettered type of the white race.

THE GOVERNMENT NATIVE POLICY

The fear complex that exists in the minds of the politicians is responsible for the contradictory and indecisive manner in which the South African Statesman handles problems affecting race relations. Take for instance the following questions:

Segregation. The same people who cry out against the Native and farming areas, who say that the Native must be segregated to prevent the stealing of stock, also say that the conditions of segregation must be such as will not prevent him coming out to work in towns and on the farm.

The same people who cry out against the "Barbarous practice of giving bride-prices for wives" as they call it, also say that "Lobola" must be made a stimulus to make the Native leave his home and come to town to look for work.

Education. The same people who say that Native Education must progress to enable him to buy European goods, also say that Native Education must not develop in him ideas of citizenship and parliamentary representation.

Franchise. The same people who say that the Native must have separate representation by Europeans in Parliament, also say that those representatives are turning the Natives into agitators. When they fight for our rights they are told that they are putting wrong ideas into our minds.

Land. The same people who shout "Take the Native back to the Reserves and let him develop along his own lines" are the same who cry against the waste of good money by buying land for Native settlement.

152

Religion. The same people who say that Missionaries must teach the Native the principles of the Christian Religion, also say that there can be no equality between the Black and White in Church and State.

Labour. While the usual pick and shovel work is usually styled as Kaffir work, yet when it comes to giving it to Poor Whites to the exclusion of Africans, the same work is regarded as civilised labour. I could go on citing instances to prove that there is no Native Policy beyond the fact that the Europeans are prepared to do anything to assure their permanent supremacy which at present nobody disputes although some of us would have liked them to try to preserve it morally and thus win the respect of the subject races without resorting to bullying measures.

THE NON-EUROPEAN FRONT

At Capetown I was asked at one of the public meetings what was the policy of the A.N.C., and what was its attitude towards the Non-European United Front.

I have observed that Transvaal and the Western Province have formed an organisation known as "The Non-European United Front", and I note with pleasure that the Indians are thinking of throwing in their lot with Bantu and Coloured. Good luck to them.

My experience is, that while the ordinary racial groups do not yet recognize their own leaders, it is no use calling upon the masses to unite even in such an attractive organisation as "The African People's Rights Protection League", or the Communist Party.

Those who served in the front ranks of the Non-European Conference between the years 1927 and 1933 understand what I mean. Although personally I am not against new organisations being formed, I think, however, the time is too critical for us to divide our forces.

If our Bantu, Coloured and Indian Africans could not keep to an association led by Dr. Abdurahman and Professor Jabavu, I fail to see how they can follow other leaders. I firmly believe that the policy of the Congress is the best, and if the African people, more especially, would support it loyally, they would find that it would carry them through their difficulties.

I can only end up by saying that the Presidents . . . and myself are agreed on pursuing a policy of reconciliation.

We were disappointed to find that there [were . . .] obvious conflicts between our views of South African problems and those of the Government. That state of affairs must not be allowed to continue without a check, or else it will lead the country over a precipice.

We believe the Joint Council Movement is [along proper] lines and should be extended to official bodies [since] the interests of the Black and White people

153

of this country are interwoven. It is impossible to run two parallel systems each opposed to the other in this land. While I find no fault with those who preach purity of race, nevertheless I am of the opinion that the ultimate development of this country depends entirely on each individual, irrespective of colour or creed, being allowed full right and privilege to make his contribution to the welfare of the country to his fullest capacity.

That is the aim of the Congress. We claim the right of full citizenship in the land of our forefathers.

NKOSI SIKELEL'I AFRIKA.
JAMES A. CALATA

Document 19. Resolutions of the ANC Annual Conference, December 15-18, 1939.

1. This conference of the African National Congress respectfully requests the Union Government to repeal all differential legislation so that the African is ruled under the General laws of the country.

2. This conference strongly urges the Government of the Union of South Africa to give the trade unions of African workers the same recognition and rights under the Industrial Conciliation Act as prescribed for European, Indian and Coloured workers.

The proposed basis of recognition as submitted by the Government is totally unacceptable to organised African labour, as the conference is fully convinced that the only form of recognition which can be accepted is such as to give these organizations the legal right to negotiate directly with employers for wages and conditions of employment and to make agreements which may be concluded to have force of law.

3. NATIVE EDUCATION

This conference resolves that in order to provide sufficient funds for Native education the budget should be on a per capita basis and that the Government should be responsible for buildings and for adequate equipment for Native schools.

4. FEEDING OF SCHOOL CHILDREN

That responsible authorities be required to provide milk and soup kitchens for African children as they do for Indian, Coloured and European school children.

5. RE PROVINCIAL CABINETS ....

6. Congress strongly protests against the action of certain municipalities in making wholesale evictions of Africans from proclaimed European residential areas without providing alternative accomodation.

7. WAR.

That unless and until the Government grants the African full democratic and citizenship rights, the African National Congress is not prepared to advise the Africans to participate in the present war, in any capacity.

8. NON-EUROPEAN UNITED FRONT

That this conference of the African National Congress now assembled, in Durban, accepts the principle of the Non-European United Front movement.

9. LODGERS' PERMITS

This conference resolves that lodgers' fees and lodgers' Permits must be abolished because:—

(a) They disorganise and disrupt family life and family discipline;

(b) They impose further direct taxation on the Head of the family as boys and girls of 18 years of age, who are under these regulations prohibited to live with their parents, are still minors and juveniles;

Conference therefore instructs its branches and other affiliated bodies to work for the abolition of such regulations.

10. RAILWAY AND HARBOUR WORKERS

That this conference gives every support to the S.A.R.& H. Workers' Union, (Non-European), in their demand for increased wages and an improvement of working conditions for the thousands of Non-European Railway and Harbour workers in South Africa.

This conference, whilst appreciating the endeavours of the Union Government in setting up a regulated minimum wage standard for the unskilled workers in a large number of industries, deplores the fact, the Union Government itself being the largest employer of unskilled Non-European labour in South Africa has turned down the demands put forward by the S.A.R. & H. Workers' Union. This conference urges the Union Government to give due consideration to the thousands of workers concerned.

Document 20. Minutes of the ANC Annual Conference, December 15-17, 1940

11 a.m. DEVOTIONAL OPENING AND NATIONAL SERVICE

A Telegram was read from the Senior Chaplain Revd. A. S. Mtimkulu apologising for his absence and asking the Revd. J. A. Calata to act for him. This was accepted by the Conference and the National Service was conducted by the Revd. J. A. Calata.

3 p.m. OFFICIAL OPENING

A letter was read from Revd. Z. R. Mahabane, President General, apologising for his inability to be present at the official opening and giving full authority to the Speaker, Mr. T. M. Mapikela, M.R.C. and the Secretary General to take charge of the proceedings of the Conference till he came. Conference agreed and elected Revd. J. A. Calata Temporary President General.

Mr. Mapikela apologised for the Mayor Mr. Sutton who was unable to attend to open the conference through illness, he then called upon the Police Sergeant in charge of the Location to welcome the Conference.

The Sergeant in opening the Conference expressed appreciation to the loyal assistance given to the Government and local officials by members of the Congress and wished the Conference success in its deliberations in Bloemfontein.

The thanks of the conference were expressed by the Speaker and Acting President.

PRELIMINARIES:

Press Secretary: Mr. S. Mac. Lepolesa was elected.
Interpreter: Mr. B. E. Mnyobo was elected.
Official Language: Mr. S. M. Bennet Ncwana seconded by Mr. J. Malangabi moved: That only African Languages such as Xhosa, Sesutho, Zulu, or Sechuana be used at this Conference and that European Languages be used only when it is necessary and then as secondary languages.

Mr. S. Oliphant seconded by Mr. J. L. Lobere moved as an amendment that the procedure for discussion shall follow the usual tradition of this house which allows freedom to individuals to use the language best understandable to him and the Conference.

A long discussion followed, the speaker supporting the original motion. The Acting President ruled that the matter await the arrival of the President-General Revd. Mahabane.

CREDENTIALS of the delegates were scrutinised by Messrs S. Oliphant and Mr. S. Mac. Lepolesa and the quorum of 25 members having been found present the Speaker declared the Conference duly constituted.

The following were then elected as the Resolutions Committee upon whom would devolve the question of submitting findings on a resolution from the Cape African Congress asking for the final settlement of the Western Province and C.A.C. dispute:
Revd. Z. R. Mahabane, Revd. J. A. Calata, Messrs. Champion, Malangabi, Gula, Baloyi, Marks, Kotane, Ncwana, Oliphant, Thubisi, Lepolesa, Lobere, with power to add to the number. The Committee to meet in the Board Room at 8 p.m. Conference adjourned at 5:45 p.m.

MONDAY, DECEMBER 16th:

9:30 a.m. Conference resumed.

Revd. J. A. Calata reported the previous day's proceedings and handed over to President General Mahabane.

President General introduced Professor Jabavu the President of the All African Convention and called upon him to address the conference.

156

Professor Jabavu in a few remarks said that every black man desired to see the success of the Congress conference.

President General thanked Professor Jabavu on behalf of the Conference.

President General then introduced Advocate Molteno M.P. for Cape Western Circle.

The President General moved a vote of condolence to Dr. A. Abdurahman's family for their bereavement through the death of Dr. Abdurahman—carried.

The conference rose in silence.

The Native Commissioner for Bloemfontein then addressed the conference. He dealt at length with the war situation. He was interrupted by members of the conference when he spoke of the unswerving loyalty of the Congress to the Government.

Mr. Z. K. Matthews of Fort Hare moved the vote of thanks and explained to the Native Commissioner that the interruption to his remarks were not due to disloyalty to the Government on part of the members but that they did not want the officials to interpret African loyalty as allowing the Government to carry on its repressive policy as before.

NATIONAL COUNCIL OF AFRICAN WOMEN:

Resolved that Mr. Baloyi and Mr. Lobere send greetings of the African National Congress to the National Council of African Women also sitting in Bloemfontein at the same time as the Congress.

The Bishop of Bloemfontein, Dr. Howe-Browne then addressed the Congress. He spoke on the progress the Africans had rapidly made and exhorted them to adopt the Festina lente policy in their undertakings.

Dr. A. B. Xuma thanked the Bishop on behalf of the conference and stressed the importance of the fact that if Europeans regarded Africans as a child race which had still to grow they must remember that one of the duties of the parents to children was to remove all obstacles in the way in order to hasten the development and progress of the child.

Votes of Condolence were passed to the Barolong Tribe on the death of Chief P. J. Moroka and Chief S. Moroka the conference rising in the usual way.

Conference adjourned at 12:30 p.m.

Conference resumed at 2:30 p.m.

Mrs. Nothandile Kuse conveyed the greetings from the National Council of African Women.

Miss Palmer replied on behalf of the Conference and stressed the need for closer co-operation between the two bodies.

3:00 p.m. PRESIDENTIAL ADDRESS.

This was read in English by the President General. Copy of the Address is attached to these minutes.

Mr. S. Oliphant seconded by Mr. P. Phahlane, Sergeant at arms, moved the acceptance—agreed.

157

Mr. Nkomo seconded by Mr. J. B. Marks moved the vote of thanks—Agreed.

Advocate Molteno M. P. Western Circle, Cape, then addressed the Congress. He first gave apologies for Senator Rheinallt-Jones whom he expected to arrive on Tuesday, and for Senator Malcomess and Mrs. Ballinger who could not attend. He gave a very inspiring address in which he explained how and why they decided to support General Smuts on the War issue. That did not commit the representatives to supporting the Government policy on Native Affairs. They were not satisfied that the African should not be given something to fight for. They wished to see much more social equality and much more economic equality after this war.

Mr. Champion seconded by Revd. E. E. Mahabane moved a vote of thanks—Carried.

LANDS:

Mr. A. W. Champion, Secretary for Lands and Locations read a very interesting paper giving account of his stewardship.

This was accepted by the Conference.

PROVINCIAL REPORTS:

The Cape African Congress report was read by Mr. J. O. Sitela of Cradock.

The O. F. S. Report was ready by Mr. J. Nkoane.

The Western Province report was read by Mr. S. Oliphant.

No reports came from Transvaal and Natal.

EXECUTIVE REPORTS:

The Secretary General read the Executive Report.

The Treasurer General read the Financial Statement.

Both reports were accepted. Copies of same are attached to these minutes.

6:30 p.m. ELECTION OF THE PRESIDENT-GENERAL:

Mr. R. G. Baloyi seconded by Mr. J. Malangabi moved the name of Dr. A. B. Xuma, M.D. etc.

Mr. A. Thubisi seconded by Mr. P. Phahlane moved the name of Revd. Z. R. Mahabane, the retiring President.

The Secretary General was asked to state whether both candidates' names had been submitted to him according to the constitution. He replied in the affirmative in the case of Dr. Xuma's name only but that it lay with the conference to accept further nominations.

Both names were then put. Voting was by ballot. Dr. Xuma—21, Revd. Mahabane—20. Dr. Xuma was declared elected. Revd. Z. R. Mahabane then addressed the conference promising his support and wishing Dr. Xuma success.

Dr. A. B. Xuma thanked the conference for electing him. He spoke on the urgent need of organisation then ended up by a confession of his creed: "I believe that an African is a human being. I believe that he should have the same rights politically, educationally, and economically as every one else, and believing that every man and every woman should work hard so as to make this belief a reality I call upon every African to be up and doing and we shall have a place in South Africa." Applause.

Conference adjourned at 7:15 p.m.

9:00 p.m. A Reception concert and Dance was held in honour of the delegates.

TUESDAY 9:30 a.m. Conference resumed.

In the absence of the Speaker Mr. T. M. Mapikela the Reverend Z. R. Mahabane took the chair and the conference discussed the resolutions presented by the Resolutions committee and passed the following:

1/40 THE WAR:

This conference re-affirms the resolution passed by the Joint Executive Committees of the African National Congress and the All African Convention on the 7th July 1940—the resolution reads as follows: [see document 61, below].

2/40 MILITARY RATES OF PAY:

This conference views with great concern the attitude of military authorities in discriminating among the military rates of pay for African and Coloured war recruits.

3/40 SUBVERSIVE CONDUCT—TRADE UNIONS:

This conference disagrees and strongly opposes the view that it is wrong for Non-Europeans to pay attention to their economic and political grievances during the war. It asserts that Non-European demands for democratic rights and trade union organisations cannot be separated from the world-wide struggle for freedom and social justice.

Conference views with dissatisfaction the absence of a clear definition by the Government, of the words "subversive conduct". It therefore urges that a clear definition of these words be made and guarantees be given that the organisation of Africans into trade unions, the organising of campaigns for increased allowances for dependents of Non-European soldiers and for economic, political and social advancement will not be regarded as subversive or in conflict with the Government's war policy.

4/40 CONDITIONS OF SERVICE:

In view of the fact that Africans have been called to make this supreme sacrifice for the prosecution of the war, this Congress respectfully requests the Government to explain why conditions of service for Africans on active service are not placed under the same category as those of other sections of the population of this country who are also on active service.

5/40 CAPE AFRICAN CONGRESS & WESTERN PROVINCE A.N.C.:

This 29th conference of the African National Congress held at Bloemfontein on 15th to 16th December 1940, having reviewed the differences of the adherents of the A.N.C. in the Western Province takes this opportunity to appeal to the loyalty of the community at large to accept the decision of this conference, namely, "One Province for the Cape Province as a whole."

6/40 LODGERS' PERMITS:

This conference resolves that Lodgers' fees and lodgers' permits must be abolished because,
(a) they disorganise and disrupt family life and family discipline;
(b) they impose further direct taxation on the head of the family as boys and girls of 18 years of age who are under these regulations prohibited to live with their parents are still minors and juveniles. Congress therefore instructs its branches and other affiliated bodies to work for the abolition of such regulations.

7/40 AFRICAN WAGES:

Whereas the attention of Congress has been drawn to the fact that representations made by Africans for increase and stabilisation of their wage levels have in many places met with no response, the African National Congress respectfully requests the Minister of Labour to instruct the Wage Board to visit not the larger centres of labour only, but also the smaller centres and there make or give effect to the wage determination in all spheres of employment.

8/40 REDUCTION OF CATTLE:

That the African National Congress respectfully requests the Government to leave the question of the provisions of the Cattle Improvement Act to the discretion of the chief or headman and his people who may, if they so desire request the application thereof in that particular area or locality.

9/40 NATIVE SERVICE CONTRACTS:

The African National Congress respectfully requests the Government to remove the illogical and anomalous provisions contained in the Masters and Servants Acts whereby a contract made and entered into by the father becomes binding on all members of his family including those who have been tacitly emancipated by the Government by reason of their being taxpayers.

10/40 SOCIAL SERVICES:

In view of the incontestable fact that very serious and urgent social problems have arisen amongst the African urban population, the African National Congress should create a separate portfolio for Social Welfare; the holder thereof will investigate and report on the Welfare of children, the blind, physically handicapped (cripples), aged and infirm persons, and other matters handled by the Government Department of Social Welfare.

11/40 MEMBERSHIP CARD:

This conference re-affirms the previous resolution that there should be a uniform membership card for all the Provinces of the Congress. To curtail printing expenses this conference favours the issue of membership cards whose duration will be for a least three years.

12/40 AFRICAN ORGANISATIONS:

That this Conference of the A.N.C. realising that the Political situation calls for a united effort on the part of the African people recommends the advisability of appointing a Joint committee of the A.N.C. and the A.A.C. to consider the relationship of these two bodies.

13/40 NYANGA AND AFRICAN DINGAKA ASSOCIATIONS:

This conference approves of the aims of the Nyanga association as presented in the Memorandum before it and recommends
1. the deletion of section 4. (d) and substituting the following "To claim the African inherent right of practising in his own methods the art and call of Medical Science."
2. The creation of an African Medicinal Fraternity and the Registration of same.

The conference resolves to reconsider the whole Memorandum from African Dingaka Association in conjunction with that from the Bantu Nyanga Association at the next conference.

Revd. Z. R. Mahabane reported on the Conference of the National Child Welfare Association which he attended on invitation.

The President General then nominated his cabinet as follows:
The Governor of the House of Chiefs: Chief G. S. Kama
The Speaker: Mr. R. V. Selope Thema M.R.C.
Senior Chaplain: Revd. Z. R. Mahabane
Secretary General: Revd. J. A. Calata
Treasurer General: Cr. R. G. Baloyi
Secretary for Chiefs: Dr. P. Ka I. Seme, B.A., L.L.D.
Secretary for Law: Lionel Mtimkulu
Secretary for Labour: E. T. Mofutsanyana
Secretary for Lands and Locations: A.W.G. Champion
Secretary for Education: Prof. Z. K. Matthews, M.A.
Assistant Secretary General: To be appointed later.
Deputy Speaker: S. Mac. Lepolesa

Serjeant at arms: Peter Pahlana

Asst. Serjeant at Arms: James Mpinda

Mr. S. Oliphant seconded by Mr. W. F. Nkomo B.Sc., moved the election of the nominated cabinet. Agreed unanimously.

Resolved: That the President and Cabinet should elect Representatives for the Mendi Memorial Scholarship Association.

Resolved: That the following form a Committee to revise the Constitution:

President-General Dr. Xuma (Convenor)

Secretary General J. A. Calata

S. Oliphant

J. Malangabi

L. Mtimkulu

Prof. Z. K. Matthews

Rev. Z. R. Mahabane

VENUE OF NEXT CONFERENCE:

Mr. S. M. Bennet Ncwana moved and Mr. J. Malangabi seconded that the next conference be held at Bloemfontein—Carried.

MOTIONS OF THANKS:

To Revd. Z. R. Mahabane for the successful way in which he piloted the Congress during his three years of Presidency.

To Mr. T. M. Mapikela for the able manner in which he performed the onerous duties of a Speaker for the last 28 years of the life of the African National Congress.

To Mr. Nkoane, Mrs. Mohlakoana and other members of the working Committee of the Bloemfontein Branch for the able manner in which they had discharged their duties.

The President General made a few remarks and the conference closed at 11 p.m.

Document 21. "An Address at the Mendi Memorial Celebration, Bantu Sports Grounds, Johannesburg." By Dr. A.B. Xuma, February 23, 1941

Fellow Countrymen,

On the eleventh hour, the eleventh day of the eleventh month in 1918 an armistice was signed bringing to an end what was known as the "Great War" or "World War". The aims of that war were stated in various ways. It was declared to be a war fought to make the world safe for democracy, and to make democracy safe for the world; a war to give self-determination to smaller or weaker nations; a war to end war. Tacitly, in these pronouncements, individual freedom and social justice were held out as the coveted prize and just reward for mankind if the allied arms were victorious in the struggle.

That promise, that noble ideal fired the imagination of men of many Nations, races, colours and creeds. They answered the call of their respective countries.

In South Africa, along with other-countrymen white and non-white, the African volunteered and served in theatres of war in Africa and on the continent of Europe. With other South African soldiers and servicemen he faced bullets and pestilence in the defence of freedom of the State and of the boundaries of the Union of South Africa in the hope that he and his own with others who survive, might enjoy the freedom of the State as well as liberty in his own country.

At the beginning of the "World War", the African had a genuine grievance arising from the evictions and privations resulting from the operation of the provisions of the Natives Land Act—1913. But, because of his deep sense of honour and responsibility, the African through his Chiefs and leaders recognized as his first and foremost duty the preservation of the State. Thus from every Province thousands of Africans joined the colours, risked their lives and many died in the service of Africa—their Country.

The Africans' record of loyalty and faithful service is excelled by that of no other section in South Africa. They are no fair-weather loyalists. They are true South Africans indeed. They know no other loyalties but hope to work out their salvation through negotiations and mutual understanding with their white fellow-citizens here.

Today, we have gathered together once more to commemorate the tragic death of those 615 Africans who went down the English Seas with the transport-ship Mendi, in 1917. They left their loved ones, their kith and kin. They dared and braved enemy submarines, mines, battleships and sea-raiders to perform the dangerous service their country had assigned to them. They died, they paid the supreme sacrifice. They met their fate heroically as disciplined men. We are proud of their memory. They died, that others, their kith and kin, might be free to share fully in the fruits of democracy; namely, personal and individual freedom and social justice.

Can a race which is willing to make such sacrifices and which produces men of such courage, dependability and devoted service to King and Country in the hour of greatest need be denied any rights and privileges at the gift of the State? I answer emphatically, NO! It may be so for a single while, but not always.

I recognise that fear, sometimes, drives people to commit certain acts of violence and/or injustice to others on the plea of self-preservation. I, nevertheless, believe that in the calm that permits reflection after the storm, moral courage and a sense of justice will ultimately prevail.

South Africa is rich in natural wealth. Her gold and her diamonds, in quality, have been graded among the best in the world. But, South Africa's most valuable, precious and priceless jewel is the African himself. At present, the African is looked down upon as brawn without brain. It is true that through lack of training and development his brain in the main, may be likened to diamonds

163

in the rough or unwrought gold. However, if the African's brain were polished and developed by a process of liberal education with unrestricted opportunities to function according to ability and capacity without restriction on account of race and colour, South Africa would have tapped within her borders an oasis of material, mental and spiritual power which would make her truly independent and self-contained indeed with home markets for her produce and manpower to contribute to her full development.

There is much evidence to show that even with the limited opportunities or with no special training the African has a valuable natural native mental endowment as shown by achievement of Africans with or without training. At the risk of being criticised and misunderstood for mentioning certain names of Chiefs and people who merit inclusion in the following list of random examples, I shall mention but a few as time is limited. For instance, in Chief Moshoeshoe, she produced a great statesman and nation-builder, in Tshaka, a great dictator, organiser of men and strategist. In the educational world, our John L. Dubes, the Reginald Cingos and others, to mention just a few, give us hope of a great future in educational administration. In law, the Mangenas, Semes, Poswayos and others gave a spark of brilliant legal minds who were handicapped by circumstances beyond their control. Among the medical men, our Sogas, Molemas, Morokas, Bokwes and others we have men who, given facilities that encourage continuous growth and development in the practice of their profession, could have established national and international reputations for themselves. In scholarship our Zachariah Matthews, Don Mtimkulu, and young Mokuena, recently a matriculant at St. Peter's Secondary School, show that the African brain is as good as the best among other races. Our young Medical students are doing well overseas. Dr. Andries Sipo Qunta of the Transkei was given a graduate scholarship at Edinburgh University on merit. He is now serving, in the present war, as a Ship's Surgeon of his Majesty's Royal Navy. Mr. Bikitsha, of the Transkei, also a medical student at Edinburgh University has distinguished himself in sports and in scholarship. He represented Edinburgh University in the inter-British University Sports and won places for his University. He received the Edinburgh blue in recognition of his achievements. In his examinations, he took 'firsts' in midwifery, Gynecology and Forensic Medicine. These achievements were accomplished among and against students of all colours and various races. This and other successes by Africans, at home and abroad, indicate that given an opportunity the African will measure up and take his rightful and God-given place among the members of the human family.

By the way, this record sets our mind at ease about the South African Native Trust scholars who have begun their full course of study in medicine in South Africa. They are no more a problem to teach than any other student. Their brothers before them have studied medicine and passed their examinations with honours and merit in some of the leading Universities of England, America and Germany. Our South African standard in medical education may be as good, but cannot be any higher.

After mentioning the Union Native Affairs Medical Scholarships for African students, I would have failed in my duty if I did not express publicly the African people's appreciation of this gesture of good will on the part of the Government. This is a step in the right direction—the spending of public taxes for the training of enlightened leaders of the African race. If the Union Government address themselves towards encouraging the high aspirations of the Africans for progress, good and enlightened citizenship as we have every hope they will, and urge them to, they will have earned for themselves and the European section as a whole the everlasting gratitude of the African people. Nothing but good-will, better race relations, and increasing confidence in the good intentions and justice of the white fellow-countrymen, can come out of such moves.

Today our country is engaged in another war, a war that threatens to destroy all the finer qualities that man seems to have acquired through the ages. And, as during the last "World War", along with his fellow country-men European, Coloured and Indians, the African is with the Union Colours—having offered to serve anywhere even at the front line. We have no doubt that, as all these men of various races are making equal and like sacrifices in the defence of their common country, they will enjoy the full privileges and immunities laid down in the Defence Act of the Union of South Africa and share in the full benefits of the Moratorium Act. And, further, we hope that their separation allowances and pensions will be reasonably sufficient enough not to make them anxious for their dependents—wives, children and mothers as the case may be.

We realise the difficult task of the Government arising out of the state of emergency in the country. Reports from other countries show that men are offering a strange prayer "God help us, devil help us" depending on the trend of successes in the struggle in the hope that their prayer will be answered and they will be well received whichever side wins the war. Many responsible people, therefore, have been anxious about the dangers of anti-state propaganda among the Africans. If I were permitted to advise the authorities in this delicate situation, I would suggest, that if all statutory regulations and technical offences which are crimes for Africans only were removed and employment offered, and a living wage established for all including Africans, no amount of propaganda from any source would be effective among the Africans.

As I speak here, South Africa's sons of all races are spilling their blood to keep her free. They have staked their all to protect those they leave behind. South Africa is fighting for noble and high ideals—for Christian democracy and human decency. And because of these ideals South Africa dare not discriminate against any section of her population on account of race or colour and be true to her ideals.

It seems to me, therefore, that in memory of the men who died in the Mendi and of thousands of others of all races who lost their lives during the World War as well as in honour of white and non-white men who are keeping

South Africa's boundaries inviolate in the North and from the high seas, South Africa can build no more valuable or a lasting monument for them than to maintain and operate during the war her democratic institutions and to grant, now, and henceforth freedom in the state and social justice for all her people irrespective of race, creed or colour. This is not merely winning the war, this is winning peace.

This done, these brave dead will not have died in vain. Thus South Africa will have done herself great honour and brought glory to her name.

Document 22. "Mass Meeting, Africans Shot in Cold Blood." Flyer issued by Transvaal African Congress, for meeting on June 26, 1941

TRANSVAAL AFRICAN CONGRESS

MASS MEETING

AFRICANS SHOT IN COLD BLOOD

A Mass Meeting of the Transvaal African Congress will be held at Newtown Market Square Johannesburg, on Thursday the 26th June, 1941, at 5 p.m. sharp.

This meeting is called for the purpose of protesting against the shooting and killing of two Africans in Sophiatown, whilst another African was seriously wounded. All this was done by a European constable.

During the usual nerve-wracking police raids in the locations an African woman was arrested for beer and savagely assulted by the police. The African woman thus attacked is in the family way.

Africans rally to this meeting in your thousands and raise your protest against this cold blooded shooting of innocent people and put a stop to it!

Convened by the organisers of the T.A.C.

E. T. MOFUTSANYANA and
S.M. MOEMA.

Document 23. Report of a Deputation from the ANC to the Minister of Justice, on July 8, 1941, [n.d.]

At 2:30 P.M. July 8th., 1941, a deputation of the African National Congress led by Dr. A.B.Xuma, President-General waited on the Honourable the Minister

166

of Justice. The deputation was the result of telegraphic protests and letter representations made by the President-General of the Congress about relations regarding the shooting and killing of Africans by police, Police raids, and relation of Police and Africans in general. Dr. Xuma was communicated with by telephone from the Department of Justice and advised to form a deputation of three with himself. He quickly made arrangements with Mr. S. P. Matseke—President Transvaal Congress—and Mr. R. V. Selope Thema M.R.C. as other members of the deputation. Unfortunately, three hours before the deputation was due at the Palace of Justice, Mr. Thema declared his inability to join the deputation, consequently, Mr. Edwin Mofutsanyane substituted for Mr. Thema.

The deputation then met the Minister at 2.30. The members were introduced to the Honourable the Minister by Dr. Xuma who also led the representations made. He, at once, expressed appreciation of the Congress to the Minister for his courtesy and public-mindedness in meeting a deputation of Africans who can give him certain aspects of any question in Native Affairs which no non-African is capable of. In the forty-five minutes that ensued various aspects of Police and the Africans were discussed, such as

(1) Police Raids on African homes and African people.
   (a) The method in which they are conducted.
   (b) Need and reasons for their abolition.

(2) Reckless use of fire-arms by police on unarmed Africans
   (a) Shooting, killing of two Africans and wounding one African at Sophiatown, June 15th., 1941.
   (b) Police raid and shooting near Roodepoort on Sunday, July 6th., 1941.

(3) Treatment and arrest of certain cases at Benoni and elsewhere.

(4) Police Raid at Western Native Township, Johannesburg on the 22nd., June, 1941, and the following Thursday.

(5) Alleged assault of Pregnant woman by police at Sophiatown.

(6) Difficulty for Africans to prove allegations of assault by police.

(7) Raiding and arresting Africans for Native Beer when the municipalities are allowed to brew and sell beer to Africans.

(8) Abuse of the right to use fire-arms in self-defence or alibi of action taken in the lawful prosecution of duty.

These and other questions formed the basis of the discussion.

The deputation was most sympathetically received by the Minister, who expressed appreciation of the spirit in which the deputation came, and stated that he expects the police to be exemplary in their conduct and not to break the law in its enforcement. He further stated that where evidence was conclusive he would take severe disciplinary measures against any policemen. It was his desire, he said, that no section of the community be singled out for ill-treatment. In conclusion, he urged the deputation to draw a memorandum along the lines of their representations and submit the same to him for substantiation and action.

Dr. Xuma again thanked the Minister for his sympathetic and patient hearing of the deputation's representations as well as for his appreciation of the good intentions of the deputation.

I understand that the deputation is now engaged in the preparation of their memorandum for the Minister as requested.

Document 24. "The Policy and Platform of the African National Congress." Statement by Dr. A.B. Xuma in *Inkululeko (Freedom)*, August 1941

The African National Congress is the mouth-piece of the African people of the Union of South Africa.

It stands for racial unity and mutual helpfulness and for the improvement of the African people, POLITICALLY, ECONOMICALLY, SOCIALLY, EDUCATIONALLY AND INDUSTRIALLY.

A. *RACIAL UNITY AND MUTUAL HELPFULNESS:* Congress aims

(1) To work and unite Africans for common action.

(2) To educate Bantu people on their rights, duties and obligations to the state and to themselves individually and collectively; and to promote mutual help, feeling of fellowship and a spirit of brotherhood among them.

(3) To encourage mutual understanding and to bring together into common action as one political people all tribes and clans of various tribes or races and by means of combined effort and united political organisation to defend their freedom, rights and privileges.

(4) To discourage and contend against racialism and tribal feuds or to secure the elimination of racialism and tribal feuds, jealousy and petty quarrels by economic combination, education, goodwill and by other means.

(5) To be the medium of expression of representative opinion and to formulate a standard policy on Native Affairs for the benefit and guidance of the Union Government and Parliament.

(6) To educate Parliament and Provincial Councils, Municipalities, other bodies and the public generally regarding the requirements and aspirations of the Native people; and to enlist the sympathy and support of such European Societies, Leagues or Unions as might be willing to espouse the cause of right and fair treatment of coloured races.

B. *POLITICALLY:*

(1) Right of Franchise to Africans.

(2) Participation of Africans in the building of a Union Policy acceptable to all sections including the African.

(3) Representation of Africans in all Government Chambers and other Governing Departments.

C. *ECONOMICALLY AND INDUSTRIALLY:*

Removal of all industrial and commercial restrictions against the African.

(1) Living wage and better working conditions.

(2) Right of all classes of African workers to organise into Trade Unions.

(3) Recognition and registration of African Trade Unions under African leadership by the Union Labour Department with all rights, privileges and immunities appertaining to such organisations.

(4) Right to learn skilled trades and engage in them.

(5) Trading rights for Africans.

D. *SOCIAL WELFARE:*

(1) Eligibility of Africans to enjoy all benefits from Social Welfare Departments of the Union Government on same principles as other sections.

(2) Pensions for aged and physically disabled Africans.

(3) Adequate hospital facilities for general and special purposes.

(4) Full extension of public health and preventive health measures to Africans.

(5) Permanent married quarters within walking distance from work for large groups of workers, such as miners, domestic servants, railway workers in larger centres, etc.

E. *LAND:*

(1) Adequate land for Africans in rural and urban areas.

(2) Right of Africans to acquire freehold title to land from any seller in rural and urban areas:
  (a) Right of Africans to buy land and acquire freehold title individually or as groups or syndicates inside or outside released areas.
  (b) Freehold title areas in every urban area must be available to Africans.
  (c) Land Bank facilities to assist African farmers.

F. *REMOVAL OF SPECIAL DISABILITIES:*

(1) Abolition of Pass Laws.

(2) Abolition of Lodgers' Permits and Fees.

(3) Abolition of Special Native Taxation based on Native Development and Taxation Act (1925) and substitution of it by taxation based on ability to pay as is the case with all other sections, (b) Abolition of all punishment or penalty for inability to pay tax.

(4) Repeal of Masters and Servants Act.

(5) Abolition of Municipal Beerhalls to be replaced with licence of Beer Stores or Home Brewing for those who desire such facilities.

(6) Mere possession of Native Beer to be no crime.

(7) Abolition of Police Raids.

G. *EDUCATIONALLY:*

(1) Participation by Africans in the best educational system planned by the State and enjoyment of the best educational facilities provided by the State.
  (i) Financing of the education of the Africans on a *per caput* basis from General Revenue based on the number of children of school going age.
  (ii) Sufficient annual grants to meet current needs and allow for expansion.

(iii) State responsibility for erection of school buildings and supplying equipment.

(iv) Adequate salaries for African Teachers to maintain a decent standard of living and leadership.

(v) Direct representation of African parents and teachers in education and school boards.

(vi) Appointment of qualified Africans into any post in African Educational Institutions.

H. *ADMINISTRATION:*

Africans should be trained and employed in graded positions in Civil Service and Public Service according to standards and qualifications required of other sections.

Fellow Africans,

GREETINGS.

I place before you in concrete form a few things upon which I want you to organise, unite, close ranks, work and fight for. They are things that other sections enjoy in greater measures. They are the rightful claims of a citizen in any country that calls itself Christian or Democratic. They are moderate claims.

I know you want these things but you always ... and expect a benevolent Government to imagine that you want these, or for well-intentioned white friends to mediate for you, that is why these good people have sometimes been unfairly charged as "busy bodies" and "putting foreign ideas into the native's mind."

Remember that this world is not a charitable ... disposed to give alike to everyone. People have to ask for, work for, even fight for, what they want. South Africa is big enough for both white and black to enjoy her wealth and live in peace, prosperity and mutual helpfulness. South Africa stands for freedom, democracy and Christianity. And, if she is true to her ideals, and I cannot believe she can be otherwise and maintain her national honour, she must, therefore, open these institutions to ....

We have a God-given opportunity to use every constitutional means now and henceforth to press our claims along the lines I have suggested and thus help South Africa attain her ideals.

I urge men and women, young and old, to join or organise Congress Clubs in all areas.

We are ready to sacrifice for you."FREEDOM NOT SERFDOM" is the Motto of Congress.

Yours for Freedom,
Dr. A. B. Xuma
President - General
African National Congress

Documents 25a-25c. ANC Annual Conference of December 14-16, 1941

Document 25a. "Presidential Address" by Dr. A.B. Xuma

Fellow Countrymen,

If you may ever need comfort, courage and inspiration for the difficult yet manly task I am going to urge you to assume, I advise you to pin on the walls of your hearts the wise words of our Prime Minister, the Right Honourable Field-Marshal J. C. Smuts who said recently, "Do not mind being called agitators. Let them call you any names they like but get on with the job and see that matters that vitally require attention, Native Health, Native Food, the treatment of Native Children and all those cognate questions that are basic to the Welfare of South Africa are attended to."

In the founding of the African National Congress in 1912, African leaders of that day displayed a great vision and laid a broad and deep foundation upon which to build the superstructure for African freedom and liberty in the land of their forefathers. They proclaimed through the organization they set up and the efforts they made, that, only through unity and concerted action of all leaders from our various races and classes may we hope to achieve our freedom and obtain justice and a fair play in South Africa. They made sacrifices and suffered privations in the cause of African freedom. Some went to gaol and became unpopular with power and influence but remained loyal and true to the cause of their people. Thus they were the architects of our salvation. Thus they pointed the way for us. They showed that freedom is precious and a heavy price must be paid to obtain it.

With our State Native Policy and the racial attitude in general, to serve your people honestly and sincerely; to take an uncompromising stand on their behalf, is to become unpopular in certain high and influential quarters.

You and I are inheritors of these great traditions. We are debtors to their fine examples. We are called upon to copy their fine example of sacrifice. We are urged not only to build upon the foundation they laid but also to improve and modernise the plan of their structure. To do this it requires the best African brains, and I believe we have them at this Conference. It calls for the greatest effort and sacrifice from every man and woman of our race. It means for all of us wherever we are and whoever we are to do our duty. Congress claims us. Congress demands our best service for our people.

Since Congress was founded and made its initial spectacular success it has experienced periods of inactivity because you and I thought and believed that organizations led by non-Africans were more dignified than African organizations and thus we abandoned our organizations and surrendered our leadership to others. We, especially the intellectuals, so-called, have been more loyal to this new leadership. We are better trained than the founders of Congress but we do not seem willing to think and act for ourselves as did these old stalwarts.

To-day you and I, the better trained we are, seem more disposed to work under orders and direction of others against and away from African organizations. Someone said to me one day, with some degree of truth, "We uneducated Africans feel that the educated African is lost to us. He is afraid to identify himself with his own people. When crisis arises, he is either silent or joins the forces against his own people. We do not know whether the education you get puts fear in you." I was dumbfounded; but was somewhat ashamed because you and I, outside our jobs for which we are paid, have not done the best we can to assist our people. Fellow Countrymen, this is a challenge. Shall we not pick up the gauntlet? South Africa, white and black, needs us. We must pull our full weight; we must make our real contribution to the building and the progress of South Africa to the full benefit, mutual helpfulness and happiness of all sections, white and black.

Let us stand for, and with, our people as long, as we are in the right.

Our position and place is what it is in South Africa and will remain what it is until you and I realise that no race can save another. Each people must rise through the efforts and leadership of its own members. Others can and must help.

In spite of this I am very much encouraged to find that during the past year Congress has received the support and co-operation of all African groups and organizations. The representations that Congress made before Government Commissions have been supported and adopted by most responsible groups. We are, therefore, proud and happy at the evidence of this unity which means strength and hope for our people.

It will not be amiss here to remind you of the aims and objects of the Congress as enunciated by its founders....

Thus the African National Congress is the mouthpiece of the African people of the Union of South Africa. All its efforts are and must be concentrated upon raising the status of the African people from their semi-serfdom to citizenship. To work for this end and to achieve it, the leaders of Congress cannot hope to be popular with any of those who would exclude the African from citizenship rights.

We cannot go on blindly and hope to achieve our goal. We must have a plan; we must have a programme of action.

REPRESENTATION

In a democratic country all members of the State must be part of the policy moulding machinery. They must have a voice and a vote in the affairs of the State. However, in South Africa the African has no vote and, therefore, no voice in South African affairs. He has ingeniously been disfranchised and put in differentiated pseudo-franchise which disfranchise the most qualified people under any fair, just, and equitable system of franchise. Under the Representation

173

of Natives' Act, the individual educated person is victimised. In rural areas only the chiefs under the influence of the Native Commissioners are voters. In urban areas, the Advisory Boards, some under the influence of the Superintendents are voters. The professional man, the teacher, the minister, the property owner outside locations, have no vote, and, therefore, cannot choose a representative either to the Native Representative Council, to the House of Assembly, or to the Senate except in the Cape Province. In a country in which two-million Europeans are represented in Municipal Councils, Provincial Councils besides 150 members in the House of Assembly and 40 in the Senate, there are only three members in the House of Assembly and 4 Senators to represent six to eight million Africans. There are no members in the House of Assembly to represent Africans in the Free State, Transvaal and Natal. The Transvaal and the Free State on the one hand and Natal on the other are represented by one Senator respectively. In the Native Representative Council there are 12 members elected by Chiefs in Rural Areas and by Advisory Boards in Urban Areas, and 4 members nominated by the Government with 5 Chief Native Commissioners and the Chairman representing the Government. The Council has only advisory functions and no legislative power. The Representation of Natives' Act not only gives inadequate representation but also excludes the best qualified Africans from being voters. It may justly be called the Mis-Representation of Natives' Act. We must work for:-

(1) Adequate representations and right of franchise for Africans.

(2) Participation of Africans, as voters and citizens, in the building of a Union Policy acceptable to all sections including the African.

(3) Representation of Africans in all Government chambers and Government departments.

LAND

The fundamental basis of all wealth and power is the ownership and acquisition of freehold title to land. From land, we derive our existence. We derive our wealth in minerals, food, and other essentials. On land we build our homes. Without land we cannot exist. To all men of whatever race or colour land, therefore, is essential for their wealth, prosperity, and health. Without land-rights any race will be doomed to poverty, destitution, ill-health and lack of all life's essentials. In South Africa all our legislation aims at depriving the African of all right and title to land, in both rural and urban areas. He is made a perpetual and eternal tenant of the State and Municipalities so that he may forever be dependent for existence and wages upon Europeans who are, alone, entitled to get as much land as they can use and even more than what they

174

can use but may hold it for future speculation while Africans are landless, homeless, destitute, and starving.

The over-crowding of the reserves is no accident. Generations of young men come of age in many of these areas but no land is available for their occupation so that tens of thousands of them are squatting on their fathers' limited areas. As many as 2 to 4 families squat on such little plots in surveyed areas.

Much of this over-crowding of stock we hear so much about is a misrepresentation of the position. Few people have as many as 5 head of cattle or more. The problem is over-population due to limited land space. The solution is not limitation of stock as it is often officially urged even though no one would object to the improvement of the quality of stock. The solution will be the opening up of more land for occupation by Africans through all forms of tenure possible for them, that is, freehold, lease-hold, and rental, as the case may be.

The provisions of the Natives' Land Act (1913) and the Natives' Land Trust Act Amendment (1936) do not tend to solve the land problem in the rural areas. They tend to aggravate and confuse the situation. The land is available to be held communally under restricted conditions and rent must be paid in perpetuity. The land, under the conditions of the Land and Trust Act is bought at highly inflated prices and thereby increases the rentals. These poor people must carry a heavy financial burden in rents.

Under this Act no land is available for sale to individuals or groups of Africans who wish to buy. Further, no facilities are available to them, such as the Land Bank to assist them to acquire or improve their land.

The whole land policy has been of benefit to European farmers who have made unheard of profits for the sale of farms in their names without any real improvements having been effected by them.

In fact, the over-crowding of the reserves, the lack of facilities to encourage the acquisition of freehold title by Africans are not an accident or an insoluble problem. They are part of a studied land policy which aims at providing an uninterrupted flow of cheaply paid labour and an absence of independent self-sufficient African farmers who would be under no European control.

In urban areas, under the Urban Areas Act, 1923, provisions are only made for accommodation of those Africans who are potential labourers for Europeans. These Africans must be accommodated in locations or hostels. Even though the idea of Native villages is provided for under the Act, it has not been encouraged in practice. No provision is made for the acquisition of freehold titles by Africans generally except in townships that were allowed before the Act came into force. Here, also, over-crowding exists because areas available to Africans and Non-Europeans in general are very limited and, therefore, become slums.

In all this land policy the worst and most dangerous clause is the restriction that provides that no Native may buy land from a non-Native except with

175

the Governor-General's approval to the transaction. The provision is universally acceptable in government and European quarters because the native generally speaking has no land to sell. This ensures that there is little chance for Africans securing more land and therefore, independence.

Congress must, therefore, work and negotiate for:-

(1) Adequate land for Africans and for Africans to acquire freehold title to land in rural and urban areas.

(2) The right of Africans to secure freehold titles to land individually or collectively or as syndicates inside or outside released areas.

(3) Right of Africans to purchase land from any seller anywhere in rural and urban areas.

(4) Land Bank facilities to assist African farmers to purchase land to improve it.

Every effort must be made, now, during the war, to get adequate land for Africans as over-crowding and starvation are undermining the health and physique of our people for generations to come. The present conditions of land occupation and available land for Africans unfit them physically, mentally and even morally for survival.

ECONOMIC AND INDUSTRIAL WELFARE

The African is the worker of South Africa. However, because of his lack of political power and because of the existence of many statutory restrictions against him such as the Pass Laws, the Natives Service Contract Act, the Masters and Servants Act, the Natives' Labour Regulations, the African finds himself debarred from benefits of certain labour awards. For instance, the Pass Laws restrict his freedom of movement, limit his bargaining power, expose him to exploitation by a certain type of employer and exclude him from enjoying benefits to be derived from the Industrial Conciliation Act. The African is paid wages far below the cost of living. He is debarred from skilled trades. He is a pawn between the white worker and the employer. He is forced to live below the bread line. Besides African wages are further depressed by the uneconomic system of recruiting and importation of African labour which exempts the mines from the operation of economic and industrial laws, supply and demand so far as Africans are concerned. He is allowed to trade on sufferance and under great restrictions. The African is a great producer and consumer of goods. He should, therefore, be allowed to trade freely according to his means and ability to help raise his economic status. To achieve our ends in this direction, Congress must work for :-

(1) Removal of industrial and commercial restrictions against the African.

(2) Living wage and better working conditions.

(3) Right of all classes of African workers to organise into Trade Unions.

(4) Recognition and Registration of African Trade Unions under African leadership by the Union Labour Department with all the rights, privileges and immunities appertaining to such organizations under the Industrial Conciliation Act.

(5) Right of Africans to learn skilled trades and engage in them.

(6) Trading rights for Africans anywhere.

(7) Abolition of Pass Laws, Natives' Service Contract Act, The Masters' and Servants' Act, and other Special Disabilities.

(8) Abolition of Recruiting and Importation of African labour from outside the Union.

All of us, whatever our status or calling, must join hands with all other classes in this fight for existence.

POLICE, CIVIC GUARDS AND THE AFRICAN

Recently the African has suffered severely at the hands of the police. During police raids not only assaults on Africans have taken place but, in the course of such raids, Africans have been actually shot dead. The situation in cities like Johannesburg has been aggravated by the appearance, as special constables, of the Civic Guards. They are more worry and a greater horror in the already harassed life of the African. Some of them do not seem to use much judgment in carrying out their duties. They seem to have no regard either to time, circumstances or persons. Some of them search all and sundry. Any questions or reluctance on the part of the African often leads to man-handling of the victim. These high-handed methods of both the police and the "civic guards" do not tend to arouse a spirit of good race relations. One feels that there are many people under these circumstances who are given authority over the African without the necessary discipline and training for the task. The Pass Laws and

177

Police Raids in general must be abolished in justice to the African and as a measure of relief to him.

Those who want to fight should go to the various battlefronts instead of attacking defenceless and unarmed Africans.

SOCIAL WELFARE

Africans in South Africa are the worst paid and consequently the poorest section of the community. Generally speaking they have no margin from their earnings to set aside for a rainy day; consequently, during old age, disablement and non-employment they find themselves with nothing with which to support themselves. As a group Africans are more in need of benefits from the Social Welfare Departments than any other section in South Africa. The Africans, therefore, should be eligible to receive all benefits from Social Welfare Departments. It should be the task of the African National Congress to work for:-

(a) Old age pensions for Africans.

(b) Disability and Disablement pensions.

(c) Extensions of provisions of the Children's Act to meet social requirements of destitute African children—adequate maintenance grants.

HEALTH REQUIREMENTS

Africans in South Africa have the highest Infant Mortality rate, highest mortality and morbidity rates, than any section. The causes are not racial but economic. The people are poverty stricken with low wages, lack of adequate food, semi-starvation, bad housing and therefore, low resistance to disease and consequent ill-health and premature death.

Adequate hospital accommodation is desirable but hospital accommodation required can be reduced if the people are paid good wages to relieve them from poverty in order to buy their health through sufficient food, good housing and other amenities. We must work for:-

(1) Adequate well-equipped and adequately staffed hospitals—General and Special.

(2) Full extension of public health and preventative health measures to Africans.

(3) The training of Africans in medicine, surgery and public health and cognate subjects, training of health visitors, health inspectors and

nurses, and their eligibility for public employment on basis of ability and training and recognised professional rates and conditions.

EDUCATION OF THE AFRICAN

Man is not born with well-developed instincts like most animals. Unlike other animals he requires a long period of care and education. He must be taught.

Under the present conditions Native Education is not State-Controlled. It is only State-Aided. The missionaries establish the schools and provide the buildings. The Government through the Provincial Education Departments, pays the teachers' salaries. Native Education is at present financed from a block grant made up of £340,000 from the general revenue and the rest a sum voted from revenue accruing from Native Taxation under the Native Taxation and Development Act, 1925.

Only about one-third of the African children of school-going age are accommodated in these schools which are always overcrowded and under-staffed.

The African teachers are the most overworked and paid the deplorable salary of £4.10.0d to £5.19.0d a month.

So far there has never been enough funds to meet the requirements of even the one-third of school population now accommodated in schools. As a consequence many of our children are growing wild without an opportunity of school education and discipline. They get their education on the streets and back-alleys from where they graduate into reformatories and finally gaols and many people wonder why there is a high and increasing rate of African Juvenile Delinquency. The Government must be asked for adequate funds but it is difficult to expect the Government to distribute lavishly public funds over a system of education over which they have no control. How can we expect them to satisfy the numerous competing mission groups?

We thank the missionaries for pioneering in, and laying the foundation of African Education. However, time and circumstances have changed.

Congress, therefore, urges for:-

(1) Free Public School system of education controlled by the Government through the various Provincial Education Departments.

(2) Provision of School Buildings and equipment by the State.

(3) Financing of Native Education on a per caput basis from the General Revenue based on the number of children of school-going age.

(4) Higher salaries for the African Teacher with Civil Service Status and pension rights compatible with the requirements of their profession under modern conditions.

179

(5) Unlimited opportunities for scholastic education and technical training for employment in Civil Service and skilled trades without colour or racial restrictions.

(6) Formation of school boards with direct representations of Africans on such boards.

(7) Appointment of qualified Africans into any post in African educational institutions.

ADMINISTRATION

Almost all Departments of State deal with African Affairs. In all these departments the candidates for the graded positions have to undergo some training and apprenticeship. Africans contribute directly and indirectly for the upkeep of these departments. We welcome the recent move by the Native Affairs Department for the appointment of Africans to certain senior posts. We urge the training of Africans and the employment of them generally in all Civil Service and Public Service other than Native Affairs. Africans must be employed in the administration of the country like others in increasing numbers and with adequate pay and pensions.

DISABILITIES UNDER THE NATIVE ADMINISTRATION ACT

I now come to a question that affects our people vitally especially in rural areas. It affects Chiefs and people alike. I refer to the operation of the Native Administration Act. Under this Act the Governor General who in this case, is the Native Affairs, has absolute dictatorial powers over our people. He may remove tribes, appoint and depose chiefs at will if it is thought of course by some Native Commissioner that such action is in the interest of good government whatever that may mean. He may deport a member or members of the tribe. Such member or members of the tribe may not be tried before a Court of Law. It is suggested that such powers are derived from African law and custom and the Governor-General exercises them as "Supreme Chief of the Africans in the Orange Free State, Transvaal and Natal." In his high office as the Viceroy we bow to the Governor-General; but on the basis of African law and custom he cannot be recognized as Supreme Chief of the African. There can be no Supreme Chief in Native law and custom who acts without the advice of other chiefs; who does not express the wish and will of the people. The most controlled person in African society is the chief. He is controlled by his family, his councillors, headmen and sub-chiefs and finally by the people. The people express their will first and the Chief speaks it out for them. He is their mouthpiece.

This distortion of Native Law and Custom was copied by Europeans from the rule of Great Chaka. He was a dictator and a despot. He was not deposed because there is no deposition in African custom. He went the way such un-controlled Chiefs go in African society. He had his head cut off.

There is no deportation of members of the tribe. If a man is unruly, the Chief "eats him up", that is, fines him until he runs across the border by night. This deportation clause does not even recognise the rule of law in English law, namely, that an accused person cannot suffer penalty without trial. The Native Administration Act is tyranny invoked in the name of customary law. We must fight for the revision of this abuse and misrepresentation of African customs.

NOMINATIONS UNDER REPRESENTATION OF NATIVES' ACT

I take up now a question that interests all of us but which is, nevertheless, not essential. I refer to the nomination of candidates under the Representation of Natives' Act. Sometime ago the Provinces received a letter from the Secretary-General asking for nominations under this Act. I have since, however, studied the question and its implications in relation to our organisation and have come to the conclusion that for the present, Congress must not sponsor any candidates either nationally or provincially. Any nominations, therefore, made in any Province will be made by qualified voters in that Province and not by the Provincial Congresses. This, however, does not preclude any voters, as such, exercising their choice; but such nominee or nominees are not endorsed by Congress either nationally or provincially. To Congress we must be loyal and true. For Congress, we must forget any personal or sectional interests or gain. We must put the cause and the interests of the people before any expediency.

My ruling is in the interests of the Congress and all genuine supporters and well-wishers of this organization will abide by it. To be true leaders, we must put the interests and welfare of our people above our own.

THE AFRICAN AND MILITARY SERVICE

The last point I would like to discuss with you is the problem of military service and the African in the Union of South Africa.

We are thrilled at the exploits of African forces from other parts of Africa. West Africans and the King's African Rifles from Central Africa have dis-tinguished themselves in the campaign against Fascist Italy. We are proud of their record in the fight to destroy the Italian African Empire. We learn that 90,000 of them took part in this campaign that is now history. West Africans are flying in Great Britain. Some have been commissioned in the Royal Air Force. South Africa and South Africans, black and white are safer to-day because these black African soldiers with their white comrades at-arms have barred the way.

Our own people have volunteered to serve King and country anywhere and in anyway; but our Government has restricted their service to manual labour. Their pay has been deplorably low. In fact, that one shilling and sixpence a day for unmarried African soldiers is just six-pence more than the allowance which, I understand, was given to internees, enemies of the State, whose dependents were receiving £ 2.10.0 to £ 5.0.0 allowance in addition, and that, for working against the Government. Our African soldiers in the Union unlike Coloureds and Indians cannot rise higher than the position of Sergeant and it seems that there have been attempts to differentiate and humiliate them further in certain directions. They are not receiving the extra shilling a day allowed for doing extra work such as clerical work, training transport drivers, and so on. There is also the problem of the disabled soldier and the discharged soldier. All these matters tend to discourage the enthusiasm of our people to join and put African leaders in a most embarrassing position.

While it is our desire to see our people armed and fighting like other soldiers, Lord Gort's memoirs, recently published, seem to indicate that if the training of Africans for active service was begun now it may not be until 1943 before they are fit to take their part safely and efficiently in a campaign under modern war conditions.

It would be a sign of irresponsibility on my part to discuss publicly all the causes of reluctance of the African to join. I feel, therefore, without disclosing some of the more delicate questions, that Congress must take steps for representations to be made to the Right Honourable the Prime Minister, Minister of Defence—Field Marshal J. C. Smuts and the Deputy Prime Minister and Minister of Native Affairs—Colonel Deneys Reitz, on these questions of ARMY SERVICE, REPRESENTATION, LAND, EDUCATION, WAGES AND RECOGNITION AND REGISTRATION OF TRADE UNIONS, THE NATIVE ADMINISTRATION ACT AND THE PASS LAWS.

Our actions of loyalty do not mean contentment and happiness on our part. We are very much dissatisfied with the lot and status of our people. We want these improved immediately. But we realise that if our present State is taken over by a foreign nation, there will be new problems. Our condition may or may not be worse. We would rather fight for, and correct, the evils of our present State and incorporate in her legislation and administration all that is best for the advancement and happiness of our common humanity.

A question may arise in the minds of some of us whether these problems of LAND, REPRESENTATION, EDUCATION, WAGES AND PASS LAWS ETC. should not wait until after the war. I reply NO! Emphatically NO! These are urgent matters clammering for immediate solution. They are essential, now for the health, well-being, and happiness of the African people as for other sections. South Africa is fighting for freedom, for democracy, for Christianity, and for human decency, and these must be enjoyed by all who will, irrespective of race, creed or colour. At home, Africans have given from their meagre earnings, from their dire poverty, more than their proportionate share towards the various war funds. As in the past when king and country were at war, the Africans' loyalty now is not and never has been excelled

182

by any section in South Africa, white or black, notwithstanding their hope-destroying disabilities under our State policy and practice. Africans are no fairweather loyalists or democrats. They have not anywhere committed acts of sabotage against the State. They have volunteered to serve anywhere and in anyway, so that, to-day, European boys and African boys, from South Africa, are falling together on the same battleground. In Sidi Rezek, Lybia, enemy bullets made no distinction on basis of colour or duties being performed. White men and black men suffered the same death, sustained the same wounds and others were taken prisoners. African men, even as stretcher bearers, died attempting to save lives of wounded European compatriots at the battle line. These Africans, whatever service they are assigned to do, are doing a man's job. They are protecting white and black women in South Africa, and all those men who either are unfit for service, those who are exempted from service, or those who expect freedom to be a gift from somewhere not worth fighting for or dying for. African boys are dying in defence of freedom, democracy, Christianity and human decency in South Africa. They are making this supreme sacrifice so that we, their Kith and Kin, may enjoy these privileges as well. They hope that we, at the home front, will defend their inherent rights and see that full justice is done to their wives and dependents so that they will not have died in vain. South Africa must play the game with the Africans now. If she gives them their legitimate right of citizenship thus more to fight for, she will get the Africans' quota for service without recruiting.

As long as these grave disabilities and glaring inconsistencies exist and are not adjusted or settled, they will continue to kill, disable, and handicap more Africans and bring more unhappiness to as many more African families than the deaths and disablement that this war will bring to South Africa. This is the battle of the home front. It must be fought and won now before the war is over as a basis for real peace.

In the past South Africa has legislated and governed for the benefits of the Europeans, the privileged group and upper cast of South Africa. Because she claims to be fighting for the ideals we have just mentioned, and also in memory of, and as a monument to, the lives of black boys who are falling and will fall in various battle fronts in her defence, South Africa must begin now to legislate for the welfare and benefit of all South Africans irrespective of race, creed or colour but must be based on human worth. Thus and thus only may South Africa win peace.

This is Congress Policy. This is the African's charter in South Africa. This is the New Order for which he is dying up North, for which he must live and work. It can only be achieved through hard work on our part, through serious thinking, careful planning, great personal sacrifices and self-denial on the part of all people, particularly Africans who would like to see the African given an opportunity to develop and use without let or hindrance, his God-given gifts and talents.

In conclusion, in the words quoted recently by our Prime Minister, Field Marshall J. C. Smuts, "I challenge you and all men of vision and goodwill of whatever race or colour to abandon the policies of the past for faith, for hope, for trust in each other. Take each others' hand and move forward to the destiny which is yours."

Thus South Africa may well adopt our Congress motto— "RIGHT NOT MIGHT. FREEDOM NOT SERFDOM."

Document 25b. Report of the Secretary-General

Until the Provinces send in their statistics showing their numerical and their financial strength, the Executive Report will always be found wanting. No Province has been able to fulfil this obligation as yet. Acting on the information received from the Cape African Congress conference last June I report six branches which fulfilled their status by having at least 25 fully paid members for the year. I know that some centres had doubled the number but as I have not got the statistics with me I shall say the Cape has about 200 members. The Cape Western Province blame the Treasurer-General for not sending the tickets to them.

I have had no reply from the other Provinces. I know, however, that they have been working hard, organising themselves, and that Provincial conferences have been held.

The President–General Dr. A. B. Xuma has exerted himself almost to breaking-point in assisting Congress to organise in various ways. His Memorandum containing the Platform and Policy of the Congress has been very useful to many organisers, for it placed the point of view and the aims and objects of the Congress in a short form, and made it easier for people to join. The President has followed up the memorandum by a personal visit to centres such as Kimberley, Cradock, East London, and Port Elizabeth, and addressing meetings and interviewing groups of local leaders.

The President–General has spoken on important social and political questions as a true leader. He has submitted evidences to the Beer Commission and to the Commission which enquired into the life and conditions of our people. His memoranda fully represented the African's point of view.

The President–General has taken up certain matters with the Government Officials and members of the Cabinet. He has approached the Department of Justice for instance and interviewed the Minister in connection with the treatment meted out to our people by the police. He has come to the assistance of the Workers and helped them to present their case to the Department of Labour.

The Secretary–General also visited the Transvaal in January and attended and took part in the opening of the Conference which was held in Alexandra Township. He accompanied Dr. Xuma throughout his tour in the Cape Province. He visited Bloemfontein in May and had a series of meetings in preparation for this conference.

The Secretary also visited Capetown and there also attended a series of meetings held by adherents of both Provinces of the Congress in the Cape.

The Question of Farm Labourers and that of the recent appointment of Advisory Boards on Farm Labour has been delegated to Advocate Molteno M. P., and he is carrying on negotiations with Government Officials with good results in certain centres. At Cradock, for instance, Mr. Akena has been invited by this Board to give evidence and also to visit certain farms in the district with a view to presenting the facts to the Congress Branch as well as help to create a better understanding between the Farmers and the Africans in general.

Some 20 families of people ejected from the farms and squatting on the Cradock Commonage have been arrested by the Council and sentenced to a month's imprisonment or 2 pounds fine to take effect as from the first day of January 1942. The matter has been referred to Senator Malcomess who is interviewing the Native Affairs Department on it.

The Executive owes a very deep debt of gratitude to the African Representatives in the Senate, House of Assembly, Provincial Council, for the indefatigable way in which they have co-operated with the Congress in fighting against injustice and Colour prejudice and class discriminations against our people.

The members of the Representative Council also deserve our full appreciation for bringing before the Government questions that might in the ordinary course have been treated as mere conference resolutions and put away in Government shelves.

The following is the reply of the Secretary for Native Affairs to our resolutions on the War:

Sir,

Resolutions of the African National Congress.

With reference to your letter of the 31st ultimo in the above connection, I have the honour to append hereto replies to the four points detailed therein:

(1) The declared intention of the Government is that Union Natives will not be armed.

(2) The conditions of Military Service, which were published in the Bantu Press early this year, were most carefully considered by the Defence authorities acting in consultation with Senators and members of Parliament representing the Natives.

It was agreed that, generally speaking, the scales of pay and other benefits were reasonable, though the opinion was expressed at the time that further provision should be made for families of recruits permanently residing, at the time of recruitment, in those urban areas where rents and the cost of living justified additional assistance. The latter suggestion has been met by extending to Bantu soldiers and their dependents the right of participation in the benefits

185

of the Governor–General's National War Fund. Such benefits will of course be available even after the War in cases of necessity.

The possibility of paying an extra duty allowance to those doing skilled work is at present under consideration.

(3) The co-operation of native leaders in stimulating recruiting by way of propaganda will be welcomed. The Defence Department has, however, intimated that the existing machinery for actual recruiting is adequate and that further expenditure upon salaried recruiters would not be justified.

(4) The possibility of revising and modifying the Pass Laws is a matter which is still engaging attention and no pronouncement in this regard can yet be made.

For information in regard to low wages and the colour bar in industry, I would suggest that you communicate with the Wage Board and the Mines and Labour Departments respectively.

Yours faithfully,

Howard Rogers
for SECRETARY FOR NATIVE AFFAIRS.

Document 25c. Resolutions

1/41 WOMEN'S SECTION:

That this Conference recommends to the parent body the necessity of reviving the women's section of the Congress in terms of the provision of the Constitution. Further that women be accorded the same status as men in the classification of membership. That the following means be made to attract the women (a) to make the programme of the Congress as attractive as possible to the women, (b) a careful choice of leadership.

2/41 RESOLUTION 5/40:

That the subject matter on resolution 5/40 [see document 20 above] be left for settlement by the Executives of the two Provinces affected as negotiations have reached a stage from whence a final settlement seems very possible.

3/41 GRIEVANCES OF THE BATLOKOA CHIEFS:

That the General Secretary send a copy of the grievances of the Batlokoa Chiefs at Vrede in connection with land to the Senator, and M.R.C.'s of the Transvaal-Free State area for investigation.

4/41 POST-WAR RECONSTRUCTION:

That Congress appoint in collaboration with all national organizations an African National Committee for Post war Reconstruction which shall study and prepare an African plan of reconstruction for submission to the next conference of the Congress which should devote most of its time to the important subject.

5/41   That the question of the Chamber of Mines' deferred pay be referred to the President.

6/41   That the question of the Bantu Welfare Trust and its activities be referred to the Trustees concerned.

7/41   That the question of Purchased Farms under the Native Trust and Land Act be referred to our M.P.'s, Senators, and M.R.C.'s.

8/41 TEACHERS' SALARIES:

That in view of the gross underpayment of African Teachers, Congress records its full support of the claims put forward by the African Teachers for an equitable scale of salaries and calls on authorities to recognize these claims.

9/41 APPOINTMENT OF A SOCIAL WELFARE SECRETARY:

That in order to encourage the support or formation of bodies whose object is to promote the welfare and to look after the interests of handicapped Africans Congress appoints a Social Welfare Secretary whose duty, among others, shall be to study the question of Social Welfare work among Africans and to bring to the notice of Congress the needs of this important work.

10/41 OFFICIAL ORGAN:

That Congress consider the need for an official organ of the African National Congress and take steps towards its establishment.

11/41 THE WAR & THE PRIME MINISTER:

That Congress reiterates its last year's resolution on the war and congratulates the Prime Minister of the Union on his recent promotion by His Majesty the King as the 13th Field-Marshall of the British Empire.

12/41 PRESIDENT–GENERAL'S PLATFORM AND POLICY:

That Congress desires to place on record its profound appreciation of the President-General's platform and policy and resolves that a committee be appointed to study the programme and make it the basis for the laying down of further principles for which Congress shall always labour.

13/41 CO-OPERATIVE TRADING SOCIETIES:

That Congress supports the formation of Co-operative Trading Societies.

14/41 D.R.C. & NATIVE TRADING RIGHTS:

That this Conference of the African National Congress assembled at Bloemfontein from the 14th to 16th December 1941, desires to place on record its profound sense of gratitude to the Orange Free State Dutch Reformed Church for its recommendation to the Government Economic, Social and Health Commission that Native Trading be allowed in the Free State Locations. Congress strongly endorses this recommendation.

Document 26. Report of a Deputation from the ANC to the Deputy Prime Minister and Others on March 4, 1942, by Dr. A.B. Xuma [n.d.]

The African National Congress, the political mouthpiece of Africans in the Union of South Africa and the recognised champion of their cause and status, has been watching the trend of events since the outbreak of the present world war. They have closely studied South Africa's native policy in general, and found that it not only affects the African adversely, economically, industrially, politically, educationally, socially, physically and physiologically, as well as morally; but it also affects most seriously and alarmingly their attitude towards the war effort. It damps their zeal to do their full share in the defence of South Africa. Most Africans feel and declare that they have not only nothing to fight for, but nothing to fight with. Even many of those who had volunteered and answered the call became disillusioned when they discovered the unsatisfactory, humiliating, discriminating conditions they have to serve under.

Some Africans feel that they did their bit for King and Country during the first world war, within the limits of service set for them by South African colour prejudices. For this, they claim, they received scant consideration after peace was restored. They feel, therefore, that "Once bitten, twice shy."

Congress, however, fully realizing their responsibility as well as their duty to the State, as leader of thought, for the seven or eight million Africans resolved, at the instance of their President-General, in his Presidential address at the Annual Conference held at Bloemfontein during December 14th-16th, that "Congress must take steps for representations to be made to the Right Honourable the Prime Minister and Minister of Native Affairs, Colonel Denez [Deneys] Reitz, on the questions of Army Service and the African Representation; Land; Education; Wages and Recognition and Registration of African Trade Unions; the Native Administration Act and the Pass Laws."

Communications were sent to both the ministers accordingly, by the writer, and a reply came through Mr. D.L. Smit, Secretary for Native Affairs, as follows:

"General Smuts has asked me to inform you that, owing to the onerous burdens cast upon him by reason of the war, it will unfortunately not be possible for him to receive you personally but he has asked Colonel Reitz, in his capacity as Deputy Prime Minister and Minister of Native Affairs to meet the deputation."

"I have discussed the matter with my Minister and he has fixed 10 a.m., Wednesday 4th March, 1942, as the date upon which the interview should take place."

188

At 10 a.m. on March 4th, 1942, the African National Congress deputation composed of the following members:

(1) Mr. R.H. Godlo M.R.C., President - Advisory Boards Congress and Advisor on Urban Affairs, African National Congress;

(2) Mr. Z.K. Matthews M.A. LL.B., President - African Teachers' Federation and Advisor on Education, African National Congress. Alice, C.P.;

(3) Mr. T.M. Mapikela M.R.C., President - O.F.S. African Congress and Vice-President, African National Congress;

(4) Mr. S.J. Sililo M.R.C., (Durban) Secretary Natal Native Congress and Advisor on Social Welfare, African National Congress;

(5) Rev. Jas. Calata (Cradock) Secretary-General, African National Congress;

(6) Mr. R.G. Baloyi M.R.C. (Johannesburg) Treasurer-General African National Congress;

(7) Mr. Qamata M.R.C., member of the Bhunga, Transkeian Territories. (Cala);

(8) Mr. D. Gosani, Secretary Non-European Council of Trade Unions. (Johannesburg),

met the Deputy Prime Minister, with some heads of State Departments, and some members of Smit's Committee which recently enquired into the Economic conditions of the African people.

The European Representatives of Africans in Parliament attended as spectators.

We sat from 10 o'clock a.m. until about 6 p.m. breaking up only for lunch....

LAND POLICY

On Land Policy we pointed out that neither the Natives' Land Act of 1913 nor the Native Land and Trust Amendment Act, 1936, was ever intended to solve or satisfy the African's land hunger. The provision and policy of these Acts seem to have caused less land available for the lawful occupation by African people in rural areas than was available before the passing of the Original Act. A similar situation for urban Africans has been created by the Natives Urban Areas Act, 1923, and its amendments. We called attention to extreme overcrowding in the so-called reserves. For example, in areas like the Transkei about half the population is landless, and contrary to popular and unsympathetic offical opinion, have no root with their families in the land but depend on wages earned away from home, and are mere squatters in these areas. In the Ciskei conditions seemed to be so much worse that, as I was told from reliable sources, when then the Chief Native Commissioner received the applications for released land, he made no allotments to any applicant, stating that he was embarassed because there were many times more applicants than available land. This seems to be almost a common experience in many areas.

Besides, under the policy of the Trust Land, landless people may not squat as in the reserves. The allotments in both are not sufficient for all family needs so that even owners of plots of land in African territories must supplement their produce with wages away from home. Only tax-payers may acquire land on Trust land.

The Trust land, we pointed out, was bought generally at highly inflated prices without improvements justifying such prices. Besides, in certain areas, the seller was allowed to remain for varying periods up to a year, thus having an opportunity to plow and reap a crop on Trust land, besides getting the huge apparently unearned price.

This point drew heat from the Secretary of Native Affairs who pointed out that everything was being done to make adjustments in certain....We were, however, not convinced as the farms referred to seem to be exceptions rather than the rule; and we made this point clear.

The whole policy we emphasized drove the people to towns. And we further observed, no land policy with increasing industrialisation could prevent Africans, like other races the world over, from moving into towns to become permanent dwellers and workers, and to us, this was not an undesirable and unnatural trend. We, therefore, recommended for adequate land made available for purchase and/or leasing by Africans with Land Bank facilities for Africans to improve such lands in rural areas.

For industrialized and urban Africans, we urged for better wages and free-hold title to land and near the areas where people are earning their living so that African families may be kept together for wholesome social and moral reasons.

REPRESENTATION "UNDER THE REPRESENTATION OF NATIVES ACT"

Under this Act we found, except in the Cape Province, that the people who should be qualified to vote under democratic conditions, such as professional men, ministers, teachers, clerks, property owners, businessmen and taxpayers, or contributors to State coffers, were not eligible to cast their individual votes. Besides, we have sixteen African members of the Native Representative council standing for about seven million people, one Senator representing the Transvaal and Orange Free State, another representing the whole province of Natal. The two Senators represent between them about four million Africans.

The resolution of the deliberations of the Native Representative Council do not seem even to catch the attention of Parliament.

Taking it all in all we cannot help calling this Act the ''MisRepresentation of Natives Act.''

We, therefore, recommended that there should be delimitation of smaller constituencies so that there may be more representatives who may and can contact members of their constituencies; all qualified persons as mentioned above, including every poll tax-payer (even though we are against the present form of African taxation) should nominate candidates and cast individual votes in place of this present communal vote which is exercised, by Chiefs in rural areas, apparently likely to be under the influence of certain European Native Commissioners in some areas in favour of certain candidates, and, Advisory Boards, in urban areas, some of whom do not always seem free from influence of Location Superintendents as some of these Advisory Board members being Council nominees.

Finally, we recommended statutory powers for the Native Representative Council.

The last recommendation seems to have created a little excitement from Government representatives who feared the creation of another Parliament.

While we could not say what limitation of these powers are going to be, we allayed the fears of all concerned by saying as [sic] they may deal with the funds of the South African Trust Funds and questions that are of African interest purely and simply, if such questions do exist.

SOCIAL WELFARE

We pressed, on principle, for the application of full benefits of Social legislation to the Africans according to the human needs of the individual and not on racial or colour basis. We urged the extension of the benefits of the Children's Act to African children, the application of Disablement pensions, Blind pensions and Old age pensions to Africans.

When we asked why the regulations under the Children's Act discriminated against African children, we were told that it was the policy of the Department of Social Welfare not to give the indigent African child more than he would receive on the basis of his father's wages of about three pounds (£ 3). Besides, we were told that it was the intention of the department not to take away the urge on the part of the mother to go out to work for her child. We then asked if it was not a fact that the Honourable the Deputy Prime Minister had stated publicly that the African lived below the bread line. This being admitted, we were anxious to know whether then the policy was a deliberate attempt on the part of the Government to keep the Africans below the bread line.

191

What had the essential and physiological requirements of an African child to do with a State policy which was morally, ethically and scientifically unsound.

It was admitted that this was a matter for careful review by the authorities.

We asked for better facilities of all desirable types of education for African children for discipline and outlets for employment of African juveniles to prevent delinquency and vagrancy.

We urged for the training of African Social workers with facilities of such training being provided at Fort Hare College as a climax.

THE AFRICAN AND MILITARY SERVICE

In approaching this subject we realise that war service is not a service in which people either get rich or derive huge profits for themselves and their dependents. The soldier volunteers and risks his life and his all for a principle, namely the defence of the rights he and his own enjoy, as well as the protection of his family in the hope that during his period of service or in case of death in service, the State will make ample provisions for his dependents. Besides, the conditions of service, the Status and treatment of the soldier during such service and the consideration the ex-soldier receives after discharge or demobilisation or disablement, may encourage or discourage those and their friends who were otherwise contemplating joining the service.

For instance, it is the consensus of opinion among African people of all classes in the Union, both urban and rural, that the condition of service for the African soldiers and the pin-pricks and humiliations he is subjected to at times, apparently to put an inferiority complex in him, tend to discourage the African people from joining the Native Military Corps and cognate units.

Africans now are not trained to be fighting men. They are merely as a race prepared to be batmen, transport drivers and stretcher-bearers. Dangerous jobs all these are, as they expose these men to death and make them objectives of enemy fire without the Africans being able to defend themselves. They have no arms with which to fight. They are expected to fight aeroplanes, tanks and enemy artillery with knob-kerries and assegais. What mockery! This seems to be 'inhumanity of man to man.'

The pay of the African soldiers is deplorably low and compares most unfavourably with even that of other Non-European soldiers not to mention that of white soldiers. It is argued that this pay compares favourably with peacetime African wages - starvation wages which have brought untold misery to the Africans, filthy surroundings, ill-health, moral degradation, morbidity and premature death. The dependents of Africans, generally speaking, cannot keep even a minimum physiological standard on the allowances given them.

Further, so far as we know no satisfactory arrangements have been made to safe-guard the interests of the discharged, disabled, or demobilized African soldier. He is more like an orange sucked of all its juice and ready to be cast into the garbage can to be food for swine or to be taken to a dump heap.

192

Naturally, it would be ridiculous to expect pensions based on this paltry pay to mean anything but starvation to the dependents of African soldiers.

Although other soldiers receive special pay for special services such as clerical work, instruction to motor drivers etc., Africans, so far as our knowledge goes, do not receive such allowances.

Even leave regulations are framed to put the African soldiers to great disadvantage as compared with others. Europeans get 30 days or a month a year, which [sic] the African soldier gets only twelve days. We realise that army leave is not a right but a privilege; but we feel that all the soldiers deserve it.

To appease racial superiority more pin-pricks and humiliation have been poured upon the African soldier's head. It seems as though his service is neither appreciated nor wanted. He may not rise in rank beyond a sergeant. To satisfy the pride of certain Europeans at one time, an order was issued calling upon African N.C.O.s to turn their stripes downwards so that they do not appear to be the same as those worn by European N.C.O.s and so that the European private will feel less embarassed in the presence of these African N.C.O.s.

The reply to this point was that the order had been rescinded. But our point is, how much harm was done by this absurd order, before its rescission.

Finally and more recently, it has been ordered that "In the event of an emergency, any European private shall have command of the Non-European personnel irrespective of rank."

European Chaplains and European officers are in command in the "Native Military Corps" in order to keep the 'native' under European control and to avoid giving him commissions so that he may lead and direct his own people, in the service of King and Country.

The Africans have men who are capable of qualifying for any army rank and get the best out of their men as officers and N.C.O.s. It would be a matter of indifference to Africans whether or not they are saluted by a European. They have no desire to inconvenience or embarass European Officers, N.C.O.s or Privates.

Why not train Africans fully, equip them and give them all commissions in the Native Military Corps. This would solve the problem of our Chaplains who would receive proper rank in the Native Military Corps and attend to the spiritual needs of our men in Service.

The British army has commissioned officers in the King's African Rifles, men like Lieutenant Kwagwa. Africans hold commissions in the R.A.F. We do not lack more capable or men of equal ability.

Since enemy bullets have no colour bar and are killing the unarmed, non-combatant Africans as quickly as they will an European, we would urge that there should be no discrimination in the soldiers' pay, allowances to their dependents, leave privileges, disablement benefits, satisfactory provisions for discharged, and demobilisation as well as pension rights.

We cannot maintain these peace-time discriminations in the army and expect the victims of such discriminations or their friends and relatives to rush in their thousands to the army to defend them.

We have come here as responsible leaders of the African people to tell the government, in the interest of all concerned, that the disabilities we have mentioned under which the Africans live tend to strain their loyalty or at least to make them indifferent to the fate of the country and the outcome of the conflict. Their loyalty so far is not happiness or contentment. They ask what must we fight for? What rights and privileges have we? Everything worth while in South Africa is a privilege of the white man.

To us, as leaders, this is a tragic situation. Danger is looming from the North and from the East. To us, this is not a war of colours that is why black Indians, yellow Chinese and black Africans are fighting the allied cause. They are fighting a war of ideologies, nazism, fascism, dictatorship and all other enemies of the State, of Christianity, of democracy and of human decency, externally and internally, that is, in South Africa.

To achieve total war effort, we urge the government to take courage in both hands and give the Africans something to fight for by removing the many disabilities and discriminations against them as well as giving them something to fight with.

If Africans are to be trained and be prepared and ready for the hour of danger and defence of their country, now is the time to begin that training in all phases, of modern warfare and in the use of all modern instruments and weapons of warfare.

To wait until the enemy is at our gates is to let South Africa go the way of other countries that looked upon the aboriginees as greater enemies than the invaders.

Given something to fight for and something to fight with, as suggested above, Africans will automatically have acquired the will and the heart to fight. They will make South Africa a costly prize for any enemy of the State.

We hope common sense will prevail over the obsolete, irrational and blind sentiments and prejudices which are the arch-enemies of South Africa internally and are preventing her total defence.

EDUCATION

On this subject we pointed, with appreciation, that, whereas in 1923 the four provinces were spending £ 340,000 on Native Education, the latest estimates at the meeting of the Native Representative Council were £ 1,1780,000 [sic] and that another £ 230,000 will be available as a result of the budget speech of the Minister of Finance who allotted 5/6 the Native Taxation revenue to Native Education. However, the latter amount would merely balance the deficit which might have accrued on the basis of the year's estimates and there was nothing left to bring relief to the underpaid and desperate African teacher on the salary of £ 4-10-0 to £ 5-10-0 per month for qualified teachers. We felt

... 6/6 must be paid over to the Native Education in order that a beginning can be made on annual increments on teachers salaries.

We futher pointed out that whereas "the State in 1939 spent over 10½ million pounds on the education of 417,000 white children, and £ 965,000 on the education of 165,000 Coloured and Indian children, that is £ 21-10-0 and £ 5-5-0 per head per pupil respectively, only £ 934,000 was spent on the education of 450,000 African children or £ 2-7-0 per African child per head. This amount is based on the one-third African children of school going age who are actually at school. The position becomes even more depressing when it is realised that on the basis of the total number of African children the per caput grant would be only 16/-per pupil. Besides, this money is from direct taxation of the Africans themselves, the poorest section of the Union population.

We finally emphasized that this inelastic source of revenue for Native education and Social Welfare was now exhausted, thereby making it imperative that a new formula for financing must be found. To us, it is clear that the only sound, national and equitable formula is the per caput grant based not on the African children now in school but on the total African population of school going age. We suggested as a minimum per caput grant of the same school going age scales as for Coloured and Indian children, namely Five guineas per caput. We pointed out that the needs and requirements of Native Education as well as the aspirations of African people far now exceeded the resources of the missions who had for so long borne the burden. It was now high time for the State to take over Native Education, finance and control it according to the best standards and requirements of sound educational policy without regard to race or colour. We urged for financing of Native Education from General revenue on a per caput basis with African teachers given professional and civil status and pension rights based on remunerations and salaries compatible with their high duties and service to the State and the community. We urged for the training of Africans for all spheres and trades and professions they are capable of mastering in order to be able to serve their people and their country in all capacities. Technical training and engagement in skilled trades should be open to all. Qualified Africans should have preference in all posts in African Schools and in all services that cater for Africans only under the country segregation policy. If there are no qualified Africans for any such posts, facilities must be created for their training immediately.

We hold that education is essential for the intelligent participation in the Affairs, by every adult member, of a democratic State.

PASS LAWS

An interesting and enlightened discussion took place on the Pass Laws. It was remarkable to find how practice or custom especially in a department
195

like the Native Affairs seem to enslave some people's attitudes even though they have no sound or rational basis for their continuance.

We pressed for the abolition of Pass Laws. We argued that they served no good purpose and protected neither the European public nor the African community. They operate and function as an instrument of oppression and repression of African people straining the relation between the police and the whites in general. They restricted the movement of the African from place to place, and, therefore, his bargaining power with his labour. The African, in pass bearing Provinces, may not remain for more than twelve days in the same area for purpose of seeking employment. If he remains he is liable to arrest subject to conviction with seven days or 10/- fine or more as the case may be. If he goes to gaol, he is stamped as a criminal as few prospective employers will believe his story that his gaol term was for contravention. He may be ordered to go to another area to seek employment. Having no money, he may decide to put into practice some of the lessons he learnt while in contact with real criminals in gaol or in cells before trial. He tries to "live on his wits" and may find this more profitable than honest work. The State law for "Natives Only" has made a criminal of him and he develops a sense of grievance and anti-State attitudes and becomes anti-social in outlook.

A pass bearing African is no employee in the terms of the Industrial Conciliation Act and as a result his trade Union cannot be registered. If he strikes, he can be prosecuted. He is being constantly harassed and embarassed by the police who may stop and ask him for his pass which he must have in his person at all times. Failure to produce the document there and then is a criminal offence for which he is arrested and charged before a magistrate even though he may have had his pass in a coat at home, or at his place of employment. Many Africans have been assaulted or even shot and wounded arising out of disputes and arrests for passes. These passes are demanded at the Railway station so that many Africans have been left by long distance trains only because one had forgotten a pass at home, while Europeans, Chinese, Indians and others are not called upon to produce such documents.

Arguments were advanced that the passes were necessary to prevent crimes committed by Africans, to protect Africans in their contracts with employers. We pointed out that criminals are always provided with passes so that they may meet the police without fear of suspicion. On the suggestion of identifying the African and protecting his contract of service, we argued that this, to us, indicates that either the European employers in the O.F.S. and the Transvaal are dishonest with regard to their contracts with Africans or we, the Africans of these provinces, are stupid, of inferior intelligence to Africans in the Cape or Natal where no contract of service - identity pass and special pass are necessary.

We illustrated that a Xosa can walk from Umzimkulu to Cape Town without being lost. An African in Natal or in the Cape requires a pass only on leaving or on entering these Provinces.

If the passes are of any value against crimes of honouring contracts of service or crimes in general, the Government in justification of the pass laws should first establish that there is more crime in the non-pass bearing provinces.

As for a single identification certificate euphoniously referred to as a pass-port, we replied that it was obsolete because it was recommended by the Interdepartmental Committee in 1920 as being suitable for that generation. This is another generation and progress has been made. So far as using this single certificate as a passport, the Africans, we declared, are not prepared to carry passports in their own home country while other South Africans do not carry such a passport.

We are prepared to carry our passports if and when we must travel abroad.

To us it seems, judging from the convictions under Pass Laws, 87,566 and 101,309 men in 1938 and 1939 respectively, that the pass laws are to be classed among the factories of crime among the many such factories created in South Africa by the Union Government 'Native Affairs.' The Pass Laws administration takes valuable time of both Police and Magistrates leading to mass arrests, mass trials and inevitable miscarriage of justice resulting in a contemptuous attitude on the part of the officers of Justice towards the African as a moral being and a feeling of despair on the part of the African to expect blind justice and fair play in the hands of the police and many magistrates in lower courts.

The exemption, so-called, we pointed out was no exemption at all; it was another form of special pass. The bearer of the special pass was subjected to the same indignities as those who carry contracts of service and other types of specials. He may be stopped anywhere and everywhere by any policeman even if it is merely to annoy him. They may and do demand it. If he does not have it on his person, he is subject to arrest and liable to a fine and/or imprisonment like any other African.

As an instrument of identification, the exemption is the most ridiculous and stupid document. It merely has one's name, no address and does not even identify the bearer from any one else.

To any fairminded and honest person of any race except as an instrument of exploitation, repression, and humiliation, and a source of revenue, the pass laws serve no good purpose either to European or African nor to employer or employee.

Much abuse has been perpetrated under the guise of enforcing the Pass Laws.

Congress stands for the total abolition of pass laws in all forms as a gesture towards regaining the confidence of the African in the justice of the whiteman towards him.

After all the arguments in favour of the Pass Laws had failed, the Deputy Prime Minister declared that the figures we gave haunted him more than any other argument and that he believed that the pass laws were the cause of more ill-feeling between European and Africans than anything else he knew of. He asked for suggestions for methods of abolition without arousing adverse European public opinion. He promised to write a memorandum on the Pass Laws for its consideration by General Smuts and the Cabinet.

We must from now on organize our people everywhere and educate them about the evils of this discriminating and humiliating legislation and fight for their abolition.

I am sure we can count upon the support of all sincere, honest and fairminded whites.

Document 27. Letter from Paul R. Mosaka, Newly-elected Member of the Natives' Representative Council, to Dr. A.B. Xuma, November 11, 1942

Stand 1515 Orlando Township,
JOHANNESBURG.
11th November, 1942.

Dr. A. B. Xuma, M.D.;
President African National Congress,
Toby Street,
Sophiatown,
JOHANNESBURG.

Dear Sir,
You will have received by now news of my success in the Native Representative Council. That success, though it is the cause for some jubilation, is certainly not the source for self-elatedness on my part. In seeking the "Honour" of the Native Representative Council I have sought to place myself at your service and at the service of the African people generally.

Unfortunately I have cause to think that during these elections, notwithstanding your promise to me, you have denied me the encouragement and support which had I received I would much have valued. There are no doubt personal and cogent reasons for your attitude towards me.

You as President of the African National Congress whose paramount interest is the welfare of the African people will no doubt realise that much as you wished otherwise, I have been elected to serve that same people and in order that I might be an instrument in your hands for the furtherance of the cause which is as much yours as mine. For that reason I should like to assure you of my willingness to receive your advice and assistance and indeed to act on the instructions of your Congress so that at all times I act as one who enjoys the confidence of his people and the backing of the one and only organisation that can serve and save the African people, the African National Congress.

You need no further assurance from me of my good-will towards you and of my readiness to place the interests of my people above matters of personal and selfish gain than this request for free and helpful cooperation.

.

With kind regards,
Yours sincerely,
Paul R. Mosaka

Document 28. Resolutions of the ANC Annual Conference, December 20-22, 1942

1/42 ATLANTIC CHARTER.

That this Congress gives the President General power to appoint a committee to go into the question of the Atlantic Charter and to draft the Bill of Rights to be presented to the Peace Conference at the end of the Present War.

2/42 PRESIDENTIAL ADDRESS.

That this most inspiring address delivered by the President General be printed in a pamphlet form by this house in order that it may be sold to all Africans.

3/42 CONDOLENCE GENERAL PIENAAR.

That this general annual conference of the African National Congress now assembled at Bloemfontein is shocked at the reported death of General Pienaar, one of the great and promising leaders of our soldiers and requests the Prime Minister to accept the sincere condolence and sorrow of the African people represented here. (Despatched by telegram.)

4/42 CONFIDENCE PRESIDENT GENERAL.

This thirtieth general annual conference of the African National Congress hereby notes with great pride the fact that Dr. A.B. Xuma, the President General, has achieved a unique success in the history of this National organisation by securing for the leadership of the Congress and the guidance of the African people the co-operation and the confidence of the leaders of all shades - distinguished University Graduates, and the most noted professional men among the African people today. This Conference sees in this achievement the opportunity to raise the influence and the power of the African National Congress and therefore the Conference hereby authorises the President General and his National Executive Committee to start a vigorous campaign of organising in the whole of South Africa a membership of one million Africans in Southern Africa.

5/42 NATIVES REPRESENTATION ACT 1936.

That this Conference of the African National Congress held at Bloemfontein in December 1942 appeals to the Government to so amend the Natives Representation Act of 1936 that the Communal system of voting be replaced by a system of individual voting and that the number of electoral areas be increased.

6/42 REPRESENTATION ON MUNICIPAL COUNCILS.

That this Congress urges the Union Government to put into immediate effect the expressed wish of Africans in favour of direct Representation on Municipal Councils.

7/42 WAR POLICY.

That this Congress requests the Government (1) to consider immediately the arming of the Non-European soldiers in order that they may play their rightful part in the defeat of Fascism and (11) to admit Non-Europeans into skilled industry in order that our South African Army may be adequately equipped. Congress re-affirms its previous resolution on the war issue which was to this effect.

8/42 BEER HALLS & POLICE RAIDS.

This Congress resolves that the Liquor Act be so amended as to abolish Municipal beer halls and police raids and to introduce home-brewing and to grant permits to those who want to obtain liquor.

9/42 SOLDIERS' DEPENDANTS' ALLOWANCES.

In view of the hardships experienced by soldiers' dependants in receiving their allowances, this conference urges the Government to instruct Commissioners to travel from place to place for the purpose of paying the said allowances. Alternatively that such allowances be posted directly to each and every such dependant. This resolution is to be recommended to the members of the Native Affairs Department immediately.

10/42 NATIVE EDUCATION.

That this Conference of the African National Congress requests the Government to finance Native Education on a per capita basis.

11/42 MIDDAY MEALS FOR SCHOOL CHILDREN.

That this conference of the African National Congress requests the Government to include African School Children in its recent midday meal scheme.

12/42 MINIMUM WAGE FOR UNSKILLED LABOURERS.

This conference views with grave concern the starvation wages recommended by the Wage Board for unskilled work in the 34 trades and industries affected on the Witwatersrand and in Pretoria; and requests the Hon. the Minister of Labour to have the recommendations altered in such a manner as would meet the requirements of the workers. Further, this conference supports fully the minimum wages of £2. per week for all unskilled labourers put forward by the Council of Non-European Trade Unions.

13/42 RAILWAY ACCOMMODATION.

That this Conference should make representations to the Minister of Railways regarding additional 1st and 2nd class accommodation especially at week ends and holidays and that platforms be so extended as to serve all passengers.

14/42 TRADING RIGHTS.

That this conference requests the Government to repeal that section of the Native Urban Areas Act which restricts the Trading Rights of Africans in Urban Areas.

15/42 PERMIT SYSTEM AND LODGERS TAX.

That the Administration be requested to abolish the Permit Systems in the locations as well as the Lodgers' Tax.

16/42 INKULULEKO.

This Conference views with serious concern the banning of the Inkululeko newspaper in Basutoland, Bechuanaland, and Swaziland and regards it as an infringement of the Freedom of the Press, and urges the High Commissioner to lift the ban immediately.

17/42 MANAGEMENT OF NATIVE SCHOOLS.

That the present system of managing African Primary Schools through Superintendants be abolished and be replaced by Committees of Management in which Africans are directly represented.

18/42 GOVERNMENT AND SCHOOL BUILDINGS.

That the Government should take responsibility for the building of schools for African children.

19/42 BOARD OF NATIVE EDUCATION.

That the time has come when the Board of Native Education should be constituted in such a way as to give the Africans direct representation of not less that 50%.

20/42 LAND TENURE IN URBAN AREAS.

That Conference requests Parliament to grant Africans freehold rights to land in Urban Areas.

21/42 SECRETARY OF TRADE AND INDUSTRY.

That in view of the growing importance of the Trading and Business movement among Africans, Congress should take steps to create within its Secretariat a Secretary for Trading and Business Activities.

22/42 NATIVE LAND AND TRUST ACT.

That the African National Congress requests the Government to amend the regulations under the Native Land and Trust Act of 1936 so as to make it possible for African tenants in released areas (i) to have a larger morgenage of land available for cultivation (ii) to be granted better grazing and other rights (iii) and to permit squatters on European farms to plough land on the "Ploughing-on-Shares" principle as was the case prior to the commencement of the Act.

23/42 ORGANISATION OF CONGRESS.

This Conference of the African National Congress, recognising that further progress in building the Congress into a powerful National Movement is gravely hampered by lack of full-time employees to attend to the organising work and the taking up of the burning issues of the people

(a) instructs Congress to open an office at its National Headquarters and emply one or more paid organisers without further delay;

(b) recommends to all Provincial Congresses to take similar steps.

(c) to take all steps to raise the necessary funds to give effect to this resolution.

24/42 SUSPENSION OF BETHANY AND RAMOKGOPA TEACHERS.

That this African National Congress in Convention at Bloemfontein views with alarm the growing autocratic manner in which the teachers in the Transvaal are being dealt with by the Transvaal Education Department in that they are being suspended for failure to collaborate with superintendants in their desire to retain superintendancy of African Schools such as Bethany and at Ramokgopa. This conference therefore requests the Transvaal Education Department to reinstate these teachers.

25/42 ALEXANDRA TOWNSHIP.

That this annual conference of the African National Congress held in December 1942 views with alarm and desires to place on record its emphatic protest against the proposed removal of the Alexandra Township.

This conference desires to endorse the recommendations of various commissions of Enquiry such as the Young Report, the Thornton Report, the Feetham Report, and the Native Affairs Commission Report which reported against the abolition of the Township and in favour of Government assistance of the inhabitants of the township to improve their social and health conditions.

The Conference desires to commend the Government Departments concerned for the steps recently taken to approach this problem through consultation with representatives of all interested parties, including representatives of the African people directly concerned.

26/42 NORTHFIELD COLLIERY.

In view of the disgraceful conditions under which the workers concerned were employed as disclosed by the evidence and by the remarks from the Bench, the African National Congress desires to appeal to the Minister of Justice to allow a review of the matter of the severe sentences imposed on the 42 Africans charged with public violence at the Northfields Colliery in Natal.

27/42   This Conference of the African National Congress views with alarm the growing strike wave among the African workers, which it declares to be due, above all, to the terribly low wages of these workers, especially in relation to the sharply rising living costs. Congress protests strongly against the repressive emergency regulations introduced by the Government, making strikes by African workers illegal and giving the workers no say in the appointment of an arbitrator to settle disputes. In order to meet the just demands of the workers and to avoid stoppages of work which are harmful to the Country's war effort, this conference calls upon the Government -

(a) to repeal these emergency regulations;

(b) to grant immediate and full recognition to African Trade Unions, such recognition to be under the Department of Labour and not under the Department of Native Affairs;

(c) to introduce by emergency regulations a minimum wage of not less than £ 2. per week for all unskilled workers.

28/42 CONGRESS ORGANISATION.

This Conference hereby authorises the President General to employ all the means in his power to carry into effect all the resolutions of this Conference as well as the suggestion which he brought forward in his Presidential address. The authority of this House includes the power to raise the initial fund necessary to begin the important work of organisation with the view of enrolling one million members of Congress in Southern Africa to be the new foundation of our greater Congress.

29/42 CONGRESS YOUTH LEAGUE.

That this Annual Conference of the African National Congress authorises the Executive to institute a Youth League of the African National Congress to include students at Fort Hare.

30/42 SECRECY AT NATIVE ELECTIONS.

That this Congress requests our Parliamentary Representatives to take up with the authorities the question of the procedure adopted by the Returning Officers in the 1942 elections under the Native Representation Act with a view to establishing the fact as to whether the provisions of the electoral Act of 1918 as amended relating to secrecy apply to the Native Elections.

Document 29a. Constitution of the ANC

1. *NAME:* The name of the organisation shall be the African National Congress.

2. *OBJECTS:* The aims of the Congress shall be:

(a) To protect and advance the interest of all Africans in all matters affecting them.
(b) To attain the freedom of the African People from all discriminatory laws whatsoever.
(c) To strive and work for the unity and co-operation of the African people in every possible way.
(d) To strive and to work for the full participation of the African in the Government of South Africa.

3. *MEMBERS:*

(a) *Individual Bodies:* Any person over 17 years of age who is willing to subscribe to the aims of Congress and to abide by its Constitution and rules may become an individual member upon application to the nearest Branch.
(b) *Affiliated Members:* Any organisation whose aims are in harmony with the aims of Congress may become an affiliated body upon application, in the case of a Provincial or local organisation, to the Provincial Committee and in the case of a National Organisation, to the Working Committee.

The Executive reserves the right to refuse an application without giving reasons.

4. *BRANCHES:*

(a) Branches may be formed with the approval of a Provincial Committee in any locality within its Province.
(b) A Branch shall consist of not less than 20 individual members.
(c) Each Branch shall hold an Annual General Meeting at which it shall elect a chairman, a secretary, treasurer, and not less than two committee members.

5. *PROVINCIAL CONFERENCE:*

(a) The Provincial Conference shall be the highest organ of Congress in each Province.
(b) An annual provincial conference shall be held in each of the provinces of the Union of South Africa. Special provincial conferences may be convened at such other time as the provincial committee may deem fit, and

shall be convened upon the requisition addressed to the Provincial Committee, of branches and/or affiliated organisations representing *at least one-quarter of the total number of delegates* entitled to be present at a Provincial Conference.

(c) Each branch shall be entitled to be represented at the provincial conference by one delegate for every 100 members or in the proportion laid down by the provincial conference from time to time.

(e) [sic] No branch or affiliated body shall be represented by more than 10 delegates at a provincial conference.

(f) The provincial conference in each province shall be responsible for the affairs of congress in that province subject only to the general supervision and control of the National Executive Committee and the Working Committee.

6. *PROVINCIAL COMMITTEE:*

(a) The annual provincial conference shall elect a provincial committee consisting of a president and 11 committee members of whom the president and not less than 5 committee members shall be resident within 50 miles of the Provincial headquarters designated from time to time by the provincial conference.

(b) The provincial committee shall elect a secretary and a treasurer from amongst its members resident as provided in the foregoing section.

(c) The provincial committee shall meet at least once in every 3 months and at such other times as it deems necessary. It shall be the executive body of the provincial conference and shall administer the affairs of Congress within the province between provincial conferences, and shall convene provincial conferences at the times provided herein.

(d) The provincial committee shall submit an annual report of the Congress organisation work and finances in the province to the provincial conference and the working committee not later than 6 weeks before the annual national conference. On failure on the part of any provincial committee to function in terms of this constitution, the working committee may convene a provincial conference to elect a new provincial committee and may form a Committee to carry on Congress work in the province during the interim period.

7. *NATIONAL CONFERENCE:*

(a) The National Conference shall be the supreme body of Congress and shall determine its general policy and programme.

(b) An annual national conference shall be held once a year at a time and place decided upon at the preceding annual national conference. Special national conferences may be convened at such other times as the national

Executive Committee may deem fit, and shall be convened upon requisition addressed to the working committee by two or more provincial conferences.
(c) The provisions of clauses 5 (c), (d) [sic] and (e) shall apply, mutatis mutandis, to the election of delegates to the National Conference.

8. *NATIONAL EXECUTIVE COMMITTEE:*

(a) Once every three years the national conference shall elect a national executive committee consisting of a National President, a National Secretary and a National Treasurer, and not less than 15 committee members.
(b) The N.E.C. shall meet on the day of its election and thereafter at least once in 6 months and at such other times as it may be convened by the Working Committee.
(c) The N.E.C. shall be responsible for the activities of Congress between National Conferences and shall supervise and review the work of the Working Committee.
(d) The N.E.C. shall submit to the annual national Conference full report of the work, organisation and finances of Congress during the preceding year which report shall be made available to provincial Committees, branches, affiliated members not later than one month before the date of the annual conference.
(e) Provincial Presidents shall be ex officio members of the National Executive.

9. *WORKING COMMITTEE:*

(a) At the meeting of the N.E.C. held on the day of its election the N.E.C. shall appoint a Working Committee of not less than 7 persons who shall be persons resident within 50 miles of the National headquarters designated by the National Conference from time to time.
(b) Members of the Working Committee shall be chosen in the first place from amongst members of the N.E.C. having the necessary residential qualification and in the event of there being fewer than 7 so qualified, the remaining members of the Working Committee shall be chosen from amongst Congress members in general who have the requisite residential qualifications.
(c) The National President shall ex officio be a member of the Working Committee. The President shall appoint an assistant National Secretary for the Working Committee.
(d) Between meetings of the N.E.C., the Working Committee shall enjoy the full Executive powers of the N.E.C. and shall carry into effect the policy and programme laid down by the National Conference, convene National Conferences and meetings of the N.E.C. as provided herein. It shall remain responsible to the National Executive Committee.

(e) The Working Committee shall meet once in every month and at such other times as it may deem necessary.

(f) The Working Committee shall place before every regular meeting of the N.E.C. a report of its activities and of the work, organisation and finances of Congress in general. The Working Committee shall take steps to publish a report of the proceedings of all National Conferences within three months after the termination of such conference.

10. *FINANCE:*

(a) Every individual member shall upon applying for membership and thereafter at the beginning of each year pay to the Branch concerned a subscription of 2/6d. There shall be no reduction in the subscription to be paid by members joining in the course of the year.

(b) Affiliated bodies shall upon application and thereafter at the beginning of each year pay to the Provincial Committee or the Working Committee, as the case may be, a sum representing one-fiftieth of the ordinary subscriptions or dues collected from its own membership in the preceding year.

(c) Affiliated bodies shall submit a constitution and an annual financial statement.

(d) Each branch shall pay to the provincial Executive Committee two-thirds of the subscription received by it and the Provincial Executive Committee shall pay to the Working Committee one-half of the income received by it.

(e) Funds of Congress shall be raised through membership fees, subscriptions, levies, donations and through functions and entertainments.

(f) All such funds shall be deposited at a recognised bank or post office savings bank immediately they are received at the Branch, Provincial or National Office.

(g) Branch Committees, Provincial Executive Committees and the Working Committees, shall keep full and proper records of all income and expenditure and shall present annual financial statements to the branch, provincial conference, and national Conference as the case may be. The Working Committee shall take steps to have a regular audit of its accounts and of the accounts of Provincial Committee, where the provincial Committee fails to do so.

11. *DISCIPLINE:* Every Committee of Congress shall have the power to take such disciplinary action as it may deem fit against any member within its jurisdiction who acts in breach of the Constitution or rules of Congress, violating its decisions or behaving in a way which is prejudicial to the interests of Congress or of the African people, provided that there shall be a right of appeal against

disciplinary action to the Provincial Conference and in the case of a decision of the Working Committee of the N.E.C. to the National Conference.

12. *RULES:*

(a) The N.E.C. shall have the power to frame rules or approve rules framed by the Working Committee not inconsistent with this constitution for regulating all matters connected with Congress.

(b) Each Provincial Conference shall have power to frame rules not inconsistent with this constitution for regulating the affairs of Congress within its own Province, which rules shall come into operation only with the previous sanction of the Working Committee.

13. *DECISIONS:* All decisions, save amendments to the constitution, taken by bodies or Congress, including the election of office-bearers and Committees shall be taken by majority vote.

14. *VACANCIES:*

(a) The office of a member of a Congress Committee shall be vacated by resignation, death, expulsion or removal as a disciplinary measure.

(b) Such vacancy shall be filled by co-option by the Committee.

15. *AMENDMENTS:* Amendments to this constitution may be made by two-thirds majority vote of the delegates present and voting at a National Conference provided that three month's notice of proposed amendments shall have been circulated prior to such National Conference, to the provincial affiliated bodies.

16. *GENERAL:* Congress shall have perpetual succession and the power, apart from its individual members, to acquire, hold and alienate property, enter into agreements and all things necessary to carry out its aims and objects.

(Sgd.)   A. B. XUMA
PRESIDENT GENERAL

(Sgd.)   JAMES A. CALATA
SECRETARY GENERAL

AFRICAN NATIONAL CONGRESS

BLOEMFONTEIN
16th December, 1943
ABX/ARM

Document 29b. *Africans' Claims in South Africa,* **Including "The Atlantic Charter from the Standpoint of Africans within the Union of South Africa" and "Bill of Rights," Adopted by the ANC Annual Conference**

PREFACE

In the following pages the reader will find what has been termed *"Bill of Rights"* and *"The Atlantic Charter from the African's Point of View."* This document was drawn up after due deliberations by a special committee whose names appear at the end of this booklet. Their findings were unanimously adopted by the Annual Conference of the African National Congress at Bloemfontein, on the 16th of December, 1943. We realise as anyone else the apparent inappropriativeness and vagueness of the expressions when adopted by us. We have, however, adapted them to our own conditions as they give us, the most dynamic way of directing the attention of our Government in the Union of South Africa, the European population of our country to the African position and status in this land of our birth—South Africa—because the Government and the European section alone have the absolute legislative and administrative power and authority over the non-Europeans. We know that the Prime Minister of the Union of South Africa and his delegation to the Peace Conference will represent the interests of the people of our country. We want the Government and the people of South Africa to know the full aspirations of the African peoples so that their point of view will also be presented at the Peace Conference. We want the Government of the United Nations to know and act in the light of our own interpretation of the "Atlantic Charter" to which they are signatories. This is our way of conveying to them our undisputed claim to full citizenship. We desire them to realise once and for all that a just and permanent peace will be possible only if the claims of all classes, colours and races for sharing and for full participation in the educational, political and economic activities are granted and recognised.

Already according to press reports there seem to be differences of opinion as to the applicability of the 'Atlantic Charter' as between the President of the United States of America and the Prime Minister of Great Britain. It would appear that President F. D. Roosevelt wanted the Atlantic Charter to apply to the whole world while the Prime Minister, Mr. Winston Churchill, understood it to be intended for the white people in the occupied countries in Europe.

In South Africa, Africans have no freedom of movement, no freedom of choice of employment, no right of choice of residence and no right of freedom to purchase land or fixed property from anyone and anywhere. Under the guise of segregation, they are subjected to serious educational, political and economic disabilities and discriminations which are the chief causes of their apparent slow progress.

We urge that if fascism and fascist tendencies are to be uprooted from the face of the earth, and to open the way for peace, prosperity and racial good-will, the 'Atlantic Charter' must apply to the whole British Empire, the United States of America and to all the nations of the world and their subject peoples. And we urge that South Africa as a prelude to her participation at the Peace Conference in the final destruction of Nazism and Fascism in Europe, must grant the just claims of her non-European peoples to freedom, democracy and human decency, as contained in the following document since charity must begin at home, and if to quote B.B.C. Radio News Reel: "We Fight for World Democracy."

The soldiers of all races Europeans, Americans, Asiatics and Africans have won their claim and the claims of their peoples to the four freedoms by having taken part in this war which can be converted into a war for human freedom if the settlement at the Peace Table is based on human justice, fairplay and equality for opportunity for all races, colours and classes.

We deliberately set up a committee composed exclusively of Africans in South Africa to deal with this matter so that they can declare without assistance or influence from others, their hopes and despairs. The document that follows is their deliberate and considered conclusion as well as their conviction. Others who believe in justice and fairplay for all human beings will support these rightful claims from Africans themselves.

The list of names of the members of the committee who produced this document tells a story for those who would understand. These fruits of their labours are a legacy, nay a heritage which they will leave behind for future generations to enjoy. For it, and to them, we are all forever indebted.

As African leaders we are not so foolish as to believe that because we have made these declarations that our government will grant us our claims for the mere asking. We realise that for the African this is only a beginning of a long struggle entailing great sacrifices of time, means and even life itself. To the African people the declaration is a challenge to organise and unite themselves under the mass liberation movement, the African National Congress. The struggle is on right now and it must be persistent and insistent. In a mass liberation movement there is no room for divisions or for personal ambitions. The goal is one, namely, freedom for all. It should be the central and only aim for [sic] objective of all true African nationals. Divisions and gratificational [sic] of personal ambitions under the circumstances will be a betrayal of this great cause.

On behalf of my Committee and the African National Congress I call upon chiefs, ministers of religion, teachers, professional men, men and women of all ranks and classes to organise our people, to close ranks and take their place in this mass liberation movement and struggle, expressed in this Bill of Citizenship Rights until freedom, right and justice are won for all races and colours to the honour and glory of the Union of South Africa whose ideals—freedom, democracy, Christianity and human decency cannot be attained until all races in South Africa participate in them.

I am confident that all men and women of goodwill of all races and nations will see the justice of our cause and stand with us and support us in our struggle.

If you ever feel discouraged in the struggle that must follow remember the wise and encouraging words of the Prime Minister, Field Marshal the Right Honourable J. C. Smuts who says: "Do not mind being called agitators. Let them call you any names they like, but get on with the job and see that matters that vitally require attention, Native health, Native food, the treatment of Native children and all those cognate questions that are basic to the welfare of South Africa are attended to."

A. B. XUMA,

President-General of the African National Congress
Secretary-Organiser Atlantic Charter
Committee, South Africa.

THE ATLANTIC CHARTER AND
THE AFRICANS.

1. The Atlantic Charter, agreed upon by the President of the United States and the Prime Minister of Great Britain in their historic meeting of August 14, 1941, and subsequently subscribed to by the other Allied Nations, has aroused widespread interest throughout the world. In all countries this summary of the war aims of the Allied Nations has aroused hopes and fired the imagination of all peoples in regard to the new world order adumbrated in its terms.

2. For us in South Africa particular significance attaches to this document because of its endorsement on more than one occasion by Field-Marshal Smuts, who has announced that the post war world will be based upon the principles enunciated in the Atlantic Charter. The Honourable Deneys Reitz, speaking on behalf of the Government, to the African people, when he opened the sixth session of the Natives Representative Council in December, 1942, indicated that the Freedoms vouchsafed to the peoples of the world in the Atlantic Charter were indicated for the African people as well.

3. In view of these pronouncements and the participation of Africans in the war effort of various Allied Nations, and to the fact that the Atlantic Charter has aroused the hopes and aspirations of Africans no less than other peoples, the President-General of the African National Council decided to convene a conference of leaders of African thought to discuss the problems of the Atlantic Charter in its relation to Africa in particular and the place of the African in postwar reconstruction. In other words, the terms of reference of the conference were to be:—

(a) To study and discuss the problems arising out of the Atlantic Charter in so far as they relate to Africa, and to formulate a comprehensive statement embodying an African Charter, and

(b) to draw up a Bill of Rights which Africans are demanding as essential to guarantee them a worthy place in the post war world.

4. The President-General accordingly invited various African leaders to become members of the Atlantic Charter Committee which would meet in Bloemfontein on December 13 and 14, 1943 to perform this important national duty, as he saw it. At the same time the President-General called upon those invited to submit memoranda on different aspects of this subject for the subsequent consideration of the whole committee on the dates indicated above.

5. The response to the President-General's invitation as indicated by the number of well prepared and thought provoking statements submitted from different parts of the country was proof that his action was timely and in line with the thinking of Africans on the vital subject of post war reconstruction.

6. The Committee met at Bloemfontein and deliberated on Monday and Tuesday, December 13 and 14, 1943. The Committee elected Mr. Z. K. Matthews as Chairman and Mr. L. T. Mtimkulu as Secretary, and a Sub-Committee consisting of Messrs. S. B. Ngcobo, M. L. Kabane and J. M. Nhlapo, with the chairman and the secretary as ex officio members, to draft the findings of the Atlantic Charter Committee. Throughout its deliberations the committee acted under the able guidance of the President-General, Dr. A. B. Xuma.

7. As already indicated above, the work of the committee fell into two parts, viz., (a) the consideration and interpretation of the Atlantic Charter, and (b) the formulation of a Bill of Rights. In dealing with the first part of its work the Committee discussed the articles of the Atlantic Charter one by one and made certain observations under each article.

8. In considering the Charter as a whole, the Committee was confronted with the difficulty of interpreting certain terms and expressions which are somewhat loosely and vaguely used in the Atlantic Charter. Among the terms or words to which this stricture applies are 'nations,' 'states,' 'peoples' and 'men.' Whatever meanings the authors had in mind with regard to these terms, the Committee decided that these terms, words or expressions are understood by us to include Africans and other Non-Europeans, because we are convinced that the groups to which we refer demand that they shall not be excluded from the rights and privileges which other groups hope to enjoy in the post-war world.

9. The Committee noted with satisfaction that the twenty-six other nations which subscribed to the Atlantic Charter on January 2, 1942 made it quite clear that the freedoms and liberties which this war is being fought to establish in countries which have been victims of aggression in this war, must be realised by the Allied Powers "in their own lands as well as other lands." This is the common cry of all subject races at the present time.

10. The articles of the Atlantic Charter and the observations of the Committee under each are as follows:—

THE ATLANTIC CHARTER

From the standpoint of Africans within the Union of South Africa.

First Point—No Aggrandisement.

"Their countries seek no aggrandisement, territorial or otherwise."
In this article there is very important assurance which is intended to exonerate the Allied Nations from the charge of having entered into this war for territorial gains or imperialistic reasons. With that understanding we support the principle contained in this article and hope that the rejection of aggrandisement in the War Aims of the Allied Nations is genuine and well meant. Having regard, however, to the possible danger of aggrandisement in the form of the extension of the Mandates System which was instituted after the last Great War, in spite of similar assurances in President Wilson's *FOURTEEN POINTS*, and also to the possibility of 'annexation' of certain African territories through their economic strangulation under veiled forms of assistance, we have deemed it necessary to make these three reservations.

Firstly, the status and independence of Abyssinia and her right to sovereignty must be safeguarded, and any political and economic assistance she may need must be freely negotiated by her and be in accordance with her freely expressed wishes. Abyssinia should be afforded a corridor into the sea for purposes of trade and direct communication with the outside world.

Secondly, we urge that as a fulfilment of the War Aim of the Allied Nations namely, to liberate territories and peoples under foreign domination, the former Italian colonies in Africa should be granted independence and their security provided for under the future system of World Security.

Thirdly, there are the anxieties of Africans with regard to British Protectorates in Southern Africa. It is well known that the Union of South Africa is negotiating for the incorporation of the three Protectorates of Bechuanaland, Basutoland and Swaziland and that incorporation might be pressed during or after this present war as part of South Africa's price for participation in this war. The schedule to the South Africa Act of 1909 did envisage the transfer, under certain conditions, of the territories to the Union of South Africa, but Africans were not contracting parties to these arrangements and they do not regard the provisions of the schedule as morally and politically binding on them. They would deprecate any action on the part of Great Britain which would bring about the extension of European political control at the expense of their vital interests. Africans, therefore, are definitely opposed to the transfer of the Protectorates to the South African State.

Second Point—No Territorial Changes.

"They desire to see no territorial changes that do not accord with the freely expressed wishes of the peoples concerned."

This statement is intended to refer to territorial changes which have been brought about in Europe by military aggression. It is clear, however, that territorial changes are also being discussed in regard to other parts of the world. We are mainly concerned with such changes in so far as they relate to the African continent, and in this connection mention has to be made to the suggested territorial changes in regard to West Africa, East Africa and Southern Africa under a system of regional regrouping as outlined in the recent speeches and writings of Field Marshal Smuts.

We hope that the mistakes of the past whereby African peoples and their lands were treated as pawns in the political game of European nations will not be repeated, and we urge that before such changes are effected there must be effective consultation and that the suggested changes must be in accord with the freely expressed wishes of the indigenous inhabitants. Further, where territorial changes have taken place in the past and have not resulted in the political and other advancement of the Africans living in those territories or colonies it would be a mistake to continue to maintain the *status quo* after the war. The objective of promoting self government for colonial peoples must be actively pursued by powers having such lands under their administrative control, and this objective should also be a matter of international concern more than has been the case in the past.

Third Point—The Right to Choose the Form of Government.

"They respect the right of all peoples to choose the form of government under which they will live; and they wish to see sovereign rights and self government restored to those who have been forcibly deprived of them."

The principle of Self Determination made famous by President Wilson in his *FOURTEEN POINTS* on behalf of small nations has been reaffirmed by this article of the charter. This principle of self determination necessarily raises not only issues relating to the independent existence of small nations besides their more powerful neighbours but those also concerning the political rights and status of minorities and of Africans now held under European tutelage.

In the African continent in particular, European aggression and conquest has resulted in the establishment of Alien governments which, however beneficent they might be in intention or in fact, are not accountable to the indigenous inhabitants. Africans are still very conscious of the loss of their independence, freedom and the right of choosing the form of government under which they will live. It is the inalienable right of all peoples to choose the form of government under which they will live and therefore Africans welcome the belated recognition of this right by the Allied Nations.

We believe that the acid test of this third article of the charter is its application to the African continent. In certain parts of Africa it should be possible to

214

accord Africans sovereign rights and to establish administrations of their own choosing. But in other parts of Africa where there are the peculiar circumstances of a politically entrenched European minority ruling a majority European population the demands of the Africans for full citizenship rights and direct participation in all the councils of the state should be recognised. *This is most urgent in the Union of South Africa.*

Fourth Point—The Open Door Policy in Trade and
Raw Materials.

"They will endeavour, with due regard for their existing obligations, to further the enjoyment of all states, great and small, victor or vanquished, of access, on equal terms, to the trade and to the raw materials of the world which are needed for their economic prosperity."

There is envisaged by this article an Open Door Policy in regard to trade and the distribution of the world's resources. Africa has figured prominently in the discussions on the better distribution of the world resources and of free international trade because of her rich raw materials most of which have not as yet been fully tapped. The exploitation that is suggested by the above article, judging by past experiences and present economic evils, raises in our minds considerable misgivings as likely to bring about a continuation of the exploitation of African resources to the detriment of her indigenous inhabitants and the enrichment of foreigners.

We are, however, in agreement with the necessity for the technical and economic utilisation of a country's resources with due regard for the human welfare and the economic improvement of the indigenous inhabitants. The primary obligation of any government is to promote the economic advancement of the peoples under its charge and any obligation, agreement, contract or treaty in conflict with this primary obligation should not be countenanced.

In our view it is essential that any economic assistance that might be rendered to weak and insufficiently developed African States should be of such a nature as will really promote their economic progress.

Fifth Point—Economic Collaboration and Improved
Labour Standards.

"They desire to bring about the fullest collaboration between all nations on the economic field with the object of securing for all improved labour standards, economic advancement and Social Security."

This article of the charter has reference to the International Labour Office as the machinery by which nations shall collaborate in economic affairs. The Governments of African states have fully participated in the deliberations and

215

exchange of ideas in regard to the promotion of improved living standards and industrial peace. For this reason Africans are vitally interested in the decisions and conventions of the International Labour Office.

But it is regrettable that conventions dealing with the welfare of African labour — Forced Labour, Migrant or Recruited Labour, Health and Housing, Wage Rates — that have been drawn up at Geneva and accepted by the majority of civilised states have, for selfish reasons, been either rejected or half-heartedly applied by African governments whose protestations at being civilised have been loudest. Thus Africa has not to any large extent felt the beneficent influence of the International Labour Organisation.

Hitherto the International Labour Organisation has been representative mainly of the interests of Governments and the capitalist class. We claim that collaboration between all nations in the economic field must include consideration of the interest of labour as well as of capital, and that all workers, including African workers, must be fully and directly represented in this collaboration. In order to make participation by the workers effective it is essential that their right to collective bargaining should be legally recognised and guaranteed.

We shall understand, 'improved labour standards,' 'economic advancement' and 'social security' as referred to in this article to mean the following:— (a) the removal of the Colour Bar; (b) training in skilled occupations; (c) remuneration according to skill; (d) a living wage and all other workers' benefits; (e) proper and adequate housing for all races and colours.''

The policy of economic collaboration is probably more applicable to economic relations between sovereign states rather than to relations with weak and insufficiently developed states or territories. In our view it is essential that any economic assistance that might be rendered to weak and insufficiently developed African territories should be of such a nature as will really promote their economic improvement and not pauperise them.

The Sixth Point— The Destruction of Nazi Tyranny.

"After the final destruction of the Nazi tyranny, they hope to see established a peace which will afford to all nations the means of dwelling in safety within their own boundaries, and which will afford assurance that all men in all lands may live out their lives in freedom from fear and want."

Africans are in full agreement with the war aim of destroying Nazi tyranny, but they desire to see all forms of racial domination in all lands, including the Allied countries, completely destroyed. Only in this way, they firmly believe, shall there be established peace which will afford to all peoples and races the means of dwelling in safety within their own boundaries, and which will afford the assurance that all men in all lands shall live out their lives in freedom from fear, want and oppression.

216

The Seventh Point—The Freedom of the Seas.

"Such a peace should enable all men to traverse the high seas and oceans without hindrance."

We agree with the principle of the freedom of the seas.

Eighth Point—The Abandonment of the Use of Force

"They believe that all the nations of the world, for realistic as well as spiritual reasons, must come to the abandonment of the use of force. Since no further peace can be maintained if land, sea or air armaments continue to be employed by nations which threaten or may threaten aggression outside of their frontiers, they believe, pending the establishment of a wider and permanent system of general security, that the disarmament of such nations is essential...They will likewise aid and encourage all other practical measures which will lighten for peace-loving peoples the crushing burden of armaments."

We are in agreement in principle with the idea of the abandoning of the use of force for the settlement of international disputes, but we do not agree with the idea envisaged in this article of the character concerning the armament of some nations and the disarmament of other nations as this policy is provocative of future wars. As a preliminary, steps must be taken to nationalise the armament industry.

While recognising the necessity for the use of force within a country as part of its policing machinery, we must nevertheless deplore the fact that force, especially in South Africa, is frequently resorted to as a method of suppressing the legitimate ventilation of their grievances by oppressed, unarmed and disarmed sections of the population.

BILL OF RIGHTS.

Full Citizenship Rights and Demands

We, the African people in the Union of South Africa, urgently demand the granting of full citizenship rights such as are enjoyed by all Europeans in South Africa. We demand:—

1. Abolition of political discrimination based on race, such as the Cape "Native" franchise and the Native Representative Council under Representation of Natives Act, and the extension to all adults, regardless of race, of the right to vote and be elected to parliament, provincial councils and other representative institutions.

217

2. The right to equal justice in courts of law, including nomination to juries and appointment as judges, magistrates, and other court officials.
3. Freedom of residence and the repeal of laws such as the Natives (Urban Areas) Act, Native Land Act and the Natives Law Amendment Act that restrict this freedom.
4. Freedom of movement, and the repeal of the pass laws, Natives Urban Areas Act, Natives Laws Amendment Act and similar legislation.
6. [sic] Right of freedom of the press.
7. Recognition of the sanctity or inviolability of the home as a right of every family, and the prohibition of police raids on citizens in their homes for tax or liquor or other purposes.
8. The right to own, buy, hire or lease and occupy land and all other forms of immovable as well as movable property, and the repeal of restrictions on this right in the Native Land Act, the Native Trust and Land Act, the Natives (Urban Areas) Act and the Natives Laws Amendment Act.
9. The right to engage in all forms of lawful occupations, trades and professions, on the same terms and conditions as members of other sections of the population.
10. The right to be appointed to and hold office in the civil service and in all branches of public employment on the same terms and conditions as Europeans.
11. The right of every child to free and compulsory education and of admission to technical schools, universities, and other institutions of higher education.
12. Equality of treatment with any other section of the population in the State social services, and the inclusion on an equal basis with Europeans in any scheme of Social Security.

Land.

We demand the right to an equal share in all the material resources of the country, and we urge:
1. That the present allocation of 12½% of the surface area to 7,000,000 Africans as against 87¼% to about 2,000,000 Europeans is unjust and contrary to the interest of South Africa, and therefore demand a fair redistribution of the land as a prerequisite for a just settlement of the land problem.
2. That the right to own, buy, hire or lease and occupy land individually or collectively, both in rural and in urban areas is a fundamental right of citizenship, and therefore demand the repeal of the Native Land Act, the Native Trust and Land Act, the Natives Laws Amendment Act, and the Natives (Urban Areas) Act in so far as these laws abrogate that right.

3. That African farmers require no less assistance from the State than that which is provided to European farmers, and therefore demand the same Land Bank facilities, State subsidies, and other privileges as are enjoyed by Europeans.

Industry and Labour.

(1) We demand for the Africans—

    (1) equal opportunity to engage in any occupation, trade or industry. In order that this objective might be realised to the fullest extent, facilities must be provided for technical and university education of Africans so as to enable them to enter skilled, semi-skilled occupations, professions, government service and other spheres of employment;

    (2) equal pay for equal work, as well as equal opportunity for all work and for the unskilled workers in both rural and urban areas such minimum wage as shall enable the workers to live in health, happiness, decency and comfort;

    (3) the removal of the Colour Bar in industry, and other occupations;

    (4) the statutory recognition of the right of the African worker to collective bargaining under the Industrial Conciliation Act.

    (5) that the African worker shall be insured against sickness, unemployment, accidents, old age and for all other physical disabilities arising from the nature of their work; the contributions to such insurance should be borne entirely by the government and the employers;

    (6) the extension of all industrial welfare legislation to Africans engaged in Agriculture, Domestic Service and in Public institution or bodies.

Commerce.

(1) We protest very strongly against all practices that impede the obtaining of trading licences by Africans in urban and rural areas, and we equally condemn the confinement of African economic enterprise to segregated areas and localities.

(2) We demand the recognition of the right of the Africans to freedom of trading.

Education.

(1) The education of the African is a matter of national importance requiring state effort for its proper realisation. The magnitude of the task places it beyond the limits of the resources of the missionary or private endeavour. The right of the African child to education, like children

219

of other sections, must be recognised as a State duty and responsibility. We, therefore, demand that—

(a) the state must provide full facilities for all types of education for African children.

(b) Education of the African must be financed from General Revenue on a per caput basis.

(c) The state must provide enough properly built and equipped schools for all African children of school-going age and institute free compulsory primary education.

(d) The state must provide adequate facilities for Secondary, professional, technical and university education.

(2) We reject the conception that there is any need of a special type of education for Africans as such, and therefore we demand that the African must be given the type of education which will enable him to meet on equal terms with other peoples the conditions of the modern world.

(3) We demand equal pay for equal educational qualifications and equal grade of work for all teachers irrespective of their race or colour. We also urge that pensions, conditions of service, and other privileges which are enjoyed by European teachers should be extended to African teachers on equal terms.

(4) We claim that the direction of the educational system of the African must fall more and more largely into the hands of the Africans themselves, and therefore we demand increased and direct representation in all bodies such as Education Advisory Boards, School Committees, Governing Councils, etc., which are responsible for the management and the shaping of policy in African schools, Institutions and Colleges and/or adequate representation in all bodies moulding and directing the country's educational policy.

Public Health and Medical Services.

(1) We regard it as the duty of the state to provide adequate medical and health facilities for the entire population of the country. We deplore and deprecate the fact that the state has not carried out its duty to the African in this regard, and has left this important duty to philanthropic and voluntary agencies. As a result of this gross neglect the general health of the entire African population has deteriorated to an alarming extent. We consider that the factors which contribute to this state of affairs are these:—

(a) the low economic position of the African which is responsible for the present gross malnutrition, general overcrowding, higher mortality and morbidity rates;

(b) the shortage of land resulting in the congestion in the reserves and in consequence the bad state of the African's health and the deterioration of his physique;

220

(c) the slum conditions in the urban areas;

(d) neglect of the health and the general education of the Africans;

(e) neglect of the provision of water supplies, proper sanitary and other conveniences in areas occupied by Africans both in urban and rural areas.

2. To remedy this state of affairs we urge and demand—

(a) a substantial and immediate improvement in the economic position of the African;

(b) a drastic overhauling and reorganisation of the health services of the country with due emphasis on preventive medicine with all that implies in modern public health sense.

3. We strongly urge the adoption of the following measures to meet the health needs of the African population.—

(a) the establishment of free medical and health services for all sections of the population;

(b) the establishment of a system of *School Medical Service* with a full staff of medical practitioners, nurses and other health visitors;

(c) increased hospital and clinic facilities both in the rural and in urban areas;

(d) increased facilities for the training of African doctors, dentists, nurses, sanitary inspectors, health visitors, etc;

(e) A co-ordinated control finance of health services for the whole Union;

(f) the creation of a proper system of vital statistics for the whole population including Africans;

(g) the appointment of District surgeons in rural areas with a large African population.

Discriminatory Legislation.

1. We, the African people, regard as fundamental to the establishment of a new order in South Africa the abolition of all enactments which discriminate against the African on grounds of race and colour. We condemn and reject the policy of segregation in all aspects of our national life in as much as this policy is designed to keep the African in a state of perpetual tutelage and militates against his normal development.

2 . We protest strongly against discourteous harsh and inconsiderate treatment meted out to Africans by officials in all state and other public offices and institutions. Such obnoxious practices are irreconcilable with Christian, democratic and civilised standards and are contrary to human decency.

We, therefore, demand—

(a) the repeal of all colour-bar and/or discriminatory clauses in the Union's Constitution, that is the South Africa 1909 Act;

(b) the repeal of the Representation of Natives Act 1936;

(c) the repeal of the Natives' Land Act 1913 and the Natives Land Amendment and Trust Act 1936;

(d) the repeal of the Pass Laws, Natives Urban Areas Acts as amended, the Natives Administration Act 1927;

(e) Repeal of the "Colour Bar" Act or Mines and Works Act 1926, Natives Service Contract Act, Masters and Servants Act, the Natives Labour Regulation Act and the amendment of all discriminatory and disabling clauses against African workers contained in the Industrial Conciliation Act.

In short, we demand the repeal of any and all laws as well as the abandonment of any policy and all practices that discriminate against the African in any way whatsoever on the basis of race, creed or colour in the Union of South Africa.

LIST OF MEMBERS OF THE COMMITTEE.

(1) Mr. R. G. Baloyi, Treasurer-General, African National Congress.

(2) Dr. R. T. Bokwe M.B., Ch.B., Medical Practitioner, Executive Member A.N.C., Additional District Surgeon, Middledrift.

(3) Rev. James Calata, Priest, Secretary-General, African National Congress.

(4) Mr. R. H. Godlo, Member of Native Representative Council. President Location Advisory Board, Executive Member A.N.C.

(5) Mr. M. L. Kabane, B.A., Teacher, President O.F.S. African Teachers' Association.

(6) Mr. Moses Kotane, Secretary S.A. Communist Party, Member of the African National Congress.

(7) Mr. S. Mac. Lepolisa, Trader, Organiser O.F.S. African National Congress, Deputy Speaker, A.N.C.

(8) Rev. Z. Mahabane, Minister, Chaplain, A.N.C.

(9) Mr. G. Makabeni, Trade Unionist, President Council of non-European Trade Unions, Johannesburg.

(10) Mr. T. M. Mapikela, Honorary Life Speaker, A.N.C., Executive member of African National Congress.

(11) Mr. Z.K. Matthews, M. A., LL.B., Lecturer, Fort Hare College, member of the Representative Council, Executive member A.N.C.

(12) Mr. C. Mbata, B.A., Teacher, Chairman African Study Circle, Johannesburg.

(13) Mr. G. A. Mbeki, B.A., B.Com., Trade Secretary, Federation of Organised Bodies, Transkei.

(14) Mr. M. T. Moerane, B.A., Secretary, Natal Bantu Teachers' Association.

(15) Mr. E. T. Mofutsanyane, member National Executive African National Congress.

(16) Dr. S. M. Molema, M.B., Ch.B., Medical Practitioner, Executive member of the African National Congress.

(17) Dr. J. S. Moroka, M.B., Ch.B., Member of the Native Representative Council, Treasurer All African Convention.

(18) Rev. Mpitso, Mendi Memorial Fund, Secretary-Organiser African Ministers Association, Executive Member A.N.C.

(19) Rev. Abner Mtimkulu, Minister, Acting-President, Natal A.N. Congress.

(20) Mr. Don. Mtimkulu, M.A., President, African Teachers' Federation.

(21) Mr. Leo. Mtimkulu, Attorney.

(22) Mr. J. M. Nhlapo, B.A., Wilberforce Institution, Executive member, A.N.C.

(23) Mr. Selby Ngcobo, B.A., B.Econ., Principal Loram Secondary School.

(24) Dr. I. P. Ka Seme, B.A., LL.D., Attorney at Law, Congress National Executive.

(25) Dr. R. Setlogelo, M.B., Ch.B., Medical Practitioner.

(26) Mr. R. V. Selope-Thema, Editor, *Bantu World*, Member Native Representative Council, Speaker African National Congress.

(27) Mr. B. B. Xiniwe, Member Native Representative Council.

(28) Dr. A. B. Xuma, M.D., B. Sc. (U.S.A.), L.R.C.P., L.R.C.S. (Edin.), L.R.F.P. & S. (Glas), D.P.H. (Lond.), Medical Practitioner, Medical Officer of Health Alexandra Health Committee, Physician-in-Charge Cragman Community, Clinic, Evaton.

Document 30. "Africans and San Francisco." Statement by Dr. A.B. Xuma, May 8, 1945

Many people have written me and others have asked me personally what part the African National Congress is taking to bring to the attention of Allied Nations and [the] outside world the back-breaking and hope-destroying restrictions and disabilities of the Africans. Many are just now desperately catching at every straw that something must be done. There is a scramble for all sorts of makeshift activities for celebrating V Day. It has just dawned upon them that the order to cease fire in Europe may be given by Marshall Stalin and General Eisenhower any day, any hour and any minute now [document revised in ink to read: "cease fire in Europe has been given now"].

The African National Congress, your leaders, who believe in method and planning instead of patchwork grabbing at every straw have long anticipated all these events. They have not been caught napping. As far back as December 1943 they prepared and submitted a document, *"The African Claims"* which was adopted at the national conference.

This document was delivered to the Prime Minister, General Smuts, whom we know to be the Constitutional leader of the South African delegation to any Peace Conference as things are at present. It was made clear to him in a covering letter that these were the claims of the African people and that they were an essential and honest basis for any just and permanent peace.

These "African Claims" deal with Land, Labour, Education, Political Status and other problems of the status of the African.

In order to know the truth and be intelligent about the Congress demands on behalf of our people order the booklet "African Claims" 1/3 post free.

Some dishonest and unthinking people may endeavour to mislead you that this document was drawn up by your leaders without the masses. Tell them that in every part of the world the leaders and representatives of the people and not the mob think and plan for them. General Smuts alone will commit the whole of South Africa, black and white, in San Francisco. Dr. Soong will speak for the 400 millions Chinese, Mr. Anthony Eden for Great Britain and the Empire, Mr. Edward Stetinius for 130 millions in America while Mr. Molotov stands for nearly 200 million Russians.

Consequently in ordered world and interracial affairs Africans must depend and place their full confidence upon their true leaders to champion their cause and protect their interests. In order to futher allay your anxiety I wish to state that besides handing over the African Claims to the Prime Minister we have sent that document and another entitled "San Francisco and the Africans" which appeared in the Democrat 5th May, 1945 to our overseas connections, England, America and other countries. Still further, we want you to realize that the San Francisco Conference is not the last word. It is only one of the necessary but important steps toward the final Peace Conference. In other words, there is still opportunity to continue pressing your claims for full freedom as human beings.

Demonstrations on Victory Day must be merely a stage in this fight for freedom. The struggle must be continued, intensified until the peace is won including full and human benefits for the African soldiers, ex-soldiers and their families.

The battle for the full freedom, for the winning of the peace calls for every African man, woman and child to join the ranks of the African National Congress and take part in this noble cause.

Yours for freedom for all,
A.B. Xuma
President-General, A.N.C.

THE FAILURE OF THE NATIVES' REPRESENTATIVE COUNCIL, 1946-1947

Document 31. *Reasons Why the Native Representative Council in the Union of South Africa Adjourned* [*on August 14, 1946*]. **Pamphlet by Professor Z. K. Matthews, published in November 1946**

The Natives Representative Council was established in 1937 in terms of the Representation of Natives Act 12 of 1936. That Act formed part of the Bills which the late General Hertzog had placed before Parliament in an attempt to arrive at what he considered might be a comprehensive solution of the Native problem. In dealing with the problem of the political representation of Africans in the Union, the Act provided for the establishment of a Council consisting of partly nominated and partly elected African members whose function would be to advise the Government on legislation and other matters affecting African welfare.

Since 1937 the Council has met regularly once or twice a year. Occasionally special sessions have been held to deal with urgent legislation which was not ready for presentation to the Council at its ordinary session or which, one or other Minister had introduced into Parliament without previous consultation with the Council as required by law.

At first high hopes were entertained in certain quarters that the Council would develop into an important part of our constitutional machinery for the Government of the Union and would give Africans a real share in shaping their own destiny in the land of their birth. Admittedly these high hopes were not shared by the African people themselves who strenuously opposed the Hertzog Bills from the time when they were adumbrated by the General in his famous Smithfield speech in 1925 until they reached the Statute Book in 1936. But that the African also surmised that the Council might have its uses as a platform for the education of the Government and the European public on their legitimate demands is proved by the fact that at one of the largest African gatherings held at that time under the auspices of the All African Convention a proposal to boycott the Council was defeated and a decision taken to give the Council a trial.

ABLEST MEN ELECTED

At two elections the African people have elected to the Council some of their ablest men among both chiefs and commoners.

Year after year since 1937 the councillors have submitted for the consideration of the Government resolutions on various aspects of African welfare, and have discussed these in debates which not infrequently have been of a very high order. In select committees appointed in Council they have made detailed recommendations on draft legislation referred to the Council by the Government or by the Provincial Councils. They have prepared reports on such aspects of Native administration as the system of political representation for Africans provided for in Act 12 of 1936, the policy embodied in our laws relating to Natives in urban areas and the system for the administration of Native Affairs provided for in the Native Administration Act for 1927. They have asked Parliament to legislate on such matters as the recognition and registration of African trade unions, the proper financing and control of Native Education, etc. They

225

have given evidence on behalf of the African people before important Government commissions appointed to investigate and report upon various aspects of African life in the Union.

The question naturally arises as to what were the reasons which led the members of the Council to take the drastic step of adjourning the Council indefinitely when it is apparently engaged on such important work. What is the meaning which must be attached to this action which is unprecedented in the history of the public bodies such as local councils, general councils, Native advisory boards, which have been established in order to give Africans a voice in the affairs of their country?

This deterioration in the relations between the Government and the Council may be attributed to a variety of factors of which only a few can be mentioned here.

OPTIMISTIC HOPE

When the Council was first established Field-Marshal Smuts himself expressed the hope that it might develop into a "Native Parliament." That was of course an over-optimistic estimate of the potentialities of this body for it would be impossible to have two parliaments in one country, but what Field-Marshal Smuts probably had in mind was that with the passage of time this advisory body would, as far as matters affecting African welfare is concerned, be accorded a weight of authority and responsibility second only to that of the supreme legislature. This obviously implied at the very least that no important decision, legislative or otherwise, affecting African welfare directly or indirectly would be taken either by Parliament or by a Provincial Council without prior consultation with the Council, and that the views of the Council, when obtained would be given serious consideration by those in whom ultimate responsibility for action was vested. A perusal of the section of the Natives Representation Act defining the functions and powers of the Council will show that the foregoing is no unwarranted estimate of what the African people were led to expect. It must be remembered that the Council was put forward by the European as a substitute for Parliamentary representation for the African, as an institution which would provide adequate machinery for giving effect to the equitable principle of consulting the African regarding legislative measures concerning his welfare—a principle which had been given statutory form as far back as 1920 in the Native Affairs Act of that year. In local matters in Native areas the principle of consultation had found expression in the extention of the local Council system and in urban areas in the system of Native Advisory Boards.

ACID TEST

The Natives Representative Council purported to be a body which would on the higher level of policy and on a Union-wide basis do for the African population as a whole what these other organs of government did in the narrower

226

sphere of purely local matters. This was to be the acid test of the policy of segregation to which European South Africa paid so much lip service. One would have thought that in the circumstances this product of Union political philosophy would be accorded by the Government such respect that its prestige would have been enhanced and the validity of the Union's political creed demonstrated to those who from the outset had no faith in it as a solution of our political problems.

How has the Government treated this product of her political genius. In the first place, although the Council is a body expected from the nature of things to consider and report upon matters of policy in Native Affairs, the persons responsible for laying down policy in this country have not considered it part of their duty to attend its sessions. Field-Marshal Smuts himself has only once deigned to appear before the Council. That was at its first meeting in 1937. The Minister of Native Affairs makes occasional appearances to open a session and to give formal address to which, as the members of the Council have been warned by a senior official of the Native Affairs Department, they are not expected to reply unless such a reply is couched in flattering terms of gratitude more suited to a primitive despot than to a Minister in a democratic State addressing the elected representatives of the people.

COUNCIL IGNORED

This conception is apparently based on the view that the Minister of Native Affairs is the Supreme Chief of the Natives. The Ministers of other Departments of State, although their departments touch African welfare at so many points —Labour, Justice, Social Welfare, Education, etc.—seem completely unaware of its existence. As for the ordinary Members of Parliament—the greatest protagonists of segregation—unless they happen to be members of the Native Affairs Commission, ignore this institution of their creation completely. The result of this is that the Council has developed into a meeting with senior officials of the Native Affairs Department who not unnaturally are beginning to regard the Council as part of the set-up of their Department and the members as Government servants like themselves. Year after year they have to listen to comments, caustic and otherwise, on matters of Union Native policy for which they are not ultimately responsible. They can make no reply on points raised except to defend or attempt to justify the legislative and administrative measures which have been entrusted to them by higher authority.

Not only do the Ministers and Members of Parliament not attend meetings of the Council, but the verbatim reports of the proceedings of the Council are not tabled in Parliament. By law the Minister of Native Affairs is required to table a report of the proceedings of the Council. What he does is to table the resolutions of the Council but not the debates on the resolutions which alone can give something approaching a true reflection of the views of the Council concerning its resolutions. A record is, of course, kept of the debates

227

in the Council, but this verbatim report is a rare document which is cyclostyled and published in a very clumsy form. No Afrikaans translation of it is provided, in spite of Section 137 of the South Africa Act. This reduces the activities of the Council to a kind of hole-in-the-corner business for information about which the public has to depend upon the scanty reports of a not too sympathetic Press.

URBAN AREAS

But even more serious than this is the fact that the Government has not shown sufficient evidence, in the opinion of the Council, of a desire to take its advice seriously when obtained, or of readiness to seek that advice on matters affecting African welfare. Bills affecting the African population directly or indirectly are introduced into Parliament without previous reference to the Council for consideration and report as required by law. A recent example was the Native Urban Areas Consolidation Act of 1945. There is probably no law which affects the interests of Africans as much as this law relating to Natives in urban areas, but the Minister refused to refer this Act to the Council on the ground that it was merely a consolidating measure which did not bring about any fundamental changes in our urban Native policy! Another example was the Financial Relations Extension Act of 1945 under which the burden of taxation on Africans was extended by empowering Provincial Councils to impose a hospital tax on all Natives liable for poll tax and a further tax on the incomes of Natives liable to income tax. It was only after this Bill had reached Parliament that it suddenly dawned on the Government that its provisions were likely to affect the African population. The Council was therefore hurriedly summoned to Pretoria to give its views on the matter on a Friday, to be taken to Cape Town by an emissary who was expected to reach that place on Monday.

Furthermore, the Council, as it is empowered to do by law, has asked the Government to introduce into Parliament legislative measures dealing with matters of great importance to the African people. On some of these matters promises have been made that something would be done, but these promises remain largely unfulfilled.

LEGISLATION REQUESTED

Thus the Council has asked for legislation according recognition to African trade unions in order to bring African workers within the scope of existing legislative machinery for the pacific and orderly settlement of industrial disputes between them and their employers. Action on this matter was promised years ago, but year after year the Government's proposals in this regard have failed to materialise, while industrial disputes between African workers and their employers have been on the increase and have culminated in the recent tragedy on the gold mines.

Pleas have been made for a revision of our system of Native taxation so that the principle underlying the system should be progressive rather than regressive, as it is at present, and in order that the methods of collecting this tax might be improved so as to reduce the number of Africans annually sent to gaol for failure to pay tax or failure to produce their tax receipts on demand. Far from heeding the advice of the Council the Government, as already indicated, has tacked on to the poll tax a hospital tax based on the same principle and to be collected in the same way.

The Council has advised the Government that the system of political representation for Africans provided for under Act 12 of 1936 is full of glaring anomalies which ought to be removed if the system is to fulfill even the limited objectives which the legislature had in mind when the Act was passed. The Council was led to believe that its representations had got the ear of the Government because a Recess Committee of the Council was appointed to consider the whole scheme and to make recommendations for its improvement. These recommendations were referred to Native local councils, general councils and advisory boards throughout the country. It looked as if something was certainly going to be done about the matter when the item "Amendment of the Native Representation Act" appeared on the agenda of one of the sessions of the Council. At that stage instructions were given for the withdrawal of the item from the agenda, and there as far as we know the matter rests.

REPORT DISCUSSED

Another piece of legislation on which a select committee of the Council was appointed was the Native Administration Act which was passed as far back as 1927 and which in the view of the Council embodies an attitude towards Native Administration which is in need of revision in order to bring into line with the facts of modern African social life. The committee's report was discussed and adopted by the full Council and referred to the Government. No action has been taken on the matter.

The council has submitted to the Government a closely reasoned memorandum calling for a revision of our urban Native policy in the light of industrial and other developments which have taken place since the original Act was passed in 1923. Admittedly in this connection the Government has recently appointed a commission—the Fagan commission—to investigate and report upon our laws relating to Natives in or near urban areas. Would it not have been a fine gesture if the Minister of Native Affairs had announced his decision to appoint this Commission in the Council or had consulted it about the personnel or the terms of references of the Commission? For some reason or other he did not think it fit and proper to do so.

PASS LAWS

To the Fagan Commission has also been referred the question of pass laws, about the abolition of which the Council has had a great deal to say ever since its inception. The African people are practically unanimous in regarding

229

the pass system as one of the greatest curses of African life in South Africa. No amount of white-washing of the system by any commission will change their views about it, especially as this matter has been dealt with by previous commissions such as the Native Economic Commission and the Inter-Departmental Committee on the Pass Laws, whose recommendations in favour of a simplification of the system fell on deaf ears. Abolition of the pass laws is the watch-word of all African organisations. The mounting figures for convictions under the pass laws in all their ramifications are a sufficient condemnation of the system.

In and out of season the Council has condemned the Municipal Beer Hall system and particularly the use of beer hall profits to relieve municipalities of their responsibility to provide ordinary amenities in the Native Locations. The question was investigated by the Native Affairs Commission which confirmed the views of the Council that urban local authorities looked upon the beer hall more as a profit-making concern than as a method of fighting the drink evil among Africans in urban areas. Legislation was actually put on the Statute Book prohibiting local authorities from using beer profits except for social or recreational activities for Africans in the urban area. This legislation had the full support of the Council, but the Municipalities were not to be done out of this lucrative source of revenue. Some argued that they had entered into certain commitments in the expectation that beer profits would help them to meet such obligations. Others argued that the profits from beer could not possibly be exhausted by expenditure on social welfare for Africans! So pressure was brought to bear on the Government to appoint another Commission on the use of beer profits. This Commission has recommended a reversal of the policy supported by the Council and by the Native Affairs Commission.

COMMON COMPLAINT

One of the commonest complaints of the African people repeatedly brought to the notice of the Government by the Council is the inequitable distribution of land as between Native and non-Native in the Union. It is common knowledge that under the Native Land and Trust Act of 1936 the Government undertook to purchase additional land for Native occupation so as to relieve congestion in the scheduled Native areas whose inadequacy to meet the present and future needs of the African population was recognised as far back as 1913. The Government's proposals for the purchase of land which had raised the hopes of many landless people in the Reserves was for various reasons suspended during the war, although the purchase of land for European settlement was apparently not suspended for the same reason. This suspension of the purchase of land for Native occupation caused grave disappointment in the Native areas, especially as the settlement of people on farms already bought was for various reasons not proceeded with as rapidly as the people desired. Some of the farms bought, instead of being thrown open for peasant settlement and cultivation were set aside for experimental purposes, for milk schemes, for bull camps, for semi-urban villages, for grazing European-owned stock on payment of a grazing fee, etc. One farm which has been bought and paid for has not yet been taken over because a European school is situated on it. Meantime a number of Trust officials has been appointed to manage these farms and to carry on the work of agricultural development in the areas concerned. Chiefs and headmen in different parts of the country complain that many of these officials are not always as sympathetic and tactful as people who are engaged on what is primarily an educative process might be. The master-servant attitude of which the average European in South Africa finds it so difficult to divest himself is completely foreign to the educative process, and the Council has repeatedly urged that the greatest care must be exercised in the personnel that is appointed to deal with any part of our Native administration.

REHABILITATION SCHEME

Towards the end of the war the Government launched an ambitious scheme for the development and rehabilitation of the Reserves which carried with it proposals for the reduction of the number of people dependent on land in the Reserves and the rigid limitation of stock to the carrying capacity of the Native locations. Admirable as the scheme appears on paper, it has rightly or wrongly come to be looked upon by the people as a further encroachment on their already limited land rights and a further entrenchment of the system of migratory labour, and in spite of its acceptance by such public bodies as the United Transkeian Territories General Council and the Ciskeian General Council, it has not aroused that enthusiasm among the common people which alone can guarantee its success. The Council has expressed its views on the scheme and made suggestions for its improvement in various directions if it is to become acceptable to the people, with little or no effect.

But not only has the confidence of the Council in the Government's intentions towards the African people been undermined by sins of omission, but a sense of despair and frustration has been induced in them by the increased output of restrictive and discriminatory legislative and administrative measures and by the increasingly provocative utterances of Members of Parliament, both from the Opposition and Government benches. As examples may be cited:

(a) The prohibition of meetings of more than 10 Natives except by permission of the Native Commissioner in the Northern Provinces.

(b) The extension of the pass system in the form of registration of service contracts in the urban areas under the Natives Urban Areas Consolidation Act of 1945, coupled with the handing over of the control of this system to the urban local authorities.

(c) Discrimination against Africans in social security measures such as Old Age Pensions, Pensions for the Blind, Invalidity Grants, etc., coupled with the unsympathetic administration of these measures by some administrative officers.

231

(d) The attempt to control the inevitable drift of Africans from the congested Native Reserves to the towns by empowering the Railways to refuse to sell them tickets unless they produce written evidence that they have already obtained employment in the urban area to which they wish to travel to search for work.

(e) The use of force by the Government to settle industrial disputes between African workers and their employers so tragically exemplified in the recent mine labourers' strike.

Sufficient has been said to indicate some of the reasons which have gradually produced in the members of the Council that sense of frustration and irritation which culminated in the collapse of the recent session of the Council. It is wrong to suppose, as has been done in some quarters, that the action of the Council was the result of a sudden decision brought about solely by the mine labourers' strike. The Government's handling of the latter situation was typical of its attitude towards the Council. Here were the elected representatives of the African people assembled at the administrative headquarters of the Union—Pretoria—only a few miles away from Johannesburg, where a major disturbance involving 50,000 of the people they represent some of whom had lost their lives or had suffered injuries in the trouble, and the Government had absolutely nothing to say to the Council about the matter. Neither the Minister of Native Affairs—to say nothing of any other Minister—nor the Secretary for Native Affairs appeared at the meeting nor thought it necessary to give the Council an official account of a situation which meant life or death to many of their people, at a time when sensational and obviously tendentious reports were appearing in the local Press and rumours of all kinds were rife. The Prime Minister was "not unduly concerned," as he told, not the Council, but the Head Committee of the United Party. To call upon the Councillors, Nero-like, to play the fiddle while Rome was burning, as it were, as the Deputy-Chairman was apparently instructed to do, was provocative, to say the least. It demonstrated, if proof were wanted, that after nine years of patient work the Council had not yet succeeded in impressing its existence upon the consciousness of the powers that be. The same indifference of the Government towards matters which the African people regard as highly important was shown when questions were asked by Councillors about the disturbance at the Lovedale Institution at which discipline had collapsed so completely that a serious riot had broken out as a result of which over 150 men students who had taken part in the affair were taken into custody. No official statement was available although it turned out afterwards that official report has been sent by the local Native Commissioner to the Chief Native Commissioner, King William's Town. The Council took the opportunity to point out that it had previously called upon the Government to appoint a commission to inquire into and report upon the administration of the Native educational institutions with a view to finding the causes and suggesting appropriate remedies for the disturbances which have become all too frequent at these seats of learning which it is becoming apparently impossible to conduct without the aid of the police. No action has been taken on the matter.

COUNCIL'S ACTION SUPPORTED

The patience of the Council was obviously near breaking point and an adjournment of the Council for an indefinite period until the Government showed evidence of its intention to give more serious consideration to the views of the Council seemed the least drastic action that the Council could take.

The question may be asked as to whether the action of the Council has the support of the African people. Those who are in touch with African opinion as expressed in African organisations and by leaders of African thought will know that the reputation of the Council has suffered as the result of the Government's attitude towards it. *The view has been expressed that this experiment in political segregation has been given a fair trial by the African people during the last decade, and that the time has come for them to recognise that the experiment has failed and to embark upon a boycott of the scheme.* This is mentioned to indicate that the councillors are not in advance of their people in drawing the attention of the Government in the way they did on August 14 to the fact that all is not well in the relations between the Government and the "Black House," as the Zulu would put it.

Document 32. Report of Interview by Some NRC Members with Prime Minister Jan C. Smuts; Verbatim Report of the Proceedings; Press Conference Remarks by Paul R. Mosaka and Professor Z.K. Matthews; and Statement by Professor Matthews, May 8-9, 1947

1. Last week the following members of the Native Representative Council were invited by the Prime Minister, Field Marshall the Rt. Hon. J.C. Smuts, to meet him in Cape Town at 9 a.m. on Wednesday, May 7th, 1947:-

    (a) *Councillor Chief Mshiyeni ka Dinizulu*, nominated member representing the electoral area of *Natal*,

    (b) *Councillor Chief Victor Poto*, nominated member representing the electoral areas of the *Transkei*,

    (c) *Councillor Chief Maserumule*, nominated member representing the electoral area of the *Transvaal and the Orange Free State*,

    (d) *Councillor R.V. Selope Thema*, elected member representing rural areas in the electoral area of the *Transvaal and the Orange Free State*,

    (e) *Councillor P.R. Mosaka*, elected member representing urban areas in the electoral area of the *Transvaal and the Orange Free State*,

    (f) *Councillor Professor Z.K. Matthews*, elected member representing rural areas in the electoral area of the *Cape excluding the Transkei*.

233

2. By Tuesday, May 6th, all the invited members had arrived in Cape Town. It then transpired that, owing to other pressing engagements, the Prime Minister had been compelled to postpone the interview to 11 a.m. on Thursday, May 8th.

3. Although the six Councillors found it impossible to arrange for a special meeting of their own for the purpose of deciding upon a common line of action, it was agreed informally among those who were able to contact one another that, in the absence of the other members of the Council, no considered reply should be given to any proposals which the Prime Minister might place before the invited group, as indeed no other course was open to them.

4. The first interview took place in the Prime Minister's office at the appointed time, the following representatives of the Government being present:-
    (a) The Prime Minister, Field Marshal Smuts.
    (b) The Minister for Native Affairs, Major P.V.G. van der Byl.
    (c) The Secretary for Native Affairs, Mr.W.J.G. Mears.
    (d) The Secretary for Labour. [Brigadier General Buchanan]
    (e) The Deputy-Chairman of the Native Affairs Commission, Dr. D.L. Smit.

5. A verbatim report of the proceedings which, it is hoped will later be available for distribution, was taken down. The following is a summary of the address of the Prime Minister which was given to the Press by Cr. P.R. Mosaka and myself:- ....
[The verbatim report follows:]

The Prime Minister: I welcome you here to this informal discussion intended as an exchange of views.

I have felt the need for some time of meeting you and having an exchange of ideas with you over the relations between our European and African peoples.

You will remember that in former years, that is long ago when I was Minister of Native Affairs and when I combined the post of Prime Minister with that of Native Affairs, I had the opportunity and the time to keep in fairly close touch with Native Affairs and with developments as affecting our Native people, and I could visit the Native people.

But since then, matters have changed.

For long years I was out of the Government, and when I became Prime Minister again some years ago, the country was in grave trouble, and the pressure was heavy on me. I had very little time to keep in close touch with Native developments.

During the war, it has been practically impossible for me to move much among the people and get into touch with various sections of our people, including our Native population. But I hope that it may be possible for me, in future, as the tension of public affairs relaxes, to get once more in touch with our Native population.

I know of the difficulties that have arisen. Some of these difficulties have arisen in connection with the Natives Representative Council, and during these last ten years that the Council has been functioning, a very difficult situation has arisen.

I don't want to go into the past. There is no profit in it for us.

I rather wish to look at the position as it is now and as it may be developing in future.

I do believe that a great deal can be done to get on right lines once more, and it is with a view to that that I thought it would be useful to have a discussion with Native leaders who must also feel a responsibility for the situation.

At present, the position in the Natives Representative Council is very unfortunate. The Council has adjourned *sine die*. There is an impasse existing. It looks like a strike—a sit-down strike, and we must get out of it. We must get things on the move again and I am very anxious to help in that respect.

We must all fairly and sincerely make our contribution in that direction. The Government is prepared to make its contribution and we may fairly call on our Native friends also to make their contribution.

The problems before us in this country call for a spirit of goodwill. These problems can only be solved in a spirit and in an atmosphere of goodwill between the various sections of our people. There must be understanding and sympathy; there must be patience. Otherwise the situation may become an insoluble problem.

I think it would be a mistake to indulge in blame and recriminations. They are not helpful. Mistakes may have been made. Mistakes may still be made. Human nature is like that. The world will always be like that, but we have to be patient and practise a spirit of goodwill and understanding towards each other and try to make a fresh start and a fresh move to right things.

You must remember that the situation in South Africa is changing very rapidly and on a very large scale.

Look at what has happened the last ten years in our relations. When the late General Hertzog got his legislation through Parliament ten years ago, he thought he had settled our whole Native policy. He thought that the laws that he had passed for Native segregation and for the Natives Representative Council would fill the bill.

But what has happened in these last ten years since then? We have seen, in spite of his legislation, a great migration of the Native population to the great urban centres. Quite new problems and a new situation have arisen. It has not been possible to segregate the Natives into reserves. The Native Reserves have proved only a very partial solution of the problem, and one of the most pressing problems today before us is how to deal with this immense influx of Native people into the urban and industrial centres of the Union.

Now, let us look at the other part of his legislation—the Natives Representative Council. His intention was that the Natives Representative Council, as then constituted, would give an outlet for the expression of Native opinion and that

235

the Natives Representative Council would make its contribution towards guiding public opinion and the opinion of Parliament into right channels.

How has this idea worked out in practice?

The Natives Representative Council was given no responsibility. It was simply a debating chamber. It became simply a platform from which to express grievances. It passed resolutions. It passed resolutions year after year, many of which Parliament didn't carry out; some of which Parliament couldn't carry out. It is very easy to ask: it is more difficult to give. And the Natives Representative Council was put in this position that it could make demands and representations to Parliament without themselves taking part in the fulfilment of them.

The result of that has been a spirit of dissatisfaction and of frustration among the Native people themselves. They see that they express their opinions and pass their resolutions, but apparently no attention is paid to them. And instead of the position being improved, it naturally gets worse, and the result is such as we see now—that the Natives Representative Council sulks and thinks that it is a useless body and it does not want to proceed with its task.

This is the unfortunate position in which we are landed today and out of which we must get.

No doubt, there are people who will say—'Well, scrap the Natives Representative Council. Do away with this body which is just a talking shop.' It would suit them to get rid of the Natives Representative Council.

The Government takes quite a different view. We are not for going backward, but for going forward. We don't want to break down the Natives Representative Council, but we want to improve it, to strengthen it. It was intended to be a real aid and help to our Native policy. You cannot ignore Native opinion in this country. You cannot have good government in this country and ignore the opinion of this vast mass of people in it.

It would, in my opinion, be a fatal step to abolish the Natives Representative Council, and it is almost just as bad to let it sit down in a strike. It must be made a real working institution, helpful to the good government of this country; and the problem before us is to make this forward move—to make the Council the reality it was intended to be.

Well, Gentlemen, it is there where I want to be helpful. It is there where I want to make a contribution towards the solution of this trouble, and I want to sketch to you in broad outline and tentatively today the lines on which my own mind is working.

I think the time has come to place a measure of responsibility on the Natives Representative Council. I think some executive authority must be given to it.

I should like to give the Natives Representative Council a 'bone to chew at'. It is no use merely talking. One gets tired of talking and then sits down on strike.

Now, what is running in my mind is this: We have set aside these Native Reserves for the development of our Native population. They are intended

236

to provide scope for Native development and progress in their own natural conditions; and the question I ask myself is this: 'Isn't it possible to give the Natives Representative Council a measure of responsibility and authority—executive authority—in regard to the development of these Reserves?' Instead of the Natives Representative Council then being merely a debating chamber and a talking shop, it will have real authority. It ought to be made possible for the Government to devolve a measure of executive authority to the Natives Representative Council in respect of these Reserves.

A beginning may be made with such a devolution, and it might be increased as time goes on and the Natives Representative Council does its task properly. It would be an increasing measure of executive devolution as time goes on. The leaders of our Native people would then get their proper training in the management of their own affairs. Instead of keeping Native Administration exclusively in the Native Affairs Department, a greater measure of devolution could thus take place and the beginnings of a substantial forward move may thus be laid down. Let them have a good substantial share in running their own Native Reserves.

That is the first step that we should consider taking. It will be a real advance on the legislation of 1936.

Secondly I think that it ought also to be possible to make the Natives Representative Council an all-Native body, make all the members elective: don't nominate Europeans as members to this Council, but let them have their own organisation and their own Native staff. It may even be possible for them to have their own Executive Committee to do the Executive and administrative part of their task. The numbers of the Council may be enlarged. Representations have been made, I know, from time to time, for the enlargement of the Council, and I think that could be done.

I think that on these lines we shall make more of a reality of the Natives Representative Council, make it a real power for Native development and make it a real instrument of executive progress in Native Affairs.

I think the time has come, probably, when such a development has to take place. It will help the self-respect of our Native population. They will feel that they have a real part in the management of their own affairs and that they are not being run solely by the European community. They will feel that they are carrying weight in the South African community.

Thirdly, let me now mention another aspect of this same matter.

We have now this situation which has developed in the great centres, where you have the Natives flocking in large numbers into the industrial and the urban centres. You know the way in which we have so far dealt with this matter, and it has not proved quite satisfactory.

In regard to these Native townships and locations in the urban areas we have established local Advisory Boards; in a large number of places you have the Native Advisory Boards—I believe this is the general system now.

The question arises whether we should not link up this great development

237

also with the Natives Representative Council—link up these local Advisory Boards into a larger body which will constitute, as it were, a general Congress or Conference of these Boards, which will keep a general supervision over them and secure for them representation also in the Natives Representative Council.

You will then have the Natives Representative Council, as it were, the central bond of all these various organisations which are helping in the management of Native Affairs.

You will have a system of Native Government which will be unified for the whole country. You would increase the usefulness of the Natives Representative Council and you will tie them all up together—all these various Native representative bodies and their General Councils—into one big organisation.

You will understand that this idea raises a number of very difficult questions. The Central Government is concerned in them, and so are the Provincial Governments, and also the local authorities. They will all have to be consulted in working out this larger scheme of Native Administration for the whole country. I have not approached any of them yet. I have simply this idea which I have been revolving in my own mind on which a practical plan might be worked out. In due course they will be approached and the question in all its bearings will be discussed with them to see how far effect can be given to it.

I want you to think over it too and discuss it among you.

I ask for no expression of opinion today. These are big matters which you must have time to consider, but in due course we can meet again and discuss them. I shall have to discuss them also with the European authorities I have mentioned—with the Central Government, Parliament, Provincial Councils, Town Councils, and so on.

My idea is that the child is growing up. This young child, South Africa, is growing up and the old clothes do not fit the growing boy. You must make some new clothes. The fashion also changes. We have to move with the times. It is no use standing still, or sitting down, as you are doing in the Natives Representative Council now!

I want us all, both Natives and Europeans, to have this thought, that this child is growing and is moving and is on the march.

It is not only the European people and their opinions that are advancing. It is Native opinion that is advancing too—it is the whole country that is fast moving forward. The pattern which we followed in cutting our clothes has changed and the time has come for us to change our clothes too.

Please don't think that in these matters the Government is standing still. Our ideas are not stationary. We know that a forward movement is taking place and must take place and that we must carry our whole population of all colours and races with us in this forward movement.

238

Well, so much about these matters—the general set up of Native organisation as I have described to you in broad outline.

I know that there are a number of particular problems which trouble you very much. They are problems like the Pass Laws. They are problems arising from this migration to the towns and the satellite Native Townships which are arising round the white townships.

The Government is anxious to provide a proper place for our Native people in these urban centres.

Our policy is to keep the two sections of our South Africa separate in their own residential areas. They will work together, they will have their economic interests very much together, but for their own peace, they prefer—both of them—to dwell apart among their own people.

This raises quite a new set of very difficult problems in South Africa. We have referred both these difficult problems of pass laws and migration—one of the past and one of the future—to the 'Fagan Commission'. The questions of the Pass Laws and the migration to the urban centres have both been referred to this Commission. They are now making inquiries and I hope that their inquiries might be helpful to us in dealing with these difficult problems. So that I do not wish to discuss these matters today. I only mention them as grave and difficult problems which are before us and before you too, and will claim our serious attention.

There is one problem to which the Government has already given a good deal of attention, and it is urgent and it must be dealt with now. It is the question of Native Trade Unions. The Native people are asking for recognition of their own labour trade unions. There are already many of these unions—almost a hundred of them—unrecognised, unauthorised, but in existence, and they are all asking for Government recognition.

A bill for the purpose has been drafted by the Government and it will be published almost immediately. The Government is anxious to introduce it into Parliament this Session still. But, of course, according to the law, we have to refer it first to the consideration of the Natives Representative Council, and the Council will be called together for the purpose. I hope they will not continue their sit down strike. I wish them to be helpful.

It is big and an urgent question—urgent both from the Native and from the European point of view, and for that purpose the Council will be called together, and I hope it will give its consideration to this Bill, so that we may introduce it into Parliament as soon as possible.

I may just say, for your information, that the Native Trade Unions will be recognised generally on the same lines as laid down in the Industrial Conciliation Act already in the Statute Book. There will be separate trade unions for Europeans and Natives so that the Natives won't be mixed up with the Europeans, but, otherwise, the scheme is very much the same.

The Bill excludes the Mines from its scope. A very large percentage, I believe, of our Native mine workers are not Union Nationals. They come from abroad; they come from foreign territories. They come and they go and they do not fit into a scheme of settled labour for which you can have trade unions such as we propose.

For that reason, the Native mine workers will not have unions such as will be recognised for all other industries.

The Native Affairs Department proposes a different scheme to help them, the mine workers—and that is to have an efficient Inspectorate on the mines looking after the Natives' interests there. A number of inspectors, with the status of Senior Native Commissioners, will be appointed on the mines, with a number of Native assistants who will work among the Native miners to keep in close touch with them and watch their interests, the interests of the Native miners.

That is the best solution that we have been able to find for this knotty problem in regard to mining labour.

For the rest, the Bill as I have said follows the machinery of the Conciliation Act. It provides for conciliation on the usual lines between the workers and the employers; and if the conciliation does not work—if there is no agreement by way of conciliation—then the Bill provides that there will be arbitration and the matter will be settled by arbitration.

The result will be that disputes will be finished and no strikes can legally take place. If conciliation does not lead to settlements, there will be impartial arbitration between the workers and the employers to finalise the differences.

Gentlemen, I have put before you matters of grave importance. I call for your contribution and your influence in these matters. I do not want us merely, either on the European or on the Native side, to adopt the attitude of critics, of fault-finding and blaming. I want us both to play our part.

I have put our cards on the table and told you the moves that we are contemplating and I want you to be helpful, you who are the leaders and who have a great responsibility of your own for the welfare of your peoples. I call on you to be helpful in these matters.

They are not easy. The movement forward may not be as fast as we wish, but let the spirit be good. Let there be a spirit of understanding and goodwill between us, and when we bump up against great difficulties, I am prepared to discuss with you these questions which affect the Natives of this country.

The worst thing which could happen, both for European and Native South Africa, would be a spirit of antagonism and estrangement to grow up between them. One hand must wash the other. That is the only way that both hands can be clean.

Let us move on in that spirit. Let us be patient. Let us not get angry with each other. Let us appreciate the good faith of each other. Among responsible South Africans of both races there should be a clear understanding on that point. We must work together. There is no other way. Providence has put both of us here. Bantu and European came to this country at the same time. That wonderful century in history—the seventeenth century—brought both of us here. You came from the North by land, we came from the farther North by sea, and here we both are, and here we shall both remain. It is our country; it is your country. We must try and build up a human society that will be happy as far as human beings can be happy.

You can make your contribution. I think Bantu South Africa can make a great contribution to the future of this continent, and the Europeans naturally will make their contribution too. Let us face the future in hope and faith and charity. Hope and faith and charity—there is no other way for us humans.

These fears that people have in South Africa, the one section of the other, in my humble opinion are quite unreasonable. The African need not fear the European. There is a great fount of goodwill among the Europeans. The Europeans are again in fear of the Africans, and that too is quite wrong.

I am not afraid of them. We are all together in one society, and we both have qualities that ought to carry us over the rough places.

I have been over other parts of the world. I have watched these other countries where there are only Europeans or all of the white races. Their troubles are just as great as ours, and so I don't despair of our position here.

I am now an old man—the oldest of you all. I have grown up among these conditions in South Africa. I have seen a steady forward movement all the time.

When I compare the conditions of our Native people as I knew them sixty years ago and more, and I look at their conditions today, then I say an almost incredible advance has been made.

When I was a youngster I went to Stellenbosch to what is now the Stellenbosch University—that was in the eighties of the last century—and we had a number of students there, some of them got their degrees there; and to me it was a wonderful thing. Then, just before the war, I went to Fort Hare, and I saw that Native University College there. Large numbers of graduates, students who had gone through all their studies, taking their degrees there. Today Fort Hare, a Native University College, is one of our largest and best in this country. In fifty years all that progress has been made and when you look away from Fort Hare in all other directions you see the same immense progress being made among our Native people almost everywhere and in all walks of life.

I have been over other African Territories. I know of conditions all over this continent, and I know this—that the real progress, the real advance, is steadier, more continuous here in South Africa than in any of the other African Territories. And, therefore, I say to you, don't let us sit down in despair; don't let us be disheartened. Don't let us be despondent. Things are moving everywhere along all lines of advance. Things may move slower than we wish, but there is a great forward movement that we must maintain and accelerate if possible.

Understanding and good faith and good will—let those be our watch words here in South Africa. Don't let us look on each other as the enemy. Let us look on each other as friends. As that black nurse has carried the white baby, so the white baby, as it grows up, must in turn look after that black nurse.

That is the spirit in which South Africa will achieve success. Let us do away with this idea of antagonism and opposition. Let it be a spirit of co-operation.

Gentlemen, that is what I wanted to talk to you about—from my heart. I don't want any misunderstanding in this country between our two peoples. We ought to talk to each other and consult with each other and we ought to realise and understand the position of each other. On that basis only can we go into the happy and prosperous future of both our two peoples.

Prof. Matthews: I would like to say a few words. I want to say that we as members of the Natives Representative Council and as leaders of the African people in different parts of the country welcome the step that has been taken by the Prime Minister to try and bring about a termination of this deadlock between the Council and the Government. As you know only a few of us are here.

Prime Minister: Please convey to the others the message that I could only speak to a few of you here and they must not look upon their exclusion from this meeting as an affront.

Prof. Matthews: Thank you. But we hope that it will be possible for the Prime Minister at some stage in the future to meet the whole Council as you have met us here today, Sir. We appreciate the step taken by the Prime Minister. I want to emphasise that.

We can naturally, as you have rightly indicated, not this morning express any final opinions about the far-reaching implications you have disclosed today.

Prime Minister: I don't call for it either.

Prof. Matthews: We would like, however, to take the opportunity to say that the African people have been very disturbed over developments during the last few years.

The Government is well aware of the fact that there is a sense of frustration, a sense of loss of hope among the African people which we, as leaders of the people, are very anxious to see pass away. We realise that there can be no progress in this country unless there is co-operation between the Government and the people. After all, the Government exists for the benefit of the people, and where there is no mutual confidence between the Government and the people, there can never be anything else but trouble.

We would like a statement of what you have said to us this morning as we would like to take that back to our people—and while you are conducting consultations with the Government, the Provincial and local authorities, we would like to have similar consultations with our people so that when we are called upon to give our final opinion in due course on these measures, we shall have consulted our people and also the rest of the members of the Council.

The other people present would, I am sure, also like to say a few words but I do feel on this large question that you have raised, and also on the specific issues to which you have made reference, that these matters affect the African people very closely indeed. Also I feel that the Europeans in this country should not lose hope as far as the African is concerned. We would like to feel that at any time when we express the opinion or point of view of our people that we should not be regarded as people who think in any other light except that we want also to make a contribution to the Government of this country. And we feel that this contribution can only be made by giving us a greater measure of recognition in the various Councils of the State.

I do not wish to appear to be giving any reply now to the issues raised by you, Sir, because we have to have consultation with our people first, but we do welcome the step taken by the Prime Minister in taking us into his confidence in regard to the measures that he is thinking about. We think that it is only right that he should do so, that the Prime Minister should, when a measure of vast implications for the African people is being contemplated, is about to be taken, consult the leaders of the African people as we have been consulted here today.

I also feel that I must say that the deadlock between the Council and the Government—the sit down strike to which you have referred—is something that we would like to see terminated, but we want to see it terminated on conditions which will leave us with the necessary self-respect.

We realise the very great responsibility which we carry as leaders of the Native people, but we don't want to put ourselves in a situation where our people will lose confidence in us; just as you, Sir, have to carry your own people with you, we want to be able to carry our own people with us.

What has worried us is that the Native people have steadily lost confidence in the Natives Representative Council. The Council is regarded as an ineffective body. If the Government is now considering steps by which they can make the voice of the African people felt to a greater extent in the affairs of the nation, that will be all to the good.

The other Councillors will, I am sure, like to say a few words.

Councillor Thema: I have been listening to what the Prime Minister has said and although I am not as old as the Prime Minister himself, I think I have lived in this country long enough to know and understand the position. The progress to which you refer, Sir, has been made. We have made that progress and whether the white people want it or not, we are making it, but I am just wondering where this progress—in education, at the universities, etc.—is going to end. Although the people are being allowed to progress with their education, they are being restricted by segregation. I do not complain about the progress myself, but where is that progress going to lead us? I wonder whether it is in the interests of our South Africa—that applies to both of us, white and black—that we should make this progress and then find that there is no scope

243

for it. What will be the end of it? The majority of my people don't want to come to Parliament—I want that, but not the majority of my people—but they want something done which *they* can feel. If the Pass Laws, for instance, had been abolished, they would have been satisfied. It is things like that which make our people unhappy. My people won't feel as though they have gained anything very much if the Natives Representative Council is improved, but if the restriction of their movements is removed, they will be happy—and unless and until that is done they will never understand.

As Prof. Matthews has said, we are not going to reply to the suggestions made, but we appreciate very much your calling us here and making that statement to us here. We would like that statement in writing so that we can tell our people. But I do feel one thing that the Government can do to make our people happy is to abolish the Pass Laws even today. We don't know what the Fagan Commission will recommend and we know that before Commissions have been appointed and have investigated this matter. I was here in 1920 and I heard you, Sir, in the House when you moved the Second Reading of the Native Affairs Act. I had just returned from England then and at that time even you mentioned that you wanted to set up machinery to go into the question of the Pass Laws so that you could see whether they couldn't be done away with. This speech you will find in Hansard. And the position is just like that today.

In conclusion I want to say that I don't want the white people in this country to think that we are their enemies. If there is ever a people who must be thankful for other people who came into their continent, it is the African people. We would never be here today if the whiteman hadn't come here. And I don't think that there is a single blackman—African—who wants the European away from this Country. But we want a fair deal, a square deal. We want to feel that we belong to this nation. We want to say that there must be unity. We agree that we don't look alike, but it is not our fault that we are black, neither is it your fault that you are white. We have no intentions against the white people, but if they go on like this, we don't know what will happen. A better foundation on which to build a firmer South Africa might be laid now. Then we will be able to tell our people that we are all one nation, the white people and ourselves. We want to be part of this nation, we want to be part and parcel of this nation so that if other people come and invade us, we want to defend our country together with the white people of this country. We don't want to feel that the newcomers might help us against the white people of this country, but that we can be part of the same nation as the white people of this country, to defend it together with them against such newcomers. You can make us feel that way if you treat us fairly.

You might say that 50 years ago we were barbarians. As you say we have progressed and we are here today and we want to be part and parcel of one nation with the white people here and I think this is possible if you want it, as we are prepared on our side to co-operate.

Councillor Mosaka: I want to say that we greatly appreciate your opening remarks in regard to this big problem.

You have stated that during the years that have past, by reason of the pre-occupation of war problems and other more pressing duties, you haven't been in such close touch with Native Affairs as was the case in earlier years when you joined the portfolios of Premier and Native Affairs. Your mind is too virile, too active to have allowed, if you were in close touch with the Natives, the deplorable state to which Native Affairs has fallen during the years that have passed. I feel certain that whichever way Native policy might have gone, during the years that have passed, it would certainly not have remained static under your guidance and that you would have made a forward move. And I take it that this meeting marks the beginning of an interest which you are now reviving in Native Affairs, and it will, therefore, auger well for the future of the whole country, not only Native Affairs but also the industrial progress with which the Native policy is closely linked.

Secondly, I want to indicate that the adjournment of the Natives Representative Council must not be misunderstood. It is true that because the Natives Representative Council was a 'talking shop', it was more likely that its members would suffer from a sense of frustration and despair. If the Council were given a certain amount of executive power, it may not be so.

But it should be understood that the adjournment of the Council was on the question of policy. If you ask the African people—the Councillors, the Advisory Boards or other bodies—to help in the administration of Native Affairs today, what are you in fact asking them to do? You ask them to carry out a policy which they don't accept; you ask them to be policemen. I am not saying anything new when I say that the changes which are taking place in this, our country, necessitate a change of policy—a big change. The big feature of the present legislation, as far as the Africans are concerned, and which is properly reflected in the 1936 legislation, is a check on the townward movement of Africans. But it is admitted by all that this townward movement is desirable in a country which is rapidly becoming industrialised. The nerve-centre of the country is not in the rural areas, but in the towns and the nerve-centre of African development will also be in the towns and not in the country and from that point of view the one thing which, I think, will give relief is if you will remove this nightmare fear of uncertainty and insecurity. The need which we have felt in recent years more than in the past is for a policy which gives us this forward move, which shows that there is scope for the talents of the African, and, more than that, that there is a home for the African in this country. We have never felt so homeless as we do today both in the town and in the country and we want a measure of security. And anything designed to give that feeling of security in our own country, anything which will let the common man as he moves about feel that way, will go a long way to give stability of thought on which to build a better future.

I mention this matter because I feel that in various other directions the
245

country is moving on very rapidly. I come from Johannesburg where we feel these forces daily. And I feel that in this very sincere attempt to make better feelings and to end the deadlock in the Council, the right approach to the council should be made.

During the war period you and our Minister of Native Affairs, Maj. van der Byl, and Mr. Smit, the then Secretary for Native Affairs, did a good deal to create a new hope and faith in the mind of the Native people. We felt that new forces were at work as industry swept through the country during the war causing the movement of people from one place to another. And when the enemy was being beaten, we also felt that a new world was in the making. And the survey which the then Secretary for Native Affairs conducted into the social and economic conditions of urban Natives made us also feel that something was at last going to be done for us, but subsequent legislation disillusioned us. We saw a spirit of fear growing among the white people. We do not fear the white people—the Police, yes, because of the beer raids and the passes—but ordinarily we haven't the same fear of the white people as the white people have of us. Throughout the later stages of the war a lot of legislation was passed which made things more and more intolerable for us.

I want to say that we would like that hope which had been created in our hearts, but which has resulted in frustration because we have seen the Government take a backward step, not honouring its promises, to be set ablaze again. We would like things to be done, a new policy to be outlined which will give us hope and make for a better foundation for the future—a hope for better things to come.

Mshiyeni ka Dinizulu: I would like to say how fortunate I feel we are about the Prime Minister's decision to call us here, and that we have had the opportunity of meeting the Prime Minister. We thank you very much for the way in which you led the country during the war period and led us to victory, and also for what you did in bringing their Majesties the King, Queen and the Princesses to this country on a visit.

You have said that the matters that you have raised we should take back to our people to consider. You have mentioned the fact that it is necessary for a spirit of goodwill and co-operation to be established between the Africans and the European people of our country. I would like to say that we very much appreciate the spirit in which you have spoken to us this morning. We will take back the matters that you have raised before us and consider them at more leisure at our own homes. We are very thankful indeed that we have seen you and had the opportunity of hearing you speak to us. We want to remind you that we have no other parent in this country except the Prime Minister. The manner in which you have spoken to us has created a very deep impression. You have the key of the affairs of this country.

You have mentioned the fact that you are a much travelled man and have seen many countries. We are not anxious to see the Natives Representative Council abolished. There, we are eyes and ears of the people. The people

246

are looking to us to express to the Government their grievances. We would like the true purpose and function of the Natives Representative Council to be fulfilled, namely that it should be the mouthpiece of the African people and should bring about better co-operation between the Government and the African people.

I am very pleased to see Dr. Smit, Mr. Mears, our Secretary, and our Minister here. The presence of all these gentlemen is a matter which pleases me a great deal indeed.

There are only six of us here and it may be that those of our Council who have not been invited to this meeting will not be pleased about it. Many people throughout the country may get the impression that we are coming to sell our people by coming here. That is what will be said by those who envy us the opportunity of being here today, but I think it is our good fortune and we are going to tell them what we have heard here today.

Prime Minister: Tell them that we were 5 and you were 6.

Chief Poto: I would also like to add my word of appreciation that the Prime Minister decided to invite us here today. You have placed matters of a far-reaching nature and importance before us here today and we are particularly thankful that you have not called upon us to make an immediate decision upon the matters that have been placed before us. We came here not knowing what was going to be put before us and we would have been put in a very difficult position if we had been called upon to make a definite decision immediately.

These matters that have been raised here today touch the affairs of our people at many points. The African people I like to think are like the English people—they believe in loyalty to their Government and to their Chiefs. Since the coming of the white man to this country, the Chiefs of the African people have rather lost their influence and prestige. In course of time the white people realised that they could not effectively govern the Native people except by making use of their Native chiefs. Although there may have been a great deal of progress among the African people during the last 50 years, I want to remind you that a considerable proportion of our people are still backward and have not made that progress. That section of the population still, in a large measure, looks to their chiefs and headmen for leadership and guidance, and I feel, Sir, that the position of the Chiefs could be strengthened so that they should provide the necessary leadership for this vast mass that has not yet made the progress to which you have referred.

I would like, when you are considering measures for the improvement of our general system of Native Administration, that attention should also be given to the place of the Chiefs in such a development and possibly measures might be devised to give them greater powers; that in their areas, over which they have jurisdiction, they might be given more responsibility and more authority.

I want to say that even in regard to the people who are in the urban areas who may be regarded as detribalised, they still have a great regard for their chiefs. Those people in the urban areas have not left the reserves because they have no respect for the chiefs and their authority, but they have left because they have no way of making a living in the reserves. And although they are away from their homes, they still retain their regard and respect for their chiefs under whom they have grown up.

I make these few remarks for your consideration and I too would like to add my appreciation for the opportunity you have given us, Sir, to be here today and to hear us.

Chief Maserumule: I thank you, Sir, for what you have said this morning. I am also pleased that the Prime Minister hasn't asked us for our decision today, but has just told us his view. We are very glad we have met you, that you have called us here today so that we can talk about the affairs of the white people and the black people.

In the Council we have always had a Chairman, but we have always thought that if all the members of the Cabinet could be there in the Council, then perhaps things would go right. That is just what it should be. We are very pleased we have seen you today. We are also very thankful to you for inviting the Royal Family here to South Africa. You are the first person to have done so. But rightly or wrongly we have thought that when the son of Queen Victoria came here, we would have freedom - we thought freedom was coming when the King came.

Minister van der Byl: I would just like to be sure that there will be no mis-understanding.... I have to introduce a Bill during this Session. This Bill has been cut down tremendously, but it was submitted to the Natives Representative Council but you wouldn't deal with it. And I don't want you to go away and say that we didn't consult you before introducing this Bill. It is the Bill to amend the position in regard to Kaffir Beer profits and so on, but it has been cut down from amending about 10 Acts to 4 Acts. But it was very necessary to have this Bill.

The Prime Minister: I thank you for what you have said. What we have been talking about today I want you to go and talk about with your people. I want the people who are outside to start talking about this and I think the best course is to inform the public of what we have been saying here today and publish a record for all the people to read.

Thank you for what you have said and the way you have said it.

[End of verbatim report.]

[Professor Matthews' report continues:]

On the following day at 12 noon Councillors Chief Mshiyeni, Thema, Mosaka and Matthews had a further interview with the Prime Minister for the purpose of asking for a clarification of certain points in the scheme he had outlined the previous day. In particular they sought enlightment on:-

    (a) the relation of this so-called improved Representative Council to other governing bodies in the country, such as Parliament, the Provincial Councils and the urban local authorities and the representation of the African people on such bodies.

    (b) the nature and the scope of the powers which it was proposed to give to the Council under the new scheme.

(c) the date when the full Council was likely to be summoned for a full discussion on the Prime Minister's proposals.

(d) whether it was intended to pass the new Trade Union Bill this session in view of reports that the session was likely to close at the end of May.

In connection with (a) and (b) the Prime Minister indicated that he was not yet prepared to go into details about his proposals which had not yet reached concrete form and about which he had not yet completed the necessary consultations with other bodies whose rights might be affected. He gave the Councillors at this interview the following statement which he thought would put in proper perspective the views he had expressed the day before:-

1. "There is no definite set of concrete proposals submitted for consideration yet. There is only a general tentative statement of the direction in which the Prime Minister thinks the next advance in Native policy should be made. He wishes this tentative indication of policy to be thought over and discussed by our European and African public, and meanwhile more definite proposals will be worked out by the Government for submission as early as possible to Parliament and the Native Representative Council.

2. All that is at present definitely before the Native Representative Council and Parliament will be the Bill for the recognition of Native trade unions, and this is being immediately published.

3. Summarised in a few words, the tentative plan of the Prime Minister is as follows:-

   (a) The Native Representative Council should be enlarged and become an all-Native elective body to whom, in addition to their present functions, will also be progressively delegated by the Government an increasing measure of executive authority in the development of the Reserves. The Native Representative Council will have its own officials and may have its own Executive Committee for this purpose.

   (b) The Local Advisory Boards in urban locations and Native satellite towns now arising in urban and industrial areas will also be mainly elective, and grouped into a general Conference and linked up with the Native Representative Council.

   (c) The legislative, executive and taxing powers which may be entrusted by law to the Native Representative Council will be exercised subject to the authority of Parliament and government who will retain the final say.

   (d) The General Council system will be developed and will also exercise administrative functions as at present provided by the Native Affairs Act, and will do so under the general supervising power of the Native Representative Council.

4. There will thus be a general unified pattern of Native Administration

in which the Natives will share, under the authority of the government and Parliament. The working out of the practical plan will be done by the government and Parliament in consultation with the Provincial and local authorities and will be proceeded with as early as possible, but must inevitably take some time''.

As regards (c) and (d) the Prime Minister indicated that he was anxious to summon the full Council as early as possible, especially to get its views on the Trade Union Bill which he intended to put through Parliament before the end of the present session in fulfilment of the promise made by Mr. J.H. Hofmeyr, then Acting Prime Minister, to the Council at its last session. He would take the opportunity at the same time to put his tentative plan regarding our future Native policy before the Council. This ended the interview which lasted about an hour.

Before they left Cape Town, Councillor Mosaka and Matthews gave a brief interview to the Press on their reaction to the Prime Minister's proposals in view of the apparently enthusiastic reception which the Press had given the new scheme. The following is the substance of the interview as it appeared in the "Argus" of 9th May:-

"The proposals made by the Prime Minister yesterday to members of the Native Representative Council were described today by two members of the Council, Professor Z.K. Matthews and Councillor P.R. Mosaka as 'constituting no radical departure from the established Native policy of the country as we know it'. Professor Matthews and Councillor Mosaka said these views could not be described as the views of the Council as a whole, which had not yet met. The Prime Minister, they said, had promised them to summon the whole Council of sixteen members at an early date when the proposals would be fully discussed.

"They did not entertain any great hopes that the Council would find in the new 'bone to chew' that assurance of cooperation on a new basis for which they had hoped. The hungry masses of the African people would have to be offered more than 'a bone to chew' if their fears for their future in this country were to be allayed.

" 'The only concrete proposal that emerged from the Prime Minister's suggestions', said Professor Matthews, 'was a type of recognition for African trade unions which [would] not in fact give the African worker the right of collective bargaining, and which would not be in the interests of either the African worker or, in the long run, the European worker. The African workers wanted recognition of their trade unions and not merely supervision and control.'

"It was also in his opinion unfair to have legislation which would make strikes by African trade unions illegal. To do so would be robbing the African worker of his most effective weapon in his struggle for better working conditions.

"The exclusion of the African mineworkers from the scope of the recognition contemplated would also come as a profound dissappointment to the African

250

people. The mineworkers constituted the largest single group of African wage-earners. To leave them to the tender mercies of an inspectorate of the Native Affairs Department without giving them organisations which they themselves could control, would not satisfy their demands.

"As regards the promised legislative and executive powers for the Council, no concrete details were given by the Prime Minister. The acceptance or otherwise of the scheme would be dependent upon the scope of these powers. It was, moreover, not clear how this scheme would be related to the functions and powers of other governing bodies in the country such as Parliament, the Provincial Councils, and the urban local authorities. It was in these bodies that the final decisions on matters affecting the African people would be made. 'Unless the Africans are given effective representation in these bodies', said Councillor Mosaka, 'they will not feel that their interests are adequately safeguarded'.

"The statement made by the Prime Minister was remarkable for what it omitted in Native policy. It made no reference to economic and industrial policy which would be followed in the future, nor did it deal with the social problem of housing in the urban areas.

"It was hoped, Professor Matthews and Councillor Mosaka said, that at the meeting with the whole Council the Prime Minister would bring forward concrete proposals".

Councillor Mosaka and myself also prepared another statement in which we endeavoured to set out briefly our reaction to the Prime Minister's specific proposals, namely, the improvement of the status of the Native Representative Council and the recognition of African trade unions looked at from the point of view of principle and policy, and [not] merely that of expediency. The following is the statement to which I refer: -

COUNCILLORS' REACTION TO SMUTS' PROPOSALS.

1. In the interview which took place yesterday between Field-Marshal Smuts and six members of the Native Representative Council, the Prime Minister outlined government proposals presumably designed to end the deadlock created by the adjournment of the Council last year.

2. Briefly stated, the Premier's "New Deal" for the African people consists of:

(a) certain changes in the Constitution and in the functions and powers of the Council and

(b) proposals regarding the form of recognition to be accorded to African trade unions.

In addition, on the burning issues of the Pass Laws and the system of migratory labour, the Prime Minister offered no direct promise of immediate relief on the ground that these matters were the subject

251

of special investigation by the Fagan Commission whose report was awaited.

3. The Councillors to whom these proposals were made consisted of THREE out of the TWELVE elected members and THREE out of the FOUR nominated members of the Council. In the circumstances the Councillors made it clear that they could not make a definite reply to the statement of the Prime Minister who indeed indicated that he himself did not expect such a reply at this stage.

4. It will obviously be necessary for the Prime Minister to summon the whole Council in order to place these proposals before them and to hear their considered views on the matter.

5. Without committing the rest of the members of the Council, we should like to make a few observations on the scheme as outlined.

6. In our opinion the proposals of the Prime Minister do not go to the root of the matter in dispute between the Council and the Government. The main submission of the Council has been and continues to be that the conditions of modern African life demand a re-orientation of the whole of our Native policy, and not a mere tinkering with the framework of existing Native policy.

It seems necessary to repeat the principal defects of our present Native policy, viz:

(a) It does not safeguard the legitimate rights of the African people in any aspect of their life.

(b) It holds out no hope to them of a possible change for the better in the foreseeable future.

(c) It is not calculated to integrate the African people into the general life of the country; on the contrary, it is based upon the principles of permanent separation which engenders a spirit of hostility and racial bitterness between black and white as against that of mutual co-operation in the interests of both sections and of the country as a whole.

(d) It is undermining the confidence of the African people in the government of the country and is making increasingly impossible that collaboration between the government (and its representatives) on the one hand and the African people on the other without which no schemes intended for them can succeed.

(e) It is static and apparently unalterable, whereas the actual conditions under which the African people are compelled to live, are changing more and more rapidly and cannot be adequately dealt with by a policy inspired by the outworn ideas and practices of 1936.

(f) It even lags behind European opinion as expressed in reports of Commissions appointed by the Government itself to investigate various aspects of native affairs, or in studies by competent scholars

252

or in utterances by leaders of industry and commerce and of progressive farming and mining interests. While they may not see eye to eye with one another in the details of native policy, all political parties, except the one in power, also seem agreed on the necessity for a new Native policy.

In our view what is required is a policy which will give the African people a sense of security in the land of their birth, a policy which is flexible and can readily be adopted to changing conditions and varying circumstances; in short, a policy which recognises that Africans are citizens of this country and not things apart.

This new outlook on Native Policy was conspicuous by its absence in the specific proposals made by the Prime Minister. Coming as they did from the head of the Government to us, it will occasion little surprise if these proposals are received with widespread disappointment by the African people. Nor indeed do we entertain any hope that the Council will find in the new "bone to chew", as the Prime Minister described his scheme, that assurance of co-operation on a new basis for which they had hoped.

The hungry masses of the African people will have to be offered more than "bones to chew at" if their fears about their future in this country are to be allayed.

In conclusion, in my capacity as Chairman of the Caucus I should like to submit for the consideration of members some observations on the pronouncement of the Prime Minister and to make one or two suggestions regarding the line of action which we should adopt.

In the first place I think it would not be incorrect to say that the personal intervention of the Prime Minister in the dispute between the Government and the Council has taken the whole problem a stage further and has lifted it out of the morass of administrative quibbles in which it has been bogged for the last 10 years on to the plane of principle and policy. It will be remembered that when the Acting Prime Minister, Mr. J.H. Hofmeyr, addressed the Council last November, our chief complaint about his approach to the problem was that he had failed to grasp the significance of our adjournment. As we put it then: "To us it (i.e. his statement) seemed to be merely an apologia for the status quo, apparently oblivious of the progressive forces at work not only in the world in general, but even in South Africa itself. The statement makes no attempt to deal with some of the burning questions of the day such as the Pass Laws, the colour bar in industry, the political rights of non-Europeans in the Union, etc., and in effect it raises no hopes for the future as far as the African people are concerned. The resolution of the Council was intended as a challenge to the Government to indicate to what extent, if any, it was prepared or preparing to adjust its Native policy to the changed and changing conditions of the African people. In his statement the Acting Prime Minister virtually denies that the Native policy of the Union is in need of revision, and proceeds to justify the policy of segregation and discrimination on the ground of its supposedly protective character''.

In the preliminary remarks which the Prime Minister made before he went on to deal with his specific suggestions for the improvement of the situation, however, he seemed to us to admit quite frankly that our present Native Policy was out of date and did not fit in with the changed and changing conditions of African life today. That is a significant admission made at the Ministerial level by the first citizen of the State. To my mind that is a definite gain. It ought to mean that in future it will no longer be necessary for us to debate the question as to whether there is any need for a change in our present Native policy. That battle has been won, and the present government, at any rate, is committed to finding a new direction for Union Native Policy.

But although we may have succeeded in getting the Government through the Prime Minister to agree to set our Native policy upon a course different from that of the past, we shall have to scrutinise with the utmost care any specific proposals designed to give effect to this so-called new policy. We must be on our guard against being fopped off with something which superficially has the appearance of change when in fact it is substantially the same as what we have already condemned. Change is not always in the direction of progress, and we are not interested in change for the sake of change. Nor must we allow ourselves to be satisfied with promises unaccompanied by tangible evidence of how, when and whether they will be fulfilled. The African people have experienced so many disappointments in the history of their relations with South African governments that a certain amount of scepticism on their part must be expected. This is not so much a question of looking a gift horse in the mouth as one of fearing the Greeks even when they appear to be coming loaded with gifts.

On the other hand we must not allow the caution dictated by ordinary prudence to develop into a mere stubborn refusal to consider proposals put before us on their merits. We owe it to the people we represent to state without fear or favour precisely what it is we condemn or approve in schemes intended for them. We are engaged in delicate negotiations on behalf of our people and we must conduct them with a due sense of responsibility.

It is in the light of these considerations that we must examine the two concrete proposals which the Prime Minister has, through the medium of the six invited Councillors placed before the country, namely,

 (a) his tentative plan regarding the constitution and the functions of the Native Representative Council,
 (b) his Bill for the recognition of African trade unions.

As regards (a), it will be remembered that over two years ago a Recess Committee of the Council was appointed to examine the Native Representation

Act and to make recommendations and suggest improvements regarding the system of representation for Africans provided for in that Act. The Report of that Committee was sent to all Native Local Councils and General Councils in the rural areas and to the South African Native Location Advisory Boards Congress for consideration and report. Finally the Report was discussed in full Council and, with various amendments, was adopted and passed on to the Government for consideration and action. That Report had behind it the united voice of the African people as expressed by the accredited representatives in official African public bodies. The principal recommendations of the Recess Committee were as follows: -

(a) The extension of Assembly representation for Africans to the Northern Provinces.

(b) The extension of Provincial Council representation to the Northern Provinces.

(c) The increase of representation for Africans in the Senate up to the limit provided for in the Act.

(d) The extension of the individual vote to the Northern Provinces and the adoption of the system of individual voting for all elections under the Act.

(e) The grant of legislative and executive powers to the Native Representative Council.

(f) The increase of the African members of the Council from 16 to 60.

(g) The extension to Africans of representation in urban local authorities.

These demands were, in the opinion of the Council, by no means extravagant, especially as they merely called for the removal of obvious anomalies in the existing system of separate representation, and did not raise the issue of a return to representation on the basis of a common roll on equal terms with other sections of the population, which, of course, remains the ultimate goal for which Africans will continue to strive until they achieve it.

What has been the response of the Government to these modest demands? After a tantalising delay during which we were informed by no less a person than the Minister of Native Affairs that this matter was receiving the serious consideration of the Cabinet and the Native Affairs Commission, the Prime Minister has come forward with proposals relating only to the Native Representative Council. A veritable case of the mountain going into labour and producing a mouse.

As the Premier himself points out, the Council will exercise its new functions and powers "subject to the authority of Parliament and government who will retain the final say". It seems obvious that, unless the African people are adequately represented in the body or bodies which retain the final say, there is no guarantee that the Council will be allowed to exercise its new found powers to the advantage of the African people. Experience has taught the African people that the grant of socalled legislative and executive powers to official public bodies established for them does not necessarily mean that those higher up in the hierarchy of government will respect the exercise of these powers. Those acquainted with the working of the Native Local Councils established under the Native Affairs Act which are supposed to possess these powers, will scarcely gainsay the fact that in practice these Local Councils are nothing more than bodies advisory to the Native Commissioner by whom alone the powers of the Local Council are in fact exercised. The mere paper delegation of responsibility to the Council will achieve nothing unless it is accompanied by that change of attitude on the part of government officials in dealing with African bodies which we have looked for in vain in the past. Nor must it be forgotten that the primary demand of the African people is for a change in the nature and content of our Native policy and not for a share in giving effect to a policy with whose fundamental principles they are in total disagreement. We shall have to know a lot more about the fate of the other recommendations of our Recess Committee before we can regard what has so far been revealed as a step in the right direction.

As regards the recognition of African trade unions, this is also a matter which has been the subject of repeated representations by the Council and, on the face of it, it may appear as if the end of this particular battle is in sight. But the type of recognition foreshadowed in the proposed Bill has certain fundamental defects.

1. It will provide for separate trade unions for African workers. The European trade union movement has split on this issue, a number of unions in favour of separate unions for Africans having walked out of the South African Trades and Labour Council. The remaining body of trade unionists believe, I think rightly, that the common economic interests of workers engaged in the same occupation are of greater importance than the differences in the pigmentation of their skins, and have taken their stand on a united front of all workers in protecting their interests against the employers. Separate trade unions for Africans will lead to a conflict of interests between European and African workers which the captains of industry will naturally exploit to the detriment of the workers both white and black. The white advocates of separate trade unions for Africans will, I think, live to rue the day when they took that decision.

2. Under this Bill it will be illegal for African workers to strike. The primary object of establishing machinery for the orderly settlement of disputes between employers and their employees is to obviate strikes, not to make them illegal. The right of the worker to withhold his labour when he is not satisfied with his conditions of employment, without fear of being bludgeoned into ac-quiescence, is the only effective weapon he has in his struggle for the betterment of his working conditions. To compel the African worker to submit to a system of compulsory collective bargaining without the right to withhold his labour if he is dissatisfied with the decisions of a Conciliation Board on which he will not be represented, is to give him the shadow instead of the substance of recognition.

256

3. African mineworkers are to be excluded from the scope of the machinery for conciliation to be established under the proposed Bill. This is justified on the ground that a large proportion of the labour on the mines comes from foreign territories. The alternative machinery that will be provided for dealing with the problems of mineworkers, namely, an inspectorate functioning under the Department of Native Affairs, will presumably take care of the interests of both foreign and Union Natives. It is asking for too much to expect the African people to believe that this new inspectorate, whatever the grade of officers appointed, will make a better job of protecting the interests of the mineworkers than the inspectorate has done in the past. The African mineworkers demand the right to protect themselves through the medium of their own recognised and registered organisations.

In the near future the Government is going to summon the Council to consider and report upon the Industrial Conciliation (Natives) Bill, and it will be for the Council to decide then whether the Prime Minister's tentative plan for future Native policy, his proposals in connection with the Council and his Bill for the recognition of African trade unions, taken either jointly or separately, provide a basis for a fresh start with the work of the Council.

Document 33. Statement on the Prime Minister's Proposals, by Dr. A.B. Xuma for the ANC, May 11, 1947

We have examined the tentative proposals of General Smuts as appeared in the press on the native policy as presented to the six invited members of the Native Representative Council at Cape Town on the 7th [sic] May, 1947, and find them vague and disappointing in that the Prime Minister seems to have side-stepped the main cause of the deadlock—namely—the demand of the Native Representative Council for the repeal of the discriminatory colour legislation against the Africans and the consequent council resolution to adjourn indefinitely until such demands have been complied with. The country has been waiting for a direct reply to the Council's resolutions which has not been forthcoming in the Prime Minister's statement.

To the uninformed the Prime Minister's reported proposals might appear to be generous and to be an improvement on the present political status of the Africans, but in fact it is a retrogressive step in that as long as the present discriminatory legislation remains on the statute book, the Africans are being in effect asked by the Prime Minister in his proposals to administer their own domination, discrimination and oppression under the cloak of giving Africans responsibility and participation in the administration of their own affairs. We wish to submit that this is a false position created, because there is no such thing as native affairs apart from South African national affairs. In fact there can be no truly representative Government or Parliament within any state in which all members of the state are not directly represented. In other words,

257

we do not accept any proposal that does not provide for direct representation of all sections of the community in all legislative bodies.

The proposed Bill dealing with the so-called Recognition of African Trade Unions is unacceptable because it maintains the principle of racial and colour discrimination and domination as well as excludes the African mineworkers, the largest working group of Africans. The presence of African workers from outside territories should not be used to deprive African workers of their industrial rights. The proposal gives the workers or their Trade Unions no active part in settlement of industrial disputes in which they are concerned and denies them the fundamental right of workers, namely, collective bargaining and the enforcement of the workers' demands by means of the strike weapon.

My Working Committee supports the Council's resolutions to adjourn indefinitely until their demands have been complied with and submits as evidence of earnestness and sincerity on the part of the Government the following [virtually identical with the program set forth in Document 40, a flyer issued by Dr. Xuma on March 21, 1947]:

1. Removal of the political colour bar in the South Africa Act, and direct representation of Africans in all legislative bodies, national, provincial and municipal.
2. Abolition of the Pass Laws.
3. Removal of land restrictions against Africans in urban and rural areas.
4. Recognition of African Trade Unions under the Industrial Conciliation Act, and adequate wages for African workers including African mineworkers.
5. Adequate Housing facilities for Africans and adequate mass training facilities for Africans as builders and in other trades with outlets for employment as skilled workers.
6. Extension of the system of free, compulsory education to all African children of school going age.
7. The re-establishment of the status of the African chiefs in our national affairs.

Document 34. Statement on the Prime Minister's Policy toward the NRC, by the Caucus of the NRC, November 1947

(a) At the May conversations in Cape Town the Prime Minister at the request of the six Councillors, promised to call together the whole Council to expound before it what he considered proposals designed to end the deadlock between the Government and the Council and to launch a new era in Union Native Policy. Not only has the Prime Minister failed to fulfil his promise but the Government has gone further and decided not to convene the normal statutory meeting of the Council which was due to have taken place in November. Further, instead of meeting the Council which by its adjournment in 1946 precipitated the negotiations for a revised Native Policy, the Prime Minister has decided to suspend all negotiations until a new Council has been elected.

The Councillors feel entitled to surmise that this has been done in the hope that the new Council will have a substantially different complexion from the present one so as to ensure a relatively easy passage for the new proposals. It may also be hoped by the Government one of the results of the boycott movement at present on foot among the African people will be the elimination from the Council of the so-called "sit down strikers" and the election of a body of men more amenable to government control and guidance. Whatever may have been in the mind of the Government in deciding upon these tactics, the Councillors desire to place on record their disapproval and condemnation of this further example of the Government's breach of faith in dealing with this body of its own creation and are determined to take appropriate measures to ensure that the primary object of their adjournment in 1946, namely to get the Government to undertake a genuine and fundamental revision of its Native Policy is not defeated by the new Council on which the Government has apparently decided to pin its faith.

(b) As regards the proposals themselves the Councillors find that they are described as being "not final in either form or substance." The tentative character of the proposals is further emphasised by reference to the report of the Fagan Commission which it is suggested must be awaited before the Government's policy is properly formulated. For this reason it is not inconceivable that the final shape which the proposals will take may be substantially different in form or substance from what has been placed before us. These factors have naturally made it difficult if not impossible for us to arrive at a final conclusion as to what view to take of these proposals.

(c) We can however state at once that the proposals in their elaborated form do not go to the root of the matter in dispute between the Council and the Government. The main submission of the Council has been and continues to be that the conditions of African modern life demand a re-orientation of the whole of our Native Policy. It seems necessary to repeat the principal defects of our present Native Policy, viz: - ... [See above, statements a through f, page 252.]

In our view what is required is a policy which will give the African people a sense of security in the land of their birth, a policy which is flexible and can readily be adopted to changing conditions and varying circumstances; in short a policy which recognises that Africans are citizens of this country and not things apart. This new outlook on Native Policy is conspicuous by its absence in the specific proposals made by the Prime Minister. But apart from the question of principle and policy the proposals fall far short of the principal recommendations of the recess committee of the Council on representation which are as follows: - ... [See above, statements a through g, page 255.]

With regard to the proposed grant of Legislative and Executive powers to the council, it is obvious that these are in effect negatived by the proviso

259

that they shall not "affect the South African Native Trust or its functions nor shall the powers of the Governor-General to legislate for Native areas be affected."

(d) The question of the subordination of Local Councils, General Councils and Advisory Boards to the Native Representative Council as indicated in the proposals is not one which was raised by this Council and is irrelevant to the main issues raised by the adjournment resolution.

(e) In our opinion the Prime Minister's proposals would be more relevant to a situation in which our main communities black and white were divided into a sort of Hindustan and Pakistan, a state of affairs which the white would be less ready to bring about than the African.

(f) The African people who have endorsed the action of their representatives in the Council whose term of office now expires are as determined as ever to work for the objectives envisaged in the Council's adjournment resolutions, and in the forth-coming elections we would advise our people if they do elect, to elect a Council which will pursue this policy until its aims and objects have been achieved.

(g) As regards the boycott movement at present on foot among certain sections of the African people the Councillors believe that it represents the natural impatience of a long suffering people with the makeshift solutions of their problems dictated by a bankrupt and outmoded Native Policy. The movement is not deserving of the negative condemnation which it has met in some quarters, official and otherwise but rather of more sympathetic understanding and practical support among the African people. Having regard however to present circumstances among the African people, the Councillors are not prepared at this stage to advise them to refrain from voting.

The attention of the Councillors has been drawn to the address of the Secretary for Native Affairs delivered at the recent session of the Ciskeian General Council in which he intimated that the Government is determined to introduce compulsory limitation of stock in the Native Reserves.

We would be failing in our duty if we did not warn the Government that any ill advised step touching the land and stock of the people may lead to widespread disturbances for which the Government will have to bear full responsibility. We desire to point out that the Government has only recently begun to educate the people on the question of the improvement of the reserves which, on their own admission, are overcrowded and this process of education will have to be conducted more vigorously and with more understanding if better results are to be achieved. In many Native Areas the African people have already accepted the principle of betterment areas and it is the complaint of the people that the Government has itself failed to carry out its side of the programme of the improvement of the agricultural conditions of the reserves.

Further the Councillors take strong exception to the remarks of the Secretary for Native Affairs in which he took it upon himself to criticise the African

260

political and other leaders in the discharge of their functions as accredited representatives of their people. The African people, we feel sure, will deplore this attitude which will not improve relations between them and the head of the department.

We would be failing in our duty if we did not protest against these provocative utterances of the Head of a department which is not entirely free from blame in this matter about which the African people not unjustifiably feel so strongly throughout all the Native Reserves.

The Councillors welcome the speedy action which the government took to appoint a Commission of Enquiry into the Moroka Incident in which three constables were killed, and it is hoped that the recommendations of the commission will lead to the improvement of the bad housing conditions and administration in the Urban Areas to which the Council has repeatedly drawn attention.

The Councillors desire to urge the Government to institute a similar commission of Enquiry into the circumstances surrounding the incident at Middledrift, Cape Province, in which three African Constables lost their lives.

The Councillors urge the Government to publish without delay the report of the committee appointed to inquire into disturbances at Native Educational Institutions which continue to take place and supply the members of the Council with copies of the report.

THE POSTWAR AFRICAN NATIONAL CONGRESS UNDER DR. XUMA, 1946-1949

Document 35. Statement on the African Worker, by Dr. A.B. Xuma, January 14, 1946

The backbone and the mainstay of both the Gold Mining Industry and Secondary Industries is the Native Labour so called. In Gold Mining alone over 300,000 African men are employed. They are a class by themselves. They are recruited and engaged under a contract system and housed in compounds for men only. Their wages are partly in cash and partly in kind. They are separated from their families for their women and children are left in the reserves and there is no doubt that the general effect is to lessen family ties and to rob the reserves. At the same time it is true that these Africans are contributing greatly, not only to the Mining industry but to the economic welfare of the country as a whole. And their contribution deserves greater recognition than it has had up to now.

In other industries the number of African workers has also increased tremendously during the War period and large numbers have been doing work requiring a higher degree of skill and intelligence than they had ever done before. They have proved that the African is capable of skilled work and of contributing more effectively to the wealth of the country.

Although here and there, there have been improvements in wages through Wage Board Determinations and the cost of living allowance, the African workers still remain not only underpaid, but still below the bread line because the rise in cost of living has outpaced any improvements and awards that have come his way.

The African worker is becoming more conscious of his needs and of his rights and is becoming to understand the value of Trade Union Organization and collective bargaining. As a result there are now many African Trade Unions with a membership running into six figures. The exclusion of Africans from being termed "employees" under the industrial conciliation act is now out of date and the sooner this mistake is rectified the better, for it will benefit the African workers themselves and improve industrial relations. The Wage Board cannot under the Wage Act discriminate on grounds of race or colour and even under the Industrial Conciliation Act the Minister of Labour has the power, on the application of an Industrial Council, to extend the provisions of an agreement to all persons in the industry or occupation concerned, including Africans. Extensive use has been made of these powers to the benefit of all workers.

We urge that the African urban labour must be stabilized to increase its efficiency, skill and productivity. This can only be achieved by the abandonment of the system of migratory labour. Naturally the success of this stabilization process calls for the improvement of Natives' reserves and the release of more land for occupation by the African people through all forms of tenure. The conditions under which Africans now live and work in urban areas have made the pass laws also out of date. Their effect is to increase the numbers of Africans who come up against the Police and who unnecessarily gain experience of gaol. The result of all these things is that the African worker has become bitter and sullen. These acts of discrimination and segregation are objected to by men and women on both sides of the colour line in South Africa because they sow seeds of racial bitterness and antagonisms which are undermining all the ideals of South Africa, namely—Democracy, Christianity, and human decency.

Document 36. Cable to the United Nations Opposing Incorporation of South-West Africa, by Dr. A.B. Xuma, January 1946

The Chairman
General Assembly
United Nations Organisation
West Minister
London

Africans South Africa Protest against [proposed] incorporation South West Africa into Union. Pray urge control Territory by UNO Trusteeship Council. Mandate over territory was under Article 22 Covenant League of Nations.

Africans South West Africa no share in Government therefore take no part in incorporation negotiations. South Africa itself denies political and economic rights her 8,000,000 Africans.

83 percent Land reserved for 2,000,000 Europeans only less than 17½ per cent for 8,000,000 Africans.

Only 40 per cent African Children accommodated in mission schools.

95 per cent Africans are imprisoned under discriminatory regulations against Africans only. South Africa must first remove colour bar, restrictions, discriminations at home.

(Sgd) - A.B. Xuma
President - General
South African National Congress

Note: Moses Kotane wrote to Dr. Xuma on January 30, 1946, to congratulate him on his cable regarding South West Africa. "My quarrel with you and Congress," he wrote, "has been over the fact that you and Congress leadership generally let things go by default, that you do not speak up when you should and when it is necessary that you should. However, well done this time, sir. The Government will gnash its teeth but the Africans will appreciate your action deeply."

Document 37. Resolutions of the ANC Annual Conference, December 14-17, 1946

1) Congress congratulates the delegates of India, China and the Soviet Union and all other countries who championed the cause of democratic rights for the oppressed non-European majority in South Africa, and pays tribute to those South Africans present in America, particularly Dr. A. B. Xuma, Messrs. H. A. Naidoo, Sorabjee Rustomjee and Senator H. M. Basner, for enabling delegates to UNO to obtain first-hand information and data which provided the nations of the world with reasonable grounds for passing a deserving judgment against the South African policy of white domination.

   Conference desires to make special mention of the Council of African Affairs for its noble efforts to defend the fundamental human rights. Congress reiterates its pronouncement of full and complete confidence in Dr. A. B. Xuma as its President General.

2) Further this Conference hails the decision of the United Nations General Assembly on the treatment of the Indian minority in South Africa and

the rejection of the Union's claim to annex South West Africa as a condemnation of the South African Government's policy of white supremacy as a flagrant violation of the UNO Charter and the principles of justice and human rights.

3) Conference further pays tribute to the gallant men and women of the Indian community and their leaders who have by their great passive resistance campaign resisted the Ghetto Act and who by their sacrifice directed the attention of the world to the policy of race discrimination.

4) Conference places on record its profound admiration for those national heroes—the African Miners of the Witwatersrand—who fell in the face of ruthless terror as martyrs in the cause of freedom and for the improvement of the working conditions of African Miners in particular.

5) This Congress rejects the much-vaunted publicised contention of the gold mines that the African Mineworkers should be excluded in any scheme for the recognition of African Trade Unions on the ground that they are tribal natives. On the contrary, Congress demands that all workers should be accorded the rights of collective bargaining on equal terms with other sections of the population. In the view of Congress the much-vaunted principle of European trusteeship is a thinly-veiled disguise for the continued exploitation of the African people.

6) This Conference further congratulates the members of the Native Representative Council for their firm stand and insistence on the Government undertaking to abandon its policy of discrimination and supports the decision to adjourn the Council for the second time.

7) In these circumstances, this Conference of the African National Congress hereby declares its firm determination to continue the struggle against white domination until such time as Congress shall have won for Africans democratic rights equal to those enjoyed by white sections of the South African population and to this end Conference instructs the incoming National Executive Committee to consider the possibilities of closer cooperation with the national organisations of other non-Europeans in the common struggle.

8) To this end in view, Conference instructs the incoming National Executive Committee to conduct a powerful and nationwide campaign for: -

   a) a boycott of all elections under the 1936 Act and a demand for representation on municipal councils, provincial councils and parliament through a common franchise;

b) abolition of the Pass Laws;

c) recognition of African Trade Unions including the mines and agriculture, and improved conditions of African farm labour;

d) land and property rights in rural and urban areas;

e) educational facilities including improved teachers' pay;

f) better health services;

g) adequate social security benefits;

h) equality before the law.

9) That it be an instruction to the incoming National Executive Committee to provide a machinery for the carrying out and speeding up of the realisation of the programme of action set forth by means of setting up a council of action with power to create wherever necessary centres of activities, the raising of funds for the purpose, campaigning with the co-operation of such bodies and individuals as may be likely to reinforce its efforts, and to organise for the production of literary propaganda matter and other effective agencies for the intensification of the campaign.

10) This Conference is convinced that the campaign envisaged can only be rendered possible by the establishment of a fighting fund as follows: -

a) a special levy of 1/-. per member per month in urban and industrial areas and 6d. per month per member in rural areas, organised and controlled by the Council to be;

b) voluntary contributions towards the fighting fund.

11) Congress directs that the council-to-be as its first act appoints full-time organisers under a properly arranged system and effective methods of control.

12) Conference is deeply dissatisfied with the manner in which the Anti-Pass Campaign has been conducted, and expresses no confidence in the National Anti-Pass Council and the Action Committee of that Council.

13) That the Acting President General be requested to submit and secure the co-operation of the South African Native Advisory Boards Congress at its annual Conference due to assemble in East London on the programme of action embodied in Resolutions 7 and 8.

14) That the emergency conference referred to in the President General's cablegram be confined to Provincial officials and members of the National Executive Committee at which arrangements for the tour of the President General round the important centres of the Union would be drawn to implement Resolutions 7 and 8 hereof.

15) It is desirable that Congress should have Provincial full-time organisers. Therefore this Conference directs that Provincial bodies should make every effort to bring about this essential service.

16) This Conference is alarmed at the increasing hardships and chaotic conditions existing among African farm labourers and the homeless-houseless Africans in urban areas. Congress is convinced that this state of affairs is caused by the reactionary and repressive policy of the Union Government motivated by the desire to bolster up white supremacy.

17) As a protest against the barbarous policy of the Union Government of denying the elementary democratic rights to Africans and in view of the fact that these injustices are perpetuated and maintained in the name of His Majesty King George VI of the Union of South Africa, this Conference instructs the incoming Executive Committee to devise ways and means likely to bring about the abstention of the Africans from participation in the welcoming of the Royal Family during its tour of the Union.

18) The Notice of Motion submitted at the Kimberley Conference of Congress in 1944 anent membership subscriptions, viz:-
   a) Every individual member who resides in a city or urban area shall pay a subscription of one shilling (1/-) per month.
   b) Every individual member who resides in rural area or rural town shall pay a subscription of three shillings (3/-) per calendar year.
   c) There shall be no reduction in the subscriptions to be paid by members in terms of (b) above joining in the middle of or towards the end of the year.
   d) Affiliated members shall upon application and thereafter at the beginning of each year pay to the Provincial Committee or National Executive Committee as the case may be, a sum representing one fiftieth of the ordinary subscriptions or dues collected from its own members in the preceding year.
   now be adopted and the Constitution be amended accordingly.

Document 38. Minutes of the National Executive Committee of the ANC, February 1-2, 1947

SATURDAY - 1st FEB. 1947, 8 P.M.

PRESENT:
   Dr. A.B. Xuma (in the chair) Messrs. J.B. Marks, C.S. Ramohanoe, R.G. Baloyi, J.E. Malepe, L.K. Ntlabati, A.M. Lembede, S.P. Sesedi, A.P. Mda, Mrs. A.M. Jacobs, Cllrs. A.W.G. Champion, R.V. Selope

Thema, Z.K. Matthews, Dr. R.T. Bokwe, Messrs. J.N. Jacobs, H. Selby Msimang, James A. Calata (Secy. Gen.) D. Tloome (Secy. B.) and J.S. Mpinda (Sgt.-at-arms).

1. *APOLOGIES:*

Apologies for their absence were received from Mrs. M. Xuma and Mr. M.M. Kotane.

IT WAS DECIDED:

"That minutes of the last Executive be deferred until the arrival of the Secretary-General"

2. *CONFERENCE RESOLUTIONS:*

The chairman reported that the Working Committee had considered the resolutions [of December 1946] and made certain recommendations which were in the hands of members.

On a motion by Mr. Ntlabati, seconded by Mr. Ramohanoe,
IT WAS DECIDED:
"That letters of congratulations be addressed to the delegations of the countries referred to in resolution No. I, which championed the cause of democratic rights at UNO, for the oppressed Non-European majority in South Africa"

After a motion by Mr. Msimang, seconded by Mr. Baloyi, calling for the rejection of the Working Committee's recommendation, pledging full active support to the struggle of the Indians, had been debated, *IT WAS DECIDED:*
"That resolutions 2 and 3, hailing the decisions of the United Nations General Assembly, on the treatment of the Indian minority in S. A.; and paying tribute to the Passive Resistance campaign by the gallant men and women of the community, be deferred until a decision had been arrived [at] on the question of co-operation with the other non-European national organizations."

RESOLUTIONS 4 AND 5
IT WAS DECIDED:
"That the working committee's recommendation that a considered statement on Recognition of African Trade Unions be issued, be adopted, giving expression to the inclusion of the African mine workers and agricultural workers"

267

RESOLUTION 7:

Co-operation with other non-European national groups.

At this stage a letter from the Joint Passive Resistance Council was read. A lengthy debate ensued on this issue, ranging from the question of unhappy relations between the Indians and the Africans in certain areas, resulting from the attitude of the Indians towards the Africans economically, to that of the need to fight with all non-Europeans on a common ground for full citizenship.

RESOLVED:

"That this meeting of the national executive hereby resolves that the working committee, with powers to co-opt, be delegated to arrange the venue and date, within the month of February, for a meeting of representatives of the three national groups for exploration of the basis for co-operation"

THE MEETING ADJOURNED AT 11:30 P.M.

SUNDAY 2ND FEBRUARY - 9:45 A.M.

4. UNOPPOSED MOTIONS

Motions of condolence were moved to the following:

A. To the family of the late Mr. S.P. Akena by the Secretary-General.
B. To the family of the late Mrs. Lutuli, by Mr. R.G. Baloyi
C. To the family of the late Mr. Kgosana, by Cllr. R.V. Selope Thema.
The Secretary-General apologized for the absence of the minutes of the previous meeting, as he had treated this meeting as a special executive.

THE APOLOGY WAS ACCEPTED.

At this stage *it was agreed*, on a motion by Mr. Ntlabati, seconded by Mr. Malepe that the President-General give his report.

5. REPORT BY PRESIDENT GENERAL:

Delivering his report the President-General thanked members of the executive for their good work during his absence, as well as members of the N.R.C. for the stand they had taken. He gave a brief outline of the proceedings at UNO reflecting the debates on the complaint of the S.A. Indians and the proposed annexation of S.W. Africa by the Union Government.

268

He reported that in the course of his efforts in America, he submitted a memorandum on behalf of the A.N.C. to the Secretary-General of the United Nations, outlining the following African disabilities in South Africa:

A. Freedom of movement.
B. The status of the African Chiefs.
C. Political rights.
D. Economic Disabilities.
E. Social Services: health and housing.
F. Education.

After a lengthy discussion and comments on the report of the President General, Cllr. Thema moved a vote of thanks to the report of the President-General on behalf of the executive.

RESOLUTIONS (continuation)
   Resolution 8: Boycott of the Elections.
   The following resolution was moved by Mr. Msimang:
   "This national executive committee interprets the resolution directing a boycott of all elections under the 1936 Act, as an ideal dependent for its success entirely on a powerful and nation wide campaign, or as a weapon to be resorted to after all constitutional means have been exhausted in the struggle for the attainment of full political rights in accord with the first part of resolution No. 7 and, therefore, resolves to demand for full political rights i.e. Direct representation in all councils of State-Parliamentary, Provincial and Municipal representation. It is convinced that the kind of representation provided by the 1936 Act is a fraud and a deception."

Mr. Marks felt that the mover of the motion was now trying to reverse the decision of conference, an attempt which was a distortion of the spirit of the resolution.
   Dr. Bokwe said that there was great confusion in the country about the boycott. There was no time stipulated for the beginning of the boycott and the people did not know what methods should be followed.
   Cllr. Champion said Congress had never attempted to put forward candidates for the elections of the N.R.C. The stand taken by the members of the N.R.C. was the initiative of the Councillors themselves. It appeared the executive wanted to dictate to the Councillors. In his opinion it would be advisable that Congress consult with the chairman of the N.R.C. caucus and obtain the full facts. He therefore suggested fall back to its old policy of watching the N.R.C. at a distance.

   This view was supported by Mr. Baloyi.

The Secretary-General felt that the resolution by Mr. Msimang was a solution to the problem. There was a strong opinion that some members be returned in order to avoid people with lack of experience coming into the council.

Prof. Matthews said he agreed with Cllr. Champion that this meeting was embarrassing members of the N.R.C. The tactics they had used in the council was to continue the adjournment in order to make the council unworkable. The councillors were prepared to carry on the war of nerves, which the Government detested. He, however, felt that there was no option but to carry out the resolution, but was not sure whether the result of the campaign would enhance or lower the prestige of Congress.

Mr. Lembede said the masses were ready to act, but the leaders were not prepared to lead. It was a misrepresentation to say people were not ready. He was almost sure if an appeal was made, fifty per cent of the people would follow the lead.

Mr. Ntlabati stated it was remarkable that members should fear to implement the resolution before the attempt was even made. To his mind it was futile to say we should wait until the people were ready.

After a lengthy discussion, *IT WAS RESOLVED*, on a motion by Mr. Ramohanoe, seconded by Mr. Malepe,

"That this Executive resolves to stand by the resolution adopted by conference."

Mr. Msimang's motion was defeated.

RESOLUTION NO. 9

Mr. Lembede pointed out that it was not necessary to create a council, but that the executive was competent to take over the campaign. It was, however, essential to solicit the co-operation of the Trade Unions.

RESOLVED:

"That the Working Committee be delegated with powers to conduct the campaign."

Dr. Bokwe suggested, as a token of sympathy, that Congress vote a sum of money to aid the fighting fund of those members who were facing a case of sedition.

AGREED.

RESOLUTION NO. 10. FIGHTING FUND.

Mr. Malepe pointed out that an awkward situation had been created by the Transvaal Province, by having initiated a campaign for a freedom fund which was started already. He felt that such a step would cause much overlapping in carrying out resolution 10.

Mr. Ramohanoe, the Provincial President of the Transvaal, explained that the freedom fund started in the Transvaal was intended to provide funds for the Province. This was a scheme that had been...financial committee of the Province for raising funds.

THE MEETING ADJOURNED AT 2:30 P.M.

3:30 P.M. THE MEETING RESUMED

Mr. Jacobs suggested that it be a policy of Congress that all appeals sent out for donations to the fighting fund must be signed by the President-General.

The chairman explained that constitutionally the provinces had the right to raise funds, but it was considered more advisable that there should be consultation in order to co-ordinate the work and avoid friction and overlapping. He, therefore, suggested that the Working Committee be empowered to go into the matter for the purpose of making suitable arrangements.

After a lengthy discussion *IT WAS DECIDED*, on a suggestion by Mr. Ntlabati,

"That in order to avoid heavy taxation on the people, resolution No. 10 be adopted and 18 be suspended."

RESOLVED.

"That in order to carry out the spirit of resolution 10, Congress resolves to start a campaign to raise a fighting fund of £ 10,000 for a period of ten months."

REDUCTION OF THE EXECUTIVE

At this stage Prof. Matthews raised the question of reducing the size of the executive in order to keep down the expenses of the organisation. He pointed out that the financial position of Congress could not meet the expenses of so large an executive.

Prof. Matthews accordingly moved, and *Mr. Msimang* seconded;

"That notice of a motion be given by the executive for the next conference, to amend the constitution to make it possible for the reduction of the executive of not more than seven members."

A counter motion was moved by Mr. Marks seconded by Mr. Baloyi:

"That the size of the executive be not reduced and the relevant clause in the constitution be not amended."

On being put to the vote the two motions were 8 votes for, and 8 against.

IT WAS DECIDED
"That both motions be submitted to the next annual conference."

RESOLUTIONS 11 and 15   *FULL TIME ORGANIZERS*

The chairman made a brief explanation on the need for appointing full time organizers to cover the provinces under a suitable scheme. This resolution was debated at length with various opinions expressed by members on how such a scheme could be put into operation.

After some discussion *IT WAS DECIDED* on a suggestion by Cllr. Champion, as a compromise,
"That resolution No. 11 be adopted and 15 to be suspended."

THE MEETING TERMINATED AT 7 P.M.

Document 39. "Joint Declaration of Cooperation." Statement by Dr. A.B. Xuma of the ANC, Dr. G.M. Naicker of the Natal Indian Congress, and Dr. Y.M. Dadoo of the Transvaal Indian Congress, March 9, 1947

This Joint Meeting between the representatives of the African National Congress and the Natal and Transvaal Indian Congresses, having fully realised the urgency of co-operation between the non-European peoples and other democratic forces for the attainment of basic human rights and full citizenship for all sections of the South African people, has resolved that a Joint Declaration of co-operation is imperative for the working out of a practical basis of co-operation between the National Organisations of the non-European peoples.

This Joint Meeting declares its sincerest conviction that for the future progress, goodwill, good race relations, and for the building of a united, greater and free South Africa, full franchise rights must be extended to all sections of the South African people, and to this end this Joint Meeting pledges the fullest co-operation between the African and Indian peoples and appeals to all democratic and freedom loving citizens of South Africa to support fully and cooperate in this struggle for:

1) Full Franchise

2) Equal Economic and Industrial rights and opportunities and the recognition of African Trade Unions under the Industrial Conciliation Act.

3) The removal of all land restrictions against non-Europeans and the provision of adequate housing facilities for all non-Europeans.

4) The extension of free and compulsory education to non-Europeans.

5) Guaranteeing freedom of movement and the abolition of Pass Laws against the African people and the Provincial barriers against Indians.

6) And the removal of all discriminatory and oppressive legislations from the Union's Statute Book.

This Joint Meeting is therefore of the opinion that for the attainment of these objects it is urgently necessary that a vigorous campaign be immediately launched and that every effort be made to compel the Union Government to implement the United Nations' decisions and to treat the non-European peoples in South Africa in conformity with the principles of the United Nations Charter.

This Joint Meeting further resolves to meet from time to time to implement this declaration and to take active steps in proceeding with the campaign.

Document 40. "To All Africans and Friends of Justice." Flyer issued by Dr. A.B. Xuma, March 21, 1947

TO ALL AFRICANS AND FRIENDS OF JUSTICE.

The Africans are the underdog of all underdogs in South Africa. The discriminations and restrictions as well as humiliations against them should challenge them to rise as one man in a campaign to remove all their disabilities. All other races and national groups with their friends are moving on fighting for their freedom. The time has now come that all self-respecting Africans—men & women must join in the struggle for their own liberation. All liberty loving people, men and women of good-will of [all] races must join in this struggle. Here is a minimum programme on which you must organise and educate public opinion.

(1) Removal of political Colour Bar in South Africa and direct representation of Africans in all legislative bodies—National, Provincial and Municipal.
(2) Abolition of the Pass Laws
(3) Removal of Land Restrictions against Africans in urban and rural areas.
(4) Recognition of African Trade Unions under the Industrial Conciliation Act and adequate wages for African workers.
(5) Adequate Housing facilities for Africans and adequate mass training facilities for Africans as Builders and in other trades with outlets for employment as skilled workers.
(6) Extension of the system of free compulsory Education to all African children of school going age.
(7) The re-establishment of the Status of the African chief in our national affairs.

Organise mass meetings in your areas and solicit the co-operation of all local organisations and people in the campaign. If you are intelligent enough to realize that racial and colour discrimination and domination undermine our progress and well-being, you must join the struggle and play your part. Remember! Talkers don't work, and workers don't talk.

Your friends in South Africa; your friends abroad and among the United Nations are watching your conditions and struggles with intelligent interest.

If you do not take the campaign vigorously and seriously you will have failed yourselves, your children and your friends all over the world.

Issued by A.B. XUMA
President-General African National Congress,
104 End Street, Johannesburg.
March 21st 1947.

Document 41. Statement at Press Conference on Coming General Election, by Dr. A.B. Xuma, April 5, 1948

The coming General Election for white South Africa for the election of Europeans only and voted for by a white electorate, in the main emphasises the anomalous idea of democracy in South Africa. Judged by world standards there is no democracy in South Africa. The authority of the state is vested in an oligarchy—a despotic colour oligarchy—a white oligarchy which has established the aristocracy of the white colour of the skin as the emblem of supremacy. Their philosophy and the basis of their national policy in race and colour relations is that white is might and white is right. Put in the language of the former South African republics in their Grondwet, "There shall be no equality between black and white either in Church or in State". This expression is not a mere "wish being mother to the thought". It is a fait accompli—an accomplished fact. It is practice; it is the bedrock of the South African native policy in Church and in State. The Apartheid policy of the Nationalist Party is nothing new and should be nothing surprising to any honest and serious student of colour relations. It is a mere elaboration, a natural and logical growth of the Union Native Policy with improvements and progressiveness by proposing the inclusion of Indians and Coloured people. It is, perhaps, to plagiarise the Union Prime Minister, General Smuts, a "Holism" in Union Non-European affairs.

There is evidence abundant that all concerned realise that we are living in a changing world under changing circumstances. The world outlook and world thought has been affected by silent revolution associated with the recent war. The Non-Whites or Non-Europeans in South Africa like other peoples have not escaped the influence of this world revolution of thought, ideas and outlook. They served "King and Country" during the war and are now thursting [sic] for progress and advancement as well as an opportunity to live as free men and to develop according to their God-given abilities and capacities without lack or hindrance. Ruling white South Africa, however, is not at all prepared to give equality of opportunity to Non-Europeans. There may be some small measures of relief, but no release. For themselves and their children they (the Europeans) look forward to a future of progress but for Non-Europeans they look backward. They want to divide the Non-Europeans into separate controllable and exploitable entities thus unwittingly limiting the Non-European's potential contribution nationally in the hope that such a policy will help maintain "Western Civilisation" or "White Supremacy" whatever that means. They would rather commit this national economic suicide since the educational and economic restrictions and disabilities imposed upon the majority of Non-Whites at present undermine national efficiency and the productivity of the country. The national income is thus reduced and progress of the country retarded socially, educationally economically and politically in proportion to the degree equality of opportunity is denied Non-Europeans in all spheres of national activity.

274

To mention just a few points of illustration, Africans are debarred from skilled employment and may not be apprenticed. They are not recognised as employees under the Industrial Conciliation Act—the Charter of White workers in South Africa. Their trade unions therefore, are denied statutory recognition under the industrial act. Only a third of African children can be admitted into overcrowded Mission schools. But for this laudable effort of Mission bodies there would hardly be any education for Africans while education for Whites in all its aspects is a State responsibility. Education for Non-Europeans, especially Africans, is not a State responsibility, it is only subsidised by the State to a limited extent.

Mention was made before about the queer coming General Election. Attention of those concerned must be drawn to just a few anomalies to remove the camouflage of South Africa being called a *democracy*. A new House of Assembly—the law-making chamber of South Africa—is to be elected but only the Whites or Europeans have a full franchise. Even the few Coloured people and Indians who will participate in the Cape Province have a loaded franchise. They must meet an educational, property and/or income qualification. The European does not need such a qualification. He or she must be 21 years of age or over and must have a white skin entitling him or her to be recognized as of European descent and therefore a citizen.

During this election not a single African is entitled to participate not even under the loaded franchise. Eight million Africans are supposed to have three European members to represent them in a house of 150 representatives for 2 million Europeans. They have four European senators as representatives as against 40 senators for Europeans. Some of those senators are supposed to represent between one million and four million Africans each. This appears more like misrepresentation than representation. This arrangement was forced upon the African population, it was not a wilful surrender of their citizenship rights for something else. They rejected the proposal which nevertheless became law because the European Parliament needed it in order to establish "White Supremacy".

South African minds in colour relations have watertight multi-compartmented minds with outlooks not of principal but of expediency. For instance Mr. H.G. Lawrence, Minister of the Interior and Justice, in commenting on Apartheid is reported as saying: "I know of [no] greater betrayal of any community than is contained in this policy." I do not believe any decent people will rectify and approve a document and policy which consists not only of a betrayal but is a grave injustice to a section of the people which had served South Africa faithfully and well in peace and in war.

"A betrayal and great injustice" had been made to the Africans in the 1936 Acts and to the Indians in the Asiatic Act in 1946. These communities have served South Africa faithfully and well in peace and war. A betrayal and injustice are habits that crop up when one would like to act decently. Fed on them in African and Indian affairs, the Coloured section is in immediate danger and in fact certain white minorities might be next. No country can busy itself in trying to establish four grades of citizenship without resorting to practices which can hardly be looked upon as fair, just and honest.

Having accomplished political and residential apartheid between Europeans and Africans, the Asiatic Act in 1946 extended the same policy to the Indians in South Africa. The Apartheid-report including the Coloured people is a logical suggestion of a growing colour policy. Here the Nationalist Apartheid-report introduces nothing new. They are merely playing the part of Doctor Rosenberg in Hitler's Germany who philosophised in justification of the policy that already existed.

The existence of political Apartheid or segregation between Europeans and Africans in the past twelve years has widened the gap between Africans and Europeans. It has suggested increasing clash instead of community of interests. The handful of so-called "Native Representatives" have found themselves constantly opposed to the views of the majority of Parliament because most of the legislation in Parliament is either intended to exclude Africans from certain benefits or to deprive them of certain benefits or freedoms. This situation has created an apparent clash of interest and consequent deterioration of race relations between Europeans and Africans.

The passing of the Asiatic Act in 1946 has merely aggravated a worsening situation and added dimension if not more cause to the tension in colour relations. Apply Apartheid to the Coloureds and the vicious circle is complete.

Apartheid, segregation or separation—call it what you may—on a colour basis is political fraud. Any of these words is a mere euphemism for exploitation. Trusteeship as used in South African politics is another abused word. The so-called trustee, the European Government, is self-appointed and administers the estate in their (the Europeans) own interest and not that of the so-called ward. He has appropriated three quarters of the land, all political, educational and economic advantages for himself. The so-called ward—the Non-European is thus deprived of full facilities and incentives to progress. In fact, the whole policy of administration is intended to assure everlasting trusteeship and perpetual wardship. A ward that never grows.

General Smuts, speaking in Kimberley the other day is reported as saying, "South Africa is considered to be one of the best governed countries in the world." This the Right Honourable Prime Minister might accept as an expedient because to him South Africa has a population of eleven million during the war when the country requires the services of all to die in defence of South Africa, and only a little over two million white citizens when peacetime enjoyment of privileges prevails. I say any other people who will accept such a statement as was made by General Smuts can only say so if they do not know the treatment of the Non-Europeans in South Africa. They may only know South Africa through General Smuts and his agents. He seems to be one man at home and another abroad. Perhaps the recent distinguished American visitors composed of publishers and journalists fit the description. They met General Smuts, Mr.

276

Lawrence and perhaps other Government dignitaries. They were in the country about 8 or 10 days not travelling through it but flying over it. Perhaps the nearest to Africans was with riksha boys. Notwithstanding this when they gave their impression of South African colour relations, one wondered which South Africa they spoke of.

I have great sympathy with these distinguished visitors. I presume they were a charming lot of men. They made perfect guests for their host although they seem to have shown innocence, honest lack of correct information of local race relations in their farewell interviews.

The African National Congress at its last annual conference voted for the reelection of the retiring members of the Native Representative Council as far as possible not because we thought the Council a useful body. We did so to enable the Government to meet most of the same men whom the Government deliberately side-stepped in 1947 by not calling the statutory meeting of the Council because these men had twice adjourned in 1947 in protest against the Government's discriminatory legislation and demanded the abolition of such legislation. In doing this they were carrying out and supporting the policy of the African National Congress. We wanted them to hold this Government machinery from being captured by collaborators. We admire them and congratulate them for their stand and solidarity. We expect them to use this machinery in the cause of national freedom and full citizenship. I have been asked as to what guarantee I had that they will be loyal to the implications of the resolution of the African National Congress. My answer is, I have none. I however, have faith and confidence in their course of responsibility and loyalty to our cause and ideal. Their own stand since August 1947 is indisputable evidence of such responsibility and sincerity. Any change of attitude on their part will be a betrayal of the peoples' cause and a surrender of their principle if they abandon their resolution.

In conclusion, I may state that soothing phrases and paternal advise from those who would urge us to bear our oppression a little longer by saying "Rome was not built in a day" make no impression on thinking Non-Europeans. They know what they want and more than that, they know that the present policy is not in the best interest for South Africa, and future generations of both colours will not thank us for it.

Good feeling, mutual respect and cooperation is impossible of attainment in South Africa until we return to the old Cape principle of a common voters role. All the other systems that are in operation or are projected by the ruling class will only aggravate the present tense situation.

Even the Fagan Commission report is a truly typical South African political and legalistic document which recognises the facts of the situation but avoids recommending the obvious remedy. It merely wants to palliate with the system within the framework of policy. It lacks the detached, scientific, social approach which alone would be constructive.

The Union Parliament and Governments of the future must be made truly

277

representative of the whole population. Members of Parliament must be rendered responsible and responsive to all the sections and colours alike. The authority of the State must be exercised in the interest of all and not for the powerful white minority. This can only come about if a common franchise is established for all.

Indians, Coloured and Africans must play their full part in the interest of future generations of white and black in South Africa, to save South Africa from committing national suicide. They must realise that democratic rights are not a free gift. They are to be earned. They must organise their respective communities for this campaign for right and justice. They must not fight Europeans or Whites. They must fight the policy of discrimination and differentiation.

All men and women of goodwill of all races in South Africa must organise public opinion in order to attain common citizenship for all races and to put in the language of the Charter of the United Nations to establish in South Africa "respect for human rights and fundamental freedom for all without distinction as to race, sex, language or religion."

Document 42. "Presidential Address" by the Rev. J. A. Calata, ANC (Cape), July 1948

Ladies and Gentlemen, I welcome you all to this thirty-sixth annual session of the Provincial conference of the African National Congress (Cape). I know what personal sacrifices each and all of you have undergone to be here. I would indeed have been surprised not to see a good attendance of branches as I know how seriously the African is looking at the period through which the country is passing just now.

THE DEATH OF PROFESSOR JAMES THAELE:

Please allow me to speak to you shortly about Prof. James Thaele of Cape Town who passed away on the 3rd June 1948. I was extremely sorry not to be able to attend his funeral, but I am happy to know that the message I sent was read at his funeral.

Although Prof. Thaele's last days were spent outside Congress, he, nevertheless is worthy of all the respect we can give him, for during the period of his presidency over the Western Province the African National Congress was a live organization in that part of the country. His name and that of the late Kenneth his brother will always be connected with the properties which Congress branches bought and in which today there are buildings used by those branches. I refer to the property at Jansenville and I have heard recently from Dr. Xuma that there is another Title deed which has come into the Head Office through Mr. Runeli Hugenot. It is possible that there are other such properties waiting for Congress to release the title deeds and Mrs. K. Thaele may help to enable us to get them. Surely the contribution of Professor Thaele in this

278

respect is unique and worthy of remembrance. He was one of the few Africans who served with deeds more than with words.

CONGRESS AND RURAL AREAS:

This is the first time for Congress to hold its Provincial conference in this town since 1930 when I took up leadership and I desire therefore to ask you to pay attention to Rural problems for here we are in the centre of Rural areas and East London is the key to both Transkei and Ciskei rural areas. This should provide an opportunity for the organisation of Congress in the Reserves for the people of the reserves need our assistance. The powers of our chiefs need strengthening. I am sure we all welcome the granting of the right to try civil cases to Chief Matanzima. Chief Matanzima has led the way for education among the chiefs and the Government in thus recognizing him has taken a step in the right direction.

Another note-worthy step is that of appointing Mr. Mbuli at Mtata assistant Prosecutor. This will alter the translation of the term Prosecutor to another word which will not mean persecutor. This will surely change the whole attitude of the African people towards South African law courts. It will assist the new movement for Penal Reform which is gaining ground among Europeans, and restore the confidence of the Africans in Magistrates and the police. We may well hope to see before long African Magistrates and Commissioners in the reserves and African Superintendents of Town locations.

LAND FOR AFRICANS:

I saw a report of a certain meeting the other day in which an important official of the Government suggested that with regard to land the African needed education in the use of the land he possessed before he got additional land. While I agree with the necessity for this kind of education, I feel, however, that it should not be in the way of the fulfilment of the promises made under the 1936 Land Act.

I do not think that we as the African National Congress are satisfied with the wholesale townward drift of our people. Those of us who have lived in towns most of our lives know that it is not a healthy sign, although we would not support prohibitive measures, still I think we ought to do all we can to support the strengthening of our rural population by supporting all progressive measures which the Government will from time to time put forward provided such measures are for the benefit of our people.

Sometimes by our desire to show sympathy we may hinder progress. Please do not take me to be pro Government in its so called Reclamation and Rehabilitation schemes. I am only making a lead for discussion by which we shall learn more about what is actually happening in the carrying out of these schemes. There is no doubt that the inadequacy of land for Africans is to a great extent responsible for the townward drift of our people and for the breakdown of morals and religion.

I think I can say without fear of contradiction that the breakdown of morals and religion amongst our people is caused by detribalisation which is the natural result of multi-racial contacts in urban areas, combined with economic difficulties and backed by the system of migratory labour [which] recurs in the rural areas and makes the task of administration harder for the headmen and chiefs.

I have lived more than twenty years in the Cape Midlands and my work has taken me to many farms in the districts of Cradock, Somerset East, Pearston, Hofmeyr and Middleburg. One thing seems to stand out more clearly to me and that is the state of the farm usually reflects the life of the labourers. Good farmers who provide their labourers with facilities, health, education and religion usually get better fruits of labour. I have come to the conclusion that factors which contribute to the breakdown of health and moral and religious lives of communities are detrimental to pastoral and agricultural people. Soil erosion is very often the result of soul erosion.

THE CHANGE OF GOVERNMENT:

The change of Government has been received with a certain amount of excitement and anxiety by Africans. The African press has asked our leaders to confer and on Friday the 25th June Dr. Xuma and I discussed the position and decided to call the National Executive for the 1st of August at Bloemfontein.

It is, however, a mistake to think that we have any power to influence the Government. I was surprised to notice that the press regarded the three European members of Parliament representing Africans as part of the United Party on national issues, for they are not supposed to ally themselves with any political party. Their duty and our duty now is to strengthen the African Congress which will give them power to wield the singular balance caused by the narrow majority between the two major parties in Parliament. However we must not lose sight of the fact that there is very little difference between the policies of the two parties as far as we are concerned and many United Party members are nearer the Nationalists than say Mr. Hofmeyr their Deputy leader. The African National Congress is gaining ground and last year our membership was about 7,000, with Transvaal and Natal having over 2,000 each. The leaders of the African National Congress have succeeded in getting the co-operation of the Members of the Native Representative Council and the members of the Native Representative Council have gained the full recognition of leaders of their people by the people. This was due to the bold step of adjourning themselves when they realised that the Government did not afford them the same recognition which they got from those they represented. Their aim as well as ours is to make the Government realise that the African is an integral part of the body politic of South Africa. This talk of White South Africa is just as bad for the country as any talk of Black South Africa because there can be no divided South Africa. Apartheid in concrete form is not possible. General Smuts with his sharp political eye saw the new political situation de-

280

veloping among Africans and immediately set about some way to meet it. He met six M.R.C.'s and made certain suggestions to them, one of which was to meet the whole council and put his proposals to them. Some African politicians had already planned a passive resistance campaign beginning with the boycott of all elections under the 1936 Act. This step appeared to be too fast and likely to divide the people instead of uniting them and the Congress resolved to proceed with the elections of the N.R.C.'s but not to abandon the Boycott issue. The Cape is to be congratulated in its following the leadership of the Congress and returning Professor Matthews, Messrs Godlo and Xiniwe unopposed. The African National Congress felt that the wisest course lay in keeping our organisation intact and giving General Smuts the chance he needed to fulfill his promises to the members of the Representative Council. This is what caused the excitement over the change of Government after the elections.

You will remember, however, that in my Presidential address last year at Cradock I pointed out the possibility of the Nationalists winning the elections. I had the 1924 experience at the back of my mind and I remembered the Nationalists' Black Manifesto of 1928 which gave them greater popularity in 1929.

South Africa is a funny country in that its rulers are full of fear. They fear the Black people who out number them by 3:1. It is supposed to be part of the British Commonwealth of Nations and yet it can have an anti-British Government. It is a country of many races, yet it is possible for it to have a Cabinet composed of men of one race. This signifies that the problem of race relations is not easy to solve and that is why South Africa cannot stand before the United Nations Organisation with a Government policy that is acceptable with regard to its treatment of non-European and African races.

THE NATIVE POLICY OF THE NATIONALISTS' GOVERNMENT:

Dr. Malan has told the country what the attitude of his Government is going to be. His Government would follow the policy of Apartheid. What that means in actual practice is hard to understand; but in theory Apartheid for the Non-European means a large measure of independence through the growth of their self reliance and self respect, and at the same time the creation of greater opportunities for free development in conformity with their own character and capacity.

For the European it means a new sense of security resulting from the safeguarding of their own identity and future. For both races it means peaceful mutual relations and co-operation for their common weal, declared Dr. Malan in his first speech as Premier broadcast from Pretoria. He further went on to say that the Government will with fixed determination endeavour to achieve the realisation of this felicitous state of affairs.

Then suddenly he remembers that he is responsible not only to his party nor to the European people of South Africa alone for his declared policy but also to God The Almighty and then he said: In South Africa's Constitution

281

the Sovereignty of God in the destiny of our country is specially acknowledged and in exercising our Governmental functions we wish to act in conformity with that confession. Lastly he appealed to the Church to give him support.

Well, his Church has advised him not to court disfavour by careless administration of Native Affairs. Even apart from that Dr. Malan will not risk another election before his term is over through his administration of Native Affairs.

AFRICANS NEED NOT FEAR:

As I have said before we are not wedded to any political party. No party cares for our support. We have to accept the Government that is in power and find a way to co-operate with it in promoting our welfare. If Dr. Malan expects the Church to support him he must abandon his apartheid policy for the Church of God should not be a party to a policy of Colour Bar.

Our chief trouble is going to be the small officials who will serve the public behind the counter at the stations, Post Office, and such like Government controlled establishments, for already some of us have met with some of the uncultured young Afrikaans-speaking officials who think that their chance has come to play the fool. Such people should just be reported to their head Office and they will certainly lose their jobs. You, leaders of the people, must not allow the people to fall a prey to the unscrupulous officials.

I know that when the late Tielman Roos was Minister of Justice we appealed to him against the indiscriminate shooting of our people and we received satisfactory attention and support from him. Dr. Jansen, the Minister of Native Affairs, is not new to this post and may not be worse than Dr. Van der Byl by any means.

Mr. Erasmus has already removed our anxiety by stating that he does not want African soldiers, for those soldiers who fought against Robey Liebrandt and his Nazi friends would not find it easy to fight under his direction in this country. We plead with our people to be careful in the future when our country is threatened with an outside invasion and not to present themselves for any war service blindly as they have done before. Let us adopt a strict neutrality policy; neither to cause trouble ourselves nor be concerned in any party trouble which may involve the country in bloodshed.

Don't worry about Mr. Schoeman's statement on the training of African Building Artisans. It will not have any effect. Just go about your work as usual as if nothing had happened and you shan't notice any difference in the treatment except the usual pinpricks you would expect under this Government, which should not be beyond your ability to face.

THE BEST OPPORTUNITY FOR CONGRESS:

I want to stress the importance of organisation and unity of action. If we are united we shall make the work of our Parliamentary Representatives easier in bargaining for our rights. There is a strong feeling among some leaders that we must boycott the election of our European Parliamentary Representatives. I still maintain that it would be wiser for us to wait for the action of the Nationalist Government who have already said that they are going to abolish this form of Representation. Perhaps who knows when the Act is revised it may turn out better than it actually is. I do not think it wise for us to meet trouble, let us wait for it to show itself and then face it.

We know what the Nationalists have been saying about us when they wanted the votes of the Europeans and we can use those statements very successfully for rallying our people round our organisation. It will be easy for them to join so that by the time we have to face the foe we shall be strongly united. If we remain divided we shall never be strong.

Please do not take my remarks to mean that we are never to co-operate with this Government. I do not want us to adopt an anti-Nationalist attitude for such an attitude could easily lead to our alliance with one or other of the parties that are not in power. I am aware of the great respect we have for men like Mr. Hofmeyr. I know how we love the people of British descent because of what we owe them, but we must not overlook the fact that there are many Nationalists who are good men and women.

Mr. Bekker of Cradock is a strong Nationalist in Politics but a real gentleman as a farmer. Sometimes I am tempted to suggest we should look for an Afrikaner for one of our Parliamentary Representatives and not only have English speaking people.

THE FAGAN COMMISSION REPORT:

When the Stellenbosch University Professors criticized this report, Justice Fagan went to Stellenbosch and explained it to them. After reading his address to the Professors of Stellenbosch I felt that a man like him might not be a bad choice as our Representative in Parliament if he could offer himself. Justice Fagan is a Nationalist and was at one time Minister for Native Affairs. Today it is he who defends the urban African and goes out of his way to show other Nationalists why Urban Africans must be regarded as co-citizens with the other sections of the Urban population. His Commission's Report offers useful suggestions regarding the Pass laws although they do not say they must be abolished altogether. They see that they are a source of unnecessary irritation to African people, and recommend some modification.

I cannot say that I agree with them for I want to see a total abolition of the pass but anyway some modification of the present system might help our people. Men of Justice Fagan's standard of education know that the world opinion must be taken into serious consideration and that what is known as the Native problem is after all the problem of Colour which is by no means peculiar to South Africa.

SOUTH WEST AFRICA:

I believe this conference is aware that this Government is already moving by consultation with the Authorities in South West Africa, and there is no doubt that they will try to perform what they had been saying, that is annex South West Africa without necessarily fulfilling the requirements of the United Nations' Organisation. It was clear from reports that Representatives of the Commonwealth at U.N.O. did not wish to offend South Africa by supporting those who were against incorporation, however, the Trusteeship Council has submitted its questions to South Africa and some of them concern the treatment of Africans. We must watch the outcome.

THE SOUTH AFRICAN CONSTITUTION:

General Smuts admitted at the Transvaal United Party Congress at the end of last year that the South African Consitution needed a thorough overhauling. May we hope that this overhauling of the Constitution will be proceeded with as soon as possible. If 40 years ago it was necessary to have a colour bar clause in the Act of Union to prevent Africans from taking their full share of responsibility in the shaping of the destiny of this land, it certainly is wrong now after the efforts to educate them have been so abundantly rewarded. Surely it cannot be right to refuse direct representation to the original inhabitants of this country in Parliament for all time. Such a policy is not only wrong but dangerous, for Africans will in the long run start their own parallel institutions and follow the example of the Burmese.

If the Europeans of this country shut their eyes to the fact that the non-white races of the world are dissatisfied with the attitude of the White people against them and are drawing closer together in order to resist White domination everywhere, then they must be strange people indeed. They will wake up one day when it is too late and their children will curse their graves.

I am one of those who have been preaching that Christianity is a world brotherhood, and that a European Christian is a nearer person to me than an African Mohammedan, but I am beginning to wonder if my European brethren preach a similar doctrine to their people. Well there is your chance Reverend Dr. Malan. Prove to the world that you stand by the principles of Christianity which involve the Fatherhood of God and brotherhood of man.

GOD BLESS AFRICA

James A. Calata
President

Document 43. Cable to the United Nations, by Dr. A.B. Xuma, November 25, 1948

Press reports Mr. Louw, Union delegate, as saying in Fourth Committee on sixteen November that Mr. Rathebe told meeting of Johannesburg Joint

Council Europeans and Africans that "Natives" would accept apartheid if it was total segregation. This was apropos Polish delegate's anticipation of racial conflict resulting from Union's discriminatory policy and meant to show that Africans like Rathebe supported apartheid. Regret to say that what Rathebe said was opposite. Mr. Louw dared not tell delegations of Trusteeship Committee that among other things Rathebe said, "Africans tried to be subservient and had done all menial work of the country, but in spite of this they had not been able to satisfy the Europeans. They realized that they needed the guidance of Europeans who had the advantages of education and an older civilization, but felt that because of their own contribution in labour to the country's wealth they should be given equality of opportunity. They were no longer willing to be regarded as serfs or articles for exploitation, they wanted to be considered equal partners in the land of their birth. If this could not be achieved then *total* apartheid would be welcomed by them. But they knew that the apartheid envisaged by the Nationalists was quite different from that for which they hoped. The Nationalists wanted them to continue as hewers of wood and drawers of water. Africans were well aware that it was futile to try and quarrel with Europeans, as they had the machine guns, for this reason and because they were so frustrated, they thought the only way to achieve harmony with the Europeans who possessed eighty-seven percent of the land [was for the Europeans] to give them territory and let them go their own way and build up their own civilization, with the help of Europeans of goodwill." Rathebe continued, "At the back of every person's mind was the desire for freedom—European countries were endeavouring to regain freedom they had lost during war; Indonesia, India and Palestine were all striving for it and Africans too longed for a state of their own where they would no longer suffer under oppressive laws." Rathebe continued, "Africans hoped that UNO would not be influenced by South African Government's attempts to prevent the discussion of Union's domestic affairs at its meeting. Naturally they felt that the rest of the world should know of the racial discrimination in South Africa." I beg you in interest of justice to backward peoples of Union of South Africa who are unrepresented in Assembly to circulate this cablegram to all members so that wrong impression may be corrected before debate in General Assembly. On twenty-third instant I cabled Mr. Louw requesting him to correct misrepresentation.

Document 44. Joint Statement on the Durban Riots, by A.W.G. Champion of the ANC (Natal) and Dr. G.M. Naicker of the Natal Indian Congress [n.d.]

The African National Congress and the Natal Indian Congress appeals to the African and Indian people of Durban to do everything in their power to prevent any further disturbances of the like which occurred yesterday.

We are deeply grieved that there should have been such a disturbance and that violence and disorder were prevalent to the detriment of large numbers

285

of innocent African and Indian people. We strongly condemn the violence and sincerely appeal to our people to be calm.

We call upon our people to avoid congregating in the streets and public places and to remain indoors as far as possible, and to go straight to their homes after work in the normal manner. There should be no panicking, and no violence and provocation must be resorted to.

We sincerely appeal for greater tolerance and understanding between our peoples.

We sympathise with all those Africans and Indians who received injuries as a result of yesterday's unfortunate incidents.

As leaders we appeal to our respective followers to assist in trying to discourage the wild and false talk which brought about this trouble.

Document 45. Statement on the Durban Riots, by the Working Committee of the ANC, signed by Dr. A.B. Xuma, January 20, 1949

The Working Committee of the African National Congress wishes to express the appreciation of the President General Dr. A.B. Xuma for his timely visit to Durban during the riots, and for his co-operation and consultations with African leaders in Natal in their efforts to bring the race riots between Indians and Africans to an end.

While deeply deploring the wanton destruction of life and property during the rioting, and the further loss of life caused by the use of firearms by the police, naval and/or military units in their intervention, the Working Committee wishes to point out and to emphasise that notwithstanding the incident of the assault of an African youth by some Indian, the Union policy of differential and discriminatory treatment of various racial groups is the fundamental contributing cause of racial friction and antagonisms. It has rendered the African the football and servant of all which he silently resents. It has given him an accumulation of grievances and a sense of frustration which find expression in unpredictable actions of violence or otherwise, to which no section is immune. Violence is the law of the jungle; it solves nothing; it arouses tempers and suspicions; it breeds hatred.

The Working Committee therefore urges all to avoid violence as far as possible, and to endeavour to find other more humane methods for the solution of the various problems.

The Durban situation, in the opinion of this Committee, is a grave challenge to the Union Government, with its racial and colour policy, to take immediate steps to review the differential and discriminatory policy in consultation with leaders of the non-European communities.

In view of the prevailing tension the Working Committee appeals to the African people not to allow themselves to be involved in actions similar to those which occurred recently in Durban, or to be used by other people who desire to further their own political ends at the expense of the African by fostering race hatred. At this stage the Working Committee appeals to the leaders of the Indian community to restrain their own people from doing anything that may lead to similar incidents and clashes between the two communities. Further the Working Committee is of opinion that the situation demands a round-table conference of African and Indian leaders including representatives of Indian commercial groups.

Finally the Working Committee would like to make it clear to all concerned that Africans claim themselves to be entitled by right of birth to receive their full share of all the rewards, the benefits and the opportunities for advancement which the Union of South Africa offers.

Document 46. "Statement Issued by Joint Meeting of African and Indian Leaders" [For Closer Co-operation], February 6, 1949

This historic joint meeting of the representatives of the national organisations of the African and Indian people, representing the Executives of the African National Congress and the South African Indian Congress, and other leaders held in Durban on this 6th day of February, 1949, expresses its regret shock and horror at the recent tragic happenings in Durban and elsewhere in Natal, during which there has been considerable loss of life and destruction of property of members of both the African and Indian communities.

This meeting extends its deep and heartfelt sympathy to the relatives of all the victims of the unhappy tragedy and to all those who have suffered.

Whatever are the immediate causes which may have precipitated the outburst, and which are receiving the attention of this meeting, this meeting is convinced that the fundamental and basic causes of the disturbances are traceable to the political, economic and social structure of this country, based on differential and discriminatory treatment of the various racial groups and the preaching in high places of racial hatred and intolerance. Any disturbances such as the recent Riots are therefore the fruits and results of such a policy as well as the responsibility of those who create and maintain such an artificial social framework.

In the light of this, this meeting calls upon our respective peoples—

(a) to view our problems in this perspective.
(b) to devise ways and means for closer co-operation and mutual understanding through their national organisations.
(c) to stand together in their fight for national liberation and their mutual political, economic and social advancement and security.

This meeting therefore directs its constituent bodies particularly the African National Congress (Natal) and the Natal Indian Congress to constitute a joint council and to establish thereunder local committees to advance and promote mutual understanding and goodwill among our respective peoples.

For *African National Congress*.

Dr. A. B. Xuma, President General.
A. W. G. Champion, President (Natal)
C. S. Ramahanoe, President (Transvaal)
R. G. Baloyi, Treasurer-General.
H. Selby Msimang, J. B. Marks, J. Malangabi, G. Makabeni, Moses M. Kotane, L. K. Ntlabati, O. R. Tambo.

For *South African Indian Congress*.

Dr. G. M. Naicker, President.
A. I. Meer, Joint Hon. Secretary.
J. N. Singh, Joint Hon. Secretary.
Dr. A. H. Sader, Joint Hon. Treasurer.
George Singh, Joint Hon. Treasurer.
I. A. Cachalia, T. N. Naidoo, V. Lawrence, I. C. Meer, M. D. Naidoo, Debi Singh, Nana Sita, Y. Cachalia, G. H. I. Pahad.

Other Indian and African leaders.

Professor D. D. T. Jabavu.
Rev. Z. R. Mahabane of the Orange Free State.
N. Mkele, Observer, All African Convention.
D. W. Moshe.
S. B. Ngcobo.
S. R. Naidoo (Cape).
T. B. Gwala.
E. O. Msimang.
A. N. Ntuli.
J. G. Mgadi.

Document 47. Minutes of the Annual Conference of the ANC, December 15-19, 1949

1. Conference opened at 10:10 a.m. on the 15th December, 1949. In the absence of the Senior Chaplain the Speaker, Cr. R. V. Selope Thema, called upon Rev. J. A. Calata to lead devotions.
2. The Speaker then introduced the Manager of the Non-European Affairs Department, Bloemfontein, Mr. Viljoen. The Manager welcomed all the delegates to Bloemfontein. He declared that good relations existed between his administration and the local Branch. Here there was none of that spirit of mutual distrust and suspicion experienced in other places. He hoped delegates would have a happy stay and wished Conference great success.

Professor Matthews proposed a vote of thanks to the Manager. He thanked the Manager especially for refraining from the usual giving of advice to delegates. It has become traditional for officials to give a plethora of pieces of advice to our people often resulting in merely confusing our people. Africans must learn to rely on their own advice if they hoped to win freedom.

3. *CONFERENCE PRELIMINARIES* ....

4. *MINUTES OF THE LAST CONFERENCE*

.... Mr. P. Motsita seconded by Mr. Nthaja moved the adoption of the Minutes.

At this stage Mr. D. Mji required an explanation from the Chairman as to whether or not all the members then assembled in Conference, Black and White, were accredited members of the A.N.C., whether with regard to the members of the Press, the A.N.C. approved of the reports usually published by the independent press after such members had covered Conference, especially in view of a misleading impression that could have been gathered from the Press reports of last year's Conference; whether Conference would not rather rely upon its own reporters, and finally Mr. Mji begged leave to move that Conference should go into Committee and all non-members should be excluded.

A short discussion ensued on these points after which the Speaker ruled Mr. Mji's motion out of order ....

Mr. N. Mokhehle desired to know whether it was the policy of the A.N.C. to distribute the delegates' badges to all and sundry indiscriminately and, more particularly, he objected to the sale of the badges to the members of the White press.

At this stage Conference adjourned for 15 minutes in order to enable the Credentials Committee to complete and present its report.

Conference resumed at 12 Noon.

5. *REPORT OF CREDENTIALS COMMITTEE*

Mr. G. I. M. Mzamane reported accredited delegates present at Conference as follows: ....[101 names are listed, including 12 members of the National Executive, 23 from Cape Province, 41 from the Transvaal, 2 from Natal, and 23 from the Orange Free State.]

Mr. R.G.Baloyi then required to know why his name did not appear on the National Executive. The General-Secretary explained that Mr. Baloyi had been suspended last year and Mr. Makabeni was acting for him and that at a later stage the President-General would give a fuller explanation.

Mr. Mokhehle again insisted on a defined policy on the badges. Rev. Calata explained that the Badges were printed and distributed always by the local Committee to supplement its funds and this matter had always remained in their hands. The Speaker ruled the matter out of order.

Mr. Pitje asked why Mr. Mbobo was recording the proceedings of Conference whereas he was not a delegate according to the Credentials Committee's report.

Mr. Resha moved that Mr. Mbobo should be replaced by a bona fide delegate. Messrs Maseko and Tloome explained that their Provincial-Secretary would only arrive in the evening when Conference would then know whether Mr. Mbobo was a delegate or not and pleaded that pending the arrival of their Secretary Mr. Mbobo should continue to record the proceedings. Mr. L.K.Ntlabati added that pending the arrival of the Transvaal Secretary it was difficult to accept any Transvaal Credentials as true or not. Mr. Pitje seconded by Mr. W.Mbete moved the name of J.A.Mokoena to replace Mr. Mbobo. The General-Secretary, supported by Mr. Selby Msimang, G. Radebe and V.M.Kwinana, deposed that constitutionally the Executive had to carry out its functions and was at liberty to do that through any functionary in whom they had confidence. The Speaker then ruled that Mr. Mbobo should continue to record Conference proceedings.

Conference adjourned for lunch.

6. *PRESIDENTIAL ADDRESS:*

Conference resumed at 2.30.p.m. and Dr.A.B.Xuma, President-General, delivered his presidential address ....

7. *DISCUSSION OF PRESIDENTIAL ADDRESS:*

Mr. A.P.Mda moved that Conference should go into Committee for the purpose of discussing the presidential address and in this regard endorsed remarks made by Mr.Mji earlier about press reports of Conference. He was seconded by Mr.L.K.Ntlabati.

The Secretary-General read messages of goodwill sent by telegram from Messrs. R.H.Godlo, M.J.Sipamla, Nyasaland African National Congress, and the S.A. Indian Congress through Dr. Naicker.

Mr. Mtwesi deposed that Mr. Selope Thema was also a member of the press and should be excluded from Conference. A motion by him of no-confidence in the Speaker [Selope Thema] failed by reason of no seconder.

With Mr. Makabeni in the Chair discussion on the presidential address took place. Mr. H.S.Msimang said that the position of the African was so rapidly deteriorating that a time had arrived when the ability of our leadership was to be put on a true test. The great object now was for all of us to find the best way out. Mr.G.I.M.Mzamane deplored the silence of our leadership during times of crises, to wit, when the bona-fides of Rev. Michael Scott were queried by the South African press, also during the recent happenings of Lovedale Hospital and at St. Matthews College.

Mr. G.Radebe said Congress stood in dire need of a re-orientation of policy and a departure from the beaten track of speeches to which he had listened for the past 15 years.

Mr.A.P.Mda spoke at length by popular consent on this need for re-orientation of policy. It was imperative that Congress, as a National Liberation Movement, should set itself a goal, an ideology towards which every member should strive, and this, he submitted, can only be found in the doctrine of African Nationalism and the instrument with which to achieve this ideal could be none other than Boycott. The following also spoke, Messrs M.P.Ntlabati, J.G.Mtwesi, D.J.Mji, N.C.Mokhehle, J.Kotsokoane, Mac.Maseko.

At 5.p.m. the hour scheduled for adjournment some dozen names were still on the list due to speak. Mr. Msimang, seconded by Mr. E.C.Duma, moved that these people should speak when the question of the Programme of Action is discussed at a later stage and there was to be no further discussion on the presidential address as such.

It was announced that Conference would on 16th assemble at 8.30.a.m. and then march to the Market Square to hear a public declaration of a considered statement by the African National Congress.

Conference adjourned at 5.20.p.m. in order to allow the Congress Youth League to hold their own Conference for the rest of that evening.

16TH DECEMBER:

Conference resumed on the second day, 16th December, 1949, at 9.a.m. 8. The Rev.L.Soga led the Devotions. Rev. J.A.Calata explained the significance of raising the right thumb when singing the African National Anthem. The first four fingers symbolised Unity, Determination, Solidarity and Militancy, while the thumb was raised as a supplication for Africa to come back to us. The symbol was first introduced by the C.Y.L. at the Cape and it has been found meet to adopt it universally in Congress. [In *A Short History of the African National Congress* prepared by Calata during the early stages of the treason trial of 1956-1961 (8 mimeographed pages, 8/2/57), he wrote regarding "the Africa Salute": "In June 1949 the Provincial Conference of the A.N.C. (Cape) adopted a THUMB-UP Sign by which Congressites might recognise and salute each other. Its meaning was presented as: a) The closed four fingers denoted Unity, Determination, Solidarity, and Militancy. b) The Thumb resembled the sharp point in Central East Africa known as Cape Guardafui, which the Africans regarded as THE HORN of Africa. This had the significance that all Africans in South Africa recognise themselves as the inhabitants of Africa. This sign was then adopted later by the National Conference the same year."]

9. Minutes of the previous day were read and adopted ....

10. STATEMENT ON VOORTREKKER CELEBRATION:

The President-General being absent at this stage, the house required that he should report at Conference and lead the march down to the Square when a Statement on the Voortrekker Celebrations was to be read in public. Upon the arrival of the President, Mr. Letlaka seconded by Mr.L.K.Ntlabati moved that the Conference should go into Committee in order to consider the Statement before adopting it.

Dr.A.B. Xuma then read the Statement. Mr. N.Mokhehle stated that he felt the statement did not properly reflect the African point of view, the whole approach[ed] did not evince the spirit of the African, on the contrary the Statement

291

rather inclined towards the Whiteman's point of view. A long discussion ensued in which the following participated and introduced various amendments:-
Messrs. N. Mokhehle, G. Radebe, Prof. Mathews, M. Kotane, G. Mzamane, L.A. Gama and J.S. Mtwesi. In its re-cast form, the statement was then adopted.

Orders were then given on the manner of marching down to the Square with Mr.E.Manyosi appointed as man in charge. At the Square the Speaker, Cr.Selope Thema made an introductory speech and then called upon the President-General to read the Statement.

Mr. A.P.Mda, the President-General of the C.Y.L. was called upon to second the National-President. He declared that an action in this connection signified not only our challenge to the Whiteman's point of view but also an inflexible determination on the part of the African to struggle for National Freedom, and that in spite of the odds heavily loaded against the African by an enemy highly organised and armed with a perfected technique of domination.

Cr. Thema in his closing remarks said that in short we had come to dedicate our lives to the cause of those heroes who fell 100 years ago and to leave as a heritage to our children the fighting spirit of our erstwhile heroes like the Dingaans, Ndlambes, Moshoeshoes and Sekukunis.

11. Conference resumes at 2.25.p.m. and the President briefly replied to matters which had been raised by those members who had spoken on his Presidential address ....

12. *PROVINCIAL REPORTS ON PROGRAMME OF ACTION:* ....

Discussion followed on the reports. At this stage the National Council of Women paid Conference a visit. The President introduced the members and welcomed them. Then Miss M.Soga briefly addressed Conference. She said their presence there was an expression of goodwill. They did not believe in physical warfare. They believed in commanding rather than demanding justice. Miss Soga was seconded by Mrs. Nkomo.

Mr. Leshoai of Bloemfontein led a collection that brought in the sum of 15/6d ....

After certain announcements with regard to Conference Reception and a session of C.Y.L. at 7.30.p.m. at the B.S.I., conference adjourned at 5.10.p.m. till 9.a.m. the next day.

17TH DECEMBER:

Conference resumed on the third day, the 17th December, 1949 at 9.25.a.m. Devotions were led by the Chaplain Rev.J.J. Skomolo.

The Secretary-General announced the death in Durban of Mr.P.Mngadi, once an organiser of Congress, and the house rose in silence for a minute.

Minutes of the previous day were read and confirmed. The reply to the question as to the collection of 15/6 the previous day was that this had gone to Congress coffers. Prof. Matthews suggested that if the matter of raising right thumb in singing the National Anthem was to be regularised it had to come as a Resolution.

Secretary-General read the Agenda for the day.

14. *PROVINCIAL REPORTS:* ....

REPORT OF CO-ORDINATING COMMITTEE OF PROGRAMME OF ACTION:

The Executive retired for consultation and the house then heard the report given by Mr. Mzamane on the Programme of Action. The Programme was thoroughly scrutinised paragraph by paragraph and amendments made, the following participating, Dr.Molema, Dr. Njongwe, Sobukwe, Dr.Moroka, M.P. Ntlabati, Sisulu, Mzamane, Phooko, Mokhehle, Mtwesi and Rev. J. J. Skomolo. The Programme was then accepted in its amended form unanimously and it was pointed out that only those people who signified their willingness to carry out this Programme should be elected into the incoming Executive. [The Programme of Action is Document 60.]

EXECUTIVE REPORT:

At 9.30. p.m. the Executive returned to the house and the General-Secretary presented their report. The National Offices were now at 2/3 New Court Chambers, Johannesburg, where there was a full-time typiste. Mr. Tambo was the Honorary Secretary of the Working Committee. The Executive had taken into hand the situation in Durban during the riots of January, 1949, and Joint Councils of Goodwill consisting of Africans and Indians had been established....

On the question of the unity between A.A.C. and A.N.C., a joint meeting had been held in April, 1949 by Executives of the two bodies, but no agreement could be reached and the matter has been shelved sine die....

RECOMMENDATIONS:

1. That the Executive was far too large and should be reduced to seven (7) elected members in addition to the Office Bearers.
2. There should be an Inner Executive consisting of the President, Treasurer, Secretary, plus the 4 Provincial Presidents.
3. Constitution should be amended with a view to creating proper machinery for dealing with disciplinary matters....

FINANCIAL REPORT:

Financial Report was read by the Acting Treasurer Mr. G. Makabeni, Prof. Matthews in the chair. Explanation was made that much difficulty had been experienced by the whole Office and the Acting Treasurer owing to the failure of the ex-Treasurer to hand over the seals of his office. The last financial statement had been presented in 1947, and Conference had refused to accept same as it was not audited. The then incumbent was required to present same audited in 1948, but, on the contrary, was not even present at Conference, hence the appointment of an Acting Treasurer. The matter had now been amicably settled and next Conference the audited statement would be presented. The Report showed a deficit of £ 219.6.4. which had been met by drawing on a Reserve A/C. A/C No. 2 had now £ 471 and No. 1 A/C £ 20.

Discussion followed in connection with the Cape not having forwarded the share of the National Executive, and it was explained that this was no dereliction of duty but a cautious step due to lack of confidence in the Treasury Department in the light of explanations referred hereto above. The Report was adopted.

ELECTIONS:

A motion to defer elections for a year on account of the state of Finance Department was defeated.

Messrs. Motili and J. Hlekani were appointed scrutineers, the Programme of Action was re-read for benefit of prospective candidates.

RESULTS OF ELECTIONS:

OFFICE BEARERS:

President-General: Dr. J. S. Moroka.
Secretary-General: Mr. W. M. Sisulu.
Treasurer-General: Dr. S. M. Molema.

COMMITTEE:

1. Dr. A. B. Xuma.
2. Dr. R. T. Bokwe.
3. Rev. J. A. Calata.
4. Mr. A. P. Mda.
5. Rev. J. J. Skomolo.
6. Mr. L. K. Ntlabati.
7. Mr. O. R. Tambo.
8. Dr. J. L. Z. Njongwe.
9. Mr. G. Radebe.
10. Mr. J. A. Mokoena.
11. Mr. G. M. Pitje.
12. Mr. D. Tloome.
13. Mr. M. M. Kotane.
14. Mr. R. G. Baloyi.
15. Mr. V. V. T. Mbobo.

Dr. Xuma presented the new President to Conference, saying he wished him the best of luck in his term of office. When he first took on nine years back, Conference hardly made a total of 40 delegates and there was nothing in the treasury. He thanked all those who had served with him and given him unstinted loyalty.

Dr. Moroka assured Conference that he would do his best for success of aspirations of Congress and hoped that neither he nor they should live ever to rue the day when he was elected.

Prof. Matthews replied that Kotane was co-opted to the Resolutions Committee as Msimang had left.

The Annual National Service would be held in this Hall at 3.p.m. 18th. December, 1949.

THE MATTER OF ELECTION:

Council of Action would be appointed on the 18th December, 1949.
The new Executive had to meet by Constitution on day of election.
Conference would resume at 10.a.m. the next day.
Conference then rose at 2.30.a.m....

18TH DECEMBER:

Conference resumed on the 18th December at 11.30.a.m....

At this stage Mr. L. A. Gama moved a vote of thanks to the retiring Executive and spoke in glowing terms of the wise and patient leadership of the retiring President, in particular of his magnanimous act of true statesmanship in agreeing to serve on the new Executive. He mentioned also the General-Secretary and the Speaker for his guidance and control of the House even when difficulties arose.

The Executive then retired into consultation. The session then was devoted to the Youth League....

Conference adjourned until 2.30.p.m.

RESOLUTIONS COMMITTEE REPORT:....

RESOLUTIONS:

1. (a) That this Conference of the A.N.C. rejects the conception put forward by the Union Government that the problem of the relations between Black and White in S. A. is merely one of domestic jurisdiction and states that U.N.O. has a right to intervene in this matter, which, unless dealt with in accordance with the principles of the U.N.O. Charter, will ultimately lead to armed conflict between the races in this country.

   (b) This Conference does not accept the contention that the representatives of the Union Government in U.N.O. in any way express or represent the views of the African people, because both by legislation and otherwise the African people are not accorded citizenship rights in the Union.

(c) Therefore this Conference claims the right to choose its own representatives to express the views of the Africans in international councils, and accordingly directs the National Executive to seek ways and means of implementing this resolution.

2. This Conference views with serious concern and alarm the deterioration which has taken place in the position of the African people as a result of the application of the policy of apartheid within the last eighteen months as indicated by the following:—

(a) The abolition or reduction of Trust Medical Scholarships.

(b) The threat to introduce compulsory academic segregation in Universities.

(c) The implied threat to Africans contained in the terms of reference of the Native Education Commission.

(d) The reduction of School Feeding for Africans while allowances are being increased for Europeans.

(e) Reduction of funds for rehabilitation in the Reserves.

(f) Expulsion of thousands of Africans from Urban Areas because of temporary unemployment.

(g) Retrenchment of Africans in accordance with the so-called Civilised Labour Policy.

(h) The refusal to register even employed Africans on the grounds that they happen to reside outside the area of jurisdiction of the Municipality.

(i) The bringing of undue pressure on Africans to take up farm labour and mining.

(j) The reduction of old age pensions, invalidity grants and other social security benefits for Africans while they are being increased for Europeans.

(k) The reduction of funds for housing Africans.

This Conference is uncompromisingly opposed to the policy of apartheid as preached and practised not only by the present Government but also by previous Governments, whatever the name they choose to call it by. The African people are resolved to fight it until we achieve the objective set out in our Programme of Action.

3. *CONGRESS SIGN:*

This Conference resolves that in future during the singing of the National Anthem the sign of the clenched right hand with the thumb pointing to the right shoulder should be used as a symbol which stands for Africa and is a sign of Unity, Determination and Resolution.

4. *AFFAIRS IN AFRICAN INSTITUTIONS:*

This Conference instructs the Executive to investigate:

(a) The state of affairs adumbrated in the announcement by the "Association of Heads of Native Institutions" that Sesotho-speaking school children are not to be admitted in Institutions in the Xhosa-speaking areas and vice versa.

(b) The basic cause of school riots in our Institutions by the appointment of an African Commission of Enquiry.

(c) The fate of the Malcomn Commission Report of 1943.

(d) The fact that minor children are made to sign declarations.

DISCUSSION:

There was discussion on the attitude to adopt towards the new Syllabus in schools. Mr. Mokhehle suggested that teachers should be called upon to refuse to teach the said syllabus as soon as it came into force and Mr. Kotsokoane added that children and parents should be organised to resist the syllabus.

It was also pointed out that children from the Protectorates were now being refused admission into Union schools. It was generally felt that apartheid was being applied even outside the boundaries of the Union and that the Protectorates were willing to close ranks with the Union inhabitants, as was demonstrated by the telegram from Chief Sobuza. It was suggested that Congress should make positive contacts with the Protectorates and that at the next Conference a report on such contacts should be made. Some members felt that these contacts should extend over all other African territories like Gold Coast, Nigeria, etc....

It was decided to send a reply of thanks to Chief Sobuza for his message and Dr. Molema was requested to draft same, which was adopted.

The resolution on the question of U.N.O. was referred to the Executive for a thorough discussion and implementation.

ALEXANDRA BRANCH VS. MESSRS. BALOYI, MODISE AND GUMEDE:

Prof. Matthews gave the Report of the Executive in 1948 during the elections of European representatives to Parliament on behalf of Africans. Messrs. Baloyi, Gumede and Modise participated as agents of certain candidates belonging to the Nationalist Party. The Alexandra Branch decided to take disciplinary measures against all three on the grounds that they had committed a breach of the Constitution and gave them various periods of suspension from membership. They then appealed to the Transvaal Provincial Executive and later to the Transvaal Provincial Conference and both bodies upheld the decision of the Branch. All three then appealed to the National Executive, the fourth body; the only other body above this and the highest according to the Constitution, was the National Conference.

The Transvaal Executive had objected to the appeals being entertained by the National Executive on the grounds that the Constitution made no such provision, but this objection had been overruled as it was based upon a false interpretation of the Constitution.

The facts in favour of the Appellants were that they claimed that they had participated in the elections because no direction had been given as to the attitude to be adopted by Congress members and they were accordingly free to support whom they pleased.

At the 1948 Conference one of the Branches had brought a similar case and the ruling of Conference was that, until Congress had laid down a definite policy with regard to supporting or otherwise of the various political parties in this country, no disciplinary action should be taken against anybody. Prof. Matthews said that Mr. Baloyi invoked this ruling in his favour, but the defence had to fail because his offence had been committed prior to this ruling. Moreover, Mr. Baloyi had been present when the National Executive drew up a statement, stating in unequivocal terms Congress's opposition to apartheid and all its protagonists. This statement was issued in July, 1948 and Mr. Baloyi's offence was subsequent to that date.

In October, 1948, prior to the said elections, the Transvaal Provincial Conference resolved that none of its members should support a Nationalist candidate and called upon its members to support one Mr.W.G.Ballinger.

Mr. Baloyi had argued that he had called upon the Working Committee to clarify the fog surrounding a definite policy as to what candidates to support. There was, however, no documentary evidence in support of this contention.

The Transvaal Executive, now Respondents in this appeal, had dismissed the appeal on the following grounds:—

(a) Appellant's act was prejudicial to interests of Africans as laid down in the Constitution.

(b) It was a direct and flagrant violation of their resolution at the Pretoria Conference.

Prof. Matthews said that the Executive frankly admitted that there had been much confusion among the most loyal of Congress members owing to the vacillating policy of Congress on this question. But the Executive had met in July, 1948 and issued a Statement in which they condemned apartheid in unequivocal terms. Mr. Baloyi was aware of this statement. He could not then go scot-free.

Prof. Matthews said that the other appellants, Modise and Gumede, were not present to present their cases. However, as the times of suspension they had been given had already expired, no useful purpose would be served by considering their appeals.

Prof. Matthews then read the written judgement of the Executive against which Mr. Baloyi was now appealing to Conference.

"We condemn the action of Mr. Baloyi in principle as being politically prejudicial to the interests of Congress, having regard to its declared policy towards apartheid. While we are satisfied that the lower Courts of Congress which dealt with this case acted in good faith, we are of the opinion that the sentence imposed was too severe and we accordingly reduce the sentence from three years to six months from the date of his lodging the appeal, i.e. 30th November, 1949."

Among those who participated in the discussion that followed on this were Messrs. Mokhehle, Manyosi, Radebe and Z. Matthews. It was agreed that Conference accepted the information constituting the case, that Conference should then constitute a court to deal with the case, the members of the Executive not to stand on the Committee that might be elected for this purpose, and then Mr. Baloyi should be called upon to present his case. Conference then adjourned and was to resume for this purpose at 9 p.m.

19TH DECEMBER:

Conference resumed at 9.50.a.m. Devotions were led by Rev.J.J.Skomolo.

The Speaker then explained that Conference had adjourned the previous night at 8 p.m. to resume at 9 p.m. He and other members, mostly members of the C.Y.L. had remained in the Hall till 12.15.a.m., and Mr. Baloyi was there all the time. It had been decided against hearing Mr. Baloyi's appeal in the absence of the National Executive and the Transvaal Executive, the respondents in the case. Accordingly it was decided to hold the last session of Conference on this day, especially in view of the fact that Conference had not been formally closed. When Conference had adjourned the previous night it was to have resumed at 9.p.m. especially to hear Mr. Baloyi's appeal. He had been there, but the Transvaal, the Respondents, had failed to turn up. Prof. Matthews explained that it was only fair that Conference had decided to extend the time of the Respondents in which to appear until 9.30.a.m. on the following day. But the Respondents had still defaulted. Mr. Mbobo then moved that in view of the absence of the Transvaal Executive this Conference resolves to give the Appelant Absolution from the instance. Mr. Kongisa seconded the motion, which was adopted unanimously.

Mr. D.Mji moved that the incoming Executive be empowered to elect the Council of Action. This was seconded by Mr. Moleleki. Mr. Mzamano pointed out that it would be competent to co-opt any bona-fide member of Congress into the Council of Action.

Prof. Matthews moved a vote of thanks to Speaker for conducting Conference smoothly. He also thanked the local Committee for all arrangements for our happy stay at Conference and thanked our hosts and hostesses whose hospitality has almost become proverbial. Mr. Mji moved a vote of thanks to the out-going Executive.

Mr. Mbobo sounded a warning to Conference that as a result of the adoption of the Programme of Action serious developments should be expected and clearly bitter times lay ahead and an Emergency Conference during the year should not be ruled out of possibility.

The new President thanked conference for electing him. He said it was not his intention to antagonise the other sections of our mixed population. On the contrary he intended to strengthen friendly relations with the Coloureds and Indians, but when it came to the question of the rights of his people, then there was no room for compromise. He thanked his predecessor for his statesmanship in being so willing to serve on the Executive. He was fully aware how difficult was the task which he had taken upon his shoulders. But he enjoined all of us to enter the struggle ahead with courage and fortitude. Above all also he would devote himself to the task of unifying the African people.

The Chaplain, Rev. Skomolo, led the House in closing prayers and Conference ended its business at 11.15.a.m.

V.V.T.Mbobo
Conference Recorder.

THE RISE OF THE AFRICAN NATIONAL CONGRESS YOUTH LEAGUE AND ADOPTION OF THE PROGRAMME OF ACTION 1943-1949

Document 48. "Congress Youth League Manifesto." Issued by the Provisional Committee of the Congress Youth League, March 1944

PREAMBLE

WHEREAS Africanism must be promoted i.e. Africans must struggle for development, progress and national liberation so as to occupy their rightful and honourable place among nations of the world:

AND WHEREAS African Youth must be united, consolidated, trained and disciplined because from their ranks future leaders will be recruited:

AND WHEREAS a resolution was passed by the conference of the African National Congress held in Bloemfontein in 1943, authorising the founding and establishment of the Congress Youth League,

WE therefore assume the responsibility of laying the foundations of the said Youth League.

STATEMENT OF POLICY

South Africa has a complex problem. Stated briefly it is: The contact of the White race with the Black has resulted in the emergence of a set of conflicting living conditions and outlooks on life which seriously hamper South Africa's progress to nationhood.

The White race, possessing superior military strength and at present having superior organising skill has arrogated to itself the ownership of the land and invested itself with authority and the right to regard South Africa as a Whiteman's country. This has meant that the African, who owned the land before the advent of the Whites, has been deprived of all security which may guarantee him an independent pursuit of destiny or ensure his leading a free and unhampered life. He had been defeated in the field of battle but refuses to accept this as meaning that he must be oppressed, just to enable the Whiteman to further dominate him.

The African regards Civilisation as the common heritage of all Mankind and claims as full a right to make his contribution to its advancement and to live free as any White South African: further, he claims the right to all sources and agencies to enjoy rights and fulfill duties which will place him on a footing of equality with every other South African racial group.

The majority of Whitemen regard it as the destiny of the White race to dominate the man of colour. The harshness of their domination, however, is rousing in the African feelings of hatred of everything that bars his way to full and free citizenship and these feelings can no longer be suppressed.

In South Africa, the conflict has emerged as one of race on the one side and one of ideals on the other. The Whiteman regards the Universe as a gigantic machine hurtling through time and space to its final destruction: individuals in it are but tiny organisms with private lives that lead to private deaths: personal power, success and fame are the absolute measures of values; the things to live for. This outlook on life divides the Universe into a host of individual little entities which cannot help being in constant conflict thereby hastening the approach of the hour of their final destruction.

The African, on his side, regards the Universe as one composite whole; an organic entity, progressively driving towards greater harmony and unity whose individual parts exist merely as interdependent aspects of one whole realising their fullest life in the corporate life where communal contentment is the absolute measure of values. His philosophy of life strives towards unity and aggregation; towards greater social responsibility.

These divergences are not simplified by the fact that the two major races are on two different planes of achievement in the Civilization of the West. This is taken advantage of to "civilise" the African with a view to making him a perpetual minor. This obstruction of his progress is disguised as letting him "develop along his own lines." He is, however, suspicious of any "lines" of development imposed on him from above and elects to develop along what the Natives Representative Council recently called the "lines of his own choosing."

In practice these divergences and conflicts work to the disadvantage of the African. South Africa's 2,000,000 Whites are highly organized and are bound together by firm ties. They view South African problems through the perspective of Race destiny; that is the belief that the White race is the destined ruler and leader of the world for all time. This has made it imperative for the African to view his problems and those of his country through the perspective of Race. Viewing problems from the angle of Race destiny, the Whiteman acts as one group in relations between Black and White. Small minorities view South African problems through the perspective of Human destiny. These number among their ranks the few Whites who value Man as Man and as above Colour. Yet these are so few that their influence on national policies is but little felt.

301

The advantages on the side of the Whites enable 2,000,000 Whitemen to control and dominate with ease 8,000,000 Africans and to own 83% of the land while the Africans scrape a meagre existence on the remaining 17%. The Whiteman means to hold to these gains at all costs and to consolidate his position, has segregated the African in the State, the Church, in Industry, Commerce etc., in all these relegating him to an inferior position where it is believed, the African will never menace White domination.

TRUSTEESHIP

To mislead the world and make it believe that the Whiteman in South Africa is helping the African on the road to civilized life, the Whiteman has arrogated to himself the title and role of Trustee for the African people.

The effects of Trusteeship alone have made the African realise that Trusteeship has meant, as it still means, the consolidation by the Whiteman of his position at the expense of the African people, so that by the time national awakening opens the eyes of the African people to the bluff they live under, White domination should be secure and unassailable.

A hurried glance at legislation passed by the Trustees for the African during the last forty years shows what a bluff Trusteeship is. The very Act of Union itself established as a legal right the claim of the Whiteman to dominate the man of colour. It did not recognize the African as a citizen of the then newly-formed Union; it regarded him as a beggar at the gate.

This was followed by the 1913 Land Act which deprived the African of Land and Land Security and in that way incapacitated him for that assertion of his will to be free which might otherwise have been inspired by assured security and fixed tenure. The Act drove him into urban areas where he soon made his way to skilled trades etc. But the Trustees had not brought him to urban areas to civilise him by opening to him avenues to skilled work. They had brought him so that he might be a cheap and nearby reserve of unskilled labour. This was finally established by the Colour Bar Act which shut Africans from skilled trades etc., thereby blocked their way to Civilisation via these channels.

In 1923 the Trustees passed the Urban Areas Act and this measure as amended warned Africans clearly that they were bidding farewell to freedom.

This Act imposed forms of control on the Africans which would have stirred into revolt any other section of the population. But because the Africans were not organized they yielded to more oppression and allowed themselves to be "controlled" from birth to the grave. This control had the effect of forcing Africans to remain impotent under unhealthy urban conditions which were set up to add their due to the ruining of the African's resistance to disease. The legalized slums, politely called Native Locations, were one aspect of these conditions.

302

But the Trustees were not satisfied with the emasculation of an entire community. In the 1927 Native Administration Act, they established the White race as the Supreme Chief of the African people. The conquest of the African was complete.

As the African accepted none of these measures to "civilise" him without a struggle, the Trustees had always been worried by his prospects as long as the Cape Franchise remained. With little compunction, in 1936 the last door to citizenship was slammed in the face of the African by the Natives Representation Act which gave us 3 Whitemen to represent 8,000,000 Africans in a house of 150 representing 2,000,000 Whites. At the same time a Land Act was passed to ensure that if the 1913 Land Act had left any openings for the African, then the Natives Land and Trust Act would seal them in the name of "humanity and Modern Civilisation."

The 1937 Native Laws Amendment Act closed up any other loophole through which the African could have forced his way to full citizenship. Today, Trusteeship has made every African a criminal still out of prison. For all this we had to thank the philosophy of Trusteeship.

While Trustees have been very vocal in their solicitations for the African their deeds have shown clearly that talk of Trusteeship is an eyewash for the Civilised world and an empty platitude to soothe Africans into believing that after all oppression is a pleasant experience under Christian democratic rule. Trusteeship mentality is doing one thing and that very successfully, to drive the African steadily to extermination. Low wages, bad housing, inadequate health facilities, "Native education," mass exploitation, unfixed security on land and halfhearted measures to improve the African's living conditions are all instruments and tools with which the path to African extermination is being paved.

But the African rejects the theory that because he is non White and because he is a conquered race, he must be exterminated. He demands the right to be a free citizen in the South African democracy; the right to an unhampered pursuit of his national destiny and the freedom to make his legitimate contribution to human advancement.

For the last two hundred years he has striven to adapt himself to changing conditions and has made every exertion to discover and derive the maximum benefits from the claims of the Whitemen that they are his Trustees. Instead of meeting with encouragement commensurate with his eagerness and goodwill he has been saddled with a load of oppression dating from the unprovoked wars of the last century and now containing such choice discriminating legislation as the 1913 Land Act and such benefits of Trusteeship as official harshness which recently attempted to hang an African under the very roof of the very State Department established to protect him and guide him on his way to civilisation just because he could not answer questions as quickly as the impatience of the Pass Office Trustees wanted.

303

In this very war South Africa is fighting against oppression and for Freedom; a war in which she has committed herself to the principle of freedom for all. In spite of this however it would be the highest folly to believe that after the war South Africa will treat the Africans as a citizen with the right to live free. South African blood...of Whites and Africans alike...has been shed to free the White peoples of Europe while Africans within the Union remain in bondage.

For his loyalty to the cause of human freedom and for his sacrifices in life, cash and kind, he has been promised a "Suspense Account"...another way of telling him that in spite of all he has done for his country in its hour of darkest need, for him there will be no freedom from fear and want.

LOSS OF FAITH IN TRUSTEESHIP

These conditions have made the African lose all faith in all talk of Trusteeship. HE NOW ELECTS TO DETERMINE HIS FUTURE BY HIS OWN EF-FORTS. He has realised that to trust to the mere good grace of the Whiteman will not free him as no nation can free an oppressed group other than that group itself.

Self-determination is the philosophy of life which will save him from the disaster he clearly sees on his way...disasters to which Discrimination, Seg-regation, Pass Laws and Trusteeship are all ruthlessly and inevitably driving him.

The African is aware of the magnitude of the task before him but has learnt that promises no matter from what high source, are merely palliatives intended to drug him into yielding to more oppression. He has made up his mind to sweat for his freedom; determine his destiny himself and, THROUGH HIS AFRICAN NATIONAL CONGRESS IS BUILDING A STRONG NATIONAL UNITY FRONT WHICH WILL BE HIS SUREST GUARAN-TEE OF VICTORY OVER OPPRESSION.

THE AFRICAN NATIONAL CONGRESS

The African National Congress is the symbol and embodiment of the Afri-can's will to present a united national front against all forms of oppression but this has not enabled the movement to advance the national cause in a manner demanded by prevailing conditions. And this, in turn, has drawn on it criticisms in recent times which cannot be ignored if Congress is to fulfill its mission in Africa.

The critics of Congress attribute the inability of Congress in the last twenty years to advance the national cause in a manner commensurate with the demands of the times, to weaknesses in its organization and constitution; to its erratic

304

policy of yielding to oppression, regarding itself as a body of gentlemen with clean hands and to failing to see the problems of the African through the proper perspective.

Those critics further allege that in that period Congress declined and became an organization of the privileged few...some Professionals, Small Traders, a sprinkling of Intellectuals and Conservatives of all grades. This, it is said, imparted to the Congress character taints of reactionism and conservatism which made Congress a movement out of actual touch with the needs of the rank and file of our people.

It is further contended by the critics of Congress that the privileged few who constituted the most vocal elements in Congress that they strongly resented any curtailment of what they considered their rights and, since the popularisation of the Congress character would have jeopardised or brought about the withdrawal of those rights by the Authorities, Congress was forced to play the dual role of being unconscious police to check the assertion of the popular will on the one hand and, on the other, of constantly warning the authorities that further curtailment of the privileges of the few would compel them, the privileged few, to yield to pressure from the avalanche of popular opinion which was tired of appeasing the Authorities while life became more intolerable.

These privileged few, so the critics of Congress maintain, are not an efficiently organized bloc. Their thinking itself lacks the national bias and this has made Congress a loose association of people who merely react negatively to given conditions, able neither to assert the national will nor to resist it openly. In this connection, Congress is accused of being partly suspicious of progressive thought and action, though it is itself unable to express correctly the views of the mass of the people.

Finally, the critics say that because the privileged few who direct Congress are poorly organized and have no marked following, Congress cannot openly defy popular wishes; hence to maintain its precarious existence, it is compelled to be very vocal against legislation that has harsh effects on the African underdog while it gives no positive lead nor has any constructive programme to enforce the repeal of all oppressive legislation.

CHALLENGE TO YOUTH

Some of these criticisms are founded on fact, it is true, but it does not advance the national cause if people concentrate on these while little or no effort is made to build Congress from within. It is admitted that in the process of our political development, our leadership made certain blunders. It was inevitable that this should have been the case, encompassed as the African people were and still are with forces inimical to their progress. But it does no good to stop at being noisy in condemning African leaders who went before us. Defects in the organisation of the people against oppression cannot be cured

305

by mouthing criticisms and not putting our heads together to build what has been damaged and to find a way out of the present suffering.

Both the oppression and the causes that give rise to the criticisms of Congress cannot be allowed to go on indefinitely. Soon the point must be reached when African Youth, which has lived through oppression from the cradle to the present, calls a halt to it all. That point, happily is now reached...as witness some of the clear-cut national demands by Youth at the Bloemfontein conference and the formation of Youth movements and political parties. All this is proof that youth wants action and is in sympathy with the rank and file of our oppressed people. It is all a challenge to Youth to join in force in the national fight against oppression.

In response to the demands of the times African Youth is LAYING ITS SERVICES AT THE DISPOSAL OF THE NATIONAL LIBERATION MOVEMENT, THE AFRICAN NATIONAL CONGRESS, IN THE FIRM BELIEF, KNOWLEDGE AND CONVICTION THAT THE CAUSE OF AFRICA MUST AND WILL TRIUMPH.

CONGRESS YOUTH LEAGUE

The formation of the African National Congress Youth League is an answer and assurance to the critics of the national movement that African Youth will not allow the struggles and sacrifices of their fathers to have been in vain. Our fathers fought so that we, better equipped when our time came, should start and continue from where they stopped.

The formation of this League is an attempt on the part of Youth to impart to Congress a truly national character. It is also a protest against the lack of discipline and the absence of a clearly-defined goal in the movement as a whole.

The Congress Youth League must be the brains-trust and power-station of the spirit of African nationalism; the spirit of African self-determination; the spirit that is so discernible in the thinking of our Youth. It must be an organisation where young African men and women will meet and exchange ideas in an atmosphere pervaded by a common hatred of oppression.

As this power-station the League will be a co-ordinating agency for all youthful forces employed in rousing popular political consciousness and fighting oppression and reaction. It will educate the people politically by concentrating its energies on the African homefront to make all sections of our people Congress-minded and nation-conscious.

But the Congress Youth League must not be allowed to detract Youth's attention from the organization of Congress. In this regard, it is the first step to ensure that African Youth has direct connections with the leadership of Congress.

Circumstances call upon African Youth to make the League specialise in championing the cause of Africa; and to serve this end best, the League will sponsor a Congress political bloc, the Congress Progressive Group within the national movement. This will be the wing of the Youth League entrusted with the duty of organizing Youth with a view to enabling it to make it accept the view that young people may organise and express better their political wishes outside of Congress; hence the formation of the bloc within Congress.

The Congress Progressive Group will stand for certain clear-cut national ideals within Congress; it will stand for specialisation within the national movement, to reinforce the latter's representative character and to consolidate the national unity front; it will keep a vigilant eye on all un-national tendencies on the national unity front and in Congress policies.

We must be honest enough to realize that neither Congress nor the African people can make progress as one amorphous mass. At a certain stage we must cultivate specialized political attitudes. Failure to recognize this will wreck Congress and encourage revolts from it until it ceases to be a force in national politics.

By recognizing this fact, Youth does not confess sympathy with those who revolted against the national movement. These failed to realize that the formation of parties out of Congress was a serious weakening of the national unity front. They recognized the fact that Congress is a national liberation movement but were not sufficiently experienced politically to form their party within the national fold and to develop opposition from within, while strengthening the national unity front.

The result of their inexperience has been the creation of serious rifts and splits on the national unity front. For this, there can be no pardon because we cannot afford to cause any rift on the national unity front at this critical moment. By weakening the national unity front we invite more oppression for Africans after the war. By strengthening the national unity front, we are preparing a strong front against onslaughts that will be made on their real aims of the national struggle and on its significance and makes the co-ordination of our political activities difficult, with the result that the African cannot take advantage of situations which, if intelligently exploited on time, may bring the African nearer full and free citizenship.

Congress is destined for a great purpose and mission, but shortsighted policies will cripple and make it unable to rise to its destiny. To prevent this and therefore the setting back of the clock of African progress, African Youth must join the League in their numbers to strengthen the national movement in view of the fact that divisions just now are being sown among the people by sections of the so-called privileged few, while no convincing effort is made to narrow down and finally eliminate the gulfs that divide our people even by those who clamour loudest for national unity. Those who sow these divisions direct their activities against the national unity front in order to make the national movement incapable of expressing the wishes of the people effectively; they are the enemies of a free Africa.

The Congress is the symbol of the African people's common hatred of all oppression and of their Will to fight it relentlessly as one compact group. Youth recognizes the existence of specialised attitudes and where these lead to differences of opinion, that must be strictly a domestic matter within the national liberation movement and must in no way be allowed to interfere with the national unity front.

THE IDEAL OF NATIONAL UNITY MUST BE THE
GUIDING IDEAL OF EVERY YOUNG AFRICAN'S LIFE

OUR CREED

a.) We believe in the divine destiny of nations.

b.) The goal of all our struggles is Africanism and our motto is "AFRICA'S CAUSE MUST TRIUMPH."

c.) We believe that the national liberation of Africans will be achieved by Africans themselves. We reject foreign leadership of Africa.

d.) We may borrow useful ideologies from foreign ideologies, but we reject the wholesale importation of foreign ideologies into Africa.

e.) We believe that leadership must be the personification and symbol of popular aspirations and ideals.

f.) We believe that practical leadership must be given to capable men, whatever their status in society.

g.) We believe in the scientific approach to all African problems.

h.) We combat moral disintegration among Africans by maintaining and upholding high ethical standards ourselves.

i.) We believe in the unity of all Africans from the Mediterranean Sea in the North to the Indian and Atlantic Oceans in the South...and that Africans must speak with one voice.

OUR PROGRAMME.....THE THREE-YEAR PLAN

a.) Drafting and framing of the Constitution.

b.) Improving and consolidating our financial position.

c.) Establishing the Congress Progressive Group.

d.) To win over and persuade other Youth Organisations to come over to the African National Congress Youth League, i.e. to create national unity and consolidate the national unity front.

e.) To win over and persuade other African Organisations to come over to and pool their resources in the African National Congress, i.e. to create national unity and consolidate the national unity front.

f.) To work out the theories of African urbanisation and the system of Land Tenure.

g.) To make a critical study of all those forces working for or against African progress.

Document 49. "Trumpet Call to Youth" [announcing meeting of September 10, 1944]. Flyer issued by the Provisional Executive Committee of the Congress Youth League

The hour of youth has struck! As the forces of National Liberation gather momentum, the call to youth to close ranks in order to consolidate the National Unity Front, becomes more urgent and imperative.

1944 marks an epoch in the struggle of the Black peoples of South Africa. A dramatic turning-point in the history of mankind, signalled by the global war now being waged, presents a clarion call to the youth of the Sub-Continent, to rally round the banner of the National Liberation Movement, so as to galvanise and vitalise the National Struggle.

The CONGRESS YOUTH LEAGUE, therefore, summons all youth from the Reef, the Transvaal and neighbouring regions, to a mass YOUTH CONFERENCE to be held at the Bantu Men's Social Centre, Eloff Street Extension, at 10 a.m. on Sunday, 10th September, 1944.

A United African Youth Front should be achieved.

The speakers will be:

1. Dr. A. B. Xuma.	"The place of youth in the National Stuggle."
2. Mr. R. V. Selope Thema, M.R.C.	"Origin and History of Congress."
3. Mr. J. M. Nhlapo, B.A.	"Education in our National Struggle."
4. Miss Ncakeni,	"The part of Women in our struggle."
5. Mr. D. Tloome.	"Youth and trade unionism."
6. Mr. C. S. Ramohanoe,	"The Anti-Pass Struggle."
7. Rev. A. Mahabane.	"Christianity and Youth Problems."
8. Mr. O. R. Thambo.	"Our Congress Youth League."

The agenda will include
(a) Discussion and Adoption of Rules and Regulations,
(b) Election of office-bearers.

AFRICAN YOUTH! DO NOT MISS THIS OPPORTUNITY!! COME IN YOUR HUNDREDS!

"The fault is not in our stars,
But in ourselves that we are underlings."

Document 50. Constitution of the ANC Youth League, 1944

I

NAME:

The name of the Organisation shall be "African National Congress Youth League" hereinafter styled: C.Y.L.

II

AIMS:

(a) To arouse and encourage national consciousness and unity among African Youth

(b) To assist, support and re-inforce the African National Congress, in its struggle for National Liberation of the African people.

(c) To study political, economic and social problems of Africa and the world.

(d) To strive and work for educational, moral and cultural advancement of African Youth.

III

OFFICIALS:

(a) Officials shall be as follows:-
 President, Vice President, Secretary, Vice-Secretary, Treasurer and Officer of Organisation and Propaganda (herein styled O.P.O.)
(b) Honorary Officials: Speaker and Deputy Speaker.

DUTIES, RIGHTS AND POWERS OF OFFICIALS:

(a) *President:*
 (i) He shall preside in the Executive meetings.
 (ii) He shall be responsible for due performance of duty by each official.
 (iii) He shall supervise the carrying out of the decisions and resolutions of the Executive Committee as well as those of the Conference.
 (iv) He shall be co-signatory of all cheques.
(b) *Vice President:*
 In the unavoidable absence of the President, the Vice President shall enjoy the same rights, exercise the same power and discharge the same duties as the President.
(c) *Secretary:*
 (i) He shall call all meetings by letter or any other approved method.
 (ii) Shall take and keep the minutes of the Conference as well as of the Executive Committee meetings.
 (iii) He shall read the minutes of a previous Conference or meeting and move that such minutes be accepted by the Conference or meeting as a correct record of a previous conference or meeting.
 (iv) He shall receive and keep all letters etc. addressed to C.Y.L. and write and dispatch all letters to the press, individuals or bodies but those dealing with organisational matters must go through the Officer for Propaganda and Organisation.

310

(v)

(i) He shall read in Conference or meeting official letters received.
(ii) He shall keep copies of all official letters written unless and until the Executive decides otherwise.
(iii) He shall immediately hand over to the Treasurer all monies received on behalf of the C.Y.L.
(iv) He shall be a co-signatory to all cheques.

(d) *Vice-Secretary:*

In the unavoidable absence of the Secretary the Vice Secretary shall enjoy the same rights, discharge the same duties, exercise the same powers as the Secretary.

(e) *Treasurer:*

(i) He shall collect, receive and bank all monies belonging to the C.Y.L.
(ii) He shall issue receipts to all payers.
(iii) He shall lay before the meeting of Conference plans for raising funds for the C.Y.L.
(iv) He shall sign all cheques on behalf of the C.Y.L.
(v) He shall present to the Executive Committee at the end of each year an audited revenue and expenditure account and a balance sheet made out for the year; the same shall be presented to the Conference by the Executive Committee.

(f) *O. P. O.:*

(i) He shall see to it that the true attitude and policy of the C.Y.L. is well reflected in the press and in public.
(ii) He shall send articles at least once a month to the press unless the executive deems it harmful or prejudicial to the interests of the C.Y.L.
(iii) He shall organise the branches of the C.Y.L. and report in the Executive Committee meetings, in conference and in the press about his organisational activities.
(iv) He shall hand over to the Treasurer all monies that he may receive on behalf of the C.Y.L.

IV

THE EXECUTIVE COMMITTEE:

(a) *Constitution:*

The Executive Committee shall consist of the Officials and five additional members; all shall be elected by Conference. Vacancies shall be filled by co-option by the Executive Committee.

(b) *Duties of the Executive Committee:*

(i) To promote and implement the aims of the C.Y.L.
(ii) To initiate and speak on measures and proposals and to arrange a definite programme and agenda before Conference.

(iii) To carry out the wishes and decisions of the Conference.

(iv) To report all its activities in every general Conference.

(v) To appoint or elect officials other than the President from among the 10 elected members of the Executive.

(vi) To expel, or cause to resign, any official if it deems it aright in the interests of the C.Y.L.

(vii) The Branch and Provincial Executive Committees shall meet every second week of the month. The National Executive shall meet once every three months. Emergency meetings may be convened at any time.

V

CONFERENCE:

(a) Provincial Conference will meet twice a year and the National Conference, annually.

(b) Only members shall have the right to vote;

(c) Conference shall discuss anything connected with the C.Y.L.

(d) If the Conference has lost confidence of the President, he and his Executive Committee must resign and the Speaker must immediately conduct election.

(e) Conference shall elect the President and his Committee.

(f) Conference shall be presided over by Speaker or deputy-Speaker.

(g) Conference shall make rules for the running and management of the meetings.

VI

MEMBERSHIP:

(a) Membership is open to all African men and women between the ages of 12 and 40.

(b) Members shall pay a registration fee of 2/- for Adults, 6d. for children under 17, who have read and understood and made pledge to abide by the C.Y.L.'s creed.

(c) Those above the age of 40 may be honorary members with no right to vote.

(d) Young members of the other sections of the community who live like and with Africans and whose general outlook on life is similar to that of Africans may become full members with age limits as in (a).

(e) There shall be a ceremony for admitting new members.

(f) Members above 17 years of age become automatically members of the African National Congress and become liable to 2/6d. annual subscription of that body.

(g) Annual subscriptions are due in January of each year and a member who is in arrears with his or her annual subscriptions for the current year ceases to be a member on the sixth day of April of that year.

VII

FINANCE:

(a) Registration Fee 2/ - paid by each member on joining the C.Y.L.

(b) Annual subscription per member shall be 2/6d. which is due in January of each year; out of the 2/6d, 1/-accrues to the African National Congress and the C.Y.L. retains the 1/6d.

(c) Funds may also be raised by donations, street collections, concerts, dinner parties, bazaars.

(d) The Branches are entitled to 6d out of the 2/6d annual subscription of each member.

(e) The National Executive Committee shall appoint, at its first meeting of the year, an auditor.

(f) Treasurer shall appoint a Financial Committee from among the Executive to plan ways and means of raising funds. This Committee shall be answerable to the Executive and shall have power to co-opt persons outside the Executive.

VIII

C.Y.L. BRANCHES:

(a) 15 members or more may found a Branch of the C.Y.L.

(b) In any area where a branch of the African National Congress exists, a branch of the C.Y.L. may be established, provided

(i) the finances of the A.N.C. Branch concerned are not disturbed or adversely affected;

(ii) C.Y.L. members shall not pay any additional annual subscription except a registration fee of 2/- paid once on joining the C.Y.L.

(c) C.Y.L. members *under the age of 17* shall pay an annual subscription of 2/6d to the C.Y.L.

(d) In an area where no A.N.C. branch exists a C.Y.L. branch shall for purposes of finance, be taken and regarded as an A.N.C. branch.

(e) Should an A.N.C. branch be later established in an area described in sub-section (d) the provisions of subsections (a), (b) and (c) shall apply.

(f) In any locality where there exists several branches, a District Committee may be formed from the executives of respective branches to act as a co-ordinating committee, providing always that the approval of the C.Y.L. Executive is acquired.

(g) Each branch shall be entitled to be represented at a provincial conference by one delegate for each 25 members or part thereof; but not less than 15 members. Only delegates shall have a right to move resolutions or to vote.

(h) Each province shall send 1 delegate for every 10 branches to the National Conference and, in addition, a branch may send 1 delegate for every 50 members in the Branch.

IX

WORKING COMMITTEE:

(a) The National Executive Committee shall immediately upon election instruct the President to appoint a Working Committee of seven members provided that the said members of the Working Committee are resident within 50 miles radius of the President's place of abode and provided further that where a sufficient number cannot be obtained from the members of the National Executive, the President, with or without consultation with other Executive Committee Members shall have the right to co-opt additional C.Y.L. members to make up the required number.

(b) The Working Committee shall be responsible to the National Executive.

(c) The Working Committee shall be given by the National Executive an outline policy and programme of action and immediately upon receipt of this, the Working Committee shall set to work to carry this or these out.

(d) The Working Committee shall submit the reports to the National Executive once every three months.

(e) The Working Committee shall hold its routine meetings once every month but may meet at any other time should circumstances demand.

X

RESIGNATION:

If any member wishes to resign from the Executive Committee, he shall give a written notice of his resignation to the Executive except in the case of a vote of no confidence in which case an immediate resignation is the result.

XI

AMENDMENT:

Two-thirds majority of vote by members in a special session of the National Youth Conference shall be required for any amendment or repeal of this Constitution.

XII

GENERAL:

If any matter arises for which this Constitution makes no provision, the constitution of the African National Congress shall be used to provide for the necessary information.

Document 51. "Some Basic Principles of African Nationalism." Article by A. M. Lembede, in *Inyaniso*, February 1945

a) The Philosophical Basis: This can be stated by quoting the words of a famous American writer, Thompson, "The materialistic conception of History that conceives of Man as essentially an economic animal—Communism—and

the biological interpretation that conceives of him as a Beast of Prey—Nazism—
are false. Man is body, mind and spirit with needs, desires and aspirations
in all three elements of his nature. History is a record of humanity's strivings
for complete self-realisation.

b) The Scientific Basis: Charles Darwin, the eminent and famous scientist,
pointed out the profound significance of the law of variation in Nature. One
can never find two leaves of plants that are exactly and in all respects the
same, nor two stems, nor two flowers, nor two animals, nor two human beings,
nor two nations. Each nation has thus its own peculiar character or make-up.
Hence each nation has its own peculiar contribution to make towards the general
progress and welfare of mankind. In other words each nation has its own divine
mission. Think, for instance, of the contribution made by the Greeks (science
and philosophy), Romans (law and politics), Jews (Christian religion and
theology), French (modern democracy), English (spread of Western civilisation
among non-Europeans through the world), Germans (modern science), Russians
(modern economic theories), etc., etc., and Africans (?) 'Ex Africa semper
quid novi'—From Africa always comes something new—said an ancient Latin
writer.

c) Historical Basis: It was Paul Kruger who in the gloomy days of the
Transvaal Republic said, 'Wie zich een toekomst scheppen wil, mag het verleden
niet uit het oog verliezen.' One who wants to create the future must not forget
the Past. These are words of deep human wisdom. We Africans have still
to erect monuments to commemorate the glorious achievements of our great
heroes of the past, e.g. Shaka, Moshoeshoe, Hintsa, Sikhukhumi, Khama,
Sobuza, and Mosilikazi, etc. In their times and environment and under the
circumstances in which they lived, these men served their people and did their
duty nobly and well. 'Lives of great men all remind us'.

d) Economic Basis: The fundamental structure of Bantu Society is socialistic.
There was for instance no individual ownership of land in ancient Bantu society.
There were no landlords or the so-called 'absentee' landlords. Land belonged
virtually to the whole tribe and nominally to the King or Chief. Socialism
then is our valuable legacy from our ancestors. Our task is to develop this
socialism by the infusion of new and modern socialistic ideas.

e) Democratic Basis: In ancient Bantu Society, the worth of a man was
not assessed by wealth. Any man could rise to any position, e.g., of Induna
or Captain or General by the virtue of the qualities of courage and ability
which were possessed by such man. In our Councils of Khotlas any citizen
could take part in discussions, and if a case was being tried, anyone could
ask questions and cross-examine the accused. The main point is the assessment
of human value by moral and spiritual qualities. This is a legacy to be preserved
and developed and highly treasured in our hearts.

f) Ethical Basis: The ethical system of our forefathers was based on ancestor
worship. People did certain things or refrained from doing certain things for
fear of punishment by the spirits of dead ancestors. We must retain and preserve
the belief in the immortality of our ancestors but our ethical system today has

to be based on Christian morals since there is nothing better anywhere in the world. Morality is the soul of society. Decay and decline of morals brings about the decay and decline of society—so History teaches. It is only African Nationalism or Africanism that can save the African people. Long live African Nationalism!

Document 52. Letter from the ANC Youth League (Transvaal) to the Secretary [Ruth First] of the Progressive Youth Council, March 16, 1945

Dear Madam,

We beg to acknowledge the receipt of your letter of the 9th instant with enclosures, for which we are gratefully indebted to you.

Regarding your request or invitation that we affiliate with your Council, we wish to state in reply that: (a) We are the African National Congress Youth League and as such we are bound to keep within the precincts of the policy of the African National Congress. We cannot without the sanction and approval of the African National Congress enter into any affiliation, alliance or entente cordiale with any other Youth organisation. (b) We fear that there is a yawning gulf between your policy or philosophic outlook and ours. We are devoting our energies to the preparation for the greatest national struggle of all time, the struggle for national liberation. Our stupendous task is to organise, galvanise and consolidate the numerous African tribes into one homogeneous nation. We are alarmed and startled by the bitter and painful realisation that these 150,000,000, African blacks have for centuries slumbered or lain dormant in this dark Continent. We consider that the hour has now struck that these black African masses as an organised powerful force be made effective or that their voice be heard and felt in international affairs.

We support the co-operation of all Non-Europeans on certain issues in this Country. But we maintain that Africans can only co-operate as an organised self-concious [sic] unit. Hence co-operation at the present juncture or stage is premature. It can only result in chaos, ineffective action and mutual jealousies, rivalry and suspicion. In consequence, therefore, and by reason of the premises, we do not see our way clear towards affiliation with your Council.

These observations, however, are not meant to incapacitate us from sending a delegate or two, as interested spectators to your World Youth Week Celebrations on the 23rd instant.

Thanking you.

We beg to remain,
Yours truly,
[no signature shown on copy]
316

Document 53. "Policy of the Congress Youth League." Article by A. M. Lembede, in *Inkundla ya Bantu*, May 1946

The history of modern times is the history of nationalism. Nationalism has been tested in the people's struggles and the fires of battle and found to be the only effective weapon, the only antidote against foreign rule and modern imperialism. It is for that reason that the great imperialistic powers feverishly endeavour with all their might to discourage and eradicate all nationalistic tendencies among their alien subjects; for that purpose huge and enormous sums of money are lavishly expended on propaganda against nationalism which is dubbed, designated or dismissed as 'narrow', 'barbarous', 'uncultured', 'devilish' etc. Some alien subjects become dupes of this sinister propaganda and consequently become tools or instruments of imperialism for which great service they are highly praised, extolled and eulogised by the imperialistic power and showered with such epithets as 'cultured', 'liberal', 'progressive', 'broadminded' etc.

All over the world nationalism is rising in revolt against foreign domination, conquest and oppression in India, in Indonesia, in Egypt, in Persia and several other countries. Among Africans also clear signs of national awakening, national renaissance, or rebirth are noticeable on the far-off horizon.

A new spirit of African nationalism, or Africanism, is pervading through and stirring the African society. A young virile nation is in the process of birth and emergence. The national movement imbued with and animated by the national spirit is gaining strength and momentum. The African National Congress Youth League is called upon to aid and participate in this historical process. African nationalism is based on the following cardinal principles:

1) *Africa is a blackman's country*. Africans are the natives of Africa and they have inhabited Africa, their Motherland, from times immemorial; Africa belongs to them.

2) *Africans are one*. Out of the heterogeneous tribes, there must emerge a homogeneous nation. The basis of national unity is the nationalistic feeling of the Africans, the feeling of being Africans irrespective of tribal connection, social status, educational attainment or economic class. This nationalistic feeling can only be realised in and interpreted by [a] national movement of which all Africans must be members.

3) *The Leader of the Africans will come out of their own loins*. No foreigner can ever be a true and genuine leader of the African people because no foreigner can every truly and genuinely interpret the African spirit which is unique and peculiar to Africans only. Some foreigners Asiatic or European who pose as African leaders must be categorically denounced and rejected. An African must lead Africans. Africans must honour, venerate and find inspiration from African heroes of the past: Shaka, Moshoeshoe, Makana, Hintsa, Khama, Mzilikazi, Sekhukhuni, Sobhuza and many others.

(4) *Cooperation between Africans and other Non-Europeans on common problems and issues may be highly desirable*. But this occasional cooperation

317

can only take place between Africans as a single unit and other Non-European groups as separate units. Non-European unity is a fantastic dream which has no foundation in reality.

5) *The divine destiny of the African people is National Freedom.* Unless Africans achieve national freedom as early as possible they will be confronted with the impending doom and imminent catastrophe of extermination; they will not be able to survive the satanic forces, economic, social and political unleashed against them. Africans are being mowed down by such diseases as tuberculosis, typhus, venereal diseases etc. Infantile mortality is tremendously high. Moral and physical degeneration is assuming alarming dimensions. Moral and spiritual degeneration manifests itself in such abnormal and pathological phenomena as loss of self confidence, inferiority complex, a feeling of frustration, the worship and idolisation of white men, foreign leaders and ideologies. All these are symptoms of a pathological state of mind.

As a result of educational and industrial colour bars, young African men and women are converted into juvenile delinquents.

Now the panacea of all these ills is National Freedom, in as much as when Africans are free, they will be in a position to pilot their own ship and, un-hampered, work toward their own destiny and, without external hindrance or restriction devise ways and means of saving or rescuing their perishing race.

Freedom is an indispensable condition for all progress and development. It will only be when Africans are free that they will be able to exploit fully and bring to fruition their divine talent and contribute something new towards the general welfare and prosperity of Mankind; and it will only be then that Africans will enter on a footing of equality with other nations of the world into the commonwealth of nations; and only then will Africans occupy their rightful and honourable place among the nations of the world.

6) *Africans must aim at balanced progress or advancement.* We must guard against the temptation of lop-sided or one-sided progress. Our forces as it were, must march forward in a coordinated manner and in all theatres of the war, socially, educationally, culturally, morally, economically, and politically. Hence the Youth League must be all inclusive.

7) *After national freedom, then socialism.* Africans are naturally socialistic as illustrated in their social practices and customs. The achievement of national liberation will therefore herald or usher in a new era, the era of African socialism. Our immediate task, however, is not socialism, but national liberation.

Our motto: *Freedom in Our Life Time.*

Document 54. "The African Mine Workers' Strike—A National Struggle." Flyer issued by the ANC Youth League, August 1946

The African Mine Workers have risen in revolt against the most brutal, callous and inhuman exploitation of man by man in the history of mankind.

Their struggle is a challenge to the whole economic and political structure of South Africa.

Huge profits from cheap Native Labour are misappropriated by the whites and applied to the perpetuating of white Domination and supremacy in this country and to the tightening of their stranglehold of oppression and suppression on the voiceless toiling and teeming African millions.

The stings of Colour Bar and race discrimination are felt by Africans in all spheres of life—as mine workers, as municipal workers, as railway workers, as domestic servants, as industrial and commercial workers, as farm workers, as teachers, as business men and Africans.

Events are moving towards a climax. Pressure from above is evoking pressure below. Africans—a brave and vigorous race—cannot be kept in subjection for ever. As a matter of fact no human race can be kept in a state of slavery and serfdom forever—so History teaches.

The African National Congress Youth League calls upon all Africans—in all spheres of life and occupation—and employment—to lend active support to the mine workers' struggle. The African Mine Workers' struggle is our struggle. They are fighting political colour bar and economic discrimination against Africans.

Then Brethren, on to the struggle! Although we are physically unarmed yet we are spiritually fortified. We are struggling for a just cause, the very fundamental conditions of human existence. We must remember that in all spheres of human activity it is the spiritual forces that lead the W O R L D.

We demand a living wage for all African Workers!!!!

Document 55. Letter on the Youth League, from A. P. Mda to G. M. Pitje, August 24, 1948

Sir,

I must first apologise for replying so late. My reasons are as follows:
1. I have not been well of late.
2. I had to have detailed consultations with the National Executive of the Youth League, stationed in Johannesburg.

Now, my old comrade, I can give you a detailed reply. Fort Hare is just the place to start a Youth League. The young people there are the intellectual leaders to be, and a growing consciousness of their role in the national liberation struggle will add new vigour and force to the struggle for national freedom. Therefore your suggestion to form a Youth League there is most welcome. Now here are a few facts about the Congress Youth League:
1. It was founded in 1944 by youths such as the late Lembede, in order to strengthen the National Movement, and give youth scope for training as the future leaders of their people. The Congress Youth League was

formed as the result of a Resolution passed by the National Conference of the A.N.C. in 1943 at Bloemfontein, "That Congress Youth Leagues and Womens' Leagues be formed." The Transvaal is the first Province to take up the work of organising the Youth League. Now, Natal has followed suit. We hope the Cape and the O.F.S. will do the same soon, so that some time next year we might have a South African Youth Congress, which can in clear terms set a new pace to the politics of South Africa.

2. The political philosophy which we profess is that of African Nationalism. This inter alia implies:

   (a) That the black people of Africa have a divine destiny, that is to say, that they are destined to rise and play their part in the advance of humanity to a better life.

   (b) That they suffer an alien and foreign oppression. Africa is the black-man's continent, the African peoples are groaning under a foreign oppression, because their country has been colonized by foreign powers, and its resources and their labour are being exploited not for their benefit, but for the benefit of the conquerors and the exploiters.

3. The Africans are a conquered race, their oppression is a racial oppression, in other words, they do not suffer class oppression. They are oppressed by virtue of their colour as a race—as a group—as a nation! In other words they are suffering national oppression.

4. As a colonial people suffering national oppression we can overthrow foreign domination, and win national freedom by organising a powerful national liberation movement. The Congress provides a good frame-work for the task of building a national liberation movement. Hence the Youth League aims at training and mobilising Youth, so that Youth should be seasoned for the tasks of leadership, and orientate the entire politics of the African people in South Africa, as they do not seek to undermine the forces of African Nationalism. We are ready to co-operate and join hands with them in fighting oppression and in attacking the common enemy. Again, we realise that pending the creation of a really militant national liberation front, many youths have identified themselves with divers movements in order to find expression for their desire to free their people. We cannot debar such youths from joining the Congress Youth League, precisely because the League aims at creating an all-in national liberation front. But then once they join the Youth League they should do so with the full determination to serve its cause with vigour and unquestionable devotion. On that basis we welcome all African Youth in the League. Once having joined the League, the League comes first and foremost. Youths who join the League and still attach themselves devotedly to other groups had little right to remain as true Leaguers.

Second Question:— "What happens in the event of a clash between the Senior Congress and the Youth League, as for instance over the question of the Boycott?"

The clash is inevitable, because the Congress Senior leadership reflects the dying order of pseudo-liberalism and conservatism, of appeasement and compromises. The Youth League reflects the new spirit of a self-conscious Africa, striving to break age-old oppression and liberate the national forces of progress.

Postscript:—

African Nationalism

Please note that our Nationalism has nothing to do with Fascism and National-ism Socialism (Hitleric version) nor with the imperialistic and neo-Fascist Nationalism of the Afrikaners (the Malanite type). Ours is the pure Nationalism of an oppressed people, seeking freedom from foreign oppression. We as African Nationalists do not hate the European—we have no racial hatred:—we only hate white oppression and white domination, and not the white people themselves! We do not hate other human beings as such—whether they are Indians, Europeans or Coloureds. When we have won our "National Freedom," we shall establish a "People's Democracy" where all men shall have rights and freedoms merely because they are men.

Document 56. Letter on the Youth League, from A. P. Mda to G. M. Pitje, September 10, 1948

Dear Sir,

You will find enclosed a badly printed copy of our 1944 Manifesto, in which we set out the immediate and long-range objectives of the Congress Youth League. You will easily notice from it that our organisation is based on the belief in the first instance that the African National Congress provides a good basis for the building of a militant and powerful National Front. Therefore the immediate task of the Congress Youth League is to overhaul the machinery of the A.N.C. from within by mobilising youth throughout South Africa, and building a powerful core of militant African Nationalism in order to arouse the masses and win our National freedom.

You will notice also that the Congress Youth League is only now beginning to unfurl its sails and to move out into open organisation by establishing Branches in Natal and the Cape. This will lead inevitably to the formation of an all-South Africa Youth League, which will be the rallying point of all nationally-minded youth in the developing struggle for the overthrow of white domination!

321

Of course, our manifesto was issued at a time (1944) when the National Movement was threatened by the splinter organisation, the African Democratic Party. Some parts of it, at least, are out of date if not too unwieldly. It will be necessary in the near future to re-word our Manifesto so that it becomes a clarion call to all Africa to rise and smash the shackles of foreign domination.

Now as regards your questions I shall answer them one by one.

"Are members of other political groups allowed to join the Youth League?" *Here is the answer:* - The Youth League professes African Nationalism, an outlook which must ultimately embrace every African. Our goal is the creation of a single powerful African National Front which will include Africans from all ranks and all walks of life. From that point of view therefore every African is eligible. But here is the rub. No serious-minded person joins a political organisation unless he believes in the validity and genuineness of its methods, principles and programme. If he believes in these he devotes almost all his energies to the furtherance of the interests of his political party and for the achievement of its ideals. It is therefore inconceivable that any serious-minded person would belong to two parties at the same time, unless he believed that they were interchangeable, which is nonsense. Therefore we of the Youth League encourage a singleness of purpose in our members, in the sense, of course, of undivided devotion to the cause of African Nationalism and National freedom. That is particularly so at this time when we are laying a solid foundation for creating a revolutionary national front upon the proper basis. If we allowed members of all political parties to join the Youth League we would soon have an amorphous body with no clear-cut political orientation and with no proper direction, because it would endeavor to accommodate all conflicting groups. That in short is our attitude. But this attitude is further qualified in two ways. The Communist Party, the Unity Movement, the Trotskyist Group, the A.D.P. etc. are all bent on fighting oppression. We are therefore not hostile to any of them as long ... [line missing] These are the cardinal features in the broadest outline of our Nationalism—such as we profess it in the Congress Youth League.

However, we shall in the very near future, supply you with copies of our Constitution and our Youth League Manifesto. Meanwhile you could do the following: -

1. Get together a small nucleus and soak them in our Nationalistic outlook and indicate to them the need for youth to train for a greater leadership. These will form the core of the Movement at Fort Hare. Once there is such a core of convinced and faithful Youth Leaguers there will be no chance of the Youth League at Fort Hare dying out.

2. Then call or let somebody call a meeting of those interested and launch a Youth League Branch at Fort Hare. But such a Branch should work hand in hand with the National Executive stationed in Johannesburg, and of which

the General Secretary is N.R.D. Mandela Esq. B.A., a law student. At that meeting an Executive should be formed. Subscription fees for students amount to only 6d., and 2/6 per annum for ...[incomplete]

Document 57. "Basic Policy of Congress Youth League." Manifesto issued by the National Executive Committee of the ANC Youth League, 1948

The African National Congress Youth League established in April 1944 aims inter alia:—

(a) At rallying and uniting African youth into one national Front on the basis of African Nationalism;

(b) At giving force, direction, and vigour to the struggle for African National Freedom, by assisting, supporting and reinforcing the National Movement —A.N.C.

(c) At studying the political, economical and social problems of Africa and the world;

(d) At striving and working for the educational, moral and cultural advancement of African youth.

In order to rally all youths under its banner, and in order to achieve the unity necessary to win the national freedom of the African people, the Congress Youth League adopts the following basic policy, which is also a basis for its political, economic, educational, cultural and social programme:—

SUMMARY OF CONTENTS.

1. African Nationalism.
2. End of political action.
3. *Economic Policy:*–
    (a) Land.
    (b) Industry.
    (c) Commerce.
    (d) General National Economy.
4. Educational Policy.
5. Cultural Policy.
6. Congress Youth League and other organisations.
7. Conclusion.

I. African Nationalism.

The African people in South Africa are oppressed as a group with a particular colour. They suffer national oppression in common with thousands and millions of oppressed Colonial peoples in other parts of the world.

African Nationalism is the dynamic National liberatory creed of the oppressed African people. Its fundamental aim is:—

(i) the creation of a united nation out of the heterogeneous tribes,

(ii) the freeing of Africa from foreign domination and foreign leadership,

(iii) the creation of conditions which can enable Africa to make her own contribution to human progress and happiness.

The African has a primary, inherent and inalienable right to Africa which is his continent and Motherland, and the Africans as a whole have a divine destiny which is to make Africa free among the peoples and nations of the earth.

In order to achieve Africa's freedom the Africans must build a powerful National liberation movement, and in order that the National movement should have inner strength and solidarity, it should adopt the National liberatory creed—African Nationalism, and it should be led by the Africans themselves.

2. Goal of Political Action.

The Congress Youth League believes that the goal of political organisation and action is the achievement of true democracy,

(i) In South Africa and

(ii) in the rest of the African continent.

In such a true democracy all the nationalities and minorities would have their fundamental human rights guaranteed in a democratic Constitution. In order to achieve this the Congress Youth League and/or the National Movement struggles for: -

(a) the removal of discriminatory laws and colour bars,

(b) the admission of the Africans into the full citizenship of the country so that he has direct representation in parliament on a democratic basis.

3. Economic Policy.

The Congress Youth League holds that political democracy remains an empty form without substance unless it is properly grounded on a base of economic, and especially industrial democracy.

The economic policy of the League can therefore be stated under the following headings: -

(a) *Land:*—The League stands for far-reaching agrarian reforms in the following directions: -

    (i) The re-division of land among farmers and peasants of all nationalities in proportion to their numbers.

    (ii) The application of modern scientific methods to, and the planned development of, Agriculture.

    (iii) The improvement of land, the reclamation of denuded areas and the conservation of water supplies.

    (iv) The mass education of peasants and farmers in the techniques of agricultural production.

(b) *Industry:*–The Congress Youth League aims at:—

    (i)   The full industrialisation of South Africa in order to raise the level of civilisation and the standard of living of the workers,

    (ii) the abolition of industrial colour bars and other discriminatory provisions, so that the workers of all nationalities should be able to do skilled work and so that they should get full training and education in the skill and techniques of production,

    (iii) establishing in the Constitution the full and unhampered right of workers to organise themselves in order to increase their efficiency and protect and safeguard their interests, particularly the workers would reap and enjoy benefits of industrial development and expansion

(c) *Trading and Cooperation:*– In order to improve the lot of the people generally and to give strength and backbone to the National Movement, the League shall:—

    (i)   encourage business, trading and commercial enterprises among Africans,

    (ii) encourage, support and even lead workers, peasants and farmers, intellectuals and others, to engage in cooperative saving, cooperative trading etc.

(d) *General National Economy:*-Generally the Congress Youth League aims at a National Economy which will

    (i)   embrace all peoples and groups within the state.

    (ii) eliminate discrimination and ensure a just and equitable distribution of wealth among the people of all nationalities.

    (iii) as nearly as possible give all men and women an equal opportunity to improve their lot.

    (iv) in short give no scope for the domination and exploitation of one group by another.

4. *Educational Policy.*

(A) The ultimate goal of African Nationalism in so far as education is concerned, is a 100% literacy among the people, in order to ensure the realisation of an effective democracy. Some of the means to that end are:—

    (i) Free compulsory education to all children, with its concommittants of adequate accommodation, adequate training facilities and adequate remuneration for teachers.

    (ii) Mass adult Education by means of night schools, adult classes, summer and winter courses and other means.

(B) All children should have access to the type of education that they are suited for. They should have access to academic, aesthetic, vocational and technical training.

(C) The aim of such education should be:—

(i) to mould the characters of the young.

(ii) to give them high sense of moral and ethical values.

(iii) to prepare them for a full and responsible citizenship in a democratic society.

5. Cultural Policy.

(A) Culture and civilisation have been handed down from nation to nation and from people to people, down to historic ages. One people or nation after another made its own contribution to the sum-total of human culture and civilisation. Africa has her own contribution to make. The Congress Youth League stands for a policy of assimilating the best elements in European and other civilisations and cultures, on the firm basis of what is good and durable in the African's own culture and civilisation. In this way Africa will be in a position to make her own special contribution to human progress and happiness.

(B) The Congress Youth League supports the Cultural struggle of the African people and encourages works by African Artists of all categories. The Congress Youth League stands for a coordinate development of African cultural activity.

(C) African works of Art can and should reflect not only the present phase of the National liberatory struggle but also the world of beauty that lies beyond the conflict and turmoil of struggle.

7. [sic] Conclusion.

The foregoing policy is largely one of ultimate objectives in general terms; although here and there it throws light on the immediate and/or near-range objectives of the National Movement.

Whilst the general policy remains fixed and unalterable, the programme of organisation and action, may and shall be modified from time to time to meet new situations and conditions and to cope with the ever changing circumstances.

By adopting this policy the Congress Youth League is forging a powerful weapon for freedom and progress.

The Position of African Nationalism.

In view of misunderstanding and even deliberate distortions of African Nationalism, it has become necessary to re-state the position of our outlook.

1. Historical Basis of African Nationalism.

More than 150 years ago, our fore-fathers were called upon to defend their fatherland against the foreign attacks of European Settlers. In spite of bravery and unparalleled heroism, they were forced to surrender to white domination. Two main factors contributed to their defeat. Firstly, the superior weapon of the white man, and secondly the fact that the Africans fought as isolated tribes, instead of pooling their resources and attacking as a united force.

2. The Birth of the African National Congress.

Thus the year 1912 saw the birth of an African National Congress. The emergence of the National Congress marked the end of the old era of isolated tribal resistence, and ushered in a new era of struggle on a national rather than on a tribal plane. The A.N.C. became the visible expression of inner organisational plane. However imperfectly it did it, the A.N.C. was in fact an outward expression of the African people's desire for a National Liberation Movement, capable of directing their resistence to white domination and of ultimately winning the African's national freedom.

Yet from the very outset, the A.N.C. suffered from serious defects. The founders, great patriots no doubt, had no grasp of the concrete historical situation and its implications, and they were obsessed with imperialist forms of organisation. As a result the A.N.C. had defects both of form and of matter and as long as these remained the A.N.C. could not (i) create an effective organisational machinery for waging the national liberatory fight; (ii) put forward a dynamic Nationalistic programme which could inspire and cement the tribes, and be a motive power and driving force in the militant struggle for national freedom.

In spite of these serious defects, however, the event of 1912, had provided a solid basis for tribal solidarity, and for a nationally organised struggle against white domination. It was for the more politically advanced rising generations to give Congress such form and substances as would suit the organisation to its historic mission.

3. Recent Tendencies - Their Significance.

Far reaching changes have taken place in the African National Congress within recent times. During Dr. A.B. Xuma's regime, a policy of centralisation has been followed and an attempt made to correct, at least in form, some of the mistakes of 1912. The result has been the gaining of ground of the idea of the National Congress, with dependent provincial branches (Transvaal, Cape, Natal, O. F. S.). Doubtless there is room for more drastic and revolutionary changes in the organisational form of Congress if this organisation is to live up to the people's expectations. As far as the matter and substance of Congress' outlook is concerned, the year 1944 saw a historic turning point, when the Congress Youth League came into life. From the very outset, the Congress Youth League set itself, inter alia, the historic task of imparting dynamic substance and matter to the organisational form of the A.N.C. This took the form of a forth right exposition of the National Liberatory outlook—African Nationalism—which the Youth League seeks to impose on the Mother Body. The first clear exponent of African Nationalism was the late Anton Muziwakhe Lembede [died July 1947].

4. Basic Position of African Nationalism.

The starting point of African Nationalism is the historical or even pre-historical position. Africa was, has been and still is the Blackman's Continent.

327

The Europeans, who have carved up and divided Africa among themselves, dispossessed, by force of arms, the rightful owners of the land—the children of the soil. To-day they occupy large tracts of Africa. They have exploited and still are exploiting the labour power of Africans and natural resources of Africa, not for the benefit of the African Peoples but for the benefit of the dominant white race and other white people across the sea. Although conquered and subjugated, the Africans have not given up, and they will never give up their claim and title to Africa. The fact that their land has been taken and their rights whittled down, does not take away or remove their right to the land of their forefathers. They will suffer white oppression, and tolerate European domination, only as long as they have not got the material force to overthrow it. There is, however, a possibility of a compromise, by which the Africans could admit the Europeans to a share of the fruits of Africa, and this is inter alia:—

(a) That the Europeans completely abandon their domination of Africa.

(b) That they agree to an equitable and proportionate re-division of land.

(c) That they assist in establishing a free people's democracy in South Africa in particular and Africa in general.

It is known, however, that a dominant group does not voluntarily give up its privileged position. That is why the Congress Youth puts forward African Nationalism as the militant outlook of an oppressed people seeking a solid basis for waging a long, bitter, and unrelenting struggle for its national freedom.

5. Two Streams of African Nationalism.

Now it must be noted that there are two streams of African Nationalism. One centres round Marcus Garvey's slogan—"Africa for the Africans". It is based on the 'Quit Africa' slogan and on the cry "Hurl the Whiteman to the sea". This brand of African Nationalism is extreme and ultra revolutionary.

There is another stream of African Nationalism (Africanism) which is moderate, and which the Congress Youth League professes. We of the Youth League take account of the concrete situation in South Africa, and realise that the different racial groups have come to stay. But we insist that a condition for inter-racial peace and progress is the abandonment of white domination, and such a change in the basic structure of South African Society that those relations which breed exploitation and human misery will disappear. Therefore our goal is the winning of National freedom for African people, and the inauguration of a people's free society where racial oppression and persecution will be outlawed.

6. Forces in the Struggle for African Freedom.

(a) Africans: They are the greatest single group in South Africa, and they are the key to the movement for democracy in Africa, not only because Africa is their only motherland, but also because by bringing the full force of their organised numbers to bear on the national struggle, they can alter the basic position of the fight for a democratic South Africa. The only driving force

328

that can give the black masses the self-confidence and dynamism to make a successful struggle is the creed of African Nationalism, which is professed by the Congress Youth League of South Africa. The Congress Youth League holds that the Africans are nationally-oppressed, and that they can win their national freedom through a National Liberation Movement led by the Africans themselves.

(b) Europeans: The majority of Europeans share the spoils of white domination in this country. They have a vested interest in the exploitative caste society of South Africa. A few of them love Justice and condemn racial oppression, but their voice is negligible, and in the last analysis count for, nothing. In their struggle for freedom the Africans will be wasting their time and deflecting their forces if they look up to the Europeans either for inspiration or for help in their political struggle.

(c) Indians: Although, like the Africans, the Indians are oppressed as a group, yet they differ from the Africans in their historical and cultural back-ground among other things. They have their mother-country, India, but thousands of them made South Africa and Africa their home. They, however, did not come as conquerers and exploiters, but as the exploited. As long as they do not undermine or impede our liberation struggle we should not regard them as intruders or enemies.

(d) Coloureds: Like the Indians they differ from the Africans, they are a distinct group, suffering group oppression. But their oppression differs in degree from that of the Africans. The Coloureds have no motherland to look up to, and but for historic accidents they might be nearer to the [Africans] than are the Indians, seeing they descend in part at least from the aboriginal Hottentots who with Africans and Bushmen are original children of Black Africa. Coloureds, like the Indians will never win their national freedom unless they organise a Coloured People's National Organisation to lead in the struggle for the National Freedom of the Coloureds. The National Organisations of the Africans, Indians and Coloureds may co-operate on common issues.

7. South Africa: A Country of Nationalities.

The above summary on racial groups supports our contention that South Africa is a country of four chief nationalities, three of which (the Europeans, Indians and Coloureds) are minorities, and three of which (the Africans, Coloureds and Indians) suffer national oppression. When we talk of and take that as the most urgent, the most immediate task of African Nationalism. At all events, it is to be clearly understood that we are not against the Europeans as such—we are not against the European as a human being—but we are totally and irrevocably opposed to white domination and to oppression.

8. Fallacies and Diversions that must be expected

(a) African Nationalism and Racialism: There is a common accusation that African Nationalism is a one-sided, racialistic out-look. The accusation is based

on ignorance of African Nationalism. Ours is the sanest and at the same time the most practical and realistic view. We do not hate other racial groups. We are the overwhelming majority and at the same time, who are a down trodden people.

(b) Pseudo-Nationalism: African Nationalists have to be on the lookout for people who pretend to be Nationalists when in fact they are only imperialist or capitalist agents, using Nationalistic slogans in order to cloak their reactionary position. These elements should be exposed and discredited.

(c) Fascist Agents: Still another group that should be closely watched, and wherever possible, ruthlessly exposed, is that section of Africans who call themselves "Nationalists", but who are in fact agents and lackeys of Nazi and Fascist organisations. Genuine African Nationalists should be (practically) perpetually vigilant and spare no effort to denounce and eventually crush these dangerous vipers.

(d) Venders of Foreign Method: There are certain groups which seek to impose on our struggle cut-and-dried formulae, which so far from clarifying the issues of our struggle, only serve to obscure the fundamental fact that we are oppressed not as a class, but as a people, as a Nation. Such whole-sale importation of methods and tactics which might have succeeded in other countries, like Europe, where conditions were different, might harm the cause of our people's freedom, unless we are quick in building a militant mass liberation movement.

(e) Tribalism: Some people mistakenly believe that African Nationalism is a mere tribalist outlook. They fail to apprehend the fact that nationalism is firstly a higher development of a process which was already in progress when the white man arrived, and secondly that it is a continuation of the struggle of our fore-fathers against foreign invasion. Tribalism itself is the mortal foe of African Nationalism, and African Nationalists everywhere should declare relentless war on Centri-fugal tribalism.

Conclusion drawn from Above Exposition.

The historic task of African Nationalism (it has become apparent) is the building of a self-confident and strong African Nation in South Africa. Therefore African Nationalism transcends the narrow limits imposed by any particular sectional organisation. It is all-embracing in the sense that its field is the whole body of African people in this country. The germ of its growth was first sown within the bosom of the African National Congress, and it found its clear crystalisation in the Congress Youth League. It should now find concrete expression in the creation of a single African National Front. The strength, solidarity and permanence of such a front, will, of course, depend not on accident or chance, but on the correctness of our stand, and on the political orientation of our front. Granting that this would be anchored on African Nationalism, we should build the most powerful front in our history.

The position of African Nationalism has been made as clear as possible. It remains for us to stress the fact that our fundamental aim is a strong and self-confident nation. Therefore our programme is, of necessity, a many-sided one corresponding to the varied activities and aspirations of our people, and to the various avenues along which they are making an advance towards self-expression and self-realisation. Our great task is to assist and to lead our people in their herculean efforts to emancipate themselves and to advance their cause and position economically, culturally, educationally, socially, commercially, physically and so on. But, of course, the most vital aspect of our foreward struggle is the political aspect.

Therefore African Nationalists should make a scientific study and approach to the problems of Africa and the world, and place themselves in a position to give the African people a clear and fearless political leadership.

Document 58. Address on Behalf of the Graduating Class at Fort Hare College, delivered at the "Completers' Social," by M. R. Sobukwe, October 21, 1949

Prof. Dent, Ladies and Gentlemen, I intend to follow in my opening remarks the conventional pattern. And for that reason I will give a very brief review of our doings within the College this year. We saw at the beginning of the year the implementation of the Students' Constitution, whereby six members of the S.R.C. [Students' Representative Council] were elected by secret ballot at a mass-meeting of the students and whereby also certain powers were delegated to the Council. Of that arrangement the worst I can say is that it seems to be working well. We witnessed also at the beginning of the year the promotion of Prof. Dent to the position of Principal of the S.A.N.C. [South African Native College]. He was succeeding a man who was highly esteemed, Dr. Kerr. But I do not think we lament the change, for we are concerned not with personalities, but with policies, and there has been no change in this respect. Moreover, however much we may disagree with Prof. Dent on certain issues, we cannot say that he has ever refused students a chance to state their case. And I believe it is due to this fact that there has been no trouble in the College this year. After all, even the minor demonstration we had last term was not a reaction against the administration of the College. The stimulus came from outside.

But that does not mean that all is well in the College. I had occasion last year and also at the beginning of this year to comment on some features of our structure of which I do not approve. It has always been my feeling that if the intention of the trustees of this College is to make it an African College or University, as I have been informed it is, then the department of African

331

Studies must be more highly and more rapidly developed. Fort Hare must become the centre of African Studies to which students in African Studies should come from all over Africa. We should also have a department of Economics and of Sociology. A nation to be a nation needs specialists in these things.

Again I would like to know exactly what the College understands by *"Trusteeship."* I understand by *"Trusteeship"* the preparation of the African ward for eventual management and leadership of the College. But nothing in the policy of the College points in this direction. After the College has been in existence for 30 years the ratio of European to African staff is 4 to 1. And we are told that in ten years time we might become an independent University. Are we to understand by that an African University predominantly guided by European thought and strongly influenced by European staff?

I said last year that Fort Hare must be to the African what Stellenbosch is to the Afrikaner. It must be the barometer of African thought. It is interesting to note that the theory of "Apartheid" which is today the dominating ideology of the State was worked out at Stellenbosch by Eiselen and his colleagues. That same Eiselen is Secretary for Native Affairs. But the important thing is that Stellenbosch is not only the expression of Afrikaner thought and feeling but it is also the embodiment of their aspiration. So also must Fort Hare express and lead African thought. The College has remained mute on matters deeply affecting the Africans, because, we learn, it feared to annoy the Nationalists' Government. What the College fails to realise is that rightly or wrongly the Nationalists believe that the Fort Hare staff is predominantly U.P. So that whether we remain mute or not the government will continue to be hostile towards us. So much for the College.

Sons and daughters of Africa, harbingers of the new world-order. What can I say to you? As you see, for the first time since the practice was started, we do not have the nurses with us on this momentous night—completers' Social. And the reason? the battle is on. To me the struggle at the Hospital is more than a question of indiscipline in inverted commas. It is a struggle between Africa and Europe, between a twentieth century desire for self-realisation and a feudal conception of authority. I know, of course, that because I express these sentiments I will be accused of indecency and will be branded an agitator. That was the reaction to my speech last year. People do not like to see the even tenor of their lives disturbed. They do not like to be made to feel guilty. They do not like to be told that what they have always believed was right is wrong. And above all they resent encroachment on what they regard as their special province. But I make no apologies. It is meet that we speak the truth before we die.

I said last year that our whole life in South Africa is *politics*, and that contention was severely criticised. But the truth of that statement has been proved in the course of this year. From the pulpit in the C.U. we have heard responsible and respectable preachers deplore the deterioration of race-relations in this country and suggest co-operation as a solution. Dr. Bruce Gardner and Rev. Mokitimi are but two of a large number. Professor Macmillan and a number of speakers in our Wednesday assembly, have condemned this "naughty spirit of Nationalism and non-cooperation" and have told us of the wonderful things that have been done for us, forgetting, of course, that what they say has been done for the Africans the Africans have achieved for themselves in spite of the South African Government. The point I am trying to make is that that was *politics*, whether we loved it or not. So that we can no longer pretend that there is a proper place and a proper occasion for politics. During the war it was clearly demonstrated that in South Africa at least, politics does not stop this side of the grave. A number of African soldiers were buried in the same trench as European soldiers. A few days afterwards word came from the high command that the bodies of the Africans should be removed and buried in another trench. "Apartheid" must be maintained even on the road to eternity.

The trouble at the Hospital then, I say, should be viewed as part of a broad struggle and not as an isolated incident. I said last year that we should not fear victimisation. I still say so today. We must fight for freedom—for the right to call our souls our own. And we must pay the price. The Nurses have paid the price. I am truly grieved that the careers of so many of our women should have been ruined in this fashion. But the price of freedom is *blood, toil, and tears*. This consolation I have, however, that Africa never forgets. And these martyrs of freedom, these young and budding women will be remembered and honoured when Africa comes into her own.

A word to those who are remaining behind. You have seen by now what education means to us; the identification of ourselves with the masses. Education to us means service to Africa. In whatever branch of learning you are, you are there for Africa. You have a mission; we all have a mission. A nation to build we have, a God to glorify, a contribution clear to make towards the blessing of mankind. We must be the embodiment of our people's aspirations. And all we are required to do is to show the light and the masses will find the way. Watch our movements keenly and if you see any signs of "broadmindedness" or "reasonableness" in us, or if you hear us talk of practical experience as a modifier of man's views, denounce us as traitors to Africa.

We will watch you too. We have been reminded time and again that fellows who, while at College, were radicals, as soon as they got outside became the spineless stooges and screeching megaphones of "white Herrenvolkism" or else became disgruntled and disillusioned objects of pity. My contention is: those fellows never were radicals. They were anti-White. And, as Marcus Garvey says: "You cannot grow beyond your thoughts. If your thoughts are those of a slave, you will remain a slave. If your thoughts go skin-deep, your mental development will remain skin-deep." Moreover a doctrine of hate can never take people anywhere. It is too exacting. It warps the mind. That is why we preach the doctrine of love, love for Africa. We can never do enough for Africa, nor can we love her enough. The more we do for her, the more we wish to do. And I am sure that I am speaking for the whole of young Africa when I say that we are prepared to work with any man who is fighting for the liberation of Africa *WITHIN OUR LIFE-TIME.*

To the completers among whom I number myself, my exaltation is: *RE-MEMBER AFRICA!* I thought last year that the position was bad. I realise it is worse this year. This is a difficult period to analyse. It is a confused period, such as only a Mqhayi, or Bereng, or Dickens could describe. We are witnessing today the disintegration of old empires, and the integration of new communities. We are seeing today the germination of the seeds of decay inherent in Capitalism; we discern the first shoots of the tree of Socialism. In married life we see a reversal to what the Missionaries condemned when they first got here—*Polygamy*. But this time it is not the African who is the culprit, and the third party is not a second wife, but a mistress. We are witnesses today of cold and calculated brutality and bestiality, the desperate attempts of a dying generation to stay in power. We see also a new spirit of determination, a quiet confidence, the determination of a people to be free whatever the cost. We are seeing within our own day *the second rape of Africa;* a determined effort by imperialist powers to dig their claws still deeper into the flesh of the squirming victim. But this time the imperialism we see is not the naked brutal mercantile imperialism of the 17th and 18th centuries. It is a more subtle one—financial and economic imperialism under the guise of a tempting slogan, "the development of backward areas and peoples." At the same time we see the rise of uncompromising "Nationalism" in India, Malaya, Indonesia, Burma, and Africa! The old order is changing ushering in a new order. The great revolution has started and Africa is the field of operation. Allow me at this juncture to quote a few lines from the Methodist Hymn-book:

> Once to every man and Nation
> Comes the moment to decide,
> In the strife of truth with falsehood
> For the good or evil side—
>
> Then to side with truth is noble
> When we share her wretched crust,
> Ere her cause bring fame and profit
> And 'tis prosperous to be just.
>
> Then it is the brave man chooses
> While the coward stands aside,
> Till the multitude make virtue
> Of the faith they had denied.

The cowards are still standing aside and the brave have made their choice. We have made our choice. And we have chosen African Nationalism because

334

of its deep human significance; because of its inevitability and necessity to world progress. World civilisation will not be complete until the African has made his full contribution. And even as the dying so-called Roman civilisation received new life from the barbarians, so also will the decaying so-called western civilisation find a new and purer life from Africa.

I wish to make it clear again that we are anti-nobody. We are pro-Africa. We breathe, we dream, we live Africa; because Africa and humanity are inseparable. It is only by doing the same that the minorities in this land, the European, Coloured, and Indian, can secure mental and spiritual freedom. On the liberation of the African depends the liberation of the whole world. The future of the world lies with the oppressed and the Africans are the most oppressed people on earth. Not only in the continent of Africa but also in America and the West Indies. We have been accused of blood-thirstiness because we preach "non-collaboration." I wish to state here tonight that that is the only course open to us. History has taught us that a group in power has never voluntarily relinquished its position. It has always been forced to do so. And we do not expect miracles to happen in Africa. It is necessary for human progress that Africa be fully developed and only the African can do so.

We want to build a new Africa, and only we can build it. The opponents of African Nationalism, therefore, are hampering the progress and development not only of Africa, but of the whole world. Talks of co-operation are not new to us. Every time our people have shown signs of uniting against oppression, their "friends" have come along and broken that unity. In the very earliest days it was the Missionary (we owe the bitter feelings between Fingoes and Xhosas to the Christian ideals of the Reverend Shaw). Between 1900 and 1946 it has been the professional Liberal. Today it is again the Missionary who fulfills this role. After maintaining an unbroken and monastic silence for years while Smuts was starving the people out of the Reserves, the Missionaries suddenly discover, when the Africans unite, that the Africans have not had a fair deal. In the same stride, so to speak, they form a "Union wide Association of Heads of Native Institutions" for the purpose of regimenting the thoughts of the students. A Missionary Hospital closes even though the people are dying in its neighbourhood, and there is a dearth of Nurses throughout the country. I am afraid these gentlemen are dealing with a new generation which cannot be bamboozled. "What you are thunders so loudly that what you say cannot be heard."

Let me plead with you, lovers of my Africa, to carry with you into the world *the vision of a new Africa, an Africa re-born, an Africa rejuvenated, an Africa re-created, young AFRICA.* We are the first glimmers of a new dawn. And if we are persecuted for our views, we should remember, as the African saying goes, that it is darkest before dawn, and that the dying beast kicks most violently when it is giving up the ghost so to speak. The fellows who clamped Nehru into jail are today his servants. And we have it from the Bible that those who crucified Christ will appear before Him on the judgment day. We are what we are because the God of Africa made us so. We dare not compromise, nor dare we use moderate language in the course of freedom. As Zik puts it:

"Tell a man whose house is on fire to give a moderate alarm; tell a man moderately to rescue his wife from the arms of a ravisher; tell a mother to extricate gradually her babe from the fire into which it has fallen; but do not ask me to use moderation in a cause like the present."

These things shall be, says the Psalmist: Africa will be free. The wheel of progress revolves relentlessly. And all the nations of the world take their turn at the field-glass of human destiny. Africa will not retreat! Africa will not compromise! Africa will not relent! Africa will not equivocate! And She will be heard! *REMEMBER AFRICA!*

Document 59. Prayer delivered at the Annual Conference of the ANC Youth League, by the Rev. I. C. Duma, December 15, 1949

1. *LET US PRAY FOR THE GUIDANCE OF THE HOLY SPIRIT:-*

Our Heavenly Father, we thank Thee that thou hast permitted us to meet here in Conference. Pour into our hearts Thine Holy Spirit, so that by Him we may be wisely guided in our deliberations, and through Him we may be bound together in fellowship and brotherly love. May His wisdom be so bestowed upon us that the programme now about to be unfolded to us, may be majestic in range, practical in detail, scientific in form and Christian in spirit. Amen.

2. *LET US PRAY FOR THE LEADERS OF AFRICAN THOUGHT:-*

Eternal Father, as we assemble here at the opening of these sessions, we would commend to Thee the leaders of African thought and opinion. Endue them with the Power of the Holy Spirit, so that they may boldly interpret Thy will for this land, and that they may so direct the deliberations of these sessions as to give wise judgments; but above all, that in them, Christ may be manifested. Amen.

3. *LET US INTERCEDE FOR OUR LAND:-*

Father of Mankind, while we are conscious of our shortcomings, because we have done those things which we ought not to have done, and left undone those things which we ought to have done; therefore there is no life in us. Hence the chaotic state of our fair land. But with Thee, our Father, as Helper, we would not despair of working for its redemption. Help us, therefore, to make the Supreme Sacrifices towards this end; teach us to unite and to rediscover ourselves as a people; so that the redemption of our fair land may be for the glory of Thine Holy name. Amen.

4. *LET US MAKE INTERCESSION FOR THE AFRICAN RACE AS A WHOLE:-*

Thou, Heavenly Father, art continuing to lift us up from the sinks of impurity and cesspools of ignorance. Thou art removing the veil of darkness from this race of the so-called "Dark Africa". The rays of Thine light have risen in the 'Eastern Horizons' of the highways of learning and Christianity. Here we are, bowing as it were, in fresh rededication of ourselves to Thine Service and to the Service of mankind in general, and for the African race in particular. We are painfully conscious that in the past, we have fallen victims of petty prejudices of this world; we have shown bitterness, hatred, anger, ill-feeling, suspicions and neglect of duty. We have committed sins of intolerance under the cloak of Christianity. We have disregarded the down-trodden masses in order to satisfy our selfish ends. We ask Thee to so guide us that we may be of service to the African race, that the decisions we may arrive at here, may be for the good of the race. Accept our supplications, Oh Lord, and let us bless Thine Holy name, through Him who died for us, Jesus Christ Our Lord and Redeemer. Amen.

Document 60. "Programme of Action." Statement of Policy adopted at the ANC Annual Conference, December 17, 1949

The fundamental principles of the programme of action of the African National Congress are inspired by the desire to achieve National freedom. By National freedom we mean freedom from White domination and the attainment of political independence. This implies the rejection of the conception of segregation, apartheid, trusteeship, or White leadership which are all in one way or another motivated by the idea of White domination or domination of the White over the Blacks. Like all other people the African people claim the right of self-determination.

With this object in view in the light of these principles we claim and will continue to fight for the political rights tabulated on page 8 of our Bill of Rights such as:-

(1) the right of direct representation in all the governing bodies of the country—national, provincial and local, and we resolve to work for the abolition of all differential institutions or bodies specially created for Africans, viz. representative councils, present form of parliamentary representation.

(2) to achieve these objectives the following programme of action is suggested:-
    (a) the creation of a national fund to finance the struggle for national liberation.

(b) the appointment of a committee to organise an appeal for funds and to devise ways and means therefor.

(c) the regular issue of propaganda material through:-

    (i) the usual press, newsletter or other means of disseminating our ideas in order to raise the standard of political and national consciousness.

    (ii) establishment of a national press.

(3) appointment of a council of action whose function should be to carry into effect, vigorously and with the utmost determination the programme of action. It should be competent for the council of action to implement our resolve to work for:-

(a) the abolition of all differential political institutions the boycotting of which we accept and to undertake a campaign to educate our people on this issue and, in addition, to employ the following weapons: immediate and active boycott, strike, civil disobedience, non-co-operation and such other means as may bring about the accomplishment and realisation of our aspirations.

(b) preparations and making of plans for a national stoppage of work for one day as a mark of protest against the reactionary policy of the Government.

(4) *Economic*.

(a) The establishment of commercial, industrial, transport and other enterprises in both urban and rural areas.

(b) Consolidation of the industrial organisation of the workers for the improvement of their standard of living.

(c) Pursuant to paragraph (a) herein instructions be issued to Provincial Congresses to study the economic and social conditions in the reserves and other African settlements and to devise ways and means for their development, establishment of industries and such other enterprises as may give employment to a number of people.

(5) *Education*.

It be an instruction to the African National Congress to devise ways and means for:-

(a) Raising the standard of Africans in the commercial, industrial and other enterprises and workers in their workers' organisations by means of providing a common educational forum wherein intellectuals, peasants and workers participate for the common good.

(b) Establishment of national centres of education for the purpose of training and educating African youth and provision of large scale scholarships tenable in various overseas countries.

338

(6) *Cultural*.
>   (a) To unite the cultural with the educational and national struggle.
>   (b) The establishment of a national academy of arts and sciences.

(7) Congress realises that ultimately the people will be brought together by inspired leadership, under the banner of African Nationalism with courage and determination.

[signed by G. I. M. Mzamane and D. W. Bopape]

THE ALL AFRICAN CONVENTION AND EFFORTS AT WIDER UNITY

Document 61. Resolution on the War. Adopted by the National Executive Committees of the AAC and the ANC, July 7, 1940

The Executive Committees of the All African Convention and the African National Congress in joint meeting held at Bloemfontein on the 7th July, 1940, gave their considered opinion and expressed concern at the developments that have taken place in the war which is now raging in Europe. The Executive expresses loyal sympathy with the British Commonwealth of Nations in the difficult task that has been thrust upon it as a result of recent developments. The Executive notes with deepest concern that the struggle has now entered Africa and that African soldiers are being employed by some of the combatants.

The Joint Committees desire to place on record their conviction that the time has arrived when the Union Government and Parliament should consider the expediency of admitting the Africans of this country into full citizenship in the Union with all the rights and duties appertaining to that citizenship.

With this end in view the Joint Committees consider that the territorial integrity of the Union of South Africa can only be effectively defended if all sections of the population were included in the defence system of the country on equal terms, and that those who are, and may be eligible for service should receive full military training in all its aspects, and be fully armed. Further, that those who are being recruited for whatever military service should be placed under regular conditions of such service involving adequate support for their dependents during and after the war. In this regard we would urge the authorities to enlist the services and co-operation of African leaders in addition to those of Chiefs and Headmen.

With regard to subversive propaganda the Joint Committees are convinced that the removal of grievances such as Pass Laws, Low Wage Levels, Industrial

339

Colour Bars, the refusal of trading rights to Africans, and so forth, will go a long way to counteract mischievous doctrines that are being disseminated among Africans.

Further, the Joint Committees respectfully urge the Government to take immediate and adequate steps for the guidance, organisation, discipline, and protection of the people against any emergency that might arise out of, and as a result of the present conflict.

[Note: This resolution was re-affirmed by the ANC National Conference of December 15-17, 1940. See Document 20.]

Document 62. Address by I. B. Tabata, AAC Conference, December 16, 1941

I must admit at the outset that when we first met in this hall six years ago, we and our people, who looked spell-bound at Convention, were full of great hopes for the future of this Assembly. In the midst of the onslaught then being made upon our people, and fully realising the hazardous task before us in staving off this onslaught, we were still confident. Little did we think then that six years later we should have to admit that not only have we failed to achieve any positive results in the struggle for the liberation of our people, but that we meet today in conditions far worse than at that time. We have not been able to avert the defeat. The Bills have become law. Instead of advancing on the road to political rights and consequently economic betterment, instead of acquiring the vote for our people in the North, instead of extending this vote to our women, instead of lightening the chains tying down the African —the Colour Bar Laws, the Pass Laws and the Poll tax—we have been driven back to a position of being completely without rights. From what they termed political minors, we have become political outcasts in our own country, tolerated only as servants who accept unconditionally the "divine" rights of the white masters to rule over us.

Six years ago, on the eve of the Convention, its secretary, Selby Msimang, published what can be termed a declaration of faith to which every African man and woman, young and old, subscribed. "Unless Bantudom realises this danger ... the inevitable destiny of her children and posterity will be one of perpetual slavery." But today we must admit that nothing has been done by the Convention to implement this declaration of deeds. Is it surprising that while six years ago the whole Bantu race looked with hope and expectation, fixed its eyes and ears on the deliberations of the Convention, breathlessly waiting for guidance and for a lead, today hardly a stir is produced by the Convention meeting? Is it because the people have become resigned to the conditions of serfdom? Is it because the people have become reconciled to the old master and servant relationship, and are satisfied with the lot of a serf and with the working of the new segregation laws? Is it because the people have lost all interest in their liberation? Is it because our people have no guts for the struggle, have no pride in themselves and have turned into knaves? Or is it because our people are *bitterly disappointed,* because they feel that once more their leaders have let them down?

It is quite probable that many people, bitterly disappointed with the results of these six years, or with the lack of results, are pinning the blame on to the Convention. Now there is one organisation quick to utilise this disappointment for its own party political aims, namely, Congress. For the outset it was lukewarm towards the Convention and reluctantly joined it. The more people become disillusioned with Convention, the bolder becomes Congress in their propaganda against it. So that today we can hear them openly shouting: "Away with Convention!" I shall deal with this question in full later.

But those who are in the struggle, who like myself are taking an active part in the Convention since its beginning, know, that the fault is not with the Convention as such, but with its leadership. It is not the organisation itself, but what we make of it! The most ideal institution with the best programme and ideas can achieve nothing if its leadership is faulty, incapable or dishonest, or even vain and selfish. In our conditions the Convention is and remains the most suitable organisation for the Africans in the struggle for liberation. To appreciate this we must return to that time when we formed the Convention and consider what was its meaning and purpose.

Before the Native Bills were introduced into Parliament, not many Africans were fully aware that they have no voice in the government of the country where they are born, where they slave and suffer and die; that they are not citizens of their country; that they have no country. They were lead to believe that some day they would become full citizens. In short they thought what the Coloured man still thinks today. They did not realise that the Government, the administration, and the Parliament, all belong to the white man who has no intention of ever giving the Africans even the least small avenue for advancement, for voicing his grievances and aspirations, and for acquiring his full and rightful place in civilisation. And that is the firm intention of the white rulers, to keep the black man in perpetual slavery. But with the introduction of the Segregation Bills by Hertzog this sinister intention was openly proclaimed for all the world to hear, and the policy of sweet promises for the future was finally discarded. It came as a terrific shock to the Black man. The African people suddenly found that from now on they had no one to rely on, except themselves. This shook, and the realisation that they had been thrown out of the community to which they thought they belonged, brought them instinctively together. Like all people in face of a catastrophe, they drew closer together. They instinctively felt that if they were not to go under and be silenced forever, they must forget the factional strife, the religious bickering, the rivalry of the chiefs, the divisions into North and South, into tribalised and detribalised, into

341

town and country, into petty political parties and groups. They realised that they must come together and unite against a common danger.

This feeling of national unity crystallised itself in the form of a national organisation embracing the whole oppressed race. Thus the All African Convention came into being. It was to be this national, all-embracing organisation to defend the Africans against the coming onslaught and to fight for their national and political rights. The All African Convention was to be the national forum from where the voice of the African could be heard. And if the ruling classes decide that the Parliament belongs to the White man and that there is no place for the Black man, then the All African Convention will naturally become the Parliament for the Africans. When it became clear that the Africans were going to be completely disfranchised, the logical conclusion was for this Convention to become a permanent body until such time as they will obtain their full rights and a full share in the legislative, administrative and judicial institutions of their country. To the builders of Convention it was obvious that no single organisation or party can fulfil such a task, but an organisation of all organisations and parties. No single party can claim to represent all African workers, farm labourers, peasants, liberal professions, the town and the country, the Reserves and the detribalised Africans. Neither the I.C.U. nor Congress, both of whom after flourishing for a time lost all influence and broke up into small groups and cliques, could claim for a moment such a place. In fact they did not. But all organisations were invited to come together, and did come together, to build the All African Convention—the African Parliament, to fight for African rights and freedom, land and decent living.

This meaning and this purpose still remain the same, and will remain until the goal of African liberation is achieved.

When we now look back at these six years of disappointments and failures, setbacks and outright defeats, we can in each case trace the cause of them. The fault was not with the masses. Wherever it was in their power they gave unmistakable proof of their militancy. Almost all mass meetings held by government officials, or the Native Affairs Department, were a failure for the oppressors. Neither with threats nor with sweet promises could they break the hostility and non-confidence of the masses. Look at the people and the question of the war, for instance. All war meetings were a flop. The masses did not wait for Convention to decide that it is not *their* war. From the first moment they made it unmistakably clear to the government officials that the time when the rulers could bluff them with promises is over. And they don't care two straws if the N.R.C. crawls on its belly begging the government to include the Africans in the after-war schemes and it magnanimously agrees to consider the question. The masses will have nothing to do with the war, because they know by experience what this democracy is, for which South Africa is fighting. As for the threat of fascism, rightly or wrongly they think that no terror can be greater than the present terror under which they are living. Vereeniging,

Black Maria, the Pass Laws, the police raids—there is no security from these terrors day or night. An African can consider himself extremely lucky if he gets out with his limbs intact from any police station. And however peaceful, law-abiding and careful he may be, he is never safe from not getting in the way of a white man and consequently of the police. And so long as he remains an outcast in the country of his birth, hunted down like an animal, and is conscious of it, no threat of fascist terrors, forced labour, concentration camps, can hold any terror for him. Similarly no babble about Atlantic charters or new deals can be a bait for him any more. He knows well, too well, the meaning of their fair play!

Therefore it is not the masses who can be blamed for these six years of defeats, but the leaders. Whenever anything depended on the spontaneous action of the masses it was all right. Whenever anything depended on the "wise" deliberation of the leaders, it was all wrong. Even in those few cases when the Convention did the right thing, this was due to the pressure of the masses upon the leaders and not to the lead given by the leaders....

Throughout these six years we can see two distinct traits in the Convention; knavish submission to the ruling classes and fear for their own people. In order to retain the goodwill of the authorities the leaders must see to it that the people do nothing that will really improve their lot, or challenge the status quo. For it is their political task to bring about conciliation between the oppressed and the oppressor, not conflict. It is their task to bring about the acceptance of oppression, not the determination to overthrow it.

Their submission is obvious. The second point, fear as far as their own people are concerned, deserves particular consideration. They, the leaders, knew that only by becoming a mass organisation, i.e. rooted in the masses, can the Convention become a real Convention, an African Parliament. But that is precisely what they, the leaders, didn't want it to become. They thought of the Convention as a manoeuvre, even as a threat, but when they discovered that it was something real, something big, they became frightened. The ruling class took notice of the Convention. There were free railway passes, negotiations with the Prime Minister, and quite a lot of publicity of a national forum. This was going too far. And they silently worked during six years to kill the Convention, or at least to make it harmless and innocuous. They failed to kill, they have succeeded on the second point, to emasculate Convention. The same General Secretary, Mr. Msimang, who came out so boldly with the pamphlet, "The Crisis"—"Rather death than slavery!"—later tried to place the Convention under the tutelage of the N.R.C.

It was not only the Congress leaders who sabotaged and tried to wreck the Convention from inside and outside. (I shall come to this later.) All the leaders were afraid of its becoming a mass organisation. They advocated no branches, a Federal constitution, meetings every three years. And when Convention adopted a resolution that didn't suit the leaders, it was simply brushed

343

aside, and repudiated, like the 1935 resolution by Xuma, or conveniently buried in the archives by the secretaries, like the one about approaching the Trade Unions last year. Add to this the dictatorial manner of running the Convention meetings, the bureaucratically imposed agenda, the stifling of any criticism from the floor by the chair. Add all these factors together and you will understand why today, not only is there not a word about the Convention in the press of the ruling class, but not even in our own Bantu press. You will understand why there are not 400 delegates as in the first session, why the people don't talk Convention, and why they have lost faith in it. . . .

Can anyone who advocated giving the legislation a trial, come forward and say that conditions in the Reserves have improved, or that the people have received more land as they were so lavishly promised, or that the ban on the export of cattle has been lifted and irrigation schemes carried through and soil erosion eliminated? Can they point to an improvement in the miserable lot of squatters, labour tenants or farm Labourers as a result of the new representation in Parliament and the N.R.C.? Are they able to say that our people are receiving more sympathetic consideration in the law courts or at the hands of the police? Can they point to better schools and improved education? Can they claim that life is easier in any way or that there is one ray of hope for the future?

You have had five years of this experiment. What have your representatives in Parliament done for the people they are supposed to represent? They did plead for the Africans, admitted. But how did they plead? In the same way that any White liberal, churchman or Joint Council man pleads. The African is your greatest asset, so it is not wise to waste it so recklessly and kill the hen that lays the golden eggs. That is their plea. We hear the same arguments about the gold mines, the forests, the rain-waters and other natural assets used and exploited by man. As if the African was brought into the world by Providence (also the monopoly of the White man) to serve the needs of the White man like any other natural asset. Not that I have anything against Mrs. Ballinger or Mr. Molteno. They are only members of their class. They are liberals and as such they are unable to see the African really as an equal. They are not better nor worse than their leader, Hofmeyr, who would like to see the African treated more humanely, again of course from the point of view of their greatest asset. He indignantly repudiated in Parliament any idea of equality between White and Black, maliciously attributed to him by the Nationalists. What an impudence, equality for the Africans!

I maintain that one has first to be in the skin of the oppressed and feel and suffer as an African does, if he wants to represent him. This representation therefore is a farce. Even if there were, not three White Representatives of six and a half million Africans, but thirty, it would still be a sham representation. If today I bring up this question of Parliamentary representation, it is not because I have any illusions or have changed my opinion about this fraud which is called Representation, but because I want the Convention to expose this fraud and tell the African people the truth! I want the Convention to tell the people that they have nothing to expect from this sham representation and whether they elect these three members or other three, they will not get higher wages or land or houses or education, but they will remain slaves as long as they accept and submit to this slavery legislation.

If you cannot agree to the idea of the boycott of the elections (and such a boycott today would be less effective than five years ago) at least do something to enhance the prestige of the Convention and show unmistakable African unity to the oppressors. Let Convention agree on the nominations, if nominations there must be, in the name of all Africans and not only of the Cape. Our people in the North have just as much right to representation as those in the Cape. If we demand equal representation for all citizens of the Union, it is because we believe in democratic rights for all, White, Black or Brown, North, South, East or West. Today we Africans are deprived of democratic rights. Let us show the oppressor that we shall struggle for them as a united people and that we have more sense of democracy and solidarity than they think. They are intentionally trying to divide us in order the more easily to break our resistance to oppression. Therefore it is all the more imperative for us to unite and even in this sham representation nominate as a united people.

In a still greater degree this applies to the N.R.C. If Parliamentary representation is a sham, the N.R.C. is worse. It is a complete dud. It is neither Native nor Representative nor Council. And besides, it presents such a sorry spectacle, that it is today the most humiliating insult for the Africans. They robbed us of our land and of our rights. They shouldn't mock us by forcing twelve men to play the role of jesters who kiss the whip that is lashing us. It is simply disgusting to read the proceedings of the Council once a year, the meek, humiliating language in which the Native Representatives speak, and the way the ruling class treat their deliberations and resolutions. Did Parliament ever discuss them? Of course not. It is just a farce at the expense of the Africans, providing many jokes for the oppressors: the Pondo Chief asking for an aeroplane ride, or Quamata seconding the vote of thanks, saying: "I am sure we have all enjoyed this session." (A session, by the way, when Clause 4 of the Land Bill was proclaimed, increasing servitude from 90 to 180 days.) Or A.M. Jabavu showing his appreciation at sitting in the Pretoria City Hall where "no Native has ever put his foot." A still greater joke was provided by Thema this year when he humbly begged the Minister for Native Affairs to include the Africans in the Government post war schemes. Surely they will be included—as usual. As cheap Native labour, as hewers of wood and drawers of water. The African is always in the Government schemes. That is what White South Africa is fighting for. You will tell me that the Convention is now powerless to do anything about it. That may be so. But

345

there is still one thing the Convention can do. Tell our people the truth about the N.R.C. Tell them what it is and what it stands for. In exposing deception it can do the greatest service to our people.

You are all aware of the agitation going on in the country concerning Convention and Congress. Everywhere Congress officials are busy putting forward their propaganda for scrapping the Convention. Wherever necessary influential leaders are approached privately and won over to Congress by means of promises and baits. It was clear already to me during the last session of Convention that some underground propaganda was being carried on in the Convention itself. The silent rivalry extending over six years expressed itself in various ways. Although Congress was given a very prominent place in the leadership, the executive and all other committees of the Convention, they were never satisfied, because they did not want Convention to exist at all. *Their* position was more important than national unity. No wonder, then, that they are not satisfied today with their work of emasculating the Convention. They are out to kill it. Then, so they think, they will hold the position they held 23 years before the beginning of Convention. Today they come out openly: Congress or Convention. On the other hand Convention seems to do nothing to counteract the pernicious propaganda.

To me it is clear that this propaganda is playing right into the hands of our oppressors, Nothing would please them better than the end of Convention. For even if today it is weak and harmless, it forms a potential threat to become some day a real African Parliament. Congress is no threat to them at all. For 29 years they have dealt with Congress and are pleased with the results. Its whole history, with its corruptions and embezzlement of funds, its petty feuds of little leaders—all feared this is a sufficient guarantee to the ruling class that nothing is to be feared from that quarter. In the Cape alone there are three organisations each pretending to be the National Congress. Outside Johannesburg, its influence is nil. I am convinced that it can never become a national organisation, able to replace Convention.

It may succeed by fifth column methods to kill the Convention, which is still very weak as a result of the wrong leadership and a faulty constitution, but it can never replace it and become an all-embracing organisation. In political practice, an organisation which has once proved bankrupt, cannot hope to flourish again and win the confidence of the people. But even if Congress could achieve the impossible and reach its former heights, it can never be more than a political party that practises fishing in the political backwash, full of petty intrigues and above all guilty of reaction.

Congress belongs to the past. Convention is a national organisation of all parties and stands for the future! In the Convention there is a place for all organisations; in the Congress for none. Convention wants to unite all in the struggle for the liberation of all Non-Europeans.

Document 63. Statement on the Atlantic Charter, by Professor D.D.T. Jabavu, June 26, 1943

Our representatives in the Native Representative Council last November rightly pressed the government for a clear interpretation of the Atlantic Charter. The reason for this pressure is not far to seek. The original terms of the Charter are couched in grandiose language that easily satisfies complacent communities that find this world a fairly comfortable place to live in. But in the case of the Black races that inhabit South Africa, this charter can mean something great and epochal if given a close and conscientious interpretation by the rulers that be. On the other hand it may amount to nothing more than empty words if the government of this land intends to stop at the reply given at Pretoria last November. The questions that naturally arise are these:-

(1) Does this charter apply only to peoples who governed themselves before the present war, or does it include those under the domination of imperial countries by reason of having been defeated in previous wars?

(2) Will this charter work for the inclusion of Africans at the peace conference or conferences?

(3) Will the opinions of Africans be recognised under the terms of the Third Article "the right of all peoples to choose the form of government under which they will live"?

(4) Will Africans be allowed to participate in legislative councils?

(5) Does the fifth point "improved labour standards, economic adjustment and social security" include land rights, betterment of agriculture, industry, health services and training of Africans for these objectives?

(6) How far will racial attitudes towards peoples who are not of European descent undergo a new orientation in the direction of the elimination of racial discrimination?

If these questions cannot be satisfactorily answered by the authors of the charter and other national leaders who profess to follow the lead of the British Prime Minister and the President of the United States, then the charter is an empty shell so far as Africans are concerned.

Document 64. "A Call to Unity." Manifesto adopted by the National Executive Committee of the AAC, August 26, 1943

When a man finds that he has taken the wrong road and is heading for an abyss, he turns and tries to find the right road. The same happens in the life of a people. Eight years ago, we, the African people, found ourselves on a new road. True, we did not choose this road; we were pushed on to it. But now, after travelling this road for eight years, we find that we are heading for the abyss, so we have to turn back and look for a way out. Now is not the time to start with recriminations as to who was responsible, whether it was the failure of the leadership or the apathy of the masses. It is of far greater importance for us to realise our mistakes, to learn from them and to find a way out.

At that time some people might have believed that the policy of segregation decided upon by the White man would eventually benefit us, because nothing, they thought, could be worse than the rut in which we were then. They were taken in by the White man's catch-phrase: "Developing on our own lines." They believed that once the White man had eliminated us from any say in the affairs of the country, and therefore had no need to fear us, he would give us land and liberty to lead our own lives as we please.

For eight years we have been "developing on our own lines." For eight years we have been fooling around with dummies, with meaningless mock-elections and mock-councils. AND HAVE WE GOT MORE LAND TO-DAY, MORE JOBS FOR OUR THOUSANDS OF YOUNG MEN? ARE WE BETTER OFF? Not even the White man would say so. Even he has to admit that our position has catastrophically deteriorated. But we do not need to look for his testimonies. No longer can anyone conceal the crying plight of our people. Soil erosion is devouring the last bit of land left to us—not to live on, but to die on. Our people are starving. The White man calls it by the fancy name of "malnutrition." This may sound better in his ears. But it is our babies and children who are dying before they have a chance to grow up. It is our cattle which the White man has always begrudged us and which today are no longer cattle but only the shadow of cattle. Whether in the towns, or in the Reserves, our poverty and misery are beyond description. While we have to pay double for everything we buy, the earnings of the people have not increased and the tax-burden has not been lightened.

Of what use is it to us when a few far-sighted Whites are worried over our terrible plight, because "the Native", as they say, "is the backbone of our economy and we must not waste our greatest asset"? Of what use is it to us when they admit that "the Non-Europeans are treated worse than slaves. Under the old Cape slave laws we could not ill-nourish a slave or allow him to become a public burden. In Africa today the Native was allowed to become a source of danger and infection—for economic purposes."

Of what use is it to us that these few ask the question whether they should "allow the Native to go on carrying us on his back without allowing him food to keep him from falling down from exhaustion? The hopeless inefficiency of driving the willing horse without giving him a mouthful of oats, must prove that we none of us think about the sane development of our country ..."? Of what use is it to us if all they think of is to give some oats to the willing horse so as to keep him in harness? Of what use is it to us when the S.A. Medical Association devotes a special number to the Transkei territories describing the horrible conditions under which our people live, presenting a picture

348

of a "slowly degenerating Native community where half of their children never grow up and a third die before they reach the age of three years"?

Of what use is it to us if this empty talk leaves us without the land to produce or the means to buy the milk, the meat and the mealies that can save our babies and the grown-ups from sickness and premature death? Of what use is it to remind us that we need more doctors, clinics, maternity hospitals, if the White man makes laws that our young sons and daughters must not be doctors, but only labourers in the mines and on the farms, and servants in the towns?

For eight years we have been learning the true meaning of this policy of "developing on our own lines." And now everyone is convinced that it leads us to ruin. Those who advocated "giving it a trial" are just as convinced of the pernicious results as those who expected real segregation into a Black man's country and a White man's country. Now we all know that this "development on our own lines" is just another name for our enslavement by the White man. Now we all know that eight years ago we were cheated with promises of land and misled by "developing on our own lines."

Then came the war and we were called upon to help to defend our country. The same White rulers who have decided that we are not a part of the S.A. community, who decided that we should only be servants and not citizens, issued a call to us to march together and defeat Fascism, the enemy of freedom, to defeat Hitlerism, the creed of race superiority. We dropped our misgiving and answered the call in our usual spirit of self-forgetfulness.

Again great promises were given us. The poll tax system was to be investigated and the gaoling of defaulters was to be stopped. The pass system, which was later to be abolished altogether, was to be relaxed immediately on the Rand. Our Trade Unions were to be recognised by law, and the same laws that protect the White workers were to apply to our workers. These promises were made by the Prime Minister, General Smuts, by the Minister for Native Affairs, Colonel Reitz, by the Minister of Labour, the Hon. Madeley, and other responsible ministers of the Crown. The Prime Minister and the Secretary for Native Affairs, Mr. Smit, publicly acknowledged that the segregation policy had failed and they promised a new deal for the Africans. That was a time of great promises by the Rulers and of great hopes by the Non-Europeans.

But again we were bound to be disappointed more bitterly than before. As soon as the enemy was thrown out of Africa, all talk of these promises ceased altogether; but even before then it became obvious that they were empty promises never to be fulfilled. Tens of thousands of our people are still being imprisoned for their inability to pay the heavy tax, or even for failing to produce the receipt. The pass system is today as vicious, tyrannical and humiliating as it ever was. Thousands upon thousands have been rounded up in the Rand alone. Today General Smuts no longer says that segregation has failed. The new Minister for Native Affairs denies that it ever was the government's intention to do away with the pass system. The African trade unions are still illegal and the government has decided not to recognise them. African workers were shot in Pretoria when they ventured to strike because they were denied their rightful wages. African workers have been imprisoned for protesting against intolerable quarters, food, wages. This, then, is our reward for loyalty to the country, for our great war effort, for our sacrifices in blood—the blood of our sons.

Where can we find redress? Where can we find relief? Not in appeals to our Rulers, not in appeals to the government. Some African leaders have been making such appeals in the Native Representative Council for the last six years in the most "modest, respectful, statesmanlike" manner. But nobody takes any notice of their appeals and the resolutions of the dummy Council.

From time to time the few Whites representing the six and a half million Africans in Parliament also make a few fine speeches and appeals which are simply ignored by the government and parliament of the White man and for the White man. These fruitless speeches and appeals are useful only to the Rulers in that they give the appearance of voicing our grievances, and our being represented. Even more important than this, they are useful because they lull us to sleep. We get promises, commissions of enquiry, inter-departmental commissions, wage commissions, and it all ends with white-washing the culprits and condemning the victims.

We ask for bread and we get stones. We ask for relief and get commissions. It is no use appealing to the government, because it is not our government but the government of the White man. It is no use appealing to parliament, because it is not our parliament but the parliament of the White man. It is no use appealing to the law courts, because the law is made by the White man against us.

These eight years of the segregation policy have proved to us that we have travelled along the wrong road, a road that is leading us to an abyss. These eight years have proved to us that "development on our own lines" is a fraud, and that the representation is a fraud. These eight years have proved to us that if we continue along this road we shall perish, as many slaves have perished before.

We cannot resign ourselves to slavery and death. Therefore there is only one way open for us: to fight for our rights as citizens of our country. Therein lies our freedom and our future. These eight years, and especially the years of the war, have proved to us that we are not the only ones to discover the road to freedom, that everywhere the people have to fight for their rights and for their freedom. We have also learned that not only we, but the Coloured people and the Indian people in South Africa have travelled the same wrong road, although separately. The White man wants this country for himself, with all the Non-Europeans as servants and slaves. The same policy that applied to us in 1935 is now being applied to the Indian and the Coloured people.

350

But they are not repeating our mistakes and they are fighting back. The Coloured people are uniting behind what they call the Anti-C.A.D. movement, a kind of federal organisation like our All African Convention. The Indian people are also uniting behind their federal organisation, the S.A. Indian Congress.

It should be obvious that if all these Non-European peoples are struggling to obtain the same thing—the rights of full citizenship, it would be foolish of them to stand separately, while they have a better chance of success if they join forces. It is very pleasing to note that both organisations, the Coloured and the Indian, have already appreciated this need for unity. They have adopted resolutions empowering their executives to enter into negotiations for a unification of all Non-European peoples in the struggle against segregation, a struggle for full citizenship rights. We, on our part, welcome these decisions of our cosufferers in South Africa and we recommend to the coming conference of the A.A.C. the adoption of the Unity resolution. This is the first step towards the new road.

But there are other tasks facing us at the Convention. The war is nearing its end and the military outcome is a foregone conclusion—a victory for the United Nations. Still, this does not mean that Hitlerism, the creed of race superiority, is defeated. The people will have to see that they are not robbed of the fruits of victory, as they were after the last war. Freedom will not be presented to us on a platter. We shall have to fight for it. The White rulers of South Africa, especially, with views so similar to Hitler's race theories, will not voluntarily give us our freedom and our rights. From the pronouncement of the Prime Minister after the General Election, we can see two things. He wants to unite all White people for a final settlement of the relations between Black and White, meaning, of course, all Non-Europeans. He also looks to the North for a Pan-African Empire as South Africa's fruits of victory. He thinks of much more than the Protectorates, but they are surely figuring in his plans.

We need only to recollect that this was the Hertzog plan for completing segregation and making South Africa safe for the White man, to realise the danger for us and our brothers in the Protectorates contained in these plans of the government, the danger to all Non-Europeans in South Africa. We must therefore decide on our answer. The representatives of the Coloured people, of the Indian people and of the Protectorates should be present at the Convention for the deliberations on this important question.

When the war is over, a Peace Conference will deal with the various claims of the oppressed peoples to self-determination and freedom. Not only the oppressed peoples of Europe, but also of Asia and Africa, will present their claims. The government of South Africa, which represents only the White people, cannot speak for us. They have rejected our constitutional claim to citizenship and representation, so that we cannot entrust our claims and our future to them. The eight million Non-Europeans of South Africa have a right to be heard at the tribunal of Nations, at the Peace Conference. Nobody can present our case but ourselves.

Thus the Convention will be called upon to make the following decisions:

(1) The rejection, after the experience of eight years, of the policy of trusteeship and segregation.

(2) The turning from the old road of passivity to the new road of leadership.

(3) The demand for full citizenship rights and representation.

(4) The realisation that the striving for freedom of all the oppressed people in South Africa, the Africans, the Coloured, and the Indians, is identical in aim and methods.

(5) To give effect to the widespread demand for the unity of all Non-Europeans in South Africa. The representatives of the other two groups have been invited by the Executive as guests to the Convention.

(6) A conference of the three groups should be convened immediately after the Convention in Bloemfontein, in order to save time and expense.

(7) The decision on the Protectorates to be reaffirmed and made known.

(8) The question of the form of representation to the coming Peace Conference to be decided upon.

From the foregoing it is clear how important the coming Convention is for our people, for all the oppressed people and for South Africa as a whole. It may mark a turning point in our history.

This time the leaders must not fail their people. This time there should be determination, resolution and unanimity. There is no place for personal bickering, for intrigues, for personal aggrandisement. We must sink our differences for the sake of the great task in front of us. The Convention must become the mouthpiece of the Africans, not only in name, but in deed and action. It must give the lead for which the people call.

But it is also necessary to realise that the people must play their part in making the Convention a success. No leadership can be successful without the support and enthusiasm of the people. Our appeal therefore goes out to the people to rally round the Convention, their Convention, and make the Conference of 1943 a memorable one in the history of our people in South Africa.

Document 65. "Draft Declaration of Unity" [including 10-point Programme]. Statement Approved by the Continuation Committee of the Preliminary Unity Conference of Delegates from the AAC and the National Anti-C.A.D., December 17, 1943

PREAMBLE

These three organisations of the Non-Europeans, which in themselves are not political parties, but federal bodies embracing various political, economic and social organisations and parties of all shades of opinion from every walk of life, have met together in Conference upon 17th December at Bloemfontein.

After frank and friendly deliberations on questions affecting all Non-Europeans in South Africa, the Conference has come to the following conclusions:

I.   That the rulers of South Africa, who wield the economic and political power in this country, are deliberately keeping the Non-European people in economic and political oppression for the sake of their own selfish interests.

II.   That the entire constitutional and economic structure, the legislative, educational, fiscal, judicial and administrative policy, is designed to serve the interests of the European ruling classes (the minority) and not the interests of the people of the country as a whole.

III.   That despite protestations to the contrary, it is the firm determination of this ruling class to prevent the economic advancement and upliftment of the Non-Europeans.

IV.   That during the thirty-three years since the formation of the Union, the promises of the rulers (who have assumed the self-appointed role of 'trustees') that they would use the economic resources of the Union for the benefit of the under-privileged (those in trust) have been flagrantly broken. Instead of a process of civilisation, of reforms leading to a greater share in self-government and government, to a greater share in the national income, to a greater share in the material and cultural wealth of South Africa, to a more equitable distribution of the land—these thirty-three years have been marked by a process of cumulative oppression, of more brutal dispossession of the Non-Europeans, of more crippling restrictions in every sphere.

V.   That not only the future welfare of the Non-Europeans in South Africa, but their very existence as a people demands the immediate abolition of 'trusteeship'', of all constitutional privileges based on skin colour, privileges which are incompatible with the principles of democracy and justice.

VI.   That the continuation of the present system in South Africa, so similar to the Nazi system of Herrenvolk, although it may lead to the temporary prosperity for the ruling class and race, must inevitably be at the expense of the Non-Europeans and lead to their ruination.

VII.   That the economic prosperity and all-round advancement of South Africa, as of other countries, can only be achieved by the collaboration of free people: such a collaboration can only be possible and fruitful as between people who enjoy the status of citizenship, which is based on equality of civil and political rights.

VIII. The recognition that segregation is an artificial device of the rulers and an instrument for the domination of the Non-European is at the same time the recognition that the division, strife and suspicion amongst the Non-European groups themselves are also artificially fostered by the ruling class. From this it follows:

(a) That no effective fight against segregation is possible by people who tacitly accept segregation amongst themselves;

(b) That the acceptance of segregation, in whatsoever form, serves only the interests of the oppressors;

(c) That our fight against segregation must be directed against the segregationists within as well as without, and

(d) That the unity of all Non-European groups is a necessary precondition for this total fight against segregation.

IX. As representatives of the African, Indian and Coloured People, we have come together in the full recognition of the above, in order to lay the foundation for real unity amongst the Non-Europeans. As the purpose of this unity is to fight against segregation, discrimination and oppression of every kind and to fight for equality and freedom for all, such a Unity Movement cannot and must not, for one moment, be considered as directed against the Europeans (an Anti-European Front). It is an Anti-Segregation Front and, therefore, all those European organisations and societies which are genuinely willing to fight segregation (as distinct from those who profess to be against segregation but in reality are only the instruments of the ruling-class) are welcome to this anti-segregation Unity Movement.

X. In view of the heavy legacy of the past still in the ranks of the Non-Europeans, the task of this movement will be the breaking down of the artificial walls erected by the rulers, walls of mistrust and suspicion between the Non-Europeans. This breaking-down must start from the top and come right down to the bottom. This is the organisational task of Unity. Provincial Committees must follow, then Regional Committees and finally Local Committees, where this Unity will be a living reality.

XI. Indeed, all Non-Europeans suffer under the same fundamental disabilities—the lack of political rights. This lack of political rights is the main cause of the poverty of the Non-Europeans, the main impediment to their progress and future. It is through lack of political rights that laws were passed, Land Acts were passed, depriving the Non-European of his land, prohibiting him from buying land and forcing him to stay on the land as a semi-labourer and semi-serf.

354

It is through lack of political rights that laws were passed making it virtually impossible for a Non-European to become a skilled worker (the White Labour Policy, the Apprenticeship Acts, etc.) and keeping unskilled and semi-skilled labour on the very lowest plane, and even below the minimum subsistence level. It is through lack of political rights:

    (a) That his education is deliberately starved;

    (b) That he is starved of medical facilities, hospitals, maternity homes and clinics;

    (c) That he is forced to live in locations, bazaars, hovels and sheds;

    (d) That he is forced to carry passes and cannot move freely;

    (e) That the system of taxation is unjustly applied against him, and

    (f) That he is not allowed to form Trade Unions.

XII. In view of the fact that all the above disabilities, economic, educational, social and cultural, all flow from the lack of political rights, the struggle for full democratic rights must become the pivotal point of our struggle for freedom. But while recognising that our struggle is chiefly a political struggle, we must not neglect any other form of struggle so long as it serves the cause of Liberation. Thus it is the duty of every organisation in the Unity Movement to unfold to the people the meaning of the following programme, a programme not for bargaining but representing the minimum demands and fundamental needs of all sections of the people.

PROGRAMME

The aim of the Non-European Unity Movement is the liquidation of the National Oppression of the Non-Europeans in South Africa, that is, the removal of all the disabilities and the restrictions based on grounds of race and colour, and the acquisition by the Non-Europeans of all those rights which are at present enjoyed by the European population.

Unlike other forms of past society based on slavery and serfdom, democracy is the rule *of* the people, *by* the people, *for* the people. But, as long as a section of the people are enslaved there can be no democracy, and without democracy there can be no justice. We Non-Europeans are demanding only those rights for which the Europeans were fighting more than a hundred years.

These democratic demands are contained in the following Ten Points:

I.   The Franchise, i.e. the right of every man and woman over the age of twenty-one to elect, and be elected to Parliament, Provincial Councils and all other Divisional and Municipal Councils.

355

II.   Compulsory, free and uniform education for all children up to the age of sixteen, with free meals, free books and school equipment for the needy.

III. Inviolability of person, of one's house and privacy.

IV.   Freedom of speech, press, meetings and association.

V.   Freedom of movement and occupation.

VI.   Full equality of rights for all citizens without distinction of race, colour and sex.

VII. *Revision* of the land question in accordance with the above.

VIII. *Revision* of the civil and criminal code in accordance with the above.

IX.   *Revision* of the system of taxation in accordance with the above.

X.   *Revision* of the labour legislation and its application to the mines and agriculture.

EXPLANATORY REMARKS ON THE PROGRAMME.

I.   This means the end of all political tutelage, of all communal or indirect representation, and the granting to all Non-Europeans of the same, universal, equal, direct and secret ballot as at present enjoyed by Europeans exclusively.

II.   This means the extension of all the educational rights at present enjoyed by European children, to all Non-European children with the same access to higher education on equal terms.

III. This is the elementary Habeas Corpus right. The present state of helplessness of the Non-European before the police is an outrage of the principles of democracy. No man should be molested by the police, nor should his house be entered without a writ from the magistrate. This same right to inviolability and privacy at present enjoyed by the European should apply to all Non-Europeans. All rule by regulation should be abolished.

IV.   This point hardly needs explanation. It is the abolition of the *Riotous Assemblies Act*, directed specifically against the Non-European. It embodies the right to combine, to form and enter Trade Unions on the same basis as the Europeans.

356

V.   This means the *abolition* of all *Pass Laws* and restriction of movement and travel within the Union, the right to live, to look for work wherever one pleases. It means the same right to take up a profession or trade as enjoyed by Europeans.

VI.   This means the abolition of all discriminatory colour bar laws.

VII.   Relations of serfdom at present existing on the land must go, together with the *Land Acts,* together with the restrictions upon acquiring land. A new division of the land in conformity with the existing rural population, living on the land and working the land, is the first task of a democratic state and Parliament.

VIII.   This means the abolition of feudal relations in the whole system of justice—police, magistrates, law courts and prisons—whereby the punishment for the same crime is not the same, but is based upon the skin colour of the offender. There must be complete equality of all citizens before the law, and the abolition of all punishment incompatible with human dignity.

IX.   This means the abolition of the *Poll Tax,* or any other tax applicable specifically to the Non-European or discriminating between Europeans and Non-Europeans. There should be one, single, progressive tax, and all indirect taxation that falls so heavily upon the poorer classes should be abolished.

X.   This means specifically the revision of the Industrial Conciliation and Wage Acts, the elimination of all restrictions and distinctions between a European worker and a Non-European worker, equal pay for equal work, equal access to apprenticeship and skilled labour. This means the liquidation of indentured labour and forcible recruitment, the full application of Factory Legislation to the mines and on the land. It means the *abolition* of the *Masters and Servants Act* and the establishment of complete equality between the seller and buyer of labour. It also means the abolition of payment in kind, and the fixing of a minimum wage for all labourers without distinction of race or colour.

Document 66. "A Declaration to the Nations of the World." Statement of the Non-European Unity Movement, signed by the Rev. Z.R. Mahabane, Dr. G. H. Gool, and E. C. Roberts, July 1945

We address this Declaration to all the Nations of the world, to all the peoples who fought against the tyranny of Hitlerism and who fight against every form of tyranny. This Declaration speaks for the 8 million Non-Europeans

357

of the Union of South Africa, Bantu, Coloured and Indian—the preponderant majority of this country.

The defeat of Hitlerism in Europe marks the end of a dark chapter in human history. And because we are confident that the peoples in the world share our conviction that the suffering and the travail of the last ten years were endured so that a new beginning might be made, a new chapter opened, we address ourselves to them. For if the peoples of the world are to eradicate forever those dark forces of Fascism which spread like a scourge over three continents, from Ethiopia in Africa to China in Asia, and Spain in Europe, then it is of prime and urgent import that the ills of tyranny assailing every country and every people should be brought into full light before the forum of the Nations of the World.

Moreover, these ten years of bloodshed and war have taught us that peace is indivisible, that there can be no real peace when tyranny is eliminated in one continent but left undisturbed in another. If a new beginning is to be made, if the foundation of the peaceful world is to be secure, then the scourge of Hitlerite tyranny must be uprooted not only in Europe but also in South Africa and every corner of the globe.

The peoples of the world who were horrified by the inhuman record of Nazism may be unaware of the fact that the Non-Europeans of South Africa live and suffer under a tyranny very little different from Nazidom. Lest it may seem to people far removed from South Africa, that this comparison is either an exaggeration or a figurative expression, we shall demonstrate in more concrete form how closely the life of the Non-European in South Africa is akin to the suffering under Nazi tyranny.

The main characteristics which distinguish the Hitler tyranny from all the tyrannies of the past, may be briefly summarised as follows:

    a) the Herrenvolk ideology which transformed itself into a mania;

    b) the ruthless trampling underfoot of all human rights;

    c) the erection of one system of law and of morality for the Aryans and a different system of law and of morality for the Non-Aryans.

The Union of South Africa, although it is represented abroad as a democracy with a system of parliamentary government, manifests itself essentially the same characteristics as the three enumerated above.

Nazi Germany provided a classic example to the world of how a people could become obsessed with the idea of their racial superiority and divine mission to rule. What originated as a cunning propaganda design by the Nazi leaders to divert the attention of the people from their real enemies and to make scapegoats of the Jews and other minorities, eventually grew into a malignant obsession with a large section of the German people. The duped masses, drugged by the incessant propaganda from school, pulpit, wireless and press, began to believe in the Messianic mission of the German, the Aryan, to rule over all Non-Aryans—their ordained slaves. This is the very essence of the Herrenvolk ideology, the doctrine of 'thinking with your blood'.

358

No less classic, although less known to the outside world, is the case of South Africa. From earliest childhood the poisonous racial arrogance of the Herrenvolk ideology is assiduously injected into the White people of this country by School and Church and State. From the cradle to the grave, every phase of life is consciously regulated and moulded in order to preserve and perpetuate the division of the people of South Africa into the European—the Herrenvolk, and the Non-European—the slave, divinely ordained to minister to all his needs. So deeply has the poison of racial superiority been infused into the life of South Africa, that it has reached the very vitals, and no single phase of public or private life remains untainted by it. And it is a tragic fact that even those who might have been expected to display more fellowship towards the Non-European as a natural ally, namely, the Labour Party, and the Trade Unions, are no less contaminated by the Herrenvolk mentality. While they may speak abroad of equality for all and opportunity for all, they do not for a single moment include the Non-Europeans. For, at home, they *act* in full accord with the Herrenvolk creed of South Africa. The success of this racial in-doctrination may be measured by Field-Marshall Smuts' claim in the House of Assembly on 14th March, 1945, that *all* in South Africa are agreed upon the mission of the Europeans to rule over the Non-Europeans in perpetuity, *all*—except those who are 'mad, quite mad'. Indeed, to such a pass has this Herrenvolk ideology reduced South Africa, that every European who does not conform to it is vilified as insane; everyone, European or Non-European, who in any way attempts to effect racial harmony by eliminating the artificially fostered racial prejudices and artifically erected barriers of race hatred, is branded and hounded as a disturber of the peace who is sowing hostility between the races. In a word, the Herrenvolk mentality of South Africa in no way lags behind that of Nazi Germany.

But it is when we compare South Africa with Nazi Germany in respect of the second characteristic of Nazism, the ruthless trampling underfoot of human rights, that the essential similarity between the two becomes even more palpable. If in Nazi Germany it was the Jew who had to distinguish himself as an outcast by wearing a yellow patch, in South Africa a brown or black face makes the patch unnecessary; but in addition the Non-European is stigmatised by having to carry not one, but many 'passes' of different kinds—one proving he has paid his taxes, one permitting him to walk in the street, one permitting him to look for work, one for the day and another for the night! An outraged world recoiled in stupefaction at the trampling underfoot of all human rights in Nazi Germany, so that the Jew was debarred from education, the professions and skilled trades; he was denied the right to own property, the right to trade, to serve in the army; he was prohibited from entering places of entertainment, from cultural institutions and the like. But the world has yet to learn that all of these outrages have been, and are still, characteristic of the normal, everyday life of South Africa. The Non-European is debarred from education. He is denied access to the professions and skilled trades; he is denied the right to

359

buy land and property; he is denied the right to trade or to serve in the army—except as a stretcher-bearer or servant; he is prohibited from entering places of entertainment and culture. But still more, he is not allowed to live in the towns. And if it was a crime in Nazi Germany for an "Aryan" to mix with or marry a Non-Aryan, it is equally a criminal offence in South Africa for a member of the Herrenvolk to mix or marry with the slave race. When a man is denied the right to hire or build a dwelling for himself and his family, the right to sell his labour on the free market; when a man is stripped of all other elementary human rights in his own country, then there can be no two opinions but that he is living under a Nazi-like tyranny.

No less complete is the similarity between the two systems in regard to the third characteristic of Nazism, the erection of one system of law and of morality for the Aryans and a different system of law and morality for the Non-Aryans. In the majority of instances there is a separate law for Europeans and a separate law for Non-Europeans; in those rare cases where one Act legislates for both, there are separate clauses discriminating against the Non-Europeans. While it is true that there are no Buchenwald concentration camps in South Africa, it is equally true that the prisons of South Africa are full to overflowing with Non-Europeans whose criminality lies solely in the fact that they are unable to pay the Poll-tax, a special racial tax imposed upon them. But this law does not apply to the Aryan; for him there is a different law which makes the non-payment of taxes not a criminal, but a civil offence for which he cannot be imprisoned. But if there is no Buchenwald in South Afica, the sadistic fury with which the Herrenvolk policeman belabours the Non-European victim, guilty or not guilty is comparable only to the brutality of the SS Guards. Moreover, the treatment meted out to the Non-European in the Law Courts is comparable only to the fate of the Non-Aryan in the Nazi Law Courts. But the fundamental difference in law and morality is not only expressed in the different paragraphs of the Legal Statutes, it lies in the fundamentally different concept of the value of the life of a Non-European, as compared with the value placed upon the life of a European. The life of a Non-European is very cheap in South Africa. As cheap as the life of a Jew in Nazi Germany.

From the foregoing it is clear that the Non-Europeans of South Africa live and suffer under a tyranny very little different from Nazism. And if we accept the premise—as we hope the Nations of the World now do—that peace is indivisible, if we accept that there can be no peace as long as the scourge of Nazism exists in any corner of the globe, then it follows that the defeat of German Nazism is not the final chapter of the struggle against tyranny. There must be many more chapters before the peoples of the world will be able to make a new beginning. To us in South Africa it is indisputable that there can be no peace as long as this system of tyranny remains. To us it is ludicrous that this same South African Herrenvolk should speak abroad of a new beginning, of shaping a new world order, whereas in actuality all they wish is the retention of the present tyranny in South Africa and its extension

360

to new territories. Already they speak of new mandates and new trusteeships, which can only mean the extension of their Nazi-like domination over still wider terrain. It is impossible to make a new start as long as the representatives of this Herrenvolk take any part in the shaping of it. For of what value can it be when the very same people who speak so graciously abroad of the inviolability of human rights, at home trample ruthlessly underfoot those same inalienable rights? It is the grossest of insults not only to the 8 million Non-Europeans of South Africa, but to all those who are honestly striving to shape a world on new foundations, when the highest representative of the Herrenvolk of South Africa, Field Marshall Smuts, who has devoted his whole life to the entrenchment of this Nazi-like domination, brazenly speaks to the Nations of the World of 'the sanctity and ultimate value of the human personality' and 'the equal rights of men and women'.

We, the Non-Europeans of South Africa and the majority of the population, are the ones who are vitally concerned and genuinely determined that there shall be a new beginning. We declare emphatically before the peoples of the world that we have no territorial demands. We seek no aggrandisement and we do not covet any territories. On the contrary, we who have fought against German Nazism and Italian Fascism to the fullest extent that we were permitted, declare unequivocally that we are opposed to the handing over to the inclusion in the Union, of the Protectorate of Bechuanaland, Basutoland, and Swaziland. We are opposed to such inclusion on principle and on the grounds that it will be detrimental both to the people of the Protectorates and to the Non-Europeans in the Union. For, however intolerable the conditions under which the people in the Protectorates live, there can be no worse fate than their falling under the domination of the South African Herrenvolk. Therefore we dissociate ourself from all such claims on the part of our rulers.

Nevertheless we have demands. But our demands are not at the expense of other peoples. Our demands can only advance the cause of building a peaceful world on new beginnings. We are a peace-loving people. We have no enmity or malice towards the Europeans, for we wish to live side by side with them in peace and harmony. Yet we can only live side by side with them in peace and harmony as equals and not as inferiors. We are also a constitutional people. And if we make this Declaration directly to the Nations of the World and not through the Government of the Union of South Africa, it is because it must be clear from all the foregoing that it would be both ludicrous and futile to appeal against the tyrants through the tyrants. *Our* demands are that the Herrenvolk ideology be eradicated in South Africa, that there shall be an end to this system whereby the rights of the people are trampled underfoot by a small minority, and that there shall no longer be one system of law and morality for the Non-Europeans and a different one for *the Herrenvolk*. To effect these it would require the practical application of the following 10 fundamental human rights: ....

[10-point program follows]

Document 67. Letter ["On the Organisations of the African People"], from I.B. Tabata to Nelson Mandela, June 16, 1948

80 Harrington Street,
Cape Town.
16th June, 1948

My dear Mandela,

. . . .

Now to the discussion on the question of organisation, which is every day assuming greater importance. Let me state from the outset that I do not support the idea of organising the people for the sake of organisation. People can be organised for good or evil. This on the face of it may seem a childish platitude. But my experience has taught me—as you, too, must have perceived if you have pondered over it—that it is absolutely necessary for every individual to ask himself the question: What purpose does this or that organisation serve? It is not what the members say or think about an organisation that matters. It is not even a question of the good *intentions* of the leaders. What is of paramount importance is the programme and principles of the organisation. To put it another way, it is not the subjective good-will of the leaders that matters, but the objective function of the organisation, what effect it has on society. In other words, the question to ask is: *Whose interests does the organisation serve objectively?* This is the only correct approach to the discussion on the present organisations.

I ask you to use this test. Apply it to yourself and the organisation to which you belong. If you use it honestly and rigidly, without prejudice and without any emotion, you are bound to arrive at the correct conclusion. You will remember that when you were here I asked you the following question: Can you give me any good reason, political reason, why you joined Congress?—apart from the fact that your father or your father's father belonged to it and it was supposed to be an organisation for African people—an argument that is purely sentimental and falling outside the realm of politics.

I have said above that people can be organised for good or evil. I can have no quarrel with any organisation which is built for the purpose of fighting for liberty. Such an organisation, if it is true to its principles, will seek to unite the oppressed people and will at the same time follow a course of non-collaboration with the Government. But I am totally opposed to any organisation whose policy is to collaborate with the Government and disunite the people. And this is the crux of the question.

Let me state here that when I talk of the African National Congress I exclude the Youth League. Politically it does not belong to Congress. It is one of those peculiar anomalies which arise in a political situation where there is lack of crystal clarity in political thinking. If the League followed its political principles to their logical conclusion it would land itself *outside* the fold of Congress, so that, though you regard yourselves as Congress, I am more correct from a political standpoint in drawing the distinction. In fact, the essential difference between Congress and the Youth League is that Congress is rooted in the past whereas the League is the product of modern conditions, with a modern outlook. It is not my purpose, however, to develop this point at this stage. I am more concerned with giving you an appreciation of the development of our present organisational difficulties. In other words, I am concerned with posing the problem of organisation in the proper way. My task is not a difficult one because recent political events which have taken place amongst the African people have served to open the eyes of many who have laboured under past illusions. All the same, I feel it necessary to give you a résumé of the past, for I am conscious of the fact that, because of your youth, you did not have the opportunity of living through the events leading up to the 1936-1948 period. You have therefore been dependent on information from the older men who are all too prone to give you a distorted picture of the events and the issues involved. They do this, not because of any innate propensities for lying, but because of the necessity to justify their personal political position.

Let us therefore briefly recapitulate the past. The beginning of this century closed a chapter in our history—the end of the resistance of the Blacks by military means. It opened a new chapter with new forms of struggle, the political form of struggle. This manifested itself in the formation of Imbumba and Ingqungquthela. These were federations of tribes, natural enough in tribal communities. The year 1912 saw the first creation of an African organisation on an individualist basis, with the breaking up of tribalism. This was a progressive step, i.e. Congress was progressive as compared with the past. Though in form Congress had broken with the past, it did not mean that it had shed completely the tribalist outlook. It could not be otherwise, for an organisation is the product of its time. It ushered in a new outlook more in keeping with the times and therefore deserved the support of all progressives.

As a result of this outlook many other organisations sprang up on an individualist basis of membership. There were the political organisations, professional organisations, trade union organisations and civic bodies, all of which had one purpose, the fight for freedom. The rise of the organisations showed a further progress in the development of the people. But the fight for freedom was undertaken by each organisation in isolation from the rest. The struggle was unco-ordinated and this led to disaster, so that by the 1930s all the African organisations had disintegrated and become completely atomised. The characteristic feature of this stage of development was a mutual suspicion, rivalry and hatred between the various organisations. It became the duty of the leaders of one organisation to denounce all others, not because of the difference in political policies or principles, not because they could not brook any rivalry in the leadership. Each one felt that the other organisations were not necessary

363

and that everybody should join the particular organisation where he was the leader. Thus all political fights degenerated into personal squabbles and the leaders exhausted all their energies in fratricidal strife.

Then came 1935, which opened up a new chapter. (It was the year of the notorious Hertzog ''Native'' Bills.) By now it was evident that the organisations which had sprung up had come to stay. All of them were neccesary in their various spheres. But what was needed was a body that would co-ordinate their struggles, create a unified leadership which could give direction to their multifarious activities.

The African people spontaneously created the ALL-AFRICAN CON-VENTION. The political exigencies of the time and the crisis (of the new slave Bills) forced the people to organise on a nation-wide scale. So without any premeditated theory the people spontaneously gave birth to a form of organisation which could knit together a whole people into a single compact unit, a fighting force. The predominant idea at the time was *unity*. This was one higher political level. The predominant thought in everyone's mind was how to remove competition and eliminate all rivalry between the organisations. Each leader was to bring his followers to this body and he together with leaders of other organisations was to form a single leadership with a common aim and a common purpose. The interests of each constituent part were identical with the interests of the whole. Mutual antagonisms and rivalry were replaced by the spirit of co-operation. The leader who jealously guarded his personal position was replaced by a unified leadership and petty sectional considerations gave way to a form of thought which embraced the whole race.

This was a turning point in the organisational history of the African people. That is, 1935-36 was the highest point of development in organisation affecting the African people as a group. It was expected that this would constitute a point of departure for all our activities and that any further political development would have as its basis the form adopted in 1935. I have said above that the African people spontaneously created this form of organisation. Not even the leaders themselves had at any time stopped to examine theoretically and evaluate its possibilities. In other words, they did not fully appreciate the potentialities and the full value of their discovery.

The ruling class, however, was fully alive to the danger to itself inherent in this development. It was not the form of organisation per se that worried them so much, but a further development which was bound to follow from it. *It could prove the basis for a new outlook*. They are aware of the interconnection of the form of organisation and a political outlook. This cleared the road for a national outlook which would prove the logical outcome of this stage of development. A national outlook of an oppressed people constitutes the first stage of a threat to white domination. Such an outlook had to be stopped by the ruling class at all costs. What I am trying to emphasise to you is this, that if the African people had progressed from 1935 as a unit, they would by now have reached a stage whereby their whole outlook, their propaganda and their agitation, their energies and their manual resources would have put them in a position to challenge the existence of the Herrenvolk.

It was to stop this that the Herrenvolk did their best to sow confusion amongst the African people. The idea of the All-African Convention had to be smashed at its birth. It was comparatively easy for the rulers to succeed, at least in part, for the idea had not yet become part and parcel of the people's thinking. They found a willing stooge in the person of the late Dr. Dube, at that time, Mr. Dube, a principal of some secondary school in Natal. He was the first one to break away from Convention, and with him went practically the whole of Natal. The white Press acclaimed him as a great statesman, a moderate, a practical politician and in fact an epitome of all virtues. They crowned him with a halo of greatness and conferred a doctorate on him. It was as Dr. Dube that he led the Zulus back to tribalism, where they still stagnate to-day.

This was a brilliant move on the part of the oppressors. Seeing the rewards and honours heaped upon Dube, the Themas and others of the same brand followed suit. But still these people could not smash the All-African Convention by the mere fact of breaking away and asking others to follow suit. For this deed an organisation was necessary. Thus Congress was resuscitated by these very individuals. At that time they held out to the people that Congress was going to be used to gather the unorganised masses and bring them into Convention. But once Congress had gathered to itself a fairly respectable number of people, they wrenched the organisation away from the All-African Convention. By this time, Dr. Xuma, an ex-president of Convention, was head of Congress. The white Press picked him up, built him up as a great leader, a great champion of the cause of the African people. This they did with an end in view.

The young intellectuals who left school at the end of the thirties or the beginning of the forties and who entered the political arena at this time, found Dr. Xuma as the proclaimed leader of the African people, and without asking any questions they threw in their lot with him. He shouted unity from the house-tops. The press helped him to unite people under Congress. Why? Because to unite people in a splinter organisation is to foster organised disunity, and that was the surest way of disuniting the African people. The oppressors had to foster and support, by every means at their disposal, an organisation which sets itself up in opposition to the All-African Convention in order to kill the very spirit of real unity on a higher plane, for it was this that had given rise to the All-African Convention. What the rulers succeeded in doing—and this the younger intellectuals do not know—was to plunge the African people back to the pre-1935 period, that whole epoch in which the struggles of the people were reduced to a stale-mate by fratricidal strife.

I know that you have often wondered why we are so intransigent and yet we say we want unity. In fact, I suspect you think we are just plainly bigoted and obstinate. The truth of the matter is that we are defending a position which was conquered by the African people in 1935. We want unity on that basis, i.e. real unity on the basis of the existing organisations, in such a way that the interests of each are the interests of the whole, a unity in which the growth of a part automatically means the strengthening of the whole, a unity which will serve as the basis for a further development leading to a truly national movement, nationalism. And this is the very antithesis of sectionalism or racialism.

If you consider the ground already covered by the African people in their development, and if you visualise what might have been accomplished by this time, if this retrograde step had not been taken, then you become aware of the enormity of the crime committed by Congress against a whole people.

Up to now I have not said anything about the divergence of political outlook between Congress and Convention, the yawning gap that separates the two organisations in the matter of principles. This is not because I think political differences are of lesser importance, it is simply because I want to give you some idea of the past history of our political development. As it is, the letter has become too long, so I propose to postpone this aspect to a later date, if you wish to discuss it any further.

At the moment I can only add that those organisations which are affiliated to Convention are facing in one direction while Congress is facing in the very opposite direction. The first group have rejected the superiority of the White race over the Black; they have rejected trusteeship with all that it implies: segregation, sectionalism and tribalism. The Convention has openly stated its policy, which is in line with this outlook, and it is following a clearly defined course without any concessions, compromises or deviations. Congress, on the other hand, is doing the very opposite of all these things. Many critics of Congress often say: "The trouble with Congress is that it has no policy." There could be nothing further from the truth than this statement. Congress has a *definite* policy. Only it is not openly stated for it cannot bear examination. Those who are interested can only divine this policy by watching the activities of Congress over a long period. They will find that at every critical moment Congress has played into the hands of the Government, either by directly siding with the Government against the people (e.g. in the case of the Boycott) or by sowing confusion in the ranks of the people to such an extent that all efforts at gathering them together for a concerted fight against the Government are rendered ineffectual. The history of the Congress in the last five years is too well known to require recapitulation. It is too painful even to contemplate. What I consider as the most despicable deed is the fact that some of the Congress leaders are not merely satisfied with sowing confusion within the African section. They now seek to extend their wrecking tactics to a broader plane and are bringing disruption and confusion amongst the ranks of the Non-Europeans who are striving to come together.

366

To mention only two examples: Xuma's pact with the two Indian doctors, and now there is the Votes For All Assembly. Anything and everything to create excitement for the moment. It does not avail the Mosakas and the Xumas to deny any connection with this new hoax, the Votes For All Assembly. They must take the blame for it. The Press has proved conclusively that Mosaka was one of the sponsors, by publishing the facsimile of the document with his signature. Xuma was cute enough not to sign anything, but he made a silly slip-up in connection with the funds. If you examine the financial statement published in the minutes of this august assembly, you will find that there is an item of expenditure amounting to £ 22.17.6. for Dr. Xuma's Press Conference. Let Dr. Xuma explain this away. But, apart altogether from these lesser connections, there is the bigger connection, a political tie-up between Xuma and the organisers of the Assembly. There has been a flirtation going on between them for the past few years. Naturally they depended on his help to go through with this fraud.

To make myself clear, let me put it this way. If Xuma and "his" Congress had been in the Convention and therefore working in harmony with the Non-European Unity Movement, on the basis of a principled programme, the 10-Point Programme, nobody would have even dreamed of asking him to support such fraudulent schemes. In point of fact, the organisers of the "Votes For All" would not have found it possible even to contemplate starting such a move. The Communist Party would not have had a foothold amongst the African people, who are to-day used as a cover for all the nefarious deeds of all the careerists and opportunists.

I have brought up these various points for your serious consideration. You have to take up your stand in this light. Finally, let me mention one aspect of your position which I feel sure you have not considered. You and all your fellow-members of the Youth League are talking with two voices at one and the same time. As members of the Youth League you speak the language of the modern intellectual—progressive, independent, rejecting inferiority. But as members of the African National Congress your language is the very negation of all these things. You accept the theory of inferiority and trusteeship with all its political manifestations, e.g. segregated institutions like the Native Representative Council, Advisory Boards, the Bunga, etc.

I can hear you already protesting that never at any time did you and the Youth League accept these things. Yes, you may not have done so in words, but you have done so in fact and in deed. The Youth League is part and parcel of the organic body of Congress, which does these things. That fact alone speaks more emphatically than words themselves. It is no use you protesting that the Youth League was originally organised by Congress. Granted that it makes its public statements on events, proclaims its policy and passes its own resolutions on the fundamental questions of the day, all of which are diametrically opposed to the policy and actions of Congress. Nevertheless it remains an entity within Congress, voluntarily. This puts you in the position of being political Januses, with two heads facing in two different directions at one and the same time. This in politics is known as *opportunism* and opportunism is the worst disease that can infect any political organisation. In fact it is the canker that has claimed the greatest toll of all our organisations up to the present day.

It is possible that you are not aware of your contradictory position or if you are aware of it you excuse yourselves by some such argument that you want to keep the people together, that you want unity and are opposed to splitting tactics. But this kind of argument is the essence of opportunism. Any attempt at unity without a *principled basis (programme)* can only lead to confusion and political paralysis and end in ultimate disunity. Principles are the backbone of any movement. To put it another way, any organisation which is not founded on the solid rock of principles is a prey to every wind that blows. It was the failure to recognise this important fact that was primarily responsible for the fall of so many of our organisations in the past. We have had large organisations which were at first hailed with enthusiasm. But they have vanished away, leaving no trace behind.

Now, Mandela, it's time I gave you a rest, and incidentally myself, too. If you curse me for having written so long a letter, remember that you have yourself to blame. I have added this last page because I think it is of paramount importance for a man, and especially a young man entering politics, to establish the habit of basing his actions on principles. He must be ready if necessary to swim against the stream. Thus armed, he is protected against the temptations of seeking popularity and ephemeral success.

I hope to hear from you soon,

Yours sincerely,

I. B. Tabata.

Document 68. "A Call for African Unity." Statement signed by Xuma, Jabavu, Moroka, Matthews, Bokwe, Godlo, Mosaka, Baloyi, Champion, Selope Thema, Ntlabati, and Mahabane, October 3, 1948

We, the undersigned, having met in Bloemfontein on this the 3rd day of October 1948, considered the political situation in the Union of South Africa in so far as it affects the interests of the African people.

Having regard to all the facts, we are convinced that in recent times there has been a marked deterioration in the plight of the African in all aspects of his life.

We are alarmed and strongly protest against the callous disregard of the fundamental rights of the African by the Government, largely with acquiscence of European public opinion.

The determination to deprive Africans of all political and other human rights, the grave threat to all African Organisations implied in Proclamation No. 1890, the insidious threat to facilities for education including higher education, the increased restrictions of freedom of movement of the African, the denial of land and residential rights for Africans in urban and rural areas and the restrictions of employment or occupational facilities for the Africans to mention but a few, have given the Africans a sense of frustration and insecurity in the land of their forefathers and has undermined any confidence they might have had in the justice of most white men, in the promises and solemn pledges made by various Union Governments from time to time.

The situation constitutes a challenge which cannot be ignored by the African people.

The primary necessity in meeting the challenge is unified action on the part of the African people.

We are convinced that the preliminary step in this direction is the Unification of the main African political organisations—the African National Congress and the All African Convention into "THE ALL AFRICAN NATIONAL CONGRESS", united and inspired by common principles and a common programme of action for the achievement of the liberation of the African people.

We consider it our duty at this time of crisis to call upon leaders and members of the Organisations concerned to take immediate steps to bring about this unification. In this connection we urge that December 16th, 1948, be the day fixed for the bringing about of this Unified National Political Organisation.

We suggest that the conference at which it is expected this national unity will be achieved must be held at Bloemfontein, on the 16th December, 1948.

We urge putting aside all questions of personal and organisational prestige, differences of the past and any other private business or programme on the part of the organisations concerned and concentrate their efforts and attention on the achievement of national unity of the African people.

We have now reached a period of crisis in the national life of the African people occasioned by the Union's Native Policy.

The situation calls for clear, constructive thinking as well as calculated and bold actions on our part as the people.

We therefore, most earnestly appeal to all Africans, Chiefs, Ministers of Religion, Leaders, men and women, young and old to rally to the call for African Unity, and make December 16th, 1948, a turning point in African political history.

Signed: A. B. Xuma (Convenor), D. D. T. Jabavu, J. S. Moroka, Z. K. Matthews, R. T. Bokwe, R. H. Godlo, Paul R. Mosaka, R. G. Baloyi, A. W. G. Champion, R. V. Selope Thema, L. K. Ntlabati, Z. R. Mahabane.

Document 69. Minutes of the Joint Conference of the ANC and the AAC, December 16-17, 1948

A. THURSDAY 3 P.M., 16TH DECEMBER, 1948.

1. ATTENDANCE:

One hundred and sixteen delegates represented the African National Congress and about thirty delegates the All-African Convention. Well over 50 people attached to neither of these two bodies also attended [in the Community Hall, Batho Location, Bloemfontein].

2. CHAIRMAN OF CONFERENCE:

Professor D. D. T. Jabavu, the President of the A.A.C. presided over Conference jointly with Dr. A. B. Xuma, the President-General of the A.N.C.

3. PURPOSES OF CONFERENCE:

1. "A direct attack on democracy has accelerated the desire of all of us to come together" said Dr. Xuma in outlining the history of the unity negotiations, "We must speak with one voice. The statement issued on the 3rd October last was a result of long planning and negotiations dating as far back as August, 1943." Dr. Xuma went on to show how he negotiated from stage to stage with the officials of the A.A.C. for the unification of the two Premier Bodies until the meeting of the 12 leaders who issued a statement calling upon the African People to unite against the threat of apartheid and initiated the joint Conference.

2. "We have been criticised" concluded Dr. Xuma, "because we did not consult the provinces. Mistakes in details and in the manner of approach to the question may have been made but we feel we were justified in this move; the defects cannot be of greater moment than the urgent question of consolidating and deploying our forces against the present political situation; the cause of Democratic South Africa is greater than any man."

4. POSTPONEMENT OF JOINT CONFERENCE TO THE 17/12/1948:

Professor Jabavu associated himself with the remarks and explanations made by Dr. Xuma. He informed Conference that the majority of the members of the A.A.C. were still meeting at a Conference of the African Voters' Association in Queenstown so that the A.A.C. could not commence discussions on the question of Unity. This was due to a misunderstanding regarding the date of the Joint Conference. Professor Jabavu then asked for a postponement of Conference until the afternoon of the 17th December, 1948.

Dr. Xuma suggested an acceptance of the request made by Professor Jabavu in the light of the explanation made.

5. DISCUSSION ON POSTPONEMENT OF JOINT CONFERENCE:

Messrs. G. Makabeni, L. S. Phillips, L. K. Ntlabati and D. W. Bopape took part in discussing the matter.

Mr. S. Elias, seconded by Mr. H. A. Schultz, moved

"That, in view of Professor Jabavu's explanation, the Joint Conference of the A.N.C. and the A.A.C. be deferred to the afternoon of the 17th December, 1948."

Agreed.

Conference then adjourned at 3:50 p.m.

B. FRIDAY 3 P.M. 17TH DECEMBER, 1948:

6. PRELIMINARY MEETING:

1. Cr. A. W. G. Champion, who had been presiding over the A.N.C. Conference made some noteworthy remarks before he vacated the Chair at a preliminary meeting to the Joint Conference. He said that the policy of the Nationalist Government made every white man an enemy of the African who would do everything possible to obtain his liberation from white oppression. The Africans, concluded Cr. Champion, would welcome assistance of any nation or race, be they Russians or Japanese or Indians.

2. The following delegates were chosen to speak at the Joint Conference on behalf of the A.N.C.: Professor Z. K. Matthews, Cr. A. W. G. Champion, Cr. R. V. Selope Thema, Cr. R. H. Godlo, Dr. R. Setlogelo, Mr. A. P. Mda, Mr. M. M. Kotane, Mr. H. Selby Msimang and Mr. J. B. Marks.

7. OPENING OF JOINT CONFERENCE:

When the Conference opened at 3.30 p.m. the All-African Convention was now represented by over 40 delegates. Professor Jabavu jointly with Dr. Xuma, presided over the Conference.

8. WELCOME OF DELEGATES:

Dr. A. B. Xuma, as Convenor of the Joint Conference, welcomed the delegates of the two bodies. "We are not gathered here to fight against the whites but to join hands and fight for fundamental rights to contribute freely to the enrichment of world civilisation", said Dr. Xuma after he had covered the same ground of the history of unity negotiations as he had done the previous day.

9. READING OF THE MINUTES OF THE PREVIOUS DAY'S PROCEEDINGS:

Rev. J. A. Calata read the minutes of the proceedings of the previous day.

Mr. W. S. Sisulu, seconded by Mr. E. Kongisa, moved

"That the minutes be adopted as a correct record of the previous day's proceedings."

Agreed.

10. *OFFICIAL INTERPRETERS:*

Messrs. A. B. Malunga and C. S. Ramohanoe were elected Xhosa and Sesuto interpreters respectively.

11. *INTRODUCTORY REMARKS BY LEADERS:*

1. "Your response to this call is an indication of your seriousness and sincerity about the issue at stake. If difficulties there are, they will be *fundamental difficulties* and *not superficial and personal ones.* Is the distress of your people less important than your personal differences here? That is the test of our political maturity as a race," said *Dr. Xuma* in addressing Conference. He then called upon his Senior, Professor D. D. T. Jabavu, to address Conference.

2. *Professor D.D.T. Jabavu* addressed Conference. "Whilst I identify myself with Dr. Xuma's outlook on this matter, I want us to address our attention to the *essentials.* I have no doubt that our spirit, desire and sentiment are one but *we have to see that the foundation we build is one of cement,*" remarked Professor Jabavu.

3. *Rev. Z. Mahabane* also addressed Conference. Rev. Mr. Mahabane traced the history of the franchise of the African since 1909 up to date. He showed that gradual whittling away of the franchise was going on all along until now the Nationalist Government was threatening to take away that *vestige* of it which yet remained. "It is time we said to the Europeans of this country 'Thus far, and no farther'. A state of emergency exists. Urgent measures must be adopted. The call is 'To Arms', not by taking weapons but by coming together and speak with one voice and act as one man," concluded Rev. Mr. Mahabane.

Mr. Mda, seconded by Mr. J.N. Hlekani, objected to long and eloquent speeches.

12. *MR. I. TABATA OPENS DEBATE:*

1. Mr. Tabata lead the discussion on behalf of the A.A.C. He argued very ably that the federal character of the A.A.C. was a source of strength and not weakness. He said that the Herrenvolk parties were united in their oppression of the Non-Europeans, and there was intrinsically no difference between them. On May 26th "the velvet glove was replaced by the brutal, mailed fist. For us it produces the same kind of blow."

2. Mr. Tabata informed Conference that the A.A.C. had decided to give Congress a given percentage of the seats on the Executive of the proposed

Convention of the two bodies. He placed before Conference the conditions under which the A.A.C. would agree to unity, namely:

1. It should be based on the Convention's 10-point Programme. The ten points were read to Conference.

2. The federal structure of the Convention should be retained.

3. The Unity should be based on the acceptance of the principle of the unity of all the Non-Europeans.

4. It should be based on a policy of "non-collaboration with the oppressor." The reference here was to Bodies like the Bunga and the Native Representative Council.

3. "We must say we do not want separate institutions. We want to go to the only Councils recognised in the land - Parliament, Provincial and Municipal Councils," ended Mr. Tabata.

13. *PROFESSOR Z.K. MATTHEWS:*

1. Professor Matthews impressed that it was necessary to *keep to the essentials and fundamentals* of the issue and feared that long speeches might cloud the important and real issue.

2. The cause of trouble between the two bodies was similarity rather than difference of objectives. Both organisations claimed to be the mouthpiece of the African people; they spoke one thing with different voices causing confusion among the people.

3. "To the average Congress person the proposal of the A.A.C. seems to mean that one mouthpiece of the African people (the A.A.C.) is wanting to swallow up the other mouthpiece (the A.N.C.), " suggested Professor Matthews.

4. Professor Matthews then spoke for the Congress view point as embodied in the resolution which read as follows:

"That (a) the principle of unity between the A.N.C. and the A.A.C. be accepted; that

(b) a Steering Committee be appointed to facilitate the process of giving effect to unity; and that

(c) The Steering Committee be instructed to approach, to interest and, as far as it may extend its activities, to open negotiations with any other African organisations for the consummation of a national unity of African organisations."

Professor Matthews felt that unity could not be achieved overnight, and that there were also other organisations which should be drawn into the process of unification.

14. *MR. MOSES M. KOTANE (A.N.C. CAPE TOWN).*

Mr. Kotane said that the two groups appeared to have different conceptions of unity. He did not agree that a federal body was necessarily a strong one.

"In order to eliminate conflicting directions, interests and ideologies," Mr. Kotane went on, "we want one political organisation that will speak for the individual members of the organisation. A federal organisation tends to be an organisation of different interested bodies that come together to consult but have always to go back to their executives for directions."

15. CR. A.W.G. CHAMPION, (A.N.C. DURBAN).

Cr. Champion felt that no useful purpose would be served by arguing as to the best character of the proposed Convention at this stage. These were details which could be thrashed out by the Steering Committee. "Was the A.A.C. agreeable to the setting up of the Steering Committee?" he queried.

16. MR. W.M. TSOTSI (A.A.C. PORT ELIZABETH).

1. Mr. Tsotsi felt that the differences between the two bodies were basic and fundamental. He said that the people wanted to know whom to follow; they wanted to know why the A.N.C. did not join the Non-European Unity Movement, and whether or not the A.N.C. subscribed to the boycott movement which the A.A.C. preached to them.

2. "Unity is not an end in itself. Unity of individuals is not enough. People must follow a common policy. They must agree to unite on a programme and a policy. Congress is an old organisation but its membership is low. This shows that the people do not see salvation in it,' concluded Mr. Tsotsi.

17. MR. A.P. MDA (HERSCHEL, C.P.).

Mr. Mda said that the basis of unity must be African Nationalism—the liberation of Africans as a race from European domination. He maintained that differences in the conceptions of the best form of organisation acceptable to both bodies must not stand in the way of unity. The differences existing between the two organisations must be reconciled.

Mr. Mda added that the A.N.C. accepted the ten-point programme as read to Conference by Mr. Tabata; in fact there was nothing new in it. The points were all covered by the Constitution of the A.N.C.

18. MR. D. KOZA (A.A.C. JOHANNESBURG).

Mr. Koza maintained that unity had to be achieved at the Conference. The fundamental differences of the two bodies had not been fully explored and the ground on which unity could possibly be laid had not been prepared. "We are not going to take the dangerous step of appointing a Committee and giving it a blank cheque", said Mr. Koza.

19. *MR. I. TABATA 'S APPEAL.*

Mr. Tabata rose to appeal to the House to discuss the basic issue and leave alone technical difficulties which could be solved at a later stage.

20. *MR. R.S. CANCA (A.A.C. CAPE TOWN).*

Mr. Canca said that immediate and fundamental essentials had to be tackled at the Conference. He said that the A.A.C. had come forward with a definite programme and it was for the A.N.C. to accept or reject that programme. He did not subscribe to the liquidation of the organisations; the delegates had come to build, and not to destroy. "But white domination we must do away with. That is why we are here," said Mr. Canca.

21. *MR. R.H. GODLO (A.N.C. EAST LONDON).*

Mr. Godlo appealed for the acceptance of the Steering Committee and said that trying to score debating points would not get the Conference anywhere. It was a healthy sign to see the adoption of the principle of Unity by the two bodies. The details could be safely left in the hands of the Steering Committee. Moreover, the ten-point programme was embodied in the African Claims issued by the A.N.C.

22. *MR. R. SELLO (KROONSTAD).*

"Am I to understand that the principle of unity is acceptable to both organisations?" questioned Mr. Sello. *The House Agreed.*

23. *MR. H. SELBY MSIMANG (A.N.C. PIETERMARITZBURG).*

Mr. Msimang said that the A.A.C. wanted the A.N.C. to wash its dirty linen in public. The best course was that recommended by the A.N.C. - the matter should be left in the hands of the Steering Committee.

24. *MR. MDA MDA (A.A.C. UMTATA).*

Mr. Mda said that there had been some misunderstanding as to what the two bodies met at Bloemfontein for. "Are we here to perpetuate the N.R.C. and the Bunga?" he asked. He maintained that the A.N.C. aimed at swallowing the different organisations in the Transkei. In his opinion what divided the two major bodies was a clear difference in conceptions in regard to important and national issues. 'Non-collaboration with the oppressors' was the principle on which to base the national struggle. "The Ballingers and the rest of them must have no place in our midst", emphasised Mr. Mda.

25. MR. A.C. JORDAN (A.A.C. CAPE TOWN).

Mr. Jordan said that his objection to the matter being left to the Steering Committee was that the differences between the two bodies had not been fully discussed and disclosed. It was necessary for the rank and file to express its opinion on the matter. He argued in favour of a federal body. In such a body, he said, one finds the best brains of different walks of life unifying their struggle and co-ordinating their resources for common interests.

26. MR. J.B. MARKS (A.N.C. JOHANNESBURG).

Mr. Marks said that whatever differences existed between the two bodies, it was evident from the speeches made that Africans demanded nothing short of equality in all walks of life. The differences were therefore subsidiary and subordinate to the real and main objective: freedom from white oppression. His experience as Head of the Trade Union Movement convinced him that a federal organisation was difficult to get to act quickly as and when need arose. The opinion of affiliated bodies had to be solicited whilst the situation deteriorated. "We want to have such a body as can take IMMEDIATE action. Under the iron heel of the present Government, the people are being crushed whilst we complacently quibble about technical difficulties," thundered Mr. Marks.

27. MR. S. JAYIYA (A.A.C. CAPE TOWN).

Mr. Jayiya accused the A.N.C. of insincerity. He said that the spokesmen of the A.N.C. accepted the ten-point programme whereas the first point in that programme demanded full democratic rights. Only on the basis of 'non-collaboration with the oppressors' could the A.A.C. agree to unite with the A.N.C. "If the members of the N.R.C. are sincere in this move and honest with their people, they must resign forthwith", demanded Mr. Jayiya.

28. CR. P.R. MOSAKA (JOHANNESBURG).

Cr. Mosaka said that there was a definite need for both a unitary and federal body. "But the A.A.C. suffers from a serious obsession. Their policy is a negative one - they do not want this or that. I am agreeable to the policy of non-co-operation, but where and when is it going to be carried out? The A.A.C. have decided their 'where and when' in pursuance of this policy of non-co-operation with the Whites. Now they want to force their will on everybody. I cannot agree to this form of dictatorship," said Cr. Mosaka.

29. MR. A.C. JORDAN.

Mr. Jordan interpolated and said that the teachers, unlike the members of the N.R.C., had not canvassed for their posts nor for travelling in coaches specially reserved for Africans.

30. *PROFESSOR D.D.T. JABAVU'S SUGGESTION REJECTED TWICE BY THE A.A.C. DELEGATION.*

Professor Jabavu urged Conference to adopt the statement of the 3rd October last. He said, "We could not reach finality in our deliberations this afternoon. I am desperate. Let us at least go away having said something." He then read the statement to the Conference so as to guide it. The A.A.C. delegation rejected this suggestion. He then put the same issue differently. He urged that he and Dr. Xuma be empowered to issue another statement drawn up in the light of the discussions of joint Conference. This also was unacceptable to the A.A.C. delegation, chief spokesman on the matter being Mr. R.S. Canca.

31. *REV. Z. MAHABANE'S MOTION.*

Rev. Z. Mahabane *moved*
  (1) "That the principle of unity be adopted"—*carried unanimously.*
  (2) "That a Committee be appointed to go into the question of unity and to report to Conference". This was also unacceptable to the A.A.C. delegation until Dr. G.H. Gool moved an amendment "That the Committee should consist of the two Executive Committees." Then the amendment was *carried unanimously.*
  (3) Rev. Mr. Mahabane again moved that the statement of the 3/10/48 be adopted and that another statement be issued by a Committee of 4, consisting of Dr. A.B. Xuma and Professor Z.K. Matthews on the one side and Professor D.D.T. Jabavu and Mr. I. Tabata on the other side. The A.A.C. delegation rejected this motion.

32. *PROFESSOR D.D.T. JABAVU'S SUGGESTION AGAIN PUT TO CONFERENCE.*

Ignoring the members of the A.A.C. delegation, who were sitting on one side of the House, Professor Jabavu put his suggestion to adopt the statement of the 3/10/48 to Conference for the third time. When the House agreed to it, he shouted "It is carried".

33. *CLOSING OF CONFERENCE.*

Conference was declared closed at 6 p.m.

Ntabetemba,
CRADOCK, C.P.

J.A. CALATA,

SECRETARY-GENERAL.
RECORDING SECRETARY

DOCUMENTS 70a-70c. Joint Meeting of the National Executive Committees of the ANC and the AAC, April 17-18, 1949

Document 70a. Minutes, signed by C. M. Kobus [of the AAC], Recording Secretary

A meeting of the above committees was held in the Board-room at the Batho Location, Bloemfontein, on Sunday morning. 17th April, 1949, at 10 a.m.

Present were:-

African National Congress.

1. Messrs. J. B. Marks; 2. A. P. Mda; 3. R. V. Selope-Thema; 4. L. K. Ntlabati; 5. Moses Kotane; 6. J. Malangabi; 7. G. Makabeni; 8. L.S. Phillips; 9. O.R. Tambo; 10. Prof. Z.K. Matthews; 11. Dr. A.B. Xuma.

All-African Convention.

1. Messrs. R. M. Canca; 2. Mda Mda; 3. A. K. Mazwai; 4. S. A. Jayiya; 5. I. B. Tabata; 6. Leo Sihlali; 7. W. M. Tsotsi; 8. Jas. Mdatyulwa; 9. Rev. Z. R. Mahabane; 10. Dr. G. H. Gool; 11. Mrs. Elizabeth Benjamin; 12. Mr. Robert Sello; 13. Mr. C. M. Kobus.

The meeting was under the joint chairmanship of Mr. W. M. Tsotsi, President of the All-African Convention, and Dr. A. B. Xuma, President of the African National Congress.

The meeting was opened with prayer by the Rev. Mahabane. Dr. Xuma in his opening remarks welcomed the delegates and expressed the hope for a successful meeting. In his remarks Mr. Tsotsi said that unity could be approached from two angles. It could be approached from the emotional as well as from the rational angle. The ordinary man's approach was emotional. We were all oppressed, he argued, and therefore we should all unite. But there were real differences which could not be ignored. Unity was a means to an end. It could also be a source of weakness if there was no common aim. We wanted unity in the fight against oppression and therefore we should be prepared to accept as allies all those people who were fighting the common enemy. There were those who did not accept road of struggle because of the travail through which the road led. We had therefore to define unity. Unity for what? Some were stumbling blocks to unity, and others, through a mistaken analysis, took the road to oppression for the road to unity and freedom. We should waste no time on the form of the organisation we intended to build, but first of all we should discuss the principles upon which unity is to be based.

The meeting decided that the principle upon which the proposed unity was to be based be discussed first.

In leading the discussion on Non-collaboration, Mr. I. B. Tabata said that we should agree that we reject inferiority and therefore we reject the institutions created for an "inferior" race and demanded full democratic rights and only those institutions which were recognised in democratic government. By non-collaboration, he said, we meant an unwillingness on our part to work those

378

institutions which were created for our own oppression. A collaborator was one who voluntarily supported and worked political institutions created for the oppression of the Black man. We should support the freely created organisations of the people. That was what we meant by Non-collaboration.

Speaking for the African National Congress, Mr. J. B. Marks said that there were fundamental differences between the All-African Convention and the African National Congress. We knew the strength of our armies and we had to unite eight million people. We should have in mind the immediate and ultimate aim of the struggle. For instance a demand for unity on the basis of socialism would be absurd where the position was not ripe. It would be wrong to stigmatise as collaborators those who did not agree with Non-collaboration at this stage.

Mr. R. V. Selope-Thema, M. R. C., supported Mr. Marks and said that if the Convention delegates advocated a boycott of Government institutions then they should carry out their policy to its logical conclusion. Did the delegates believe that they could tell the people of the Transkei to abolish the Bhunga? (Several Transkei delegates replied "Yes"!) Some of them believed that they could fight these institutions; that was why the government was afraid of the Native Representative Council. If we accepted the policy of Convention then we should have nothing to do with Europeans. If a lawyer who defended an African in a European Court was not collaborating but earning a living, then the M. R. C.'s were not collaborating. The people did not appreciate the demand for parliamentary representation, what the people wanted was land. We should think of the eight million Africans who still wanted these things. The Bhunga had done many things. It had granted bursaries and planted trees. If he were to go to his own area Pietersburg and tell the people to have nothing to do with the Bhunga, they would think he was mad. We sat in our various homes and cried "Don't collaborate," while in the meantime the people accept these things. Non-collaboration was alright as a long term policy. These things could not be overthrown overnight. We were all agreed. The difference was merely one of approach.

With regard to unity Mr. Thema said that if by unity we meant the unity of all the oppressed, then we might as well go home. They regarded the unity of the African people of primary importance. Charity began at home. They, the Africans, wanted to unite in their economic and social life, and therefore they had to unite as a race. If we wanted to unite with other people, we could form an alliance with them. We had a purpose to fulfil as a united African race. Our aims might be opposed to those of other people, it did not matter. We should follow the law of self preservation. We should love each other first before we loved other people.

Mr. R. M. Canca, explaining the meaning of collaboration, said that laws were not enough to rule. Institutions had to be created to create a mental attitude of acceptance of the laws. These institutions were the N.R.C., the Bunga and Advisory Boards. A collaborator was one who contested a seat in one of the above institutions. He was engaged in a mental swindle. He knew participation in these institutions could not free the African, yet he pretended that it could. The delegates should not confuse issues. A teacher in a segregated school and an African boarding a reserve coach in a train could not be called collaborators because they had no choice in these things.

Mr. G. Makabeni felt that policy was most important. The word "Non-collaboration" was vague. They represented the masses and were concerned with freedom and not with words. The expression was meaningless, it was not honest and it would not rally the people. The duty of a trade-unionist was to represent the interests of the people wherever those interests were. Trade unionists had to state their case before Gov. Commissions when necessary. They had to present the case of the people honestly. We should unite and not weed out leaders even before we had formed an organisation. If we could not look at realities then there was no point in further discussion.

Mr. Moses Kotane said that they could not reply by "Yes" or "No" to the question of acceptance or non-acceptance of Non-collaboration. They were fighting for freedom. Congress did not want to collaborate. The worker in production was operating the machinery of oppression, but he formed another instrument whereby the same instrument could be overthrown through strikes and revolutions. Congress did not want to collaborate, but the people were not ready. We could not carry out "Non-collaboration." The A.A.C. itself had not been able to carry out "Non-collaboration." In some cases non-collaboration might be possible, determined by the preparedness of the people at the particular time. Congress stood for Non-collaboration—when the people were ready. They went into the N.R.C. to abolish it from within. They could not accept an inflexible term.

Rev. Z. R. Mahabane replied that the analogy of the worker did not apply. Non-acceptance of collaboration because the people were not ready was defeatism. Words were vehicles of ideas which the world eventually followed. Democracy was first a word and then a reality. It was the Apartheid term which had brought Malan into power. We should not drop the term because the people do not follow it. People were already beginning to accept non-collaboration. It was the intention of the Government to establish tribal councils, and we should express ourselves unequivocally against the system. Until the Africans were represented in parliament by their own people they could not abolish their oppression.

Mr. A. P. Mda said that there was much weight in what Convention said on Non-collaboration. There was also much weight in what Congress said. But we shall all be forced in time to accept Non-collaboration. The discussion should boil down to whether Congress was prepared to accept Boycott as long term policy. In 1946 the African National Congress had resolved to boycott the N.R.C. and Advisory Boards. In 1947 there was a slight change in the attitude of Congress. They advocated the election of "Boycott candidates." They felt that the time was not ripe and that the present instruments should be used to further the boycott weapon. We should decide whether we were going to accept boycott or not, and when we were going to apply it. Some thought we should boycott now, others thought we could use these institutions to teach the people boycott. Mr. Mda felt that not sufficient work had been done to educate the masses. He proposed the acceptance of the boycott weapon on principle.

Mr. O. Tambo said that it had not been suggested that getting into these institutions to wreck them was collaboration. We should accept the principle and then decide when to apply it and where. Unity should not break on acceptance or non-acceptance of non-collaboration.

Mr. I. B. Tabata then moved: the following resolution for the All-African Convention:

> In view of the political crisis facing the African people today, in view of the urgent necessity to unite the people to fight oppression and for full democratic rights, this joint session of the All-African Convention and the African National Congress executive committees meeting in Bloemfontein this 17th day of April, 1949, resolves that this unity be based on:
> 1. A demand for full citizenship rights equal to those of the European.
> 2. A rejection of inferior status as expressed in the segregated and inferior political institutions created for a so-called child race and for the perpetuation of white domination, viz, the N.R.C., the Bhunga; Location Advisory Boards; and any other institution of a similar nature which may be created to substitute, supplement or strengthen existing institutions.
> 3. The acceptance of Non-collaboration, i.e. the rejection of the N.R.C.; Bhunga; Local Advisory Boards; The Natives Representation Act, etc.

In moving this resolution Mr. Tabata said that the term "Non-collaboration" was open to many interpretations. We, the African people, had decided to use it in this particular sense. We were not concerned with the dictionary meaning of the term in our interpretation of it. He did not understand what the Congress speakers meant by long-term policy. The duty of leadership was the interpretation of the aspirations of the people. We should go out to the people therefore and preach Non-collaboration, and not wait for the people to lead us. We want to eliminate internal strife by agreeing now. We could not accept the statement that the people did not want to go to parliament. If the question were properly put to them they would all say they wanted to go, because that was what they were used to. They were used to making laws in their own Inkundlas, and it is surprising to hear anybody say African men did not want to go to a National Inkundla. That was why we wanted to be agreed on the question. Convention has come to Congress because we realise that unless responsible

381

organisations agree on the boycott it will be difficult for the people to follow. They were suspicious of Government institutions, but it was the intellectuals who went to the people and asked to be elected. The intellectuals must therefore be agreed on non-collaboration. If the position were to be reversed, and Europeans were to elect three Black men to represent them in parliament, they would not accept the position. We must create such an attitude of mind as will make these institutions stink in the nostrils of the people. The people will follow if the leadership gives expression to the aspirations of the people.

This resolution was seconded by Mr. S. A. Jayiya.

Mr. R. V. Selope-Thema said that so far as [*sic*] the meeting had not discussed policy but a programme. He proposed the appointment of a committee.

Mr. L. K. Ntlabati said that we should be agreed on the principle of non-collaboration, but if we found that it would serve our purpose to contest seats in these government institutions we should not be called collaborators.

Mr. Moses Kotane wanted to know whether, if the policy was accepted, it would be carried out immediately.

Dr. G. H. Gool replied that the government would always find quislings to sell the people. We should let them know that all those who went into those institutions would be nailed on to the wall as traitors. He appealed to the delegates to be open with each other.

Mr. R. M. Canca said that we could not support something against which we spoke. There was a school of psychologists who doubted the mentality of the Africans. They don't understand how the African can put up with so much oppression. If we decided to boycott we should boycott.

Mr. Thema said that unity would be destroyed by non-collaboration as a basis. We should merely agree on the principle of unity, i.e. non-co-operation with the authorities and not mention the institutions to be boycotted.

Professor Z. K. Matthews said that para. 1 of the resolution was comprehensive. It dealt with the political, economic and social institutions. Para. 2 and 3 were not consistent with para. 1. They narrowed the question to the political aspect. The joint resolution should incorporate the desire of Congress to broaden the definition. We have to be consistent.

Dr. G. H. Gool explained that we brought in the political aspect because if we succeeded in that field all else would follow. In India Gandhi had advocated the boycotting of government schools. It had failed. The argument was merely a red-herring to confuse the issue more and more.

Mr. C. M. Kobus said that the acceptance of Non-collaboration meant the carrying out of non-collaboration straight away, not at some dim and distant future. We would not speak of fighting segregationist institutions from within, because we could not accept Non-collaboration and still help to work segregationist institutions.

Rev. Z. R. Mahabane moved the acceptance of the original resolution as moved by Mr. Tabata. The resolution was accepted.

Leading the discussion on the structure of the proposed body, Mr. A. P. Mda said that the time had come for the establishment of a basis for total struggle against oppression. We should lay such foundation as would make the force gain momentum as struggle continued. The most effective way of appealing to the Africans would be to appeal to them as oppressed people. We should base our appeal on colour. The basis of the organisation should be nationalistic. We could meet oppression by organising on the basis of African Nationalism. This pre-supposed a unitary organisation. The advantages of this would be first of all that we would be able to mobilise the majority of the people in a language they could understand. Secondly, there would be no contradictions within the body caused by groups which may place certain interpretations on certain principles because of differences in political outlook. There was a danger in admitting different groups in the same organisation, particularly was this the case when major decisions had to be made. The Miners' strike confusion was as a result of this weakness. We should appeal to Africans as such, to unite as Africans. An African united front would not be opposed to an alliance with other oppressed groups organised in their national organisations.

Mr. W. M. Tsotsi wanted to know whether if Mr. A. P. Mda was speaking for Congress, as his speech seemed to be contrary to the Congress resolution.

Messrs. A. P. Mda, Dr. Xuma and Moses Kotane stated that Congress had intended the resolution to mean unitary organisations. It meant that other organisations were to be invited to disband themselves and join the unitary organisation.

Dr. G. H. Gool, in reply said that it would be the ideal thing to have a unitary organisation. There had been such in the past, e.g. the I.C.U., but these could not carry the country with them, hence the adoption of the Federal structure in 1935. If in 1935 we had established a unitary organisation we would have been charged with competing with local organisations for membership. There were old organisations long established in their own areas, hence the decision of the Anti-CAD to form a federal organisation, so as to be able to accommodate other organisations. Convention was prepared to guarantee the leadership of the new organisation to Congress by granting a certain number of seats in the executive of the new federal body, to Congress.

Mr. I. B. Tabata: Creating a unitary organisation would mean creating one mass political party dictating to the African population. We would be arrogating to ourselves the right to dictate that no African shall have ideas different from our own. We should fight that, for who would determine this outlook? We wanted the greatest amount of unity among the Africans, and we could achieve this only by inviting other organisations to come in and work with us. No political party could dictate to all the people. We should agree on the minimum demands, then the people would not run away from us because they feared competition. When people wanted to fight they formed federal organisations. That was what had been done in the past e.g. the bus strike. We should have a permanent structure because we were in a state of permanent emergency. A mouthpiece should represent all strata of society. We did not want to see Congress abolished. We wanted to see it strengthened. We should all go out to organise together. Where Congress existed, we should let people join Congress. But these organisations should meet in a federal organisation. This would eliminate mutual competition. If one unitary party were formed, another would crop up. No single party could be a mouthpiece. The mouthpiece of the whites was parliament and we should build a similar organisation.

Mr. L. K. Ntlabati said that by a unitary organisation Congress did not mean a political party. We were dealing with national organisations to fight for freedom. The All-Indian Congress was mainly a unitary organisation, until India achieved independence. Only where people had attained national autonomy could they form political parties. When the Dutch fought the English, the Dutch had different shades of opinion, but they were united in their aim of fighting the English. It had been claimed that Convention had been formed to accommodate different shades of opinion. A political body formed to fight for political rights would object to bringing in Teachers Associations in a political body. We should not have a conglomeration of organisations which were not political. He would concede the inclusion of Voters Associations and Vigilance Associations, but teachers should not discuss politics as teachers organisations. They should join political parties.

Mr. O. R. Tambo said that the danger in the suggestion of a federal structure was that it opened up avenues for division. The masses could be united on the fact that they were oppressed because they were black. We should recognise our strength. We should not preach to the masses divisions which did not exist in their minds. The unitary was the strongest form of organisation, he said.

Mr. W. M. Tsotsi said that the discussion was in the air. The Congress had been a unitary organisation since 1912, and yet it had not built up a worthwhile following. The mere fact that an organisation was unitary and black was no guarantee that we would have a following. The people formed their organisations for local purposes, and Convention had shown that it was possible to politicise these organisations and show them that their disabilities flowed from the general oppression. We should build on what existed and not on a unitary organisation whose future we did not know. Mr. Leo Sihlali pointed out that even where there is one political party one does find splits on personalities. Even women's organisations split on personalities, e.g. the East London Congress split into two and both groups wanted to affiliate to the Provincial Congress. We wanted to appeal to organisations because we could not appeal to the people in vacuo. It had been said that organisations had specific interests. Could not these organisations be orientated? Ordinary leaders of organisations were not going to accept competition. We could not force the people to disband their organisations, moreover, people would not be prepared to join new organisations, as these would mean more subscriptions.

Mr. G. Makabeni complained that the delegates were not serious. When the president of the A.A.C. said we were not oppressed because we were black, then we wondered whether we were serious. All forces should be centred in one place, namely, a unitary body. He was not sure what the nature of the proposed federation was going to be, but he wanted the Africans to be taught African nationalism and be taught to fight as Africans.

Mr. A. K. Mazwai said that a unitary organisation was not practical. We could not have all Africans owing allegiance to one organisation.

Mr. Moses Kotane said that the Congress was committed to advocate that the organisation be unitary. The point raised, that Congress, a unitary organisation, did not have a large membership was irrelevant, because the small membership was not due to its unitary structure. There could be no stability in a federal organisation because interest in the federal structure remained only while there was a burning question. Why should even ping-pong players be brought into a political organisation? There would be the difficulty of being unable to decide important issues because the constituent organisations had no mandate. In our crisis we wanted a unitary organisation which would be a source of strength. We should have one mouth-piece. The question was not the structures of the two bodies, but which body was to be the mouth-piece. The people should be instructed to one organisation.

Mr. S. A. Jayiya said that it would not be easy to disband local organisations. The people formed their local organisations to fight local questions. This was alright as long as they linked up with other organisations in a federal body to fight the bigger issues.

Mr. R. V. Selope-Thema said that it seemed that the two sections had conflicting mandates and there was no spirit of give and take. Would both the A.A.C. and the A.N.C. retain their respective identities? The League of Nations had gone to pieces and the United Nations was also going to pieces. We could not encourage divisions by allowing separate organisations to exist. According to its new constitution Congress demanded 50% of the funds of an affiliating organisation.

Dr. G. H. Gool said we should try to create such an organisation as would make it possible for Congress and Convention to work together. All the organisations in the All-African Convention would have to be brought into the new organisation. The question of the name was unimportant.

Mr. L. K. Ntlabati said that it would be a sad spectacle if we were to go back to the people without concrete decisions. People were not interested in structure. They wanted to see unity. The country was expecting some form of unity, America was a federation, so had South Africa some federal features. We should come to some compromise, so as to inspire the ordinary man with confidence, we should form a unitary organisation with federal features. There had been no mention of destroying existing organisations. Farmers organisations had a purpose, but they should not be brought into politics. Mr. Ntlabati then moved that:

Unity be accepted on the unitary organisation with federal features.

The motion was seconded by Mr. O. R. Tambo. When asked what the federal features would be, the movers said that some organisations would be allowed to affiliate, but the new organisation would decide which organisation to affiliate and which not to affiliate.

The Convention delegates wanted to know the basis on which the deciding would be made, and Mr. R. M. Canca, seconded by Mr. I. B. Tabata moved as an addendum:

Organisations accepting the policy of the new organisation would be allowed to affiliate.

The Congress delegates refused to accept this addendum, whilst the Convention delegates felt that the Congress resolution left as it was would lead to an arbitrary cutting out of certain organisations from the new body, even if they accepted its policy.

As no agreement could be arrived at, Rev. Mahabane proposed that the joint-committee should meet before the next conference to continue the discussion. This proposal was not accepted by Congress.

Mr. I. B. Tabata proposed that we report to the joint conference. Mr. O. R. Tambo felt that we could not report to the joint conference until an agreement between the two executives had been reached.

The conference was adjourned sine die, at 3:30 a.m. on the 18th day of April, 1949.

(Sgd) C. M. Kobus.
Recording Secretary Joint Meeting

Document 70b. Letter reporting on this meeting, from Moses Kotane to Professor Z. K. Matthews, May 8, 1949

P.O. Box 2098
Cape Town
8th May, 1949

Dear Professor,

I am writing to thank you for your letters of the 23/4/49 and 5/5/49, as well as the telegram of 30/4/49. I shall now wait for a word from you advising me of your arrival.

About the joint meeting of the Executive Committees of the All African Convention and the African National Congress, briefly this is what happened:

1. We continued the discussion on the form of organisation after you people left till about 3:30 a.m. on the 18/4/49.

386

2. Negotiations broke down at about 2 a.m., an hour and a half before the representatives of the All African Convention left.

3. Earlier we had *all agreed* on a compromise formula. But when the chairman called for the next item, some representatives of the All African Convention at the instigation of Mr. Tabata—on the pretext of not having clearly understood the formula—went back on their word. Rev. Mahabane was strongly for the formula and Mr. Mda Mda [not A.P. Mda] did not go back on his word.

4. The formula was:- "That this joint session of the Executives of the A.A.C. and the A.N.C. agrees on a unitary form of organisation with federal features."

Yes, Mr. Tabata and Mr. Canca agree with this formula but they felt it needed amplification. Otherwise they felt it was dangerous because it gave the leaders of the new organisation the right to exclude some organisations or refuse their applications for affiliation.

5. These gentlemen then moved that the following sentence be added to the resolution:-

"That is, all organisations which agree with its policy shall have the right to affiliate to it."

6. After we had shown unmistakably that we would rather break off negotiations than accept the addendum and after we had pointed out that the effect of the addendum would be to make the proposed organisation federal in character with unitary features, Rev. Mahabane made a special appeal to Messrs. Tabata and Canca to accept the formula as it was and drop their amendment.

7. Before making his special appeal to Tabata and Canca, Rev. Mahabane stated that if they did not listen to his appeal he would "chuck up the sponge." His appeal was treated with contempt.

8. As we could not reach agreement on the formula, the negotiations broke down. We then said that as negotiations have broken down on this important point *all that which were done or agreed to previously are null and void*, and that we would report accordingly to the Congress.

But it was felt that it would be bad politically to announce that unity negotiations between the two organisations have broken down. We then agreed on the statement published in the African Press and the Guardian. The statement was actually drafted by Mr. Mda Mda. It was merely a public face saving statement—a statement which covered up the truth.

I was surprised to read the report in the Torch of the 25/4/49. I am convinced that we cannot come to an understanding with the conventionites, especially if they still have Dr. Gool, Mr. Tabata and Mr. Tsotsi as their leaders.

Their "non-collaboration" policy is in one sense a cover or pretext for not doing any practical work. While I am strongly for the boycotting of the inferior institutions set-up to perpetuate the oppression and exploitation of the

387

African people, I nevertheless do not agree that the boycott should be carried out without regard to the support we have for it.

Yours Sincerely,

Moses M. Kotane

Document 70c. Review of this meeting, in Minutes of the Annual Conference of the AAC, December 1949

From the very beginning it was obvious that some of the Congress delegates had no genuine desire for unity. They had to pretend they wanted unity because the masses wanted unity, and they did not want to appear responsible for the non-consummation of unity, lest they lost their following. The Convention delegates introduced as the first thing to be discussed, the policy of the proposed organisation. We knew that the Congress delegates would not dare break with us on the question of policy, because they would thus stand exposed to the country as collaborators. At the same time they would be committing themselves if they accepted non-collaboration, and they did not want to commit themselves. After a discussion lasting almost all day the Convention resolution on Non-collaboration was accepted. This acceptance of Non-collaboration by the Congress delegates, it appeared later, was a tactical move and not genuine acceptance. They had hoped that since they had conceded a point in accepting non-collaboration, we would also be sporting enough to concede a point on the structure of the organisation. They wanted a unitary organisation, membership to which would be determined by the whim of whosoever had the power so to do. In other words they merely wanted a re-juvenated Congress with no A.A.C. to embarrass it by advocating Non-collaboration. Having killed the A.A.C. they would conveniently forget about the Non-collaboration resolution.

Unfortunately for them, the Convention delegates refused to be hoodwinked. They demanded that in the new organisation there should be provision for the admission of all organisations which accepted its policy. On this point the meeting broke down. The Congress delegates refused to guarantee the acceptance of such organisations, while the Convention delegates refused to accept unity without this assurance.

The Congress delegates now wanted to repudiate even that part of the proceedings on which agreement had been reached, i.e. they wanted to repudiate the agreement not to collaborate. As this was discussed and decided, however, we have no choice but to report what did happen.

The meeting was adjourned, sine die, and it is not likely that unity will be effected in the near future with the A.N.C., at least as long as it has its present leadership.

388

OTHER NON-EUROPEAN OR LEFT-WING ACTIVITY

Document 71. "Arms for Non-Europeans." Flyer issued by the Non-European United Front of South Africa, March 18, 1942

ARMS FOR NON-EUROPEANS

MASS MEETING

IN THE

CITY HALL (GRAND HALL) CAPE TOWN
ON WEDNESDAY EVENING 18TH MARCH 1942

8 P.M.

under the auspices of the Non-European United Front of S.A.

(1) Arms for non-European Soldiers

(2) Equal pay, promotion, pensions and military allowances for Non-European soldiers

(3) Withdrawal of Regulation 9(b) placing non-European Soldiers and N.C.O's under European privates.

Speakers:

Councillor Mrs. Z. Gool	Rev. F. J. Tladi
Rev. Dr. F. H. Gow	Mr. D. B. Molteno, M.P.
Councillor Ahmed Ismail	Mr. I. Baboo
Right Rev. Bishop J.W. Lavis	Mr. W. Stoutz

SOUTH AFRICA IS IN DANGER!

NON-EUROPEANS—SEE THAT YOUR HOMES AND LIVES ARE PROPERLY PROTECTED

8,000,000 Non-Europeans Fully Mobilised and Armed will Lessen the Danger for All!

Loud Speakers

Issued by the Non-European United Front of S.A., Box 389, Cape Town. Printed by the Stewart Printing Co. (Pty.) Ltd., 15-19 Mechau Street, Cape Town.

Document 72. "Non-European Peoples' Manifesto." Adopted at Non-European Conference Convened by the Non-European United Front, June 28, 1942

The danger which faces South Africa is greater than ever before. This fact is admitted by all shades of opinion with the sole exception of the conscious adherents of the Nazi system, the leaders of the Nationalist Party and the Ossewabrandwag. This critical situation in the history of our country faces the Non-Europeans with an urgent task. The more so in that in spite of oppression and national humiliation, the love of their country remains undaunted.

The Non-European people cannot remain passive or indifferent to the future of South Africa, the country in which we were born and in which, in common with our fellow South Africans of European descent, we have to struggle to build a decent society of progress, freedom and justice.

We recognise that the danger with which South Africa is faced is not merely the horrors of total warfare but also the imposition of a barbarous system which regards the struggles for justice and national liberation as a crime, the penalty for which is death.

The European Population Alone Cannot Defend South Africa.

This threat to South Africa is a threat to the whole population. Participation in the defence of South Africa is the right and duty of all South Africans, irrespective of colour.

That is why our main demand to the Government today is that the Non-Europeans must be allowed to play their full share in the armed struggle for the defence of their country. The continued failure, in spite of progressive Governmental statements, to arm the Non-Europeans, to raise army pay and improve the conditions and terms of enlistment of Non-European soldiers, in the face of the increasing threat from the Nazis, must be accounted as a weakening of our war effort and a menace to the country.

This Conference of Non-European organisations requests the Government immediately to arm the Non-Europeans and to provide full military training in all branches of the Services for them; to admit Non-Europeans to the army on an equal basis with European soldiers, and to end colour discrimination in the army.

Loosen Our Hands to Defend South Africa.

The record of modern warfare shows that what is needed for the real defence of their country in an all-out people's war against Fascism is a free people to defend freedom: arms to the people, enough production of essential goods to keep the fighting forces and the country going.

The many oppressive and humiliating laws which in South Africa are directed against us, the Non-European people, undermine the morale, the strength and the will of the people to defend South Africa and defeat the enemy. The task of mobilising South Africa's manpower, therefore, is also one of liberating the physical and moral strength of the Non-European people.

This Conference of Non-European organisations in the Transvaal therefore request the immediate improvement of the lot of the Non-European people, by abolition of the pass laws, poll tax; and other discriminatory and harsh legislation, improved living standards for the Non-European workers, and the recognition of their trade unions under the Industrial Conciliation Act, the removal of segregationist laws which debar trading rights, the right to purchase or acquire land and other rights, on colour grounds, and the provision of adequate State services for improved education, health and housing facilities for all Non-Europeans.

All war, food and other essential production must be thoroughly organised and planned now, without regard to vested interests. This can only be done by the Non-European manpower taking its part in skilled industry and the lot of the agricultural worker being improved. The ban on Non-European workers entering skilled trades means that a large portion of the country's working population is deliberately debarred from assisting the maximum industrial output.

This Conference therefore demands that the colour bar in industry be lifted and skilled trades opened to Non-European workers; that in order to achieve maximum food production, Non-Europeans on the land be provided with adequate land, and assisted by the State to achieve maximum production.

The Non-European people dare not stand aside from the gigantic struggle which is now raging all over the world. We must throw our weight on the side of those forces which are combating the system which stands for the enslavement of nations, the worst forms of racialism and the crushing of progress. Our hearts are with the Soviet Union and the great Chinese Nation, who are in the front line of the fight for human freedom.

This Conference issues a call to all Non-European people of the Transvaal to organise themselves in a mighty united people's movement for the right of all South Africans to fight with arms for the defence of their country, for the freedom of the Non-European and the sweeping aside of all unjust colour bar laws which prevent the unity of all South Africans on an equal basis for victory and freedom.

Non-European people:

Forward to the defence of our country!

Forward to victory over the Fascist enslavers!

Forward to freedom!

Forward to a free South Africa!

Document 73. Manifesto of the African Democratic Party, September 26, 1943

PREFACE.

1.—At some time or other in the life of every nation an occasion arises when the conditions of life impose upon all the members of the group, a duty and an obligation to make a supreme effort to remove barriers and to improve their lot so as to enjoy a greater measure of happiness and freedom.

2.—Wars are outstanding examples of such occasions, unhappily attended by much misery and loss of life, for which reason, wars are an evil, and whenever and wherever they occur, they signify the failure to secure a settlement through the method of peaceful negotiation and by the spirit of give and take which is as necessary in our national and international relations as in our private lives.

3.—The present world war is at once evidence of the conflict of interests that could not be solved by peaceful methods and of the will to seek and to find a new way of life to happiness and freedom.

4.—The conflagration that has engulfed the continents and oceans of our earth in war has stirred in the hearts of men the world over, a deep desire for the ways of peace and happiness, and the masses of unprivileged humanity everywhere look to men of vision, learning and authority for a clear picture of that post-war world which will end their misery and set their feet on the paths of peace and progress.

5.—The African people share in this hope of a better post-war world. Their faith is engendered by the statements of international statesmen abroad (e.g., The Atlantic Charter), and by the forceful pronouncements of high-placed men in the Government (e.g., The anti-segregation speech delivered by General Smuts at the Institute of Race Relations Conference in 1942).

6.—Moreover the African people realise that the measure of their share and place in the new and reconstituted post-war society depends, the legislature being such as it is, largely on the readiness of European public opinion to concede what it conceives to be the legitimate claims of the African people. It must be recognised, however, that the vested interests of the ruling class will ever be limiting factors in determining the rights that should be granted to the African people.

7.—Two factors are vital in creating that readiness of European public opinion to grant democratic rights to the African people:—

(a) The first is the enlistment of that growing and powerful minority of progressive minded, justice-loving, and far-sighted European element who unfettered by colour and race prejudice, recognise that their good and that of the African people constitutes one indivisible whole. Of this class there are a good few. They are the leaven and the foundation of the happier and more prosperous South Africa of the future.

(b) The second factor is the preparedness of the African people to claim, to seize, and to use the rights which are inherently theirs and to which they are progressively entitled.

8.—In our opinion no solid advance can be made in the betterment of the conditions of the African people without the joint operation of these two factors, which are both complementary and supplementary.

9.—Of the injunctions to African leaders and their people not to alienate the sympathy of their European friends there is no lack, both in official quarters as well as in ordinary public life. There is happily evidence of the existence

392

of an increasing volume of European opinion sympathetic to African aspirations, and there is further evidence that that body of opinion is in part organised, e.g., The Institute of Race Relations, Joint Councils, The Christian Council, the Friends of Africa, etc. The impact of these institutions and of the men and women of the liberal school has indeed resulted in the slight alleviation of the lot of the African people, but has hardly effected any material change in the political and economic system under which they live.

10.—Weakness has lain all too long in the comparative unpreparedness of the African people to pull their weight in the struggle for national liberation. Far too long the fear to antagonise European sympathisers, the desire to curry favour with the ruling class have withheld African leaders from doing their work. They have failed to realise that the unity of the masses is the first preparedness for the task to claim, to seize and to use, the opportunities that make for freedom and happiness.

11.—We believe, above all, in the method of peaceful negotiation by leaders whose influence derives from the mass support of their followers and, as a last resort, we believe in the weapon of mass passive resistance.

12.—For years now we have recognised the African National Congress as the organisation around which all African people of whatever class or denomination should rally. We pledged our fullest support to its leaders and its programme.

13.—There is unhappily in the ranks of Congress to-day disorganisation, political stagnation and general inaction. The leaders quarrel while the people die.

14.—Our times call for Unity, Organisation and Action. Further delay and inaction are inexcusable and criminal. The signs of the times bode ill for non-Europeans of this country; the Pretoria Riot, the threatened removal of Alexandra Township, the failure to raise the pay of African soldiers, the continued application of harsh and oppressive laws, the curtailment of the rights of Indians and Coloured people, the reaffirmation of the policy of Segregation by the Minister of Native Affairs, all portend a new post-war world in which the rights of the masses will be studiously ignored and violated.

15.—The need for a dynamic organisation, expressive of the spirit of the times and designed to remobilise African opinion to meet this imminent danger is, therefore, a matter of the utmost urgency and importance.

ANALYSIS OF METHODS.

16.—Existing African organisations are characterised by general indecision and inactivity. This hesitancy arises not so much from divergent views on political objectives as from fundamental differences among the leaders on the "modus operandi" by which our political ends can be achieved.

17.—Two courses of action seem to present themselves:—

(a) The Method of Revolt whereby the masses decide to use force in order to effect the necessary changes in the government of the country. This method is on the whole ruled out by the African people as grossly impractical.

(b) The Policy of Appeasement. This school of thought believes that the problems of our race relations and the disabilities of the African people can only be removed by the logical presentation of facts, the persistent and courteous pleading of the down-trodden and by invoking the sympathy and the sense of justice of the ruling classes. This method of approach requires the leadership of the intelligentsia, which is often detached from the masses and fails to arouse and to enlist their interest. The policy of appeasement is the one in general use to-day in African politics. This explains the existing cleavage between African leaders and the masses. This policy is frequently and erroneously called the policy of moderation. It has the fullest support of the majority of Europeans in this country and has the special blessing of the government.

18.—In our opinion these lines of action represent two extremes and none of them can be effective in our complex South Africa. The fact that African leadership while wedded to the policy of appeasement has nevertheless called the masses to action, accounts for that lack of response, that indecision and helplessness, that sense of frustration which characterise African political organisations to-day. We cannot keep in the same political fold, the violent revolutionary and the spineless appeaser.

19.—It seems to us that the right modus operandi is a synthesis of these two extremes, whereby we shall harness the forces of reason in establishing the just claims of the African people while simultaneously exerting the necessary pressure in the right quarter through the quiet and orderly demonstrations of the masses and, where necessary, through the employment by the masses of the method of passive resistance. That rightly conceived is the Policy of Moderation, because it provides that happy and effective via media between Bloody Fight and Cheap Talk, and establishes that bond of contact between the leaders and the led, which galvanises the whole organisation into wholesome and effective action.

20.—This synthetic method is now generally recognised the world over as the Method of Peaceful Revolution—it is the method of the STRIKE used as the weapon of TRADE UNIONS throughout the world—it is the method of MASS PROTESTS and MASS DEMONSTRATIONS such as brought victory to the residents of Alexandra Township in their recent Bus dispute. This method requires for its success intelligent and disciplined leadership and the undivided loyalty and co-operation of the masses. It is not unaccompanied by sacrifices and hardships.

THE NEW PARTY—THE AFRICAN DEMOCRATIC PARTY.

21.—An African political organisation which strives to liberate the masses by the employment of this method does not exist. We believe that such an organisation is eminently necessary and that its emergence would be symptomatic of the quickened political consciousness of the African people born of the critical circumstances in which they live.

22.—Such an organisation is the AFRICAN DEMOCRATIC PARTY, which we propose to launch forthwith, as a political organisation with a definite programme and a definite method of action. We repeat that the African Democratic Party differs from other African political organisations not in the ends for which it strives, but in the method by which it hopes to attain its goal. Its programme deals with immediate and pressing claims, and its methods are militant and their execution depends on the masses.

PARTY PROGRAMME.

23.—The African Democratic Party believes that basically the so-called "Native Problem" is an economic problem that is complicated by social and racial issues, and that inasmuch as South Africa can only have one industrial economy for Black and White, the policy of industrial, territorial and political segregation is incompatible with the fullest economic development of the country and repugnant to the principles of liberty and justice.

24.—The African Democratic Party realises that the role of the African in South African industry is at present that of Labour and that the policy of the country is designed to render the African people a cheap mobile and unskilled labour force for the use of the mining and farming industries. This policy imposes intolerable hardships upon the African people and is economically, indefensible.

25.—The African Democratic Party believes it incumbent upon the African people to oppose this policy of economic enslavement, as much for the greater prosperity and well-being of all sections of the South African population as for their own good.

26.—The African Democratic Party believes that this struggle for economic emancipation involves:—

(a) The removal of the present restrictions on the acquisition of LAND by the African people and the distribution of the land on a more just and equitable basis between all sections of the population.

(b) A LIVING WAGE to be paid to all labourers both in the towns and in the country. For this purpose the African Democratic Party believes that the formation of African Trade Unions be encouraged in both town and country and that the fullest recognition under the Industrial Conciliation Act be accorded them. The Party regards a living wage as the best insurance against malnutrition and many forms of Social Insecurity.

(c) The provision of adequate EDUCATIONAL facilities for the acquisition of skill and literacy in order that the African should pull his weight in creating and increasing the national income and so that he may the more fully enjoy the fruits and benefits of civilization.

(d) The abolition of the INDUSTRIAL COLOUR BAR and all restrictions which place colour and class above merit and ability. To this end the

African should be allowed to attain to whatever rank his ability and talent qualify him.

(e) FREEDOM OF MOVEMENT—the right to come and go. This means the abolition of the Pass System in all its forms.

27.—The African Democratic Party is fully aware that there can be no settlement of the entire economic problem while the bulk of the population representing the African people remains unrepresented and in effect voiceless in the councils of the state. The Native Representation Act does not give any real representation to the African people. Accordingly the African Democratic Party believes that the struggle for economic emancipation must proceed at the same time as the struggle for a share of the political power now exclusively wielded by 20 per cent of the total population. This implies not only direct representation in the Councils of the State, but also a share in the more responsible ranks of administration.

CONCLUSION.

28.—Fundamentally, the African Democratic Party stands for the granting of DEMOCRATIC RIGHTS TO THE AFRICAN PEOPLE. In that sense it stands for Liberty, Justice and Economic Security.

29.—The party has not come to usurp the place and function of any existing organisation: it has not come to destroy but to fulfil. Within the framework of its constitution it seeks and welcomes the co-operation of persons and other organisations which are working in a like direction and for the same ends.

30.—FREEDOM comes to men as they deserve it. They deserve it when they WORK for it, PRAY for it and SACRIFICE for it. The watchwords of the African Democratic Party therefore are:—

ACTION! DEVOTION! PREPAREDNESS!

Document 74. Resolution of the National Anti-Pass Conference, May 20-21, 1944

(1) **This Conference declares** that the Pass Laws are in conflict with the high and progressive war aims for which our country, together with the other United Nations, is fighting. These laws hold the African people in conditions of abject poverty and subjection; they retard the economic and industrial development of South Africa; they hamper the growth of organisation of African workers and thus weaken the entire Labour movement; they are the cause of sharp racial friction between the peoples of South Africa; they uphold the cheap labour system which results in malnutrition, starvation and disease; they fill our gaols with innocent people and thus create widespread crime.

(2) **This Conference, therefore, calls upon** the South African Government to repeal immediately all Pass Laws, and all regulations framed in terms of those laws.

(3) In order to ensure that the Government takes heed of this call, **Conference resolves** to launch a nation-wide Anti-Pass Campaign for the repeal of the Pass Laws.

(4) As a first step in this Campaign, **Conference resolves** upon the following measures:

(a) 1,000,000 signatures be obtained to the Anti-Pass Petition by the end of August, 1944.

(b) This Petition be represented to the Government by a deputation of leaders of the African people.

(c) A National Anti-Pass Demonstration Day be held on the date of the presentation of the Petition.

(d) The Anti-Pass Badge be widely popularized as a pledge of the wearer to support the National Anti-Pass Council in all its decisions.

(e) The sum of £5,000 be raised for the furtherance of the Campaign.

(f) Factual and educational material about the Campaign be continuously published and distributed to all sections of the population both here and overseas, by means of public meetings, printed matter and articles in the press, with particular reference to winning the support of those sections of people not included in the terms of the Pass Laws.

(g) Local Anti-Pass Committees be organised in towns, villages, locations, compounds and factories throughout the Union of South Africa.

(5) To further this Campaign it is further **resolved** that a **National Anti-Pass Council** be elected by this Conference, to whom the direction of the Campaign shall be entrusted.

(6) **The National Anti-Pass Council** shall be composed as follows:

(a) Five representatives of each of the following areas elected by delegates present from those areas: Cape Western Division, Cape Eastern Division; Natal; Orange Free State; Transvaal.

(b) A further 35 members elected by a ballot of all delegates.

(7) **The National Anti-Pass Council** shall meet within 24 hours of the closing of this Conference, and shall elect a **Working Committee** of not more than 21 members, including a Chairman, Secretary, Treasurer and two trustees, all of whom shall reside within 50 miles of Johannesburg.

(8) **The Working Committee** shall exercise the functions of the National Council between meetings of the National Council.

(9) The **National Council** shall be called together immediately after the presentation of the Petition to the Government, in order to review the progress

397

made, and to take any further decisions which may be necessary regarding the conduct of the Campaign and shall, if necessary, call another **Conference.**

(10) The delegates here assembled pledge themselves to give wholehearted and unstinting support to the **National Anti-Pass Council** in all steps taken by it to carry out this resolution, and to further the **Campaign for the Repeal of the Pass Laws.**

DOCUMENTS 75a-75b. First Transvaal-Orange Free State People's Assembly for Votes for All, May 22-24, 1948

Document 75a. "Manifesto." Call to Attend the People's Assembly, [n.d.]

IN THE BELIEF THAT ALL MEN HAVE THE RIGHT TO FREEDOM

We call on representatives of all citizens in every walk of life

To the

FIRST TRANSVAAL—ORANGE FREE STATE PEOPLE'S ASSEMBLY FOR VOTES FOR ALL

Our Object:

> To rally to the Assembly delegates irrespective of race and colour from Transvaal and Orange Free State who will represent more citizens than those voting in the General Elections.

> To demand for all South Africans of all races the democratic right to vote and be elected to the governing bodies of the country.

> To challenge the election of the new Parliament by a minority of the people. To launch a campaign for the democratic principles of the United Nations Charter by promoting and encouraging

>> "respect for human rights and for fundamental freedom for all without distinction as to race, sex, language or religion."

Document 75b. "The People's Charter." Manifesto adopted at the People's Assembly

WE HERE ASSEMBLED, the elected representatives of the African, Indian and Coloured people of the Transvaal and Orange Free State, represent people in all walks of life, of all political creeds and of all religious beliefs.

WE PROCLAIM our burning belief in the ideals of democracy, in the principles of government of the people, by the people and for the people.

All history confirms our knowledge that Fascism, tyrannical and barbarous, will menace the lives and liberty of all South Africans while the privileges of democracy are limited to a minority of the people.

WE BELIEVE that in voicing the great stirrings amongst our people for democracy, we act not only in response to the mandate of those who sent us here, but defend the best interests of all our countrymen whosoever they may be.

Gathered together on the eve of the 1948 General Elections to Parliament

WE RECORD the solemn protest of the voteless people who we represent—the vast majority of our South African citizens—at the holding of elections to Parliament from which they are excluded.

WE DECLARE that this long exclusion from the councils of the nation has made our people the most poverty stricken in the land, the most illiterate, the most backward. Amongst our people is to be found the lowest wage standards, the highest incidence of disease and the greatest death rate. Our sufferings bear tribute to the disasters of exclusion from the democratic life.

WE STATE our solemn belief, strengthened by the experience of years of Government neglect, that until our people participate as equals in the governing of their own country, there will be found neither the desire nor the ability in the Government under which we live to provide all our people all the happiness and prosperity which modern society can offer.

Where there is no freedom the people perish. Raising high the banner of freedom, the banner of the liberation and the salvation of our people

WE PLEDGE that we shall not rest until all adult men and women of all races in South Africa have the right to stand for, vote for and be elected to all the representative bodies which rule over our people.

399

WE CHALLENGE the existence of a Parliament from whose election the majority of the citizens are excluded, in a country which upholds in words
the principles and practices of democracy.

WE RESOLVE to campaign for the democratic principles of Government contained in the Charter of the United Nations Organisation, namely:

*"Respect for human rights and fundamental freedoms for all, without distinction
as to race, sex, language or religion."*

PART THREE

Joint Action and
the Defiance Campaign

1950-1952

A CRUCIAL PERIOD

The years 1950-1952 were among the most crucial in the history of the African National Congress. They followed the adoption of the Programme of Action in December 1949, which abandoned the ANC's traditional reliance on tactics of moderation such as petitions and deputations. Also in December 1949, a new leadership, nurtured in the Youth League, came to power in the ANC. Walter Sisulu became secretary-general, and some half-dozen key Youth Leaguers were elected to the national executive committee, including Sisulu's successor, Oliver Tambo.[1] For the next two decades, despite bannings and some defections, the new leadership displayed a remarkable coherence and continuity.[2] The period 1950-1952 began with a commitment to militant African nationalism and mass action and to tactics of boycott, strike, and civil disobedience. It ended with the Defiance Campaign, the largest scale nonviolent resistance ever seen in South Africa and the first mass campaign pursued jointly by Africans and Indians.

The resistance also won United Nations recognition that South African racial policy is an international issue. During the campaign some 8,000 nonwhites went to jail for defying apartheid laws and regulations, and the ANC's membership rose by tens of thousands. Only toward the end of 1952, when the campaign was marred by sporadic rioting and violence and the leaders placed on trial or restricted, did it die down. On balance, the campaign was a success in some respects; in others, a failure.

The years were crucial because the Defiance Campaign was the culmination of movement in the ANC from moderation to militancy. It was the last mass effort by Africans to bring about change through nonviolent civil disobedience. Although demonstrations, boycotts, and strikes were staged during the remainder of the decade, none was to challenge white domination as directly as did the Defiance Campaign. The campaign was also a test of the efficacy of nonviolent extraparliamentary pressures. It failed to deflect the government from its course and won little sympathy from the white electorate. On the other hand, there were many grounds for judging the campaign a success, particularly in politicizing many thousands of Africans and in instilling self-confidence and discipline. Toward the end of 1952, the campaign began to spread to the rural reserves; elsewhere its progress never came near its projected stage of "industrial action," that is, general strike.

Official countermeasures had the effect of foreclosing similar campaigns in the future. The pattern of raids, arrests, bans, and trials that was increasingly to restrict the scope of nonwhite protest and to immobilize many first-string leaders became clearly apparent by 1952. Meanwhile, the Nationalist Party government was also laying the groundwork for the mass trial of the late 1950s by which it sought (unsuccessfully) to stigmatize the ANC's advocacy of equality as support for violence and high treason. Any remaining expectation within the ANC that it might seek to revive the Defiance Campaign was virtually ended in 1953 when new legislation provided severe penalties, including whipping, for persons engaging in civil disobedience as a means of political protest.[3]

The period immediately following the adoption of the Programme of Action was crucial also in shaping the alignments and issues of the Lutuli years—those years following the election in December 1952 of Albert J. Lutuli as president-general of the ANC. Multiracial developments later in the decade had their roots, of course, in earlier years. ANC leaders had cooperated with whites, Coloureds, and Indians in the 1920s; and Dr. Xuma as president-general during the 1940s had participated in multiracial programs and agreed explicitly with Indian leaders on joint action. Africans who were members of the Communist Party, and therefore allied to whites and Indians, had also been members of the ANC since the late 1920s. At the same time, Africanist opposition to multiracial tactics and orientation had even deeper roots, since a racially exlusive orientation was a minor strand running throughout the history of African political thinking. Thus the events of the early 1950s were of major importance in varied and divergent respects: in establishing the multiracial cooperation that underlay the Congress Alliance of the ANC, the SAIC, and white and Coloured groups in the mid-1950s, in making Communist influence a recurrent theme of propaganda among opponents of this trend, and in contributing to the Africanist split from the ANC and formation of the Pan-Africanist Congress in 1959.

The months immediately following the adoption of the Programme of Action saw rapid and significant changes occurring in the relationships among opponents of apartheid. The new Afrikaner Nationalist Party government was proceeding systematically to tighten and extend the forms of racial discrimination against all nonwhites. The Population Registration Act, 1950, aimed to give everyone a permanent racial classification; and the Group Areas Act (attacked as "the Ghetto Act"), to classify all areas by function and race. The government also threatened the entire extraparliamentary opposition by its vaguely worded Unlawful Organisations Bill, which was enacted in July 1950 as the Suppression of Communism Act. (In anticipation, the Communist Party dissolved itself on June 20.)[4] The common threat widened the ground upon which a common opposition could be built. Moreover, the necessity for new political initiatives became more pressing. Responding in particular to the placing of restrictions on some leaders, the radical leadership of the ANC in the Transvaal together with the Indian Congress and the Communist Party took the initiative early in 1950 in staging protest meetings and strikes.

Leaders of the Youth League were generally hostile to the role that non-Africans were playing in this apparent preemption of the Programme of Action.

But the extent of the popular response, their own new experiences of close cooperation with radicals of various races, and a reevaluation of political necessity became persuasive. By June 1950 a predominant segment of those who had founded the Youth League, notably Oliver Tambo, Walter Sisulu, and Nelson Mandela, were shifting toward acceptance of a multiracial front and cooperation with the left.

In contrast, Selope Thema, a liberal and old-guard nationalist who was anti-Communist and suspicious of Indians, overtly opposed that development in 1950 and 1951 and more particularly the role of Communists in the Transvaal ANC. More significant was the muted antagonism of men like A. P. Mda (a theoretician for the Youth League and later for the PAC) who supported the Defiance Campaign while preparing to resist anti-Africanist trends within the ANC. In the years to come, both the ANC and its exclusive opponents were to claim to be the true exponent of the philosophy underlying the Programme of Action.

Trends both in white and African alignments which were apparent at the beginning of the Lutuli years continued throughout the decade. The conflict between Afrikaner and African nationalism became more polarized. The entrenched political power of the Nationalist Party government became deeper, in part because the nonwhite protest of 1952 contributed to the Nationalist Party's victory at the general election of 1953. White opposition to the Nationalist Party reached its highest point during the constitutional crisis that began in 1951 over the government's efforts to remove Coloured voters from the Cape's common voters' roll. In 1952 a small group of white liberals who were impatient with the opposition United Party sought contact with African leaders. At the same time Africans themselves sought support from a wide spectrum of whites rather than exclusive identification with the left-wing. But although white liberals and progressives became politically more active later in the decade, their efforts to provide a bridge between white and black were frustrated by Afrikaner nationalism and events.

South Africa was far from ripe for revolution at the time of the Defiance Campaign. Despite a rise in left-wing rhetoric, the ANC retained its mainly liberal aims; and its leaders, despite some trips behind the Iron Curtain, continued to be primarily nationalists. But lingering hopes for a change in the direction of South African policy became increasingly difficult to sustain. The protest and challenge of 1950-1952 continued intermittently throughout the remainder of the decade. Not until after the outlawing of the ANC and the PAC, its newly-organized break-away rival, in 1960 did hope for peaceful change finally give way to violence.

THE PROGRAMME OF ACTION IN 1950

The Programme of Action envisaged appointment of a Council of Action to plan "a national stoppage of work for one day as a mark of protest against the reactionary policy of the Government." June 26, 1950, became that day, a "National Day of Protest and Mourning" when all nonwhites were to stay home from work and keep their children from school (Documents 82 and 83). Proclaimed as "historic" and "unique," June 26 was declared to be "the first attempt at a political strike on a national scale by the Non-European people of this country" (Document 85). Two years later the same date formally opened the Defiance Campaign. Since then, June 26 has been celebrated annually by the ANC and its allies as South African Freedom Day.

The Council of Action, a small group chaired by Dr. Moroka and with members in different parts of the country, could be expected to be the body to make plans for the day of protest. But the council's session on February 18 was its first and only meeting in 1950.[5] Preparations for June 26 were to become in practice the responsibility of a multiracial coordinating committee.

The immediate precedent for multiracial planning was to be seen in the Transvaal in March and April. The executive committee of the Transvaal ANC in cooperation with the Johannesburg District of the Communist Party, the Transvaal Indian Congress, and the provincial branch of the virtually nonexistent African People's Organisation [of Coloureds] convened a "Defend Free Speech Convention" in Johannesburg on March 26, 1950.[6] Dr. Moroka himself presided and delivered his first public address after becoming ANC president-general. At the meeting the sponsoring organizations announced they would organize a stay-at-home from work on May 1 as a day of protest against official restrictions on nonwhite leaders and in support of higher wages and other workers' demands. The restrictions referred to were bans under the Riotous Assemblies Act that had been placed on two African Communists, J. B. Marks and Moses Kotane, on the leading Indian Communist, Dr. Yusuf Dadoo, and on others.

Non-Communist supporters of the choice of May Day (which fell on Monday, always a desirable day) have defended it, in retrospect, as an international workers' day widely recognized in South Africa rather than one identified with the Communist Party. The most serious objections to the demonstration came from Youth Leaguers and other African nationalists who feared that attention was being diverted from the Programme of Action or, worse yet, that the Programme was being taken over by an ad hoc group heavily influenced by Communists and non-Africans. Thus Mandela, Tambo, and other exclusive-minded young nationalists actively opposed the mobilization of support for the May 1 demonstration.

Nonetheless the May Day appeal was heeded by a substantial number of African workers mainly in the Johannesburg area. Indeed, claims were made that more than half the African labor force stayed home. Much of the success of the work boycott was credited to Marks's organizational skills, a reaction that contributed to his election later in the year as president of the Transvaal ANC. But the heaviest impact of the day lay in its tragic ending: police intervention in clashes between returning workers and boycotting workers which resulted in nineteen dead and thirty injured in Benoni, Orlando, Alexandra, and Sophia-town (Document 85).

Local African hostility toward the police was intense. In the eastern Cape, Professor Matthews in a bitter speech on May 14 to a crowd of more than 5,000 at New Brighton, Port Elizabeth, called on all Africans to take part "in the building up of the African nation."[7] Observing from Natal and engaging in recrimination, Jordan Ngubane, unlike Matthews, attacked the Communists in the editorial columns of *Inkundla ya Bantu (Bantu Forum)* and criticized Dr. Moroka for serving as a tool in "decisions which result in the loss of African life without advancing the cause of Africa" (Document 76).

On the same day that Matthews spoke, initiative shifted from provincial to national bodies when the ANC's national working committee held a conference in Johannesburg to which it invited representatives of the national executive committees of the ANC Youth League, Indian Congress, APO, Communist Party (CP), and also the Transvaal Council of Non-European Trade Unions. The conference was an "emergency" one held in response to the introduction of the Unlawful Organisations Bill [later the Suppression of Communism Act] in Parliament on May 5. The conference attacked the bill as a "fascist" threat to all South Africans and in particular to "the underprivileged sections" and pledged to mobilize "whites and nonwhites" to offer "concrete mass opposition" (Document 77). In that spirit, the emerging multiracial popular front sponsored a "United Anti-Fascist Rally" against "Gestapo & Ghetto Bills" in Durban's so-called Red Square later in the month. At the meeting, Dr. Moroka was the main speaker (Document 79).

The ANC's national working committee, which had summoned the conference of May 14, came to play a more independently active role during Dr. Moroka's presidency and thereafter than it did under Dr. Xuma. It was composed of members of the National Executive Committee (NEC) who lived within fifty miles of the national headquarters in Johannesburg and were appointed by the NEC. While responsible to that body and with the president an ex officio member, the working committee exercised full powers between meetings of the NEC (Document 29a). Dr. Xuma himself, who lived in Johannesburg, had proposed the formation of such a committee and had presided over it. Dr. Moroka, however, could not come easily to Johannesburg since he maintained a busy practice in Thaba 'Ntchu near Bloemfontein. In any event, although he often used the long-distance telephone, he was not temperamentally as disposed as Dr. Xuma to keep close control. In practice, therefore, Walter Sisulu, the secretary-general, and some of the younger and more militant members, attained special importance and power.[8]

On May 21, the national executive committee itself met in emergency session at Dr. Moroka's home and issued its own statement that the Unlawful Organisations Bill was "primarily directed against the Africans and other oppressed people." It agreed on one concrete step of protest: a one-day national stay-at-

407

home to show "general dissatisfaction" and "mourning for all those Africans who lost their lives in the struggle for liberation" (Document 78). Thus, it was an all-African body that took the first national move envisaged by the Programme of Action, and it was Dr. Moroka who announced on June 11 that the Day of Protest would be June 26. (June 26, a Monday, had no earlier significance in African political history.)

Dr. Moroka's announcement was made, however, only after consultation with the other organizations that had taken part in earlier meetings, and his announced plans were publicly agreed to by the heads of the Indian Congress, the APO, and the CP. The intention of the African and Indian leaders at this point was to set up a coordinating committee that would be representative of those organizations and also of the trade unionists. Both the trade unionists and the APO sent only moral support, however, instead of representatives, the APO bemoaning the "precipitate" manner in which the date of June 26 had been declared and the lack of time for building up its organization (Document 84). In any case, the APO was virtually defunct, but the organizers sought to use it in an effort to build a fully multiracial alliance.[9] The CP's membership lapsed when the Party dissolved itself in June, though propaganda flyers for the Day of Protest in Cape Town and Durban retained the Party's name (Documents 82 and 83). By June 26, therefore, the alliance was formally limited to the ANC and the Indian Congress, with Walter Sisulu and Yusuf Cachalia as joint secretaries of the coordinating committee and Nelson Mandela as office manager, working in the main headquarters of the ANC.

In 1950 the Communist Party had about 2,000 members, about three-fourths of them African. Following the Party's dissolution and the end of its influence as an organization, it is not surprising that Africans who were Communists should give increased attention to the ANC. The more exclusive or racialist members of the ANC, who claimed to be the more nationalist, increasingly expressed concern about the role and influence of former Communists of all races and of Africans who might be their tools or secret supporters. (Government officials charged in later years that Communists infiltrated the ANC after their Party was banned, but these officials overlooked the long-standing involvement of African Communists in the ANC. Nor is it possible to identify Africans who were Communists but not ANC members before 1950 and then entered the ANC and reached positions of importance.)[10] Africans who were fearful of Communist influence read much significance into the election of J. B. Marks as president of the ANC in the Transvaal on November 12, 1950.[11] His personal victory did not signify, however, that the ANC either in the Transvaal or nationally was in the process of abandoning the liberal premises of African nationalism or was about to substitute class for nationalist appeals.

Some critics also charged that Sisulu and Mandela, among others, became Communists at that time, but the charge was loosely made and without convincing evidence. What is clear is that Sisulu and Mandela began to work with Communists and Indians and to move leftward, away from African exclusivism.

Their shift can be explained by their personal experiences of close cooperation and their reassessment of the need for allies in the face of threats to all opponents of apartheid. In 1950 at any rate, the shift of leading Youth Leaguers appeared due more to a growing self-assurance than to ideological reorientation.

Beneath the surface of wide African support, there was disquiet and suspicion, especially on the part of older and more conservative members of the ANC. A. W. G. Champion, the once fiery activist in the Industrial and Commercial Workers' Union in the 1920s but now the cautious president of the ANC in Natal, presided at the "United Anti-Fascist Rally" of May 28 (Document 79), but he disliked the presumptions of the Youth League, the timing of militancy, the involvement of non-Africans, and (as he complained in a letter of June 5 to Sisulu) the "drastic decisions" of the national executive committee. Ten days before the Day of Protest of June 26, the Rev. J. J. Skomolo of Aliwal North, in an emotional "private letter" to Professor Matthews, who was the Cape provincial president, made the familiar argument that Africans were not ready to bear the brunt of suffering in yet another hastily called strike. [12] He placed the blame on Communists and charged that they were seeking "to disrupt Congress from within" (Document 81).

These sentiments underlay the opposition to the new leadership expressed by R. V. Selope Thema, an ANC veteran who had been prominent in the Joint Council movement of the 1920s and who deeply distrusted both Communists and Indians. While Selope Thema shared Skomolo's feelings about June 26, the development that precipitated his establishment of the National-minded Bloc (or Nationalist Bloc), despite Xuma's discouragement, was Marks's election as president of the ANC in the Transvaal later in the year. (Moroka, like other older leaders who were uninterested in ideology and accustomed to working with Communists, supported Marks's election.) Although appearing at first to be an internal pressure group, the Bloc printed its own membership cards in 1951. R. G. Baloyi and a few others were associated with Selope Thema, but the Bloc was almost exclusively identified with him. [13] Perhaps the main significance of his disaffection was that the *Bantu World*, of which he was editor, became increasingly hostile to the ANC's leadership.

Members of the Youth League who shared the apprehensions regarding Communist influence of Skomolo and Selope Thema were not in tune with the cautious spirit of the older nationalists. In any event, their tactical judgment was to continue working within the ANC. They were in a minority in the Transvaal, where the provincial Youth League issued a fervent statement of support for the Thaba 'Ntchu decision regarding June 26. The statement, however, expressed support in characteristically Africanist language (Document 80). On the other hand, although accepting an alliance with the Communist Party, the Youth League opposed Marks's election to the Transvaal presidency.

The popular response to the appeal to stay at home on June 26 was "very poor in the Transvaal," where much support had been shown on May 1—"95% a Flop," said the *Rand Daily Mail*—although "a complete stoppage of work" was claimed at Alexandra township near Johannesburg and at Evaton near Vereeniging (Document 85). The most impressive stoppages occurred in the eastern Cape, particularly in Port Elizabeth, areas which had a long history of attachment to the ANC. "Some of the cities were just like Sunday," according to Professor Matthews. "Nobody was at work." [14] Measured by retaliation, however, Durban's stay-at-home had the most impact since about a thousand persons, including Indians, were subsequently dismissed from their jobs because of their participation.

"As a political strike," held after only two weeks' notice and "in the face of intensive and relentless police intimidation," June 26 was "an outstanding success" in the view of Walter Sisulu, writing a month later (Document 84). The report of the national executive committee to the December 1950 annual conference presented a more mixed balance sheet (Document 85). It praised the people's behavior in the face of intimidation, and their loyal support, and it spoke in general terms about the increase in membership and new branches. On the other hand, in addition to discerning "lack of faith in the struggle," the report recognized once again that in addition to the absence of free speech, free assembly, and free movement there was still the chronic lack of money, of propaganda organs, and of discipline, efficiency, and devotion to official duty. [15]

There was a lull in political activity during the second half of 1950 although the government was moving relentlessly against the extraparliamentary opposition. The Natives' Representative Council, while no longer attracting much African interest, had its final, frustrating meeting. Police surveillance became closer, and late in the year the police raided the offices of the left-wing *Guardian*. On the legislative front, the Nationalist Party cabinet moved one more step toward political apartheid when it overcame internal opposition to its policy to remove Coloured voters from the common roll. Nevertheless, despite weakness and setbacks, ANC delegates at the well-attended conference in December could look back upon a year in which there had been enough evidence of mass support and discipline to justify optimism that Africans could move forward jointly with their allies in planning civil disobedience.

MOVING TOWARD DEFIANCE

Protests by both whites and nonwhites against the Nationalist government's legislation to remove Coloureds from the common voters' roll dominated the first half of 1951. African and Indian planning of the Defiance Campaign did not get well under way until the middle of the year. In the meantime, with the focus of attention mainly on Cape Town, where Parliament was sitting and left-wing and Coloured political activity was centered, two new antigovernment bodies sponsored conferences, demonstrations, and mass processions in the streets: the Franchise Action Council and the Torch Commando.

Since coming into power, the Nationalist government had moved to transform the uneven pattern of customary segregation of Coloureds into a rigid legal form. In 1948 it had introduced apartheid on the nationally owned trains in the Cape Peninsula, where first-class coaches were traditionally unsegregated. [16] Racially mixed marriages were prohibited in 1949; and in 1950 sexual intercourse, between whites and Coloureds (prohibited between whites and Africans since 1927). The Population Registration Act and the Group Areas Act, both enacted in 1950, had also increased the apprehension felt by the small proportion of politically conscious Coloureds. Tension reached a high point early in February 1951, when the terms of the Separate Representation of Voters Bill were made public. [17]

The bill was an important step toward political apartheid. It proposed to place some 50,000 Coloured voters in Cape Province on a separate or communal roll, as had been done with African voters in 1936, thus removing them as an influence on white elections. (The Nationalists also had made clear their intention to remove from Parliament the whites elected by Africans.) But by moving to do so by ordinary majority procedures in Parliament instead of by the constitution's entrenched-clause or extraordinary-majority procedure used in 1936, the government created a constitutional crisis. The bill became law in June 1951, but without reducing either the crisis or the intense emotions it stirred among whites and Coloureds.

The Franchise Action Council, an ad hoc and coordinating body to oppose the bill, was formed in Cape Town. Coloureds on the council included those still associated with the African People's Organisation (APO) and also, in the early stages, George Golding, a school principal whose Coloured People's National Union (CPNU) was disposed to cooperate with the United Party and took a lead in challenging the Voters' Act. [18] Joined with them were representatives of the ANC, the Indian Congress in Cape Province, and some whites who had belonged to the now-banned Communist Party. Dr. Moroka, Dr. Dadoo, and S. M. Rahim of the APO addressed a conference of the Franchise Action Council in February. Impressive "political strikes" were held on March 11, 1951, in Cape Town, when some 15,000 Coloureds marched through the city, and on May 7 in Port Elizabeth and elsewhere. At a conference in May, the Franchise Action Council resolved "to press for the early achievement of united action by national organizations with a view to a nationwide resistance and struggle against the entire apartheid system." [19]

Coloureds were far from unanimous, however, as to tactics. Those belonging to the Anti-C.A.D. and the Non-European Unity Movement had urged defiance of the railway regulations in 1948 but now again attacked "spectacular" protests as unprincipled and unprepared. A lengthy NEUM statement of April 1951 declared, "How unedifying the childishness of those sporadic displays of Anti-Pass Day, Protest Day, Mourning Day and, lastly, the display of so-called

411

'unity.'" Coloured support for "anti-Unity elements," it claimed, was "negligible" (Document 97).

A spectacular series of protests against the Coloured Voters Bill was mounted by a group of white veterans who attacked the government for subverting the constitution. Their leadership gave rise in April 1951 to an extra-party mass movement, the Torch Commando. [20] Although Coloured veterans marched in some of the early torchlight processions and some of the white leaders were liberals, the presence of nonwhites proved a great embarrassment to the organization. The Nationalists accused the Torch Commando of nonracialism and of planning to enlist both Coloured and African support. Despite veiled threats of a national strike and extraconstitutional action, at no time did the Torch Commando leadership move to incorporate nonwhites within the movement. [21]

On the African front, however, new moves toward joint action were made as the 1951 parliamentary session was ending. African leaders gathered in Johannesburg on June 17 for the funeral of Dr. Seme, one of the founders of the ANC. Their readiness to engage in joint planning with non-Africans at that time was an indication that "the old exclusive Congress had been buried with Seme." [22] Meeting immediately afterward, the national executive committee discussed the recommendations of the Council of Action, presented by its secretary, Gaur Radebe, who had been active on the left and was eventually to join the PAC. Radebe's report appeared sketchy and hasty in comparison with the carefully formulated program adopted later in the year. The NEC decided to "Declare War" on the pass laws and stock limitation and to call a joint conference of the national executive committees of the SAIC and the APO, with observers from the Franchise Action Council in attendance. The minutes of the NEC meeting dealt with Coloured cooperation as follows:

> Let us not refuse to cooperate with the Coloured people for the simple reason that they have let us down in the past.... We must, therefore, call these other groups to a joint meeting and ask them to join us in unfolding our Programme of Action. We, by reason of our numbers and our claims in Africa, should initiate these moves ... the Coloured people or Fr. A. C., must come in and be made functionary within our Programme of Action. [23]

Planning for the Defiance Campaign soon began in earnest under the direction of the ANC but in close and apparently equal partnership with the SAIC. On July 29, 1951, the joint conference was held, and a five-man Joint Planning Council—a subcommittee of the two national executive committees—was constituted: Moroka, Sisulu, Marks, Dadoo, and Cachalia. Thus, two Africans and two Indians—including two Communists, Marks and Dadoo—were on the Joint Planning Council under Moroka as chairman.[24] (Exclusive-minded African nationalists were often in the future to cite the equal representation of Africans and Indians, if the chairman was not counted, as evidence of African subordination to Indians.) In a little over two months, the council issued its report, the basic

412

plan for the campaign, dated November 8, 1951 (Document 86); and about six weeks later, on December 15-17, the ANC's annual conference adopted the report and its suggested timetable after extensive discussion in committee. [25] An ultimatum was to be issued to Prime Minister Malan that if certain laws were not repealed by Februrary 29, 1952, protest meetings and demonstrations would be held on April 6, 1952, the climax of the extended white celebration of the 300th anniversary of Van Riebeeck's arrival at the Cape. The demonstrations were to be "a prelude to the implementation of the plan for the defiance of unjust laws."

The ANC's annual conference endorsed the Joint Planning Council's report with little apparent opposition although an undercurrent of disquiet persisted regarding readiness to embark on mass action. [26] Chief Albert Lutuli, who was supported by the Youth League in Natal and had defeated Champion to become provincial president on May 30, 1951, questioned his own ability to comply with the program, but only because he had not received information about plans for civil disobedience until the eve of the conference. [27]

On the other hand, H. Selby Msimang, the ANC veteran who was provincial secretary of the ANC in Natal, appealed for a postponement of action until the Marks and Selope Thema factions in the Transvaal had become reconciled. Selope Thema's group was expelled from the ANC, however, and Msimang returned to Natal "profoundly depressed in spirit and mind." In a letter published in *Ilanga Lase Natal* on January 12, 1952, he criticized the Joint Planning Council for "practically taking over the control and leadership of the African National Congress" and opposed "any form of ultimatum being issued in an atmosphere of boisterousness and bunkum" although "I fully support the programme of action adopted in 1949." He was to resign from his position as provincial secretary before the Defiance Campaign began.

Because of their commitment to the Programme of Action, A.P. Mda and his supporters in the Youth League did not oppose the adoption of the report; they supported plans for the Defiance Campaign while preparing to withstand any moves that, in their eyes, diluted the spirit of exclusive African nationalism. Mda himself was ill and could not be present at the conference, at which Cachalia (and Manilal Gandhi, editor of *Indian Opinion*) sat on the dais. He and others had opposed the involvement of Indians and Communists in planning the implementation of the Programme. They had also been disturbed by Communist language and pro-Soviet viewpoints in *African Lodestar*, the official journal of the Youth League in the Transvaal, although the journal's language was mixed with a strong emphasis on African nationalism and even some criticism of South African Communists. [28]

Late in 1951, a group within the Youth League organized a loosely knit and underground "watchdog committee" to keep the Joint Planning Council and the movement toward defiance under surveillance and to press for reliance upon exclusive African nationalism. [29] Like-minded men organized the so-called

Bureau of African Nationalism in East London in January 1952. [30] One of its publications issued before April 6, 1952, proclaimed that the struggle was "basically Africanistic." At the same time, the publication heralded the forthcoming campaign and listed the names both of members of the Joint Planning Council and of officeholders in the ANC as a group from which "National Heroes and Nation Builders" would come. [31]

In accordance with the ANC's decision, Dr. Moroka and Sisulu sent an ultimatum to Prime Minister Malan on January 21, 1952, calling for the repeal of six "unjust laws" by February 29, 1952 (Document 88). Those laws, the Joint Planning Council had said, were those "which are most obnoxious and which are capable of being defied." Two were the sources of long-standing grievances on the part of urban and rural Africans, respectively: the pass laws and "stock limitation." The latter (not strictly a law but a policy or practice) referred to cattle culling to reduce overgrazing and was opposed as a protest against the scarcity of land for Africans. The other laws were the Group Areas Act and the Suppression of Communism Act, main objects of attack in 1950, the Coloured Voters Act of 1951, and—not yet noted here—the Bantu Authorities Act of 1951, which was passed toward the end of the parliamentary session. [32]

The Bantu Authorities Act, which abolished the Natives' Representative Council, provided for a hierarchical system of tribal authorities composed of government-approved chiefs and advisers. The act's purpose, as seen by Professor Matthews, was

to delay indefinitely the development of a sense of national unity among Africans. The African people were not consulted about the Act; had they been, their leaders would have rejected it, for the efforts of all responsible leaders of the African people are directed toward welding the different tribal groups together. [33]

Although the African and Indian leaders focused their aim in the forthcoming campaign on the repeal of the six laws, the demand was always made in the context of their broader aim: equality. In the letter to the prime minister, Moroka and Sisulu spoke of "democracy, liberty and harmony in South Africa" and declared that the African people were "fully resolved to achieve them in our lifetime." ("In our lifetime" later became a phrase of crucial importance in the government's prosecution of ANC leaders in the treason trial of 1956-1961. According to A. P. Mda, the slogan "Freedom in Our Lifetime" was composed by Anton Lembede.) The reply, signed by Malan's private secretary and referring to him in the third person, was a categorical rejection of the ANC's arguments and a warning that the government would "deal adequately with those responsible for inciting subversive activities of any nature whatsoever." [34] A second letter from Moroka and Sisulu regretted that the prime minister had rejected "our genuine offer of cooperation on the basis of full equality" [35] (Document 90).

In accordance with these longer range aims, the Joint Planning Council had outlined an open-ended program of noncooperation and nonviolence, the most suitable forms of struggle (said the council's report) in the "historical conditions" of South Africa at that time. In the first of three stages of defiance, a small number of trained and disciplined persons were to break selected laws and regulations in the major centers. In the second stage, the number of volunteers and centers would increase. (The volunteers were usually to be grouped with fellow members of their organization but might sometimes be in racially mixed units.) Accelerated by resistance to the enforcement of the Population Registra-tion Act (not one of the six laws), the struggle would move into the third stage, when it would broaden out into urban and rural areas throughout the country and "assume a general mass character." "Industrial action" or strikes (sometimes referred to as "lawful industrial action") would in all probability come at a later stage although such action could be taken at any time. It was called "the best and most important weapon in the struggle." "Mass action," when that stage was reached, would be "sustained" and would

gradually embrace larger groups of people, permeate both the urban and rural areas and make possible for us to organise, discipline and lead the people in a planned manner.

Although the aims of the Defiance Campaign were clearly revolutionary in the eyes of the government, Dr. Moroka in his presidential address declared that " . . . we ask for nothing that is revolutionary" (Document 87b). In the circumstances, his address was one of moderation as well as an invocation of African nationalism that contained a slap at "the sting of inferiority" felt by Africans inside white churches. Dr. Moroka was popular with whites—Afrikaans-speaking whites were among his patients—and he spoke with genuine feeling and apparent expectation of some kind of favorable response in appealing to whites for "a change of heart."

Dr. Molema, on the other hand, in opening the conference of the South African Indian Congress on January 25, 1952, declared that nonwhites had "hoped in vain for a change of heart among the rulers" (Document 89. At this conference, the SAIC accepted the plan of action for the Defiance Campaign). His address had a bitterly passionate rhetoric that Dr. Moroka's lacked, although like Moroka he was uninterested in, if not ignorant of, ideologies. What was most remarkable about his address, however, was the unqualified denunciation of "the white man," the emphasis on unity among Africans, Indians, and Coloureds, and the absence of any recognition either of white support or nonracial aims. [36]

The two letters to Malan, unlike Molema's address, emphasized the aim of nonracial equality and the support of enlightened whites. [37] Nor did the letters contain any Marxist or revolutionary analysis or language. They spoke despairingly of forty years of patience and frustration, equally condemned "trusteeship, segregation, and apartheid," and warned that "racial bitterness and tension" were rising. But the correspondence reaffirmed the peaceful nature of the forthcoming campaign and ended on a note of hope. The second letter was not answered.

Soon afterward, the ANC issued "A Message to Every Democrat," a pamphlet printed both in English and in Afrikaans, announcing that mass meetings were to be held on April 6. "We stand on the eve of a great national crisis," it concluded. "We call on every true South African to support us."

THE DEFIANCE CAMPAIGN

On April 6, 1952, the climax of the countrywide Van Riebeeck Festival, white South Africa celebrated the tercentenary of Jan Van Riebeeck's arrival at the Cape in 1652. The ANC and the SAIC appealed to nonwhite South Africa to observe the day as a "National Day of Pledge and Prayer," a "prelude" to the Defiance Campaign. In the Transvaal, the provincial organizations issued a flyer (Document 91) calling for "protest meetings and demonstrations" and declaring, "This Van Riebeeck celebration cannot be a time for rejoicing for Non-Europeans." The flyer attacked the Malan government for glorifying 300 years of "conquest, enslavement and oppression" and for saying nothing about "the famous leaders of the Non-European peoples" or of "the noble Europeans who fought for freedom for all."

In assessing the whites' historical contribution, another flyer (appearing without attribution, in both English and an African language, and mimeographed rather than well printed like Document 91) struck a balance sheet on "300 Years of Sorrow, Sin, and Shame":

> If we have learnt to read and write, we have also lost our lands and our freedom; if we have known new spiritual flights and values, we have also learnt new spiritual depths of Sorrow and Despair. If we have acquired a knowledge of, and faith in God, we have also seen how His holy name can be taken in vain and used for plunder, deceit and murder. If Europeans have put a stop to our barbarous and suicidal inter-tribal wars, they have also introduced terrible diseases and immoralities that are killing us by the million. Poverty, Slums, Malnutrition, Scurvy, Consumption (of the Lungs), Syphilis and other killers are leaving a broad black trail of death across African homes. Altogether, we have been losers by the coming of the White man to South Africa. We have lost our Land, our Liberty and our very Life.

African adults and school children boycotted many of the festivities. On April 6 mass rallies took place without any incidents of disorder in Johannesburg, Pretoria, Port Elizabeth, Durban, East London, Cape Town, and in smaller centers.[38] Dr. Moroka was the main speaker in Johannesburg at a meeting presided over by Dr. Dadoo. In Port Elizabeth, Professor Matthews struck a tone of militant African nationalism and self-reliance. The ANC was convinced, he

416

said, that "only the African people themselves will ever rid themselves" of "political subjugation, economic exploitation and social degradation." To "our well wishers" who had suggested abandoning the forthcoming campaign, he replied that they had offered no alternative course of action. In any event, the struggle would be nonviolent since "it is obvious that in our present unarmed state it would be futile and suicidal for us to think of an armed struggle." "Freedom or Serfdom" was the choice: "AFRICA'S CAUSE MUST TRI-UMPH! " [39]

African leaders acclaimed the spirit of April 6 as proof that the people were ready for the Defiance Campaign to begin. The obvious date, if the ANC was to nurture its own anniversaries into greater significance, was June 26, the second anniversary of the 1950 "Day of Protest." The Cape ANC recommended this date at a conference on April 12. On May 31, the national executive committees of the ANC and the SAIC, with Coloureds also attending, met in Port Elizabeth and decided to open the campaign officially on the anniversary date. The gathering of leaders was a festive one. It ended with a banquet, attended by foreign journalists, in which tribute was paid to Professor Matthews on the eve of his departure for the United States. At a mass rally on the following day, a Sunday, Dr. Moroka called for 10,000 volunteers.

Matthews left South Africa on June 12 to spend an academic year in New York City as the Henry W. Luce Visiting Professor of World Christianity at Union Theological Seminary. Thus he was to miss the entire campaign, but he was to perform a potentially valuable role as the official representative of the ANC in the United States and to the United Nations. [40]

Earlier in May, the government had begun to take repressive steps against the Defiance Campaign leaders as a prelude to its own developing campaign to decapitate the nonwhite movement and quell the spread of enthusiasm for defiance. Acting under the Suppression of Communism Act, it ordered five leaders—all Communists—to resign from their organizations and to stay away from political gatherings: Moses Kotane of the ANC's national executive committee; J. B. Marks, president of the Transvaal ANC; D. W. Bopape, secretary of the Transvaal ANC; J. N. Ngwevela, chairman of the Cape Western Regional Committee of the ANC; and Dr. Dadoo, president of the SAIC. Also during May, the government banned the left-wing *Guardian*, which promptly reappeared as *The Clarion*; deprived Sam Kahn and Fred Carneson, former Communists, of their seats as Natives' Representatives in Parliament and in the Cape Provincial Council, respectively; and placed bans on Michael Harmel, a leading former Communist then active in the Transvaal Peace Council, and E. S. (Solly) Sachs, the left-wing leader of the Garment Workers' Union.

None of the banned nonwhite leaders was allowed to attend the May 31 meeting, but on that day the announcement was made that they would defy their bans and thus become "the vanguard of the volunteers." [41] Kotane spoke at a meeting on June 2 and was arrested. Within a week, Dadoo, Bopape, and

Marks spoke and were arrested. [42] Sachs and Harmel also violated their bans, but their action was not a prelude to defiance by whites, for whites were notably inactive in the Defiance Campaign except toward the end in negligible numbers. More significant was the fact that the timing of the government's bans resulted in the emergence of leading Communists in the vanguard of defiance.

The defiers who began the campaign on June 26, 1952, did so with a sense that history was being made: for the first time, Africans and Indians with a few Coloureds were engaging in joint political action under a common leadership. A national action committee, whose key members were Sisulu and Cachalia, and a national volunteer board, with Mandela as the volunteer-in-chief, conducted the campaign. Both bodies had been set up by the ANC and SAIC executive committees following the May 31 meeting. Cooperation between the African and Indian leaders was close, but the paramountcy of the African leadership in the campaign was frequently affirmed. Dr. Moroka and others traveled widely among the major centers during the early months. The national action committee worked continually to maintain direction and coordination, but the success of the campaign depended to a large extent on local leadership and organization. The fact that the eastern Cape Province was by far the most active area of defiance was partly due to the experience and commitment of local African leaders.

A so-called Day of the Volunteers on Sunday, June 22, preceded the opening of the campaign. Prayers were said, and volunteers signed the following pledge:

> I, the undersigned, Volunteer of the National Volunteer Corps, do hereby solemnly pledge and bind myself to serve my country and my people in accordance with the directives of the National Volunteer Corps and to participate fully and without reservations to the best of my ability in the Campaign for the Defiance of Unjust Laws. I shall obey the orders of my leader under whom I shall be placed and strictly abide by the rules and regulations of the National Volunteer Corps framed from time to time. It shall be my duty to keep myself physically, mentally and morally fit. [43]

A meeting of 3,000-5,000 persons took place in New Brighton, Port Elizabeth. At a much larger mass meeting in Durban, Chief Lutuli, president of the ANC in Natal, and Dr. Naicker, president of the Natal Indian Congress, publicly committed themselves to the campaign; and Nelson Mandela, having come from Johannesburg to be the main speaker, declared, "We can now say unity between the Non-European people in this country has become a living reality." [44]

Disciplined "batches" of volunteers went into action on June 26 in small numbers but with high spirits. During the campaign, the acts of defiance were often accompanied by "freedom songs," the thumbs-up sign (introduced by the Cape ANC in 1949 as a sign of unity), cries of "Afrika!" and cheers from supporting onlookers. Nana Sita, a veteran Gandhian, led fifty-two Africans and Indians, including Walter Sisulu, into Boksburg location near Johannesburg without permits. All were arrested. Mandela and Cachalia were present only as observers since they planned to avoid arrest, but that evening they happened to be among a group of Africans who were arrested in Johannesburg when they left a hall after curfew. In Port Elizabeth, thirty entered the railway station through a "Europeans Only" entrance and were arrested. A handful were arrested in Worcester in Cape Province. Others were to be arrested for entering the European sections of post offices, sitting on a bench marked for whites, or violating other apartheid regulations.

The government at first charged Sisulu and the others in Boksburg with conspiring to commit public violence but then withdrew the charge. On July 21 the Africans were convicted for being without passes and the Indians for entering a Native location. All were penalized by a fine of £1 or seven days in jail, and all but one chose jail. Sisulu delivered a short statement (Document 92), which is a prototype of many other statements that were to be made from the dock in succeeding years. [45] He noted the ANC's efforts since 1912 to use "every constitutional means" on behalf of the African people, the gradual deterioration of the African's position, the Nationalist government's closing of "all constitutional channels," and his determination to "fight" for the abolition of discriminatory laws.

Slowly the campaign spread, from Port Elizabeth and East London to the smaller towns in the eastern Cape Province, from Johannesburg to a dozen centers on the Witwatersrand, to Cape Town on August 3 and a half-dozen smaller centers in the western Cape, and late in September to Bloemfontein and Durban. (Bloemfontein and Durban were the only centers of resistance in the Orange Free State and Natal.) During the last few days of June, the campaign leaders counted 146 volunteers arrested; during July 1,504; in August (when the national executive committee of the ANC called for an intensification of the campaign after the arrest of the 20 leaders, described below), 2,015; and in September (on the eve of the United Nations session), 2,058. The campaign gained momentum until October, but during that month and in November rioting erupted. The leadership was becoming increasingly hampered, and although there were signs that the campaign was beginning to spread into the reserves, the number of defiers fell rapidly. By mid-December, however, an additional 2,334 were arrested, and the total reached 8,057. [46]

Although defiance occurred in all the major centers of the country, about 70 percent of those arrested were in the small cities and towns of eastern Cape Province. In the eastern Province, also, were to be seen the beginnings of resistance in the reserves and rural areas. Julius Lewin has suggested the following explanations:

First, the African people there are more homogeneous in tribal tradition and less divided than elsewhere. They are also better educated and more Christianized after longer contact with western civilization. Resistance in this area was marked by notable religious fervour—it was

419

often preceded by prayer—and it was supported by African clergy and by African trade unions. Secondly, the people in these parts had lost more than others since 1936 through the operation of the land and franchise laws that deprived them and their children of old-established rights. [47]

Local organizations were also generally more efficient here than elsewhere. One local center of special enthusiasm in the eastern Province was Fort Hare Native College in Alice. Some of its students, though they themselves were advised by the leaders not to defy, were active as organizers in the towns and villages of a wide area at night and during weekends. [48]

Some 5,719 were arrested in the eastern Province; 1,411, in the Transvaal; 423, in western Cape, Mafeking, and Kimberley; 258, in the Orange Free State; and 246, in Natal. Rallies in Durban attracted thousands, but the low number of defiers there, Kuper suggests, resulted from poor ANC organization, the persistence of anti-Indian sentiment among nationalist-minded Africans, and the reluctance of Indians to take the lead. More remarkable was the relatively low participation on the Witwatersrand. Professor Matthews, in reacting to accusations of Communist influence, wrote the following to an American friend:

The Campaign was strongest and best organised precisely in those areas where so-called 'Communist influence' was weakest. Anybody who knows anything about the Communist Party of South Africa knows or ought to know that its influence was strongest in Cape Town, where its headquarters were situated, in Johannesburg and in Durban. The figures of the Campaign speak for themselves . . . Cape Town providing a negligible number. The largest number came from the Eastern Cape where the 'Communist' influence was practically nil. [49]

Because offenses were minor, the penalties were usually no more than one or two months' imprisonment with the option of a fine not exceeding £7 to £10. Sometimes defiers were acquitted, most notably in the case of twenty-four who entered a railway waiting room in Cape Town and were acquitted when the magistrate found that facilities for whites and nonwhites were unequal. [50] On some occasions, the police ignored the defiers, for example, when one group walked the Durban streets for two nights after curfew. As the campaign continued, magistrates sometimes decided on whippings for defendants under the age of twenty-one, and allegations of assault and ill-treatment in prison became more frequent.

A more accurate measure of the government's concern about the campaign was the scope of its action against the leadership under the Suppression of Communism Act. On July 30, the police raided and confiscated papers in the homes and offices of ANC and SAIC officials in some sixteen centers throughout the country and in the offices of the left-wing *Clarion*. The countrywide raids were unprecedented and set a pattern that the government was to follow in later

420

years. Two weeks later, the police arrested twenty national and Transvaal leaders of the campaign and in September, fifteen leaders in the eastern Cape Province. All were charged with promoting communism and were released on bail. Four years later, some of the accused were to be arrested on charges of high treason and to be tried under an indictment covering a period that began on October 1, 1952, shortly before the first riot.

Of the twenty on trial in Johannesburg, twelve were Africans, including Moroka, Sisulu, Marks, and Mandela; seven were Indians, including Dadoo, Cachalia, and Ahmed Kathrada, president of the Transvaal Indian Youth Congress; and one was a Coloured, the chairman of the Coloured Branch of the Garment Workers' Union. The fifteen on trial in Port Elizabeth included Dr. J. L. Z. Njongwe, acting provincial president; Joseph Matthews, the son of Professor Matthews; and Tsepo T. Letlaka, who was later actively to oppose the ANC's multiracial tactics. Appearances of the accused in court were occasions for enthusiastic political rallies, but the actions of Dr. Moroka during the trial produced a sour break in the front of unity. Feeling that the other accused had not consulted him adequately and being unhappy about the role of lawyers who had been members of the Communist Party, Dr. Moroka hired his own lawyers, took the witness stand, unlike the others, and sought mitigation by stressing his anticommunism and his efforts for racial harmony. Disaffection with his conduct was to contribute to his defeat for reelection in December.

The trial of the twenty did not take place until the end of November. It was short, and on December 2 all were found guilty of what Mr. Justice Rumpff (who was later to be the presiding judge in the treason trial) called "statutory communism," in contrast to "what is commonly known as communism." Although the Joint Planning Council envisaged "a range of acts from open noncompliance of laws to something that equals high treason," according to Justice Rumpff, he accepted "the evidence that you have consistently advised your followers to follow a peaceful course of action and to avoid violence in any shape or form." [51] The accused were sentenced to nine months' imprisonment with hard labor, but this was suspended for two years. The fifteen accused in the Port Elizabeth trial also were found guilty, in 1953, and their nine months' sentences suspended for three years.

The leaders were arrested at a time when the campaign was still unmarred by violence. Before their trials were held, however, they were stunned—and a suddenly aroused white public was horrified—by rioting in Port Elizabeth on October 18, in an African hostel in Johannesburg on November 3, in Kimberley on November 8, and in East London on November 10. In confused circumstances of angry crowds, stone throwing, and firing by police, about forty persons were killed, hundreds injured, and government buildings and churches extensively damaged. About six whites, but no white policemen, were among those killed, who included a medical nun whose body was mutilated. The campaign, which the government blamed for the disorders, may have contributed to tension; but, as Kuper concludes, there was "no evidence to connect the resistance movement with the disturbances nor was violence at any time advocated by the resisters as a means of struggle." [52]

Immediately after the rioting in Port Elizabeth, the local executive committee of the ANC issued a statement (Document 93), which was published on the front page of the *Eastern Province Herald*, deploring the "ill-considered return to jungle law" and extending sympathy to black and white families which had suffered losses. (*Die Burger* in Cape Town had commented, "For a while primitive Africa ruled, stripped of the varnish of civilisation and free from the taming authority of the white man."[53]) The national working committee of the ANC claimed that the riots had been deliberately provoked. Neither that claim nor the government's charges could be proved, but the charge was repeated in a flyer issued by the national action committee after the East London riots (Document 94). Accusing the government of attempting "to cause panic among the Europeans," it called on Africans to "be peaceful, disciplined, non-violent." (Early in the treason trial of 1956-1961, the government attempted to link the ANC to the riots; ANC leaders have asserted that the attempt was abandoned because witnesses for the prosecution were revealing the government's role as provocateur.)

The rioting, and especially the murder and mutilation of the nun, excited attention from whites as the campaign itself had failed to do. The opposition English-language press called for a cessation of the campaign, and the leader of the United Party called for consultation with unspecified "moderate" African leaders. As the gulf between African leaders of some popular standing and whites appeared to widen, the small number of liberal or left-wing whites considered ways of strengthening contact with nonwhites and identifying themselves with the aims of the campaign.

Late in September, a distinguished group of twenty-two white liberals living in Johannesburg, Cape Town, and Durban issued a statement entitled "Equal Rights for All Civilized People." [54] They called for "a revival of the liberal tradition" of the nineteenth-century Cape Colony in order to "attract the support of educated, politically conscious non-Europeans by offering them a reasonable [not "equal"] status in our common society." Recognizing that the men who led the campaign were "acknowledged leaders," it asked them "to recognize that it will take time and patience substantially to improve the present position." The statement urged the repeal of measures such as the Group Areas Act, the pass laws, and the Suppression of Communism Act, thus accepting the immediate aims of the campaign. But nonracialism, it said, was necessarily a long-term aim, and all were asked to exercise "restraint."

The leaders of the Defiance Campaign welcomed white support and reaffirmation that the resistance was against unjust laws and not against whites. In order to build more active white support, the national action committee itself announced a public meeting for mid-November in Johannesburg. Over 200 whites came and heard Sisulu, Tambo, Cachalia, and others. (Replying to a question, Sisulu said he did not think that the offer of a limited franchise would have any appeal for the great majority of nonwhites.) [55] Former Communists and other left-wing whites who desired to identify themselves with the aims of the campaign took the initiative in the meeting and in the provisional committee elected by it. Eventually, late in 1953, they organized the Congress of Democrats as an ally of the ANC.

For some Africans, this course of events was disappointing since they had hoped to see the creation of a body that would generally support the ANC's aims and appeal to a wide spectrum of whites rather than to a tiny activist group that would be identified with the ANC. [56] Potentially more useful in their eyes was a body like the Liberal Party, which was organized after the 1953 general election. It was joined by many of the whites who signed the September "Equal Rights" statement, but it went beyond ANC interests when it began actively to recruit African members.

Defiance itself was the means by which a handful of whites effectively identified themselves with the Defiance Campaign. On December 8, photographers recorded the unauthorized entrance into Germiston location, and the arrest, of seven whites and some thirty Africans and Indians. On the following day four whites defied in Cape Town. Especially notable was the fact that the leader of the Germiston batch was not a left-wing activist but an anti-Communist young man, Patrick Duncan, whose father had been Governor-General. (Duncan later joined the Liberal Party and eventually the Pan Africanist Congress.) He was accompanied by Manilal Gandhi, son of Mahatma Gandhi. Later in the month Duncan was welcomed to the platform at the ANC annual conference and spoke in praise of ANC and SAIC leaders and their "true vision of the South Africa of the future." [57]

Dr. Moroka and Sisulu had claimed in their two letters to the prime minister (Documents 88 and 90) that not only enlightened whites at home but also world opinion condemned apartheid. Early in October, a group of resisters (in South Africa) identified as the first "UNO Batch" attempted to draw attention to South Africa while the United Nations was preparing to open its session. [58] Asian and Arab delegates had already asked for inclusion of an apartheid item, and soon afterward the General Assembly voted (with the Western countries abstaining) to set up a UN Commission on the Racial Situation in South Africa. Apartheid was thus added to the issues of South West Africa and the position of Indians in South Africa as a perennial concern of the United Nations.

In evaluating the impact of the Defiance Campaign within South Africa, one is struck by the breadth of its support among African leaders. Within the older generation, Dr. Xuma, who had been politically inactive after his defeat in December 1949 and was unsympathetic to the leadership of the campaign, observed that "no reasonable person who knows the conditions in South Africa can condemn the defiance movement." And, in countering United Party and other white appeals for consultation with "moderate Non-European leaders" rather than leaders of the campaign, he declared, "There is no such thing as a moderate African." [59] In a public letter, writing "as senior chaplain of my nation in this struggle," the Rev. J. J. Skomolo, who had expressed serious misgivings about premature action in June 1950 (Document 81), called for prayerful support for the campaign. [60]

Although some older leaders either opposed the campaign or failed to support it, the Youth League presented a largely united front during 1952. Occasional publications of the Bureau of African Nationalism supported the campaign with an African nationalist interpretation but also expressed the guarded apprehensiveness of men like Mda, who were to be the nucleus of the Africanist group within the ANC. Mda himself observed that white and Indian Communists were winning the confidence of some African nationalists through the intimate association engendered by the campaign; on the other hand, he also saw that African Communists were themselves being influenced by African nationalism and that they seemed to relish the opportunities for African leadership provided by the campaign. [61] Ngubane feared that Dr. Dadoo was gaining control over the national headquarters of the ANC and that Sisulu and Mandela were becoming "mere puppets." [62] (Mandela was elected president of the Transvaal ANC at its October 10-12 conference to succeed the banned J. B. Marks.) But Ngubane and others looked upon Lutuli's election as president-general at the December 18-20, 1952, conference as a victory for African nationalism.

The most articulate opponent of the campaign was R. V. Selope Thema, the elder statesman of the ANC who was the editor of the *Bantu World* and founder of the National-minded Bloc, a splinter group. Writing before the start of the campaign, he declared flatly that the Communists had captured the ANC and controlled it. Disliking Indians, whom he accused of exploiting the African, he identified "the originators and leaders" of the campaign as Indians who were Marxists and also defenders of Indian economic interests. Like the Coloured "men of the Fourth International" who controlled the Unity Movement, he said, they wanted "to make Africans international-minded before they are even national-minded." [63] Other ANC veterans who failed to support the campaign or opposed it were in Natal: A. W. G. Champion, who had been replaced by Lutuli as provincial president in 1951 and who resented the Youth League, and Selby Msimang.

The All African Convention continued, of course, to be scornful of the campaign, which it described as "yet another stunt" staged by African "Quislings" concerned with "assuring the rulers of their harmlessness, while increasing the price of collaboration." [64] At the other end of the political spectrum, the campaign was opposed by a pro-government body, the Bantu National Congress, created in February 1952 by an African herbalist—ridiculed as a witch doctor— named S. S. Benghu. Although the Afrikaans press reported that he had 400,000 followers in Natal, [65] the Bantu National Congress produced little evidence of support beyond some tribal chiefs, and Benghu himself was finally discredited when he was convicted of theft and fraud.

Meanwhile, Chief Lutuli, who was to become president-general of the ANC, was rising in prominence. During September, he was summoned to Pretoria and given a choice between continuing as an elected and government-paid chief in Natal or continuing as a provincial president of the ANC and supporter of defiance. Lutuli refused to renounce the ANC, and on November 12 the Native commissioner of Stanger announced that he was dismissed as chief. Lutuli's public statement, made immediately afterward, referred to his experiences in church organizations, Joint Councils, and the Natives' Representative Council and contained an eloquent plaint that has been widely quoted: "who will deny that thirty years of my life have been spent knocking in vain, patiently, moderately and modestly at a closed and barred door?" (Document 95) During those years, he said, the government had intensified the subjugation of the African. Lutuli warned that the people would "dismiss from their hearts" chiefs who did not cooperate with other leaders to promote "common national interests" and described a "new spirit . . . that revolts openly and boldly against injustice." He reaffirmed his support for nonviolent passive resistance as a "non-revolutionary, legitimate and humane" means to bring about "partnership in the Government of the country on the basis of equality" and expressed hope that he could continue to work with "liberal and moderate Europeans and Non-Europeans."

Shortly before Lutuli's dismissal, the government on November 7 banned fifty-two nonwhite leaders in the eastern Cape Province from attending any gathering for six months. On November 28, before the resistance by Patrick Duncan, a proclamation provided that anyone (including whites) who influenced Natives to break a law or who permitted or addressed a meeting of more than ten Africans in a Native area could be fined £300 or imprisoned for three years. Bans on travel and attendance at meetings were placed on Sisulu and Mandela on the eve of the annual conference, and at the last minute the conference was transferred from Kimberley to Johannesburg.

Although many could not come, 215 delegates from the four provinces were reported in attendance. [66] The conference reelected Sisulu as secretary-general. Dr. Moroka, however, had lost support because of his personally defensive posture in the Johannesburg trial, and he was defeated for reelection by a large majority. Lutuli, the candidate of the Natal Youth League, became president-general with the respect both of African nationalists and Marxists. In these circumstances of apprehension, facing the prospect of additional repressive legislation in the coming parliamentary session, the conference endorsed a resolution giving extraordinary powers to the national executive committee when necessary for "the continuance of the struggle in any shape or form" and constituted a committee to revise the ANC's constitution. [67]

Was the Defiance Campaign a success or a failure? The question is an impossible one to answer: participants and observers vary in the criteria they use and they vary in the span of time to which they apply their criteria. There is also the additional consideration of hidden motives: some Africans may have hoped and expected that further polarization, violence, and repression were necessary if the masses were to be made ready for militant confrontation. In this sense, the tensions out of which the riots erupted, the growing severity of police measures, the extreme legislation and penalties of 1953, the strengthening of the National- ist government in the general election of that year might all be regarded as necessary stages in the struggle. In any event, the campaign saw the beginning of systematic effort by the government to ban, prosecute, and generally immobilize the ablest and most experienced leaders. Although the leaders were to continue their activity behind the scenes, the ANC and the SAIC were damaged.

None of the laws that were the objects of the campaign was repealed; the government proceeded relentlessly in its course to tighten and extend apartheid. An unsigned memorandum of December 16, 1952, prepared for the national action committee, reviewed the "Government onslaught" and efforts to link the campaign with Mau Mau and to unite the whites against the nonwhites. But the memorandum also noted with optimism the range of white sympathy that the campaign had generated among "philosophers, liberals, university professors and other prominent people," including church leaders, the concern expressed by the Civil Rights League, the Institute of Race Relations, the Torch Commando, and similar organizations, the action [unspecified] of commerce and industry in "propagating liberal and more humane policy," and the direct participation of whites in the campaign under the leadership of Patrick Duncan. The publicizing of nonwhite grievances in a "dignified manner," the memorandum said, had been "appreciated."

Another review of the campaign (Document 96), which was in the form of a circular letter from the working committee of the ANC in Cape Province, signed by Mokxotho [Robert] Matji, did not note gains among Whites, although it listed as one achievement the introduction of South African policy "into the arena of world politics." [68] Otherwise, what was claimed were gains among Africans themselves—in organization, unity, heightened self-confidence, and the "good riddance" of "pleading, cowardly and hamba-kahle [go slow] leaders." "Great achievements," however, were accompanied by "grave weaknesses": the continued lack of an ANC newspaper and of full-time organizers; defective "administration"—that is, failures in record-keeping and communication; and the need to develop "responsible, honest, sincere and militant leadership." The cir- cular letter called for "a school for Secretaries," recruitment of active and dues- paying members, and "regular fund-raising functions for the protracted struggle ahead of us."

The Defiance Campaign never approached the stage of mass resistance that had the dimensions of a general strike, but it transformed the ANC into an embryonic mass movement. The first aim of the campaign, said Lutuli later at the time of the treason trial, was "to politicize the African people." [69] Political enthusiasm was enhanced, though no measure of this is available. Songs, the thumbs-up sign, the ANC flag, armbands, cries of "Mayibuye! " and "Afrika!"—all these contributed to mass enthusiasm. Of far-reaching importance was the growth in numbers of men and women whose commitment to the movement was intensified by the experience of jail and the popular recognition it carried. The defiers became a source of future political educators and leaders.

From an estimated 7,000 to 20,000 members at the beginning of the campaign, the ANC's membership grew rapidly. Some writers have estimated that it grew to 100,000; this was, indeed, the aim set forth by the national executive committee in its report to the December 1951 conference (Document 87a). [70] Documents of late 1952 speak more modestly of expansion into "a mighty National organisation with thousands of members and thousands of Volunteers" (Document 96). Dr. Moroka has recalled that when he traveled throughout the country to speak, "I would say that easily 70-80 percent of the people were behind us, even on the farms." [71] Undoubtedly the surge of enthusiasm during the campaign increased the volume of the ANC's support, but the perennial problem remained of estimating the number of members whose dues were not currently paid-up as well as the number of adherents or sympathizers. Only the most politically conscious could be relied upon to renew their membership by paying dues each year. In December 1953, the total (presumably paid-up) membership reported was 28,900. [72]

Shortly after the Van Riebeeck day demonstrations of April 6, 1952, Professor Matthews had defined a recurring problem that the leaders faced:—the choice between action now or action later.

The importance of holding meetings of this kind from time to time cannot be overemphasized [he wrote], but the enthusiasm shown by the people will not take long to evaporate and [will] be succeeded by disappointment and disillusionment if the expected campaign is not launched, even if only on a limited scale, in the not too distant future. Nevertheless, it would be suicidal to launch the campaign unless there is evidence that our preparations have reached such a stage that the campaign will not be merely a flash in the pan, but an effort that can be sustained over a reasonable period of time. [73]

In the short run, the campaign was surely a remarkable success in demonstrating both to whites and to Africans the potential power of African leadership, organizational skill, and discipline and the readiness of Africans to cooperate with other nonwhites. The leaders, in turn, were encouraged by the readiness of large numbers to set examples of personal sacrifice and by signs of movement toward national solidarity. Yet the campaign came to a standstill by the end of the year. [74] The supply of volunteers had declined and family hardships had intensified; in the aftermath of the riots some time for reassessment was needed. Had the campaign begun too early or perhaps too late? Might a more solid basis for future militancy have been laid if it had been exclusively African? Should (or could) it continue? These questions of timing and tactics divided African political leaders and in the new period that began in 1953 produced sharper divisions. At the same time, the half-century quest for unity which for many Africans had culminated in the Defiance Campaign was reinforced during the next decade by the ever-increasing impact of white domination.

NOTES

1. In addition to Tambo, the new national executive committee included the following Youth League men: A. P. Mda, Dan Tloome, James Njongwe, Victor Mbobo, Godfrey Pitje, and Joseph Mokoena. Both Tambo and Mda had filled vacancies and served on the national executive committee before December 1949. Also elected were Dr. Xuma, the Rev. James A. Calata, and Moses Kotane.

   (The composition of the national executive committee at a particular time is sometimes difficult to determine because of changes of membership due to vacancies. Letters written on ANC letterheads are sometimes unreliable sources on officeholders because letterheads might be out of date. The names listed here are taken from the minutes of the ANC Annual Conference of December 1949 (Document 47). For a somewhat different membership of the national executive committee during "1949-52," see Duma Nokwe, "The Great Smear: Communism and Congress in South Africa," *Africa South in Exile*, October-December 1961, pp. 5-7.)

   Mbobo, Pitje, and Mokoena became politically inactive, and Mda later parted company with Sisulu and Tambo. But other like-minded younger men who joined the national executive committee later and continued on it for all or most of the decade included Wilson Conco, Duma Nokwe, Robert Resha, Dr. Arthur Letele, and M. B. Yengwa. Also prominent were Nelson Mandela and Joseph Matthews.

2. Many decades of experience were represented in the small national executive committee of nine members elected at the ANC conference of April 1969 held at Morogoro, Tanzania. The committee included Oliver Tambo, Acting President-General, J. B. Marks, Moses Kotane, and Joseph Matthews. *Mayibuye*, May 1969, no. 10.

3. Not until 1960 was mass civil disobedience again attempted, but the effort was then made by the ANC's breakaway rival, the Pan Africanist Congress, and was abortive, ending with fateful shootings at Sharpeville and the outlawing of both the PAC and the ANC.

4. In addition to outlawing the Communist Party, the act greatly enlarged ministerial power to ban an individual from an area, from membership in an organization, or from attendance at "gatherings." Such action could be

taken, subject only to extremely limited judicial review, if the minister of Justice was satisfied that the person was encouraging or likely to encourage any act or omission to further "the achievement of any of the objects of communism." "Communism" in the act included any doctrine "which aims at bringing about any political, industrial, social or economic change within the Union by the promotion of disturbance or disorder, by unlawful acts or omissions or by the threat of such acts or omissions." This legislation also gave the minister wide powers over assembly and publication if he expected that the objects of "communism" would be furthered.

5. According to the report of the council, which has been deleted from Document 87a. But Document 85 says two meetings.

6. C. S. Ramohanoe, the Transvaal provincial president, was reluctant to support the initiative of his executive committee. Conversation with David Bopape. Also see Document 85.

7. Z. K. Matthews, unpublished manuscript.

8. Not surprisingly, a branch that was dissatisfied with policies adopted by national headquarters could blame the working committee. Thus, the Kimberley Branch wrote to Professor Matthews on June 19, 1950 to charge that the working committee was running the ANC and calling strikes without consultation. It urged a constitutional amendment requiring the working committee to consult each member of the NEC by mail.

9. The most articulate Coloured leaders did not participate in the joint efforts but continued their association with the AAC and the NEUM. Nonetheless, representatives of the AAC sought to attend the meeting of May 14 as observers but were refused admission (Document 85).

10. The number of known Communists holding office in the ANC was very small before and after 1950. Communists who served on the national executive committee at some time during Xuma's presidency, before December 1949, were Moses Kotane, J. B. Marks, and Edwin Mofutsanyana; under Dr. Moroka, Kotane, Marks, and Dan Tloome.

   In the Cape Province and especially in Cape Town, where white Communists were prominent and Kotane was based, leading ANC members accepted Communists as members of the ANC but were strongly opposed to their holding office. Kotane, however, was a member of the ANC's national executive committee; and Professor Matthews, Cape provincial president after June 1949, considered him "more of a Nationalist than a Communist." Conversation with Z. K. Matthews.

11. The ANC's national executive committee decided in the December 1950 conference that the meeting of November 12 at which Marks was elected was improperly constituted. Beginning on April 1, 1951, administration and

429

control of the Transvaal was vested in the national working committee. At the Transvaal conference of September 30—October 1, 1951, Marks was unanimously reelected president in the Transvaal and David Bopape was elected secretary. (The NEC reviewed the dispute in its report of December 1951—Document 87a—but this review has been deleted from the document.)

12. The executive committee of the AAC said of May 1 and June 26, "Both these demonstrations, unprepared, unorganized and unco-ordinated, with the resultant loss of life, arrests, dismissals and feelings of frustration and futility, can only be called acts of criminal irresponsibility, for which the A.N.C. should be called to account." The real motive of the organizers was "to obtain [from the government] a higher price for their collaboration." Statement appended to *Minutes of the Conference of the All African Convention . . . 15th-16th December, 1950.*

13. Dr. S. M. Molema, the treasurer-general at the time, said in 1964, "It was such a small group that I cannot remember another man of standing [other than Selope Thema] who was a member."

14. Interview with "Worldover Press," Press Release, February 6, 1953.

15. A sharp contrast between money on hand or expended and money being appealed for was evident in 1950. A circular letter of June 2 to the national executive committee estimated that £75,000—or, to begin with, £7,000—was required "to mobilize the masses" for June 26. Sisulu's report on June 26 said that the ANC had paid £25 to the coordinating committee (Document 84). Sisulu also reported that a campaign had been launched to raise a £30,000 "Liberation Fund" to aid the persons victimized on June 26. A letter of July 6 from Sisulu and Cachalia to Professor Matthews noted that Dr. Molema, the treasurer-general and director of the "Liberation Fund" campaign had himself donated £253. A letter of August 5 signed by Mandela for Molema and addressed to Matthews described "our present position of financial embarrassment and general chaos of our affairs" and the impossibility of the NEC meeting that month to plan the December conference. But in December, the NEC reported that the coordinating committee had spent more than £10,000 on the June 26 campaign, most of it in aid of persons victimized. The NEC also repeated a suggestion made earlier: that membership dues should be raised from a half-crown (two shillings and sixpence) per year to one shilling a month for urban members and sixpence a month for rural members.

16. Discussed in an article criticizing Document 97, in *Discussion: Being Lectures Delivered and Discussion Held at the Forum Club, Lansdown, Cape Town*, Vol. I, No. 4, December 1951, pp. 24-35.

17. On the legislation of 1949-1951, see Carter, *op. cit.,* Chapters 3 and 4.

18. In a conversation in 1964, Golding, who styled himself a "moderate," recalled that the APO had become "completely defunct" and that its old leaders had called on him to take the lead. In later years, the CPNU tended to cooperate with the government.

19. Quoted in a memorandum by defense counsel in the treason trial of 1956-1961.

20. Seeking both Afrikaans-speaking and English-speaking support, the Torch Commando condemned as constitutionally immoral any change of the entrenched Coloured franchise by ordinary majority procedures. The movement organized processions and meetings (of up to 35,000 people on one occasion) throughout the country and in 1952 attracted nearly a quarter million members. See Carter, *op. cit.*, Chapter 12.

21. Indeed, in March 1952 they appealed for an abandonment of plans for the Defiance Campaign. Instead, the Torch Commando swung into the party battle. During April 1952 they formed a "United Democratic Front" with the United Party and the Labour Party. After the defeat of the United Party in the 1953 election, the Torch Commando lost its impetus and soon died out, although a few of its members went into the new Liberal Party.

22. Anthony Sampson, *The Treason Cage: The Opposition on Trial in South Africa* (London: Heinemann, 1958), p. 85. Sampson is in error on the date of the funeral.

23. *Minutes of a Meeting of the Executive Committee of the African National Congress . . . on the 17th June, 1951* [mimeographed]. The NEC noted that there was "sharp" controversy within the ANC regarding cooperation with the Franchise Action Council, which was organizing branches throughout Cape Province and gave signs that it might extend its activities to issues other than the franchise. Moroka appeared to believe that the Youth League supported cooperation with the council; Professor Matthews declared that the Youth League was opposed.

24. I. A. Cachalia, D. Tloome, and D. W. Bopape signed the "Recommendations of the Joint Planning Council's Sub-Committee on the Million Shillings Scheme" [undated]. This was a scheme to raise £50,000 by the end of March 1952 by selling shilling stamps.

25. The report of the Joint Planning Council "as amended by the National Executive and accepted by the Conference" was reproduced in the *Quarterly Bulletin* of the ANC (Cape), Vol. 3, No. 2, February 1952. That text is virtually identical with the report dated November 8—Document 86—and is reproduced in this volume with the minor changes in wording that appear in the *Quarterly Bulletin*.

26. The report was accepted by "a large majority," according to Sampson (*op. cit.*, p. 86), who was present. The first letter to the prime minister, Document 88, said that the conference had acted "unanimously." According to another source, only M. T. Moerane voted against adoption.

27. Conversation with Lutuli. H. Selby Msimang, in his letter referred to below, complained that the Joint Planning Council's report had not been referred to the provincial bodies and that "even members of the National Executive had seen it at the Conference for the first time."

28. Coincidentally, the Transvaal Peace Council was formed at a conference of April 28-29, 1951, in Johannesburg, convened jointly by the ANC (Transvaal), APO (Transvaal), Transvaal Indian Congress, and a Provisional Committee for a South African Peace Movement. Speakers included Dr. Molema, Yusuf Cachalia, the Rev. D. C. Thompson, and Michael Harmel, a leader of the former Communist Party. *Agenda* and *Resolutions.*

29. Conversation with the PAC Presidential Council, 1964.

30. Among those associated with the Bureau of African Nationalism and writing under pseudonyms for its occasionally published mimeographed sheets were Mda, Sobukwe, T. T. Letlaka, and J. N. Pokela. The Bureau's publications were succeeded in 1953 by *The Africanist.* That periodical circulated more openly out of Orlando, Johannesburg, than it had in East London, although the writers still used pseudonyms.

31. "Bureau of African Nationalism, The Order of the Day," two-page mimeographed newsletter "issued by Africus," undated. Youth League leaders listed were President-General: N.R.D. Mandela; Secretary-General: J. G. Matthews; President and Secretary in the Cape Province: T. T. Letlaka and S. K. Ngqangweni; President and Secretary in Natal: J. K. Ngubane and M. B. Yengwa; President and Secretary in the Transvaal: D. J. Mji and J. G. Matthews.

32. During 1950-1951, African leaders were awaiting the results of the deliberations of the Government's Commission on Native Education, which met during 1949-1951. Dr. Moroka in his presidential address in December 1951 (Document 87b) criticized the possibility that African education might be transferred from mission and provincial control to the Department of Native Affairs rather than to the preferred Department of Education. The fear was realized by the enactment of the Bantu Education Act of 1953.

33. Z. K. Matthews, "The African Response to Racial Laws," *Foreign Affairs,* Vol. 30, No. 1, October 1951, p. 97.

34. The full text of the reply (addressed to "The Secretary" of the ANC on

January 29, 1952, and signed by M. Aucamp, Private Secretary to the Prime Minister) is as follows:

Dear Sir,

I am directed to acknowledge the receipt of your undated letter addressed to the Prime Minister and to reply as follows: —

It is noted that your submission is framed in terms of a resolution adopted at its recent session in Bloemfontein of the "African National Congress." Resolutions adopted by the African National Congress at its annual meetings were, in the past, sent to and dealt with by the Minister of Native Affairs and his Department. On this occasion, however, there has been a definite departure from the traditional procedure in as much as you have addressed yourself directly to the Prime Minister in order to present him with an ultimatum. This new approach is probably accounted for by the recent rift or purge in Congress circles, after which it is doubtful whether you can claim to speak authoritatively on behalf of the body known to the Government as the African National Congress.

The Prime Minister is, however, prepared to waive this point and to reply to various points raised by you and also to your ultimatum as he feels that the Government's attitude in the matter should be clearly stated.

The first point which stands out clearly in your letter is that your organisation maintains that since 1912, although no Government in the past has even been able to consider this, the objective has been the abolition of all differentiating laws. It now demands such abolition as well as consequential direct representation in Parliament, provincial and municipal councils in all Provinces, and in all councils of State as an inherent right.

You will realise, I think, that it is self-contradictory to claim as an inherent right of the Bantu who differ in many ways from the Europeans that they should be regarded as not different, especially when it is borne in mind that these difference are permanent and not man-made. If this is a matter of indifference to you and if you do not value your racial characteristics, you cannot in any case dispute the Europeans' right, which in this case is definitely an inherent right, to take the opposite view and to adopt the necessary measures to preserve their identity as a separate community.

It should be understood clearly that the Government will under no circumstances entertain the idea of giving administrative or executive or legislative powers over Europeans, or within a European community, to Bantu men and women, or to other smaller non-European groups. The Government, therefore, has no intention of repealing the long-existing laws differentiating between European and Bantu.

You demand that the Union should no longer remain a State controlled by the Europeans who developed it to the advantage of all groups of the population. You demand that it should be placed under the jurisdiction of the Bantu, Indian and other non-European groups together with Europeans without any distinction whatsoever, and with no restriction on the possible gradual development of a completely mixed community. Nevertheless you apparently wish to create the impression that such demands should be regarded as a generous gesture of goodwill towards the European community of this country. It is quite clear that the very opposite is true. This is not a genuine offer of co-operation, but an attempt to embark on the first steps towards supplanting European rule in the course of time.

Racial harmony cannot be attained in this manner. Compliance with such demands must inevitably lead to disaster for all population groups. Not only temporary racial tension, due to misunderstanding, but worse would follow, and the Bantu would suffer first and most. For instance, if the latter were to be exposed to full competition, without their present protection, they would soon lose the land now safeguarded and being increased for them. The masses would suffer misery indeed, if they lost the many privileges which the Union of South Africa—in contrast to other countries—provides for them. They would pay the price in order to satisfy the political ambitions of the few who are prepared to tear loose from the background of their own nation. The road to peace and goodwill lies in the acceptance of the fact that separate population groups exist, and in giving each group the opportunity of developing its ambitions and capacities in its own area, or within its own community, on its own lines, in the service of its own people.

Your third point is that the differentiating laws are of an oppressive and degrading nature. This again is a totally incorrect statement. The laws are largely of a protective nature. Even those laws which are regarded as particularly irksome by the Bantu people, have not been made in order to persecute them, but for the purpose of training them in the performance of those duties which must be fully observed by all who wish to claim rights. The fact that you refer to a betterment law (Stock Limitation) as being one of the oppressive laws, is a clear indication of your failure to understand that the function of such laws is to protect the interests and the land of the Bantu Community, both present and in future.

It is even more significant that you should condemn the Bantu Authorities Act, which was designed to give the Bantu people the opportunity for enlightened administration of their own affairs in accordance with their own heritage and institutions, adapted to modern conditions. It should be clearly understood that while the Government is not prepared to grant the Bantu political equality within the European community, it is only too willing to encourage Bantu initiative, Bantu service and Bantu administration within the Bantu community, and there to allow the Bantu full scope for all his potentialities.

I must, now, refer to your ultimatum. Notwithstanding your statement that your Congress has taken the decision to present its ultimatum to the government in full appreciation of the consequences it entails, the Prime Minister wishes to call your attention to the extreme gravity of pursuing the course indicated by you. In the interests of the Bantu he advises you to reconsider your decision. Should you adhere to your expressed intention of embarking on a campaign of defiance and disobedience to the Government, and should you in the implementation thereof incite the Bantu population to defy law and order the Government will make full use of the machinery at its disposal to quell any disturbances and, thereafter, deal adequately with those responsible for inciting subversive activities of any nature whatsoever.

The Prime Minister has instructed me to urge you to let wiser counsels prevail and to devote your energies to constructive programmes of development for the Bantu people. This can be done by [using] the opportunities offered by the Government for building up local Bantu government and administration within all spheres of Bantu life.

This could be co-operation in the real sense of the word. Your organisation could render a lasting service to the Bantu population of South Africa, by helping the Government to carry out this programme of goodwill. The Prime Minister trusts that you will take these words to heart, and that you will decide to work for the welfare of your people in a constructive way.

Yours faithfully,

35. The SAIC also wrote to the prime minister but only after the ANC's correspondence was concluded. For the text of the SAIC letter, see Leo Kuper, *Passive Resistance in South Africa* (London: Jonathan Cape, 1956), pp. 242-247.

36. In the spirit of unity, Molema visited Selope Thema while in Johannesburg for the Indian Congress Conference and wrote to Msimang shortly afterward to express agreement with Msimang's effort to bring about a reconciliation between disputing groups in the Transvaal. Molema also appealed to Msimang to recognize that the ANC was "a one party organism" and that he should feel bound by majority vote. Dr. S. M. Molema to H. Selby Msimang.

37. The reply to Malan had been carefully considered at a special meeting of the national executive committee, and Professor Matthews had played a major part in drafting it.
    A sharp contrast with the ANC statements, that is, the Moroka and Molema addresses and the two letters to Malan, is to be seen in I. B. Tabata's address opening the first conference of the Society of Young Africa (SOYA) on December 20, 1951. (Document 98. The address is greatly abridged in this volume.) The AAC organized SOYA as a rival to the Youth League. It opposed the Defiance Campaign. Three-fourths of the students at Fort Hare may have been members of the Youth League or SOYA in 1952. The Youth League had the support of a majority and dominated the students' representative council.

38. The ANC claimed that 100,000 persons participated nationally (National Executive Committee Report, December 1954), and Professor Matthews (unpublished manuscript) estimated some 60,000 in Cape Province. A detective sergeant who observed the Johannesburg meeting in "Freedom Square," Fordsburg, estimated an attendance of 2,500-3,000. Transcript of Preparatory Inquiry, Regina v. Sisulu, p. 164.

39. Z. K. Matthews, unpublished manuscript. According to Mda, Lembede composed the slogan "Africa's Cause must Triumph! "

40. Sisulu and Cachalia signed a statement, "To Whom It May Concern," January 20, 1953, certifying that Professor Matthews was "the accredited representative and plenipotentiary" of the ANC and the SAIC in dealing with the General Assembly's fact-finding commission on South Africa.
    Matthews returned to South Africa on May 16, 1953. Among his published writings during this period were the following: "South Africa: A Land Divided Against Itself," *Yale Review*, June 1953, pp. 513-528; "The Crisis in South Africa," *Christianity and Crisis: A Bi-Weekly Journal of Christian Opinion*, November 10 and 24, 1952, pp. 146-149, 154-159; "The African Response to Racial Laws," *Foreign Affairs*, October 1951, pp. 91-102; "The Black Man's Outlook," *The Saturday Review of Literature*, May 2, 1953, pp. 36-41; "Apartheid Forum" [articles by Z. K. Matthews, J. J. van Schaik, and M. H. H. Louw], *International House Quarterly*,

Summer 1953, pp. 170-183; "Apartheid—Another View," *Journal of International Affairs*, VII: 2, 1953, pp. 145-150; and "Africa Today and Tomorrow" (Inaugural Address as Henry W. Luce Visiting Professor of World Christianity), Union Theological Seminary, n.d., 18 pp. *Life* asked Matthews to write an article for its "Africa" issue of May 1953 but did not print it.

41. "Statement Issued by the Joint Meeting of the Executive Committees of the African National Congress and the South African Indian Congress held at Port Elizabeth on Saturday, 31st May, 1952," Annexure "A.3" to the *Secretarial Report to the Twenty-First Conference of the South African Indian Congress, July 9-11, 1954*.

42. On July 15-16, after a trial that had attracted large crowds in the courtroom and in the street, Kotane, Marks, and Bopape were sentenced to four months' hard labor, Dadoo (who had previous convictions on his record because of his participation in the passive resistance campaign of 1946) to six months, and all were released on bail pending appeal. Over two months later, the Supreme Court upheld Kotane's appeal on narrow grounds. By then, however, all four were involved in the larger trial against 20 leaders.

43. Mimeographed form headed "National Volunteer Corps (African National Congress)."

44. *The Clarion*, June 26, 1952, p. 2.

45. *The Clarion*, July 24, 1952, reports the Sisulu trial and contains extracts of statements from the dock made on July 15-16 by Kotane, Marks, Bopape, Dadoo, and Sachs. Other extracts are in Kuper, *op. cit.*

46. These figures are taken from an unsigned memorandum of December 16, 1952, much of which is reproduced in the 1954 Secretarial Report of the SAIC. According to the report, an additional 200 persons were arrested in September and an additional 300 in October. These 500 persons were all identified as having been arrested in the Transvaal.

47. *Politics and Law in South Africa: Essays on Race Relations* (London: Merlin Press, 1963), p. 47.

48. Conversation with Tennyson Makiwane.

49. Z. K. Matthews to Dr. George Haynes, June 8, 1953. Matthews was responding to an inquiry about an interview with Max Yergan, a right-wing American Negro, published in *U.S. News and World Report*.

50. Nonwhites did not take advantage of the decision by flooding white waiting rooms. Kuper, *op. cit.*, p. 145. The magistrate was upheld by the appellate division in 1953, a few weeks before the general election, to the National-

ists' benefit. Later in the year, Parliament nullified the decision by enacting the Reservation of Separate Amenities Act. See Carter, *op. cit.*, pp. 96-97, and Kuper, *op. cit.*, p. 59.

51. The judgment is "Annexure A. 7" in the 1954 Secretarial Report of the SAIC.

52. Kuper, *op. cit.*, p. 133.

53. Quoted in *People's World*, October 23, 1952, p. 1.

54. The full text of the statement, published in *The Forum*, October, 1952, is as follows:

"We have watched with dismay the situation that has developed from the growth of the non-European movement of passive resistance against unjust laws.

"This movement clearly is no sudden impulse. It bears all the signs of careful thought and planning over many months by men who are acknowledged leaders among Africans and Indians, and who have organised it with a full appreciation of all it implies.

"The movement has met with a very remarkable response both from the mass of the people and from those to whom it appeals for voluntary personal support, and for substantial courage and sacrifice.

"In these circumstances it is clear that we South Africans face a double challenge. It is a challenge to those who hold the reins of government; and it is, not less, a challenge to all who participate in the exercise of political power, i.e., the whole white community. The challenge comes primarily from those who are excluded by reason of their race or colour from any real form of citizenship.

"Considering the movement in this light, we are sure that no good can come from merely condemning it and denouncing its leaders.

"We Europeans must frame an answer and adopt an approach to the movement that holds within it constructive possibilities.

"Otherwise we foresee a progressive worsening of race relations and an even deeper bitterness than is already visible in our country in the relations between its peoples.

"We believe that it is imperative that South Africa should now adopt a policy that will attract the support of educated, politically conscious non-Europeans by offering them a reasonable status in our common society. This can be done by a revival of the liberal tradition which prevailed for so many years with such successful results in the Cape Colony. That tradition, an integral part of South African history, was based on a firm principle, namely, *equal rights for all civilised people and equal opportunities for all men and women to become civilised.* In our opinion, only the acceptance of that fundamental principle can provide South African government with the moral basis it now lacks.

"We believe that the wise and steady application of this principle will gradually remedy the worst grievances and disabilities which non-Europeans now suffer, since their deepest feelings are stirred by the fact that our laws are not based, as they should be, on tests of civilisation and education but on race and colour.

"On their side, we ask the African and Indian leaders to recognise that it will take time and patience substantially to improve the present position. We ask them to accept the principle we have indicated as a long-term aim, and we do so in the hope that it will make negotiations possible and their success probable.

"As an immediate short-term programme of reform, we urge all who sincerely desire racial peace and harmony in our country to concentrate on demanding the repeal of the most mischievous measures on the statute book. These are measures such as the Group Areas Act, the pass laws, and the Suppression of Communism Act in its present form—measures which offend the human sense of justice as well as the canons of good government.

"Finally, we appeal to all concerned to express themselves with restraint at this disturbing time and to refrain from doing or saying anything that might aggravate the present unhappy situation."

The signatories were Margaret Ballinger, W. G. Ballinger, Edgar H. Brookes, Herbert Coblans, George W. Gale, H. J. Hanson, Ellen Hellmann, A. Winifred Hoernle, Trevor Huddleston, Ambrose Reeves, A. M. Keppel-Jones, Julius Lewin, D. McK. Malcolm, J. S. Marais, Leo Marquard, Donald B. Molteno, Mabel Palmer, Hugh Parker, Alan Paton, L. I. Rabinowitz, Saul Solomon, and J. B. Webb.

55. *Advance*, November 27, 1952, p. 7.

56. Conversation with Joseph Matthews.

57. *Advance*, December 18, 1952, p. 3.

58. *Drum*, November 1952.

59. Quoted in *Advance*, November 20, 1952, p. 4.

60. *People's World*, October 9, 1952, p. 7.

61. Conversation of Gail M. Gerhart with A. P. Mda, January 1, 1970.

62. Unpublished manuscript. Nevertheless, Ngubane wrote in *Drum* (December 1955, pp. 61-63) of the "breadth of vision and genius for statesmanship . . . during the early stages of the resistance campaign."

63. R. V. Selope Thema, "Non-European Political Moves in South Africa," *African World*, May 1952, pp. 11-12; "African National Organizations," *South African Outlook*, May 1, 1952, pp. 70-72.

64. W. M. Tsotsi, Presidential Address at AAC Conference, December 1952. "In spite of the attempts of the U.P. Press to boost the campaign and create the impression of a landslide, only a few thousand out of a population of ten million Non-Europeans have been persuaded to take part." Tsotsi expressed "admiration for the physical courage" of the defiers but condemned the ANC and SAIC leaders as criminals for demanding sacrifice without proper organizational and theoretical preparation.

65. *People's World*, September 18, 1952, p. 4. According to *People's World*, October 9, 1952, p. 1, Benghu hoped to visit the United Nations to demand repatriation of the Indians. In a cable to the UN, he said: "The defiance of 'unjust' laws and the passive resistance which is now under way do not come from the hearts of the millions of Bantu whom we represent, but out of the distorted ideas of the so-called leaders who have been bought by rich Indians and are afraid of the Group Areas Act." The government refused permission for him to go since it considered the Indian question a matter of domestic jurisdiction. *Ibid.*, October 16, 1952, p. 7.

66. *Advance*, December 18, 1952, p. 1.

67. *Ibid.*, December 18, 1952, pp. 1, 3.

68. The memorandum of December 16, 1952, prepared for the national action committee, also declared that "tremendous support" had come "from important and influential organisations in Britain, U.S.A., and in Arabian, Asian and African countries." (In the United States a small group of liberal sympathizers organized "Americans for South African Resistance," which became in 1953 the American Committee on Africa.)

69. "Statement Taken from Chief Albert J. Luthuli" [in preparation for his testimony].

70. "Our aim must be one hundred thousand members during this year, 1951 [sic]."

71. Conversation with Dr. Moroka.

72. This total was reported at the ANC's annual conference in December 1953 and was broken down as follows: Cape Province, 16,000; Transvaal, 11,000; Natal, 1,300; Orange Free State, 600. Report of the ANC Annual Conference, December 18-20, 1953.
    Some persons, having taken out a membership card, thought they had paid for life. In Cape Province, for example, members were expected to pay one shilling per month in addition to two shillings and sixpence.

73. Report by Z. K. Matthews to ANC (Cape) on April 6, 1952, in unpublished manuscript.

74. After his election in December, Lutuli attended a meeting outside Johannesburg at which an appeal for volunteers to defy produced virtually no response. "Shortly afterwards," he has written, "we brought the Campaign to an official end, rather belatedly. Its back had been broken well before this, by the skill with which the riots were engineered, and by the blatant exploiting of the riots thereafter." Albert Luthuli, *Let My People Go: An Autobiography* (London: Collins, 1962), p. 130. Nevertheless, Professor Matthews could write to two American friends on June 8 and July 9, respectively, that the campaign was in "a lull just now" and "in abeyance at the present moment." Z. K. Matthews to George E. Haynes and to George M. Houser.

DOCUMENTS – PART THREE

THE PROGRAMME OF ACTION IN 1950

Document 76. "Post-Mortem on a Tragedy." Editorial on the events of May 1, by Jordan K. Ngubane, in *Inkundla ya Bantu*, **May 20, 1950**

The unhappy events in Johannesburg on May Day have had the effect of introducing unfortunate division in our ranks at a time when we, as a community, cannot afford to weaken ourselves in the face of the aggressive mood in which the forces of oppression are in.

The Communists apparently are satisfied that they have, by stampeding our people into the May Day demonstrations, at least gained a major propaganda victory for Communism. After years of obstructing the struggle of the African people, one way or the other, now that they are about to be banned they want to go down having at least summoned a little courage to convince Moscow that they are not always the lackeys of the oppressors.

The May Day demonstration was not meant to advance the cause of the African. It is a thousand pities that Dr. Moroka, the President-General of Congress, did not realise this. The May Day demonstrations were intended to be part of a world campaign engineered by the Communists to help advance the cause of Communism and not of the oppressed African. Knowing that the African is now in mood to challenge oppression, the Communist took advantage of this and came with the idea of the demonstrations.

They have now got what they wanted. But something else now follows. They are trying to sow division in the ranks of Congress. Everybody knows that Congress has its own difficulties, which it is trying courageously to resolve. Apparently this courage does not suit the Communists. They are now attacking those who opposed their rash actions and, in the well-known Communist style, are calling them names. What are they going to gain by this?

First, most probably they might remain satisfied in the knowledge that in Dr. Moroka they have a very valuable tool. Valuable because he will ignore his own committees and followers and lead in taking decisions which result in the loss of African life without advancing the cause of Africa.

441

Secondly, for a few months there might be a little confusion in the Transvaal Congress. But the question comes up immediately: What are the African Nationalists going to do about it? The easiest thing at the moment is to attack the Communists and stop there. But the African Nationalists should go farther than that. Communism and apartheid are two similarly vicious evils. The most dangerous of those at the moment is apartheid. The African Nationalists will do well to exercise a little more statesmanship and realise that they can carry their fight against the Communists only up to a certain point if they are not going to play right into the hands of Malan. The present Government is going to finish off the Communists first, but let no one be mistaken about its real intentions. Next on the Government list is the African National Congress. Let us be quite clear about that. In view of this, it is more important to exercise statesmanship in our dealings with the Communists than to help the Malanites by weakening their political enemies.

Communism is a lesser evil to us at the moment. It will be something to deal with effectively when we rule the country with the other South Africans.

On the Congress side, it is quite clear that Dr. Moroka has started off very badly as a national leader. The very first act of leadership he took as President-General of Congress was a major blunder; it landed the Africans in disaster; it left him isolated, with the majority of his followers not with him. If he has the consolation that he is very popular with the Communists, he should also be very worried that he has shaken African confidence in himself.

In these circumstances, it will not do Congressmen much good to let the world see all the dirty washing that is being washed in the Congress backyard at present. It certainly is not good for the morale of the African masses—who await only a pointed lead against oppression. Congress has excellent machinery for resolving differences within itself—the national conference. We should like to urge all Congressmen to demand that a special conference should be called where the differences that seem to be developing inside Congress will be ironed out. Otherwise we shall have endless Press campaigns of vilification and the only people who will be helped will be the Malanites. For this reason we urge Dr. Moroka to call a special conference of Congress where his followers will present a truly united front against oppression.

Document 77. Resolution adopted at a Conference of Representatives of the Executive Committees of the ANC, South African Indian Congress, African People's Organisation, ANC Youth League, Communist Party, and Transvaal Council of Non-European Trade Unions, May 14, 1950

This emergency conference of representatives of: THE AFRICAN NATIONAL CONGRESS, THE SOUTH AFRICAN INDIAN CONGRESS, THE AFRICAN PEOPLES ORGANISATION, THE AFRICAN CONGRESS YOUTH LEAGUE, THE COMMUNIST PARTY OF SOUTH

AFRICA, THE TRANSVAAL COUNCIL OF NON EUROPEAN TRADE UNIONS, meeting in Johannesburg on Sunday, 14th May, 1950, under the auspices of the African National Congress, after careful and serious consideration, of the full implications of the UNLAWFUL ORGANISATIONS BILL, is of the emphatic opinion that this bill is the most serious threat to the civil liberties of the eleven million people of the country.

The introduction of this bill in Parliament by the present Government fully confirms our viewpoint that the Government of Dr. Malan is out to establish a totalitarian regime in the country, a regime, under which the freedom of organisation, freedom of speech, freedom of assembly and the freedom of the press will be totally destroyed. In fact with this Bill on the Statute Book, South Africa will become a fully fledged fascist state with all opposition to the racialist policy of the Government declared unlawful at the instance of the Cabinet or a Minister. In particular, this Bill is directed against the underprivileged sections of the population, whose demand for justice and equality is sought to be stifled by this far reaching measure.

It is our solemn belief that liberty is the primary right of man and that it is the privilege of no racial group to prescribe limits or apportion shares in the distribution of it. Consequently it is the bounden duty of every South African who believes in basic human rights to express his strongest condemnation of this Bill which will bring further world condemnation of South Africa, our country.

This country makes an urgent call to all South Africans, white and Non-White to take each and every effective measure for the withdrawal of this Bill. The whole country must meet this grave challenge with unity of purpose and determination so that freedom is not totally extinguished in this country of racial oppression.

The NATIONAL ORGANISATIONS present here jointly pledge themselves to take immediate steps to mobilise all sections of the South African people to offer concrete mass opposition to this vicious Bill with the aim of defeating it.

Document 78. Statement of the National Executive Committee of the ANC in an Emergency Meeting on May 21, 1950

An emergency meeting of the National Executive of the African National Congress was held at Thaba 'Nchu on Sunday, May 21st 1950, to discuss the attitude of the African National Congress to the Unlawful Organisations Bill now before Parliament, and to consider ways and means of organising and directing the opposition of the African people to the proposed legislation.

It was unanimously decided to issue the following statement:

1. Although the Unlawful Organisations Bill purports to be directed against Communism in general and the Communist Party of South Africa in

particular, the A.N.C. Executive is satisfied, from a study of the provisions of this Bill, that it is primarily directed against the Africans and other oppressed people, and is designed to frustrate all their attempts to work for the fulfilment of their legitimate demands and aspirations. The Bill is a further example of the determination of the white people of this country to keep the African in permanent subordination.

It goes without saying that the African people are equally determined that they are not going to remain in that position forever.

The A.N.C. is resolved to oppose this and other measures of a similar nature by all means at its disposal.

2. As a first step it was agreed to launch a campaign for a national day of protest. It is suggested that, on this day, to mark their general dissatisfaction with the position in this country, the African people should refrain from going to work, and regard this day as a day of mourning for all those Africans who lost their lives in the struggle for liberation. The actual date on which this protest will be held, will be announced in due course. Preparations for the day will, however, commence immediately.

Document 79. "United Anti-Fascist Rally." Flyer announcing rally in Durban on May 28, 1950, to be addressed by Dr. J.S. Moroka, [n.d.]

FIGHT
GESTAPO & GHETTO BILLS

THEY THREATEN YOUR LIVES

ATTEND
UNITED ANTI-FASCIST RALLY
SUNDAY 28TH MAY - 2.30 P.M.

RED SQUARE

Convened Jointly by:

African National Congress (Natal), Natal Indian Congress, A.P.O. (Coloured People's Organisation), African National Congress Youth League, African Women's Association, Communist Party (Durban District).

Councillor A. W. G. CHAMPION, President of Natal African Congress, will introduce Dr. J. S. MOROKA, President-General of African National Congress.

WHAT THEY MEAN

THE GESTAPO BILL
(The Unlawful Organisations Bill)

is designed to silence all opposition to the Nationalists' Apartheid policy. If the Bill becomes law all organisations, persons and publications who disagree with the Government will be banned and all who defy the law will be thrown into jail. A Fascist Republic will be set up where all freedom of speech and assembly will be crushed and where police rule will terrorise the people.

THE GHETTO BILL
(The Group Areas Bill)

is designed to create overcrowded and neglected ghettoes in which the African, Indian, and the Coloured peoples will be forced to live under most intolerable conditions. The Ghetto life will make it impossible for the Non-European to make any economic progress whatsoever. Severe unemployment and disgraceful slums will be the order of the day! These follow on the Native Lands Segregation Laws, which have disgraced this country in the eyes of the world.

WE MUST DEFEAT THESE BILLS!

Document 80. Statement on a National Day of Protest, by the Central Executive Committee of the ANC Youth League (Transvaal), May 31, 1950

The Youth League stands solidly behind the decision taken by the Executive of the African National Congress on May 21st, at Thaba 'Nchu, viz that a National Day of Protest be organised throughout the Country.

This decision to us has a special significance. Our stand is uncompromising opposition to the "UNLAWFUL ORGANISATIONS BILL", which is the precipitating cause for the unprecedented step we intend to take. The protest is to us a manifestation of all those divine stirrings of discontent of the African people since 6th, April 1652, onward—through the period of the so-called Kaffir Wars, through the days of Dingana, through the days of Moshoeshoe, through the days of Sekhukhuni against the Grondwet, through the days of the Treaty of Vereeniging, through the days of the White Union Pact of 1910.

To add insult to injury, the oppressors were yet to rob us of the land—The Natives Land Act of 1913; and as one sin leads to another:

> COLOUR BAR ACT!
> NATIVES ADMINISTRATION ACT!
> NATIVES URBAN AREAS ACT!
> INDUSTRIAL CONCILIATION ACT!
> NATIVES REPRESENTATION ACT!

RIOTOUS ASSEMBLIES ACT!
"POLL TAX ACT"
"PASSES ACT"
"LIQUOR RAIDS ACT"
"LOCATION SUPERINTENDENTS ACT"
"NATIVE COMMISSIONERS ACT"
"MINISTER OF NATIVE AFFAIRS ACT"
"STARVATION AND DISEASES ACT"
"SHANTY TOWNS ACT"
"FARM PRISONS ACT"
"STOCK LIMITATIONS ACT"
"BAASSKAP ACT"
"TRIBAL AREAS ACT"

and last SIN of all the
"UNLAWFUL ORGANISATIONS BILL"—which, interpreted simply, means that anyone who complains of HUNGER and VERMIN in a BREEZE—BLOCK SHELTER or HESSIAN SHACK has committed a crime against the state—a FASCIST STATE.

What is more significant to us is that for the first time since 1652 African National Leaders are going to stage SIMULTANEOUSLY a forceful opposition to our oppressors. If Makana, Dingana, Khama and Sekhukhuni had defended their country jointly, Africa would have been saved for posterity. Now, for the first time in the history of South Africa, the people intend to offer a joint National Opposition at all costs, even if the Government intends repeating the events that occured at *Bulhoek* and *Bondelswart*, the painful memory of which looms vividly in our minds. Even if that were to come, the African people have been nerved for it.

We want to warn the Government—especially the Department of Justice, Defence and Native Affairs—that no physical might in the world can crush the invincible spirit of a nation. AFRICA'S CAUSE MUST TRIUMPH.

The African people have pledged themselves to liberate South Africa—BLACK, WHITE and YELLOW, and to that end the impending national crisis presages the shape of things to come. The names of Organisations can be banned, leaders can be imprisoned, but the spirit and aspirations of a people can never be subdued. The scroll of the World History is littered with examples.

Our cause is just, our aspirations noble; VICTORY CANNOT BUT BE OURS.

UP YOU MIGHTY RACE!

VUKA AFRIKA!

TSOGA AFRIKA!

Document 81. Letter on plans for June 26, from the Rev. J. J. Skomolo to Professor Z. K. Matthews, June 16, 1950

St. Peter's Mission

16-6-50

My dear Chief;

I am writing you a private letter. The national executive has agreed on the sit down strike on June the 26th. My chief, let us not carry our brains in our feet. We must study the conditions and internal affairs of the nation. We are a conquered nation, this we must admit. Let us face practical truths. Through the May Day strikes, our people lost lives, properties and jobs, and have had no redress. Before these wounds are healed, we are again formulating another strike. The nation is not ready. If we are to be at the mercy of the Communist Party, take it from me, the Congress hasn't got another year to live. The Engine and brain of the Congress cannot be the communist influence.

Take these into accounts. There are poor widows by their thousands whose children do not eat until the mother comes back from the white man's kitchen carrying scraps of food left at the table. If this woman does not go to the kitchen to cook for the white boss, are we to feed her children that day? The next she finds another woman already employed; are we to give her work? There are several other instances which render this strike business of any form at present impracticable.

There are cases where we have to retreat according to plan and organise. That is strategy. We cannot achieve all over one night. There are other means by which we can make our voice heard. Remember, the strike hits friend and foe, while Swarts in the house of Parliament is scott free. He will not suffer a thing. As a member of the national executive, and you as president of this province, use all your influence that the nation is not ready. No army ever marched into the battle unarmed and untrained. That is what we are now doing. We are dividing the nation into two or several hostile camps. Chiefs under the jackboot of the ruler set against the urban labourer and the end will be that Congress will stink in the nostrils of the whole nation. Let us take into account the national groups to be used against the strikers. Africans against others.

We are now in Basutoland divided. The chiefs and the Administration arrayed against the Basuto strikers.

I will be the saddest of men if Congress is dragged into this confusing issue. I was at E.L. and the Communist Congress members invited Kotane to come by air ahead of me to disorganise my Congress meetings for which I was invited. This he tried, whenever I reached a certain part of the location I was at his heels. The people were hostile against the preaching of strikes.

I poured water and got a lot of new members. I will after the conference sacrifice my time again and organise since you, Bokwe & Mzamane are at the head of the affairs.

Yours for Africa,

J. J. Skomolo

P.S. The Communists' sinister move is to get into all Congress branches to disrupt Congress from within.

Document 82. "Monday 26th June, National Day of Protest and Mourning." Flyer issued by the Natal Co-ordinating Committee, [n.d.]

MONDAY 26TH JUNE

NATIONAL DAY OF
PROTEST AND MOURNING

PICTURE

PEOPLE'S LEADERS AT DURBAN PROTEST MEETING OF 20,000 PEOPLE ON 28TH MAY 1950.

OUR LEADERS APPEAL:

MONDAY, 26th JUNE will be observed throughout South Africa as a National Day of protest and Mourning. This decision was taken by leaders of the Non-European National Organisations after a call had been made by Dr. J. S. Moroka, the President-General of the African National Congress. Africans, Indians, Coloureds and European democrats are asked to demonstrate their opposition to the Group Areas Bill and the Suppression of Communism (Unlawful Organisations) Bill by answering this call to defend their liberties and freedom and to fight against the Nationalist Government's policy of apartheid, tyranny and oppression.

● SCHOOLS AND STUDENTS

All Schools must be closed on this day and children and students must remain at home. Parents must not send their children to School on MONDAY, 26th JUNE.

● FACTORIES AND WORKERS

Factory owners and employers must give their workers a holiday and workers must remain at home on this day of protest, mourning and prayer.

● SHOPS AND BUSINESSES

All shop-keepers, merchants, stall-holders, farmers, hawkers, tea-room owners, professionals and other business people must observe this day of Hartal and have their places of business closed on this historic day in the lives of our people.

United, We will Win Freedom!

Issued by the Natal Co-ordinating Committee on instructions from the National Protest Day Committee of the African National Congress, African Peoples' Organisation, South African Indian Congress, Communist Party of South Africa.

Document 83. "National Day of Protest and Mourning, Stay at Home on Monday, 26th June!" Flyer issued by [twelve persons], June 15, 1950

NATIONAL DAY OF PROTEST AND MOURNING

STAY AT HOME
ON
MONDAY, 26TH JUNE!

A CALL TO THE PEOPLE OF CAPE TOWN

The four leading organisations of the people in South Africa—the African National Congress, the South African Indian Congress, the A.P.O. and the Communist Party, have declared MONDAY, 26th JUNE, 1950, as a NATION-AL DAY OF PROTEST against the Group Areas Bill and the Suppression of Communism Bill, and as a DAY OF MOURNING for all those who have lost their lives in the struggle for liberation in South Africa.

In his appeal to the people of South Africa to observe MONDAY, 26th JUNE, by remaining at home on that day, Dr. J. S. Moroka, President-General of the African National Congress, stated:—

"The African National Congress and other National and local organisa-tions are required by the clear implications of the Suppression of Communism Bill to fight the last fight against the Pass Laws, against low wages, against the Urban Areas Act, the Group Areas Bill, the Riotous Assemblies Act, lack of housing accommodation, of franchise rights, of educational facilities and against every other disability which has been and is the lot of the ruled in this country."

In Durban, Johannesburg and all the main centres in South Africa the people will be staying at home on MONDAY, 26th JUNE.

We, the undersigned, call upon the people of Cape Town to play their part in the struggle for freedom, and observe MONDAY, 26th JUNE, by staying quietly in their homes, closing their shops, and keeping their children from school.

> Down with the Group Areas Bill!
> Down with the Suppression of Communism Bill!
> Down with Nationalist Tyranny!
> Long live the struggle for Freedom and Equality!

Signed:

COUNCILLOR A. ISMAIL	N. D. KOTA
J. N. NGWEVELA	COUNCILLOR S. DOLLIE
MOSES M. KOTANE	J. W. G. ALLEN
SUNDRA PILLAY	E. A. PARKER
JOSEPH NKATLO	CLR. SAM KAHN, M.P.
F. CARNESON, M.P.C.	R. NDIMANDE

STAY AT HOME FOR FREEDOM
ON MONDAY, 26th JUNE!

(Issued by F. Carneson, P.O. Box 1176, Cape Town, on behalf of the above. June 15, 1950.)
Printed by Pioneer Press (Pty.), Ltd., 27, Oxford Street, Woodstock

Document 84. "Report on the National Day of Protest, June 26, 1950." Issued by the Secretary-General of the ANC and initialed by Nelson R. Mandela, July 26, 1950

At the Emergency Meeting of the National Executive of the African National Congress held at Thaba 'Nchu on Sunday, May 21st 1950, the attitude of the A.N.C., to the Suppression of Communism Act (then called the Unlawful Organisations Bill) was discussed. It was agreed to launch a campaign for a National Day of Protest. It was suggested that on that day, to mark their general dissatisfaction with the position in this country the African people should refrain from going to work and regard that day as a Day of Mourning for all those Africans who lost their lives in the struggle for liberation. The actual date on which the Protest would be held would be announced in due course. The Secretary General was instructed to communicate with the leaders of the other National Organisations to establish a machinery for the implementation of this decision.

Following upon this resolution, and after consultation with leaders of other National Organisations, a National Day of Protest Coordinating Committee was set up with head-quarters in Johannesburg. The composition of the Committee was originally planned to consist of seven members from the African National Congress, and two representatives from each of the following organisations:—The South African Indian Congress, the African Peoples' Organisation, the Communist Party of South Africa and the Transvaal Council of Non-European Trade Unions. The Presidents of the A.N.C., the S.A.I.C., the A.P.O. and Chairman of the C.P. were to be ex-officio members of this Committee, making a total of nineteen members. Only the A.N.C., S.A.I.C. and the C.P. were actually represented on the Committee.

The African Peoples' Organisation passed the following resolutions:—

"That the A.P.O. supports the proposed Day of Mourning with the following proviso, namely, that proper organisation be carried out and that we then assess our organisational strength and, to expedite this matter, a United Front be established on the following basis:

1. Anti-Segregation.
2. Equal Rights for All.
3. Against the Bills."

Furthermore, the A.P.O. felt that the precipitate manner in which the Day of Mourning was declared left the participating bodies very little time to build up their organisation and prepare their members for the Day of Protest. The Transvaal Council of Non-European Trade Unions supported the Protest morally. They sent no representatives to the Committee. The representation of the Communist Party of South Africa automatically lapsed when the Party dissolved.

On the 11th June 1950, the President-General, acting on the authority of the National Executive, and after consulting with the other National leaders, released a Press Statement declaring Monday June 26, 1950 a National Day of Protest and called upon the African People in their united millions to observe it as such by refraining from going to work on that Day, and appealed to all South Africans of all races to respond to the call of their leaders for the observance of this unique day in the history of South Africa. The Presidents of the S.A.I.C., and A.P.O. and Chairman of the C.P. pledged the wholehearted active support of their organisations to this call and appealed to the white voters and working class of South Africa to join the struggle for the defeat of these tyrannical measures and for the extension of democracy to all.

The head-quarters of the National Day of Protest Committee were at the offices of the A.N.C., Johannesburg. Messrs W.M. Sisulu and Y.A. Cachalia were elected Joint Secretaries. Mr. N.R.D. Mandela was placed in charge of the office. Members of the National Executive and other leading members of Congress were given specific duties. Dr. J.S. Moroka and Mr. O.R. Tambo visited Natal to assist in the implementation of this decision. Mr. Sisulu toured the Eastern Province concentrating in Port Elizabeth and East London. Mr. Gaur Radebe went to the O.F.S. Messrs C.S. Ramohanoe and E. Mofutsanyana also toured the Free State. Mr. D. Tloome toured the Western Transvaal and Kimberley. Mr. Moses Kotane was instructed to organise the Western Province.

Provincial, district, regional and local Coordinating Committees were established throughout the country.

Soon after the Emergency Meeting at Thaba 'Nchu, young men and women spontaneously came forward and freely placed their services at the disposal of the National Executive. Mr. Diliza Mji, a fourth year Medical Student at the University of the Witwatersrand, gave up his studies and devoted himself full-time to the campaign. Mr. Mji was sent down to Durban where he did outstanding service.

An amount of approximately £ 150 (One hundred and Fifty pounds) was spent by the A.N.C. before the N.D.P.C.C. took over. Out of this amount £ 25 (Twenty-five pounds) was paid to the N.D.P.C.C. as a contribution by the A.N.C. towards the funds of the Committee.

As a result of the National Day of Protest a number of people were victimised especially in Durban where a large number of workers lost their jobs. The Committee had to assume the responsibility of maintaining these people. To meet this situation, a fund raising campaign has been launched with the aim of raising £ 30,000. I might mention that a big debt was incurred by the Committee in organising the campaign for a National Day of Protest and funds have to be raised to redeem this liability. With this end in view, a team of collectors has been sent out to various parts of the country to appeal for donations. An Entertainment Committee has been set up to raise funds by staging concerts, tea-parties, bazaars and similar functions.

A further report on the results of this fund raising campaign will be submitted in due course.

Having regard to the fact that the Committee had only two weeks to prepare, and in the face of intensive and relentless police intimidation, and after studying the reports from various parts of the country, I am perfectly satisfied that, as a political strike, Monday June 26, was an outstanding success. Full details regarding this fact are contained in the report of the National Day of Protest Coordinating Committee which is attached herein.

Document 85. Draft Report of the National Executive Committee of the ANC, submitted to the Annual Conference, December 15-17, 1950

INTRODUCTION:

1. The year 1950 was a turning point in the political history of the African people in this country. It was marked by a number of events which took place from the beginning of the year. These events indicated a new political outlook on the part of the African people. The events showed quite clearly that the conditions under which the African people live have become intolerable and that the masses are marching far ahead of the leadership. The gravity of the developments among the masses is no doubt a serious one to the leadership of the African people.

2. The 1949 Conference of the A.N.C. adopted a Programme of Action which was to serve as a guide to the African people in the struggle for liberation. The Programme of Action indicated a definite form of struggle for the African people and reflected a new attitude towards the oppresser and demanded the National Independence of the African people as a nation.

INTERNATIONAL SITUATION:

3. Since we met in our annual Conference last year the international situation has shown serious developments. The conflict between West and East has become sharper as never before, which conflict endangers world peace. As a result of which the Korean soil has now become the battlefield.
4. Your National Executive issued a statement on the question to the effect that the creation of the artificial "38th Parallel" was not in the interests of the Korean people. The attitude of the African National Congress is that the Korean people are competent to solve their own problems.

SOUTH AFRICA:

5. The policy of the white rulers in South Africa has undoubtedly aggravated the relations between the whites and the Non-whites. The Nationalist Government has this year gone a step further towards tyranny and the establishment of a police state by introducing two most notorious laws namely the Group Areas Act and the Suppression of Communism Act.
6. The Group Areas Act is designed to intensify the policy of Apartheid to which the Nationalist Government is wedded. It is intended to ruin the Indian community economically and to divide the African people into tribal sections thereby weakening their political solidarity in their fight for national liberation.
7. Although the Suppression of Communism Act purports to be directed against Communism in general and the Communist Party of South Africa in particular; we are satisfied from a study of the provisions of this Act that it is primarily directed against the African and other oppressed people and is designed to frustrate all their attempts to work for the fulfillment of their legitmate demands and aspirations.
8. The African people and other democrats have demonstrated their opposition against such stern measures.

COUNCIL OF ACTION:

9. The National Executive met on the 10th February 1950, in Johannesburg. The Council of Action was appointed having as its Chairman Dr. Moroka, and four others....

RIOTS:

On the 29th January, the police raided Newclare and assaulted some Africans and arrested certain others. This was resented by the people of Newclare. Consequently a fight ensued resulting in the death of two Africans. President General and a number of members of the National Executive visited the area and addressed a big meeting. On the same date a riot also took place in Benoni and in Durban. A statement was issued by the WORKING COMMITTEE on these incidents. On the 13th February another riot occurred in Newclare which also resulted in the death of one African. On this day some shops were burnt. This second riot took a turning point against Asiatics. Members of the Working Committee worked very hard with the co-operation of the other Provincial and Local leaders. A Telegram demanding the withdrawal of the Police was sent to the Minister of Justice after which the District Commandant summoned a meeting between his Department and the Local leaders of Newclare. The Secretary-General attended as an observer. The leaders insisted on the withdrawal of the Police. The Police were withdrawn and the trouble was over.

MAY DAY.

On the 26th of March 1950 a Conference was convened by a body called the "DEFEND FREE SPEECH CONVENTION"—a body consisting of the AFRICAN NATIONAL CONGRESS (TVL.) BRANCH, (TVL) INDIAN CONGRESS, A.P.O. and the COMMUNIST PARTY (JOHANNESBURG DISTRICT). Dr. J.S. Moroka presided at this Conference. This meeting decided, among other things, to observe "MAY DAY" as a "Freedom Day" when people were advised not to go to work in the Transvaal. On April, 1950, MR. C.S. RAMOHANOE, the Transvaal-President, issued a statement asking the Branches of the Transvaal not to participate until a ruling was given by the National Executive. On April 24th, the following statement was issued by the Working Committee:

"The Annual Conference of the AFRICAN NATIONAL CONGRESS, held in Bloemfontein last year adopted a Programme of Action to be carried out by Congress Branches throughout South Africa. There has now been established in the Transvaal the Defend Free Speech Convention, which has decided on and is carrying out its own Programme of Action."

"May Day", however, was observed.

In the afternoon of the 1st May, the Police opened fire, using stern guns and other weapons, wherein 19 Africans lost their lives and 30 others were wounded in the following areas: - BENONI, ORLANDO, ALEXANDRA and SOPHIATOWN.

NATIONAL DAY OF PROTEST AND MOURNING.

On the 14th May, 1950, an Emergency Conference was summoned by the Working Committee of the A.N.C. which was attended by the following Organisations: S.A.INDIAN CONGRESS, A.P.O., A.N.C.YOUTH LEAGUE, COUNCIL OF NON-EUROPEAN TRADE UNIONS and the COMMUNIST PARTY of SOUTH AFRICA. The delegates for the A.A.C., who attended as observers, were refused admission.

After a lengthy discussion on the "Unlawful Organisations Bill" (now "The Suppression of Communism Act") and the "Group Areas Bill", the Conference decided that the matter be referred to the respective National Executives of the Organisations represented for their considerations.

An Emergency meeting of the National Executive met at Thaba 'Nchu on May 21st,1950. After three hours discussion on the "Unlawful Organisations Bill," it was unanimously agreed that there be a National Day of Protest and Mourning, as a Protest against these Bills and other discriminatory measures. The date to be fixed by the President-General in consultation with other National Leaders who had attended the Emergency Conference on the 14th May,1950. Subsequently the President General of the A.N.C. Dr. J.S. MOROKA, declared JUNE 26TH, 1950 as a *"NATIONAL DAY OF PROTEST AND MOURN-ING"*, followed by the following leaders: -

Dr. G.M. Naicker, President of the S. A. I. C.

Mr. S.M. Rahim, President of the A.P.O. and

Mr. I. Horvitch, Chairman of the C.P. of S.Africa.

A vigorous campaign was launched throughout the country calling upon the people to observe this historic day.

A Co-ordinating Committee was formed with its Head-quarters in Johannesburg. The functions of this Committee were to direct and conduct the campaign.

While we did not achieve the desired results on this historic day, we, however, feel quite satisfied that the people of South Africa are behind us. This was demonstrated by a complete stoppage of work at Port Elizabeth, Uitenhage, Durban, Ladysmith, Evaton and Alexandra Township. Partial stoppage of work took place at the following centres:— Johannesburg and the Witwatersrand, Danhauser, Bloemfontein, Grahamstown, Capetown and other centres. In the face of such a short period hardly a month between the disastrous "May Day" and the National Day of Protest, yet the Africans responded to the clarion call of the National leaders of our Non-European people. The response was very poor in the Transvaal. Police intimidation during May Day; also, fieldworkers did not come up to expectation.

THE AFTERMATH OF THE NATIONAL DAY OF PROTEST AND MOURNING.

The people of Durban suffered most, in that about a thousand workers were dismissed from employment. The Co-ordinating Committee was responsible for the payment of maintenance grants for the victims for the first six weeks at the Unemployment Benefit rates which cost the Committee about £ 500 per week. This was well handled by the able leadership of the Natal Co-ordinating Committee. Payments are still being made to those who have recently been dismissed by the Municipal authorities. There is also the case of Chief Walter Kumalo who has been victimised by the Government because of the prominent

455

part he played during the campaign. The campaign has cost the Co-ordinating Committee more than £ 10,000, some of the liabilities thereof have yet to be met.

A number of our field workers were arrested in all parts of the country. Some of the cases are still pending. This is an indication that the struggle is not over. Our people behaved extremely well on the 26th of June in spite of the intimidation by the police. It must be taken into account that this was the first attempt at a political strike on a national scale by the Non-European people of this country. We must therefore compliment our people for their solidarity and loyalty in the cause of the struggle for liberation.

ORGANISATION

ADMINISTRATIVE WORK

Following are the number of meetings held by the various Committees during the year:

National Executive Committee, 5
Working Committee, 8
Council of Action, 2

Both the President-General and the Secretary-General have visited all the four Provinces during the year. The Treasurer-General, the Secretary for the Council of Action and some members of the National Executive have visited some of the Provinces.

Our organisation, as you all know is based on the division of the National organisation into four Provincial branches. I have pleasure to state that there has been a general increase of membership throughout the country and new branches have been established in various places.

ACTIVITIES

TRANSVAAL

This Province has handled the Compulsory Endorsement and evictions of Africans in some of the farms. The protest against the carrying of passes by women revived the women's section. The Youth League tackled the educational aspect and has played a leading part in the establishment of a National School in Sophiatown. Among other things handled this year are the riots at Newclare and also the victims of the May Day tragedy. The Youth League has started a Bulletin known as the "LODESTAR".

CAPE

This Province is fighting hard against the introduction of the pass system. Kimberley is fighting the matter in the Supreme Court. Queenstown has successfully fought against this measure and its victory has raised the prestige of Congress in the area.

The Cape has also a bulletin for educating their members, something which must be encouraged in all the Provinces. This bulletin is known as "ILIZWE LAM" (My country). The Port Elizabeth branch has been very active and wound up the year by a mammoth Youth Rally which was attended by the President-General and some members of the National Executive and also by people from various Provinces.

NATAL

Natal is on the march in spite of its internal difficulties. The Youth League has been busy throughout the year and has tackled vigorously the introduction of passes for women. It assisted the Provincial Secretary in raising funds for the case of Chief Walter Kumalo. Like other Provinces it has also started a bulletin known as "VUKAYIBAMBE" which is published in Zulu.

O.F.S.

The situation which had developed in the Free State as reported in the last Conference was settled amicably by the Province at its Conference held early in October by the election of office-bearers and Committee members. The newly elected President and Secretary are very responsive to instructions from the head office. During the Witzieshoek incident the President was on the spot.

Having dealt with all the Provinces, your Executive will be failing in its duty if it does not put on record the wonderful work which has been done by the four branches viz. Port Elizabeth, Newclare, Springs and Durban Youth League. The standard of these branches must be the example to all the branches of Congress throughout the country.

ORGANISATIONAL DIFFICULTIES

1. The machinery of Congress leaves much to be desired. A subscription of 2/6 per member per year cannot be expected to maintain an organisation like Congress. In order to carry on the struggle we require sufficient funds.
2. There is a general negligence of duty on the part of the officials of Congress. Positions are used as positions of honour, there is no response to correspondence and instructions.
3. There is lack of faith in the struggle and of course we lack propaganda organs such as the press.
4. We are denied freedom of assembly, freedom of speech and freedom of movement.

These are the difficulties which Congress has to solve sooner or later.

REMEDIES

a) A resolution to the effect that Congress members must pay a monthly subscription of a 1/- in the urban areas and 6d in the rural areas was further considered by the Executive and it is suggested that the Constitution must be amended accordingly.

b) Political education will help the co-ordination and co-operation of all branches of Congress which is necessary and essential.

c) Strict discipline must be enforced. This too must be inserted in the Constitution.

d) Congress must devise ways and means in this Conference of taking an advantage of the "Inkundla Ya Bantu" which the directors are willing to offer to us on reasonable terms.

e) On the freedom of speech and assembly, the Programme of Action provides an answer, on the item of civil disobedience. In other words, the National Executive will have to consider the question of how soon it can put this into operation, as it is the only remedy for the situation.

f) Literature to supply to Provinces and branches will have to be done by the head office. This method will not only be cheap but will be more effective. The policy of Congress must be translated into vernacular so as to enable every Congressite to know what Congress stands for and what it is.

In conclusion I submit this report on behalf of my Executive with the hope that it will receive the attention it deserves, from every delegate in this conference. I believe that if Congress is to be a force in the liberation of the African people in this country, then it must of necessity put its machinery in order. It must teach its members responsibility and the division of labour.

The gravity and the seriousness of the situation must be fully realised. Loyalty to the ideals which we stand for and the spirit of sacrifice must receive paramount importance above all else.

Africa's cause must triumph.

MOVING TOWARD DEFIANCE

Document 86. Report of the Joint Planning Council of the ANC and the South African Indian Congress, signed by Dr. J. S. Moroka, J. B. Marks, W. M. Sisulu, Dr. Y. M. Dadoo, and Y. Cachalia, November 8, 1951

To the President-General and Members of the Executive Committee of the African National Congress and the President and Councillors of the South African Indian Congress:

WHEREAS the African National Congress, at its meeting of its National Executive, held on 17th June 1951, decided to invite all other National Executives of the National organizations of the non-European people of South Africa to a Conference to place before them a programme of direct action, and,

WHEREAS a Joint Conference of the National Executives of the African National Congress and the South African Indian Congress and the Representatives of the Franchise Action Council (Cape) met at Johannesburg on the 29th July, 1951, and

WHEREAS it was resolved at the aforesaid Conference:

(1) to declare war on Pass Laws and Stock Limitation, the Group Areas Act, the Voters' Representation Act, the Suppression of Communism Act and the Bantu Authorities Act;

(2) to embark upon an immediate mass campaign for the repeal of these oppressive laws, and

(3) to establish a Joint Planning Council to co-ordinate the efforts of the National Organisations of the African, Indian and Coloured peoples in this mass campaign

NOW THEREFORE, the Joint Planning Council, as constituted by the aforegoing resolution, have the honour to report to the African National Congress and the South African Indian Congress as follows:—

1.

We the undersigned, were constituted into a Joint Planning Council in terms of the resolution adopted at the Joint Conference of the Executives of the African National Congress and the South African Indian Congress and the representatives of the Franchise Action Council of the Cape, held at Johannesburg on the 29th July, 1951. Dr. J. S. Moroka, the President-General of the African National Congress, was elected as the Chairman and of the four remaining members of the Council, two each were nominated by the Executive Organs of the African National Congress and the South African Indian Congress.

2.

We are, in terms of the resolution mentioned above, charged with the task of co-ordinating the efforts of the National Organisations of the African, Indian and the Coloured peoples in a mass campaign agreed upon at the Joint Conference for the repeal of the Pass Laws, the Group Areas Act, the Voters' Representation Act, the Suppression of Communism Act, the Bantu Authorities Act, and for the withdrawal of the policy of stock limitation and the so-called rehabilitation scheme.

3.

Having given due and serious attention to the task before us, we have great pleasure in recommending the following plan of action to the African National Congress and the South African Indian Congress for consideration and decision at their forthcoming annual Conference.

4.

The African National Congress in Conference assembled at Bloemfontein on the 15th - 17th December, 1951, should call upon the Union Government to repeal the aforementioned acts by *NOT LATER THAN 29TH FEBRUARY, 1952*. This call should be supported by the Conference of the South African Indian Congress and by all other democratic organizations which find themselves in full agreement with it.

5.

In the event of the Government failing to take action for the repeal of these Acts which cannot be tolerated by the people any longer, the two Congresses will embark upon mass action for a redress of the just and legitimate grievances of the majority of the South African people. It is our considered opinion that such mass action should commence on the *6th April, 1952*, the Van Riebeck Tercentary. We consider this day to be most appropriate for the commencement of the struggle as it marks one of the greatest turning points in South African history by the advent of European settlers in this country, followed by colonial and imperialist exploitation which has degraded, humiliated and kept in bondage the vast masses of the non-White people.

Or, alternatively,

on *June 26th, 1952*. We consider this day equally as significant as April the 6th for the commencement of the struggle as it also ranks as one of the greatest turning points in South African history. On this day we commemorate the National Day of Protest held on 26th June, 1950, the day on which on the call of the President-General of the African National Congress, Dr. J. S. Moroka, this country witnessed the greatest demonstration of fraternal solidarity and unity of purpose on the part of all sections of the non-European people in the national protest against unjust laws. The 26th June was one of the first steps towards freedom. It is an historical duty that on this day we should pay tribute to the fighting spirit, social responsibility and political understanding of our people; remember the brave sacrifices of the people and pay our homage to all those who had given their very lives in the struggle for freedom.

Although we have suggested two alternative dates, the Joint Planning Council strongly favours the earlier date as it considers that three calendar months would give the people ample time to set the machinery of struggle into motion.

6.

With regard to the form of struggle best suited to our conditions we have been constrained to bear in mind the political and economic set-up of our country, the relationship of the rural to the urban population, the development of the trade union movement with particular reference to the disabilities and state of organization of the non-white workers, the economic status of the various

460

sections of the non-white people and the level of organization of the National Liberatory movements. We are therefore of the opinion that in these given historical conditions the forms of struggle for obtaining the repeal of unjust laws which should be considered are:—

(a) defiance of unjust laws and (b) industrial action.

7.

In dealing with the two forms of struggle mentioned in paragraph six, we feel it necessary to re-iterate the following fundamental principle which is the kernel of our struggle for freedom:

ALL PEOPLE IRRESPECTIVE OF THE NATIONAL GROUPS THEY MAY BELONG TO, AND IRRESPECTIVE OF THE COLOUR OF THEIR SKIN, ARE ENTITLED TO LIVE A FULL AND FREE LIFE ON THE BASIS OF THE FULLEST EQUALITY. FULL DEMOCRATIC RIGHTS WITH A DIRECT SAY IN THE AFFAIRS OF THE GOVERNMENT ARE THE INALIENABLE RIGHTS OF EVERY INDIVIDUAL—A RIGHT WHICH IN SOUTH AFRICA MUST BE REALISED NOW IF THE COUNTRY IS TO BE SAVED FROM SOCIAL CHAOS AND TYRANNY AND FROM THE EVILS ARISING OUT OF THE EXISTING DENIAL OF FRANCHISE RIGHTS TO VAST MASSES OF THE POPULATION ON GROUNDS OF RACE AND COLOUR. THE STRUGGLE WHICH THE NATIONAL ORGANIZATIONS OF THE NON-EUROPEAN PEOPLE ARE CONDUCTING IS NOT DIRECTED AGAINST ANY RACE OR NATIONAL GROUP BUT AGAINST THE UNJUST LAWS WHICH KEEP IN PERPETUAL SUBJECTION AND MISERY VAST SECTIONS OF THE POPULATION. IT IS FOR THE TRANSFORMATION OR CREATION OF CONDITIONS WHICH WILL RESTORE HUMAN DIGNITY, EQUALITY AND FREEDOM TO EVERY SOUTH AFRICAN.

We believe that without realization of these principles, race hatred and bitterness cannot be eliminated and the overwhelming majority of the people cannot find a firm foundation for progress and happiness in South Africa.

It is to be noted, however, that the present campaign of defiance of unjust laws is only directed for the purposes of securing the repeal of those unjust laws mentioned in the resolution of the Joint Conference.

8.

Plan of Action. We recommend that the struggle for securing the repeal of unjust laws be *DEFIANCE OF UNJUST LAWS based on non-co-operation.* Defiance of unjust laws should take the form of committing breaches of certain selected laws and regulations which are undemocratic, unjust, racially discriminatory and repugnant to the natural rights of man.

461

Defiance of Unjust Laws should be planned into three stages—although the timing would to a large extent depend on the progress, development and the outcome of the previous stage. Participation in this campaign will be on a volunteer basis, such volunteers to undergo a period of training before the campaign begins.

Three stages of Defiance of Unjust Laws:-

(a) *First Stage.* Commencement of the struggle by calling upon selected and trained persons to go into action in the big centres, e.g., Johannesburg, Cape Town, Bloemfontein, Port Elizabeth and Durban.

(b) *Second Stage.* Number of volunteer corps to be increased as well as the number of centres of operation.

(c) *Third Stage.* This is the stage of mass action during which as far as possible, the struggle should broaden out on a country-wide scale and assume a general mass character. For its success preparations on a mass scale to cover the people both in the urban and rural areas would be necessary.

9.

Joint Planning Council. In order to prosecute and put into effect the plan of Defiance of Unjust Laws and in order to co-ordinate the efforts of the various national groups as well as of the various centres both urban and rural, it will be necessary for the Planning Council from time to time to make recommendations to the Executive Committees of the National Organizations who will jointly conduct, prosecute, direct and co-ordinate the campaign of Defiance of Unjust Laws as agreed upon by the Conference of the African National Congress and supported by the Conference of the South African Indian Congress. The Council must be empowered:-

(a) to co-opt members to the Council and fill vacancies with the approval of the Executive organs of the African National Congress and the South African Indian Congress.

(b) Invite representatives from non-European organisations which are in full agreement with, and active participants in the campaign, to serve as non-voting members of the Council.

(c) To frame rules and regulations for the guidance of the campaign for approval by the National Executive.

(d) To set up provincial regional and/or local councils within the framework of the existing organizations.

(e) Issue instructions for the organisation of volunteer corps and frame the necessary code of discipline for these volunteers.

10.

Under the direction of the Joint Executives, a Provincial, Regional or where possible Local Council will have the primary task of organising and enrolling volunteers into volunteer corps on the following lines:-

(a) *A leader* to be in charge of each volunteer corps for the maintenance of order and discipline in terms of the ''code of discipline'' and for leading the corps into action when called upon to do so.

(b) Corps to consist of members of both sexes.

(c) The colours of the African National Congress-black, green and gold—shall be the emblem of the Volunteer Corps.

(d) Each unit of the Volunteer Corps shall consist of members of the organisation to which they belong, viz., ANC, SAIC, FAC. The Coloured Organisations in the provinces of Natal, O.F.S. and the Transvaal participating in the campaign with the approval of the Joint Planning and Directing Council shall also be allowed to form units of the Volunteer Corps.

(e) In certain cases, where a law or regulation to be defied applies commonly to all groups, a mixed unit may be allowed to be formed of members of various organisations participating in the campaign.

11.

Laws to be tackled. In recommending laws and regulations which should be tackled we have borne in mind the Laws which are most obnoxious and which are capable of being defied.

The African National Congress.

Insofar as the African National Congress is concerned, the laws which stand out for attack are naturally the Pass Laws and the Regulations relating to Stock Limitation.

Method of Struggle on the Pass Laws:

(a) A Unit of Volunteer Corps should be called upon to defy a certain aspect of the pass laws, e.g., enter a Location without a permit. The Unit chosen goes into action on the appointed day, enters the location and holds a meeting. If confronted by the authorities the leader and all the members of the Unit court arrest and bear the penalty of imprisonment.

(b) Selected leaders to declare that they will not carry any form of passes including the Exemption Pass and thus be prepared to bear the penalty of the law.

(c) Other forms of struggle on the Pass Laws can also be undertaken depending on the conditions in the different areas throughout the country.

Rural Action.

Whilst the Volunteers go into action on the Pass Laws in the Urban Areas, the people in the rural areas should be mobilised to resist the culling of the cattle and stock limitation.

(a) Stock Limitation: People in the rural areas to be asked not to

463

co-operate with the authorities in any way in culling cattle or limiting livestock.

(b) Meetings and demonstrations to be held.

(c) Regional Conferences: Such Conferences in the rural areas should be called to discuss the problems of the people and to decide on the most suitable form of Defiance of Unjust Laws in the area.

The South African Indian Congress

Insofar as appropriate action by the South African Indian Congress is concerned, the conditions and effects of the laws vary in the three provinces, but we submit the following for the consideration of the South African Indian Congress:-

(a) Provincial Barriers

(b) Apartheid Laws such as train, post office, Railway Stations, etc.

(c) Group Areas Act—if and when possible.

The Franchise Action Council

(a) General Apartheid segregation in Post Offices, Railway Stations, trains, etc.

(b) Group Areas Act—if and when possible.

Both (a) and (b) will apply to the Coloured people in the other provinces as well.

In the Cape a strong possibility exists of having mixed units rather than having separate national organisation units.

12.

The Population Registration Act.

During the conduct of the campaign it should not be forgotten that the Government is preparing the machinery for the enforcement of the Population Registration Act. This Act is repugnant to all sections of the people and the campaign must pay particular attention to preparing the volunteers and instructing the masses of the people to resist the enforcement of this Act. The campaign on this Act may well take the struggle from stages one and two into stage three of mass action.

13.

We cannot fail to recognise that industrial action is second to none, the best and most important weapon in the struggle of the people for the repeal of the unjust Laws and that it is inevitable that this method of struggle has to be undertaken, at one time or another during the course of the struggle. We also note that in the present day South African conditions, the one-day protests on May 1st and June 26th, 1950, and the one-day protest in the Cape on May 7th, 1951 against the Separate Representation of Voters' Bill, demonstrated the preparedness of the people to undertake this form of struggle with no mean success. We are nevertheless of the opinion that in this next phase of our campaign lawful industrial action should not be resorted to immediately, but that it should be resorted to at a later stage in the struggle. In this new phase of the campaign a sustained form of mass action will be necessary which will gradually embrace larger groups of people, permeate both the urban and the rural areas and make it possible for us to organise, discipline and lead the people in a planned manner. And, therefore, contrary to feelings in some quarters, we are not keen to advocate industrial action as the first step, but only as a later step in the campaign against Unjust Laws. It should be noted, however, that our recommendations do not preclude the use of lawful industrial action during the first stage provided that conditions make its use possible on a local, regional, provincial or national scale.

14.

It is apparent that the plan of action herein outlined cannot be put into effect without the necessary funds to back it. It is also apparent that no body of men can sit down and work out a budget estimate for such a vast national undertaking. Suffice it to say that a full scale campaign will require thousands of pounds. Conscious of this essential requirement, we recommend with some confidence that if the African National Congress and the South African Indian Congress undertake to launch a *1 Million Shilling Drive* it can sustain the campaign. The Drive should be conducted under the slogan: *"1 Million Shillings by the end of March, 1952 for Freedom"*.

National Pledge

This Council is strongly of the opinion that an inspired National Pledge should be issued which could be read out at public, factory and group meetings and repeated by all those present. A special day, e.g., April 6th should be set aside so that special meetings are called everywhere, in towns, villages, and hamlets, in factories and locations, and special church services be held on this day, where the National Pledge could be publicly read out. This day or any other day which the Conference of the African National Congress sets aside for the purpose should be called *"The National Day of Pledge and Prayer"*.

(Sgd.) J. S. MOROKA
(Chairman)

Y. M. DADOO
Y. CACHALIA
(Representatives of the
South African Indian Congress)

J. B. MARKS
W. M. SISULU
(Representatives of the African National Congress)

Thaba 'Nchu
November 8th 1951

465

DOCUMENTS 87a-87b. ANC Annual Conference of December 15-17, 1951

Document 87a. Draft Report of the National Executive Committee

Mr. Speaker, Mr. President, Sons and daughters of Africa:

On behalf of the Executive Committee of the African National Congress, I have great pleasure in submitting to you, for your approval and adoption, the Executive Report for the year ending December, 1951.

The political situation has already been reviewed at length and you will no doubt agree that the review has disclosed a most serious state of affairs in our country.

During the period covered by this Report, your Executive was faced with a most difficult task and a very trying time, as the result of internal troubles, such as the situation in Natal and the dispute in the Transvaal and the financial crisis confronting the Congress since the National Day of Protest—26th June 1950.

The white rulers have concentrated all their energy with vigour and determination in tightening up their machinery for oppression. This was clearly indicated by the last session of Parliament which dealt, inter alia, [with the] amendment of the Suppression of Communism Act. This Act was bitterly opposed at all its stages by the African National Congress, supported by all democratic movements in the country, because of its undemocratic principles. We are pledged to fight this Law to a bitter end.

The Separate Representation of Voters' Act deprived the non-Europeans of the last vestige of token democratic rights.

The Bantu Authorities Act is intended to bluff the African chiefs into believing that it restores to them the original powers they enjoyed before the coming of the white man. In real fact it prevents any democratic system being extended to the Africans in the Reserves and places the chiefs into the position of Government Agents—a position which must necessarily provoke the antagonism of their people and undermine their prestige.

Under the provisions of the Group Areas Act, the Government intends to divide the African people into tribal groups in a bid to stem the rise of African Nationalism, a creed for the unification of the people of Africa into one solid Nation.

The Prevention of Illegal Squatting Act, which is a part and parcel of the forced labour policy in this country, is calculated to render thousands of our people homeless.

The Native Consolidated Amendment Bill, which was dropped due to lack of time, is as dangerous as any of the above Acts. It proposes unlimited power to the Minister of Native Affairs and to petty officers of his Department. Under the provisions of this Bill it will be possible to deport at will any African the Minister feels displeased with. The arbitrary powers proposed in this Bill can even outlaw the urban population of this country.

As far as the non-Europeans are concerned, the last Session of Parliament was a record session, it was outrageous for its concentration on the colour issue. These repressive measures clearly show the desperate position in which the Nationalists find themselves. This desperation was further demonstrated by the appointment of four sub-Cabinet Ministers under the Minister of Native Affairs. There is also established a Coloured Affairs Department under the Minister of the Interior.

From the foregoing, you will clearly see the determination of the Nationalist Government to keep the oppressed people down by all means at their disposal, and to this end they wish to crush the national democratic front that opposes them.

THE COUNCIL OF ACTION.

The various Committees appointed by the National Executive in terms of the Programme of Action have not produced encouraging results. . . .

THE JOINT PLANNING COUNCIL.

The Joint Planning Council ... consisting of Dr. J. S. Moroka (Chairman), Messrs. J. B. Marks, W. M. Sisulu, Dr. Y. M. Dadoo and Mr. Y. A. Cachalia representing the African National Congress and the South African Indian Congress respectively was duly formed, and has presented its Report to the Congress. In our opinion this Report is of utmost importance and should receive the most serious attention of the Conference.

WITZIESHOEK SITUATION.

It is to be regretted that the people of Witzieshoek, who as a result of their struggle against Stock Limitation, and whose tragedy is well known to us, have not been sufficiently assisted by the Congress. Although the National Executive gave directive to the provinces for the collection of funds for the defence of the affected persons, there was no response except from the Province of the Transvaal. The Executive has decided to establish a National Fund to defend the affected persons and to continue the struggle against Stock Limitation throughout the country.

ADMINISTRATION.

The year under review seriously strained the administering of affairs of the Congress due to financial crisis. The acute financial position is reflected in the treasurer's financial statement.

As a result of the situation referred to above we have been reluctantly compelled to terminate the services of the lady typiste, who not only served the

National Organisation with deepseated devotion, but also made highly commendable sacrifices in the national causes. Your Executive wishes to record its deep appreciation for the services rendered to the nation.

EXECUTIVE MEETINGS....

EJECTMENT OF AFRICAN FROM TOWNS UNDER THE GROUP AREAS AND THE URBAN AREAS ACTS.

Africans are required under the Urban Areas Act to obtain the Governor-General's consent before occupying any premises owned by non-Africans and in areas outside African Townships. Since 1944 the Authorities did not implement the law and therefore many Africans occupied premises without consent and without hindrance. In keeping with the trend of events under the present rule, the Authorities have suddenly taken action and have raided the office of the Congress and also offices of the trade union organisations. Upon making inquiries it was revealed by a letter from the Native Affairs Department that Africans are now required to apply to the Land Tenure Advisory Board for occupation of premises in town under the Group Areas Act. After the sanction of this Board further permission must be obtained from the Governor-General. This will create a most intolerable situation as it will hamper the work of the organisations and individuals in cities.

OBITUARY.

Your Executive notes with regret the irreparable loss sustained by the African people due to the passing of three outstanding personalities. The late Dr. P. Ka I Seme and the late Rev. Magatho were past Presidents of the African National Congress and were also its foundation members. Mr. Clement Kadalie was the founder and the leader of the I.C.U. They have served their country and as such will always be remembered by the Nation.

TRANSVAAL DISPUTES....

NATAL SITUATION....

PROVINCIAL BRANCHES.

Transvaal. The Transvaal Branch of the Congress must be complimented for its concrete work in the province. In spite of the fact that the present executive has been in office for only a short while, it has aroused tremendous enthusiasm among the people. The President, the Secretary, together with some of the members of the executive committee have toured almost the whole of the Transvaal. Many meetings were addressed and a number of new branches have been established. Today there are 25 very active branches in the province. The work of the Provincial Congress is, however, hampered by the obstacles placed in the way by Government and Municipal regulations.

468

Your executive has received a report of the existence of a group styled as the 'Nationalist Bloc', which has now printed its own membership cards, purporting to be membership of the African National Congress. This matter is submitted to the Conference for attention and instruction....

Organisational work is going on in the Province and it is the aim of the Province to establish one hundred branches in a short period. In this regard the Province proposes to employ part time organisers on a commission basis. The women section and the Youth League are to be congratulated for their splendid work.

CAPE PROVINCE.

The Cape held its Annual Conference on the 23rd June, 1951, at Cradock. At this Conference 37 accredited delegates representing 14 Branches were present....

The report of the secretary disclosed an unfortunate situation in the Cape. It appears that there is no co-ordination in the Province and even in some cases letters of direction are ignored. Although there are virile branches in the Province, the report is silent about activities undertaken by the Province and from that point of view the report seems unsatisfactory.

NATAL....

FREE STATE.

There are seventeen branches of the Congress in the Province the most active being the one in Ladybrand, which has tackled a number of local issues. The people who were arrested in this area as a result of their participation in the National Day of Protest on June, 26th, were convicted by the local Magistrate but they won on appeal.

The President and the Secretary did their best to assist the people in the Sediba Reserve, who refused to assist the authorities in the culling of the cattle in the area. The leaders were arrested and kept under custody without trial....

ORGANISATION.

The membership of the A.N.C., is undoubtedly increasing everyday. We are continuously receiving letters from various parts of the country from individuals and groups. Some inform us that they have formed themselves into branches, others seek a mandate to form such branches. The African people are very enthusiastic about Congress. They show faith and confidence. It is for us to give proper directives and co-ordinate these forces. The question of a perfect machinery cannot be overemphasised....

Whatever we do in our endeavors to liberate the African People depends entirely on the solid foundation of a National Front. The African people must be educated as to what the Congress stands for, what the Congress is, and what it is doing.

For this reason the Working Committee has agreed on the implementation of the following plan by the National Executive, Provincial Executives and Branch Organs.

The National Executive will have its Propaganda Committee as the Spearhead of this particular department. It shall be held responsible for the Political Education and arrange lectures for the above committees. These lectures will also be available to the National Executive itself. This field is intended to produce well trained men for the field.

Provinces must zone themselves into regions, each of the eleven members of the executive to be responsible for a particular zone. Branch Executives will be responsible for the creation of organs under their supervision. A place, for instance like the New Brighton, Bloemfontein, Orlando locations, could each have one hundred organs as will fully appear in the sketch herein enclosed.

The functions of the Organs will be to meet and discuss or be lectured to on what the Congress stands for, what activities the Congress is engaged in, day to day issues—National and local. There shall be regular weekly meetings, reporting fortnightly to the Branches, the Branches reporting monthly to the Provinces and the Provinces in turn reporting quarterly to the National Executive.

This will ensure the bringing of the decisions of the Congress more effectively to the people, and an effective co-ordination will be established. Above all these Organs will become recruiting ground for Congress membership. Our aim must be one hundred thousand members during this year, 1951.

There is a great need for administrative training. There must be regular meetings of secretaries of all the provinces in order that they may discuss their difficulties and receive training on how to administer their branches. This will bring about a high standard of efficiency on the part of the Congress Officials. Strict discipline must be observed, particularly by the officials so as to avoid officials deliberately ignoring instructions from above by giving flimsy excuses for failure to carry out the instructions of the Congress.

This plan must receive priority over all else, since all depends on the strength of solid and disciplined organisation.

DIFFICULTIES.

The same difficulties as reported last year in connection with the holding of meetings still exist. These restrictions on the freedom of movement and speech are calculated to stifle National aspirations of the people and cannot be tolerated any longer. We recommend very strongly that effective and concerted struggles be launched against this form of tyranny as suggested in the report of the Council of Action.

CONCLUSION.

In conclusion we thank all those who co-operated and wholeheartedly assisted in the cause of the liberation of the people of South Africa during the period under review. It is sincerely hoped that with the great and noble task that lies ahead of us every responsible [person] in the organisation will make redoubled efforts to save our country from chaos and confusion brought about by the present rulers of South Africa. We are confident that the highest spirit of sacrifice which is expected from the leadership of the organisation in the cause of liberation will be forthcoming.

NKOSI SEKELELA AFRIKA

MORENA BOLOKA SECHABA SA HESO

Document 87b. "Presidential Address" by Dr. J. S. Moroka

It gives me great joy to see so many of you gathered on this, another memorable occasion of the conference of the African National Congress. I am happy to welcome you all. You show that you have the welfare of your people at heart. You have come here not only to make numerous proposals. But you have come also to take decisions of deep and far-reaching consequence. You have come to this well-known forum to rededicate yourselves to, and to baptize your sons and daughters into, the cause of African Nationalism.

It is the duty of all Africans (especially those who by reason of their education have a clear grasp of those issues which vitally affect the Africans of this land) to show interest and to take active part in the furtherance of the welfare of the Africans. You must all realise that whilst the other people can help you in your direction towards your National ideals, upon you and you alone lies the ultimate salvation of your individual selves and of your nationhood. From this preliminary statement must be drawn the threadbare but fundamental inference that you, Africans, must be organised more and more solidly so that you may the better forge those means and instruments by which you may carve your way to your destiny.

At the outset I wish to repeat what I have so often said before. We Africans, like other sections of the population of South Africa, are painfully aware of the deteriorating relationships between the Europeans and the Non-Europeans of this our land. On behalf of my people, I wish to say quite emphatically that we are prepared to work together with the Europeans, the Indians and the Coloureds for the welfare of South Africa. We are prepared to work so together only upon terms of equal partnership. Any terms which are designed to relegate us to a position of an inferior, we stoutly scorn, and will stubbornly reject.

From the government of South Africa we ask for nothing that is revolutionary. If what we ask for is communistic, then communism is humane and Christian; it is a consummation devoutly to be wished. We ask for those things which,

471

I believe, will facilitate co-operation between the Europeans and the Non-Europeans: those things which minimise the occasions and remove the causes for bad relationships between the Europeans and ourselves.

We ask for education for the Africans. By education I mean education of the Kindergarden type, Primary Education, Secondary Education, University Education, Technical and Adult Education. I mean the provision of these educational facilities on a scale commensurate with the African population of this land, I mean such education as does not presuppose that all Africans are farmers or serfs. I mean such education as recognises the humanity of the African, the wideness of man's mental, physical and moral abilities and the true democracy of all true evidences of true knowledge.

I would like to make the following suggestions:-

(a) *Compulsory Education:* ...

There is yet another aspect of African Education to which I would like to say a word. We are all looking forward to the report of the Eiselen Commission. The Africans have said that they want African education to be placed under the government. The government of South Africa has a department of education. If Native Education is placed under the Native Affairs Department, it will mean that an African teacher serves one master in two capacities, whose demands will not always agree. He will serve as a local resident or dweller. He will also serve the same master as a professional man. What is expected of him as a teacher would not always tally with what the Native Affairs Department as an Administrative department expects of him. It would be difficult to divorce administrative business from professional principles and practice. It would be difficult also to divorce the administration of the Reserves from educational principles, problems and practice in the urban areas. There would be confusion and dissatisfaction.

(b) *Freedom of Movement:* The right to move about freely in a police state is no whit different from that allowed within the prison premises....

I am aware that the government has appointed a commission to go into the operation of the Pass Laws. I have no doubt that with open minds the gentlemen in that commission will find some evidence of what I have here hinted. They will find also that the Africans want to seek employment wherever they can find it. The Africans want to live anywhere in South Africa like the other sections of the population. The Pass laws are a denial of this elementary right of man. The Pass Laws must go if South Africa must make any progress along the path of racial harmony and peace. The Pass laws are not for the protection of the Africans. They are an iron chain forged for the enslavement of the African.

(c) *Freedom to do any kind of work:* The very idea of Africans being debarred from doing skilled work except in the Reserves is revolting. There is more skilled employment to be expected in one of the larger urban areas than in all the Reserves put together. In any case, it seems an outrageous limitation of the scope of the economic life of the African, that he cannot work where he wants to work and do the work he wants to do there.

(d) *A say in Legislation:* We Africans whatever any other have maintained, maintain that we are an integral part of the population of this country. We are part and parcel of the soil, the climate, the rugged mountains, the meandering rivers, the vast plains, the mines, the farms, the factories and the undulating deserts of this land. We love them as intensely as any here who claim to love them. No degree of illiteracy can blot out this knowledge. No artifice can sever us from the love that binds us to South Africa. In two world wars we have shed the blood of our youth. We have sacrificed with the rest of South Africa to see our country through. We therefore feel very keenly when the South African government and some Europeans like to treat us as though we were intruders and invaders in this land. We are South Africans and as South Africans, we ask for the political status of South Africans....

WE ARE RULED BY PROCLAMATION: a system of rule which denies us all right of a say in the making of the laws under which we are ruled.

WE HAVE NOT A SINGLE AFRICAN MEMBER OF PARLIAMENT.

WE HAVE NO DIRECT REPRESENTATION IN THE UNITED NATIONS ASSEMBLIES.

In the parliament of South Africa and at UNO we should be represented by our people. There are many Africans and other Non-Europeans who are fit and proper people to represent us at these assemblies ... the ultimate goal is to divide us and deal with us piecemeal. Nothing can tear the mask more forthrightly than the abolition of the Native Representative Council and its substitution by the Bantu Authority's Bill of 1951. The bill has come to divide the Africans. We are being divided by a government which has made much noise about its intentions to bring about unity and racial harmony. It is this government which is throwing a wall between us and the Europeans. It is this government which by this bill is throwing partitions between the ethnic groups of the Bantu population. This can be a source of misunderstanding and confusion amongst us. But if it is persisted in and if it should attain any measure of success the harvest which South Africa will reap in the ominously near future will be a sorry spectacle.

One of the chief aims of the African National Congress is to bring about harmony and goodwill amongst the inhabitants of South Africa. We are against the government of South Africa not because we hate White South Africa but because we are wronged. We want the Europeans to realise that we are wronged. Even the blind can now see the growing tree of African Nationalism. But we would that that plant should strike root and grow upon soil that has not been contaminated. It is one of the sad truths in the political life of this land that only a few Europeans see the need for a good soil for the growing tree.

If my words are to some Europeans meaningless the unchanging testimony of future history will yet give meaning to them....

The trade Union movement amongst the Africans will grow apace whether the government is prepared to recognise that or not. It is only to be regretted that if driven underground, it will assume a shape that will be unsightly when it comes up to the surface....

The Africans must be allowed to organise their Trade Unions without the unnecessary interference of the government. We should be free to bargain with our labour upon the free market. Otherwise our position is in all respects but name, that of slaves.

Trade in the townships and the locations is in a somewhat similar plight. Trade licences are restricted, and the traders have their hands tied behind their backs. They are powerless to help themselves, their people, the wholesale dealers and the whole fabric of the commercial and trade enterprise of South Africa....

Immigration: The question of immigration is as important to us as it is to the government of South Africa. Thousands of artisans are being recruited from overseas. They are brought into this land ostensibly to relieve labour shortage. We and the world are told that South Africa is inadequately supplied with skilled artisans. That may be so. But these people are brought from European countries to serve two purposes. They are brought here to reduce our majority over the Europeans in South Africa. They are brought here above all to provide an excuse to the government not to train us as skilled and semi-skilled artisans. There are thousands and thousands of young Africans who are willing to come forward for training. There are thousands and thousands who would acquit themselves creditably. They would be a priceless asset to South Africa.

Protectorates: Geographically the protectorates belong to South Africa and should be incorporated. But we are opposed to the incorporation of these territories without the consent of the inhabitants there. If incorporation should be thrust upon them, then it will only go to prove the foundation of the fear that this government is one that tramples upon the feelings of those upon whom it rules. It has no regard for and does not respect the opinion of the ruled.

If pledges are given they should be respected. If the South African government should try to ram incorporation down the throats of the inhabitants of these territories, if it should threaten or bully them or any other interested party into the idea of incorporation, then, from our point of view and from the point of view of the Africans in these territories, this government will have done nothing to allay our fears that there are motives other than the welfare of the Africans both in the territories and in South Africa. From the point of view of the Africans in those territories the consequences will ever be of a more serious nature. What will the Africans there (even the vast majority of the Europeans there) think of Britain's interest in the welfare of her subjects and those whom she has given her word of honour to protect?....

The United Nations Assembly: The bickering that is going on in Paris in the Chambers of UNO is not edifying. Tempers have risen very high and nerves are frayed over the question whether or not four Herero chiefs should be allowed to put their case and the case of their people before one of the chambers of that forum of nations. Some of those countries which are looked upon as the very bulwark of democracy are protesting vigorously against the personal representations of the Herero chiefs. I am amazed and disappointed. It appears to me that UNO is not concerned with the welfare of those Non-European peoples who are downtrodden.

UNO would be a great organisation, I am convinced, if it tackled its duties fearlessly and without prejudice. It should make itself interested in those countries where the majority are ruled by the minority as is the case in South Africa, and without it the world would be internationally the poorer. With open minds and great hearts, the spokesmen of the nations of the world could do a mighty job towards world peace and goodwill among men. It is in that light that this forum of nations should be regarded....

Conclusion: In conclusion I wish to sound to Africans a clarion call to unity. In unity there is indeed strength; divided we shall surely scatter like chaff before the tempest. We stand for an ideal: not for a person. Our ideal is summed up in *African Nationalism.*

I appeal to all Africans to consider a great step towards the realisation of that ideal. The step I commend to you is a consideration of the steps to be taken to establish a national church. It is in the sanctuary of your home that you come nearest to your God. It is in the fold of your nation—the African nation—that you come nearer to your God than in the foreign atmosphere of European churches. If because the Anglican church, the Methodist church, the Dutch Reformed church and the numerous other National churches all of which have their origin from the Roman Catholic church have strayed from the path of the true God of Christ because they are national, then the sooner they stopped misleading us the better. In those churches there is often the stigma and the sting of inferiority attaching to us. We are being eternally led to the light. We never seem able to walk to the light. Our African ministers don't seem to grow spiritually to show white congregations the light.

To the white people of this country I wish to emphasise that we bear them no personal malice. We fight not against persons but against the iniquity of the laws by which we are ruled. I appeal to them to reconsider their attitude towards us. Give us democratic rights in this land of our birth. I am sorry that in this fair land, this land which could set an unbeatable example for the admiration of the world, there is so much unnecessary hatred and discrimination based upon nothing else but colour. People are not judged on their merits, but on the colour of their skin.

I wish this conference all the happiness of Christmas and the abundant prosperity of the New Year.

MORENA BOLOKA SECHABA !

475

Document 88. Letter Calling for Repeal of Repressive Legislation and Threatening a Defiance Campaign, from Dr. J. S. Moroka and W. M. Sisulu to Prime Minister D.F. Malan, January 21, 1952

Sir,

In terms of the resolution adopted by the 39th Session of the African National Congress held at Bloemfontein we have been instructed to address you as follows:

The African National Congress was established in 1912 to protect and advance the interests of the African people in all matters affecting them, and, to attain their freedom from all discriminatory laws whatsoever. To this end the African National Congress has, since its establishment, endeavoured by every constitutional method to bring to the notice of the Government the legitimate demands of the African people and repeatedly pressed, in particular, their inherent right to be directly represented in Parliament, Provincial and Municipal Councils and in all councils of state.

This attitude was a demonstration not only of the willingness and readiness of the African people to co-operate with the Government but also evidence of their sincere desire for peace, harmony and friendship amongst all sections of our population. As is well-known the Government through its repressive policy of trusteeship, segregation and apartheid and through legislation that continues to insult and degrade the African people by depriving them of fundamental human rights enjoyed in all democratic communities, have categorically rejected our offer of co-operation. The consequence has been the gradual worsening of the social, economic and political position of the African people and a rising tide of racial bitterness and tension. The position has been aggravated in recent times by the Pass Laws, Stock Limitation, the Suppression of Communsim Act of 1950, the Group Areas Act of 1950, the Bantu Authorities Act of 1951 and the Voters Act of 1951.

The cumulative effect of this legislation is to crush the National Organisations of the oppressed people; to destroy the economic position of the people and to create a reservoir of cheap labour for the farms and the gold mines; to prevent the unity and development of the African people towards full nationhood and to humiliate them in a host of other manners.

The African National Congress as the National Organisation of the African people cannot remain quiet on an issue that is a matter of life and death to the people; to do so would be a betrayal of the trust and confidence placed upon it by the African people.

At the recent Annual Conference of the African National Congress held in Bloemfontein from the 15th to 17th December, 1951, the whole policy of the Government was reviewed and after serious and careful consideration of the matter, Conference unanimously resolved to call upon your Government, as we hereby do, to repeal the aforementioned Acts by *NOT LATER THAN THE 29th DAY OF FEBRUARY, 1952*, failing which the African National Congress will hold protest meetings and demonstrations on the 6th day of

April, 1952 as a prelude to the implementation of the plan for the defiance of unjust laws.

In the light of the Conference resolution we also considered the statement made by the Prime Minister at Ohrigstad on the 5th instant in which he appealed to all sections of our population, irrespective of colour and creed, to participate fully in the forthcoming Jan Van Riebeek Celebrations. It is our considered opinion that the African people cannot participate in any shape or form in such celebrations, unless the aforementioned Acts which constitute an insult and humiliation to them are removed from the Statute Book.

We firmly believe that the freedom of the African people, the elimination of the exploitation of man by man and the restitution of democracy, liberty and harmony in South Africa are such vital and fundamental matters that the Government and the public must know that we are fully resolved to achieve them in our lifetime.

The struggle which our people are about to begin is not directed against any race or national group but against the unjust laws which keep in perpetual subjection and misery vast sections of the population. In this connection, it is a source of supreme satisfaction to us to know we have the full support and sympathy of all enlightened and honest men and women, black and white in our country and across the seas and that the present tension and crises have been brought about not by the African leaders but by the Government themselves.

We are instructed to point out that we have taken this decision in full appreciation of the consequences it entails and we must emphasise that whatever reaction is provoked from certain circles in this country, posterity will judge that this action we are about to begin was in the interest of all in our country, and will inspire our people for long ages to come.

We decide to place on record that for our part, we have endeavoured over the last forty years to bring about conditions for genuine progress and true democracy.

Yours faithfully,

Dr. J. S. Moroka (President-General)

W. M. Sisulu (Secretary-General)

Document 89. "Opening Address" at Annual Conference of the South African Indian Congress, by Dr. S. M. Molema, January 25, 1952

Mr. President, Ladies and Gentlemen:

I am deeply conscious of the signal honour it is to be asked to open this 20th conference of the South African Indian Congress, and I wish to thank you for the gesture.

The Congress meets today at the zero hour of our national life as the black and despised inhabitants of this subcontinent.

Like dumb animals we have for years meekly stood still while we have been haltered and bound, and we have submissively bowed to the dull yoke of men who are nothing else than robbers and villains, traitors to the highest and noblest teachings of the Christianity which they so blatantly profess, men shockingly contemptuous of their conscience and their God, and now in a frenzy of self-adulation preparing to embrace each other and shake their bloody hands in commemoration of their three hundred years of rapine and bloodshed, and ready to commence another evil era of piracy and oppression.

It is right and fitting, as you meet in Conference under these conditions, to remember the salient, the dominant fact of South African history, namely that all the monuments, all the celebrations and all the feasts of the white man have a diametrically opposite meaning to the black man, because every monument of the white man perpetuates the memory of the annihilation of some black community, every celebration of victory the remembrance of our defeat, his every feast means our famine and his laughter our tears. Such are the Great Trek celebrations and the Voortrekker Monument; such are Dingaan's Day, Kruger Day and Union Day, and such the approaching Van Riebeeck celebrations.

Let us prepare ourselves, therefore, to behave accordingly during these months, and not be carried away like chaff before the wind,

Nor hold a candle to our shame and sorrow,
Nor flatter the rank breath of white South Africa,
Nor bow our knee to their idolatries,
Nor coin our cheek to their smiles,
Nor shout in worship of their echo.

But rather, let these sad memorials of our misfortunes spur us to gird our loins in earnest determination to reverse the dismal and tragic history of past years.

It is gratifying to note the faint glimmer of a common consciousness and the efforts at self-criticism, however meagre they still are, among the unprivileged and oppressed peoples of South Africa and the corresponding desire to throw off the shackles that have bound us so long, and a determination among us to stretch our arms and partake of the God-given fruit of life and liberty. Too long have we ourselves been the blind instruments of our undoing and the fashioners of our own degradation by our petty squabbles and disunity.

Ever since the earliest contact of the white man with Africans three hundred years ago, he has succeeded, beyond his wildest dreams in dispossessing them of their land, their liberty and their life, and ever since the meeting of the white man and the Indians, with the coming of the latter at the special behest of the European, he has regularly made harsh laws for the restriction of the Indian people.

To all this catalogue of political crimes committed against us in the form of discriminatory legislation, it is true that our separate groups have each protested individually by all constitutional methods, but still always with a remarkable display of super-human patience and slavish timidity and with never an idea of uniting their forces in a common platform of protest.

Some excuse might be pleaded for one Non-European group's apathy and ignorance of the conditions, disabilities and sufferings of another non-European group prior to the Union. For instance the Natal disenfranchisement of Indians in 1896, and the several anti-Indian Immigration Acts of Natal and the Transvaal in 1905 and 1907 might be said to be matters that concerned and are therefore hitherto only known to Indians, just as the anti-African land and labour laws of the Transvaal and the Orange Free State were peculiar worries of the Africans concerned.

But to think that the Union of South Africa, with its cynical provisions excluding all people of colour from the legitimate enjoyment of political rights was framed before our eyes, and no worthwhile united action was taken against the Act by Non-European groups is staggering. We looked on with equanimity as people dazed and paralyzed, much as donkeys and cattle look at a train approaching to destroy them. Year after year, Draconic differential legislation was enacted, whittling down to nothingness the meagre rights that had been left to us, and still we did not lift our finger in united protest. Now it was the African that was robbed and ruined by such enactments as the Natives Land Act (1913), Native Service Contract Act (1934) and Native Representation Act (1936), and now it was the Indian that was insulted and coerced by such legislation as the Immigration Regulation Act (1913), the Trading and Occupation of Land Restriction (Pegging) Act (1943), or the Asiatic Land Tenure and Indian Representation (Ghetto) Act (1946), and now it is the Eur-African—the Coloured man—that having been first inveighed into the belief that because he is a surreptitious product of the white man's loins he will be accorded all the political rights and privileges of a European, now (he) is treacherously undermined and served with a Coloured Representation Act (1951).

Some sort of excuse might even now still be pleaded for our indolence and selfishness that while these things happened to one or another Non-European group the others looked on passively or even contentedly to see it submerged by the steadily advancing tide of white exploitation and domination, little realising that it was their turn next to be similarly submerged.

All that, I say, may still be condoned. But what excuse can anyone find for the whole Non-European population acquiescing in the principle of differential legislation, with its Colour Bar Acts, Pass Laws, Group Areas Acts and Communal Representation Acts and other such diabolical laws which affect and restrict all the Non-European groups together? What excuse can there be, now, when the white man, the European of South Africa has been unmasked in his political dishonesty, and stands condemned before the conscience and bar

479

of the world for his utter contempt of the value and dignity of human rights and human personality and fundamental freedoms?

With characteristic tolerance we have waited patiently and hoped in vain for a change of heart among the rulers. Now we see that the white man's insatiable appetite for power, kingdom and glory has grown by what it has fed upon, and his political piracy will know no bounds until we bestir ourselves, stand up to bar his progress and say "Thus far and no further." Can we say that with one voice and as one organic being?

The spate of vicious, repressive and differential legislation which successive Parliaments and Governments seem to vie with each other in dishing out—are we for ever going to sit and stupidly look on while these laws are enforced to crush us?

My friends, if we have any right to life and liberty, let us prove it right now before the year 1952 is older. We have the power, but do not realise it. We have the means. We carry the weapons within us, and none can rob us of them.

The efforts that have been made recently by some of our far-seeing men to bring about mutual esteem, friendship and collaboration between the different groups of oppressed peoples, between the Indian, the African and the Eur-African or Coloured people, cannot be too highly commended, and I hope that each member of these groups represented here today, each and every one in this hall will go forth as an inspired missionary to bring about the consummation of that unity so highly to be desired—to implement the plan of defiance of unjust laws, which has already been adopted by the conference of the African National Congress and which I have no doubt this conference will consider very seriously. For I am persuaded that so long as the white man can succeed in making us believe that our interests and destinies are antagonistic, incompatible or even distinct, so long will he succeed, as he has thus far succeeded in destroying us one by one. On the contrary, if we fully realise, as we should, the identity of our lot and combine to do relentless battle for our legitimate and common rights of life and liberty, we shall save ourselves and our children, and no power on earth can prevent our success.

One of the leading prophets of the modern world has passionately cried out "Workers of the world, Unite." Earnestly I call upon you, sons and daughters of Africa and India—Unite. Passionately I call upon you men and women of colour—Unite. Prayerfully, I call upon you Coloureds, Africans and Indians—Unite.

Document 90. Letter replying to letter from the Prime Minister's Office and statement of intention to launch defiance campaign, from Dr. J.S. Moroka and W.M. Sisulu to Prime Minister D.F. Malan, February 11, 1952

Sir,

We, the undersigned, have the honour to acknowledge receipt of your letter of the 29th January, 1952.

The National Executive of the African National Congress, at a special conference convened for the purpose, has given careful consideration to the contents of your letter, and has instructed us to address you as follows:

It is noted that exception is taken in your letter to the fact that the resolution adopted by the African National Congress at its 1951 Conference was directed to the Prime Minister instead of the Minister of Native Affairs and his Department. The African National Congress has at no time accepted the position that the Native Affairs Department is the channel of communication between the African people and the State. In any event, the subject of our communication to you was not a Departmental matter but one of such general importance and gravity affecting the fundamental principles of the policy practised by the Union Government, and its effect on the relations between Black and White, that it was considered appropriate to bring these matters directly to the notice of the Prime Minister. The suggestion that we were actuated by a so-called "recent rift or purge in Congress circles" is without foundation and entirely beside the point in so far as the substance of our case is concerned.

In reply to our demand for the abolition of differentiating laws, it is suggested in your letter that there are "permanent and not man-made" differences between Africans and Europeans which justify the maintenance of these laws. The question at issue is not one of biological differences, but one of citizenship rights which are granted in full measure to one section of the population, and completely denied to the other by means of man-made laws artificially imposed, not to preserve the identity of Europeans as a separate community, but to perpetuate the systematic exploitation of the African people.

The African people yield to no-one as far as pride of race is concerned, and it is precisely for this reason that they are striving for the attainment of fundamental human rights in the land of their birth.

It is observed that your Government rejects out of hand our claim for direct representation in Parliament and other Councils of State. This is the kernel of the policy of apartheid which is condemned not only by the African, Indian and Coloured people, but also by a large section of white South Africa. It is precisely because of this policy that South Africa is losing cast in international circles.

Your letter suggests that the policy of your Government is motivated by a desire to protect the interests of the African people in various spheres of life, e.g., land rights, and unspecified privileges not enjoyed by them in other countries. The Reserve land policy has always been designed to protect European rather than African land rights, and even within the so-called Reserves, Africans hold only occupancy privileges at the discretion of the Government. These

481

Reserves are notoriously congested and overcrowded, and the so-called re-habilitation scheme, notwithstanding the protestations of just intentions with which it is camouflaged, has aggravated the misery of the people and rendered thousands destitute and homeless, and has exposed them to vexatious regimentation by Native Commissioners and petty Trust officials. In this connection we note that even the Native Laws Amendment Bill, which is now before Parliament, in spite of all its harsh and draconian provisions, has been described as a "protective" measure. There can be no doubt that, like similar measures passed hitherto, this Bill is intended to protect and advance the interests of Europeans and not those of Africans. It is those discriminatory laws that are preventing the African people from developing their ambitions and capacities, and along lines satisfactory to themselves.

As far as the Bantu Authorities Act is concerned, it is clear that this Act is part of the policy to which we are opposed, namely, that "the Government is not prepared to grant the Africans political equality", and is not, as you suggest, "designed to give the Africans the opportunity of enlightened administration of their own affairs"! Nothing contained in the Bantu Authorities Act can be a substitute for direct representation in the Councils of State.

With reference to the campaign of mass action which the African National Congress intends to launch, we would point out that as a defenceless and voteless people, we have explored other channels without success. The African people are left with no alternative but to embark upon the campaign referred to above. We desire to state emphatically that it is our intention to conduct this campaign in a peaceful manner, and that any disturbances, if they should occur, will not be of our making.

In reiterating our claim for direct representation, we desire to place on record our firm determination to redouble our efforts for the attainment of full citizenship rights. In conclusion we regret that the Prime Minister has seen fit to reject our genuine offer of co-operation on the basis of full equality, and express the hope that in the interest of all concerned the Government may yet reconsider its attitude.

THE DEFIANCE CAMPAIGN

Document 91. "April 6: People's Protest Day." Flyer issued by the ANC (Transvaal) and the Transvaal Indian Congress

APRIL 6: PEOPLE'S PROTEST DAY

The African National Congress has served notice on the Government that the Non-European people can no longer go on tolerating the ill-treatment they suffer in the land of their birth.

482

Today our people are suffering as never before under this Nationalist Government of Dr. Malan with its policy of Apartheid. Under high prices and low wages, we are starving, our cattle are being taken away. We are homeless—or if we have homes, "Group Areas" threaten to drive us from them. Every day we are jailed and sent to farm-slavery for passes—and now women and children are faced with the pass system too. We are insulted and bullied because of our colour. Under the Coloured Voters Act, the Anti-Communist Law, the Bantu Authorities Act, South Africa is being made a fascist state.

FORWARD TO FREEDOM IN 1952

This year 1952, marks three hundred years since, under Jan van Riebeeck, the first white people came to live in South Africa.

The Malan Government is using this occasion to celebrate everything in South African history that glorifies the conquest, enslavement and oppression of the Non-European people.

Nothing is said of the fact that South Africa has been built up on the sweat and blood of the working people. Nothing is said of the famous leaders of the Non-European peoples. Nor is anything said of the noble Europeans who fought for freedom for all.

This Van Riebeeck celebration cannot be a time for rejoicing for the Non-Europeans.

IT IS THE TIME TO PUT AN END TO SLAVERY
IN SOUTH AFRICA

ENOUGH

That is why, now, the African National Congress, backed by the South African Indian Congress, Coloured Organisations and other patriotic leaders of the people have decided upon a mighty campaign of mass action against unjust laws and for democratic freedom.

We demand the right to live as human beings. We want an end to all the laws that discriminate against us. We want the right to vote, to choose for ourselves who will make and administer the laws we live under. We demand Trade Union rights and freedom of organisation.

APRIL 6, 1952

On Sunday, April 6, 1952, protest meetings and demonstrations will be held throughout South Africa as a first stage in the struggle for the Defiance of Unjust Laws, for the ending of oppression: the march to freedom.

THIS IS A CALL TO EVERY MAN AND WOMAN TO JOIN THE STRUGGLE FOR FREEDOM!

Come in hundreds of thousands to the meetings and demonstrations on April 6!

483

Document 92. Statement in court by W.M. Sisulu before sentencing for pass offence, July 21, 1952

Your Worship has just pronounced his verdict in a case in which I and fifty-one other colleagues are charged with Pass Offences. Before your Worship passes sentence on me, I want to indicate that I am the Secretary General of the African National Congress, which was founded in 1912 to fight for the abolition of all discriminatory laws and for the freedom and national independence of the African people. Since this date, Congress has endeavoured by every constitutional means to bring to the notice of the Government the legitimate aspirations of the African people. Far from improving, the position of my people gradually deteriorated through the passage of such laws as the Land Act of 1913, which deprived us of our land, the Native Urban Areas Act, of 1923, which introduced the infamous Section 17 under which hundreds of thousands of innocent people are hounded by the police and gaoled every year, the Natives Administration Act of 1927, which vested the Government [Governor-General] with unbridled despotism in his government of the African people. The Representation Act of 1936, which deprived us of our Franchise Rights, and numerous other measures which are calculated to prevent the realisation of our destination. Our position has so worsened that today white South Africa has placed into office a government which has closed all constitutional channels between itself and my people and whose barbarous and Godless policies have shocked enlightened opinion all over the world. As an African, and National Secretary of the Congress, I cannot stand aside in an issue which is a matter of life and death to my people. My duty is perfectly clear—it is to take the lead and to share with the humblest of my countrymen the crushing burden, imposed upon us because of the colour of our skins. In conclusion, I wish to make this solemn vow and in full appreciation of the consequences it entails. As long as I enjoy the confidence of my people, and as long as there is a spark of life and energy in me, I shall fight with courage and determination for the abolition of discriminatory laws and for the freedom of all South Africans irrespective of colour or creed.

Document 93. Statement on violence in New Brighton, Port Elizabeth on October 18, by local ANC leaders, in the *Eastern Province Herald*, October 20, 1952

The recent happenings, in which there was needless loss of human lives, has greatly shocked the South African people.

The A.N.C., whilst dissociating itself and condemning the unwarranted use of firearms and useless destruction of property, wishes to express the sincerest sympathy of the African people towards those families, both Black and White, who have suffered the loss of their loved ones through this unfortunate, reckless, ill-considered return to jungle law.

This incident serves to bring to the notice of the public, forcibly, the danger of the doctrine of apartheid and race hatred, where differences between individuals immediately assume a racial character. The A.N.C. has, time and time again, condemned this unwise policy, pursued ruthlessly and relentlessly by successive governments in this country.

The only correct and sane policy which aims at the establishment of peace and racial harmony is that enunciated by the A.N.C. and by no European political organisation in South Africa.

The A.N.C. calls upon the African people to cease forthwith from participating in any violent action. They must rally to the call of the A.N.C., which is conducting a non-violent struggle against racially discriminatory, unjust laws.

Document 94. "Police Shootings Must Stop!" Flyer issued by the National Action Committee, ANC, and South African Indian Congress, November 1952

POLICE SHOOTINGS MUST STOP!

The police have fired on unarmed crowds at Kimberley, Denver Hostel, East London. Many people were killed. These shootings follow Mr. Swart's order to shoot and take law in their own hands.

We protest against this outrageous order.

We demand that the shootings must stop!

MALAN GOVERNMENT'S PLOT AGAINST NON-EUROPEANS

These shootings are a part of the Government's plot to weaken the DE-FIANCE CAMPAIGN and to ruthlessly oppress the non-European people.

THE GOVERNMENT WANTS:

- ★ TO CREATE race riots between European and non-European, Indian and African, and African and Coloured;
- ★ TO USE the riots and general disturbances to cause panic among the Europeans so as to drive them into the arms of the Nationalists;
- ★ TO DECLARE a state of National Emergency, to seize absolute power, to cut off the leaders from the people and to impose a fascist dictatorship on the country.

THEIR METHODS ARE:

TO SEND OUT agents among the people to provoke incidents which can be used by the police as a pretext for shooting and to incite and preach race hatred;

TO ACCUSE the Indians, blame the Africans and praise the Coloureds;

TO USE THE POLICE for the purpose of inciting racial strife between the Africans and Indians and for the distribution of literature propagating Apartheid.

BEWARE!

★ DO NOT be provoked—Do not listen to those who preach violence—Avoid rioting—Follow Congress lead—BE PEACEFUL, DISCIPLINED, NON-VIOLENT.

★ DO NOT listen to those who talk against any section of our population—Any one who speaks against the Indian, the Coloured, the Chinese, the African or European is an enemy of the people and an agent of the Government.

BEWARE!

LET US NOT ALLOW OURSELVES TO BE DIVERTED FROM THE COURSE OF ACTION LAID DOWN BY OUR CONGRESSES

..OUR DUTY. JOIN AND BE AN ACTIVE MEMBER OF CONGRESS.

ENLIST AS A VOLUNTEER IN THE DEFIANCE CAMPAIGN.

SUPPORT THE DEFIANCE CAMPAIGN

STAND BY YOUR LEADERS AND AWAIT CONGRESS CALL.

Issued by National Action Committee, African National Congress and South African Indian Congress, P.O. Box 2948, Johannesburg.

Document 95. "The Road to Freedom Is Via the Cross." Statement by Chief A. J. Lutuli, issued after the announcement on November 12, 1952, of his dismissal as chief, [n. d.]

I have been dismissed from the Chieftainship of the Abase-Makolweni Tribe in the Groutville Mission Reserve. I presume that this has been done by the Governor-General in his capacity as Supreme Chief of the "Native" people of the Union of South Africa save those of the Cape Province. I was democratically elected to this position in 1935 by the people of Groutville Mission Reserve and was duly approved and appointed by the Governor-General.

Previous to being a Chief I was a school teacher for about 17 years. In these past thirty years or so I have striven with tremendous zeal and patience to work for the progress and welfare of my people and for their harmonious relations with other sections of our multi-racial society in the Union of South Africa. In this effort I always pursued what liberal-minded people rightly regarded as the path of moderation. Over this great length of time I have, year after year, gladly spent hours of my time with such organisations as the Church and its various agencies such as the Christian Council of South Africa, the Joint Council of Europeans and Africans and the now defunct Native Representative Council.

In so far as gaining citizenship rights and opportunities for the unfettered development of the African people, who will deny that thirty years of my life have been spent knocking in vain, patiently, moderately and modestly at a closed and barred door?

What have been the fruits of my many years of moderation? Has there been any reciprocal tolerance or moderation from the Government, be it Nationalist or United Party? No! On the contrary, the past thirty years have seen the greatest number of Laws restricting our rights and progress until today we have reached a stage where we have almost no rights at all: no adequate land for our occupation, our only asset, cattle dwindling, no security of homes, no decent and remunerative employment, more restrictions to freedom of movement through passes, curfew regulations, influx control measures; in short we have witnessed in these years an intensification of our subjection to ensure and protect white Supremacy.

It is with this background and with a full sense of responsibility that, under the auspices of the African National Congress (Natal), I have joined my people in the new spirit that moves them today, the spirit that revolts openly and boldly against injustice and expresses itself in a determined and non-violent manner. Because of my association with the African National Congress in this new spirit which has found an effective and legitimate way of expression in the non-violent Passive Resistance Campaign, I was given a two week limit ultimatum by the Secretary for Native Affairs calling upon me to choose between the African National Congress and the Chieftainship of the Groutville Mission Reserve. He alleged that my association with Congress in its non-violent Passive Resistance Campaign was an act of disloyalty to the State. I did not, and do not, agree with this view. Viewing Non-Violent Passive Resistance as a non-revolutionary and, therefore, a most legitimate and humane political pressure technique for a people denied all effective forms of constitutional striving, I saw no real conflict in my dual leadership of my people: leader of the Tribe as Chief and political leader in Congress.

I saw no cause to resign from either. This stand of mine which resulted in my being sacked from the Chieftainship might seem foolish and disappointing to some liberal and moderate Europeans and Non-Europeans with whom I have worked these many years and with whom I still hope to work. This is no parting of the ways but "a launching further into the deep". I invite them

487

to join us in our unequivocal pronouncement of all legitimate African aspirations and in our firm stand against injustice and oppression.

I do not wish to challenge my dismissal but I would like to suggest that in the interest of the institution of Chieftainship in these modern times of democracy, the Government should define more precisely and make more widely known the status, functions and privileges of Chiefs.

My view has been, and still is, that a Chief is primarily a servant of his people. He is the voice of his people. He is the voice of his people in local affairs. Unlike a Native Commissioner, he is part and parcel of the Tribe, and not a local agent of the Government. Within the bounds of loyalty it is conceivable that he may voice and press the claims of his people even if they should be unpalatable to the Government of the day.

He may use all legitimate modern techniques to get these demands satisfied. It is inconceivable how Chiefs could effectively serve the wider and common interest of their own tribe without co-operating with other leaders of the people, both the natural leaders (Chiefs) and leaders elected democratically by the people themselves.

It was to allow for these wider associations intended to promote the common national interests of the people as against purely local interests that the Government in making rules governing Chiefs did not debar them from joining political associations so long as these associations had not been declared "by the Minister to be subversive of or prejudicial to constituted Government." The African National Congress—its non-violent Passive Resistance Campaign may be of nuisance value to the Government, but it is not subversive since it does not seek to overthrow the form and machinery of the State but only urges for the inclusion of all sections of the community in a partnership in the Government of the country on the basis of equality.

Laws and conditions that tend to debase human personality—a God-given force—be they brought about by the State or other individuals, must be relentlessly opposed in the spirit of defiance shown by St. Peter when he said to the rulers of his day "Shall we obey God or man?" No one can deny that in so far as non-Whites are concerned in the Union of South Africa, laws and conditions that debase human personality abound. Any Chief worthy of his position must fight fearlessly against such debasing conditions and laws. If the Government should resort to dismissing such Chiefs, it may find itself dismissing many Chiefs or causing people to dismiss from their hearts chiefs who are indifferent to the needs of the people through fear of dismissal by the Government. Surely the Government cannot place Chiefs in such an uncomfortable and invidious position.

As for myself, with a full sense of responsibility and a clear conviction, I decided to remain in the struggle for extending democratic rights and responsibilities to all sections of the South African community. I have embraced the non-violent Passive Resistance technique in fighting for freedom because I am convinced it is the only non-revolutionary, legitimate and humane way that could be used by people denied, as we are, effective constitutional means to further aspirations.

The wisdom or foolishness of this decision I place in the hands of the Almighty.

What the future has in store for me I do not know. It might be ridicule, imprisonment, concentration camp, flogging, banishment and even death. I only pray to the Almighty to strengthen my resolve so that none of these grim possibilities may deter me from striving, for the sake of the good name of our beloved country, the Union of South Africa, to make it a true democracy and a true union in form and spirit of all the communities in the land.

My only painful concern at times is that of the welfare of my family but I try even in this regard, in a spirit of trust and surrender to God's will as I see it, to say: "God will provide."

It is inevitable that in working for Freedom some individuals and some families must take the lead and suffer: the Road to Freedom Is Via The CROSS.

MAYIBUYE!

AFRIKA!   AFRIKA!
AFRIKA!

Document 96. "Circular Letter to All Congress Branches of the Province." Review of 1952 by the Working Committee of the ANC (Cape), December 1952

The year 1952 is about to end. It ends when the A.N.C. in the Cape Province has made tremendous and remarkable strides in the organisation of the African people, in the rural and urban areas and even in the reserves.

In the forty years of the existence of our National Organisation, never was the response greater to the call for a liberatory struggle as has been witnessed since the 26th June 1952, up to date. Congress has been able to lead the hesitant, to rouse the dormant, to open the horizon and to encourage those who had considered themselves too weak to think for themselves. The active struggle against tyranny, exploitation and oppression has disclosed the magnitude of the power of the African people and clarified their minds for the tasks ahead of them.

PERSPECTIVE: REVIEW OF EVENTS 1952. THE FUTURE!

It was in December 1951 that the National Conference of the A.N.C. adopted the plan for the defiance of unjust and racially discriminatory laws. At that time, in spite of the boundless faith that the leaders had in the capacity of the people to unite and struggle for their rights, there was, in certain quarters among the African people themselves, grave misgivings about the future. It was said "the people are divided"; That they would never support such a method of struggle; That the Africans were inherently prone to resort to violence, others said the sacrifices and suffering that would be demanded were such as would daunt our people early in the campaign. Malicious enemies of the African people, white detractors and believers in the outworn and discredited doctrines of white superiority predicted that the campaign would last a week and fizzle out. It was said that the African leaders did not have the necessary organising ability nor the political skill to launch a campaign of this nature; How false these hopes have been proved by the African people's readiness to maintain their solidarity against intimidation, victimisation and the violence to which the Nationalist regime has resorted in order to crush their unity and determination.

Let us but mention a few of the achievements of the Campaign during the last six months:—

(I) Congress has been able to unite the yearnings, spirits and aspirations of the African people, rural and urban, educated and un-educated in the one stream of achieving "FREEDOM IN OUR LIFETIME" under the liberatory slogan "AFRIKA!"

(II) Congress has created a mighty National organisation with thousands of members and thousands of Volunteers, ready to work and die in the defence of their rights and freedom.

(III) Congress has exposed the false and shallow doctrine of white supremacy and proved that the white man rules South Africa, not because he is fit to rule but because presently, he holds the monopoly of offensive military and police power. His rule rests not on superior moral strength, discipline or character, but upon tanks, stenguns, armoured cars and aeroplanes. That is one important lesson which our people have learnt during the campaign, that the cowardice of fascists who are inclined to be sadists is a result of fear, fear that they with their inhuman policies have no future in South Africa against the forces of progress which are emerging from the struggle of the Non-Europeans in the Country. The imperialists are no more the "inkosi" but his sten-gun, yes the sten-gun, indeed.

(IV) The campaign has thrown the question of the treatment of the African in South Africa into the arena of world politics and it is openly admitted that this question attracted the most attention at U.N.O. this year.

(V) The campaign has also proved that the policy of the A.N.C. is the only sane one that affords hope and a future to all inhabitants of South Africa. In spite of the slanderous, malicious hate campaign against our intentions, in spite of the shootings of innocent Africans, which have led to violence and riots, in some towns, we have not panicked; But, on the contrary, we have consistently, under severe hardships taught our people that we are not fighting a race but, RACIAL LAWS, that we do not hate men but "HATE THE EVIL THAT MEN DO".

We have placed before our people the ideal of a democratic South Africa in which all men, irrespective of race, colour, creed or sex, shall live a happy and free life unmarred by fear, prejudice or race hatred; This has appealed to them, thus their unreserved support for the African National Congress. Those preaching race-hatred have become more hysterical as they saw their world tumble around them; They have tried to malign the campaign in order to frighten the Europeans in South Africa to support their evil designs, which can only lead to the total destruction of what they believe to be western civilisation. The A.N.C. is the only organisation with a policy which can lead to harmonious relations between the races in this country and indeed that policy places the A.N.C. in par with progressive and civilised mankind; A policy, unlike that of the protagonists of "White supremacy or Basskap" does not use the colour or race of men as a measuring rod for men's abilities. That is left to the unscientific broederbond and its hysterical band of betrayers of civilisation; History will judge them.

(VI) The campaign has enabled the African people to shed their fears of shadows (IZITHUNZELA). The African people are today, a force to be reckoned with even by those who rear their children by teaching them to despise us.

(VII) We have got rid of pleading, cowardly and hamba-kahle [go slow] leaders who were always ready to compromise after they had been flattered by taking tea with the rulers of the people. These leaders have now been isolated and are siding with their masters to justify oppression and exploitation; GOOD RIDDANCE. These are great achievements. When we consider that for three hundred years we have been carpets to be trampled upon at the will and whim of every European, we must thank God for having travelled with us so rapidly in the path towards the promised land of freedom and a future of fearlessness and hope for mankind.

SEARCH-LIGHT ON THE A.N.C.: A SELF CRITICISM.

The campaign has helped to bring out certain grave weaknesses in our organisation. Like a search-light, it has focussed attention to certain grave defects which we have to overcome if we are to succeed in our task of leading the African people towards that glorious goal "FREEDOM AND HAPPINESS".

The first defect in our movement, placed here because it is the most difficult to solve is that of a NEWSPAPER. A NEWSPAPER, in our own languages can give official reports and state in unequivocal terms, the policy of the A.N.C. A movement like ours cannot hope to progress without a press of its own. Too often have we seen news prostituted by prejudiced owners, who fear that the African, free from racial laws constitutes a danger to interests of exploiters. Who, today amongst the African people has any faith in the "Bantu World" and "Umteteli", Umteteli indeed! for the Chamber of Mines? The enemies of our progress are spending tremendous sums of money to found papers for their lackeys; One has just been launched in Port Elizabeth, "NEW AFRICA". We suspect that several well known Europeans are behind this paper, which so stupidly advocates a return to the old Cape tradition. In their recent edition, the blind servants of NEW AFRICA, raising virtuous eyes to heaven cry,

"WE THANK THEE OH LORD THAT WE ARE NOT AS YOUNG AS ... THESE CONGRESS LEADERS." The editor incidentally is ex-Secretary of the CAPE A.N.C. (SAVE US FROM THE TEA DRINKING LEADERS) They are worth three pence a day extra to the City Council of Port Elizabeth. *The African National Congress must have a press of its own, in 1953.*

The second defect is the absence of full time organisers for the A.N.C. Our A.N.C. is truly remarkable. It has been able to achieve a lot without a single paid organiser. Many CADRES, produced by the struggle have given up their jobs in order to serve voluntarily in organising and uniting the African people. We must not expect too much from our glorious Volunteers but encourage them by looking after them in recognition of their services to the cause of the people's freedom. Finances must be obtained to create an efficient and satisfied personel to perform organisational and administrative work "FULL TIME".

A third defect, made manifest during the course of the campaign is in *ADMINISTRATION.* Many of our branch secretaries do not know the first thing about administration of an office. Letters are not acknowledged. Reports, if any, come slowly. Finances are not recorded properly nor subscriptions despatched to the right quarters, promptly and regularly. Decisions of grave importance are taken by branches and sometimes not reported to H.Q. In some areas, people think they can manage their own affairs until they find themselves in trouble, when, only then, are matters reported to H.Q. This is bad. The A.N.C. is supposed to be a properly constituted movement, its strength lies in its unity of action. It is a disciplined organisation and obtains its inspiration from the solidarity of its supporters. Any action, taken at any time by anybody must be a result of common understanding, consultation and a decision emanating from the popular will of those who have been entrusted with a mandate to make decisions. All branches must take action on the instructions sent by H.Q. in the absence of Conference. Congress needs a school for Secretaries, who must receive proper training for their duties.

The stern trials with which we are faced make it necessary for us to develop responsible, honest, sincere and militant leadership, which only arises from people participating without reservation in an active struggle. Not only do we expect our members to pay subscriptions, but they too, must work actively in building the A.N.C.; Introduce new members, there is no room for shirkers today. The quality of our members must also be improved; Members who will be able to counteract parochial and self seeking enemies of our cause; Members must be able to perceive and expose any malicious distortions of the principles and policies which we have adopted. The many undesirable and morbid features in the administration of the affairs of the A.N.C. must be overcome, NOW.

The pernicious consequences of complacency must be completely uprooted and eradicated. Congress cannot afford any more vainglorious displays or allow occasion for self-laudation. All our weaknesses, from the top-most officials downwards must be subject to constructive and objective criticism so that our faults of yesterday may not be allowed to endanger our progress tomorrow. All of us, connected with the A.N.C., however remotely, must set an example of service; We must show an objective conscientiousness in all matters affecting the African people.

In conclusion, we must look ahead at the future in our struggle for freedom. You have seen what can be achieved in a few months of active struggle, a bold leadership and confidence in the people. Today, meetings are banned by proclamation, many Sons of Africa are banned from attending any gatherings anywhere in South Africa; Twenty Leaders have received sentences of Nine months with compulsory labour; Twenty three others are awaiting trial in the Cape. Seven leaders have been arrested on allegations that they attended gatherings. These are indeed days of stern trials. The Government, not satisfied to gag leaders is threatening to send them to Concentration camps, they intend to ban Congress; Today we learn, without surprise that it is illegal to say "FREEDOM IN OUR LIFE TIME". WE HAVE A DUTY TO THE AFRICAN PEOPLE, WE MUST BE VIGILANT AND EXPOSE ALL THESE PLOTS AGAINST THE AFRICAN PEOPLE, QUICKLY AND EFFECTIVELY. WE HAVE RID OURSELVES OF CORRUPT LEADERS, LET US BE FEARLESS AND IMPLICIT IN OUR FAITH OF THE OUTCOME OF OUR PRESENT STRUGGLES: THE PEOPLE, YES THE PEOPLE, ARE WITH US, OF THAT WE ARE CONVINCED.

INSTRUCTIONS

(I) Branches are hereby instructed to order from Headquarters the "STEWARD OR LEADER CARDS". These are obtainable at fifty (50) for ten shillings (10/-). These cards are intended for branch administration and organisation and will be of great usefulness under the present restrictions imposed by Verwoerd's proclamation, to prevent the gathering of more than ten Africans. Branches shall receive instructional directions on the use of these cards upon application to the Secretariat.

(II) Branches must hold regular fund raising functions for the protracted struggle ahead of us. Already thousands of pounds have been spent on the maintenance of the dependants of our gallant Volunteers and the defence of many members, arrested under the malicious "suppression of Communism Act" but many more thousands will be needed in the new year. Do not be caught napping; PREPARE.

(III) Branches are requested to submit suggestions for the date and venue of the next Provincial Conference. This is very important as we shall have to make decisions affecting our future activities.

(IV) All branches must double their membership for 1953; Subscriptions must be sent promptly. It is not satisfactory to have twenty members in an area of ten thousand people; With a population of ten thousand, your records must show a membership of ten thousand too. The increase in membership depends naturally, upon the activity of your branch and your ability to organise is assessed by the number of people in your books. Make a resolution to take more interest in the A.N.C. in the new year. Become an asset to the organisation, not a liability. We must now make up our minds not to RETURN TO POLITICAL STAGNATION.

The President and Executive Committee of the Cape A.N.C. extend their warmest Xmas Greetings and best New Year Wishes for the determined struggle for freedom in our lifetime.

AFRIKA

Mokxotho Matji
Secretary (Cape) A.N.C.

NEUM AND SOYA

Document 97. "A Declaration to the People of South Africa from the Non-European Unity Movement." Statement by the NEUM, April 1951

THIS is a declaration to the people of South Africa. Five years ago we sent a declaration to the nations of the world (not to be confused with their Governments) informing them of the Nazi-like tyranny under which the people of South Africa live, telling them that although a World War had been fought against the pernicious creed of Hitlerism and its "Master-Race" madness and though it was supposed to have been won in Germany, yet in South Africa this creed continued to live and flourish and triumph. Since then we have had overwhelming proof that the nations of the world (not to be confused with their Governments) know about our plight in South Africa and that we can count on their warmest sympathy, fellow-feeling and goodwill in the struggle against these worshippers of Nazism, the South African Herrenvolk. On the other hand, the contempt in which the South African Herrenvolk are held by world public opinion, the rebuffs and contempt which they meet with in every forum and council outside South Africa, the scorn and cold-shouldering meted out to them individually by every decent White man and woman in Europe and America, all this demonstrates that although we have no Press and our voice is weak, while they have the most powerful means of white-washing themselves and throwing dust in the eyes of the world, yet the force of truth and right has not been crushed and WE ARE NOT ALONE.

494

But when we turn our eyes from the outside world to our own country, we realise that while there is less need to-day to address the nations of the world about our tragic plight, because they know it full well, there is more need to address our own people because it seems that we, the people, do not know it full well.

How otherwise can we explain the fact that we are making so little progress in building that Unity of the nation, without which we can never liberate ourselves? We know that the Herrenvolk are waging relentless war upon us and aim at crushing us as a people and reducing us to a soul-less, will-less, ambition-less chattel slavery. Yet we go about as if we did not know either the cause of our suffering or the remedy for it. Every new blow that the Herrenvolk inflict upon us is received first with astonishment, then with bitterness and then with frustration. Somehow the hatred of oppression that is generated by it, and even the determination to resist and fight back, is not cumulative, but is dissipated either in fruitless, isolated outbursts, or in meaningless argumentation over trifles, or in the harmless channel of appeals, resolutions and petitions readily provided by the Herrenvolk agencies. The dead weight of the past weighs heavily upon us and we seem reluctant to throw it off. We still think and act as isolated groups, each in and for his own kraal of Africans, Coloureds, Indians, Malays, and so on.

Who are the people to whom we are addressing this declaration? Who constitutes the South African nation? The answer to this question is as simple as it would be in any other country. The nation consists of the people who were born in South Africa and who have no other country but South Africa as their mother-land. They may have been born with a black skin or with a brown one, a yellow one or a white one; they may be male or female; they may be young, middle-aged or of an advanced age; they may be short or tall, fat or lean; they may be long-headed or round-headed, straight-haired or curly-haired; they may have long noses or broad noses; they may speak Xhosa, Zulu, Sotho, English or Afrikaans, Hindi, Urdu or Swahili, Arabic or Jewish; they may be Christians, Mohammedans, Buddhists, or of any other faith. So long as they are born of a mother and belong to the human species, so long as they are not lunatics or incurable criminals, they all have an equal title to be citizens of South Africa, members of the nation, with the same rights, privileges and duties. In a nation it is not necessary that the people forming it should have a common language or a common culture, common customs and traditions. There are many nations where the people speak different languages, consist of different nationalities with different cultures. The United States of America, Switzerland and the Soviet Union may be taken as examples. All that is required for a people to be a nation is community of interests, love of their country, pride in being citizens of their country.

And have not the Non-Europeans of South Africa sufficient community of interests? Are we not all crushed by the same Nazi-like racial creed? Are we not all persecuted and humiliated by the South African brand of Nüremberg laws under the hall-mark blazoning all over South Africa: "For Europeans Only"? Do we not live in constant fear of every official and policeman because, from the moment of our birth, we are branded as criminals by the colour of our skin? The prisons and cemeteries, or, as official language prefers it, the statistics of crime and death, are eloquent testimony of our community of interests. Indeed, to-day we are brutally deprived of a stake in the development of the riches and beauty of our country, a stake in its progress or in its citizenship. But we are imbued with the hope that our claim to them all will be realised in full during the present generation. And it is through no fault of ours that we have to bear before the rest of the world the shame that is now inseparable from the name of South Africa. Here, too, we are confident that the shame and blot will be erased in our generation.

But this universal concept of a nation is not shared by the criminal minds of Hitler and his Nazi followers; it is not shared by the South African Herrenvolk, who have usurped to themselves all political, economic and judicial rights, who have wielded the gun and grabbed the land in order to proclaim themselves the sole citizens of the country, the sole rulers, owners, law-makers, to proclaim themselves THE nation. It is against these usurpers who have robbed the whole nation of its rights and reduced its people to the position of outcasts thrust into reserves, locations, bazaars and sub-economic or sub-human townships and tolerated only as servants and unskilled labourers—it is against these that the nation has to unite in the struggle for its land, rights and liberty. It is therefore to all those who are against Nazism and Herrenvolkism that this Declaration of the Non-European Unity Movement is addressed. If it is primarily addressed to all Non-Europeans, it does not exclude any European who accepts unconditionally our right to full and equal citizenship and our definition of a nation.

It is common knowledge to-day that the Herrenvolk have been able to conquer the Non-Europeans and maintain their domination chiefly by their policy of "divide and rule". They have persistently and consciously followed this policy of splitting the people, playing one section off against the other and fomenting jealousy and enmity by intrigues and by seeming to vary the degree to which the screw of oppression is being applied. The policy of segregation has held not only as between White and Non-White—this is fundamental to the Master-Race creed—but among the Non-Europeans themselves in order to split them into as many sections and groups as possible and prevent them from coming together and forming a nation.

This policy has been going on unchanged up to our own day. Even now, when the screw is being turned to the breaking-point, this policy is being consistently followed: first take away from the Africans their semblance of a vote (they never had a real vote) and give them special "Native" Representatives and a Native "Representative" Council, but leave the Coloured "vote" alone. Then a little later do the same thing with the Coloured People's semblance of a vote but, in order to assure them that they are not being "reduced to

496

the same level as the Natives'', abolish the ''Native'' Representatives altogether from the House of Assembly, leaving only ''Native'' Representatives in the Senate. Still later, when the ''Coloured'' Representatives are likewise abolished from the House of Assembly, console the Coloured people with the fact that their Senate ''Representatives'' remain while those of the Africans are abolished. And so the Herrenvolk go on keeping up the appearance of preferential treatment. They must at all costs prevent the Non-Europeans from coming together and building a nation, for they know it will sound the death-knell to their domination.

The process of finding out this subtle game began to germinate in 1935-36 during the passage of the three infamous ''Native Bills'', and eventually gave birth to the Non-European Unity Movement in 1943. We need not here go into the history of the Unity Movement, the thorough and systematic working out of its federal structure so indispensable to the building of a nation consisting of many nationalities, its fundamental principles, its policy and its 10-Point Programme. What we have to stress here is that, while the policy of the Herrenvolk is chiefly directed to splitting the Non-Europeans and preventing them from building the nation, it is the fundamental policy of the Unity Movement, on the other hand, first and foremost to break the barriers of segregation between the Non-Europeans and to help in the building of a nation.

This task, however, is proving much more difficult than was at first thought. The mental barriers of segregation, built up and fortified by the Herrenvolk for generations, are proving much harder to break than what may be called the physical barriers which the insane policy of the Herrenvolk has been steadily undermining for the past fifteen years. When we pose to the people the questions: ''Do we as a nation know where we are and whither we are going? Do we as a nation realise what the Herrenvolk are scheming and whither they are dragging us?'' and when we look at the way the people have behaved during the past few years, we must in all honesty admit that the people do not know the answers. They behave as groups, think as groups, act as groups, but not as a nation. All sections of the Non-Europeans are afflicted with this segregation-germ. It puts back the clock when the leadership of the Indians can see nothing but the Group Areas Act and direct all their energy towards bringing about a Round Table Conference with India and Pakistan; or when, as one hears repeatedly at meetings in defence of the Coloured vote, it is argued that ''we shall not allow ourselves to be reduced to the level of the Natives''; or when, to the delight of the Herrenvolk and the enemies of Unity, the Africans in Natal still harbour Indo-phobia and have actually been guilty of an anti-Indian pogrom. Admittedly, the agents and lackeys of the Herrenvolk have a great deal to do with all this, but a part of the blame must be placed on the shoulders of the Non-Europeans themselves.

THE FIRST QUESTION.

When we look back over the past few years, one of the most striking things we notice is the amount of the nation's energy and time that has been wasted through the activities of the Quislings, misleaders and the cranks who may

497

unwittingly have aided and abetted the Quislings. We have a rather large number of persons who profit and prosper on the misery and oppression of the people. Some make it their only profession, while some work it as a sideline. Their task is to fasten the chains on the people, not as direct gaolers but in such a way that the people do not notice it. Naturally such persons are to be found occupying prominent positions, playing the part of "tried and tested leaders who work themselves to the bone in the service of the people". Clever and capable, they have to play a subtle game. They work the machinery of oppression: the Natives' Representative Council, the Coloured Advisory Council, the Asiatic Advisory Board, the Bungas and Advisory Boards; they are the hangers-on of the "Native" Representatives in the Assembly and the Senate, and a host of other agencies. And all because, as they claim, "we must be practical and realistic". At the same time they pacify the hostility of the people by making a few violent speeches and even pretending to be in opposition to the Herrenvolk. And when they see that the people are finding them out, they become afraid lest the rulers will drop them as being of no further use, so they try to hoodwink both sides by launching something spectacular, something that will catch the imagination of the masses and at the same time show the rulers that they are not played out yet and thus heighten their value to the masters. If the rulers are still reluctant to raise the price, there is always that useful weapon, the THREAT of unity. Now the name by which these persons are known throughout the world is—QUISLING.

The activities of the Quislings and the extent to which they have put back the clock during the past few years cannot be properly assessed until we have examined the political behaviour of certain other persons who may honestly have meant well, but whose actions have had the objective effect of assisting the work of the Quislings. For example, no one could accuse the present Indian leaders of being Quislings but, nevertheless, the end result of their practical activity has meant condoning, assisting and collaborating with the Quislings. Without the moral and material support that the Indian leaders gave to the African Quislings, there would not have been that whole sorry chapter of opportunism, adventurism and buffoonery which has cast so much shame and sorrow over the past few years. For no one can look back on the whole national scene without this sense of shame, and if it were not for the lessons we have to learn from it, we would be tempted to skip the whole chapter.

How unedifying it is to look back on the spectacle—more proper to a circus than to the struggle of an oppressed people:—the stepping in and out of the Quisling Councils, the pretence of bowing to the will of the people (in front of the curtain) by staging a revolt, by adopting non-collaboration, then flouting the will of the people (behind the curtain) by negotiations with the Herrenvolk for an enlarged Council and better pay, and then achieving the unbelievable feat of electing collaborators on a non-collaboration ticket. How unedifying it was to see grown-up people, despite the whole rich experience of the liberatory movement throughout the world, indulging in an exhibition of mysticism and

498

inviting the rulers to make them martyrs by throwing them into jail, and hoping thereby to soften the hearts of the Herrenvolk. How unedifying the spectacle of pompously sending off delegations to U.N.O. after the collapse of the mystical exhibitionism, then pleading at the bar of the House and making frantic efforts to bring about a Round Table Conference. How unedifying the childishness of those sporadic displays of Anti-Pass Day, Protest Day, Mourning Day and, lastly, the display of so-called "unity".

Not that there is anything wrong with pass-burning, protest strikes, sit-down or stay-at-home strikes—if we have the power to carry them out and when we have the nation behind the organisation. But without any proper organisation and with a complete lack of preparation, mobilisation and co-ordination, to call a strike of this nature means playing right into the hands of the enemy. It results in a shocking waste of life; it brings about dismissals, a chopping off of the militants, prosecutions and in effect throws the movement back.

It is not that there is anything wrong with unity—if it is meant honestly and not as a kind of utility unity that is mentioned only on special occasions when it is needed and does not exist at any other time. One can only blush in shame at the display of "unity" when an African doctor arrives in Durban to shake hands with his Indian colleagues on the occasion of anti-Indian legislation and when the Indian doctors reciprocate at a Johannesburg meeting on the occasion of anti-African legislation, or when African and Indian doctors travel to Cape Town to display unity of all three sections on the occasion of anti-Coloured legislation and then, having satisfied themselves that they have shown a "United Front" to the Herrenvolk, relax from unity for the rest of the year. And yet the most appalling thing about it all is not so much the comic or even the tragic side; it is the political dishonesty, the wanton playing about with the sentiments and the very lives of the people, the raising of false hopes while knowing that they will lead the people into a blind alley—and all for selfish motives, a Round Table Conference, a Gentleman's Agreement, a little more scope to the Dummy Councils, in a word, maintaining the *status quo*.

It would be wrong to underestimate the force of the Quislings and *other anti-Unity elements*. Not because they have a big following. They have not. Among the Coloured population their following is negligible. Their following among the Africans is also numerically small and only among the Indians is it at all significant. But it is as a negative force that their influence must be reckoned with, as a disruptive agency causing confusion and blocking the way to progress. Their disruptive influence is particularly pernicious and detrimental to the building of Unity and of a nation. Their habit of running around in circles and making a noise, their enthusiasm for all kinds of stunts and their propensity to flare up and rush into stupid adventures can only lead to dis- illusionment among the people; cause confusion and panic in their thinking and create despair. Desperation is indeed a bad counsellor. Consequently the great issues, the whole potential strength of the national forces and, on the other hand, the weakness of the Herrenvolk structure, become obscured from vision and in their stead the small issues loom large. Every fresh piece of anti-Non-European legislation, every fresh attack is apprehended as something out of the blue and viewed as a thing in itself, and not as part of a whole process. Instead of realising that it is all a part of the war which the Herrenvolk are constantly waging against us, we treat it as if it were an emergency, a thunderstorm out of a blue sky. But there is no blue sky; it is dark with storm and all the time we are in the midst of war.

As a result of this misconception, all we see is the new, the immediate, and the old is treated as if it were a matter of course. We fail to see ourselves as a nation, more than half-submerged. We fail to see the sum total of our economic, political and social bankruptcy, our health, our education, our future. Indeed, during the past few years we have had a rich crop of legislation directed against all sections of the Non-Europeans: the Mixed Marriages Act, the Immorality Act, the Group Areas Act, the Registration Act (Passes for all Non-Europeans), the Suppression of Communism Act. Train and Post Office Apartheid, and now the Native Building Workers Bill and the Coloured Disfranchisement Bill—to mention only the chief. Each and all of them mean fresh nails in our coffin. *Each and all of them have to be fought and resisted.* Only let us not think that these are the be-all and end-all of our lives. Let us not get into the slavish way of thinking: "Give us the good old days, the days before *Apartheid"*, for this in effect means: "Give us the good old days of segregation!"

This is precisely what the Quislings, the misleaders and cranks are driving towards. According to them the main thing is to preserve the *status quo*. If only the Group Areas Act could be withdrawn and the Disfranchisement Bill staved off, if only the Native Representative Council (N.R.C.) could be enlarged and permitted to discuss policy, all three sections would be satisfied. Then life would be normal again. We could go on having babies and burying them; we could go on filling the jails with Pass Law "offenders" and Poll Tax "defaulters"; we could go on being dragged out of bed in police raids for liquor offences or no offence at all; we could go on being chained by the farmers for fear of our sons and daughters escaping from slavery to the towns and then being brought back to the "rightful owners" by the still stronger chains of the Masters and Servants Act; we could go on happily with the Colour Bar Act, the Apprenticeship Act, the Tot System and the thousand and one Nazi laws; we could go on without land, without the right to move, without access to the professions, without education, hospitals, houses, without the right to sell our labour where we please, without the right to strike against intolerable conditions. We could do without self-respect, dignity and human rights as long as we can get 1/4½d. a shift in the mines and 5/- a month on the farms!

This question of the *status quo* is not merely an academic question of no practical importance to-day. It is a question of the highest significance in the

500

building of a nation. Is it to be based on the principle of complete freedom from all national oppression and on the demands for full and equal democratic rights, or is it to be based on bargaining for the amelioration of conditions, on bargaining for some concessions and crumbs? The Non-European Unity Movement (N.E.U.M.) is solidly built on the former; the "utility unity" on the latter. In the latter case, unity is conceived and used only as a bargaining weapon by those who are ready at any moment to betray it, to drop it, if they can gain something for themselves. That is why the Herrenvolk are not impressed, knowing as they do its value and its price. The question of the *status quo* may seem academic to-day when the Herrenvolk are waging total war upon the Non-Europeans and do not think in terms of reforms or armistice. But we are living in an epoch of wars and change. If the war that is smouldering in the East should flare up into a world conflagration, the situation might change very rapidly. The same set of conditions (the unfavourable turn of the war for the allies) which induced Field-Marshal Smuts to change face and proclaim that "Segregation has fallen on evil days! Segregation is dead!" may induce Dr. Malan in the coming war to say the same with regard to *Apartheid*. And the collaborators and Quislings will certainly not be found wanting. They will be ready to sell the Non-Europeans to Dr. Malan for a few promises, a few crumbs. The time to say it is now! Let the people learn from the lessons of the past and not treat the question of the *status quo* as academic and remote. Let them realise that all the shouting for the *status quo,* for the two-thirds majority necessary to change the Constitution and for Round Table Conferences is the forerunner to coming betrayals and sell-outs.

From the foregoing it is obvious that the people are much too slow in realising the destructiveness that the Quislings, collaborators and cranks are inflicting on the national cause. To that blight may be attributed the greatest part of the damage. Of the additional factors that have retarded progress, the chief one is the lack of co-ordination between town and country. The town worker, beset with his own load (a miserable stationary wage and a continually rising cost of living, the heartbreaking problem of shelter—called "housing"—the Pass raids and the Police Terror) still knows too little of the terrible hardship of the "peasant" without land, of the squatter and the farmlabourer whose status is something between slavery and serfdom. In general, the land problem, the most important problem with which we as a nation are faced, is too little known and appreciated by the town worker and the intellectual. They do not sufficiently realise that robbing the people of the land is the cause of the migratory labour system, the pass-laws, poll-tax, the shanty towns, the destitution, desertion, the breaking up of the family and most of the undesirable features in our social organism. The so-called Rehabilitation Scheme, the culling of stock, with its periodic Witzieshoek affairs, are only the by-products of the land problem of South Africa.

This lack of co-ordination between town and country becomes all the more serious when it is considered together with the general organisational weakness of the Non-Europeans. We are a poor people and cannot as yet afford to have numerous paid organisers who would constantly be touring the country to enlighten and organise the people. Neither do we as yet possess a centralised Press in one language, let alone the various languages of our people. But even if we had both we would not be able to make much use of them because of the lack of local organisations. Neither the spoken word not the written one can be sent out into a vacuum. In order to reach the people they must have channels through which to flow and points of support to receive them. Such points are local organisations in every dorp, village, town, location or bazaar. Without them, not even the simplest message can be effectively sent out from the centre by the national organisation. If we are serious about conducting a liberatory struggle and attaining freedom, we have got to join our existing local bodies (even in the smallest places) or build them where they do not yet exist. Without these local organisations there is no possibility of successfully conducting any resistance, no possibility of mobilising the people and consequently of marching forward. This work cannot be done from the centre. It has to be done by the more advanced people on the spot.

Another handicap to our progress is the inability of the organised workers to emancipate themselves from Herrenvolk tutelage and to play their full part in the national movement. In the so-called "mixed" trade unions they are just hanging on to the tails of the Europeans, afraid to be left alone, paying their subscriptions—and are of no use to the liberatory struggle. Since the White leaders of the trade unions, with only a few exceptions, are all good Herrenvolk henchmen, they use the slogan of "No Politics in Trade Unions", in order to allow only the politics of their masters in the trade unions. As to the purely Non-European Trade Unions, they also hang on to the tails of the South African Trades and Labour Council, as if therein lay their only salvation. While the benefits accruing to the S.A. Trades and Labour Council are obvious and tangible, it is very difficult to detect with the naked eye the benefits that the Non-European trade unions derive from this attachment. Neither official recognition nor the right to strike is the reward for submission to Herrenvolk tutelage and supervision; but on the other hand the Herrenvolk profits by keeping the Non-European workers out of the liberatory movement.

It is necessary to state clearly and unequivocally: the place of the worker is first of all in the national movement for liberation; his first duty is to his people and to himself as a part of the people. There can be no successful resistance to the Herrenvolk, there can be no action whatsoever on a national scale, until the Non-European workers, the trade unions, are fairly and squarely in the national movement, ready to play their full part alongside the peasants and the intellectuals.

This, then, is the position in which we as a nation find ourselves to-day, still disunited, still unorganised and unco-ordinated, still at the beginning of the road.

THE SECOND QUESTION.

From the point of view of the Herrenvolk we don't count at all as a people, even as a part of the nation. For them we are only an asset, a part of immovable capital, and the argument is solely whether we are a useful asset or a wasteful asset. It appears, therefore, quite natural to them to shape the policy of the country according to the interests of the Herrenvolk only. The economic policy is to squeeze out from this asset—labour—as much as possible for as small an expense as possible. The social policy is to keep the Non-European out of sight when he is not needed for service. The educational policy is to ensure that the Non-European's intellectual powers are stunted, while allowing just sufficient latitude to fit him to become a servant. And the general policy is to proclaim to the world—while they stand with both feet firmly planted on the body of the Non-European—that "He does not want to rise, the savage". The net result of this, necessarily simplified, picture is that *at every point* the interests of the Non-Europeans are diametrically opposed to the interests of the Herrenvolk. Since the policy of the Herrenvolk is directed towards their *own* good, it must at every stage be against *our* good. The external policy of a country is the continuation of its internal policy. So it should not surprise us that the Government does not consider it necessary to consult us or even to inform us what it is doing abroad in relation to other countries. That might put the idea into our heads that we are also part of the nation!

The Government of Dr. Malan, just as the Government of Field-Marshal Smuts before it, stubbornly maintains that whatever the Herrenvolk do to the Non-European people is a strictly internal affair of South Africa and concerns nobody else. In this they are merely being consistent with the Master-Race creed. Hitler also maintained that whatever the Herrenvolk of Germany did to the Jews was their own internal affairs and nobody should poke his nose into it. The attempt of India and Pakistan to alleviate the lot of the Indians of South Africa, particularly after the passing of the Asiatic Land Tenure Act and the Group Areas Act, by a direct approach to the Government of South Africa, failed. And since then the yearly farce has been going on at U.N.O.: India brings forward the accusation that the South African Herrenvolk have violated Human Rights, only to drop it at the last moment or accept a meaningless U.N.O. resolution as a compromise. However, as a result of the pressure of public opinion at home, the Indian Government recalled her High Commissioner and the relations between India and South Africa are strained.

The second act of the yearly farce at U.N.O. is in connection with South-West Africa, which South Africa has administered as a Mandate since the end of World War I, and now has decided to incorporate into the Union. Neither the yearly passing of resolutions censuring the Union nor the adverse verdict of the International Court at The Hague could stop the Herrenvolk from annexing the territory. Moreover, emboldened by the fact that the U.N.O. condemnation of the Union is meant only as a make-believe, while, behind the scenes, the

503

Union is told to go ahead, the Malan Government has adopted an openly aggressive Imperialistic policy and attitude towards affairs on the African Continent and even beyond it, in the Middle East and the Far East. The demand for the Protectorates, the casting of covetous eyes on the Rhodesias, the condemnation of the "liberal" policy of the other Imperialist powers who shared out Africa among themselves at the end of the last century, the opposition to even the slightest reforms which the Imperialist powers are forced to concede as a result of the increasing militancy of the masses and the growing liberatory movement—all these have earned for Malan's Government and the South African Herrenvolk the hatred of the masses of Africa. At the same time they annoy the old Imperialist powers, the big sharks, who resent this arrogance and swollenheadedness on the part of the bull-frog. At present a controversy is going on between the South African Herrenvolk and the Imperialists of Britain on the question of raising armies of Africans for the coming World War. The Herrenvolk are violently opposed to the arming of Africans, fearing that the Non-Europeans will turn upon their oppressors, just as the peoples of Asia did so successfully during and after World War II.

This was before the fateful days of June, 1950, when a spark in Korea set in motion what will probably be recorded in history as the prelude to World War III. During these ten months sufficient evidence has come to the fore to demonstrate that it was the U.S.A. which planned and provoked the Korean War. Stung by the success of the Chinese people in their long and arduous struggle for liberation from the yoke of America and Britain, smarting from the crushing defeat of their Quisling, Chiang-Kai-Shek, whose armies were paid and equipped with American money and ammunition and even assisted directly by the American navy and air-force; pained also by being thrown off the mainland of Asia and by the loss of what they had come to consider as their colony and preserve of raw materials and markets for their goods; bitter at the frustration of their foreign and military policy of world domination, the United States of America—those worshippers of Gold and War—skilfully planned their revenge upon the people of Asia by deliberately provoking the war with China through a war with Korea.

These ten months of war have brought many changes. First the U.S.A. suffered a series of humiliating defeats at the hands of the Koreans. Then, by throwing in half-a-million men they forced the Koreans to the very borders of China, and by boasting of their intention of going beyond the borders they compelled China to send its army in defence of its power-plants and its people. Once again the U.S.A. suffered a series of defeats, this time administered by the Chinese. Of one thing only can they boast with confidence—they have laid Korea waste by bombing, burning, raping, slaughtering. And all in defence of "peace" and "democracy".

It is important for us to note three things arising out of the war against Korea. Firstly, the rôle that U.N.O. has played in the war. Throwing off all pretence of being a League of Nations for the defence of peace and human rights, it revealed itself for all to see as a machine in the service of the Imperialist powers who "own" the colonies in Asia and Africa, hold the colonial and semi-colonial countries in chains, oppress the Non-European peoples there and prosper and batten on their labour and sweat and blood. With indecent haste and unbounded cynicism these powers, together with their satellites and Quislings under the cloak and name of U.N.O., have branded as aggressors those who defended their homes and their liberty. How familiar this is to a Non-European—to be called a law-breaker when he is defending his home, his cattle, his rights!

The second point for us to note is the utter contempt which the ideologists of the Master-Race displayed towards the Koreans and the Chinese. When things went badly for the aggressors—those who did not turn a hair at the wiping out of the civilian populations of Hiroshima and Nagasaki—they twice wanted to use the atom bomb, first against the Koreans and then against the Chinese. Only the intervention of the other Imperialist Powers, especially Britain who still has a stake in Asia and is afraid to lose her last colonial possessions there, such as Hong-Kong, Ceylon, Burma and a half-share in India, forced President Truman to desist from this dastardly step by pointing out that the Non-European peoples would interpret such a step as meaning that the atom bomb was for Non-Europeans Only.

The third point for us to note is how the South African Herrenvolk entered the war against Korea and China. At first the Government decided only to vote for the American resolution at U.N.O. and, apart from this moral support, to decline any active participation in view of the remoteness of the theatre of war from the actual sphere where "South Africa" considers herself vitally interested, namely, the Continent of Africa, the Mediterranean and the Suez Canal. This decision held only for about a week or so and then it was announced to the Herrenvolk that "South Africa" was sending an air force squadron as its contribution to the punishment of the Korean Aggressor and the fight against Communism. No one asked questions about the reasons for this sudden somersault, because everyone could guess what the U.S.A. Government told the South African Government. It might have been couched in the customary language of to-day: "Defence of the principles of Democracy and Peace against Communist Aggression", but in plain English the South African Herrenvolk were told that, being themselves the oppressors of a Non-European population, they were in duty bound to help in the crushing of the struggle of a Colonial people against foreign aggression, because if this sort of thing were allowed to spread and succeed in Asia to-day, then to-morrow it might be on the order of the day in Africa!

Now it is hardly necessary to repeat that, since we have no say whatsoever in the shaping of either the internal or the foreign policy and no voice in the affairs of the country, we cannot be held responsible for the actions of the Herrenvolk Government. We have declared war neither on Korea nor on China. We have no quarrel with the Korean people or the Chinese people, or with any other people fighting for their liberation. The Korean war drives home what we have already observed before, namely, that at any and every point, whether in peace or in war, the interests of the Herrenvolk are diametrically opposed to the interests of the people. Anyone who is well disposed towards us is considered by the Herrenvolk as an enemy. And naturally we have to conclude that anyone who is a friend of the Herrenvolk must be an enemy of ours. We want this to be grasped clearly and fully.

CONCLUSIONS.

Now, having stated what we consider important for the people to know, we wish to conclude this Declaration with the following:

There is no escaping the fact that, during the past few years, we have made very little progress on the road to liberation. We have enumerated the reasons for this and, unless we consummate these lessons, we cannot hope for any drastic change in the situation. We do not believe in miracles. There is a time for everything. There is a time for heart-searching and a time for deliberations; there is a time for decisions before the time for action comes. But we cannot remain dilly-dallying in the first stage. The Herrenvolk are waging war upon the Non-Europeans, and if we want to survive as free human beings we have to win this war. We can win it only if we are prepared to fight, to bear sacrifices and submit to discipline in the national cause. Even without arms, with the only weapon at our disposal—Non-Collaboration—we can win.

But in order to achieve victory,

We have got to build the Nation.

We have got to build the Unity of the Nation.

We have got to put the Quislings beyond the pale of the Nation.

We have got to mobilise every capable man and woman into active local organisations.

We have got to bring the organised workers, the trade unions, into the national organisations.

We have got to co-ordinate the work of town and country.

Let us not forget that battles are fought, and will be fought, over this or that position, over this or that Bill, but a war is fought over big issues. And the big issues for which we are fighting are contained in the 10-Point Programme....

Document 98. "Opening Address" at First Conference of the Society of Young Africa, by I.B. Tabata, December 20, 1951

This, the first Conference of the Society of Young Africa, is in my opinion no ordinary conference. It is a historical landmark in the arduous road that the Non-Europeans must travel in order to achieve liberation....

... another development ... found expression in the last Conference of the Non-European Unity Movement early this year—the Birth of a Nation.

The Birth of a Nation. This conception directs the population along new channels of thought. It signalises the beginning of political maturity. No longer do the Non-Europeans see themselves as a "problem to be solved". On the contrary, it is they who have to solve the problem of South Africa.... They see themselves as faced with the task of Building a Nation, a healthy, virile nation.

This is the stage which the Non-Europeans have reached in their political development. This is the atmosphere in which the new body, the Society of Young Africa, is being formed....

Like everything else that is born, the Society of Young Africa must grow, and it will grow if it adjusts itself to its environment, growing with the struggle and in turn contributing to it. By growth I do not mean merely an increase in their numbers. This is taken for granted. I refer rather to progress in the realm of ideas. The Soyan youth must integrate themselves with the movement for liberation, draw sustenance from it, expand their intellectual horizon and in turn make their contribution to the movement.... S.O.Y.A. can, for instance, assist in bringing to the consciousness of wider sections of the people the two-fold nature of oppression: national oppression and class exploitation. It is generally recognised that Non-Europeans are oppressed as nationalities and most people see the struggle simply as between the oppressed Non-Europeans and the White oppressor. It is not so commonly realised that there is another and more fundamental form of oppression, namely, class exploitation. When we consider this last, we find that in the final analysis the conflict is not basically that of colour...

The only question the Soyans ask is: What are your political convictions? Do you believe in unqualified equality, political, economic and social? In other words, do you believe in the 10-Point Programme? These are the only relevant questions. And our test is: whether or not a man applies non-collaboration. Questions of colour, race, sex or creed do not enter.

You will have noted that I lay great stress on the importance of ideas. But we must realise that ideas are not hot-house plants artificially divorced from the soil. It is when men come to grips with reality that their consciousness is heightened and correct ideas spring up.... The ideas are the weapons with which you cut your path in the barbaric jungle of South African society to-day. *We have to fight ideas with ideas....*

While the propaganda of the Herrenvolk is designed for the enslavement of the oppressed, it has a boomerang effect. Those who seek to enslave are in a way themselves enslaved. Intellectually they are rotting on their feet.

Let us take a look at that section of the White population that provides the leadership of the country.... Let us take a look at the different stages that a child belonging to this section goes through.... When the time comes for him to enter the University, what do we find? And (this is important) what kind of University do we find?... This superman, then, puts in his time at the university and emerges untouched—or shall we say, unscathed—by new ideas, spiritually stunted, intellectually bedwarfed. And at the end of it all he is let loose on society to disseminate in his turn all the racial prejudices, myths and superstitions.... But facts—harsh facts—have a habit of hammering at blind faith and at the present time they are attacking its very citadel.... The chronic state of crisis in the whole capitalist world together with the successes of the Non-White peoples in the East has produced an acute tension in the minds of the South African Herrenvolk. It has produced an intellectual crisis. Faced with problems they cannot solve, they fall into a neurosis. It is a sickness which is sapping the well-being of society. The truth is, the Herrenvolk to-day has reached a stage of spiritual bankruptcy, intellectual stagnation and, indeed, the destruction and decay of the whole moral fibre.

What is the effect of this state of affairs on their youth?... he finds himself called upon to defend Herrenvolkism and all that that implies. The unthinking and the thug find no difficulty in doing this; their training has prepared them for the job. But what of the more intelligent and the more sensitive mind? He cannot fail to see the injustice and the sheer immorality of a system that permits a few White people to batten on a whole Black population. A conflict arises in his mind. He cannot give himself wholeheartedly to a cause which his reason rejects. But he finds it difficult to cut himself adrift from his milieu, with its comforts and privileges, re-orientate his thinking and throw in his lot with the opponents of the system. This requires a strength of character of which few are capable. The vast majority of this section takes the course of least resistance and find refuge in various forms of escapism. The most common among the so—called intellectuals is called Bohemianism. I needn't paint to you the lurid picture of this world of pseudo art and moral perversities. It is an affliction that has blighted the young intelligentsia. It has taken great toll of the youth. And the Non-European intellectual, too, is being contaminated by the same disease. In one form or another all society has fallen under this blight of herrenvolkism which permeates it from top to bottom.

It is against this background that we must view the idea of the Birth of a Nation. It is against this background that the conception of Building a Nation assumes its full significance. In the full consciousness of the magnitude of our tasks, we come forward to shoulder our responsibilities. We have nothing to lose. We have a world to conquer. We, the oppressed, are the only people who can throw into the struggle all our energies, convinced of the justice of our cause. We go into the struggle, not simply to save the youth, not only to save the Non-Europeans. It is a question of the preservation of all society. Our struggle here in South Africa is part and parcel of the struggle of humanity as a whole.

To the Society of Young Africa I say: Let us get down to the task of Building The Nation!

Chronology

1935

May: Joint Select Committee of Parliament tables the Representation of Natives Bill and the Native Trust and Land Bill

October: Italy attacks Ethiopia

December: Coloured radicals form National Liberation League

December 15-18: Professor D. D. T. Jabavu and Dr. Pixley ka I. Seme call meeting of the All African Convention (AAC)

1936

February: AAC deputation meets with Prime Minister J. B. M. Hertzog

March 30: United Transkeian Territories General Council supports retention of the Cape African franchise

April 7: Joint sitting of Parliament passes Representation of Natives Bill, 169-11; Native Trust and Land Bill becomes law in May

June 29–July 2: AAC reconvenes

1937

Natives (Urban Areas) Amendment Act

Native Laws Amendment Act

Industrial Conciliation Act

June: Election for Natives' Representative Council (NRC)

December: Meeting of AAC

December: "Silver Jubilee" Conference of African National Congress (ANC); the Rev. Z. R. Mahabane succeeds Dr. Seme as president-general

1938

Afrikaner nationalist celebration of the centenary of the Great Trek

April: Formation of the Non-European United Front

May 30: General election

1939

Asiatics (Transvaal Land and Trading) Act

Formation of the short-lived National Union of African Youth in Natal

Communist Party headquarters moves from Johannesburg to Cape Town under Moses Kotane as national secretary

May 15-17: Deputation from the ANC and Congress of Urban Advisory Boards to the minister of Native affairs

September 4: House of Assembly votes 80-67 to enter World War II; resignation of Hertzog, who is succeeded by Jan Christiaan Smuts as prime minister

1940

January: Hertzog's followers merge with Daniel F. Malan's in the Reunited National Party

July 7: The national executive committees of the ANC and the AAC adopt resolution on the war

December: Meeting of a joint ANC-AAC committee
          First meeting of AAC since 1937
          ANC conference elects Dr. A. B. Xuma to succeed the Rev. Z. R. Mahabane as president-general

1941

Factories, Machinery and Building Work Act

June: Supporters of Malan draft constitution for a future republic

July 8: Deputation from the ANC to the minister of justice

August 3: Conference to rebuild the African Mine Workers' Union

August 14: Roosevelt and Churchill's Atlantic Charter

November: Formation of Council of Non-European Trade Unions

December: Special session of the AAC

1942

War Measure 145

Election for NRC

March 4: Deputation from the ANC to the deputy prime minister

June 28: The Non-European United Front convenes conference

December 28: Pretoria riot (17 killed, about 111 wounded)

1943

Trading and Occupation of Land (Transvaal and Natal) Restriction Act

February 28: Formation of Anti-C.A.D. [Coloured Affairs Department]

July 7: General election

August: Alexandra bus boycott (nine days)

September 26: Inauguration of Paul Mosaka's African Democratic Party

November: Inauguration of Anti-Pass Campaign (1943-1945)

December 4-5: Inauguration of Campaign for Right and Justice

December 16: ANC conference adopts *Africans' Claims* (including "Bill of Rights") and a new constitution; authorizes formation of a Youth League

December: Meeting of joint ANC-AAC committee

December 17: Adoption of a "10-Point Programme" by delegates from the AAC and the Anti-C.A.D. at the First Unity Conference and provisional founding of the Non-European Unity Movement (NEUM)

1944

War Measure 1,425

February 2: Meeting of youth leaders with Dr. Xuma

April 2: Inaugural meeting of ANC Youth League

May 20-21: National Anti-Pass Conference

July 8: Second Unity Conference of NEUM

September 10: Conference of the ANC Youth League (Transvaal) elects A. M. Lembede as president

November 14: Beginning of Alexandra bus boycott (seven weeks)

November: Scattered fighting between Africans and whites in Johannesburg; destruction of the *Bantu World* printing plant and offices

1945

Native Education Finance Act

Natives (Urban Areas) Consolidation Act

June: Adoption of United Nations Charter at the San Francisco Conference; Smuts' preamble calls for "larger freedom"

August: All-in Conference of nonwhite trade unions; opening address by Dr. Xuma

October: ANC representation at fifth Pan-African Congress, in Manchester

October: Dr. G. M. Naicker takes over leadership of the Natal Indian Congress

1946

Asiatic Land Tenure and Indian Representation Act

Death of the Rev. J. L. Dube; Chief Albert J. Lutuli in a by-election wins Dube's seat in the NRC

June 13: Natal Indian Congress and Transvaal Indian Congress (the latter under Dr. Y. M. Dadoo) begin passive resistance campaign (1946-1948)

June 23: Second National Anti-Pass Conference

August 12-15: African mine workers' strike

August 14-15: Meeting and adjournment of the NRC

August-September: Trial of 52 accused of aiding illegal mine strike; discharged or fined; followed by trial of Communists for sedition, November 1946-October 1948

October 6-7: Dr. Xuma, who later attends the United Nations in New York, calls "Emergency Conference of All Africans"

November 20: Acting Prime Minister Jan Hofmeyr addresses the NRC

November 26: NRC adjourns

1947

Industrial Conciliation (Natives) Bill; not enacted

March 9: Dr. A. B. Xuma, Dr. G. M. Naicker, and Dr. Y. M. Dadoo issue "Joint Declaration of Cooperation"

May 8-9: Interview by some NRC members with Prime Minister Jan Smuts

July: Death of A. M. Lembede

1948

Report of the Native Laws Commission, 1946-1948 [Fagan Report]

March: Election for NRC

May 22-24: First Transvaal-Orange Free State People's Assembly for Votes for All

May 26: General election; victory of Malan's Nationalist Party

Introduction of apartheid on trains in Cape Peninsula

October 3: Twelve African leaders issue "A Call for African Unity"

December 3: Death of Jan Hofmeyr

December 16-17: Joint conference of the ANC and the AAC

1949

Prohibition of Mixed Marriages Act

January 4-5: Notice of government's intention to abolish the NRC given at the first meeting of the NRC in over two years

January 13: Eruption of Zulu rioting against Indians in Durban: statements by African and Indian leaders (January 14-February 6)

April 17-18: Joint meeting of the ANC and AAC national executive committees

June: Professor Z. K. Matthews succeeds the Rev. James A. Calata as president of the Cape African Congress

December 17: ANC conference adopts the Programme of Action. Dr. James S. Moroka elected to succeed Dr. Xuma as president-general; new leadership comes into power, with Walter M. Sisulu succeeding the Rev. James Calata as secretary-general

1950

Group Areas Act

Population Registration Act

Immorality Amendment Act

Suppression of Communism Act

March 26: "Defend Free Speech Convention" in Johannesburg

May 1: Stay-at-home day of protest in Transvaal; police intervention (19 dead, 30 injured)

May 14: Conference of representatives of the executive committees of the ANC, South African Indian Congress (SAIC), African People's Organisation, ANC Youth League, Communist Party, and Transvaal Council of Non-European Trade Unions

May 21: ANC national executive committee decides to call a national one-day stay-at-home protest [June 26]

June 20: Communist Party declares it dissolved itself (before enactment of the Suppression of Communist Act)

June 26: "National Day of Protest and Mourning"

November 12: Election of J. B. Marks as president of the ANC (Transvaal)

November: Last meeting of the NRC

Formation of R. V. Selope Thema's National-minded Bloc

1951

Bantu Authorities Act

February: Separate Representation of Voters Bill to remove Coloureds from common roll (enacted in June) is made public

February: Conference of Franchise Action Council

March 11: Coloured political demonstration in Cape Town

April: Rise of the Torch Commando

April 28-29: Formation of the Transvaal Peace Council

May 30: Chief Lutuli succeeds A. W. G. Champion as president of the ANC (Natal)

June 17: Funeral of Dr. Seme, followed by meeting of ANC national executive committee; decision to meet with SAIC and other representatives

July 29: Joint conference of national executive committees of the ANC and the SAIC; formation of Joint Planning Council (JPC)

November 8: Report of the JPC

December 15-17: ANC conference adopts report of the JPC

December 20: First conference of the Society of Young Africa

1952

January: Exclusive-minded Africans organize Bureau of African Nationalism

January 21: Letter from the ANC to Prime Minister Malan threatening a Defiance Campaign

January 29: Reply and warning by Prime Minister Malan

February 11: Second letter from the ANC to Malan stating intention to launch Defiance Campaign

February: Formation of pro-government Bantu National Congress

April 6: Climax of Van Riebeeck tercentenary festival; ANC-SAIC protest meetings and demonstrations as prelude to Defiance Campaign

May: Ban on five Communist leaders and left-wing *Guardian*

May 31: ANC and SAIC national executive committees decide to open the Defiance Campaign on June 26

June 26: Official opening of the Defiance Campaign

514

July 15-16: Trial and sentencing of Communist leaders for defying bans

July 30: Countrywide police raids

August: Arrest of twenty African and Indian leaders of the Defiance Campaign; found guilty on December 2

September: Arrest of fifteen leaders in eastern Cape Province; found guilty in 1953

September: Statement by twenty-two white liberals

October 1: Beginning of the period covered by the indictment in the treason trial of 1956-1961

October-November: Riots in Port Elizabeth (October 18), Johannesburg (November 3), Kimberley (November 8), and East London (November 10)

November 7: Banning of 52 nonwhite leaders in eastern Cape Province

November 12: Government dismisses Lutuli as chief

November: Public meeting of whites in support of the Defiance Campaign

December 5: United Nations General Assembly decision to set up a Commission on the Racial Situation in South Africa

December 8: Patrick Duncan and other whites illegally enter African location in support of the Defiance Campaign

December 18-20: ANC conference elects Lutuli to succeed James S. Moroka as president-general

Bibliographical Data

In the preparation of the introductory essays in this volume, heavy reliance has been placed on the documents collected by the editors and the interviews conducted by them inside and outside South Africa. The documents, of which only a small proportion are reproduced here, and the transcripts of interviews may be consulted with the permission of the editors.

Much valuable material of the South African Institute of Race Relations in Johannesburg is being microfilmed and will be available from the Cooperative Africana Microform Project (CAMP) of the Center for Research Libraries in Chicago. Among its rich though uneven holdings of South African material, CAMP possesses files of *Inkundla ya Bantu (Bantu Forum)* for 1944-1951 and the left-wing *Guardian* and its successors, *The Clarion, People's World*, and *Advance*. Among other important newspapers and periodicals of the period were *Ilanga Lase Natal*, the *Bantu World, Imvo Zabantsundu (Native Opinion of South Africa), Indian Opinion, Umteteli wa Bantu, African Lodestar, Workers' Voice, Inkululeko* [Freedom], *Drum, The Forum*, and *The South African Outlook*. Also valuable are trial records, notably Regina vs. Sisulu and 19 Others, Johannesburg Magistrate's Court, August-December 1952, and the record of the treason trial of 1956-1961. The latter, in part, and certain other trial records are available from CAMP.

Only a few African leaders have written books: Jordan Ngubane, *An African Explains Apartheid* (New York: Praeger, 1963); Albert Luthuli, *Let My People Go: An Autobiography* (London: Collins, and New York: McGraw-Hill, 1962); and I. B. Tabata, *The All African Convention: The Awakening of a People* (Johannesburg: People's Press, 1950). Dr. A. B. Xuma wrote "Extracts from the Life Story of Dr. Alfred Xuma" in eleven brief installments in *Drum*, March 1954-January 1955. Because of the foresight of Benjamin Pogrund, Dr. Xuma's extensive personal papers are at the Institute of Race Relations in Johannesburg. A number of Professor Z. K. Matthews's published articles during 1951-1953 are listed in a footnote in the introductory essay to the Defiance Campaign but contain little biographical matter. Unpublished manuscripts by him and Ngubane have been useful in the preparation of this volume. R. V. Selope Thema wrote editorials in the *Bantu World*; two of his articles published elsewhere are footnoted in the section on the Defiance Campaign. Dr. S. M. Molema collected political material and correspondence that are available from CAMP.

516

A popular and sympathetic history of the African National Congress is Mary Benson's *South Africa: The Struggle for a Birthright* (New York: Funk & Wagnalls, 1969). Earlier editions are *South Africa: The Struggle for a Birthright* (Harmondsworth, Middlesex, England: Penguin Books, 1966) and *The African Patriots: The Story of the African National Congress of South Africa* (London: Faber & Faber, 1963). A much shorter history, with biographical chapters, is Anthony Sampson, *The Treason Cage: The Opposition on Trial in South Africa* (London: Heinemann, 1958). Leo Kuper, a sociologist, has analyzed the main developments in "African Nationalism in South Africa, 1910-1964," in volume two of Monica Wilson and Leonard Thompson (eds.), *The Oxford History of South Africa* (London: Oxford University Press). (Because of censorship, his chapter is not included in the South African edition.) See also his perceptive study of the Defiance Campaign, *Passive Resistance in South Africa* (London: Jonathan Cape, 1956; New Haven: Yale University Press, 1957). Julius Lewin analyzed "The Rise of African Nationalism" in an article published in 1953 and reprinted in *Politics and Law in South Africa: Essays on Race Relations* (London: Merlin Press, 1963). Ronald Segal, *Political Africa: A Who's Who of Personalities and Parties* (New York: Praeger, 1961) contains biographies of thirty-one nonwhite leaders. A valuable historical study of the ANC, not available during the preparation of this volume, is Peter Walshe, *The Rise of African Nationalism in South Africa: The African National Congress, 1912-1952* (London: C. Hurst and Co., 1970). See also his "Black American Thought and African Political Attitudes in South Africa," *Review of Politics* (January 1970, pp. 51-77).

Edward Roux's *Time Longer than Rope: A History of the Black Man's Struggle for Freedom in South Africa* (London: Gollancz, 1948; 2nd ed., Madison: University of Wisconsin Press, 1964), written by a former Communist who was politically active in the 1920s and early 1930s, has for years been the indispensable history of the wide range of radical activity in South Africa. His book is now complemented by *Class and Colour in South Africa 1850-1950* (Baltimore: Penguin Books, 1969) by H. J. and R. E. Simons, two outstanding South Africans, a political sociologist and a trade unionist, who have also been active as Communists. Their book is a richly detailed analysis of the interactions of national movements and class struggles. Briefer historical surveys are by Brian Bunting, a Communist, *The Rise of the South African Reich* (Harmondsworth, Middlesex, England: Penguin Books, 1964) and Alex Hepple, formerly leader of the now-defunct Labour Party, *South Africa: A Political and Economic History* (London: Pall Mall Press, 1966). The autobiography of Michael Scott, *A Time To Speak* (Garden City, N.Y.: Doubleday, 1958) includes his observations on the Campaign for Right and Justice.

An essential book for an understanding of South African liberalism is Alan Paton's splendid biography of Jan Hofmeyr: *Hofmeyr* (London: Oxford University Press, 1964). It has also been published in abridged form as *South African Tragedy: The Life and Times of Jan Hofmeyr* (New York: Scribner's 1965; paperback, 1970). Margaret Ballinger's *From Union to Apartheid: A Trek to Isolation* (Cape Town: Juta, 1969) is a political rather than autobiographical history of 1937-1960, the years when she sat in Parliament as a representative of the Africans of eastern Cape Province. Her book was not at hand during the

517

preparation of the introductory essays, nor was Janet Robertson, *Liberalism in South Africa, 1948-1963* (London: Oxford University Press, 1971).

For those beginning their study of South Africa, a good introduction is Leo Marquard, *The Peoples and Policies of South Africa* (4th ed., London: Oxford University Press, 1969). A more extensive analysis of white politics is Gwendolen M. Carter, *The Politics of Inequality: South Africa since 1948* (New York: Praeger, 1958, 1959). Other relevant materials are listed in the bibliographical note appearing in Volume I and in the bibliographical sections of *The Politics of Inequality* and G. M. Carter (ed.), *Five African States: Responses to Diversity* (Ithaca, N.Y.: Cornell University Press, 1963).

Index of Names

Abdurahman, Dr. Abdullah, 153, 157
Akena, S. P., 45, 185, 268
Allen, J. W. G., 450
Asher, 137
Aucamp, M., 433

Baboo, I., 389
Balfour, M., 41
Ballinger, Margaret, 75, 77, 135, 136, 158, 344, 375, 438, 517
Ballinger, William G., 100, 136, 137, 298, 375, 438
Baloyi, R. G., 82, 87, 93, 138, 141, 156-158, 161, 189, 222, 266-269, 271, 288,
     289, 294, 297-299, 368, 369
Bam, E. C., 41
Bam, L. G. E., 25, 41
Basner, Hyman M., 72, 91, 100, 111, 127, 263
Beaumont, 30
Bekker, 283
Bell, P. A. M., 41
Benghu, S. S., 424, 425, 439
Benjamin, Elizabeth, 378
Bereng, 334
Berry, Sir Bisset, 22
Bhola, Mrs., 55
Bikitsha, 164
Bikitsha, Chief H., 41
Blaxall, Rev. A. W., 137
Bokwe, Dr. R. T., 164, 222, 267, 269, 270, 294, 368, 369, 448
Bopape, David W., 101-104, 116, 124, 125, 129, 339, 371, 417, 429-431, 436
Brookes, Edgar H., 75, 438
Browne, Dr. Howe, 157
Buchanan, Brigadier General, 234

Cachalia, I. A., 288, 431
Cachalia, Yusuf A., 288, 408, 412, 418, 419, 421, 423, 430, 432, 435, 451, 458,
     465, 467
Calata, Rev. James A., 82-86, 88, 104, 110, 120, 121, 131, 138, 141, 143, 145,
     154-156, 161, 162, 189, 208, 222, 267, 278, 284, 288, 289, 291, 294,
     371, 377, 428, 513
Canca, R. M., 378, 379, 382, 386, 387
Canca, R. S., 375, 377
Carey, Bishop, 135
Carneson, Fred, 417, 450
Chaka. *See* Tshaka

Champion, Allison W. George, 41, 87, 88, 92, 93, 100, 121, 122, 124, 156, 158, 161, 266, 269, 270, 272, 285, 288, 368, 369, 371, 374, 409, 424, 444, 514
Chiang Kai-shek, 504
Chuene, Chief, 55
Chuenyane, A., 14
Churchill, Winston, 73, 87, 94, 209, 510
Cingo, Reginald, 41, 164
Coblans, Herbert, 438
Coka, Gilbert G., 5, 9, 10, 16, 44
Conco, Wilson Zami, 101, 428
Cooper, J. R., 42
Cope, John, 75
Crewe, Sir Charles, 22

Dadoo, Dr. Yusuf M., 77, 83, 91, 92, 108, 114-116, 126, 272, 406, 411, 412, 416, 417, 421, 424, 436, 458, 465, 467, 512
Dana, G., 27, 41
Darwin, Charles, 315
Dent, Professor, 331
Descartes, 106, 126
de Villiers, René, 75
Dickens, 334
Dingaan, 40, 56, 78, 292, 478
Dingana, 445, 446
Dinizulu, Chief Mshiyeni ka, 33, 246, 248
Dippa, J. M., 20, 41
Dollie, S., 450
Donaldson [Fund], 86
Donaldson, Colonel, 137
Douglas, Frederick, 17
Dube, Rev. John L., 6, 11, 41, 43, 82, 83, 88, 93, 131, 132, 164, 365, 512
Duma, E. C., 291
Duma, Rev. I. C., 336
Duncan, Patrick, 423, 425, 426, 515
Dunjwa, C., 14

Eden, Anthony, 224
Edward VII, King, 28
Eiselen, Dr. W. W. M., 98, 332, 472
Eisenhower, General Dwight D., 223
Elias, S., 371
Engels, 126
Erasmus, 282

Fagan, Henry A., 75, 79, 138, 148, 229, 239, 244, 248, 252, 259, 277, 283, 512
First, Ruth, 316
Fischer, Abram (Bram), 121
Frost, 22
Fuller, 22

Gale, George W., 438

Gama, L. A., 292, 295
Gandhi, Manilal, 423
Gandhi, Mohandas K., 69, 103, 382, 423
Gardner, Dr. Bruce, 333
Garret, 22
Garvey, Marcus, 10, 17, 105, 106, 126, 328, 333
George V, King, 33
George VI, King, 266
Gilson, L. D., 24, 25
Godlo, Mrs., 55
Godlo, R. H., 11, 20, 34, 40, 41, 45, 88, 93, 118, 138, 140-143, 188, 189, 222, 281, 290, 368, 369, 371, 375
Golding, George, 431
Gomas, John, 7, 34
Gool, Dr. G. H., 7, 40, 45, 110, 112-114, 118, 126, 129, 357, 377, 378, 382, 383, 385, 387
Gool, Jane (Janub), 56, 110
Gool, Mrs. Z., 55, 114, 389
Gort, Lord, 182
Gosani, D., 189
Gow, Dr. F. H., 389
Grobler, P. G., 40, 134, 139, 148
Gula, 156
Gumede, 297, 298
Gumede, James T., 107, 132
Gwala, T. B., 288

Hanson, H. J., 438
Harmel, Michael, 417, 418, 432
Haynes, Dr. George E., 436, 440
Hellmann, Dr. Ellen, 438
Hemming, 135
Hertzog, Prime Minister J. B. M., 3-5, 8, 9, 24, 58, 61, 69, 71, 78, 225, 234, 341, 351, 364, 509, 510
Hintsa, 315, 317
Hitler, Adolf, 99, 126, 276, 321, 351, 357, 358, 503
Hlekani, J. N., 294, 372
Hlongwane, Rev. J. Mdelwa, 14
Hoernlé, Professor Alfred, 75
Hoernlé, A. Winifred, 438
Hofmeyr, Jan H., 9, 69, 73-76, 94, 95, 116, 123, 228, 250, 253, 280, 283, 344, 512, 513, 517
Horvitch, I., 455
Houser, George M., 440
Howe-Browne, Dr., 157
Huddleston, Father Trevor, 438
Hugenot, Runeli, 278

Innes, Sir James Rose, 22, 30
Ismael, Ahmed, 389, 450

Jabavu, Alex M., 11, 41, 93, 345

Jabavu, Professor Davidson Don Tengo, 5, 6, 8-11, 15, 24, 40, 42, 48, 81, 88, 92, 93, 99, 109, 112-115, 118, 123, 126, 127, 129, 130, 136, 153, 156, 157, 288, 347, 368-372, 377, 509
Jabavu, John Tengo, 135
Jacobs, Mrs. A. M., 266
Jacobs, J. N., 267, 271
Jagger, J. W., 28
Jansen, Dr., 282
Jayiya, S. A., 376, 378, 382, 385
Jones, J. D. Rheinallt, 75, 138, 158
Jordan, A. C., 376

Kabane, M. L., 55, 212, 222
Kadalie, Clements, 6, 7, 34, 80, 81, 101, 126, 468
Kahn, Sam, 417, 450
Kajee, A. I., 113, 114
Kama, Chief G. S., 161
Kambule, J., 41
Kathrada, Ahmed, 421
Keppel-Jones, A. M., 438
Kerr, Dr., 331
Kgosane, 268
Khama, 315, 317, 446
Kies, B. M., 110, 114
Klaaste, 55
Kobus, C. M., 118, 119, 378, 382, 386
Kongisa, E., 299, 371
Kotane, Moses M., 14, 82, 88, 100, 104, 107, 108, 116, 118, 119, 123, 124, 126, 138, 156, 222, 263, 267, 288, 292, 294, 295, 371, 373, 374, 378, 380, 382, 383, 385, 386, 388, 406, 417, 428, 429, 436, 447, 450, 451, 510
Koti, Rev. E. P., 132
Kotsokoane, J., 290, 297
Koza, Dan, 111, 114, 126, 127, 374
Kruger, Paul, 315, 478
Kumalo, Chief Walter, 41, 457
Kuse, Mrs. Nothandile, 157
Kuzwayo, G. R., 111
Kwagwa, Lieutenant, 193
Kwinana, V. M., 290

Langalibalele, 17
Lavis, Rt. Rev. Bishop J. W., 389
Lawrence, H. G., 275, 277
Lawrence, V., 288
Lebere, 41
Leepile, 55
Lekhetho, J. M., 138, 140
Lembede, Anton Muziwakhe, 95, 100-103, 105, 106, 125, 126, 266, 270, 314, 317, 319, 327, 435, 512
Lepolesa (Lepolisa), S. Mac., 156, 161, 222
Lesabe, Mrs., 55
Leshoai, 292

Lesolang, S. J. J., 111
Letanka, D. S., 132
Letele, Dr. Arthur, 101, 104, 428
Letlaka, Tsepo T., 291, 421, 432
Lewanika, 17
Lewin, Julius, 419, 438
Liebrandt, Robey, 282
Likhong, Rev. J., 41
Lobengula, 17
Lobere, J. L., 156, 157
L'Ouverture, Toussaint, 17
Louw, 284, 285
Lutuli (also Luthuli), Chief Albert J., 88, 93, 94, 404, 413, 418, 424-426, 432,
    439, 440, 486, 512, 514-516
Lutuli, Mrs. Albert J., 268

Mabaso, C. S., 14
Mabeta, G. S., 14
Mabude, Saul, 93
McLeod, T., 43
Macmillan, Professor, 333
Madeley, 349
Madupuna, J., 41
Mafu, J., 138
Magatho. *See* Makgatho
Mahabane, Rev. A., 309
Mahabane, Rev. E. E., 158
Mahabane, Rev. Z. R., 4, 6, 13, 37, 41, 43, 82-84, 88, 92, 109, 110, 114, 118,
    125, 126, 129, 130, 138, 139, 141, 146, 155, 156, 158, 159, 161, 162, 222,
    288, 309, 357, 368, 369, 372, 377, 378, 380, 382, 386, 387, 510
Mahlanza, E., 14
Majombozi, Lionel, 101
Makabeni, Gana, 88, 222, 288-290, 293, 371, 378, 380, 384
Makana, 17, 317, 446
Makgatho, Rev. Samuel M., 132, 468
Makiwane, Tennyson, 436
Malan, Dr. Daniel F., 7, 70, 78, 79, 83, 91, 281, 282, 284, 321, 380, 413-416,
    435, 442, 443, 476, 480, 483, 501, 503, 504, 510, 512, 514
Malangabi, J., 156, 158, 162, 288, 378
Malcolm, D. McK., 438
Malcomess, Senator, 158, 185
Malcomn, 297
Malepe, J. E., 125, 266, 268, 270
Malunga, A. B., 372
Mama, P., 41
Mampuru, Mrs., 128
Mampuru, Self, 100, 110-112, 128
Mancoba, 55
Mandela, Nelson R. D., 101, 103, 104, 118, 125, 323, 362, 368, 405, 406, 408,
    418, 419, 421, 424, 425, 428, 430, 432, 450, 451
Mangena, 164
Manope, Chief, 19

Manyosi, E., 292, 298
Mapikela, Thomas M., 11, 14, 40, 41, 43, 44, 46, 55, 82, 93, 132, 138, 143, 145, 156, 159, 162, 189, 222
Mapitsa, 55
Marais, J. S., 438
Marks, John B., 6, 14, 38, 41, 46, 70, 81, 82, 88, 100, 108, 110, 116, 120, 121, 124, 128, 138, 156, 158, 266, 269, 271, 288, 371, 376, 378, 379, 406, 408, 409, 412, 413, 417, 418, 421, 424, 428-430, 436, 458, 465, 467, 513
Marquard, Leo, 75, 438, 518
Marx, 126
Masekela, Bigvai, 101, 125
Maseko, MacDonald, 289, 290
Maserumule, Chief, 233, 248
Mashologu, B., 45
Matanzima, Chief, 279
Matji, Robert Mokxotho, 101, 426, 494
Matlou, Johannes, 101
Matseke, S. P. (or N. S. P. Matseko), 14, 41, 44, 138, 141, 144, 167
Matthews, Joseph G., 101, 421, 428, 432, 438
Matthews, Professor Z. K., 40, 41, 83, 86, 88, 93-97, 103, 104, 110, 119, 122-127, 157, 161, 162, 164, 189, 212, 222, 224, 233, 242, 244, 248, 250, 251, 267, 270, 271, 281, 288, 292, 293, 295, 297-299, 368, 369, 371, 373, 377, 378, 382, 386, 407, 409, 416, 417, 420, 421, 427, 429, 430, 432, 435, 436, 439, 440, 447, 513, 516
Maxeke, Charlotte, 43, 44
Mazingi, A., 41
Mazwai, A. K., 378, 385
Mazwi, Rev., 24
Mazwi, J. S., 41
Mbata, J. Congress, 89, 100-102, 105, 124, 222
Mbeki, Govan A., 222
Mbelle, Horatio I. Bud., 45
Mbete, W., 55, 290
Mbobo, Victor T., 101, 125, 289, 290, 294, 299, 300, 428
Mbuli, 279
McLeod, T., 43
Mda, A. P., 100, 101, 103-106, 118, 124-126, 130, 266, 290, 292, 294, 319, 321, 371, 372, 374, 375, 378, 380, 381, 383, 387, 405, 413, 424, 428, 432, 435
Mda, Mda, 375, 378, 387
Mdatyulwa, Jas., 378
Mdolomba, Rev. E., 41, 132
Mdolomba, Rev. S., 14
Mears, W. J. G., 234, 247
Meer, A. I., 288
Meer, I. C., 288
Menelik, 17
Merriman, 22
Metcalf, 137
Mfeka, 55
Mgadi, J. G., 288
Mgudlwa, Chief I., 41

Mji, Diliza J., 289, 290, 299, 432, 452
Mkele, N., 288
Mlandu, W. P., 41
Mngadi, P., 292
Mnyobo, B. E., 156
Modise, 297, 298
Moema, S. M., 166
Moerane, Manasseh T., 89, 99, 124, 222, 432
Mofutsanyana, Edwin T., 6, 41, 88, 100, 108, 161, 166, 167, 222, 429, 451
Mohlakoana, Mrs., 162
Moikangoa, C. R., 41, 56
Mokhehle, N. C., 289-293, 297, 298
Mokitimi, Rev., 333
Mokoena (Mokuena), Joseph A., 125, 164, 290, 294, 428
Molaltou, 41
Moleleki, 299
Molema, Dr. Silas M., 41, 121, 164, 223, 293, 294, 297, 415, 430, 432, 435, 477, 516
Molotov, V. M., 224
Molteno, Donald B., 22, 75, 125, 135, 157, 158, 185, 344, 389, 438
Molteno, J. T., 30
Mopedi, Chief Charles, 19, 20
Mopeli, Chief C., 41
Moroka, Dr. James S., 6, 39, 41, 73, 88, 93-95, 97, 118, 122, 130, 164, 223, 293-295, 368, 369, 406-409, 411, 412, 414-418, 421, 423, 425, 427, 429, 431, 432, 439, 441, 442, 444, 448, 451, 453-455, 458-460, 465, 467, 471, 476, 477, 480, 513, 515
Moroka, Chief P. J., 157
Moroka, Chief S., 157
Mosaka, Paul R., 72, 88, 93, 96, 100, 111, 112, 116, 118, 127, 128, 198, 199, 233, 234, 245, 248, 250, 251, 367-369, 376, 511
Moshe, D. W., 288
Moshesh, Chief Jeremiah, 23, 41, 93
Moshoeshoe, Chief, 164, 292, 315, 317, 445
Mote, Keable, 41, 42
Motili, 294
Motshabi, 41
Motsita, P., 289
Mpanza, J., 41
Mpinda, James S., 162, 267
Mpitso, Rev., 223
Mqhayi, 138, 334
Mqubuli, S. P., 14, 41
Msimang, E. O., 288
Msimang, H. Selby, 9-11, 31, 36, 37, 40, 41, 55, 57, 93, 104, 267, 269-271, 288, 290, 291, 295, 340, 343, 371, 375, 413, 424, 432, 435
Msimang, Richard W., 132
Mtimkulu, Rev. Abner S., 31, 40, 41, 138-140, 155, 223
Mtimkulu, Don., 164, 223
Mtimkulu, Leo., 223
Mtimkulu, Lionel T., 33, 35, 161, 162, 212
Mtwesi, J. G. (or J. S.), 290, 292, 293

Muroe, I. B., 14
Mussolini, Benito, 126
Mvabaza, L. T., 14, 41
Mzamane, G. I. M., 289, 290, 292, 293, 299, 339, 448
Mzilikazi (or Mosilikazi), 315, 317

Naicker, Dr. G. M., 91, 92, 114, 272, 285, 288, 290, 418, 455, 512
Naidoo, H. A., 91, 263
Naidoo, M. D., 288
Naidoo, S. R., 288
Naidoo, T. N., 288
Ncakeni, V., 125, 309
Ncwana, B. S., 45
Ncwana, S. M. Bennet, 156, 162
Ndimande, R., 450
Ndlambe, 292
Ndlovu, W. W., 41, 132
Nehru, Jawaharlal, 53, 54
Newcastle, Duke of, 20, 134
Ngakane, W. B., 108
Ngcobo, Selby D., 41, 212, 223, 288
Ngedlane, J., 14
Ngojo, James D., 132, 138, 140
Ngqangweni, S. K., 432
Ngubane, Jordan K., 99-102, 105, 106, 124-126, 129, 407, 424, 432, 438, 441, 516
Ngwevela, J. N., 417, 450
Nhlapo, J. M., 125, 212, 223, 309
Nichollas, Heaton, 23, 60, 136, 151
Nietzche, 126
Njongwe, Dr. James L. Z., 102, 104, 293, 294, 421, 428
Nkatlo, Joseph, 450
Nkoane, J., 158, 162
Nkomo, Mrs., 292
Nkomo, William F., 99-101, 124, 125, 158, 162
Nokwe, Duma, 101, 428
Nthaja, 289
Ntintili, H., 41
Ntintili, T., 29
Ntlabati, L. K., 104, 266-268, 270, 271, 288-291, 294, 368, 369, 371, 378, 382, 384, 385
Ntlabati, M. P., 290, 293
Ntuli, A. N., 288
Nxumalo, P., 125, 132
Nyezi, 55

Oliphant, S., 138, 156, 157, 158, 162

Pahad, G. H. I., 288
Pahlana. *See* Phahlane, Peter

526

Palmer, Mabel, 157, 438
Parker, E. A., 450
Parker, Hugh, 438
Paton, Alan, 74, 94, 96, 438, 517
Payn, 24
Peter, Saint, 488
Phahlane, Peter, 157, 158, 162
Phillips, L. S., 371, 378
Phooko, 293
Pienaar, General, 199
Pillay, Sundra, 450
Pirow, Oswald, 78
Pitje, Godfrey M., 101, 103, 104, 124, 289, 290, 294, 319, 321, 428
Pitso, Rev. A. P., 132
Plaatje, Solomon T., 21, 132
Pokela, J. N., 432
Poswayo, T., 41, 164
Poto, Chief Victor, 233, 247

Qamata, E., 27, 189
Quamata, 345
Qunta, Dr. Andries Sipo, 164

Rabinowitz, L. I., 438
Raboroko, Peter, 100, 124
Radebe, Gaur, 81, 290, 292, 294, 298, 451
Rahim, S. M., 411, 455
Rajuili, 55
Ramahanoe. See Ramohanoe, C. S.
Ramailane, 41
Ramohanoe, C. S., 117, 138, 140, 266, 267, 270, 271, 288, 309, 372, 429, 451, 454
Ramutla, 55
Rathebe, 284, 285
Reeves, Bishop Ambrose, 438
Reitz, Colonel Deneys (or Denez), 182, 188, 211, 349
Resha, Robert, 289, 428
Rheinallt-Jones. See Jones
Rhodes, Cecil, 27, 43, 135
Roberts, E. C., 357
Rogers, Howard, 186
Roos, Tielman, 282
Roosevelt, Franklin D., 73, 87, 94, 209, 510
Rose-Innes. See Innes
Rosenberg, Doctor, 276
Rubin, Leslie, 75
Rubusana, Rev. Walter B., 132, 135
Rumpff, Mr. Justice, 421
Ruskin, 126
Russell, 126
Rustomjee, Sorabjee, 91, 263

Sachs, E. S., 417, 418, 436
Sader, Dr. A. H., 288
Sakwe, C. K., 11, 30, 41, 93
Sandile, Paramount Chief Velile, 20
Sauer, 22, 30
Schoeman, 282
Schreiner, W. P., 22
Schultz, H. A., 371
Scott, Rev. Michael, 115-117, 290, 517
Scully, 30
Sehloko, P., 138
Sekhukhuni (Sikhukhumi), 315, 317, 445, 446
Sekukuni, Chief, 19, 292
Sello, Robert A., 41, 375, 378
Selope-Thema. *See* Thema, R. V. Selope
Seme, Dr. Pixley ka I., 6, 12, 35, 41, 81, 82, 88, 100, 107, 131, 132, 161, 164,
    223, 412, 468, 509, 514
Sesedi, S. P., 266
Setlogelo, Dr. R., 223, 371
Shaka, 17, 315, 317
Shaw, Rev., 335
Sihlali, Leo, 378, 384
Sikhukhumi. *See* Sekhukhuni
Sililo, A. J., 138, 142
Sililo, S. J., 189
Singh, Debi, 288
Singh, George, 288
Singh, J. N., 288
Sipamla, M. J., 290
Sisulu, Walter M., 87, 98, 100, 101, 104, 125, 293, 294, 371, 403, 405, 407,
    408, 410, 412, 414, 418, 419, 421, 423-425, 428, 430, 435, 451, 458,
    465, 467, 476, 477, 484, 513, 516
Sita, Nana, 288, 418
Sitela, J. O., 158
Skomolo, Rev. J. J., 292-294, 299, 300, 409, 424, 447, 448
Skota, T. D. Mweli, 14, 41
Smit, Dr. D. L., 20, 24, 138, 143, 188, 189, 234, 246, 247, 349
Smuts, Jan Christiaan, 3, 10, 23, 27, 28, 36, 45, 58, 61, 69, 72-75, 77, 78,
    89-97, 103, 116, 123, 126, 158, 172, 182, 184, 187, 188, 198, 211, 214,
    223, 224, 226, 227, 233, 234, 247, 248, 251, 257, 274, 276, 280, 281,
    284, 335, 349, 359, 361, 392, 501, 503, 510, 512
Sobukwe, Mangaliso Robert, 102, 104, 106, 293, 331, 432
Sobuza (Sobhuza), Chief, 297, 315, 317
Socenywa, G. B., 104
Soga, Dr., 164
Soga, Miss, 292
Soga, Rev. L., 291
Solomon, Saul, 22, 30, 438
Soong, Dr., 224
Stalin, Joseph, 223
Stanford, 30
Stettinius, Edward, 224

Stoutz, W., 389
Stuttaford, R., 19
Sutton, Mayor, 156

Tabata, I. B., 86, 88, 110, 112, 114, 115, 118, 123, 126, 127, 129, 340, 362,
    368, 372-375, 377, 378, 381-383, 386, 387, 435, 506, 516
Tambo (Thambo), Oliver R., 98, 100, 101, 104, 124, 125, 288, 293, 294, 309,
    378, 381, 384, 386, 403, 405, 406, 423, 428, 451
Thaele, James, 278
Thaele, Kenneth, 278
Thaele, Mrs. Kenneth, 278
Thema, R. V. Selope, 11, 41, 82, 86, 88, 93, 94, 96, 99, 112, 116, 125, 132,
    161, 167, 223, 233, 243, 248, 267-269, 288, 290, 292, 309, 365, 368,
    369, 371, 378, 379, 382, 385, 405, 409, 413, 424, 430, 435, 438, 514, 516
Thompson, 314
Thompson, Rev. D. C., 432
Thubisi, 156, 158
Tladi, Rev., F. J., 389
Tloome, Dan, 101, 125, 267, 289, 294, 309, 428, 429, 431
Tomlinson, 75, 79
Truman, Harry S., 505
Tsala, 41
Tshaka (Chaka), 164
Tshongwana, E., 132
Tsoai, 41
Tsotsi, W. M., 109, 118, 374, 378, 383, 384, 387, 439
Tunzi, Rev. R. M., 41, 45, 55
Twala, Rev., 14
Twayi, J. B., 132

van Coller, 24
van der Byl, Piet, 96, 234, 246, 248, 282
van Riebeeck, Jan, 413, 416, 427, 460, 477, 478, 483, 514
Verwoerd, Dr. Hendrik, 98, 126, 493
Victoria the Good, Queen, 23, 29
Viljoen, 288

Washington, Booker, 17
Webb, J. B., 438
White, A. C., 41
Wilson, Woodrow, 213, 214

Xabanisa, P. T., 30, 41, 43, 45
Xakekile, J., 29
Xiniwe, B. B., 93, 223, 281
Xuma, Dr. A. B., 6, 35, 40, 41, 43, 46, 71, 72, 73, 80, 82, 84-92, 95, 97,
    100-102, 104, 105, 109-112, 114-118, 120-130, 157, 158, 162, 166-168,
    171, 172, 184, 188, 198, 199, 208, 211, 212, 223, 224, 257, 261-263,
    266, 272-274, 278, 280, 284, 286, 288, 290, 291, 294, 309, 327, 344,
    365, 367-372, 377, 378, 383, 404, 407, 409, 423, 428, 429,
    510-513, 516
Xuma, Mrs. Madie Hall, 267

Yengwa, M. B., 102, 428, 432
Yergan, Max, 436

Zik, 336
Zwide, F. H. M., 38

Index of Organizations

Adams College, 98, 124
Advisory boards. *See* Congress of Urban Advisory Boards
"African Council of Women," 39
African Democratic Party (ADP), 72, 88, 90, 91, 100, 110-112, 127, 128, 322, 391, 394, 396, 511
African Dingaka Association, 14, 161
African Mine Workers' Union, 69, 70, 77, 81, 318, 319, 510
African Ministers' Association. *See* Interdenominational African Ministers' Association
"African National Committee for Post war Reconstruction", 186
African National Congress (ANC), 4, 6, 8, 9, 11, 12, 14, 69-73, 78, 81-93, 97-105, 107-112, 114-119, 121, 122, 124, 126-133, 136, 138, 139, 145, 146, 153-155, 157-161, 166-168, 172, 173, 178, 181-189, 198-205, 209-212, 222-224, 257, 258, 261, 263-270, 272, 273, 277, 279-281, 286-300, 304-308, 310, 312-314, 316, 320, 321, 323, 327, 330, 337-343, 362, 363, 365-388, 393, 403-414, 416-433, 435, 436, 439, 441-445, 447-455, 457-460, 462, 463, 465-471, 473, 476, 481-490, 492-494, 509-514
Alexandra Branch, 297
Bloemfontein Branch, 288
Cape (Cape Native Congress, Cape African Congress), 82, 83, 85-87, 104, 131-134, 136, 145, 147, 156, 158, 184, 185, 278, 279, 281, 289, 294, 346, 384, 409, 417, 426, 429, 439, 447, 456, 457, 469, 489, 492, 494, 513
Cape Western Regional Committee, 417
Cradock Branch, 184, 185
East London Branch, 184
Kimberley Branch, 184, 429, 456
Ladybrand Branch, 469
Natal (Natal Native Congress), 82, 85, 92, 114, 121, 131, 132, 138, 158, 184, 189, 223, 280, 285-289, 409, 413, 418, 424, 425, 439, 444, 456, 457, 469, 487, 514
Newclare Branch, 454, 457
Orange Free State (Orange Free State Native Congress), 85, 131, 132, 138, 158, 189, 222, 289, 439, 456, 457, 469
Port Elizabeth Branch, 184, 422, 457
Queenstown Branch, 456
Springs Branch, 457
Transvaal (Transvaal Native Congress, Transvaal African Congress), 4, 14, 80, 81, 84, 85, 100, 102, 104, 111, 112, 117, 131, 132, 138, 158, 166, 167, 184, 271, 280, 288-290, 297-299, 404-406, 408, 409, 413, 416, 417, 424, 429, 430, 432, 435, 439, 442, 454, 456, 467, 468, 469, 482, 513
Western Province (Cape Western Province), 84, 138, 156, 158, 160, 184, 185, 278

531

African National Congress Women's League [Women's Section], 101, 186, 320, 469
African National Congress Women's League (East London), 384
African National Congress Youth League (ANCYL), 71-73, 89, 95, 98-108, 110, 111, 117, 118, 124, 125, 203, 291, 292, 295, 299, 300, 306-314, 317-330, 336, 362, 363, 367, 403-407, 409, 413, 424, 428, 431, 432, 435, 442, 444, 454, 511, 513
  Cape, 320, 321, 432
  Durban, 457
  Fort Hare, 102-104, 319, 322
  Natal (Natal Youth League), 320, 413, 424, 425, 432, 457
  Transvaal, 125, 316, 320, 409, 413, 432, 445, 456, 469, 511
"African Parliamentary Committee," 109
African People's Organisation (APO), 43, 117, 406-408, 411, 412, 431, 442, 444, 449, 451, 454, 455, 513
  Transvaal, 432
"African People's Rights Protection League," 153
African People's Union, 14
African Study Circle, Johannesburg, 222
African Teachers' Federation, 189, 223
"African Vigilance Associations," 14
African Voters' Association. *See* Cape Voters' Association
African Women's Association, 444
Afrikander Bond Party, 135
All African Convention (AAC), 6-12, 31-57, 61-66, 69, 71, 72, 81, 83, 84, 86, 88-93, 97-99, 107, 109-113, 115, 117-119, 123, 126-128, 130, 136, 146, 156, 159, 161, 223, 225, 288, 293, 339-347, 351, 352, 364-367, 369-373, 375-388, 424, 429, 430, 435, 439, 454, 509-511, 513
  Western Province Committee, 112, 118
"All African National Congress," 72, 118, 119, 369
All India Congress, 53, 384
American Committee on Africa, 439
Anglican Church, 98, 475
Anti-C.A.D. *See* National Anti-C.A.D.
Anti-Pass Council. *See* National Anti-Pass Council
Anti-Segregation Council, 114
Asiatic Advisory Board, 498
Atlantic Charter Committee, 88, 89, 104, 112, 122, 209, 210, 212, 222, 223

Bantu National Congress, 424, 425, 514
Bantu Nyanga Association, 161
Bantu Union, 14
Bantu Women's League, 14
Broederbond, 102
Bunga. *See* United Transkeian Territories General Council
Bureau of African Nationalism, 414, 424, 432, 514

Campaign for Right and Justice, 115, 129, 511, 517
Cape African Congress. *See* African National Congress, Cape
Cape African Teachers' Association (CATA), 111, 115
Cape Native Congress. *See* African National Congress, Cape

532

Cape Native Voters' Convention, 5, 9
Cape Town, University of, 73, 74
Cape Voters' Association (Cape African Voters' Association), 14, 109, 110, 370
Cape Western Congress. *See* African National Congress, Western Province
Christian Council of South Africa, 393, 487
Ciskeian General Council, 231, 260
Civil Rights League, 426
Coloured Advisory Council, 498
Coloured People's National Union (CPNU), 411, 431
Communist Party, Communists, 4-6, 11, 14, 70, 71, 81, 87, 88, 90, 99, 100,
    107-109, 111, 112, 116, 118, 119, 121, 124, 127, 129, 133, 146, 153, 222,
    322, 367, 404, 405, 406-409, 411-413, 417, 418, 420, 421, 423, 424, 428,
    429, 432, 441-443, 447-449, 451, 453-455, 510, 512-515, 517
  Durban District, 444
  Johannesburg District, 406, 454
Congregational Church, 124
Congress Alliance, 104, 404
Congress of Democrats, 423
Congress of the People, 117
Congress of Urban Advisory Boards (Location Advisory Boards Congress),
    11, 14, 83, 138, 139, 147, 189, 255, 265
Congress Progressive Group. *See* African National Congress Youth League
Co-operative Trading Societies, 187
Council of Action, 295, 299, 338, 405, 406, 412, 453, 456, 467, 470
Council of African Affairs, 263
Council of Non-European Trade Unions, 81, 89, 189, 201, 222, 454, 510

Defend Free Speech Convention, 406, 454
Domestic and Cultural Workers' Club, 124
Dutch Reformed Church, 188, 475

Federation of Organised Bodies, Transkei, 222
Fort Hare, University College of (South African Native College, Fort Hare
    Native College), 5, 98, 99, 103, 104, 110, 111, 124, 135, 192, 203, 222,
    241, 319, 322, 331, 332, 420, 435
Fourth International of Johannesburg, 127
Fourth International (Trotskyists) of South Africa, 108, 111, 112, 127, 322,
    424
Franchise Action Council, 410, 411, 412, 431, 459, 463, 464, 514
Friends of Africa, 111, 393

Garment Workers' Union, 417
Garment Workers' Union, Coloured Branch, 421

Healdtown, 98, 124

I.C.U. yase Natal, 14, 87
Ikaka la Basebenzi, 14
Imbumba, 363
Independent I.C.U., 14
Indian Congress in Cape Province, 411

Industrial and Commercial Workers' Union (I.C.U.), 4-6, 14, 81, 110, 342, 383, 409, 468
Ingqungquthela (Ngqungquthela), 132, 363
Institute of Race Relations. *See* South African Institute of Race Relations
Interdenominational African Ministers' Association, 14, 223

Johannesburg Joint Council of Europeans and Africans, 284, 285
Joint Council of Native Ministers, 14
Joint Councils, 83, 111, 137, 153, 284, 285, 344, 393, 409, 425, 487
"Joint Councils of Goodwill consisting of Africans and Indians," 92, 293
Joint Passive Resistance Council, 268
Joint Planning Council, 412-415, 421, 431, 432, 458-462, 467, 514

Labour Party, 431
League of Nations, 91, 385, 405
Liberal Party, 76, 423, 431.
Libertas Bond, 75
Libertas League of Action, 75
Location Advisory Boards' Congress. *See* Congress of Urban Advisory Boards
Loram Secondary School, 223
Lovedale Instituion, 98, 124, 232

Mendi Memorial Fund, 223
Mendi Memorial Scholarship Association, 162
Methodist Church, 124, 334, 475

Natal Bantu Teachers' Association, 99, 222
Natal Indian Congress (NIC), 103, 114, 272, 285, 287, 418, 444, 512
Natal Native Congress. *See* African National Congress, Natal
Natal, University of, 74
Natal Youth League. *See* African National Congress Youth League, Natal
National Anti-C.A.D., 72, 112, 113, 115, 116, 129, 351, 352, 383, 411, 511
National Anti-Pass Council, 116, 265, 397, 398
National Child Welfare Association, 161
National Council of African Women, 40, 157, 292
National Liberation League, 108, 509
National Union of African Youth, 99, 510
National Volunteer Corps, 418, 462, 463, 464
Nationalist Party (National Party, Purified National Party, Reunited National Party), 7, 45, 69, 70, 73-76, 78, 79, 96, 97, 103, 117, 274, 280, 281, 283, 285, 297, 298, 390, 404, 405, 410-412, 487, 510, 512
National-minded Bloc (Nationalist Bloc), 409, 413, 424, 469, 514
Native Advisory Boards' Congress. *See* Congress of Urban Advisory Boards
Natives' Representative Council (NRC), 3, 7, 10, 11, 23, 28, 34, 54, 64, 69, 70, 72, 76, 82, 88, 91-98, 103, 109, 111-113, 118, 123, 127, 136, 138, 141, 150, 174, 185, 190, 191, 198, 211, 217, 222-261, 264, 268-270, 277, 280, 281, 301, 342-347, 350, 367, 373, 375, 376, 379-381, 410, 414, 425, 473, 487, 496, 498, 500, 509, 510, 512, 513
New Era Fellowship, 110
New Order, 78
Non-European Council of Trade Unions. *See* Council of Non-European Trade Unions

Non-European United Front, 83, 84, 108, 110, 112, 126, 153, 155, 389, 390, 509, 510
Non-European Unity Movement (NEUM) (Unity Movement), 72, 90, 99, 107, 109, 112-117, 119, 126, 129, 130, 322, 354, 357, 367, 374, 411, 424, 429, 494, 497, 501, 507, 511
Nyanga Association, 161
Nyasaland African National Congress, 290

Orange Free State African Teachers' Association, 222
Orange Free State Dutch Reformed Church, 188
Orange Free State Native Congress. *See* African National Congress, Orange Free State
Orlando High School, 90
Orlando (Johannesburg) advisory board, 108
Ossewa Brandwag (OB), 78, 390

Pan-African Congresses, fifth and sixth, 91
Pan Africanist Congress (PAC), 100, 101, 104, 105, 404, 405, 412, 423, 428, 432
Pathfinder Scout movement, 137
Progressive Party, 76, 89
Progressive Youth Council, 103, 316

Roman Catholic Church, 106, 475

St. Matthews College, 290
St. Peter's [Anglican secondary school], 98
Social Studies Society, 99
Society of Young Africa (SOYA), 435, 506, 507, 514
South African Indian Congress (SAIC), 92, 112-114, 117, 287, 288, 290, 351, 404, 407, 408, 412, 415-418, 420, 423, 426, 435, 436, 439, 442, 449, 451, 454, 455, 458-460, 462-467, 477, 483, 485, 486, 513, 514
South African Institute of Race Relations, 75, 111, 150, 392, 393, 426
South African Medical Association, 348
South African Native College. *See* Fort Hare, University College of
South African Native Convention, 6
South African Native Location Advisory Boards Congress. *See* Congress of Urban Advisory Boards
South African Native National Congress, 6, 145, 146
South African Native Teachers' Federation, 62
South African Party, 45
South African Passive Resistance Council, 91
South African R. & H. Workers' Union (Non-European), 155
South African Trades and Labour Council, 502
Stellenbosch University, 283, 332
Students' Representative Council (Fort Hare), 104, 331, 435

Torch Commando, 410, 412, 426, 431, 514
Transkei Bunga. *See* United Transkeian Territories General Council
Transkei Native Congress, 82, 131, 132
Transvaal African Congress. *See* African National Congress, Transvaal

Transvaal African Students' Association, 99, 100
Transvaal African Teachers' Association, 99, 111
Transvaal Council of Non-European Trade Unions, 407, 442, 443, 451, 513
Transvaal Indian Congress, 103, 114, 117, 272, 406, 416, 432, 454, 482, 512
Transvaal Indian Youth Congress, 421
Transvaal Native Congress. *See* African National Congress, Transvaal
Transvaal Peace Council, 417, 432, 514
Transvaal Youth League. *See* African National Congress Youth League,
    Transvaal
Trotskyist Group. *See* Fourth International

United I.C.U., 14
United Nations, 74, 91, 94, 95, 262-264, 267, 268, 273, 278, 281, 284, 285,
    295, 297, 351, 385, 398, 400, 403, 417, 419, 423, 435, 439, 473-475, 490,
    499, 503-505, 511, 512, 515
United Party, 3, 23, 69, 74-78, 232, 280, 284, 405, 411, 422, 423, 431, 487
United Transkeian Territories General Council [Bunga, Bhunga], 6, 8, 11, 23-31,
    189, 231, 367, 373, 375, 379, 381, 498, 509
Unity Movement. *See* Non-European Unit Movement
University of South Africa, 106

Wayfarer Guide Movement, 137
Western Native Township, African Vigilance Association, 14
Wilberforce Institution, 223
Witwatersrand, University of, 74, 101, 452

Young Men's Ethiopian Society, 110